A DOCUMENTARY HISTORY OF COMMUNISM

Volume 1
Communism in Russia

A DOCUMENTARY HISTORY OF COMMUNISM

Revised edition

*edited, with introduction, notes
and original translations,
by* **ROBERT V. DANIELS**

Volume 1
Communism in Russia

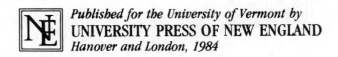

Published for the University of Vermont by
UNIVERSITY PRESS OF NEW ENGLAND
Hanover and London, 1984

Copyright 1984 by the Trustees of the University of Vermont

Printed in the United States of America

LIBRARY OF CONGRESS CATALOGING IN PUBLICATION DATA
Main entry under title:

A Documentary History of Communism.

Bibliography: p.
Contents: v. 1. Communism in Russia – v. 2. Communism and the world.
1. Communism – Soviet Union – History – Sources. 2. Communism – History – Sources.
I. Daniels, Robert Vincent. II. University of Vermont.
HX313.D64   1984   335.43'0947   83-40555
ISBN 0-87451-298-0 (set)
ISBN 0-87451-299-9 (pbk.: v. 1)
ISBN 0-87451-300-6 (pbk.: v. 2)

Design and production by Haan Graphic Publishing Services, Ltd.,
Middletown, Connecticut.

Contents
Volume 1

Preface (1960 Edition)

It would naturally be impossible in one volume of documentary materials to cover a subject as broad and complex as communism from every point of view. The careful description of political institutions, events and everyday life as they have proceeded over the years under communism would require whole shelves of source materials. The present work has been deliberately focused on the subject of Communist thought and doctrine, for reason of its commanding importance, its relative uniformity within the Communist scheme of things, and the appropriateness of the documentary approach to its elucidation. We will be primarily concerned with the evolution of top-level guiding ideas, policies and intentions among the Communists. Statements of deviators of all sorts are included along with the official line of those in power—we may regard anyone who claims descent from Lenin as equally meriting the label "Communist." Through the pronouncements of its leading figures, both those who have ruled and those who have fallen from grace, we may arrive at a reasonably approximate picture of what communism actually is, historically considered.

The problems of selecting materials for a purpose such as this never permit a fully satisfactory solution. I have attempted a fair digest and representative choice of statements expressing all the main concepts and currents in communism. Many readers, however, will find that their areas of interest are under-represented. This failing is the price that must be paid in an effort to survey the entire Communist movement in one documentary volume, and meet the needs of the student, the general reader, and the scholar who is not a specialist in this field.

The present work would never have materialized without the assistance of many people who helped in its preparation or who paved the way with their own studies. I am indebted to the many publishers who kindly permitted me to reprint selections of previously translated material (individually acknowledged under each item). Certain documentary collections which have been particularly helpful deserve special mention—the pioneering *Documentary History of Chinese Communism*, by Conrad Brandt, Benjamin Schwartz and John K. Fairbank (Harvard University Press, 1952); the *Materials for the Study of the Soviet System*, by James H. Meisel and Edward S. Kozera (The George Wahr Publishing Co., Ann

Arbor, Michigan, 1950), which brings together a wide selection of previously translated Soviet documents; the documentary compilations prepared by the Legislative Reference Service of the Library of Congress; the various collections of Soviet documents published by the Stanford University Press; and the English editions of the selected works of Lenin and Stalin, published by the Foreign Languages Publishing House in Moscow. The Harvard University Library has kindly permitted me to include my translations from a number of hitherto unpublished documents in the Trotsky Archive. For their suggestions regarding documents on Far Eastern communism I am indebted to Professors Justus M. van der Kroef and George T. Little, and to Professor Little and Professor Lewis S. Feuer I am grateful for many helpful criticisms. To Mr. Nathan Glazer I wish to express my appreciation for initially encouraging me to undertake this project, and for his editorial assistance since that time. Mrs. Joyce McLaughlin of the Inter-Library Loan Department of the University of Vermont Library rendered me invaluable service in locating and obtaining many scarce but important publications. The vast work of transcribing and assembling the documentary materials was ably done by Mrs. Madeline Chaplin, Mrs. Jean Falls, Mrs. Phyllis Reservitz, Mrs. Roberta Stetson, and my wife, Alice Daniels.

Preface (Revised Edition)

Since the publication of the original edition of this work more than two decades ago the subject of Communism has expanded in years, in territory and in complexity. In the present revision I have endeavored to respond to these changes by abridging the pre-1960 material of the first edition and adding new selections to reflect recent developments in the various Communist parties both inside and outside the Soviet Union. To facilitate the interest of users in focusing either on internal Soviet history or on the evolution of Soviet foreign policy and Communist movements outside the USSR, the new edition has been organized into two volumes, each devoted to one of these aspects of Communism and proceeding chronologically. Both original material and the post-1960 additions have been divided accordingly, and the portion of the 1960 introduction pertaining to external issues has been placed in volume 2.

With the increasing scope and diversity of the subject of Communism it has become more difficult than ever to achieve a totally satisfactory and representative selection of documents within a reasonable compass. To comply with spatial limitations, items in the original edition have been culled where their retrospective importance is not crucial in mapping the development of the Communist movement. A few new pre-1960 items have been added. Post-1960 material has been selected with emphasis on illustrating the main internal developments in the Soviet Union, the most significant events in Soviet foreign relations and the chief variants among Communist movements outside the Soviet Union. As in the original edition, statements representing the views of dissenters within Communist countries are included together with the official views of the leadership. Though many points of particular interest inevitably remain unrepresented, I hope the reader will find that the overall usefulness of this collection has been substantially enhanced.

For their support in the initiation of this revised edition I am indebted to Mr. Thomas McFarland, Director of the University Press of New England, Professor Henry Steffens of the Editorial Board of the Press and Dean Robert Lawson of the Graduate College of the University of Vermont. In the compilation of new material for this edition I have been greatly aided by the vast resources of Soviet documentation made available since the

1950's by the *Current Digest of the Soviet Press* and its companion series, *Current Soviet Policies*. I wish to thank Professor Stephen Cohen and Mr. Orest Pelech of Princeton University for locating for me the hitherto unpublished "Secret Speech" by Suslov in 1964. I am grateful to Mrs. Carolyn Perry, Mrs. Penni Bearden, Mrs. Susan Lacy, and Mrs. Claire Sheppard for their able assistance in preparing new portions of the manuscript.

Introduction
Part 1: The Evolution of the Communist Mind – In Russia

The subject of this work is the world-wide movement which was initially brought into being by Vladimir Ilich Lenin when he organized his Bolshevik faction of Russian revolutionaries in the years 1902-1904. Earlier doctrines and movements going under the name "communism" are not of concern except as they were relevant to the thinking of the specific contemporary Communist movement founded by Lenin and developed in Russia after the revolution of 1917. This applies particularly to the philosophy of Marx and Engels, of which Russian communism was by no means a simple, uncomplicated application (nor the only school of followers, for that matter). Marxism is of interest here insofar as, and only so far as, it contributed to Communist thought, policies and problems. By itself, Marxism is wholly inadequate either to define or explain the Communist movement.

THE COMMUNIST MOVEMENT AND COMMUNIST DOCTRINE

There is one essential point on which the whole matter of the correct understanding of communism rests. Contrary to every assertion, the Communist movement is not truly described by its doctrine. Broadly speaking, the doctrine is a picture of history, past, present and future, which gives the present movement that definite place which was forecast by the original authors of the picture a century ago. Very strong doubts can be cast upon the present validity of the picture as a whole. But it can be shown beyond any reasonable question that within the terms of the Marxist picture itself, the present Communist movement does not occupy the place which its official spokesmen ascribe to it. As a picture of Communist society and a map of its intentions, Communist doctrine is not a free and honest approach to the apprehension of reality, but a forced political imposition.

It is accordingly necessary for anyone who wants to understand communism to look beneath the doctrine and to question all the assumptions which it casts in the way of a clear view. The lack of correspondence between theory and reality will then become readily apparent. This divergence of statement and fact is actually one of the basic features of the Communist movement as it now exists, and it dictates in turn another prime Communist characteristic – the institution of complete control of communication and expression, in order to sustain the irrelevant theoretical picture which it is in the nature of communism to demand. The Communist mentality can be described in essence as a compulsively self-justifying opportunism, where the leaders assume full freedom of action but insist on squaring every step with the holy verities of Marxism-Leninism.

Since Communist doctrine has been so far abstracted from reality, it can well be asked why the doctrinal statements of the movement are worth studying. What, indeed, can be the value of putting forth a collection of Communist ideological pronouncements like the present one, if the real nature of the movement is neither expressed nor governed by its doctrine? Taken at their face value these doctrinal statements can be quite misleading; the reader must bear in mind the context and learn the habit – essential to every student of communism – of reading between the lines. Doctrine has always been extremely important to the Communist movement, though for a long time not in its literal sense. An awareness of the evolving use and reinterpretation of doctrine is basic in appreciating how the movement has developed. The documents are thus primarily useful for the pursuit of historical understanding, which is the only way to comprehend how the movement acquired the paradoxical characteristics which it now displays.

MARX AND THE RUSSIANS

Communist thought cannot be understood apart from Marx, but neither can it be understood on a simple, unqualified Marxist basis. The intellectual origins of the movement must be approached as an interaction of Marx's ideas and the political and intellectual setting of pre-revolutionary Russia in which they took root. The circumstances in which Marxism became popular in Russia in the 1890's belie the expectations of the theory itself. Russia was not a capitalistic country with a proletariat ripe for revolution; it was just beginning to experience the change and dislocation which accompany the initial stages of industrialization. For decades, however, Russia had possessed a class of energetic and articulate intellectuals who devotedly embraced each new radical or utopian idea that came to them from Europe. Marx himself recognized this fashion among the Russians, and commented sardonically that they "always run after the most extreme that the West can offer. . . . This does not prevent the same Russians, once they enter State service, from becoming rascals."* Revolutionary elements among the Russian intelligentsia were primed to respond to

*Marx to Kugelman, October 1, 1868, in *Letters to Dr. Kugelman* (New York, International Publishers, 1934), pp. 77-78.

any revolutionary doctrine from the West. When Marxism became known to them, they devotedly embraced it in large numbers.

The intellectual success of Marxism had nothing to do with its logical applicability to Russia. It was difficult to apply it at all, as Marx realized: "The 'historical necessity' of . . . capitalist production . . . is explicitly restricted to the *countries of Western Europe*." * Rigorously construed – as Marx's Russian disciples construed it – Marxism could give scant hope for an early proletarian revolution in Russia. The expectation for a country at the Russian stage of development was a "bourgeois-democratic revolution" and an extended period of capitalistic industrial development, before Russia would follow the socialist course that her West-European neighbors were supposed to initiate. For the immediate future Marxism would serve more appropriately as an ideological justification of capitalism, and in fact the theory did have considerable appeal in Russia on just this basis, among the so-called "legal Marxists."

Among the revolutionaries in Russia, Marxism could not appeal on logical grounds. People did not become revolutionary after an intellectual conversion to the Marxian historical analysis. They became Marxists – in Russia as everywhere else – because they were revolutionary for prior emotional reasons and because Marxism appealed to them on emotional grounds as a pseudo-scientific rationale for revolution. Logical inconsistency was no obstacle. Marxism in Russia has from the very beginning neatly fit Marx's own definition of ideology as "false consciousness" – a set of ideas used without concern for truth or consistency to rationalize the interests and aims of a particular social group. Marxism became the "ideology" of a large part of the revolutionary Russian intelligentsia. Since the revolution it has fulfilled the same function for the ruling Communist Party.

Lenin, in this context, represents simply the clearest and most extreme example of emotional commitment to Marxism in disregard of its incongruence in Russia. Lenin had grown up with the burning revolutionary ardor so familiar among the scions of the educated gentry. He embraced Marxism with religious devotion, as the ultimate word in human affairs, almost as a supernatural prophecy which no mortal could dare question or modify without committing the sin of blasphemy. Despite this dogmatism, however, Lenin was quite capable of ignoring or violating Marxian principles when it came to the actual formulation of revolutionary programs and tactics. Lenin's program and tactics did not come from Marx at all, but from his own emotional make-up as a member of the Russian revolution-

*Marx to Vera Zasulich, March 8, 1881, in Blackstock and Hoselitz, eds., *The Russian Menace to Europe* (Glencoe, Illinois, The Free Press, 1952), p. 278.

ary intelligentsia, and from the previous traditions of the revolutionary movement in Russia. Lenin's Marxism was superimposed upon his Russianism, to supply the terminology and conviction of righteous inevitability.

While we cannot understand Lenin as a Marxist, the study of his theoretical pronouncements and his tactical statements does contribute basic understanding about the Communist movement. What we have to deal with is in reality a new doctrine – Leninism – which, while observing the Marxian language and professing spiritual continuity from Marx, actually contradicted him in many vital respects. Leninism as a system of belief has had a very profound effect in shaping the Communist movement, and so it is the natural starting point for any analysis of modern communism.

THE PREMISES OF LENINISM

Lenin's political thinking rested on two cardinal assumptions, neither of which bore any logical relation to Marxism. One of these implicit beliefs was his conception of the overall nature of the historical process: that history is made in the last analysis not by classes or the forces of production, but by willful individual leaders and by ideas. This was an outlook he shared with practically all pre-Marxist Russian social thinkers. Lenin had assimilated it so deeply that he was scarcely conscious of its import, so that he could go right on resting his thought on such an assumption while he imagined himself to be a perfectly orthodox Marxist. Time and again Lenin railed against "spontaneity" and proclaimed the vital role of "consciousness." He made it abundantly clear that he never expected the working class to carry out a revolution by itself. Only the deliberate leadership of dedicated "professional revolutionaries" like himself could bring the event about.

In his emotional orientation toward revolution Lenin shared a trait with the unscientific aspect of Marx's outlook which did not follow logically from his theoretical system. This was what might be called the moral imperative of revolution. Lenin, like Marx, was dedicated to the anticipated revolution as a moral absolute, as a sort of purgative judgment day which would extirpate all the evil in the old way of life, and usher in the millenium. For both Marx and Lenin, all questions of good and evil hinged on the ultimate question of revolution. They differed, however, in the manner in which they sustained their hopes about revolution. Marx's solution was that of pseudo-scientific inevitability; having committed himself to the moral necessity for the revolutionary reconstruction of society, he proceeded to work out an elaborate, sweeping, in many respects brilliant system of social analysis which purported to prove the inevitability of that prospective upheaval: the relentless dialectic of historical materialism would sooner or later raise the chosen class of proletarians to the seats of power.

Lenin followed all this verbally, but the actual foundation which he established for his revolutionary goal was in fact diametrically opposed to Marx's. For Lenin the revolution was not inevitable at all; it had to be brought about by the deliberate action of conscious revolutionaries, *against* the natural flow of history. If the spontaneous forces of history were not interfered with, Lenin implied, the moral imperative of revolution would never become a reality. Hence it was on willful revolutionaries, sustained by a sense of moral duty, that Lenin had to rest his hopes. How guarantee, however, that the revolutionaries would keep striving in the right direction against the frustrating spontaneity of the passive herd? Lenin's answer was the same on which any religious movement relies to assure individual rectitude: the proper doctrine, the true faith.

The proper doctrine was Marxism as read by Lenin. Any questioning of the doctrine or of Lenin's own interpretation of it – in fact, any independence of mind at all – not only disqualified a member of the revolutionary movement but classified him irretrievably with the enemies of the revolution, as far as Lenin was concerned. Lenin and his followers were sustained by an absolute faith in Marx's revolutionary prophecy, with all its pseudo-science of dialectical inevitability. It mattered not that the doctrine of inevitability contradicted the philosophy of will and idea which all of Lenin's political practice implied, for the Bolsheviks were revolutionaries before they were Marxists. They displayed the Calvinistic paradox of people who believed in a foreordained future but who, thanks to this belief, were all the more vigorously determined on individual action to make that future come true. The psychological truth here is that people with a strong emotional impulse toward a given goal are irrationally inclined to embrace a doctrine that says that that goal is inevitably going to be realized.

The emotional commitment to strive mightily for a revolution that was regarded as inevitable had significant moral implications for the Bolsheviks: it allowed them to conclude without qualms that the end justifies any means. Like the Russian extremists who preceded them, the Bolsheviks regarded the revolution as the all-decisive event, the leap from the kingdom of Evil to the kingdom of Good. Nothing had any value or made any sense except in relation to the revolution. But the revolution could not be passively awaited, according to the Bolshevik philosophy; it required a total commitment and the utmost exertion by those morally committed to it to make it a reality. Therefore, it was morally binding upon the adherents of revolution to employ every expedient means, not excepting violence, false-hood, robbery and treachery, to prepare and consummate the revolution-ary victory. All such questionable tactics could be utilized with equanimity because the expected revolution would be all-decisive in governing the high moral level of the new society; it would wipe away any evil effects of evil means presently used.

The grave defect in this reasoning was the lack of assurance that the revolution – i.e., the right kind of revolution, the real revolution – would actually follow from the revolutionaries' action and offset the expedient evils employed by them. How know that the present evil means would assuredly procure the future good? For this foundation to their righteous-ness the Bolsheviks had to depend on the Marxian inevitability of the pro-letarian revolution and the classless society. However, it was precisely the lack of real conviction about such inevitability that required them to adopt evil expedients in the first place. Far from being corrected in the revolution which actually took place, the Bolsheviks' system of violent, authoritarian and deceitful expedients rapidly became an end in itself; it is now the basis of the Communist social order.

THE PARTY AS THE INSTRUMENT OF REVOLUTION

The major contribution which Lenin made to the theory and practice of communism was by way of implementing his belief in the moral impera-tive of a historically uncertain revolution. He had to have reliable means for accomplishing a problematical political goal, and he found them in a fea-ture which had been a distinguishing trait of the earlier Russian revolution-ary movements – the stress on conspiratorial organization, the revolutionary party. The party represents the essence of Leninism.

The function of the party, as Lenin conceived it, was to force the revolu-tion to occur, against all the resistance of the old order. The party would overcome the impracticality of the intellectuals and the formless spontane-ity of the masses, and drive for a victory which otherwise would never materialize. For this instrument of revolution Lenin had in mind forms of organization, dictated both by the circumstances of the political under-ground and by his own proclivities, from which he never deviated. First of all, the party was to be a narrow organization, not the mass of like-minded sympathizers, but the active and conscious minority, the professional revo-lutionaries. This was the specific issue over which the factional split of the Russian Social Democrats into Bolsheviks and Mensheviks began in 1903. For the accomplishment of its revolutionary objective Lenin required that this minority organization be constituted on military lines, with a hierar-chy of command and binding discipline upon its members. The formula which he proposed to guide the party organization was "democratic centralism," meaning the democratic determination of policy and the centralized execution of it. In practice, however, Lenin could brook no expression of policy contrary to his own thinking; anyone who differed with Lenin found himself attacked as "opportunist" or "petty bourgeois," an unreliable element if not a potential traitor to the revolutionary cause. Lenin recognized none as genuine proletarian Marxists save those who unreservedly followed his own leadership. Thus, while the notion of a one-party dictatorship was never explicitly formulated before the Bolsheviks came to power, the exclusion of all who differed had already been long implicit in the monopoly of revolutionary morality which in practice Lenin ascribed to himself.

There is irony in the fact that when the Bolsheviks took power in October, 1917, the Leninist rigor of their organization was at its lowest point, the party having been diluted with hundreds of thousands of new members and many new leaders like Trotsky who had never committed themselves to the principles of Bolshevik discipline. A spontaneous mass upheaval and the enthusiasm of the party members – forces which Lenin had distrusted or discounted – were responsible much more than organization and narrow discipline for the Bolshevik success. It was only through a step-by-step process in the years following the revolution that the organization of the party was tightened up to approximate Lenin's old ideal, with the major imposition of discipline coming in 1921, after the crisis of civil war had been weathered. The great difference now was in the function which the party had to play – not the underground conspiracy aiming to get the revolution started, but the exclusive association of people engaged in ruling the state. Never anticipated, this new role for the disciplined party was to constitute the backbone of Communist totalitarianism.

WHOSE REVOLUTION?

After Lenin had worked out his plan for the "proletarian" party as the instrument of revolution, he had to find a place for it to operate in the Marxian scheme of things as applied to Russia. The dilemma, as we have seen, was how to hold strictly to the Marxian prognosis of bourgeois revolution and still envision an opportunity to lead an anticapitalist mass revolutionary movement. Among most of Lenin's rivals in the Menshevik faction of the Social Democrats, a weaker emotional attachment to revolution was attested by their acceptance of the prospect of a "bourgeois-democratic" revolution and of a long period of capitalism after that, during which the workers' party could be nothing more than a legal opposition. Lenin, however, took the bull very boldly by the horns at the time of the revolutionary ferment of 1905, to declare that the bourgeois revolution could be carried through to its conclusion only by the party of the proletariat, because the bourgeoisie was not revolutionary enough. It did not occur to Lenin that this made mincemeat of the basic Marxian propositions governing the relationships of economic stages, class forces, and political movements. He blithely called for a "democratic dictatorship of the proletariat and peasantry," which would hold power until the capitalists prepared the industrial conditions for their own demise, after which the real dictatorship of the proletariat would confiscate the means of production and effectuate the transition to the socialist society.

There was another approach to the dilemma of Marxist revolution in Russia which avoided Lenin's violence to the doctrine and at the same time preserved the prospect of immediate revolutionary action by the workers and their leaders. This was the "theory of permanent revolution" expounded by Trotsky, a set of ideas which proved to be very important later on – in 1917 as the rationale for the Bolshevik seizure of power, and during the 1920's as a major subject of factional controversy among the Communists. Trotsky's view proceeded from the observation that Russia's economic development had been uneven, with some modern industry and a politically conscious working class surrounded by a vast majority of impoverished peasants mainly interested in owning more land. It would be natural, he suggested, for the bourgeois revolution to swing without any break in continuity (hence "permanent") into a proletarian phase where the workers as an energetic minority could temporarily take power. They would soon be in danger of falling before the "petty-bourgeois" (mainly peasant) majority, were it not for the international repercussions which Trotsky expected their momentary success to have. Supposedly the exploits of the revolutionary workers in Russia would provide the stimulus for the ripening forces of proletarian revolution elsewhere in the world, and the socialist upheaval would therefore proceed without interruption (again "permanent") on the international plane. Brotherly socialist states would hasten to succor the embattled proletarians of Muscovy and help raise the whole population of Russia to the industrial level where the advantages of socialism would be apparent to all.

Trotsky's theory gradually gained adherents in the years before 1917, and then, after the fall of the Czar in February, 1917, was startlingly borne out by events. "Bourgeois" revolution did indeed open the way for the proletarians and the party they supported to surge toward power; recognizing this, Lenin and most of the other Bolshevik leaders accepted Trotsky's reasoning in all but name. The Bolsheviks prepared to seize power in the fall of 1917, assuming that their social backing as well as the underdeveloped economy in Russia were not sufficient to sustain their program of socialist revolution, but with the conviction that their success of the moment would evoke the instantaneous response of international revolution. Some Bolsheviks (led by Zinoviev and Kamenev) were skeptical about the latter, and on this ground opposed the October coup d'état as an irresponsible gamble. Lenin, in contrast, demanded insurrection as a Russian duty to give the European workers the signal they needed. Implicit in all this was the irrational faith, inherited from mid-nineteenth-century Russian thinkers, in the efficacy of Russia's revolutionary mission to the world. The fact remains, however, that the Bolsheviks took power with a theoretical outlook which told them that their aims could not possibly be achieved in Russia without the assistance of like-minded revolutionary regimes in those advanced countries where socialism, according to Marxism, was supposed to begin first. Such help never came, and in its absence a drastic reconstruction of theory was required if the most embarrassing implications were to be evaded.

THE PARADOX OF MARXIAN SOCIALISM IN RUSSIA

It has sometimes been suggested that the successful proletarian revolution in Russia proved Marx wrong by showing that socialism could win without previous industrial development under capitalism. But if Marx's predictions cannot be relied upon, with what assurance can the revolution be described as "proletarian"? Actually the Soviet system has developed in an entirely different direction. The Marxist labels of proletarian socialism and the "workers' state" have been kept only for the sake of self-righteousness and propaganda – the "ideology" or "false consciousness" of the new post-revolutionary regime.

The step-by-step adaptations of Marxist theory after the establishment of the Soviet regime illustrate very clearly the impact of circumstances which forced the Communists to revamp their program. Within a matter of months after the October Revolution basic decisions had been made which fatally compromised the Marxian logic of the Communists' position. They kept power, but only by shifts of policy which changed the whole direction of their revolution and brought it into line with what Russian conditions permitted.

The first of these major policy changes was the decision in February, 1918, to make peace with Germany instead of proclaiming an international civil war against all the capitalist powers. The Bolsheviks' seizure of power had been predicated on the imminence of proletarian revolution in the West, which the Russian assault on the "imperialist" Provisional Government was supposed to evoke, and which in turn was presumably indispensable to sustain socialist hopes in Russia. Once in power, however, Lenin declined to gamble his position in the interests of world revolution; over the anguished protests of the left-wing utopians, he decided to make peace and buy time rather than risk losing power in Russia while attempting to set a fighting example for the European workers. In other words, his estimate of the revolutionary potential outside Russia had now dropped – but that estimate had been the only Marxist way of justifying his seizure of power in the first place. Lenin rejected the alleged possibility of immediately evoking international revolution, in the interest of holding power which could have no Marxian socialist meaning in the absence of that international revolution. This is how the Communists came to rule in a country where Marxism ruled out the success of the proletariat.

Following the peace of Brest Litovsk, during the period of civil strife and economic disruption which goes by the term "War Communism," the ranks of the Communist Party were torn repeatedly with dissension over the implications of holding power where conditions made the realization of the program of proletarian socialism, as theretofore conceived, entirely chimerical. Lenin had espoused the utopian program as firmly as anyone in the programmatic tract, "State and Revolution," which he wrote while hiding in Finland in 1917. The workers would seize power, subject the whole economy to their control, destroy the existing state machinery, and install new officials of their own choosing whose pay would be no higher than "workman's wages." The resistance of the former exploiting classes would be crushed, and the state – i.e., the organs of law-enforcement and repression – would commence to "wither away." The annihilation of authority and the apotheosis of equality were visions animating vast numbers of Russians, not excepting the Communists, during the revolutionary years.

By the spring of 1918, Lenin had turned emphatically against these attitudes on the ground of total impracticability for the foreseeable future (though the evidence of most of his career strongly suggests that he was emotionally set against anarchy and equality in any event). In the government, the army, the factories, the Communist Party, Lenin (joined by Trotsky) demanded an end to equalitarianism and collective decision-making, and called instead for the establishment of firm hierarchies of individual authority and responsibility with clear differentials of individual reward. Step by step the institutions of the new Soviet society were recast in the old mold. By 1921, with the elimination of the trade unions from industrial management, the abolition of factions within the Communist Party, and the enunciation of the "New Economic Policy" (NEP) with its concessions to the individual profit motive, the Communist leaders had completed their adaptation of a late-industrial program to early-industrial conditions.

The occasion for the introduction of the New Economic Policy was a growing state of economic crisis and mass dissatisfaction, coming to a head in armed rebellion against the Soviet regime. In the perspective of past revolutions this marked the point where the national convulsion of revolutionary emotion was subsiding in favor of growing demands for normal living. Revolutionary emotion among large numbers of people in Russia had sustained for a time the illusion that the immediate socialistic transformation of the country was still possible, whether or not strong authority and stringent controls were necessary to accomplish this. By early 1921, however, it was clear to Lenin and the more practical-minded Communists that power and program could not both be held to at the same time; again, as with the world revolution in 1918, one of these desiderata would have to be sacrificed, and again it was the program. Lenin, thanks to his compelling leadership and the strength of the party organization, was able to command the Communists to go into retreat, postpone their socialistic objectives, and come to terms with the realities of an underdeveloped country. In effect, he carried out his own "Thermidorean reaction" (by analogy with the fall of the Jacobins in France in 1794), and by adapting his party's policies from the stage of violent revolutionary emotion to the stage of post-revolutionary convalescence he was able to keep power.

This change was not effected, however, without serious difficulties within the ranks of the Communist Party. The utopians demanded that the party hew to the strictly idealist course, and began to attack Lenin for betraying the workers. Lenin, for his part, was determined to claim full Marxist justification for his compromising policy, and as was his custom, to condemn as un-Marxist anyone who took issue with him. At the Tenth Party Congress in March, 1921, Lenin used his control of the party organization to have the leftists condemned as a "petty-bourgeois" deviation, and to ban any recurrence of factional criticism.

It is interesting to note that the political and social situation in Russia after the introduction of the NEP in 1921 comes remarkably close to Lenin's old notion of the "democratic dictatorship of the proletariat and peasantry," with a self-styled party of the workers holding power but adapting its policies to the capitalistic necessities of industrial development. This arrangement, as we have seen, contradicts the basic Marxian proposition regarding the dependence of the political "superstructure" on the economic "base." The only way to salvage the Marxian analysis is to dismiss the "proletarian" label and regard the Communist politico-economic structure as an expression of industrialism in its developmental phase – not the successor of capitalism but a parallel alternative.

The transition to the New Economic Policy meant a major change as regards the vitality of Marxist theory among the Communists. Prior to this time they could still imagine that a lucky conjunction of circumstances in Russia was enabling them to proceed with the Marxian plan of proletarian dictatorship. After the "Thermidor" of 1921, when revolutionary hopes had to be suspended, the basic perspective was one of adaptation to the wrong conditions. The function of Marxist doctrine then had to shift from direct inspiration to the justification of a regime which no longer fit the requirements of the theory. In the language of Karl Mannheim, Marxism was changed from a "utopia" to an "ideology," from an inspirational illusion to a rationalization of actuality.* The defense of the "ideology" demanded stringent suppression of anyone who would again take the doctrine seriously as a "utopia" and hold it up as a challenge to the status quo; hence the necessity of rooting out the left-wing Communists and making the party line – the official interpretation of doctrine – an obligatory canon of faith. We have here, in the picture of the revolutionary party trying to explain away its conversion to a post-revolutionary role, the key to the mentality of total thought-control which was soon to become a permanent feature of the Communist system.

Although the Communist Party leaders claimed exclusive doctrinal sanction for their compromises of 1921, they remained for the time being aware that their policies were indeed expedients that did not point directly toward the ultimate socialistic goal. Concessions in the capitalistic or bureaucratic direction were recognized as such; they were simply regarded as practical necessities for the preservation of the power of the Communist Party until the industrial development of the country had proceeded to the point where the fully socialist ideal could be put into effect. The real fallacy here from the Marxist standpoint lay in the notion that there was value in the retention of power *per se* regardless of the social base with which the authorities had to operate. The concessions which the Communists had to make at the expense of their program bear out clearly the conditions which social circumstances can impose on a government. Furthermore, thanks to their habit of justifying each practical expedient in terms of basic Marxist doctrine, the Communists began to lose any clear notion of what the ultimate goal was, as opposed to the pattern of immediate expedients. As is so often the case in human affairs, it was the practical steps rather than the original intention or blueprint that determined the outcome: the means became ends in themselves.

*See Karl Mannheim, *Ideology and Utopia* (New York, Harcourt, Brace, n.d.), pp. 192ff.

SOCIALISM IN ONE COUNTRY

During the factional controversies in the Communist Party after Lenin's demise the most bitter debate raged around the theoretical implications of the anomaly of the self-styled proletarian socialist state in Russia. The Trotskyists, who had been forced out of their positions of influence in 1921-23, sought arguments to use against Stalin and the other more direct followers of Lenin who were endeavoring to follow the NEP compromise of economic leniency plus firm party control. It was easy for Trotsky and the Left Opposition to find lapses by the leadership from the strict proletarian path, and they stressed these with warnings that the isolation of the revolution in a backward country made it very difficult to sustain a socialist policy without great care and effort. They began to suggest that Stalin's leadership was the embodiment of a "Thermidorean reaction," yielding to the desires of the petty-bourgeois majority of the country.

Stalin's defense against this line of reasoning represents a major change in the intellectual status and political function of Communist doctrine, though its meaning has usually been misunderstood. To meet the challenge of the opposition Stalin looked to the scriptures for assurance that he could not possibly be in error and particularly that national backwardness was not a crippling embarrassment. He found what he sought in a statement made by Lenin in 1915, to the effect that the country first going over to socialism would stand alone and fight the others until the revolution spread. Taking this remark out of context, Stalin applied it to Russia and appealed to it as the authority for his contention that the socialist regime could stand alone in Russia whether or not it was sustained by international revolution. At the same time the party propaganda machine whipped up a storm over Trotsky's theory of permanent revolution, on the grounds of its pessimistic "lack of faith" in Russia's own revolutionary potential. Neither faction, it must be understood, rejected the world revolution as a Communist desideratum, while on the other hand neither was prepared to take great risks to bring it about. The issue in this respect was only over the implications for Russia of a delay in the world revolution: Trotsky said they were dangerous and required careful scrutiny of the existing leadership, and Stalin denied this.

The major significance of "socialism in one country" lay not with the Communist International, for which it made no difference, nor with the factional struggle among the Russian Communists, which was decided by organizational pressure, but with the meaning and role of Communist ideology as a whole. While it is pointless to debate whether Marxian socialism was really feasible in Russia (the whole experience of modern industrialism makes it appear more and more utopian), Stalin's manner of asserting the possibility of socialism is highly significant. He did not inquire empirically as to how the conditions of Russian life might be shaped in order to promote the ideal. (Bukharin did attempt this in some of his statements about the anticapitalist bent of the peasantry around the world.) Stalin preferred the scholastic method of turning to the scriptures for an authoritative statement that would give doctrinal sanction for what he was determined to do anyway. He did not base his action on an honest effort to understand and follow the doctrine as such; as his opposition critics irrefutably pointed out, he had distorted Lenin's meaning completely. Lenin had in mind the most advanced country, and had no intention of asserting the immediate possibility of socialism in an underdeveloped country. Stalin's maneuver was a purely casuistical trick, indicative of the determination which he and his like-minded associates felt to maintain absolute doctrinal justification of their rule. The new theory was a major step in the manipulation of doctrine to make it accord with action that was decided on pragmatically.

The immediate consequence of the doctrinal twisting represented by "socialism in one country" was the suppression of all criticism, political or otherwise, aimed at the leadership or its rationalizations. From the standpoint of any serious regard for the doctrine itself it was easy to expose the maneuvers of the party leadership, as the Trotskyist opposition clearly demonstrated. In fact the ideological embarrassment which the Trotskyists posed was a major reason why Stalin and Bukharin were led to the decision to expel them from the party and silence them altogether. Thenceforth, to uphold their suppression of criticism, the Soviet leaders had to assert the absolute right of the party to pass definitive judgment on any question whatsoever. In this manner the compulsive pursuit of self-justification led to the establishment of totalitarian thought-control soon after Stalin achieved personal rule in 1929.

THE INDUSTRIALIZATION PROGRAM
AND THE EASTERNIZATION OF COMMUNISM

Simultaneously with the Stalin-Trotsky political struggle and the development of Communist dogmatism, the Russian leaders were beginning to face the implications of the actual conditions under which they ruled, i.e., the economic problems of an underdeveloped country. The problems were serious and acute, and the differences of opinion which they evoked added fuel to the flames of factional controversy. As it happened, however, it was the accidents of factional politics rather than any particularly convincing analysis that governed the response to the industrialization problem which Russia made under Stalin's direction.

After the introduction of the NEP, as we have seen, both the Stalin-

Bukharin faction and the Trotsky faction were nervously concerned about the weakness of Russian society as the base for the dictatorship of the proletariat. The dominant group took the position of caution, relying on tight party controls together with a conciliatory policy toward the peasants to keep the Communists in power during the expected long period of gradual development of state-owned industry. This was the program for which "socialism in one country" was required as the doctrinal justification. On the other hand, Trotsky and his supporters, much less patient, were calling by 1923 for concerted economic planning and industrial development by the state, in order to rectify as quickly as possible the economic backwardness which, according to the earlier orthodoxy, made socialism in Russia a very insecure proposition. The Trotskyist position, however, made no more sense from the strictly Marxian point of view than did "socialism in one country"; in suggesting that the "workers' state" could rapidly create its own economic base of large-scale industry the Trotskyists turned Marx's conception of the relation of economics and politics completely upside down.

While the Trotskyist demand for deliberate, intensive industrialization defied the traditional preconceptions of Marxism, it was nonetheless of major significance for the future development of the Communist movement. Implied in the Trotsky approach was a fundamentally new conception of the historical role of the socialist organization of society. From the beginning of the socialist movement in the early nineteenth century socialist thinkers and parties had been almost exclusively concerned with the redistribution of existing wealth, the reapportionment on some more equitable basis of the proceeds from society's productive capacity. The productive capacity itself was taken for granted, either as a static quantity or (as Marx approached it) as the creature of capitalism prior to the establishment of socialism. The Trotskyists' great innovation was to apply the socialist system of a state-operated economy to the task of developing productive capacity. All previous schools of socialist thought, including Marx's and Lenin's, represented forms of what we might call "distributive" socialism. Trotsky's was the first school of "productive" socialism—the essentially un-Marxist idea that the socialist state could and should be used to promote industrialization and overcome the poverty of low productivity.

Ironically, the actual shift in the Communist movement from the distributive to the productive orientation was not accomplished by Trotsky but by his principal enemy. Until 1927, the party leadership headed by Stalin and Bukharin had steadfastly resisted Trotsky's demand for rapid, planned, tax-supported industrial development, in favor of gradual development financed mainly out of the profits made by Soviet industry while catering to the needs of the consuming public. By the end of 1927, however, when the factional struggle within the Communist Party had reached its climax with the expulsion of Trotsky and Zinoviev and their followers from the party's ranks, the party leadership had itself begun to move toward a somewhat more aggressive economic policy. Then, rapidly playing his hand with remarkable political finesse, Stalin commenced in 1928 to maneuver against his erstwhile colleagues in the party leadership, Bukharin, Rykov and Tomsky. Knowing that these men were committed to economic caution, Stalin abruptly took over the Trotskyist approach to industrialization and with it the plan of wholesale collectivization of the peasants (a step necessary to squeeze from them the unrecompensed surplus necessary to support the industrialization effort). Carefully representing his ideas as the continuation of established party policies, Stalin was able to take the protests made by Bukharin, Rykov and Tomsky as the pretext for having them condemned as a "right deviation" secretly favoring capitalism. With this Right Opposition group out of the way in 1929, Stalin found himself all-powerful but also all-responsible, and committed to an irrationally extreme program of intensive industrial development. He apparently saw no alternative except to forge ahead under the scarcely Marxian slogan "There are no fortresses which Bolsheviks cannot storm."

With the industrialization program launched by Stalin, paid for by national belt-tightening and enforced by totalitarian police controls, Soviet Russia had entered into the new productive form of socialism. This was socialism not of the overripe industrial society but of a partially backward and preindustrial country, not the successor to capitalism but the alternative to it for accumulating the industrial plant to bring the country to a modern level of economic development. Soviet socialism served not to solve the problems of industrial life, but to accentuate them and to carry them afield into virgin territory.

The Soviet economic example has proved highly infectious, because it is such a logical and effective approach to the problem of developing a backward country. Even among non-Communist circles in Asia and Africa the notion of using the authority of the state to accelerate economic development has proved to one degree or another irresistible since World War II. Under Stalin's leadership, communism was converted from an essentially Western response to Western problems of industrial life under capitalism, to an essentially Eastern response of applying despotic state authority to the pursuit of rapid industrial development and equality with the West. By viewing Russia in the early part of this century as a hybrid society, part Western and part Eastern, partially industrialized yet substantially backward, we may understand why this transitional role of converting a Western revolutionary movement into an Eastern one fell to her. The product of this Russian alchemy was a unique system of oriental state capitalism.

STALIN AND THE VIRTUE OF NECESSITY

The new productive emphasis on economic development had profound implications for other aspects of the Communist movement in Russia. It became necessary to make a wide variety of policy adjustments, converting the Western postcapitalist socialist ideal to the Eastern state-capitalist pattern. The many such adjustments already made, ostensibly as temporary concessions, had to be accepted as permanent.

Under Stalin's leadership the Communist Party adapted itself to the harsh realities of industrialization and of the industrial way of life – realities which made the social ideals professed by every Marxist up to 1917 completely utopian. Contrary to Marx's egalitarian, anarchistic expectations, industrial society does not permit a diminution of hierarchical authority to the advantage of the democratic collective – it puts all the greater premium on the hierarchical division of labor and responsibility and on maintaining complex organizations in which everyone observes instructions with unflagging discipline. It was apparent by the 1930's that the real task for Russia was not the introduction of collectivist equality but the training of responsible leaders and responsible subordinates, to convert lackadaisical peasants into disciplined troops in an industrial army. The real Russian innovation was a new organizational basis for industrial development – the postcapitalistic institutions of the "managerial" society.

Discipline and authority in political and economic life, hateful as they had been from the standpoint of the Russian revolutionaries of 1917, had been substantially restored by the end of the Civil War period. Stalin's innovation was to declare them to be in effect on a practically permanent basis as positive aspects of the socialist ideal, and he further laid it down as the official line that socialism had never meant anything else. Similarly with the ideal of equality, which to some extent had continued to be observed up until 1929, Stalin declared it to be un-Marxist and un-Leninist, and justified inequality of economic rewards as a natural aspect of Soviet socialism. Between 1931 and 1937, for reasons of political practicality or personal preference, Stalin proceeded to reverse the party line on a wide range of policy matters, ranging from education and art to religion and the family. In every case the earlier revolutionary attitude was condemned as a "petty-bourgeois" deviation from Marxism, and what the outside world regarded as the conservative norm became the standard of official Communist belief and practice (except for religion, which enjoys toleration but is still officially disparaged). Together with these adjustments Stalin overhauled the basic political theory of Marxism by asserting the long-term positive role of the state in overcoming economic obstacles and developing the socialist society, instead of withering away. Stalin simply made his theory conform to what he had actually been doing, with the characteristic twist that the new version was alleged to have been the only correct interpretation of Marxism all along.

Stalin's transformation of the aims and practices of communism was directly responsible for fundamental changes in the realm of Communist thinking, not only with respect to what was thought but with respect to the basic function of doctrine in the Communist system. The Communists faced circumstances where either the theoretical prerequisites of the old ideal were lacking (the weakness of the Russian industrial base), or where it became evident that those presumed preconditions were themselves not conducive to the ideal (the bureaucratic requirements of industry itself). Under Lenin the party made expedient adaptations to these circumstances, while still imagining that these were temporary maneuvers. Machinery of control was meanwhile set up over the channels of thought and communication, and was used to justify the necessity of the expedients. Stalin's changes were to pursue such expedients more freely, intensify the controls over public communication, and then to proclaim that his policies were not temporarily necessary deviations but the direct implementation of the revolutionary program. Instead of guiding Soviet practice, the goals of communism were redefined to conform with the trend that expedient practice had taken.

Paradoxically, as doctrine ceased to operate as a basic motive and guide, the stress laid by the Soviet regime on rigorous orthodoxy became all the greater. This has made it difficult for outside observers to appreciate how little Marxist theory really shapes Communist behavior. Its function is to provide the sense of revolutionary legitimacy which the Communist leaders since Lenin have always insisted on maintaining, and also to serve as the vehicle for party control over every aspect of life. The thoroughgoing control which requires this orthodoxy is in turn necessitated by the difficulty of bridging the vast gulf between theory and practice and suppressing the innumerable opportunities for criticizing the doctrinal manipulations in which the Communist regime has indulged. The Soviet leaders have long been committed to a self-enforcing false image of their system. In all probability they believe in this image, in a narrow-minded and defensive way, and will endeavor to sustain it at any cost, even though the real standards in their action are those of free-wheeling practicality rather than loyalty to the spirit of any theory. Communism has become wedded to a psychology of compulsively self-justifying opportunism, so dogmatically unscrupulous that it is not even faithful to its own principles.

The real meaning of communism is to be found in the pattern of evolution through expedients, in the course of which the movement was changed to deal with its circumstances. During the first two decades of the Soviet regime communism was systematically Easternized. It was converted into a system for solving the Eastern problems of rapid modernization and national self-assertion against the West, through the method of terror and compulsion wielded by an autocratic government. Subsequent replacement of leading personalities has made no fundamental difference in the system.

POSTSCRIPT: 1983

Communism as it is depicted in this revised edition is still the political movement descended from the revolutionary ideas and actions of Lenin. In the last two or three decades, however, it has become vastly more complex and varied, with the development outside Russia of numerous independent forms of Communism, whether successful or abortive. At the same time, within the Soviet Union a remarkable degree of stability was maintained during the era of Leonid Brezhnev, distinguished by a paucity of new ideas, theories or initiatives. The documentary selections for these years reflect the Soviet regime's preoccupation with administrative problems, thrown into relief in the privately circulated critiques by dissident writers. Despite the rhetoric about "building communism," official Russia has lost any vision of a new future apart from quantitative improvement in the statistical indicators.

The Soviet Union under Brezhnev continued its long-standing habit of justifying itself in Marxist terms even though it could not be meaningfully described by Marxism. The system and its official thinking became more rigid than ever, in contrast to the brief period of impulsive experimentation between Stalin's death and the fall of Khrushchev. Doctrinal statements continued to have a primarily manipulatory and legitimizing significance, and offered no prospect of a relaxation of the ideological rigidity and official unanimity exhibited ever since Stalin's day. For some Soviet dissenters, notably the historian Roy Medvedev, Marxism has been the point of departure for a penetrating critique of Soviet reality, but the dynamic development of Communism as a political program has been confined for the last quarter century to parties and governments outside the Soviet Union.

The essence of the Soviet political and social system has not changed since Stalin, though terror was moderated and economic conditions improved. Khrushchev's years in power were, in retrospect, only a temporary interlude, an aberration of abortive reform in the history of the Stalinist system of totalitarian rule. Power remains centralized and arbitrary; dissent is crushed and initiative is stifled; society is managed through the interpenetrating bureaucratic hierarchies of the party and the state; the "New Class" of officials has become an old class of self-perpetuating privilege.

Toward the end of the Brezhnev era the liabilities of the old system were becoming obvious. The command economy could not adjust to the complexities of high-technology industrialism nor could it transcend the age-old limitations of sub-arctic agriculture. Economic growth, military power and consumer satisfaction became impossible to reconcile simultaneously. At the same time the hold of ideology over the average citizen, not to mention the technical specialist, became steadily weaker. With the passage of power from Brezhnev to Yuri Andropov and from the Stalinist to the post-Stalinist generation, the question on all sides is whether the Soviet regime will try to maintain the status quo that satisfies no one, or finally launch into some kind of radical new departure and open a new chapter in the history of communism.

Volume 1
Communism in Russia

Chapter One
Leninism and the Bolshevik Party, to 1917

The background of the Communist movement was dominated by one powerful figure, Lenin. The disciplined organization, the revolutionary mission, and stern enforcement of Lenin's version of doctrinal orthodoxy were all firmly established in the Bolshevik faction of the Russian Social-Democratic Party long before 1917. The reactions of other Marxists testify eloquently to the unique impress which Lenin's personality made in the movement. When revolution came in 1917, Lenin was prepared to strike for power and hold it at any costs.

LENIN AS A MARXIST

As early as 1894, when he was twenty-four, Lenin (born Vladimir Ilich Ulyanov) had become a revolutionary agitator and a convinced Marxist. He exhibited his new faith and his polemical talents in a diatribe of that year against the peasant-oriented socialism of the Populists led by N. K. Mikhailovsky.

. . . Now – since the appearance of *Capital* – the materialist conception of history is no longer a hypothesis, but a scientifically demonstrated proposition. And until some other attempt is made to give a scientific explanation of the functioning and development of any form of society – form of society, mind you, and not the mode of life of any country or people, or even class, etc. – another attempt which would be just as capable as materialism of introducing order into the "pertinent facts" and of presenting a living picture of a definite formation and at the same time of explaining it in a strictly scientific way, until then the materialist conception of history will be synonymous with social science. Materialism is not "primarily a scientific conception of history," as Mr. Mikhailovsky thinks, but the only scientific conception of history. . . .

. . . Russian Marxists . . . began precisely with a criticism of the subjective methods of earlier Socialists. Not satisfied with merely stating the fact that exploitation exists and condemning it, they desired to *explain* it.

FROM: Lenin, "What the 'Friends of the People' Are and How They Fight the Social-Democrats" (April, 1894; in V. I. Lenin, *Selected Works*, Moscow, Foreign Languages Publishing House, 1950-52, Vol. I, book 1, pp. 110, 165-66).

Realizing that the whole post-Reform* history of Russia consisted in the impoverishment of the mass and the enrichment of a minority, observing the colossal expropriation of the small producers side by side with universal technical progress, noting that these opposite tendencies arose and became intensified wherever, and to the extent that, commodity production developed and became consolidated, they could not but conclude that they were confronted with a bourgeois (capitalist) organization of social economy, which *necessarily* gave rise to the expropriation and oppression of the masses. Their practical program was quite directly determined by this conviction; this program was, to join the struggle of the proletariat against the bourgeoisie, the struggle of the propertyless classes against the propertied, which constitutes the principal content of economic reality in Russia, from the most out-of-the-way village to the most up-to-date and perfected factory. How were they to join it? The answer was again suggested by real life. Capitalism had brought the principal branches of industry to the stage of large-scale machine industry; by thus socializing production, it had created the material conditions for a new system and had at the same time created a new social force—the class of factory workers, the urban proletariat. Subjected to the same bourgeois exploitation—for such, in its economic essence, is the exploitation to which the whole toiling population of Russia is subjected—this class, however, has been placed in a special, favourable position as far as its emancipation is concerned; it has no longer any ties with the old society, which is wholly based on exploitation; the very conditions of its labour and circumstances of life organize it, compel it to think and enable it to step into the arena of the political struggle. It was only natural that the Social-Democrats should direct all their attention to, and base all their hopes on, this class, that they should make the development of its class consciousness their program, that they should direct all their activities towards helping it to rise and wage a direct political struggle against the present regime and towards drawing the whole Russian proletariat into this struggle. . . .

THE FOUNDATION OF THE RUSSIAN MARXIST PARTY

While Marxism had been winning adherents among the Russian revolutionary intelligentsia for more than a decade previously, an avowedly Marxist party was not organized until 1898. In that year a "congress" of nine men met at Minsk to proclaim the establishment of the Russian Social-Democratic Workers' Party. The manifesto issued in the name of the congress after the police broke it up

---

*I.e., since the emancipation of the serfs in 1861—Ed.

was drawn up by the economist Peter Struve, a member of the moderate "legal Marxist" group who soon afterward left the Marxist movement altogether. The manifesto is indicative of the way Marxism was applied to Russian conditions, and of the special role for the proletariat which the Russian Marxists envisaged.

. . . Fifty years ago the invigorating storm of the Revolution of 1848 burst over Europe.

For the first time the modern working class appeared on the scene as a major historical force. With its forces the bourgeoisie succeeded in removing many antiquated feudal-monarchial systems. But the bourgeoisie quickly perceived in its new ally its most hostile foe, and betrayed both it and itself and the cause of freedom into the hands of reaction. However, it was already late: the working class, pacified for the time being, after ten or fifteen years appeared again on the stage of history with redoubled force, with matured consciousness, as a full-grown fighter for its own liberation.

All this time Russia apparently remained aside from the main road of the historical movement. The class struggle was not apparent there, but it was there, and the main thing was that it was steadily growing and maturing. The Russian government, with laudable zeal, itself planted the seeds of class struggle by cheating the peasants, patronizing the landlords, fattening up the big capitalists at the expense of the toiling population. But the bourgeois-capitalist order is unthinkable without a proletariat or working class. The latter is born together with capitalism, grows together with it, gets stronger, and in proportion to its growth is thrown more and more into conflict with the bourgeoisie.

The Russian factory worker, serf or free, has always carried on a hidden or open struggle with his exploiters. In proportion to the development of capitalism, the proportions of this struggle have grown, they have embraced more and more layers of the working class population. The awakening of the class self-consciousness of the Russian proletariat and the growth of the spontaneous workers' movement have coincided with the conclusive development of international Social Democracy as the bearer of the class struggle and the class ideal of the conscious workers of the whole world. . . . Vainly the government imagines that by concessions it can calm the workers. Everywhere the working class is becoming more

FROM: Manifesto of the Russian Social-Democratic Workers' Party, issued by the First Congress of the party, Minsk, March, 1898 (in *The Communist Party of the Soviet Union in the Resolutions and Decisions of its Congresses, Conferences, and Plenums of the Central Committee* [hereafter referred to as "CPSU in Resolutions"], 7th ed., Moscow, 1954, Vol. I, pp. 11-14; editor's translation).

demanding, the more they give it. It will be the same with the Russian proletariat. They have given in to it up to now only when it *demands*, and in the future will give it only what it *demands*.

And what does the Russian working class not need? It is completely deprived of what its foreign comrades freely and quietly enjoy: participation in the administration of the state, freedom of speech and of the press, freedom of organization and assembly – in a word, all those instruments and means with which the West-European and American proletariat improves its position and at the same time struggles for its final liberation, against private property and capitalism – for socialism. Political freedom is necessary for the Russian proletariat like fresh air is necessary for healthy breathing. It is the basic condition for its free development and the successful struggle for partial improvements and final liberation.

But the Russian proletariat can only win the political freedom which it needs *by itself.*

The farther east one goes in Europe, the more the bourgeoisie becomes in the political respect weaker, more cowardly, and meaner, and the larger are the cultural and political tasks which fall to the share of the proletariat. On its broad shoulders the Russian working class must bear and will bear the cause of the fight for political freedom. This is essential, but it is only the first step toward the realization of the great historical mission of the proletariat – towards the creation of that social order in which the exploitation of man by man will have no place. The Russian proletariat will throw off its burden of autocracy so that with all the more energy it will continue the struggle against capitalism and the bourgeoisie until the complete victory of socialism. . . .

As a socialist movement and inclination, the Russian Social-Democratic Party continues the cause and the traditions of all the preceding revolutionary movements in Russia; taking as the principal immediate task of the party the goal of conquering political freedom, Social Democracy moves toward the goal which has already been marked out by the glorious activists of the old "People's Will." But the means and the path which Social Democracy chooses are different. The choice of them is determined by its conscious desire to be and remain a class movement of the organized working masses. It is firmly convinced that "the liberation of the working class can only be its own business," and it will undeviatingly make all its action conform to this fundamental basis of international Social Democracy.

Long live Russia, long live international Social Democracy!

LENIN'S THEORY OF THE PARTY

Leaving Russia in 1900, Lenin went to Geneva to join Plekhanov's circle of older Russian Marxists in publishing a paper for the new Social-Democratic party – *Iskra*, "The Spark." In the course of this work he turned his attention to the organizational problems of the movement, and formulated what in retrospect have proven to be the fundamental ideas underlying the Communist movement – his theory of the tightly organized and disciplined party of "professional revolutionaries." This idea Lenin first developed in "What Is to Be Done?," a lengthy polemic against the "Economists" – those Marxists who preferred to stress the economic struggle of the workers rather than a separate revolutionary movement. The publication of "What Is to Be Done?" in 1902 marks the true beginning of Leninism as a distinctive political current.

. . . It is no secret that two trends have taken shape in the present-day international Social-Democracy. The fight between these trends now flares up in a bright flame, and now dies down and smoulders under the ashes of imposing "truce resolutions." What this "new" trend, which adopts a "critical" attitude towards "obsolete dogmatic" Marxism, represents has with sufficient precision been *stated* by Bernstein, and *demonstrated* by Millerand.*

Social-Democracy must change from a party of the social revolution into a democratic party of social reforms. Bernstein has surrounded this political demand with a whole battery of symmetrically arranged "new" arguments and reasonings. The possibility of putting Socialism on a scientific basis and of proving from the point of view of the materialist conception of history that it is necessary and inevitable was denied, as was also the growing impoverishment, proletarianization and the intensification of capitalist contradictions. The very conception, *"ultimate aim,"* was declared to be unsound, and the idea of the dictatorship of the proletariat was absolutely rejected. It was denied that there is any counterdistinction in principle between liberalism and Socialism. *The theory of the class struggle* was rejected on the grounds that it could not be applied to a strictly

FROM: Lenin, "What Is to Be Done?" (1902, *Selected Works*, Vol. I, book 1, pp. 207-8, 210, 227-28, 233-34, 242-44, 286-88, 322-25, 330, 336, 338-39, 347-48).

*Eduard Bernstein: leader of the "revisionist" or avowedly nonrevolutionary tendency in the German Social-Democratic Party; Alexandre Millerand: French socialist leader, the first to join a "bourgeois" cabinet (later President of France) – Ed.

democratic society, governed according to the will of the majority, etc.

Thus, the demand for a resolute turn from revolutionary Social-Democracy to bourgeois Social-reformism was accompanied by a no less resolute turn towards bourgeois criticism of all the fundamental ideas of Marxism. . . .

He who does not deliberately close his eyes cannot fail to see that the new "critical" trend in Socialism is nothing more nor less than a new variety of *opportunism*. And if we judge people not by the brilliant uniforms they don, not by the high-sounding appellations they give themselves, but by their actions, and by what they actually advocate, it will be clear that "freedom of criticism" means freedom for an opportunistic trend in Social-Democracy, the freedom to convert Social-Democracy into a democratic party of reform, the freedom to introduce bourgeois ideas and bourgeois elements into Socialism. . . .

Without a revolutionary theory there can be no revolutionary movement. This thought cannot be insisted upon too strongly at a time when the fashionable preaching of opportunism goes hand in hand with an infatuation for the narrowest forms of practical activity. . . . Our Party is only in process of formation, its features are only just becoming outlined, and it is yet far from having settled accounts with other trends of revolutionary thought, which threaten to divert the movement from the correct path. . . . The national tasks of Russian Social-Democracy are such as have never confronted any other socialist party in the world. . . . *The role of vanguard fighter can be fulfilled only by a party that is guided by the most advanced theory.* . . .

. . . The strikes of the nineties represented the class struggle in embryo, but only in embryo. Taken by themselves, these strikes were simply trade union struggles, but not yet Social-Democratic struggles. They testified to the awakening antagonisms between workers and employers, but the workers were not, and could not be, conscious of the irreconcilable antagonism of their interests to the whole of the modern political and social system, i.e., theirs was not yet Social-Democratic consciousness. In this sense, the strikes of the nineties in spite of the enormous progress they represented as compared with the "riots," remained a purely spontaneous movement.

We have said that *there could not yet be* Social-Democratic consciousness among the workers. It could only be brought to them from without. The history of all countries shows that the working class, exclusively by its own effort, is able to develop only trade union consciousness, i.e., the conviction that it is necessary to combine in unions, fight the employers and strive to compel the government to pass necessary labour legislation, etc.

The theory of Socialism, however, grew out of the philosophic, historical and economic theories that were elaborated by the educated representatives of the propertied classes, the intellectuals. According to their social status, the founders of modern scientific Socialism, Marx and Engels, themselves belonged to the bourgeois intelligentsia. In the very same way, in Russia, the theoretical doctrine of Social-Democracy arose quite independently of the spontaneous growth of the working-class movement, it arose as a natural and inevitable outcome of the development of ideas among the revolutionary socialist intelligentsia. At the time of which we are speaking, i.e., the middle of the nineties, this doctrine not only represented the completely formulated program of the Emancipation of Labour group, but had already won over to its side the majority of the revolutionary youth in Russia.

Hence, we had both the spontaneous awakening of the masses of the workers, the awakening to conscious life and conscious struggle, and a revolutionary youth, armed with the Social-Democratic theory, eager to come into contact with the workers. In this connection it is particularly important to state the oft-forgotten (and comparatively little-known) fact that the *early* Social-Democrats of that period *zealously carried on economic agitation* (being guided in this by the really useful instructions contained in the pamphlet *On Agitation* that was still in manuscript), but they did not regard this as their sole task. On the contrary, *right from the very beginning* they advanced the widest historical tasks of Russian Social-Democracy in general, and the task of overthrowing the autocracy in particular. . . . The adherents of the "pure" working-class movement, the worshippers of the closest "organic" . . . contacts with the proletarian struggle, the opponents of any non-worker intelligentsia (even if it be a socialist intelligentsia) are compelled, in order to defend their positions, to resort to the arguments of the *bourgeois* "pure" trade unionists. . . . This shows . . . that *all* worship of the spontaneity of the working-class movement, all belittling of the role of "the conscious element," of the role of Social-Democracy, *means, quite irrespective of whether the belittler wants to or not, strengthening the influence of the bourgeois ideology over the workers.* All those who talk about "overrating the importance of ideology," about exaggerating the role of the conscious element, etc., imagine that the pure working-class movement can work out, and will work out, an independent ideology for itself, if only the workers "wrest their fate from the hands of the leaders." But this is a profound mistake. . . .

Since there can be no talk of an independent ideology being developed by the masses of the workers themselves in the process of their movement the *only* choice is: either the bourgeois or the socialist ideology. There is no middle course (for humanity has not created a "third" ideology, and, moreover, in a society torn by class antagonisms there can never be a non-class or above-class ideology). Hence, to belittle the socialist ideology *in any way*, to *turn away from it in the slightest degree* means to strengthen bourgeois ideology. There is a lot of talk about spontaneity, but the *spontaneous* development of the working-class movement leads to its becoming subordinated to the bourgeois ideology, *leads to its developing according to the program* of the *Credo*,* for the spontaneous working-class movement is trade unionism, and trade unionism means the ideological enslavement of the workers by the bourgeoisie. Hence, our task, the task of Social-Democracy, is to *combat spontaneity*, to *divert* the working-class movement from this spontaneous, trade-unionist striving to come under the wing of the bourgeoisie, and to bring it under the wing of revolutionary Social-Democracy. The phrase employed by the authors of the "economic" letter in the *Iskra*, No. 12, about the efforts of the most inspired ideologists not being able to divert the working-class movement from the path that is determined by the interaction of the material elements and the material environment, *is absolutely tantamount* therefore *to the abandonment of Socialism.* . . .

We have seen that the conduct of the broadest political agitation, and consequently the organization of comprehensive political exposures, is an absolutely necessary, and the *most urgently* necessary, task of activity, that is, if that activity is to be truly Social-Democratic. . . . *However much we may try* to "lend the economic struggle itself a political character" *we shall never be able* to develop the political consciousness of the workers (to the level of Social-Democratic political consciousness) by keeping within the framework of the economic struggle, for *that framework is too narrow.* . . .

Class political consciousness can be brought to the workers *only from without*, that is, only from outside of the economic struggle, from outside of the sphere of relations between workers and employers. The sphere from which alone it is possible to obtain this knowledge is the sphere of relationships between *all* the classes and strata and the state and the government, the sphere of the interrelations between *all* the classes. For that reason, the reply to the question: what must be done in order to bring political knowledge to the workers? cannot be merely the one which, in the majority of cases, the practical [party] workers, especially those who are inclined towards Economism, mostly content themselves with, i.e., "go among the workers." To bring political knowledge to the *workers* the Social-

*The *Credo*: a statement of the views of the "Economists," 1899–Ed.

Democrats must *go among all classes of the population*, must dispatch units of their army *in all directions*. . . .

. . . The political struggle of Social-Democracy is far more extensive and complex than the economic struggle of the workers against the employers and the government. Similarly (and indeed for that reason), the organization of a revolutionary Social-Democratic party must inevitably be of a *different* kind than the organizations of the workers designed for this struggle. A workers' organization must in the first place be a trade organization; secondly, it must be as broad as possible; and thirdly, it must be as little clandestine as possible (here, and further on, of course, I have only autocratic Russia in mind). On the other hand, the organizations of revolutionaries must consist first, foremost and mainly of people who make revolutionary activity their profession (that is why I speak of organizations of *revolutionaries*, meaning revolutionary Social-Democrats). In view of this common feature of the members of such an organization, *all distinctions as between workers and intellectuals*, and certainly distinctions of trade and profession, must be *utterly obliterated*. Such an organization must of necessity be not too extensive and as secret as possible. . . .

The workers' organizations for the economic struggle should be trade union organizations. Every Social-Democratic worker should as far as possible assist and actively work in these organizations. That is true. But it is not at all to our interest to demand that only Social-Democrats should be eligible for membership in the "trade" unions: that would only narrow down our influence over the masses. Let every worker who understands the need to unite for the struggle against the employers and the government join the trade unions. The very aim of the trade unions would be unattainable if they failed to unite all who have attained at least this elementary degree of understanding, and if they were not very *wide* organizations. And the wider these organizations are, the wider our influence over them will be – an influence due not only to the "spontaneous" development of the economic struggle but also to the direct and conscious effort of the socialist trade union members to influence their comrades. . . .

. . . A small, compact core of the most reliable, experienced and hardened workers, with responsible representatives in the principal districts and connected by all the rules of strict secrecy with the organization of revolutionaries, can, with the widest support of the masses and without any formal organization, perform *all* the functions of a trade union organization, and perform them, moreover, in a manner desirable to Social-Democracy. Only in this way can we secure the *consolidation* and development of a *Social-Democratic* trade union movement, in spite of all the gendarmes.

... I assert: 1) that no revolutionary movement can endure without a stable organization of leaders that maintains continuity; 2) that the wider the masses spontaneously drawn into the struggle, forming the basis of the movement and participating in it, the more urgent the need of such an organization, and the more solid this organization must be (for it is much easier for demagogues to sidetrack the more backward sections of the masses); 3) that such an organization must consist chiefly of people professionally engaged in revolutionary activity; 4) that in an autocratic state, the more we *confine* the membership of such an organization to people who are professionally engaged in revolutionary activity and to have been professionally trained in the art of combatting the political police, the more difficult will it be to wipe out such an organization, and 5) the *greater* will be the number of people of the working class and of the other classes of society who will be able to join the movement and perform active work in it.

... The centralization of the most secret functions in an organization of revolutionaries will not diminish, but rather increase the extent and quality of the activity of a large number of other organizations which are intended for a broad public and are therefore as loose and as non-secret as possible, such as workers' trade unions, workers' self-education circles and circles for reading illegal literature, socialist and also democratic circles among *all* other sections of the population, etc., etc. We must have such circles, trade unions and organizations everywhere in *as large a number as possible* and with the widest variety of functions; but it would be absurd and dangerous to *confuse* them with the organization of *revolutionaries*, to obliterate the border line between them, to dim still more the masses' already incredibly hazy appreciation of the fact that in order to "serve" the mass movement we must have people who will devote themselves exclusively to Social-Democratic activities, and that such people must *train* themselves patiently and steadfastly to be professional revolutionaries.

Yes, this appreciation has become incredibly dim. Our chief sin with regard to organization is that *by our amateurishness we have lowered the prestige of revolutionaries in Russia*. A person who is flabby and shaky in questions of theory, who has a narrow outlook, who pleads the spontaneity of the masses as an excuse for his own sluggishness, who resembles a trade union secretary more than a people's tribune, who is unable to conceive of a broad and bold plan that would command the respect even of opponents, and who is inexperienced and clumsy in his own professional art – the art of combating the political police – why, such a man is not a revolutionary but a wretched amateur!

Let no active worker take offence at these frank remarks, for as far as insufficient training is concerned, I apply them first and foremost to myself. I used to work in a circle that set itself very wide, all-embracing tasks; and all of us, members of that circle, suffered painfully, acutely from the realization that we were proving ourselves to be amateurs at a moment in history when we might have been able to say, paraphrasing a well-known epigram: "Give us an organization of revolutionaries, and we shall overturn Russia!" And the more I recall the burning sense of shame I then experienced, the more bitter are my feelings towards those pseudo Social-Democrats whose teachings "bring disgrace on the calling of a revolutionary," who fail to understand that our task is not to champion the degrading of the revolutionary to the level of an amateur, but to *raise* the amateurs to the level of revolutionaries. . . .

. . . The history of the revolutionary movement is so little known among us that the name "Narodnaya Volya"* is used to denote any idea of a militant centralized organization which declares determined war upon tsarism. But the magnificent organization that the revolutionaries had in the seventies, and which should serve us as a model, was not established by the Narodnaya Volya-ites, but by the *Zemlya i Volya-ites,* who split up into the Cherny Peredel and Narodnaya Volya. Consequently, to regard a militant revolutionary organization as something specifically Narodnaya Volya-ite is absurd both historically and logically, because *no* revolutionary tendency, if it seriously thinks of fighting, can dispense with such an organization. The mistake the Narodnaya Volya-ites committed was not that they strove to enlist in their organization *all* the discontented, and to direct this organization to decisive battle against the autocracy; on the contrary, that was their great historical merit. Their mistake was that they relied on a theory which in substance was not a revolutionary theory at all, and they either did not know how, or were unable, inseparably to link up their movement with the class struggle within developing capitalist society. And only a gross failure to understand Marxism (or an "understanding" of it in the spirit of Struve-ism) could prompt the opinion that the rise of a mass, spontaneous working-class movement *relieves* us of the duty of creating as good an organization of revolutionaries as the *Zemlya i Volya* had, and even an incomparably better one. On the contrary, this movement *imposes* this duty upon us, because the spontaneous struggle of the proletariat will not become its genuine "class struggle" until this struggle is led by a strong organization of revolutionaries. . . .

*"Narodnaya Volya": The "People's Will," the terrorist organization which assassinated Tsar Alexander II in 1881. Its ancestor was the "Land and Liberty" party (*Zemlia i Volia*), which split in 1879 into the "People's Will" and the "Black Repartition" (*Cherny Peredel*) party of those who favored mass agitation – Ed.

LENIN ON THE PARTY SPLIT

The first true congress of the Russian Social-Democratic Workers' Party was the Second. It convened in Brussels in the summer of 1903, but was forced by the interference of the Belgian authorities to move to London, where the proceedings were concluded. The Second Congress was the occasion for bitter wrangling among the representatives of various Russian Marxist factions, and ended in a deep cleavage brought about by Lenin – his personality, his drive for power in the movement, and his "hard" philosophy of the disciplined party organization. At the close of the congress Lenin commanded a temporary majority for his faction and seized upon the label "Bolshevik" (from the Russian *bolshinstvo* – majority), while his opponents (led by Y. O. Martov) who inclined to the "soft" or more democratic position became known as the "Mensheviks" or minority. The terms stuck despite the fact that for most of the time between 1903 and 1917 the Bolsheviks were the numerically weaker group.

Following the Second Congress Lenin prepared a polemical account of the issues, in which he argued that the weaknesses shown by the "intellectuals" at the congress proved the need for the kind of organization which he advocated.

. . . It is quite natural . . . that the work of the *Iskra* and the entire work of organizing the Party, the entire work of *actually* restoring the Party, *could not* be regarded as finished until the whole Party had adopted and officially registered certain definite ideas of organization. This task was to be performed by the rules of organization of the Party.

The principal ideas which the *Iskra* strove to make the basis of the Party's organization amounted essentially to the following two: first, the idea of centralism, which defined in principle the method of deciding all particular and detail questions of organization; second, the special function of an organ, a newspaper, for ideological leadership, an idea which took into account the temporary and special requirements of the Russian Social-Democratic working-class movement amidst conditions of political slavery, on the understanding that the *initial* base of operations for the revolutionary assault would be set up abroad. . . .

. . . Martov, as is usually the case, forgot a good deal and, therefore, again muddled things up. . . .

I could not have "liked" the "idea" of paragraph one of Martov's draft,

FROM: Lenin, "One Step Forward, Two Steps Back" (May, 1904; *Selected Works*, Vol. I, book 1, pp. 452, 454-56, 468, 613-16, 618-20, 644-45).

for that draft did not contain a *single idea* that came up at the Congress. His memory played him false. I have been fortunate enough to find Martov's draft among my papers, and in it *"paragraph one is not formulated in the way he proposed it at the Congress"*! So much for the "open vizor"!

¶1 of Martov's draft: "A member of the Russian Social-Democratic Labour Party is one who, accepting its program, works actively to carry out its aims under the control and direction of the organs (*sic*!) of the Party."

¶1 of my draft: "A Party member is one who accepts its program and who supports the Party both financially and by personal participation in one of the Party organizations."

¶1 as formulated by Martov at the Congress and adopted by the Congress: "A member of the Russian Social-Democratic Labour Party is one who accepts its program, supports the Party financially and renders it regular personal assistance under the direction of one of its organizations."

It is clearly evident from this comparison that there is no *idea* in Martov's draft but only *empty phrases*. It goes without saying that Party members must work under the control and direction of the *organs* of the Party; *it cannot be otherwise*, and it is talked about only by those who love to talk in order to say nothing, who love to flood "rules" with huge quantities of verbal water and bureaucratic formulas (i.e., formulas that are useless for the matter in hand and supposed to be useful for display). . . .

. . . Comrade Martov's three years' *Iskra* training has not imbued him with disdain for the anarchist phrasemongering by which the unstable mentality of the intellectual is capable of justifying the violation of rules adopted by common consent. . . . When I say that the Party should be a *sum* (and not a mere arithmetical sum, but a complex) of *organizations*, does that mean that I "confuse" the concepts Party and organization? Of course not. I thereby express clearly and precisely my wish, my demand, that the Party, as the vanguard of the class, should be as *organized* as possible, that the Party should admit to its ranks only such elements *as lend themselves to at least a minimum of organization*. My opponent, on the contrary, wants to *lump together* organized elements and unorganized elements in the Party, those who submit to direction and those who do not, the advanced and the incorrigibly backward—for the corrigibly backward may join the organization. . . .

. . . Unity on questions of program and tactics is an essential but by no means a sufficient condition for Party unity and for the centralization of Party work (good God, what rudimentary things one has to keep repeating nowadays, when all concepts have been confused!). The centralization of Party work requires, in addition, unity of organization, which, in a party that has grown to be anything more than a mere family circle, is inconceivable without formal rules, without the subordination of the minority to the majority, of the part to the whole. . . .

. . . The point at issue is whether our ideological struggle is to have forms *of a higher type* to clothe it, forms of Party organization binding on all, or the forms of the old disunity and the old circles. . . . The proletariat is trained by its whole life for organization far more radically than many an intellectual prig. Having gained some understanding of our program and our tactics, the proletariat will not start justifying backwardness in organization by arguing that the form is less important than the content. It is not the proletariat, but *certain intellectuals* in our Party who lack *self-training* in the spirit of organization and discipline, in the spirit of hostility and contempt for anarchist phrasemongering. . . . The proletarian who has become a conscious Social-Democrat and feels that he is a member of the Party will reject *khvostism* ["tail-endism," i.e., following the masses] in matters of organization with the same contempt as he rejected *khvostism* in matters of tactics.

. . . The factory, which seems only a bogey to some, represents that highest form of capitalist cooperation which has united and disciplined the proletariat, taught it to organize, and placed it at the head of all the other sections of the toiling and exploited population. And it is precisely Marxism, the ideology of the proletariat trained by capitalism, that has taught and is teaching unstable intellectuals to distinguish between the factory as a means of exploitation (discipline based on fear of starvation) and the factory as a means of organization (discipline based on collective work united by the conditions of a technically highly-developed form of production). The discipline and organization which come so hard to the bourgeois intellectual are especially easily acquired by the proletariat just because of this factory "schooling." Mortal fear of this school and utter failure to understand its importance as an organizing factor are characteristic of the ways of thinking which reflect the petty-bourgeois mode of life and which give rise to that species of anarchism which the German Social-Democrats call Edel-anarchismus, i.e., the anarchism of the "noble" gentleman, or aristocratic anarchism, as I would call it. This aristocratic anarchism is particularly characteristic of the Russian nihilist. He thinks of the Party organization as a monstrous "factory"; he regards the subordination of the part to the whole and of the minority to the majority as "serfdom" (see Axelrod's* articles); division of labour under the direction of a centre evokes from him a tragicomical outcry against people being transformed into "wheels and cogs" (to turn editors into contributors being

---

*P. B. Axelrod: a Menshevik leader who stressed democratic party organization – Ed.

considered a particularly atrocious species of such transformation); mention of the organizational rules of the Party calls forth a contemptuous grimace and the disdainful remark (intended for the "formalists") that one could very well dispense with rules altogether. . . .

. . . Aristocratic anarchism cannot understand that formal rules are needed precisely in order to replace the narrow circle ties by the broad Party tie. It was unnecessary and impossible to give formal shape to the internal ties of a circle or the ties between circles, for these ties rested on friendship or on a "confidence" for which no reason or motive had to be given. The Party tie cannot and must not rest on either of these; it must be founded on *formal*, "bureaucratically" worded rules (bureaucratic from the standpoint of the undisciplined intellectual), strict adherence to which can alone safeguard us from the wilfulness and caprices characteristic of the circles, from the circle methods of scrapping that goes by the name of the free "process" of the ideological struggle. . . .

One step forward, two steps back – It happens in the lives of individuals, and it happens in the history of nations and in the development of parties. It would be the greatest criminal cowardice to doubt even for a moment the inevitable and complete triumph of the principles of revolutionary Social-Democracy, of proletarian organization and Party discipline. We have already won a great deal, and we must go on fighting, without being discouraged by reverses, fighting steadfastly, scorning the philistine methods of circle scrapping, doing our very utmost to preserve the single Party tie among all the Russian Social-Democrats which has been established at the cost of so much effort, and striving by dint of stubborn and systematic work to make all Party members, and the workers in particular, fully and intelligently acquainted with the duties of Party members, with the struggle at the Second Party Congress, with all the causes and all the stages of our disagreements, and with the utter disastrousness of opportunism, which, in the sphere of organization, as in the sphere of our program and our tactics, helplessly surrenders to the bourgeois psychology, uncritically adopts the point of view of bourgeois democracy, and blunts the weapon of the class struggle of the proletariat.

In its struggle for power the proletariat has no other weapon but organization. Disunited by the rule of anarchic competition in the bourgeois world, ground down by forced labour for capital, constantly thrust back to the "lower depths" of utter destitution, savagery and degeneration, the proletariat can become, and inevitably will become, an invincible force only when its ideological unification by the principles of Marxism is consolidated by the material unity of an organization which will weld millions of toilers into an army of the working class. Neither the decrepit rule of Russian tsardom, nor the senile rule of international capital will be able to withstand this army. Its ranks will become more and more serried, in spite of all zigzags and backward steps, in spite of the opportunist phrase-mongering of the Girondists of present-day Social-Democracy, in spite of the smug praise of the antiquated circle spirit, and in spite of the tinsel and fuss of *intellectual* anarchism.

MARXIST REACTIONS TO LENIN – ROSA LUXEMBURG

Rosa Luxemburg, born of a Jewish family in Russian Poland in 1870, became one of the most articulate representatives of idealistic radicalism in the Russian Marxist movement. After 1900, having acquired German nationality through marriage, she exerted her revolutionary efforts primarily in the German Social-Democratic Party, and helped found the Spartacus League which became the nucleus of the German Communist Party in 1919. She did not cease to concern herself with the revolutionary movement in Russia, and published a penetrating attack on Lenin's concept of the centralized party. Her position is significant as a Marxist stand equally as revolutionary as Lenin's, but emphatically repudiating his faith in discipline.

. . . The present book of Comrade Lenin, one of the prominent leaders and debaters of *Iskra* in its campaign preliminary to the Russian Party Congress (N. Lenin: "One Step Forward, Two Steps Backward," Geneva, 1904), is the systematic exposition of the views of the ultra-centralist wing of the party. The conception which has here found expression in penetrating and exhaustive form is that of a thorough-going centralism of which the vital principle is, on the one hand, the sharp separation of the organized bodies of outspoken and active revolutionists from the unorganized though revolutionary active masses surrounding them, and on the other hand, strict discipline and direct, decisive and determining intervention of the central authorities in all expressions of life in the party's local organizations. It suffices to note, for example, that the central committee, according to this conception, is authorized to organize all sub-committees of the party, hence also has power to determine the personal composition of every single local organization, from Geneva and Liège to Tomsk and Irkutsk, to give it a set of self-made local statutes, to completely dissolve it by a decree and create it anew, and finally in this manner to influence the composition of the highest party authority, the Party Congress. According to this, the

FROM: Luxemburg, *Leninism or Marxism* (1904; English translation, Glasgow, Anti-Parliamentary Communist Federation, 1935, pp. 6-7, 15, 17-20, 22-23).

central committee appears as the real active nucleus of the party, and all other organizations merely as its executive organs. . . .

But to desire, as Lenin does, to deck out a party leadership with such absolute powers of a negative character would be only to multiply artificially and in a most dangerous measure the conservatism which is a necessary outgrowth of every such leadership. Just as the Social-Democratic tactic was formed, not by a central committee but by the whole party or, more correctly stated, by the whole movement, so the separate organizations of the party plainly require such elbow-room as alone enables complete utilization of all means offered by the situation of the movement, as well as the unfolding of revolutionary initiative. The ultra-centralism advocated by Lenin, however, appears to us as something which, in its whole essence, is not informed with the positive and creative spirit, but with the sterile spirit of the night-watchman. His thought is patterned mainly upon the *control* of party activity and not upon its promotion, upon narrowing and not upon unfolding, upon the hemming and not upon the drawing together of the movement. . . .

. . . Social-Democratic centralization cannot be based on blind obedience, on mechanical subordination of the party fighters to their central authority; and, furthermore, . . . no absolute partition can be erected between the nucleus of the class-conscious proletariat already organized into fixed party cadres and the surrounding element engaged in the class struggle but still in process of class enlightenment. The setting up of the central organization on these two principles – on the blind subordination of all party organizations, with their activity, down to the least detail, under a central authority which alone thinks, acts and decides for all, and on a sharp separation of the organized nucleus of the party from the surrounding revolutionary milieu, as championed by Lenin – appears to us for that reason as a mechanical carrying-over of the organizational principles of the Blanquist movement of conspiratorial circles onto the social-democratic movement of the working masses. . . .

. . . It is not by adding on to the discipline impressed upon it by the capitalist State – with the mere transfer of the baton from the hand of the bourgeoisie into that of a social-democratic central committee – but by the breaking up and uprooting of the slavish spirit of discipline, that the proletariat can be prepared for the new discipline, the voluntary self-discipline of the Social Democracy. . . .

Even from the standpoint of the fears entertained by Lenin, that is, the dangerous influence of the intellectuals upon the proletarian movement, his own conception of organization constitutes the greatest danger for the Russian Social Democracy.

As a matter of fact, there is nothing which so easily and so surely hands over a still youthful labour movement to the private ambitions of the intellectuals as forcing the movement into the strait jacket of a bureaucratic centralism, which debases the fighting workers into a pliable tool in the hands of a "committee." And, inversely, nothing so surely preserves the labour movement from all opportunistic abuses on the part of an ambitious intelligentsia as the revolutionary self-activation of the working masses, the intensification of their feeling of political responsibility. . . .

In this frightened effort of a part of the Russian Social Democracy to preserve from false steps the aspiring labour movement of Russia, through the guardianship of an omniscient and omnipresent central committee, we seem to see also the same subjectivism involved by which socialist thought in Russia has frequently been imposed upon in the past. . . .

. . . Now, however, the ego of the Russian revolutionary quickly stands on its head and declares itself once more to be an almighty ruler of history—this time, in the direction of the Social-Democratic working masses. In so doing, the bold acrobat overlooks the fact that the only subject to which this role has now fallen is the mass-ego of the working class, which everywhere insists on venturing to make its own mistakes and learning historical dialectic for itself. And by way of conclusion, let us say openly just to ourselves: Mistakes which a truly revolutionary labour movement commits are, in historical perspective, immeasurably more fruitful and valuable than the infallibility of the very best "central committee." . . .

MARXIST REACTIONS TO LENIN—LEON TROTSKY

Though born only in 1879, Trotsky had gained a leading place among the Russian Social-Democrats by the time of the Second Party Congress in 1903. Like Rosa Luxemburg, he represented ultra-radical sentiment that could not reconcile itself to Lenin's stress on the party organization. Trotsky stayed with the Menshevik faction until he joined Lenin in 1917. From that point on he accommodated himself in large measure to Lenin's philosophy of party dictatorship, but his reservations came to the surface again in the years after his fall from power. His comments on Lenin in 1904 were truly prophetic.

. . . We wish that our comrades would not overlook the difference of principle between the two methods of work. . . . This difference, if we reduce it to its basis of principle, has decisive significance in determining

FROM: Trotsky, *Nashi politicheskie zadachi* (Our Political Tasks), Geneva, Russian Social-Democratic Workers' Party, 1904, pp. 50, 52, 54, 73–75, 105; editor's translation.

the character of all the work of our party. In the one case we have the contriving of ideas for the proletariat, the political *substitution* for the proletariat; in the other, political *education* of the proletariat, its political *mobilization*. . . .

The system of political substitution, point for point like the "Economists'" system of simplification, proceeds – consciously or unconsciously – from a false "sophisticated" understanding of the relation between the objective interests of the proletariat and its consciousness. . . .

In contrast to the "economists," the "politicians" take as their point of departure the *objective* class interests of the proletariat, established by the method of Marxism. But with the same fear that the "economists" have they turn away from the "distance" which lies between the objective and subjective interests of the class whom in principle they "represent." . . . Thus, if the "economists" do not lead the proletariat because they are dragged *behind it*, the "politicians" do not lead the proletariat because they themselves *carry out its obligations*. If the "economists" have saved themselves from the immensity of the task by assigning themselves a modest role – to march at the tail end of history – the "politicians" resolve the question by trying to transform history *into their own tail*. . . .

Poorly or well (more poorly) we are revolutionizing the masses, arousing in them the simplest political instincts. But to the extent that this involves complicated tasks – the transformation of these "instincts" into the conscious striving for the political self-determination of the working class – we resort in the broadest way to abbreviated and simplified methods of "contriving" and "substitution."

In the internal politics of the party these methods lead, as we shall yet see, to this: the party organization is substituted for the party, the Central Committee is substituted for the party organization, and finally a "dictator" is substituted for the Central Committee. . . .

According to Lenin's new philosophy . . . it is enough for the proletarian to go through the "school of the factory" in order to give lessons in *political discipline* to the intelligentsia, which has meanwhile been playing the leading role in the party. According to this new philosophy, anyone who does not imagine the ideal party "as a vast factory," who thinks on the contrary that such a picture is "monstrous," anyone who does not believe in the unlimited power of a machine for political education, "immediately exhibits the psychology of the bourgeois intellectual." . . .

Without fear of exhibiting the "psychology of the bourgeois intellectual," we assert above all that the conditions which impel the proletariat to collectively agreed-upon methods of struggle lie not in the factory but in the general social conditions of the proletariat's existence. . . .

Of course, "production which is highly developed technologically" creates the material for the political development and political discipline of the proletariat, just as capitalism in general creates the *preconditions* of socialism. But just as it is unfounded to identify socialism with capitalism, so is it wrong to identify the *factory* discipline of the proletariat with *revolutionary-political* discipline.

The task of Social-Democracy consists of setting the proletariat against that discipline which replaces the work of human thought with the rhythm of physical movement, and against this dead, killing discipline to weld the proletariat into one militant army – all in step and shoulder to shoulder – united by a common political consciousness and revolutionary enthusiasm. *Such* discipline the Russian proletariat does not yet have; the factory and the machine do not provide it with this quality as spontaneously as they dispense occupational diseases.

The barrack regime cannot be the regime of our party, as the factory cannot be its model. . . .

The tasks of the new regime are so complicated that they cannot be solved in any way other than by competition between various methods of economic and political construction, by way of long "disputes," by way of systematic struggle – not only of the socialist world against the capitalist one, but also between various tendencies within socialism, tendencies which will inevitably appear as soon as the dictatorship of the proletariat throws up dozens, hundreds of new, hitherto unsolved problems. And no "strong, authoritative organization" can suppress these tendencies and disagreements in order to hasten and simplify the process, for it is all too clear that a proletariat capable of dictatorship over society will not tolerate dictatorship over itself.

ORGANIZATION OF THE BOLSHEVIK FACTION

In the months following the Second Congress of the Social-Democratic Party Lenin lost his slim majority and proceeded to organize an insurgent group in opposition to the dominant "Menshevik" leadership. A group of twenty-two Bolsheviks (counting Lenin himself) met in Geneva in August, 1904, to endorse the idea of the highly disciplined party and to urge the reorganization of the whole Social-Democratic movement on Leninist lines.

Recently a private meeting was held of twenty-two like-minded mem-

FROM: Resolution of the "Twenty-two Like-minded Members of the RSDWP Who Take the Point of View of the Majority at the Second Party Congress" (August, 1904; CPSU in Resolutions, I, pp. 60-63, 65; editor's translation).

bers of the RSDWP who take the point of view of the majority at the Second Party Congress; this conference considered the question of our party crisis and the means of emerging from it, and decided to turn to all Russian Social Democrats with the following proclamation:

Comrades! The severe crisis of party life is becoming more and more involved, and its end is not in sight. Confusion is growing, creating still newer conflicts, and the positive work of the party all along the line is strained by it to the utmost. The forces of the party, which is still young and not successfully stiffened, are fruitlessly wasted to a threatening extent.

Meanwhile, the historical moment presents to the party demands which are vaster than ever before. The revolutionary alertness of the working class is growing, the ferment is increasing, and in the other strata of society, war and crisis, hunger and unemployment are with elemental inevitability undermining the roots of the autocracy. The shameful end of a shameful war is already not far off: and it unavoidably multiplies revolutionary alertness ten-fold, unavoidably drives the working class face to face with its enemies and demands from Social Democracy colossal work, a terrific intensification of effort, in order to organize the final decisive struggle with the autocracy.

Can our party satisfy these demands in the condition in which it now finds itself? Any conscientious man must without hesitation answer no!

The unity of the party has been deeply undermined; the struggle inside has gone beyond the bounds of any party spirit. Organizational discipline has been shaken to its very foundation; the capacity of the party for harmonious unified action has turned into a dream.

Nevertheless, we consider this illness of the party to be an illness of growth. We see the basis of the crisis in the transition from the circle forms of the life of Social Democracy to party forms; the essence of the internal struggle is in the conflict between the circle spirit and party spirit. Therefore, only by putting an end to this illness can our party *really* become a party.

Under the name of the "minority" in the party [the Mensheviks], heterogeneous elements have gathered, which are linked by the conscious or unconscious effort to retain circle relationships, preparty forms of organization. . . . Their allies are all those elements which in theory or practice have fallen away from the principle of strict Social-Democratism, for only the circle spirit could preserve the individuality of ideas and the influence of these elements; while party spirit threatened to dissolve them or deprive them of any influence. . . . However, the chief cadres of the opposition consisted in general of all those elements in our party which by preference belong to the intelligentsia. In comparison with the proletariat, the intelligentsia is always more individualistic, due to the basic conditions of its life and work, which do not directly give it a broad unification of its forces or a direct education in organized joint labor. Therefore, it is more difficult for intellectual elements to adapt to the discipline of party life, and those of them who are not in a position to undertake this task naturally raise the banner of rebellion against the essential organizational limitations, and elevate their elemental anarchy into a principle of struggle, incorrectly designating this anarchy as the striving for "autonomy," as the demand for "tolerance," etc.

The portion of the party which is abroad, where the circles are distinguished by their relative longevity, where theoreticians of various shades form groupings, where the intelligentsia definitely predominates—this portion of the party had to be the most inclined to the point of view of the "minority." Therefore, it quickly became an actual majority there. On the other hand, Russia, where the voice of the organized proletarians is heard more loudly, where in more vital and closer intercourse with them, the party intelligentsia is educated in a more proletarian spirit, where the gravity of the immediate struggle more strongly compels people to feel the necessity of the organized unity of work—Russia has come out determinedly against the circle spirit, against anarchist disorganizing tendencies. She has definitely expressed this attitude toward them in a whole series of manifestations on the part of the committees and the other party organizations. . . .

The majority of the party, striving however it can to preserve its unity and organizational bond, has struggled only by loyal party means and has not once made concessions for the sake of conciliation. The minority, carrying on the anarchistic tendency, has not bothered about party peace and unity. It has made each concession an instrument of further struggle. Of all the demands of the minority only one has up to this time not been satisfied—the introduction of diversity into the Central Committee of the party by way of co-opting members of the minority who are forcibly bound to it—and the attacks by the minority have become more embittered than ever. Having taken control of the Central Organ and the Party Council, the minority now does not desist from exploiting in its circle interests that very discipline against which in essence it struggles. . . .

Coming forth with this program of struggle for the unity of the party, we invite the representatives of all other shadings and all party organizations to express themselves on the question of their programs, in order to make it possible to prepare for a congress, seriously and consistently, consciously and according to a plan. A question of life, a question of honor and worth is being decided for the party: does it exist as an ideological force and real force capable of rationally organizing itself enough to come forth as the actual leader of the revolutionary workers' movement of our country? In all its manner of action the minority abroad says no! And it continues to act surely and determinedly in this sense, relying on the remoteness of Russia, on the frequent replacement of party workers there, on the irreplaceability of its leaders, its literary figures. A party is being born to us, we say, seeing the growth of the political consciousness of the progressive workers, seeing the active initiative of the committees in the general life of the party. A party is being born to us, our young forces are multiplying, and they are able to replace and outlive the old literary collegia which are losing the confidence of the party; we are more and more getting to be revolutionaries who value the sustained direction of party life more than any circle of former leaders. A party is being born to us, and no tricks or delays will hold back its decisive and final judgment.

From these forces of our party we draw the assurance of victory. Comrades! Print and distribute this proclamation.

LENIN ON THE REVOLUTION OF 1905

During the revolutionary disturbances of 1905 in Russia, Lenin endeavored to justify a major role for the workers' party, despite the Marxist consensus that Russia was ready only for the "bourgeois-democratic" revolution. Lenin solved the problem by denying the revolutionary capabilities of the bourgeoisie and insisting that the workers' party, so-called, would have to push the "bourgeois" revolution through to the end. The party would gather the land-hungry peasants under its wing, establish the "revolutionary democratic dictatorship of the proletariat and peasantry," and hold power until the opportunity arrived to implement the program of socialism.

This type of reasoning has underlain Communist aspirations to power not only in Russia but in the underdeveloped East in general: they insist on a leading role for the "proletarian" party no matter what social conditions must be faced or what strange alliances must be made.

. . . It is entirely absurd to think that a bourgeois revolution does not express the interests of the proletariat at all. This absurd idea boils down either to the hoary Narodnik [Populist] theory that a bourgeois revolution runs counter to the interests of the proletariat, and that therefore we do not need bourgeois political liberty; or to anarchism, which rejects all partici-

FROM: Lenin, "Two Tactics of Social Democracy in the Democratic Revolution" (July, 1905; *Selected Works*, Vol. I, book 2, pp. 48-51, 86-90, 104-5, 107, 142).

pation of the proletariat in bourgeois politics, in a bourgeois revolution and in bourgeois parliamentarism. From the standpoint of theory, this idea disregards the elementary propositions of Marxism concerning the inevitability of capitalist development where commodity production exists. Marxism teaches that a society which is based on commodity production, and which has commercial intercourse with civilized capitalist nations, at a certain stage of its development, itself inevitably takes the road of capitalism. Marxism has irrevocably broken with the ravings of the Narodniks and the anarchists to the effect that Russia, for instance, can avoid capitalist development, jump out of capitalism, or skip over it and proceed along some path other than the path of the class struggle on the basis and within the framework of this same capitalism.

All these principles of Marxism have been proved and explained over and over again in minute detail in general and with regard to Russia in particular. And from these principles it follows that the idea of seeking salvation for the working class in anything save the further development of capitalism is *reactionary*. In countries like Russia, the working class suffers not so much from capitalism as from the insufficient development of capitalism. The working class is therefore *decidedly interested* in the broadest, freest and most rapid development of capitalism. The removal of all the remnants of the old order which are hampering the broad, free and rapid development of capitalism is of decided *advantage* to the working class. The bourgeois revolution is precisely a revolution that most resolutely sweeps away the survivals of the past, the remnants of serfdom (which include not only autocracy but monarchy as well) and most fully guarantees the broadest, freest and most rapid development of capitalism.

That is why a *bourgeois* revolution is *in the highest degree advantageous to the proletariat*. A bourgeois revolution is *absolutely* necessary in the interests of the proletariat. The more complete and determined, the more consistent the bourgeois revolution, the more assured will be the proletarian struggle against the bourgeoisie for Socialism. Only those who are ignorant of the rudiments of scientific Socialism can regard this conclusion as new or strange, paradoxical. . . .

On the other hand, it is more advantageous for the working class if the necessary changes in the direction of bourgeois democracy take place by way of revolution and not by way of reform; for the way of reform is the way of delay, of procrastination, of the painfully slow decomposition of the putrid parts of the national organism. It is the proletariat and the peasantry that suffer first of all and most of all from their putrefaction. The revolutionary way is the way of quick amputation, which is the least painful to the proletariat, the way of the direct removal of the decomposing parts, the way of fewest concessions to and least consideration for the monarchy and the disgusting, vile, rotten and contaminating institutions which go with it. . . .

Marxism teaches the proletarian not to keep aloof from the bourgeois revolution, not to be indifferent to it, not to allow the leadership of the revolution to be assumed by the bourgeoisie but, on the contrary, to take a most energetic part in it, to fight most resolutely for consistent proletarian democracy, for carrying the revolution to its conclusion. We cannot jump out of the bourgeois-democratic boundaries of the Russian revolution, but we can vastly extend these boundaries, and within these boundaries we can and must fight for the interests of the proletariat, for its immediate needs and for the conditions that will make it possible to prepare its forces for the future complete victory. . . .

The basic idea here is the one that the *Vperiod** has repeatedly formulated, stating that we must not be afraid of a complete victory for Social-Democracy in a democratic revolution, i.e., of a revolutionary-democratic dictatorship of the proletariat and the peasantry, for such a victory will enable us to rouse Europe, and the socialist proletariat of Europe, after throwing off the yoke of the bourgeoisie, will in its turn help us to accomplish the socialist revolution. . . .

The *Vperiod* quite definitely stated wherein lies the real "possibility of holding power" – namely, in the revolutionary-democratic dictatorship of the proletariat and the peasantry, in their joint mass strength, which is capable of outweighing all the forces of counterrevolution, in the inevitable concurrence of their interests in *democratic* changes. . . . If in our fight for a republic and democracy we could not rely upon the peasantry as well as on the proletariat, the prospect of our "holding power" would be hopeless. But if it is not hopeless, if a "decisive victory of the revolution over tsarism" opens up such a possibility, then we must point to it, we must actively call for its transformation into reality and issue practical slogans not only *for the contingency* of the revolution being carried into Europe, but also *for the purpose* of carrying it there. . . . Beyond the bounds of democracy there can be no question of the proletariat and the peasant bourgeoisie having a single will. Class struggle between them is inevitable; but it is in a democratic republic that this struggle will be the most thorough-going and widespread struggle of the people *for Socialism*. Like everything else in the world, the revolutionary-democratic dictatorship of the proletariat and the peasantry has a past and a future. Its past is autocracy, serfdom, monarchy and privilege. In the struggle against this past, in the struggle against coun-

*"Forward": Lenin's paper, 1904-5 – Ed.

terrevolution, a "single will" of the proletariat and the peasantry is possible, for here there is unity of interests.

Its future is the struggle against private property, the struggle of the wage worker against the employer, the struggle for Socialism. Here singleness of will is impossible. Here our path lies not from autocracy to a republic but from a petty-bourgeois democratic republic to Socialism. . . .

A Social-Democrat must never for a moment forget that the proletariat will inevitably have to wage the class struggle for Socialism even against the most democratic and republican bourgeoisie and petty bourgeoisie. This is beyond doubt. Hence the absolute necessity of a separate, independent, strictly class party of Social-Democracy. Hence the temporary nature of our tactics of "striking jointly" with the bourgeoisie and the duty of keeping a strict watch "over our ally, as over an enemy," etc. All this is also beyond the slightest doubt. But it would be ridiculous and reactionary to deduce from this that we must forget, ignore or neglect these tasks which, although transient and temporary, are vital at the present time. The fight against the autocracy is a temporary and transient task of the Socialists, but to ignore or neglect this task in any way would be tantamount to betraying Socialism and rendering a service to reaction. The revolutionary-democratic dictatorship of the proletariat and the peasantry is unquestionably only a transient, temporary aim of the Socialists, but to ignore this aim in the period of a democratic revolution would be downright reactionary. . . .

. . . We Marxists all know . . . that the bourgeoisie is inconsistent, self-seeking and cowardly in its support of the revolution. The bourgeoisie, in the mass, will inevitably turn towards counterrevolution, towards the autocracy, against the revolution and against the people, immediately its narrow, selfish interests are met, immediately it "recoils" from consistent democracy (*and it is already recoiling from it!*). There remains the "people," that is, the proletariat and the peasantry: the proletariat alone can be relied on to march to the end, for it is going far beyond the democratic revolution. That is why the proletariat fights in the front ranks for a republic and contemptuously rejects silly and unworthy advice to take care not to frighten away the bourgeoisie. The peasantry includes a great number of semiproletarian as well as petty-bourgeois elements. This causes it also to be unstable and compels the proletariat to unite in a strictly class party. But the instability of the peasantry differs radically from the instability of the bourgeoisie, for at the present time the peasantry is interested not so much in the absolute preservation of private property as in the confiscation of the landed estates, one of the principal forms of private property. While this does not make the peasantry become socialist or cease to be petty-bourgeois, it is capable of becoming a wholehearted and most radical adherent of the democratic revolution . . . .

. . . The Russian revolution will begin to assume its real sweep, will really assume the widest revolutionary sweep possible in the epoch of bourgeois-democratic revolution, only when the bourgeoisie recoils from it and when the masses of the peasantry come out as active revolutionaries side by side with the proletariat. In order that it may be consistently carried to its conclusion, our democratic revolution must rely on such forces as are capable of paralyzing the inevitable inconsistency of the bourgeoisie (i.e., capable precisely of "causing it to recoil from the revolution," which the Caucasian adherents of *Iskra* fear so much because of their lack of judgment).

The proletariat must carry to completion the democratic revolution, by allying to itself the mass of the peasantry in order to crush by force the resistance of the autocracy and to paralyze the instability of the bourgeoisie. The proletariat must accomplish the socialist revolution, by allying to itself the mass of the semiproletarian elements of the population in order to crush by force the resistance of the bourgeoisie and to paralyze the instability of the peasantry and the petty bourgeoisie. . . .

Major questions in the life of nations are settled only by force. The reactionary classes themselves are usually the first to resort to violence, to civil war; they are the first to "place the bayonet on the agenda," as the Russian autocracy has been doing systematically and undeviatingly everywhere ever since January 9.* And since such a situation has arisen, since the bayonet has really become the main point on the political agenda, since insurrection has proved to be imperative and urgent – constitutional illusions and school exercises in parliamentarism become only a screen for the bourgeois betrayal of the revolution, a screen to conceal the fact that the bourgeoisie is "recoiling" from the revolution. It is therefore the slogan of dictatorship that the genuinely revolutionary class must advance. . . .

TROTSKY ON "PERMANENT REVOLUTION"

Trotsky's response to the revolution of 1905 and the problem of the workers' role in Russia was to predict a new upheaval in which the proletariat would temporarily find itself in power. It would depend on world revolution to sustain them, however, and rescue the Russian socialists from the backwardness of their country. Herein lay Trotsky's notion of continuous or "permanent" revolution, which

---

*January 9, 1905: "Bloody Sunday," when troops fired on demonstrators in St. Petersburg – Ed.

reconciled the predominantly backward character of Russia with the Marxists' desire to justify a revolutionary role for themselves.

... The Russian working class of 1906 differs entirely from the Vienna working class of 1848. The best proof of it is the all-Russian practice of the Councils of Workmen's Deputies (Soviets). Those are no organizations of conspirators prepared beforehand to step forward in times of unrest and to seize command over the working class. They are organs consciously created by the masses themselves to coordinate their revolutionary struggle. The Soviets, elected by and responsible to the masses, are thoroughly democratic institutions following the most determined class policy in the spirit of revolutionary Socialism. ...

Within the limits of a revolution at the beginning of the twentieth century, which is also a bourgeois revolution in its immediate objective aims, there looms up a prospect of an inevitable, or at least possible, supremacy of the working class in the near future. ...

To imagine a revolutionary democratic government without representatives of labor is to see the absurdity of such a situation. A refusal of labor to participate in a revolutionary government would make the very existence of that government impossible, and would be tantamount to a betrayal of the cause of the revolution. A participation of labor in a revolutionary government, however, is admissible, both from the viewpoint of objective probability and subjective desirability, *only in the role of a leading dominant power.* Of course, you can call such a government "dictatorship of the proletariat and peasantry," "dictatorship of the proletariat, the peasantry, and the intelligentsia," or "a revolutionary government of the workingmen and the lower middle class." This question will still remain: Who has the hegemony in the government and through it in the country? *When we speak of a labor government we mean that the hegemony belongs to the working class.* ...

Our attitude towards the idea of a "dictatorship of the proletariat and the peasantry" is now quite clear. It is not a question whether we think it "admissible" or not, whether we "wish" or we "do not wish" this form of political cooperation. In our opinion, it simply cannot be realized, at least in its direct meaning. Such a cooperation presupposes that either the peasantry has identified itself with one of the existing bourgeois parties, or it has formed a powerful party of its own. Neither is possible, as we have tried to point out. ...

FROM: Trotsky, *Results and Prospects* (1906; translated as *Our Revolution* by M. J. Olgin, New York, Holt, 1918, pp. 80, 92, 95-96, 100-03, 109-10, 132, 136-37, 142-44; reprinted by permission of the publisher).

The proletariat can get into power only at a moment of national upheaval, of sweeping national enthusiasm. The proletariat assumes power as a revolutionary representative of the people, as a recognized leader in the fight against absolutism and barbaric feudalism. Having assumed power, however, the proletariat will open a new era, an era of positive legislation, of revolutionary politics, and this is the point where its political supremacy as an avowed spokesman of the nation may become endangered.

The first measures of the proletariat—the cleansing of the Augean stables of the old regime and the driving away of their inhabitants—will find active support of the entire nation whatever the liberal castraters may tell us of the power of some prejudices among the masses. The work of political cleansing will be accompanied by democratic reorganization of all social and political relations. The labor government, impelled by immediate needs and requirements, will have to look into all kinds of relations and activities among the people. It will have to throw out of the army and the administration all those who had stained their hands with the blood of the people; it will have to disband all the regiments that had polluted themselves with crimes against the people. This work will have to be done immediately, long before the establishment of an elective responsible administration and before the organization of a popular militia. This, however, will be only a beginning. Labor democracy will soon be confronted by the problems of a normal workday, the agrarian relations and unemployment. The legislative solution of those problems will show the *class character* of the labor government. It will tend to weaken the revolutionary bond between the proletariat and the nation; it will give the economic differentiation among the peasants a political expression. Antagonism between the component parts of the nation will grow step by step as the policies of the labor government become more outspoken, lose their general democratic character and become *class policies*. . . .

Social-Democracy can never assume power under a double obligation: to put the *entire* minimum program into operation for the sake of the proletariat, and to keep strictly *within the limits* of this program, for the sake of the bourgeoisie. Such a double obligation could never be fulfilled. Participating in the government, not as powerless hostages, but as a leading force, the representatives of labor *eo ipso* break the line between the minimum and maximum program. *Collectivism becomes the order of the day*. At which point the proletariat will be stopped on its march in this direction, depends upon the constellation of forces, not upon the original purpose of the proletarian party. . . .

Political supremacy of the proletariat is incompatible with its economic slavery. Whatever may be the banner under which the proletariat will find itself in possession of power, it will be compelled to enter the road of Socialism. It is the greatest Utopia to think that the proletariat, brought to the top by the mechanics of a bourgeois revolution, would be able, even if it wanted, to limit its mission by creating a republican democratic environment for the social supremacy of the bourgeoisie. Political dominance of the proletariat, even it if were temporary, would extremely weaken the resistance of capital which is always in need of state aid, and would give momentous opportunities to the economic struggle of the proletariat. . . .

How far, however, can the Socialist policy of the working class advance in the economic environment of Russia? One thing we can say with perfect assurance: it will meet political obstacles long before it will be checked by the technical backwardness of the country. *Without direct political aid from the European proletariat the working class of Russia will not be able to retain its power and to turn its temporary supremacy into a permanent Socialist dictatorship*. We cannot doubt this for a moment. On the other hand, there is no doubt that a *Socialist revolution in the West would allow us to turn the temporary supremacy of the working class directly into a Socialist dictatorship*. . . .

The influence of the Russian revolution on the proletariat of Europe is immense. Not only does it destroy the Petersburg absolutism, that main power of European reaction; it also imbues the minds and the souls of the European proletariat with revolutionary daring. . . .

. . . The colossal influence of the Russian revolution manifests itself in killing party routine, in destroying Socialist conservatism, in making a clean contest of proletarian forces against capitalist reaction a question of the day. . . .

The Russian proletariat in power, even if this were only the result of a passing combination of forces in the Russian bourgeois revolution, would meet organized opposition on the part of the world's reaction, and readiness for organized support on the part of the world's proletariat. Left to its own resources, the Russian working class must necessarily be crushed the moment it loses the aid of the peasants. Nothing remains for it but to link the fate of its political supremacy and the fate of the Russian revolution with the fate of a Socialist revolution in Europe. All that momentous authority and political power which is given to the proletariat by a combination of forces in the Russian bourgeois revolution, it will thrust on the scale of class struggle in the entire capitalistic world. Equipped with governmental power, having a counter-revolution behind his back, having the European reaction in front of him, the Russian workingman will issue to all his brothers the world over his old battle-cry which will now become the call for the last attack: *Proletarians of all the world, unite!*

LENIN ON DEMOCRATIC CENTRALISM

Following the revolution of 1905 repeated attempts were made by the Bolsheviks and Mensheviks to restore the unity of the Social-Democratic Party. Lenin was criticized for indiscipline, and replied with a defense of the rights of minorities within the system of "democratic centralism." This formula became the official doctrine of the Communist organization, though freedom of factions disappeared very quickly.

The authors of the resolution are completely wrong in their understanding of the relation between *free criticism* within the party and the party's *unity of action*. Criticism within the limits of the *foundations* of the party program must be completely free . . . not only at party meetings, but also at broader ones. To suppress such criticism or such "agitation" (for criticism cannot be separated from agitation) is impossible. The political action of the party must be united. No "appeals" are permissible which violate the unity of actions which have already been decided upon, neither at open meetings, nor at party meetings, nor in the party press.

Obviously the Central Committee has defined the freedom of criticism inaccurately and too narrowly, and the unity of action – inaccurately and too broadly. . . .

The Central Committee's resolution is incorrect in substance and *contradicts the statutes of the party*. The principle of democratic centralism and autonomy of local institutions means specifically freedom of criticism, complete and everywhere, as long as this does not disrupt the unity of action already decided upon – and the intolerability of any criticism undermining or obstructing the unity of action decided on by the party.

We consider it a great mistake on the part of the Central Committee to issue a resolution on this important question without any preliminary consideration of it by the party press and the party organizations; such consideration would have helped it avoid the mistakes indicated by us. . . .

BOGDANOV'S PHILOSOPHICAL REVISION OF MARXISM

Lenin's outstanding lieutenant in the early years of the Bolshevik faction was Alexander A. Bogdanov – physician, economist, philosopher, sociologist, and exponent of romantic revolutionary extremism. After 1905, Bogdanov became the leader of the left-wing purists among the Bolsheviks who refused to make use of the Duma, the parliamentary body of limited power established in

FROM: Lenin, "Freedom of Criticism and Unity of Action" (June, 1906; *Sochineniya* [Works], 2nd ed., Moscow, Marx-Engels-Lenin Institute, 1928, IX: 274-75; editor's translation).

1906. At the same time he attempted an original philosophical extension of Marxism by applying the philosophy of "empirio-criticism" of the Austrian physicist Ernst Mach and the German philosopher Richard Avenarius. This was of immediate significance because it provoked Lenin's ire and a drastic shake-up in the Bolshevik ranks to enforce Lenin's standards of ideological discipline. It also had implications much later, during the second decade of the Soviet regime, because of its suggestion that truth is conditioned by classes and the class struggle.

. . . The task of cognition, according to the views of Mach and Avenarius, consists of systematizing the content of experience, since experience is both the natural basis and the natural boundary of cognition. In its own objective significance this systematization is a powerful living adaptation, an instrument for preserving life and its development. . . .

But cognition in this picture is not merely adaptation in general; it is also *social* adaptation. The social genesis of cognition, its dependence on social experience, the principled difference of value in the thinking of different people, and its constant social interaction, clearly emerge and are consciously underscored by both thinkers. . . .

Where Mach sketches out the connection of cognition with the social process of labor, the correspondence of his views with the ideas of Marx occasionally becomes quite astonishing. . . .

We arrive at this conclusion: the characteristics of "objectivity" in general cannot have as their basis individual experience. . . . The basis of "objectivity" must lie in the sphere of *collective* experience. . . .

The agreement in collective experience which is expressed in this "objectivity" can only appear as the result of the progressive concordance of the experience of different people as they express themselves to each other. The objectivity of the physical bodies which we encounter in our experience is established in the last analysis on the basis of mutual verification and the concordance in what different people express. In general the physical world is this: socially agreed-upon, socially harmonized, in a word, *socially organized* experience. . . .

Laws do not belong at all to the sphere of immediate experience; laws are the result of conscious reworking of experience; they are not facts in themselves, but are created by thought, as a means of organizing experience, of harmoniously bringing it into agreement as an ordered unity. Laws

FROM: Bogdanov, *Empiriomonism* (St. Petersburg, Dorovatovsky and Charushnikov, Book I, 2nd ed., 1905, pp. 9, 10, 25, 36, 40-41, and Book III, 1906, pp. iv-v, ix, xxiii-xxv, xxxiii, 83-84, 139-42, 149-50, 152, 159; editor's translation).

are *abstract cognition*, and physical laws possess physical qualities just as little as psychological laws possess psychic qualities. . . . The antithesis between the physical and psychic aspects of experience reduces to the distinction between socially organized and individually organized experience. . . .

. . . The social materialism of Marx presented demands to my world view which the old materialism could not satisfy. . . . It was necesary *to know one's knowledge,* to explain one's world view, and according to the idea of Marxism this could and had to be done on the basis of research on its social genesis. It was obvious that the basic concepts of the old materialism – both "matter" and "immutable laws" – were worked out in the course of the *social* development of mankind, and inasmuch as they were "ideological forms," it was necessary to find their "material base." But since the "material base" has the property of changing as society develops, it becomes clear that any given ideological form can have only a historically transitory meaning, not an objectively supra-historical meaning, that it can be a "truth of the time" (*"objective"* truth, but only within the limits of a given epoch) – but in no case can it be a "truth for all time" ("objective" in the absolute meaning of the word). . . . For me Marxism includes the denial of the unconditional objectivity of any truth whatsoever, the denial of every eternal truth. . . .

Truth is an ideological form – the organizing form of human experience; and if we know this without doubt, and know that the material basis of ideology changes, that the content of experience expands – do we have any right whatsoever to assert that this given ideological form will never be transformed by the development of its social basis, that this given form of experience will not be burst apart by its growing contents? Consistent Marxism does not allow such dogmatic and static notions. . . .

Marxist philosophy must above all be one of natural science. Of course, natural science is the *ideology of the productive forces of society,* because it serves as the basis for technical experience and the technical sciences; in concordance with the basic idea of historical materialism, the productive forces of society represent the base of its development in general. But it is also clear that Marxist philosophy must reflect the *social form* of the productive forces, relying obviously on the "social" sciences proper. . . .

Ideological forms are the *organizational adaptation of social life,* and in the last analysis (directly or indirectly), of the *technical process.* Therefore the development of ideology is determined by *necessities* in the organizational adaptations of the social process and by the *material present* for them. The viability of ideological forms depends, consequently, on the harmony and order with which they really organize the social content of labor. . . .

The world of experience has been crystallized and continues to be crystallized out of chaos. The force which determines the forms of this crystallization is the intercourse of people. Outside of these forms there is really no *experience*, because a disorganized mass of occurrences is not experience. Thus, experience is social in its very basis, and its progress is the *social-psychological process of organizing it*. The individual psychical organizing process is completely adapted to this. If, for the empiriocriticist, the experience of all humans is of equal value, which I have earlier designated as the familiar cognitive "democracy," then for the empiriomonist this experience is rather the result of the collective organizing work of all people—a sort of cognitive "socialism." . . .

Summarizing the connection and dependence between "ideology" and "technology" in the process of social development, we arrive at the following formulations:

1. The technical process is the area of the direct struggle of society with nature; ideology is the area of the organizing forms of social life. In the last analysis the technical process represents just that content which is organized by the ideological forms.

2. Corresponding to this relationship, the technical process represents the basic and ideology the derivative area of social life and social development. From the standpoint of energetics, ideology is conditioned by the technical process in the sense that it arises and develops according to that preponderance of assimilation over disassimilation which is characteristic of it. On the qualitative side the material of ideological forms also has its beginning in the technical area.

3. The development of technical forms is accomplished under the direct action of both "extra-social" selection (influences on the part of external nature) and social selection. The development of ideology is directly subordinated to social selection alone.

4. The point of departure of any social development lies in the technical process. The basic line of development goes from the technical forms through the lower organizing forms of ideology to the higher. Corresponding to this, there proceeds in the same direction an increase in the conservatism of social forms.

5. The derivative line of social development, directed from the higher organizing forms toward the lower and from ideology toward technology, is always just the continuation and reflection of the basic line. Not only does it never change the relatively greater magnitude of the conservatism of

the higher forms of ideology; it actually rests on this conservatism as its necessary condition.

6. Thus the dynamic conditions of social development and degradation, the motive forces of these processes, lie in the technical process; in ideology lie the static conditions, the limiting, regulating, and form-giving forces. . . .

We summarize the main conclusions concerning the group and class differentiation of society:

1. Both group and class divisions in society are the result of the quantitative and qualitative progress of technology. "Social groups" arise on the basis of specialization; classes, on the basis of the progressive isolation of the organizer and executive functions in society. Group and class dissociation essentially amounts to vitally important distinctions in the direction of social selection.

2. Social groups and classes acquire the definite and firm qualities of social complexes when they are provided with definitely distinct ideologies, which condition the firmly distinct direction of social selection within these collectivities. . . .

5. The ideology worked out by the organizer part of society retains full vital significance for both parts of society as long as the content which it organizes remains really common to them. When this condition is violated . . . the ideological dissociation of classes begins; the ideology of the upper class comes into contradiction with the actual experience and urges of the lower, and this contradiction is then further intensified.

6. The organizer function of the "upper" class allows it to organize the life of the "lower" class by means of norms which do not correspond with the conditions of life of the latter. For the class subordinated to them, such norms acquire the significance of external forces, like the forces of extra-social nature—hostile forces to which one has to adapt. Such a primary and basic class contradiction is the starting point for the development of any class struggle. . . .

8. . . . The organizer class, progressively removing itself from the technical-production process, in the course of time loses its real organizer function, changes into a parasite class, inevitably degenerates, and at the same time loses its social strength. . . .

10. The capitalistic type of class development . . . leads to the progressive transformation of the mass of individual working operatives into a solid collectivity, adapted to the organizer role on a scale which expands without limit. The rapid technical progress which is characteristic of this type of development stimulates the rapid development of opposed class

ideologies and the class struggle. This culminates in the downfall of the former organizer class and society's transition from class development through contradictions, to integral-harmonious development. Extrasocial and social spontaneity are both overcome by the planfully organized force of humanity, and its power over nature grows without limit. . . .

In a class society any world view is either the ideology of one definite class or a definite combination of different class ideologies. Even the most individual of them can only be a particular combination of elements of collective, class thinking. For the individual is created and defined by the social milieu—in a class society, by the class milieu.

Such being the case, the ideology of the technical process is inevitably the ideology of the class which stands in the closest relationship to the technical process, i.e., the class of "producers" in the *broad* sense of the word . . . . In the social-labor experience of the worker in machine production there exists material with basic vital significance both for the recognition in principle of the homogeneity of the "psychic" and the "physical," and for the tendency cognitively to subordinate the "psychic" to the collectively elaborated forms of the cognition of the "physical." The philosophy which organizes this material into pure finished forms and makes these forms general must be regarded as the ideology of a given class—of course, just to the extent that it really accomplishes this and does not add alien tendencies which contradict the tendencies of the proletariat. . . .

We have arrived at this characterization of the philosophical world view we are considering: the cognitive ideology of the technical process, proletarian in its tendencies, which in its general scheme reproduces the basic features of the structure of contemporary society. . . .

LENIN'S PHILOSOPHICAL ORTHODOXY

Lenin wrote his main philosophical work, *Materialism and Empiriocriticism*, as a polemical reply to Bogdanov. Here Lenin revealed his intolerance of any critical attitude toward what he regarded as the absolute truth laid down by Marx and Engels. His dogmatic assertion of an oversimplified nineteenth-century materialism remains the official philosophy for the entire Communist movement.

A number of writers, would-be Marxists, have this year undertaken a veritable campaign against the philosophy of Marxism. . . .

FROM: Lenin, *Materialism and Empirio-Criticism—Critical Comments on a Reactionary Philosophy* (1908; English translation, New York, International Publishers, 1927, pp. 9-10, 38, 121, 127-29, 335-38, 370-71; reprinted by permission of the publisher).

All these people could not have been ignorant of the fact that Marx and Engels scores of times termed their philosophical views dialectical materialism. Yet all these people, who, despite the sharp divergence of their political views, are united in their hositility toward dialectical materialism, at the same time claim to be Marxists in philosophy! Engels' dialectics is "mysticism," says Berman. Engels' views have become "antiquated," remarks Bazarov casually, as though it were a self-evident fact. Materialism thus appears to be refuted by our bold warriors, who proudly allude to the "modern theory of knowledge," "recent philosophy" (or "recent positivism"), the "philosophy of modern natural science," or even the "philosophy of natural science of the twentieth century." Supported by all these supposedly recent doctrines, our destroyers of dialectical materialism proceed fearlessly to downright fideism (in the case of Lunacharsky it is most evident, but by no means in his case alone!). Yet when it comes to an explicit definition of their attitude towards Marx and Engels, all their courage and all their respect for their own convictions at once disappear. In deed – a complete renunciation of dialectical materialism, i.e., of Marxism; in word – endless subterfuges, attempts to evade the essence of the question, to cover their retreat, to put some materialist or other in place of materialism in general, and a determined refusal to make a direct analysis of the innumerable materialist declarations of Marx and Engels. . . .

Materialism, in full agreement with natural science, takes matter as primary and regards consciousness, thought and sensation as secondary, because in its well-defined form sensation is associated only with the higher forms of matter (organic matter), while "in the foundation of the structure of matter" one can only surmise the existence of a faculty akin to sensation. Such, for example, is the supposition of the well-known German scientist Ernst Haeckel, the English biologist Lloyd Morgan and others . . . . Machism holds to the opposite, the idealist point of view, and at once lands into an absurdity: since, in the first place, sensation is taken as primary, in spite of the fact that it is associated only with definite processes in matter organised in a definite way; and, since, in the second place, the basic premise that bodies are complexes of sensations is violated by the assumption of the existence of other living beings in general, of other "complexes" beside the given great I. . . .

Bogdanov's denial of objective truth is agnosticism and subjectivism . . . . Natural science leaves no room for doubt that its assertion that the earth existed prior to man is a truth. This is entirely compatible with the materialist theory of knowledge: the existence of the thing reflected independent of the reflector (the independence of the external world from the mind) is a fundamental tenet of materialism. The assertion made by science that the earth existed prior to man is an objective truth. This proposition of natural science is incompatible with the philosophy of the Machians and with their doctrine of truth: if truth is an organising form of human experience, then the assertion of the earth's existence *outside* human experience cannot be true. . . .

. . . The Machians are subjectivists and agnostics, for they *do not sufficiently* trust the evidence of our sense-organs and are inconsistent in their sensationalism. They do not recognise objective reality, independent of man, as the source of our sensations. They do not regard sensations as the true copy of this objective reality, thereby directly conflicting with natural science and throwing the door open for fideism. On the contrary, for the materialist the world is richer, livelier, more varied than it actually seems, for with each step in the development of science new aspects are discovered. For the materialist, sensations are images of the ultimate and sole objective reality, ultimate not in the sense that it has already been explored to the end, but in the sense that there is not and cannot be any other. This view irrevocably closes the door not only to every species of fideism, but also to that professorial scholasticism which, while not regarding objective reality as the source of our sensations, "deduces" the concept of the objective by means of such artificial verbal constructions as universal significance, socially-organised, and so on and so forth, and which is unable, and frequently unwilling, to separate objective truth from belief in sprites and hobgoblins. . . .

Matter is a philosophical category designating the objective reality which is given to man by his sensations, and which is copied, photographed and reflected by our sensations, while existing independently of them. Therefore, to say that such a concept can become "antiquated" is *childish talk*, a senseless repetition of the arguments of fashionable *reactionary* philosophy. . . .

Bogdanov's attempt imperceptibly to correct and develop Marx in the "spirit of his principles" is an obvious distortion of these materialist principles in the spirit of *idealism*. It would be ludicrous to deny it. . . . The immanentists, the empirio-criticists and the empiriomonists all argue over particulars, over details, over the formulation of *idealism*, whereas we *from the very outset* reject all the principles of their philosophy common to this trinity. Let Bogdanov, accepting in the best sense and with the best of intentions *all the conclusions* of Marx, preach the "identity" of social being and social consciousness; we shall say: Bogdanov *minus* "empirio-monism" (or rather, *minus* Machism) is a Marxist. For this theory of the identity of social being and social consciousness is *sheer nonsense* and an *absolutely reactionary* theory. If certain people reconcile it with Marxism, with Marxist behavior, we must admit that these people are better than their theory, but we cannot justify outrageous theoretical distortions of Marxism. . . .

Materialism in general recognises objectively real being (matter) as independent of the consciousness, sensation, experience, etc., of humanity. Historical materialism recognises social being as independent of the social consciousness of humanity. In both cases consciousness is only the reflection of being, at best an approximately true (adequate, perfectly exact) reflection of it. From this Marxian philosophy, which is cast from a single piece of steel, you cannot eliminate one basic premise, one essential part, without departing from objective truth, without falling a prey to a bourgeois-reactionary falsehood. . . .

First and foremost, the theoretical foundations of this philosophy [empirio-criticism] must be compared with those of dialectical materialism. Such a comparison . . . reveals, *along the whole line* of epistemological problems, the *thoroughly reactionary* character of empirio-criticism, which uses new artifices, terms and subtleties to disguise the old errors of *idealism and agnosticism*. Only utter ignorance of the nature of philosophical materialism generally and of the nature of Marx's and Engels' dialectical method can lead one to speak of a "union" of empirio-criticism and Marxism.

Secondly, the place of empirio-criticism, as one very small school of specialists in philosophy, in relation to the other modern schools of philosophy, must be determined. Both Mach and Avenarius started with Kant and, leaving him, proceeded not towards materialism, but in the opposite direction, towards Hume and Berkeley. Imagining that he was "purifying experience" generally, Avenarius was in fact only purifying agnosticism of Kantianism. The whole school of Mach and Avenarius is more and more definitely moving towards idealism, hand in hand with one of the most reactionary of the idealist schools, viz., the so-called immanentists.

Thirdly, the indubitable connection between Machism and one school in one branch of modern science must be borne in mind. The vast majority of scientists, both generally and in this special branch of science in question, viz., physics, are invariably on the side of materialism. A minority of new theories brought about by the great discoveries of recent years, influenced by the crisis in the new physics, which has very clearly revealed the relativity of our knowledge, have, owing to their ignorance of dialectics, slipped into idealism by way of relativism. The physical idealism in vogue today is as reactionary and transitory an infatuation as the fashionably physiological idealism of the recent past.

Fourthly, behind the epistemological scholasticism of empirio-criticism it is impossible not to see the struggle of parties in philosophy, a struggle

which in the last analysis reflects the tendencies and ideology of the antagonistic classes in modern society. Recent philosophy is as partisan as was
philosophy two thousand years ago. The contending parties are essentially,
although it is concealed by a pseudo-erudite quackery of new terms or by a
feeble-minded non-partisanship, materialism and idealism. The latter is
merely a subtle, refined form of fideism, which stands fully armed, commands vast organisations and steadily continues to exercise influence on
the masses, turning the slightest vacillation in philosophical thought to its
own advantage. The objective, class role played by empirio-criticism
entirely consists in rendering faithful service to the fideists in their struggle
against materialism in general and historical materialism in
particular . . . .

THE 1909 PURGE OF THE BOLSHEVIK LEFT WING

The differences between Lenin and the Bogdanov group of revolutionary romantics came to a head in 1909. Lenin condemned the
latter—the "otzovists" [Russian for "recallists"] who wanted to
recall the Bolshevik deputies in the Duma, and the "ultimatists"
who demanded that the deputies take a more radical stand—both
for their philosophical vagaries which he rejected as "idealism,"
and for the utopian purism of their refusal to take tactical advantage of the Duma. The real issue was Lenin's control of the faction
and the enforcement of his brand of Marxist orthodoxy. Lenin
demonstrated his grip on the Bolshevik faction at a meeting in Paris
of the editors of the Bolsheviks' factional paper, which had become
the headquarters of the faction. Bogdanov and his followers were
expelled from the Bolshevik faction, though they remained within
the Social-Democratic fold.

a) COMMUNIQUÉ ON THE CONFERENCE

. . . The Conference declared in its resolutions that in the Bolshevik faction a tendency has been observed which in its definite tactical phys-
iognomy contradicts Bolshevism. Bolshevism is represented for us by the
Bolshevik *faction* of the party. A faction is not a party. A party can include a
whole scale of shadings, in which the extremes may even sharply contradict each other. In the German party, together with the clearly revolution-

FROM: The Conference of the Expanded Editorial Board of *The Proletarian*, Paris, June
21-30, 1909 (CPSU in Resolutions, I, 214-15, 220-21; editor's translation).

ary wing of Kautsky,* we see the arch-revisionist wing of Bernstein. This is not a faction. Within a party a faction is a group of *like-minded people* formed above all for the purpose of influencing the party in a definite direction, for the purpose of introducing its principles in as clear a form as possible into the party. For this real *unity of thought* is essential. . . .

b) RESOLUTION ON OTZOVISM AND ULTIMATISM

. . . In the course of the bourgeois-democratic revolution our party has been joined by a series of elements which were not purely attracted by its proletarian program, but which preferred its clear and energetic struggle for democracy and which adopted the revolutionary-democratic slogans of the proletarian party apart from its connection with the objective of the struggle of the socialist proletariat.

Such elements, insufficiently permeated with the proletarian point of view, appeared even in the ranks of our Bolshevik faction. Hard times cause these elements to reveal more and more their inadequate Social-Democratic endurance, and coming into sharper and sharper contradiction with the foundations of revolutionary Social-Democratic tactics, they have created in the past year a tendency to try to form a theory of otzovism and ultimatism, which actually has led in principle only to an increasingly false picture of Social-Democratic parliamentarianism and Social-Democratic work in the Duma.

These attempts to create from the otzovist inclination a whole system of otzovist policy lead to a theory which essentially reflects the ideology of political indifferentism on the one hand and anarchistic roaming on the other. With all its revolutionary phraseology the theory of otzovism and ultimatism is in fact to a significant degree the reverse side of constitutional illusions which are connected with hopes that the State Duma itself can satisfy this or that substantial demand of the people, and in essence this replaces the proletarian ideology with petty-bourgeois tendencies. . . .

By their attempts to convert individual applications of the boycott of representative institutions at this or that moment of the revolution, into the line that the boycott is the distinguishing sign of the tactics of Bolshevism even in the period of counter-revolution, ultimatism and otzovism show that these tendencies are in essence the reverse side of Menshevism, which undertakes wholesale participation in all representative institutions, inde-

*Karl Kautsky: leading theorist in the German Social-Democratic Party; later drew Lenin's ire when he opposed violent means of revolution and criticized the Soviet dictatorship – Ed.

pendently of the given stage of development of the revolution, independently of the presence or absence of a revolutionary upsurge.

All the attempts made by otzovism and ultimatism up to now to give theory a foundation of principle inevitably lead them to the denial of the foundations of revolutionary Marxism. The tactics which they have in mind lead to a complete break with the tactics of the left wing of international Social Democracy as applied to contemporary Russian conditions; they lead to anarchist deviations.

Otzovist-ultimatist agitation has already begun to cause undoubted harm to the workers' movement and to Social-Democratic work. If continued further it can become a threat to the unity of the party, for this agitation has already lead to such monstrous phenomena as the combination of otzovists and SR's* (in St. Petersburg) to carry out their refusal to help our party's representatives in the Duma, and also to certain public appearances before workers, jointly with confirmed syndicalists.

In view of all this the expanded editorial board of *The Proletarian* declares that Bolshevism as a definite tendency within the RSDWP has nothing in common with otzovism and ultimatism, and that the Bolshevik faction must conduct the most determined struggle against these deviations from the path of revolutionary Marxism.

THE ULTRA-LEFT ON LENIN'S COMPROMISES

After the split of 1909 Lenin's left-wing Bolshevik opponents organized a new Social-Democratic faction, known as the "Forward" group from the name of their newspaper. These extremists denounced Lenin for opportunism in much the same terms that he applied to the Mensheviks, but also attacked his organizational centralism. The group never attracted much rank-and-file support, and most of them found their way back to the Bolshevik ranks after the revolution.

a) BOGDANOV, "LETTER TO ALL COMRADES"

Where are we going? What is the historical fate of our generation – a new revolutionary wave or an organic development? . . .

If we are holding a course toward 'organic development,' then revolutionary-military questions and tasks simply do not exist for our gen-

FROM: Declarations of the "Vperiod" ("Forward") Group, 1910 (excerpts quoted in K. Ostroukhova, "The 'Vperiod' Group," *Proletarskaya Revoliutsiya* [Proletarian Revolution], No. 1, 1925, pp. 200-01; editor's translation).

*SR's: Socialist Revolutionary Party which stressed peasant revolution – Ed.

eration, and the tradition connected with them is a harmful survival from the past. . . . But we assert that the long 'organic development' of Russia is only an Octobrist* dream. . . .

[We must consider] sustaining the remaining militant elements in their party spirit and discipline, and accordingly educating those working-class youths who manifest an attraction in this direction; strengthening propaganda among the troops, and, if possible, re-creating the military organizations which have fallen apart. . . .

Some people among your representatives in the executive collegium – the Bolshevik Center – who live abroad, have come to the conclusion that we must radically change the previous Bolshevik evaluation of the present historical moment and hold a course not toward a new revolutionary wave, but toward a long period of peaceful, constitutional development. This brings them close to the right wing of our party, the Menshevik comrades who always, independently of any evaluation of the political situation, pull toward legal and constitutional forms of activity, toward 'organic work' and 'organic development.' But this is what has led to disagreements with those Bolsheviks who do not see in the reaction which they observe sufficient grounds for such a change of front. . . .

Bolshevism continues to exist as before. It lives not in the circles abroad, not among politically sick people who are repressed and beaten by the harsh reaction; it lives in the steadfast and healthy proletarian movement, which organizes itself instead of splitting itself up. . . .

Comrades, a glorious cause – political, cultural, social – stands before us. It would be shameful for us if leaders who have outlived their times, overcome by adversity, should prevent us from fulfilling it. But this is an impossible, absurd suggestion. We will proceed on our way according to the old slogan – with our leaders, if they wish; without them, if they do not wish; against them, if they oppose us. Our cause is the cause of the collective, not of individual personalities. . . .

b) "LETTER TO OUR BOLSHEVIK COMRADES"

. . . The Bolshevik Center has surrendered every Bolshevik position, one after another. . . . Accountable management by material means has changed into the uncontrolled freewheeling of irresponsible people; this group of people (the Bolshevik Center), which had already become ideologically Menshevik, has assumed the right of disbanding the Bolshevik faction. . . .

---

*Octobrists: conservative party standing by the constitutional concessions of October, 1905 – Ed.

The Bolshevik Center, now altered in its composition—the majority were able to get rid of the "inconvenient" members who refused to abandon the position of Bolshevism—is completely cut off from Russia, has essentially become a private circle of former Bolsheviks, and has finally ceased to take account of the opinions and inclinations of the organizations in Russia. . . .

Only the organizations themselves have the right to decide their fate. Only the Russian Bolshevik comrades themselves, those worker socialists who struggle face to face with the enemy, can and must tell the party whether its revolutionary current has really died or whether in this period of blind reaction which is preparing a new outburst of the popular struggle, it has become more essential for the proletarian cause than ever before. . . .

We, the "Forward" group, suggest that the Russian Bolshevik comrades organize in the immediate future Bolshevik conferences on as large a scale as possible, and at them consider the questions of the fundamental vital interests of Bolshevism. As opponents of the old factional forms, we will insist at these conferences on the reconstruction of the Bolshevik faction on new foundations so that its ideological solidarity will be achieved not through formal centralization, but through the living ideological link, and so that these *ideological* centers which are created for this will be under real control by the local organizations. This will prevent the possibility of such a political degeneration of the "higher-ups," of such abuses and corruption as we have witnessed. The ideological current must direct its leaders and representatives. Only the decision of the local Bolshevik organizations can be considered the real decision of a question. . . .

LENIN ON NATIONAL SELF-DETERMINATION

Early in 1914 Lenin turned his attention to the problem of the national minorities in Russia. His answer to "Great-Russian chauvinism" was the unconditional right of any minority to independent statehood, while those who remained would accept a thoroughly centralized revolutionary party and government. The actual Soviet solution was in form quite different, with the elaborate federal structure of republics embodied first in the Russian Republic in 1918 and then in the Union of Soviet Socialist Republics in 1922. Centralism has of course been maintained in practice by virtue of the power of the highly centralized Communist Party.

FROM: Lenin, "The Right of Nations to Self-Determination" (1914; *Selected Works*, Vol. 1, book 2, pp. 382-86).

. . . From the point of view of the theory of Marxism in general the question of the right of self-determination presents no difficulties. No one can seriously dispute the London resolution [of the Socialist International] of 1896, or the fact that self-determination implies only the right to secession, or the fact that the formation of independent national states is the tendency of all bourgeois-democratic revolutions.

The difficulty is created to a certain extent by the fact that in Russia the proletariat of both oppressed and oppressing nations are fighting and must fight side by side. The task is to preserve the unity of the class struggle of the proletariat for Socialism, to resist all the bourgeois and Black-Hundred* nationalist influences. Among the oppressed nations the separate organization of the proletariat as an independent party sometimes leads to such a bitter struggle against the nationalism of the respective nation that the perspective becomes distorted and the nationalism of the oppressing nation is forgotten.

But this distortion of the perspective cannot last long. The experience of the joint struggle of the proletarians of various nations has demonstrated only too plainly that we must formulate political questions not from the "Cracow," but from the all-Russian point of view. And in all-Russian politics it is the Purishkeviches and the Kokoshkins who rule.† Their ideas are predominant, their persecution of alien races for "separatism," for *thinking* about secession, are being preached and practiced in the Duma, in the schools, in the churches, in the barracks, and in hundreds and thousands of newspapers. It is this Great-Russian poison of nationalism that is contaminating the entire all-Russian political atmosphere. The misfortune of a nation, which, in subjugating other nations, is strengthening reaction throughout Russia. The memories of 1849 and 1863 form a living political tradition, which, unless great storms sweep the country, threatens to hamper every democratic and *especially* every Social-Democratic movement for many decades.

There can be no doubt that, however natural the point of view of certain Marxists of the oppressed nations (whose "misfortune" is sometimes that the masses of the population are blinded by the idea of "their" national liberation) may appear at times, *in reality* the objective alignment of class forces in Russia makes refusal to advocate the right of self-determination tantamount to the worst opportunism, to the contamination of the proletariat with the ideas of the Kokoshkins. And in substance, these ideas are the ideas and the policy of the Purishkeviches. . . .

*"Black Hundreds": armed bands of ultra-rightists—Ed.

†Purishkevich: an extreme right-wing leader in the Duma; Kokoshkin: a representative of the Constitutional Democratic Party in the Duma—Ed.

Even now, and probably for a fairly long time to come, proletarian democracy must reckon with the nationalism of the Great-Russian peasants (not in the sense of making concessions to it, but in the sense of combating it). The awakening of nationalism among the oppressed nations, which became so pronounced after 1905 (let us recall, say, the group of "Autonomists-Federalists" in the First Duma, the growth of the Ukrainian movement, of the Moslem movement, etc.), will inevitably cause the intensification of nationalism among the Great-Russian petty bourgeoisie in town and country. The slower the democratization of Russia, the more persistent, brutal and bitter will be national persecution and quarrelling among the bourgeoisie of the various nations. The particularly reactionary nature of the Russian Purishkeviches will at the same time engender (and strengthen) "separatist" tendencies among the various oppressed nationalities which sometimes enjoy far greater freedom in the neighbouring states.

This state of affairs confronts the proletariat of Russia with a twofold or, rather, a two-sided task: to combat all nationalism and, above all, Great-Russian nationalism; to recognize not only complete equality of rights for all nations in general but also equality of rights as regards statehood, i.e., the right of nations to self-determination, to secession. And at the same time, precisely in the interest of the successful struggle against the nationalism of all nations in any form, preserving the unity of the proletarian struggle and of the proletarian organizations, amalgamating these organizations into a close-knit international association, in spite of the bourgeois striving for national segregation.

Complete equality of rights for all nations; the right of nations to self-determination; the amalgamation of the workers of all nations – this is the national program that Marxism, the experience of the whole world, and the experience of Russia, teaches the workers. . . .

LENIN ON THE UNEVEN PROSPECTS OF REVOLUTION

In reply to some of his radical associates who proposed an international socialist federation, Lenin pointed out the likelihood of the first socialist countries having to fight those which clung to capitalism. This idea was of major significance in the 1920's as the starting point for Stalin's theory of "socialism in one country."

. . . A United States of the World (not of Europe alone) is the state form of the union and freedom of nations which we associate with Socialism—

FROM: Lenin, "The United States of Europe Slogan" (August, 1915; *Selected Works*, Vol. I, book 2, pp. 416-17).

until the complete victory of Communism brings about the total disappearance of the state, including the democratic state. As a separate slogan, however, the slogan of a United States of the World would hardly be a correct one, first, because it merges with Socialism; second, because it may be wrongly interpreted to mean that the victory of Socialism in a single country is impossible, and it may also create misconceptions as to the relations of such a country to the others.

Uneven economic and political development is an absolute law of capitalism. Hence, the victory of Socialism is possible first in several or even in one capitalist country, taken singly. The victorious proletariat of that country, having expropriated the capitalists and organized its own socialist production, would stand up *against* the rest of the world, the capitalist world, attracting to its cause the oppressed classes of other countries, raising revolts in those countries against the capitalists, and in the event of necessity coming out even with armed force against the exploiting classes and their states. The political form of society in which the proletariat is victorious by overthrowing the bourgeoisie, will be a democratic republic, which will more and more centralize the forces of the proletariat of the given nation, or nations, in the struggle against the states that have not yet gone over to Socialism. The abolition of classes is impossible without the dictatorship of the oppressed class, the proletariat. The free union of nations in Socialism is impossible without a more or less prolonged and stubborn struggle of the socialist republics against the backward states.

It is for these reasons and after repeated debates at the conference of the sections of the R.S.D.L.P. abroad, and after the conference, that the editors of the Central Organ have come to the conclusions that the United States of Europe slogan is incorrect.

BUKHARIN ON THE IMPERIALIST STATE

Nikolai Bukharin as a young Bolshevik theorist often criticized Lenin from the left until he became more conservative as a responsible Soviet leader after 1921. During the First World War Bukharin led a "left-Bolshevik" subfaction and wrote of the necessity for the total revolutionary destruction of the existing state. This, he warned, was necessary to forestall the development of a Leviathan of "state capitalism." Without realizing it, Bukharin prophesied the whole modern phenomenon of totalitarianism.

FROM: Bukharin, "On The Theory of the Imperialist State" (1916; published in *Revoliutsiya prava* [The Revolution of Law], Collection I, Moscow, Communist Academy, 1925, pp. 7-8, 13-16, 21, 23, 26, 27, 29-32; editor's translation).

1. The General Theory of the State

. . . From the point of view of Marxism the state is nothing but *the most general organization of the dominant classes, the basic function of which is to maintain and extend the exploitation of the suppressed classes.* . . . Insofar as there is an organization of state power set up according to a plan and consciously regulated (and this appears only at a certain stage in the development of the state), to that extent one can speak of the posing of *goals*, but these goals are defined by the interests of the *dominant* classes and *only by them.* This is not in the least contradicted by the circumstance that the state performs and has performed a whole series of functions for the common good. The latter merely provides the necessary *condition*, the *conditio sine qua non*, for the existence of the state power. The state's "activities for the common good" are thus the *conditions for maximally protracted and maximally successful exploitation of the enslaved classes* in contemporary society, above all the proletariat. . . .

In this connection it is possible to distinguish two types of relationships: either the state organization is the *direct* organization of exploitation – in which case the state stands forth as the union of the capitalists, having its own enterprises (e.g., railroads, monopoly production of certain products, etc.); or the state organization participates in an *indirect* manner in the process of exploitation, as a service mechanism to sustain and extend the most profitable conditions for the process of exploitation. In the first case – insofar as we are speaking of productive labor – the state absorbs the surplus value which is created in the sphere of its direct activity; in the second – it appropriates part of the surplus value which is produced in the branches of production that lie outside the sphere of direct state control, by means of taxes, etc. Usually the state extracts not only a part of the surplus value, but also a certain part of wages (and where other categories of "labor income" exist, part of the latter as well). In concrete actuality both these types exist simultaneously, although their proportions are subject to change and depend on the stage of historical development which has been attained.

The support and extension of the process of exploitation proceed in two directions: externally, i.e., outside the boundaries of the state's territory, and internally, i.e., within these boundaries. The *foreign* policy of the state organization expresses its struggle to share the surplus value which is produced on a world-wide scale (insofar as there is a non-capitalist world, the struggle for the surplus product), the struggle which is enacted between the various politically organized groups of the dominant classes.

The *internal* policy of the state organization reflects the struggle of the dominant classes for a share of the value (i.e., product) created by way of the systematic suppression of all attempts at liberation on the part of the suppressed classes. . . .

2. The Imperialist State and Finance Capitalism

Even the most superficial glance at social-economic life shows us the colossal growth of the economic significance of the state. This is reflected above all in the growth of the *state budget*. The complicated apparatus of the contemporary state organization requires enormous expenses, which increase with astonishing swiftness. . . .

A vast role in such an increase of the budget is undoubtedly played by militarism, one of the aspects of *imperialist* politics, which in turn stems necessarily from the structure of *finance capitalism*. But not only militarism in the narrow sense of the word. The cause of this is the growing interference of the state power in all branches of social life, beginning with the sphere of production and ending with the higher forms of ideological creation. If the pre-imperialist period – the period of liberalism, which was the political expression of industrial capitalism – was characterized by the noninterference of the state power, and the formula laissez-faire was a symbol of the faith of the ruling circles of the bourgeoisie, who all permitted the "free play of economic forces," our time is characterized by a directly opposite tendency, which has as its logical conclusion *state capitalism*, sucking everything into the area of state regulation. . . .

The *state power thus sucks in almost all branches of production; it not only preserves the general conditions of the process of exploitation; the state becomes more and more a direct exploiter, which organizes and directs production as a collective, composite capitalist*. . . . The anarchistic commodity market is to a significant degree replaced by the organized distribution of the product, in which the supreme authority is again the state power. . . .

. . . In war socialism* class contradictions are not only not eliminated, but are brought to their maximum intensity. In the ideal type of the imperialist state the process of exploitation is not obscured by any secondary forms; the mask of a supraclass institution which treats everyone equally is thrown off from the state. This fact is a basic fact, and it completely refutes the argumentation of the renegades [i.e., the prowar Social Democrats]. For socialism is the regulation of production directed by *society*, not by the state (state socialism is like soft-boiled boots); it is the annihilation of class contradictions, not their intensification. The regulation of production by itself does not mean socialism at all; it exists in any sort of economy, in any

---

*"Kriegssozialismus" – the highly mobilized German economy in World War I – Ed.

slave-owning group with a natural economy. What awaits us in the immediate future is in fact *state capitalism.* . . .

3. The Organizational Process, State Power, and the Working Class . . .

The necessities of imperialist development compel bourgeois society to mobilize all its forces, to become organized on the broadest scale: the state draws into itself the whole series of bourgeois organizations.

Here war gives an enormous impetus. Philosophy and medicine, religion and ethics, chemistry and bacteriology – all are "mobilized" and "militarized" just like industry and finance. The whole grand-scale technical, economic, and ideological machine operates more planfully as soon as the conscious organized adaptation to the "whole" has appeared – i.e., when the state in one way or another has drawn these innumerable groups into its all-over organization. . . .

The general scheme of the state's development is as follows: At first the state is the only organization of the dominant class. Then other organizations arise, whose numbers are especially increased in the epoch of finance capitalism. The state is transformed from the only organization of the dominant class into one of its organizations which exist simultaneously – an organization which is distinguished by its most general character. Finally the third stage arrives, *when the state absorbs these organizations and again becomes the only over-all organization of the dominant class, with a technical division* of labor inside it; the formerly independent organizational groupings are transformed into divisions of a gigantic state mechanism, which descends with crushing force upon the obvious and internal enemy. Thus arises the final type of the contemporary imperialist bandit state, the iron organization which with its grasping, prehensile paws seizes the living body of society. It is a new Leviathan, in the face of which the fantasy of Thomas Hobbes seems like child's play. And all the more *"non est potestas super terram quae comparetur ei"* ("there is no power on earth which can compare with it").*

We must now raise the fully natural question of the role of the workers, of proletarian organizations.

Theoretically there can be two possibilities here: *Either the workers' organizations, like all the organizations of the bourgeoisie, will grow into the state-wide organization and be transformed into a simple appendage of the state apparatus, or they will outgrow the framework of the state and burst it from within,* as they organize their own state power (the dictatorship) . . . .

---

*Epigraph to "The Leviathan" [author's note].

The immediate development of state organisms – as long as the socialist overturn does not occur – is possible only in the form of *militaristic state capitalism*. Centralization becomes barrack centralization; the intensification of the most hateful militarism among the upper groups, of bestial drilling of the proletariat, of bloody repressions, is inevitable. On the other hand, as we have already noted above, any move by the proletariat is inevitably transformed under these circumstances into a move against the state power. Hence the definite tactical demand – Social-Democracy must vigorously underscore its hostility in principle to the state power.

. . . To support the contemporary state means to support militarism. The historical task of the day is not to worry about the further development of the forces of production (they are quite sufficient for the realization of socialism), but the preparation of a general attack on the ruling bandits. In the growing revolutionary struggle the proletariat destroys the state organization of the bourgeoisie. . . .

Chapter Two
The Bolshevik Revolution, 1917-1921

The Russian Revolution was not a simple matter of the conspiratorial seizure of power, but one of the most complex events in all history. As in the
other great revolutions, in England and France, the unexpected collapse of
the monarchy's authority initiated a sequence of political convulsions, as
power passed through a succession of leading groups, with growing
extremism and violence. Stable rule by the Communists (as the Bolsheviks
renamed themselves in 1918) was not consolidated until 1921, by which
time they had lost much of their revolutionary utopianism.

During the years of the revolution the Communist Party was by no
means a single-minded force, though Lenin always exerted commanding
influence. At every stage in the revolution deviant groups arose among the
Communists to object to Lenin's course of action – some who found it too
rash, others who protested its expedient compromises. The revolutionary
period reveals the wide range of political and social alternatives which the
general standpoint of radical Russian Marxism afforded.

The years 1917-1921, during which the Communists seized power,
endured factional controversy, and fought their way to victory in a bitter
civil war, were the critical, formative period of the Soviet regime and of the
Communist movement as a whole. Communism is specifically the child of
the Russian Revolution, and its basic character – the exclusive dictatorship
of a bureaucratic party in a bureaucratic state – stems directly from the
way in which the conditions of that era selected among the political alternatives offered by the revolutionary movement.

LENIN'S RETURN TO RUSSIA

When Czar Nicholas II fell in February, 1917 (March, by the Western Gregorian calendar), Lenin and the Bolsheviks were taken by
surprise. The moderate and hopefully democratic Provisional Government which was established under Prince Lvov seemed to refute
Lenin's contention that the Russian middle class could not rule. The
Bolsheviks in Russia were confused and divided about how to
regard the Provisional Government, but most of them, including
Stalin, were inclined to accept it for the time being on condition that
it work for an end to the war. When Lenin reached Russia in April

after his famous "sealed car" trip across Germany, he promptly denounced his Bolshevik colleagues for failing to take a sufficiently revolutionary stand.

1. In our attitude towards the war, which also under the new government of Lvov and Co. unquestionably remains on Russia's part a predatory imperialist war owing to the capitalist nature of that government, not the slightest concession to "revolutionary defencism" is permissible.

The class-conscious proletariat can give its consent to a revolutionary war, which would really justify revolutionary defencism, only on condition: a) that the power pass to the proletariat and the poor sections of the peasantry bordering on the proletariat; b) that all annexations be renounced in actual fact and not in word; c) that a complete break be effected in actual fact with all capitalist interests.

In view of the undoubted honesty of the broad strata of the mass believers in revolutionary defencism, who accept the war as a necessity only, and not as a means of conquest, in view of the fact that they are being deceived by the bourgeoisie, it is necessary with particular thoroughness, persistence and patience to explain their error to them, to explain the inseparable connection existing between capital and the imperialist war, and to prove that without overthrowing capital *it is impossible* to end the war by a truly democratic peace, a peace not imposed by violence.

The most widespread propaganda of this view in the army on active service must be organized.

Fraternization.

2. The specific feature of the present situation in Russia is that it represents a *transition* from the first stage of the revolution—which, owing to the insufficient class consciousness and organization of the proletariat, placed the power in the hands of the bourgeoisie—*to the second* stage, which must place the power in the hands of the proletariat and the poorest strata of the peasantry.

This transition is characterized, on the one hand, by a maximum of legally recognized rights (Russia is *now* the freest of all the belligerent countries in the world); on the other, by the absence of violence in relation to the masses, and, finally, by the unreasoning confidence of the masses in the government of capitalists, the worst enemies of peace and Socialism.

This peculiar situation demands of us an ability to adapt ourselves to the

FROM: Lenin, "On the Tasks of the Proletariat in the Present Revolution" (the "April Theses," April 7 [20], 1917;* *Selected Works*, Vol. II, book 2, pp. 13-17).

*Russian dates are old style, with new style in brackets, up to the calendar reform effective February 1 [14], 1918; all new style thereafter—Ed.

special conditions of Party work among unprecedentedly large masses of proletarians who have just awakened to political life.

3. No support for the Provisional Government; the utter falsity of all its promises should be explained, particularly those relating to the renunciation of annexations. Exposure in place of the impermissible illusion-breeding "demand" that *this* government, a government of capitalists, should *cease* to be an imperialist government.

4. Recognition of the fact that in most of the Soviets of Workers' Deputies our Party is in a minority, and so far in a small minority, as against *a bloc of all* the petty-bourgeois opportunist elements, who have yielded to the influence of the bourgeoisie and convey its influence to the proletariat, from the Popular Socialists and the Socialist-Revolutionaries down to the Organization Committee (Chkheidze, Tsereteli, etc.), Steklov,* etc., etc.

It must be explained to the masses that the Soviets of Workers' Deputies are the *only possible* form of the revolutionary government, and that therefore our task is, as long as *this* government yields to the influence of the bourgeoisie, to present a patient, systematic, and persistent *explanation* of the errors of their tactics, an explanation especially adapted to the practical needs of the masses.

As long as we are in the minority we carry on the work of criticizing and exposing errors and at the same time we preach the necessity of transferring the entire power of state to the Soviets of Workers' Deputies, so that the masses may by experience overcome their mistakes.

5. Not a parliamentary republic – to return to a parliamentary republic from the Soviets of Workers' Deputies would be a retrograde step – but a republic of Soviets of Workers', Agricultural Labourers' and Peasants' Deputies throughout the country, from top to bottom.

Abolition of the police, the army and the bureaucracy. †

The salaries of all officials, all of whom are to be elected and to be subject to recall at any time, not to exceed the average wage of a competent worker.

6. In the agrarian program the most important part to be assigned to the Soviets of Agricultural Labourers' Deputies.

Confiscation of all landed estates.

Nationalization of *all* lands in the country, the disposal of the land to be put in the charge of the local Soviets of Agricultural Labourers' and Peasants' Deputies. The organization of separate Soviets of Deputies of Poor Peasants. The creation of model farms on each of the large estates (varying

---

*Chkheidze, Tsereteli, Steklov: Menshevik leaders in the Petrograd Soviet – Ed.

†I.e., the standing army to be replaced by the arming of the whole people.

from 100 to 300 dessiatins*, in accordance with local and other conditions, by decisions of the local institutions) under the control of the Soviets of Agricultural Labourers' Deputies and for the public account.

7. The immediate amalgamation of all banks in the country into a single national bank, and the institution of control over it by the Soviets of Workers' Deputies.

8. It isn't our *immediate* task to "introduce" Socialism, but only to bring social production and distribution of products at once under the *control* of the Soviets of Workers' Deputies.

9. Party tasks:

   a) Immediate convocation of a Party congress;

   b) Alteration of the Party program, mainly:

   1) On the question of imperialism and the imperialist war;

   2) On our attitude towards the state and *our* demand for a "commune state" (i.e., a state of which the Paris Commune was the prototype);

   3) Amendment of our antiquated minimum program.

   c) Change of the Party's name. Instead of "Social-Democracy," whose official leaders *throughout* the world have betrayed Socialism and deserted to the bourgeoisie (the "defencists" and the vacillating "Kautskyites"), we must call ourselves a *Communist Party*.

10. A new International.

We must take the initiative in creating a revolutionary International, an International against the *social-chauvinists* and against the "Centre". . . .

LENIN ON THE SOVIETS

Simultaneously with the establishment of the Provisional Government, the leaders of the Russian socialist parties – Mensheviks, Bolsheviks, and Socialist-Revolutionaries ("SR's") – organized the so-called "soviets (Russian for "councils") of workers' and soldiers' deputies." The soviets, set up in every major city on the model of similar bodies that existed during the Revolution of 1905, began to exert a strong though informal political influence – hence Lenin's expression of "dual power" shared by the more moderate Provisional Government and the more radical soviets. Lenin saw in the soviets the ideal organs of revolution; it remained only for his Bolsheviks to win paramount influence in them, which they did on the eve of their seizure of power.

FROM: Lenin, "On the Dual Power" (April 9 [22], 1917; *Selected Works*, Vol. II, book 1, pp. 20-23).

*Dessiatina: old Russian unit of land, approx. 2.7 acres – Ed.

The basic question in any revolution is that of state power. Unless this question is understood, there can be no conscious participation in the revolution, not to speak of guidance of the revolution.

The highly remarkable specific feature of our revolution is that it has brought about a *dual power*. This fact must be grasped first and foremost: unless it is understood, we cannot advance. We must know how to supplement and amend old "formulas," for example, of Bolshevism, for as it has transpired, they were correct on the whole, but their concrete realization has *turned out to be* different. *Nobody* previously thought, or could have thought, of a dual power.

In what does this dual power consist? In the fact that side by side with the Provisional Government, the government of the bourgeoisie, there has arisen *another government*, weak and incipient as yet, but undoubtedly an actually existing and growing government – the Soviets of Workers' and Soldiers' Deputies.

What is the class composition of this other government? It consists of the proletariat and the peasantry (clad in soldier's uniforms). What is the political nature of this government? It is a revolutionary dictatorship, i.e., a power directly based on revolutionary seizure, on the direct initiative of the masses from below, and *not on a law* enacted by a centralized state power. It is a power entirely different from that generally existing in the parliamentary bourgeois-democratic republics of the usual type still prevailing in the advanced countries of Europe and America. This circumstance is often forgotten, often not reflected on, yet it is the crux of the matter. *This* power is of *the same type* as the Paris Commune of 1871. The fundamental characteristics of this type are: 1) the source of power is not a law previously discussed and enacted by parliament, but the direct initiative of the people's masses from below, in their localities – direct "seizure" to use a current expression; 2) the replacement of the police and the army, which are institutions separated from the people and set against the people, by the direct arming of the whole people; order in the state under such a power is maintained by the armed workers and peasants *themselves*, by the armed people *themselves*; 3) officialdom, the bureaucracy are either similarly replaced by the direct rule of the people themselves or at least placed under special control; they not only become elected officials, but are also *subject to recall* at the first demand of the people; they are reduced to the position of simple agents; from a privileged stratum holding "jobs" remunerated on a high, bourgeois scale, they become workers of a special "branch," whose remuneration *does not exceed* the ordinary pay of a competent worker.

This, and this *alone*, constitutes the *essence* of the Paris Commune as a special type of state. This essence has been forgotten or perverted by the Plekhanovs (out-and-out chauvinists who have betrayed Marxism), the Kautsky's (the men of the "Centre," i.e., those who vacillate between chauvinism and Marxism), and generally by all those Social-Democrats, Socialist-Revolutionaries, etc., etc., who now hold sway.

They are trying to get away with phrases, evasions, subterfuges; they congratulate each other a thousand times upon the revolution, but they refuse to *ponder* over *what* the Soviets of Workers' and Soldiers' Deputies *are*. They refuse to recognize the obvious truth that inasmuch as these Soviets exist, *inasmuch as* they are a power, we have in Russia a state of the *type* of the Paris Commune.

I have underscored the words "inasmuch as," for it is only an incipient power. By direct agreement with the bourgeois Provisional Government and by a series of actual concessions, it has itself *surrendered and is surrendering* its positions to the bourgeoisie.

Why? Is it because Chkheidze, Tsereteli, Steklov, and Co. are making a "mistake"? Nonsense. Only a philistine can think so – not a Marxist. The reason is *insufficient class-consciousness* and organization of the proletarians and peasants. The "mistake" of the leaders I have named lies in their petty-bourgeois position, in the fact that instead of enlightening the minds of the workers, they are *befogging* them; instead of dispersing petty-bourgeois illusions, they are *instilling* them; instead of freeing the masses from bourgeois influence, they are *strengthening* that influence.

It should be clear from this why our comrades too commit so many mistakes when putting the question "simply": should the Provisional Government be overthrown immediately?

My answer is: 1) it should be overthrown, for it is an oligarchic, bourgeois, and not a people's government, and *is unable* to provide peace, or bread, or full freedom; 2) it cannot be overthrown just now, for it is being maintained by a direct and indirect, a formal and actual *agreement* with the Soviets of Workers' Deputies, and primarily with the chief Soviet, the Petrograd Soviet; 3) generally, it cannot be "overthrown" in the ordinary way, for it rests on the "*support*" given to the bourgeoisie by the *second* government – the Soviet of Workers' Deputies, and that government is the only possible revolutionary government, which directly expresses the mind and will of the majority of the workers and peasants. Humanity has not yet evolved and we do not as yet know a type of government superior to and better than the Soviets of Workers', Agricultural Labourers', Peasants' and Soldiers' Deputies.

In order to become a power the class-conscious workers must win the majority to their side. *As long as* no violence is used against the masses there is no other road to power. We are not Blanquists,* we do not stand for the seizure of power by a minority. We are Marxists, we stand for proletarian class struggle against petty-bourgeois intoxication, against chauvinism-defencism, phrasemongering and dependence on the bourgeoisie.

Let us create a proletarian Communist Party; its elements have already been created by the best adherents of Bolshevism; let us rally our ranks for proletarian class work; then, from among the proletarians, from among the *poor* peasants, ever greater numbers will range themselves on our side. For *actual experience* will from day to day shatter the petty-bourgeois illusions of the "Social-Democrats"—the Chkheidzes, Tseretelis, Steklovs et al.—of the "Socialist-Revolutionaries," petty bourgeois of a still purer water, and so on and so forth.

The bourgeoisie stands for the undivided power of the bourgeoisie.

The class-conscious workers stand for the undivided power of the Soviets of Workers', Agricultural Labourers', Peasants' and Soldiers' Deputies—for undivided power made possible not by dubious ventures, but by the *enlightenment* of the proletarian minds, by their *emancipation* from the influence of the bourgeoisie.

The petty bourgeoisie—"Social Democrats," Socialist-Revolutionaries, etc., etc.—vacillates and *hinders* this enlightenment and emancipation.

Such is the actual, the *class* alignment of forces that determines our tasks.

LENIN'S VISION OF THE REVOLUTIONARY STATE

After the abortive uprising of the "July Days," Alexander Kerensky became head of the Provisional Government and tried to outlaw the Bolsheviks. Lenin had to flee to Finland and there composed what is usually taken to be his main contribution to political theory, a commentary on the political program of Marx and Engels which he published under the title *State and Revolution*. The essence of the argument, in which Lenin was strongly influenced by Bukharin's ideas, was that the "bourgeois" state had to be completely destroyed and replaced by an entirely new revolutionary state on the model of the Paris Commune of 1871 (which the soviets were to provide in Russia). The new state would exclude all bureaucracy and inequality, and eventually "wither away" after the resistance of the old propertied classes was overcome.

Although this view of the revolutionary process has been fully

---

*Blanquists: adherents of the conspiratorial doctrine of the French revolutionary L. A. Blanqui—Ed.

incorporated into official Communist theory, it is obvious that it had very little relationship to Soviet practice after the revolution. How seriously Lenin took the vision when he was writing is difficult to say, but it should be noted that the anti-authoritarian emphasis expressed here offers a sharp contrast to his more characteristic disciplinarian bent both before and after 1917. On the other hand, many of Lenin's supporters, particularly in the left wing of the party, took the anti-authoritarian ideal very seriously indeed; they eventually had to be curbed or purged.

. . . The state is the product and the manifestation of the *irreconcilability* of class antagonisms. The state arises when, where and to the extent that class antagonisms objectively *cannot* be reconciled. And, conversely, the existence of the state proves that the class antagonisms are irreconcilable.

. . . The teaching of Marx and Engels concerning the inevitability of a violent revolution refers to the bourgeois state. The latter *cannot* be superseded by the proletarian state (the dictatorship of the proletariat) through the process of "withering away," but, as a general rule, only through a violent revolution. The panegyric Engels sang in its honour, and which fully corresponds to Marx's repeated declarations (recall the concluding passages of *The Poverty of Philosophy* and the *Communist Manifesto*, with their proud and open proclamation of the inevitability of a violent revolution; recall what Marx wrote nearly thirty years later, in criticizing the Gotha Program of 1875, when he mercilessly castigated the opportunist character of that program) – this panegyric is by no means a mere "impulse," a mere declamation or a polemical sally. The necessity of systematically imbuing the masses with *this* and precisely this view of violent revolution lies at the root of *all* the teachings of Marx and Engels. The betrayal of their teaching by the now predominant social-chauvinist and Kautskyite trends is expressed in striking relief by the neglect of *such* propaganda and agitation by both these trends.

The supersession of the bourgeois state by the proletarian state is impossible without a violent revolution. The abolition of the proletarian state, i.e., of the state in general, is impossible except through the process of "withering away." . . .

The overthrow of bourgeois rule can be accomplished only by the proletariat, as the particular class whose economic conditions of existence prepare it for this task and provide it with the possibility and the power to

FROM: Lenin, "The State and Revolution" (August-September, 1917; *Selected Works*, Vol. II, book 1, pp. 204, 219-20, 223-24, 243-44, 291-94, 297-98, 304-06, 313-14).

perform it. While the bourgeoisie breaks up and disintegrates the peasantry and all the petty-bourgeois strata, it welds together, unites and organizes the proletariat. Only the proletariat – by virtue of the economic role it plays in large-scale production – is capable of being the leader of *all* the toiling and exploited masses, whom the bourgeoisie exploits, oppresses and crushes often not less, but more, than it does the proletarians, but who are incapable of waging an *independent* struggle for their emancipation.

The teaching on the class struggle, when applied by Marx to the question of the state and of the socialist revolution, leads of necessity to the recognition of the *political rule* of the proletariat, of its dictatorship, i.e., of power shared with none and relying directly upon the armed force of the masses. The overthrow of the bourgeoisie can be achieved only by the proletariat becoming transformed into the *ruling class*, capable of crushing the inevitable and desperate resistance of the bourgeoisie, and of organizing *all* the toiling and exploited masses for the new economic order.

The proletariat needs state power, the centralized organization of force, the organization of violence, both to crush the resistance of the exploiters and to *lead* the enormous mass of the population – the peasantry, the petty bourgeoisie, the semiproletarians – in the work of organizing socialist economy.

By educating the workers' party, Marxism educates the vanguard of the proletariat which is capable of assuming power and *of leading the whole people* to Socialism, of directing and organizing the new order, of being the teacher, the guide, the leader of all the toilers and exploited in the task of building up their social life without the bourgeoisie and against the bourgeoisie . . . .

. . . Capitalist culture has *created* large-scale production, factories, railways, the postal service, telephones, etc., and *on this basis* the great majority of the functions of the old "state power" have become so simplified and can be reduced to such exceedingly simple operations of registration, filing and checking that they can be easily performed by every literate person, can quite easily be performed for ordinary "workmen's wages," and that these functions can (and must) be stripped of every shadow of privilege, of every semblance of "official grandeur."

All officials, without exception, elected and subject to recall *at any time*, their salaries reduced to the level of ordinary, "workmen's wages" – these simple and "self-evident" democratic measures, while completely uniting the interests of the workers and the majority of the peasants, at the same time serve as a bridge leading from capitalism to Socialism. These measures concern the reconstruction of the state, the purely political reconstruction of society; but, of course, they acquire their full meaning and significance only in connection with the "expropriation of the expropriators" either being accomplished or in preparation, i.e., with the transformation of capitalist private ownership of the means of production into social ownership. . . .

. . . Forward development, i.e., towards Communism, proceeds through the dictatorship of the proletariat, and cannot do otherwise, for the *resistance* of the capitalist exploiters cannot be *broken* by anyone else or in any other way.

And the dictatorship of the proletariat, i.e., the organization of the vanguard of the oppressed as the ruling class for the purpose of suppressing the oppressors, cannot result merely in an expansion of democracy. *Simultaneously* with an immense expansion of democracy, which *for the first time* becomes democracy for the poor, democracy for the people, and not democracy for the moneybags, the dictatorship of the proletariat imposes a series of restrictions on the freedom of the oppressors, the exploiters, the capitalists. We must suppress them in order to free humanity from wage slavery, their resistance must be crushed by force; it is clear that where there is suppression, where there is violence, there is no freedom and no democracy. . . .

Only in communist society, when the resistance of the capitalists has been completely crushed, when the capitalists have disappeared, when there are no classes (i.e., when there is no difference between the members of society as regards their relation to the social means of production), *only* then "the state . . . ceases to exist," and it *"becomes possible to speak of freedom."* Only then will there become possible and be realized a truly complete democracy, democracy without any exceptions whatever. And only then will democracy begin to *wither away*, owing to the simple fact that, freed from capitalist slavery, from the untold horrors, savagery, absurdities and infamies of capitalist exploitation, people will gradually *become accustomed* to observing the elementary rules of social intercourse that have been known for centuries and repeated for thousands of years in all copybook maxims; they will become accustomed to observing them without force, without compulsion, without subordination, *without the special apparatus* for compulsion which is called the state. . . .

. . . Only Communism makes the state absolutely unnecessary, for there is *nobody* to be suppressed – "nobody" in the sense of a *class*, in the sense of a systematic struggle against a definite section of the population. We are not utopians, and do not in the least deny the possibility and inevitability of excesses on the part of *individual persons*, or the need to suppress *such* excesses. But, in the first place, no special machine, no special apparatus of suppression is needed for this; this will be done by the armed people itself, as simply and as readily as any crowd of civilized people, even in modern society, interferes to put a stop to a scuffle or to prevent a woman from being assaulted. And, secondly, we know that the fundamental social cause of excesses, which consist in the violation of the rules of social intercourse, is the exploitation of the masses, their want and their poverty. With the removal of this chief cause, excesses will inevitably begin to "*wither away*." We do not know how quickly and in what succession, but we know that they will wither away. With their withering away the state will also *wither away*. . . .

. . . In the first phase of communist society (usually called Socialism) "bourgeois right" is *not* abolished in its entirety, but only in part, only in proportion to the economic revolution so far attained, i.e., only in respect of the means of production. "Bourgeois right" recognizes them as the private property of individuals. Socialism converts them into *common* property. *To that extent* – and to that extent alone – "bourgeois right" disappears.

However, it continues to exist as far as its other part is concerned; it continues to exist in the capacity of regulator (determining factor) in the distribution of products and the allotment of labour among the members of society. The socialist principle: "He who does not work, neither shall he eat," is *already* realized; the other socialist principle: "An equal amount of products for an equal amount of labour," is also *already* realized. But this is not yet Communism, and it does not yet abolish "bourgeois right," which gives to unequal individuals, in return for unequal (really unequal) amounts of labour, equal amounts of products.

This is a "defect," says Marx, but it is unavoidable in the first phase of Communism; for if we are not to indulge in utopianism, we must not think that having overthrown capitalism people will at once learn to work for society *without any standard of right*; and indeed the abolition of capitalism *does not immediately* create the economic premises for *such* a change.

And there is no other standard than that of "bourgeois right." To this extent, therefore, there still remains the need for a state, which, while safeguarding the public ownership of the means of production, would safeguard equality in labour and equality in the distribution of products.

The state withers away insofar as there are no longer any capitalists, any classes, and, consequently, no *class* can be *suppressed*.

But the state has not yet completely withered away, since there still remains the safeguarding of "bourgeois right," which sanctifies actual inequality. For the state to wither away completely, complete Communism is necessary. . . .

. . . The development of capitalism . . . itself creates the *premises* that *enable* really "all" to take part in the administration of the state. Some of these premises are: universal literacy, which has already been achieved in a number of the most advanced capitalist countries, then the "training and disciplining" of millions of workers by the huge, complex, socialized apparatus of the postal service, railways, big factories, large-scale commerce, banking, etc., etc.

Given these *economic* premises it is quite possible, after the overthrow of the capitalists and the bureaucrats, to proceed immediately, overnight, to supersede them in the *control* of production and distribution, in the work of *keeping account* of labour and products by the armed workers, by the whole of the armed population. (The question of control and accounting should not be confused with the question of the scientifically trained staff of engineers, agronomists and so on. These gentlemen are working today in obedience to the wishes of the capitalists; they will work even better tomorrow in obedience to the wishes of the armed workers.)

Accounting and control – that is the *main* thing required for "arranging" the smooth working, the correct functioning of the *first phase* of communist society. *All* citizens are transformed here into hired employees of the state, which consists of the armed workers. *All* citizens become employees and workers of a *single* nationwide state "syndicate." All that is required is that they should work equally, do their proper share of work, and get equally paid. The accounting and control necessary for this have been *simplified* by capitalism to the extreme and reduced to the extraordinary simple operations – which any literate person can perform – of supervising and recording, knowledge of the four rules of arithmetic, and issuing appropriate receipts.

When the *majority* of the people begin independently and everywhere to keep such accounts and maintain such control over the capitalists (now converted into employees) and over the intellectual gentry who preserve their capitalist habits, this control will really become universal, general, popular; and there will be no way of getting away from it, there will be "nowhere to go."

The whole of society will have become a single office and a single factory, with equality of labour and equality of pay.

But this "factory" discipline, which the proletariat, after defeating the capitalists, after overthrowing the exploiters, will extend to the whole of society is by no means our ideal, or our ultimate goal. It is but a necessary *step* for the purpose of thoroughly purging society of all the infamies and abominations of capitalist exploitation, *and for further* progress.

From the moment all members of society, or even only the vast majority, have learned to administer the state *themselves*, have taken this work into their own hands, have "set going" control over the insignificant minority of capitalists, over the gentry who wish to preserve their capitalist habits and over the workers who have been profoundly corrupted by capitalism – from this moment the need for government of any kind begins to disappear altogether. The more complete the democracy, the nearer the moment approaches when it becomes unnecessary. The more democratic the "state" which consists of the armed workers, and which is "no longer a state in the proper sense of the word," the more rapidly does *every form* of state begin to wither away.

For when *all* have learned to administer and actually do independently administer social production, independently keep accounts and exercise control over the idlers, the gentlefolk, the swindlers and suchlike "guardians of capitalist traditions," the escape from this popular accounting and control will inevitably become so incredibly difficult, such a rare exception, and will probably be accompanied by such swift and severe punishment (for the armed workers are practical men and not sentimental intellectuals, and they will scarcely allow anyone to trifle with them), that the *necessity* of observing the simple, fundamental rules of human intercourse will very soon become a *habit*.

And then the door will be wide open for the transition from the first phase of communist society to its higher phase, and with it to the complete withering away of the state. . . .

As far as the supposedly necessary "bureaucratic" organization is concerned, there is no difference whatever between railways and any other enterprise in large-scale machine industry, any factory, large store, or large-scale capitalist agricultural enterprise. The technique of all such enterprises makes absolutely imperative the strictest discipline, the utmost precision on the part of everyone in carrying out his allotted task, for otherwise the whole enterprise may come to a stop, or machinery or the finished product may be damaged. In all such enterprises the workers will, of course, "elect delegates who will form *a sort of parliament.*"

But the whole point is that this "sort of parliament" will *not* be a parliament in the sense in which we understand bourgeois-parliamentary institutions. The whole point is that this "sort of parliament" will *not* merely "draw up the working regulations and supervise the management of the bureaucratic apparatus," as Kautsky, whose ideas do not go beyond the bounds of bourgeois parliamentarism, imagines. In socialist society the "sort of parliament" consisting of workers' deputies will, of course, "draw up the working regulations and supervise the management" of the "apparatus" – *but* this apparatus will *not* be "bureaucratic." The workers, having conquered political power, will smash the old bureaucratic apparatus, they will shatter it to its very foundations, they will destroy it to the very roots; and they will replace it by a new one, consisting of the very same workers and office employees, *against* whose transformation into bureaucrats the measures will at once be taken which were specified in detail by Marx and Engels: 1) not only election, but also recall at any time; 2) pay not exceeding that of a workman; 3) immediate introduction of control and supervision by *all*, so that *all* shall become "bureaucrats" for a time and that, therefore, *nobody* may be able to become a "bureaucrat". . . .

LENIN'S CALL FOR AN UPRISING

By September, 1917, it was clear that mass sentiment among the workers, soldiers and peasants was shifting to the left. The Bolsheviks won control of the Petrograd and Moscow Soviets. Lenin thereupon called upon the Bolshevik Party to prepare to overthrow the Provisional Government by force.

. . . Marxists are accused of Blanquism for treating insurrection as an art! Can there be a more flagrant perversion of the truth, when not a single Marxist will deny that it was Marx who expressed himself on this score in the most definite, precise and categorical manner, referring to insurrection precisely as an *art*, and saying that it must be treated as an art, that one must *win* the first success and then proceed from success to success, never ceasing the *offensive* against the enemy, taking advantage of his confusion, etc., etc.?

To be successful, insurrection must rely not upon conspiracy and not upon a party, but upon the advanced class. That is the first point. Insurrection must rely upon a *revolutionary upsurge of the people*. That is the second point. Insurrection must rely upon such a *crucial moment* in the history of the growing revolution when the activity of the advanced ranks of the people is at its height, and when the *vacillations* in the ranks of the enemy and *in the ranks of the weak, halfhearted and irresolute friends of the revolution* are strongest. That is the third point. And these three conditions for raising the question of insurrection distinguish *Marxism from Blanquism*.

But once these conditions are present, to refuse to treat insurrection as an *art* is a betrayal of Marxism and a betrayal of the revolution. . . .

All the objective conditions for a successful insurrection exist. We have the exceptional advantage of a situation in which *only* our victory in the

FROM: Lenin, "Marxism and Insurrection: A Letter to the Central Committee of the R.S.D.W.P." (Sept. 13-14 [26-27], 1917; *Selected Works*, Vol. II, book 1, 167-68, 170-73).

insurrection can put an end to that most painful thing on earth, vacillation, which has worn the people out; a situation in which *only our* victory in the insurrection can *foil* the game of a separate peace directed against the revolution by publicly proposing a fuller, juster and earlier peace, a peace that will *benefit* the revolution. . . .

We must draw up a brief declaration of the Bolsheviks, emphasizing in the most trenchant manner the irrelevance of long speeches and of "speeches" in general, the necessity for immediate action to save the revolution, the absolute necessity for a complete break with the bourgeoisie, for the removal of the whole present government, for a complete rupture with the Anglo-French imperialists, who are preparing a "separate" partition of Russia, and for the immediate transfer of the whole power *to the revolutionary democracy headed by the revolutionary proletariat.*

Our declaration must consist of the briefest and most trenchant formulation of this conclusion in connection with the proposals of the program: peace for the peoples, land for the peasants, confiscation of outrageous profits, and a check on the outrageous sabotage of production by the capitalists.

The briefer and more trenchant the declaration the better. Only two other highly important points must be clearly indicated in it, namely, that the people are worn out by the vacillations, that they are tormented by the irresolution of the Socialist-Revolutionaries and Mensheviks; and that we are definitely breaking with these *parties* because they have betrayed the revolution.

And another thing. By immediately proposing a peace without annexations, by immediately breaking with the Allied imperialists and with all imperialists, either we shall at once obtain an armistice, or the entire revolutionary proletariat will rally to the defence of the country, and a really just, really revolutionary war will then be waged by the revolutionary democracy under the leadership of the proletariat.

Having read this declaration, and having appealed for *decisions* and not talk, for *action* and not resolution-writing, we must *dispatch* our whole group to the *factories and the barracks.* Their place is there, the pulse of life is there, the source of salvation of the revolution is there, and there is the motive force of the Democratic Conference.*

There, in ardent and impassioned speeches, we must explain our program and put the alternative: either the Conference adopts it *in its entirety,* or else insurrection. There is no middle course. Delay is impossible. The revolution is perishing.

*Democratic Conference: a semi-official meeting of various Russian political leaders, convoked by the Provisional Government in September, 1917 – Ed.

By putting the question thus, by concentrating our entire group in the factories and barracks, *we shall be able to determine the right moment for launching the insurrection.*

And in order to treat insurrection in a Marxist way, i.e., as an art, we must at the same time, without losing a single moment, organize a *headquarter staff* of the insurgent detachments, distribute our forces, move the reliable regiments to the most important points, surround the Alexandrinsky Theatre, occupy the Peter and Paul Fortress, arrest the general staff and the government, and move against the cadets and the Savage Division such detachments as will rather die than allow the enemy to approach the centres of the city; we must mobilize the armed workers and call them to fight the last desperate fight, occupy the telegraph and the telephone exchange at once, place *our* headquarter staff of the insurrection at the central telephone exchange and connect it by telephone with all the factories, all the regiments, all the points of armed fighting, etc.

Of course, this is all by way of example, only to *illustrate* the fact that at the present moment it is impossible to remain loyal to Marxism, to remain loyal to the revolution, *without treating insurrection as an art*.

THE DECLARATION OF REVOLUTIONARY INTENT – TROTSKY

The Bolsheviks' hope of seizing power was hardly secret; bold defiance of the Provisional Government was one of their major propaganda appeals. Some three weeks before the insurrection they decided to stage a demonstrative walkout from the advisory assembly known as the Council of the Republic or "Pre-Parliament." At this point, Trotsky (a Bolshevik only since August, 1917, but already the party's most articulate spokesman) denounced the Provisional Government for its alleged counterrevolutionary intentions and called on the masses to support the Bolsheviks.

. . . The bourgeois classes which are directing the policy of the Provisional government have set themselves the goal of *undermining* the Constituent Assembly. This is now the basic task of the privileged elements, to which their whole policy, domestic and foreign, is subordinated.

In the industrial, agrarian, and food-supply fields, the policy of the government and the propertied classes aggravates the natural disruption engendered by the war. The privileged classes, having provoked a peasant

FROM: Trotsky, "Declaration of the Bolshevik Fraction to the Council of the Republic" ("Pre-Parliament"), October 7 [20], 1917 (Trotsky, *Sochineniya* [Works], Moscow, State Press [1924], Vol. III, book 1, pp. 321-23; editor's translation).

uprising, now move to suppress it, and openly hold a course towards the "bony hand of famine," which is to smother the revolution and above all the Constituent Assembly.

No less criminal is the foreign policy of the bourgeoisie and its government.

After forty months of war mortal danger threatens the capital. In answer to this a plan is proposed to transfer the government to Moscow. The idea of surrendering the revolutionary capital to the German troops does not evoke the least indignation among the bourgeois classes; on the contrary, it is accepted by them as a natural link in the general policy, which is to facilitate their counterrevolutionary plot.

Instead of recognizing that the salvation of the country lies in the conclusion of peace; instead of openly throwing out the proposal of immediate peace, over the heads of all the imperialist governments and diplomatic offices, to all the exhausted nations and in this way making further waging of the war actually impossible – the Provisional Government, taking its cue from the Kadet* counterrevolutionaries and the Allied imperialists, without meaning, without strength, without a plan, toils along in the murderous harness of war, dooming to pointless destruction ever new hundreds of thousands of soldiers and sailors, and preparing the surrender of Petrograd and the smothering of the revolution. At a time when the soldier and sailor Bolsheviks are perishing together with the other sailors and soldiers as a result of others' mistakes and crimes, the so-called Supreme Commander-in-Chief continues to ruin the Bolshevik press. . . .

The leading parties of the Council of the Republic serve as a voluntary cover for this whole policy.

We, the fraction of Bolshevik Social-Democrats, declare: with this government of national betrayal and with this council that tolerates counterrevolution we have nothing in common. We do not wish either directly or obliquely to conceal even for a single day, that work, fatal to the people, which is being accomplished behind the official curtain.

The revolution is in danger! At a time when the troops of [Kaiser] Wilhelm are threatening Petrograd, the government of Kerensky-Konovalov† is preparing to flee from Petrograd, in order to transform Moscow into a stronghold of counterrevolution.

We appeal to the vigilance of the Moscow workers and soldiers!

Quitting the Council of the Republic, we appeal to the vigilance and courage of the workers, soldiers and peasants of all Russia.

*"Kadets": the Constitutional Democratic Party, from its Russian initials – Ed.

†Konovalov: a minister in Kerensky's government and acting premier at the time of the Bolshevik revolution – Ed.

Petrograd is in danger! The revolution is in danger! The nation is in danger!

The government aggravates this danger. The ruling parties help it.

Only the people themselves can save themselves and the country. We turn to the people.

All power to the Soviets!

All the land to the people!

Long live an immediate, honorable, democratic peace!

Long live the Constituent Assembly!

THE DECISION TO SEIZE POWER

On October 10 [23], 1917, Lenin came secretly to Petrograd to overcome hesitancies among the Bolshevik leadership over his demand for armed insurrection. Against the opposition of two of Lenin's long-time lieutenants, Zinoviev and Kamenev, the Central Committee adopted Lenin's resolution which instructed the party organizations to prepare for the seizure of power.

The Central Committee recognizes that the international position of the Russian revolution (the revolt in the German navy which is an extreme manifestation of the growth throughout Europe of the world socialist revolution; the threat of peace between the imperialists with the object of strangling the revolution in Russia) as well as the military situation (the indubitable decision of the Russian bourgeoisie and Kerensky and Co. to surrender Petrograd to the Germans), and the fact that the proletarian party has gained a majority in the Soviets – all this, taken in conjunction with the peasant revolt and the swing of popular confidence towards our Party (the elections in Moscow), and, finally, the obvious preparations being made for a second Kornilov affair* (the withdrawal of troops from Petrograd, the dispatch of Cossacks to Petrograd, the surrounding of Minsk by Cossacks, etc.) – all this places the armed uprising on the order of the day.

Considering therefore that an armed uprising is inevitable, and that the time for it is fully ripe, the Central Committee instructs all Party organizations to be guided accordingly, and to discuss and decide all practical questions (the Congress of Soviets of the Northern Region, the withdrawal of

FROM: Lenin, Resolution "On the Armed Uprising," adopted by the Central Committee of the R.S.D.W.P., October 10 [23], 1917 (*Selected Works*, Vol. II, book 1, pp. 189-90).

*Reference to the abortive right-wing coup attempted by the Chief of Staff General Lavr Kornilov in August, 1917 – Ed.

troops from Petrograd, the action of our people in Moscow and Minsk, etc.) from this point of view.

BOLSHEVIK OPPOSITION TO THE INSURRECTION

Fearful on Marxist grounds that the Bolsheviks did not have the mass support or the international backing to assure them success, Zinoviev and Kamenev circulated a statement endeavoring to dissuade the party from an uprising. Lenin denounced them for "strike-breaking."

A tendency is accumulating and growing in workers' circles that sees the only way out in immediately proclaiming an armed uprising. All due dates have now converged, such that if one speaks of such an uprising, he has to set the time openly, and in the next few days. In one form or another this question is already being discussed by the whole periodical press, and in workers' meetings, and it occupies the minds of a considerable circle of party workers. We, in turn, consider it our duty and our right to express ourselves on this question with full frankness.

We are most deeply convinced that to proclaim an armed uprising right now means to gamble not only the fate of our party but the fate of the Russian and international revolution as well.

There is no doubt that there occur such historical situations where the oppressed class has to recognize that it is better to go down to defeat than to surrender without a fight. Does the Russian working class now find itself in such a situation? *No, a thousand times no!!!. . .*

As a result of the tremendous growth of the influence of our party in the cities and especially in the army, such a situation has shaped up at the present time that it is becoming a more and more impossible thing for the bourgeoisie to disrupt the Constituent Assembly. Through the army, through the workers we hold a revolver at the temple of the bourgeoisie: the bourgeoisie is put in such a position that if it thought of making an attempt to disrupt the Constituent Assembly now, it would again push the petty-bourgeois parties toward us, and the hammer of the revolver would be released.

The chances of our party in the elections to the Constituent Assembly are excellent. We believe that the talk that the influence of the Bolsheviks is beginning to fall is emphatically without foundation. In the mouths of our political opponents this assertion is simply a maneuver in a political game that counts precisely on evoking a move by the Bolsheviks under condi-

FROM: Zinoviev and Kamenev, Statement to the Principal Bolshevik Party Organizations, Oct. 11 [24], 1917, in V. I. Lenin, *Sochineniya* (Works), 2nd ed., Moscow & Leningrad, State Press, 1929, XXI: 495-97 (editor's translation).

tions favorable to our enemies. The influence of the Bolsheviks is growing. Whole strata of the toiling population have just begun to be caught up by it. With the correct tactics we can win a third or even more of the seats in the Constituent Assembly. The position of the petty-bourgeois parties in the Constituent Assembly cannot be entirely the same as it is right now. Above all, their slogan, "For land, for freedom, wait for the Constituent Assembly," will be dropped. And the intensification of poverty, hunger, and the peasant movement will put more and more pressure on them and compel them to seek an alliance with the proletarian party against the landlords and capitalists represented by the Kadet Party. . . .

In Russia the majority of the workers and a significant part of the soldiers are for us. But all the rest is questionable. We are all convinced, for instance, that if the matter now reaches the point of the elections to the Constituent Assembly, the peasants will vote in the majority for the S.-R.'s. What is this – an accident? The mass of the soldiers supports us not because of the slogan of war, but because of the slogan of peace. This is an extremely important circumstance, failing to consider which we risk building all our calculations on sand. If we now take power alone and confront (as a result of the whole world situation) the necessity of waging revolutionary war, the mass of the soldiers will pour away from us. . . .

And here we approach the second assertion – that the international proletariat is supposedly now already with us, in the majority. This unfortunately is not yet so. The mutiny in the German navy has an immense symptomatic significance. The harbingers of a serious movement are present in Italy. But from this it is still very far to any amount of active support for the proletarian revolution in Russia, declaring war on the whole bourgeois world. It is extremely bad to overestimate one's forces. Undoubtedly much has been given to us and much will be asked of us. But if we now stake the whole game on one card and suffer a defeat – we will deal a cruel blow as well to the international proletarian revolution, which is growing very slowly but nevertheless growing. In time the growth of the revolution in Europe would make it obligatory for us to take power in our hands immediately, without any hesitation. In this consists the sole guarantee of the victoriousness of an uprising of the proletariat in Russia. This will come, but it is not yet. . . .

Before history, before the international proletariat, before the Russian Revolution and the Russian working class we do not now have the right to stake the whole future on the card of an armed uprising. It would be a mistake to think that a move now similar to that of July 3–5 would in the event of failure lead only to such consequences. Now the question is bigger. The question is decisive battle, and defeat in *this* battle would be defeat for the revolution.

THE MILITARY-REVOLUTIONARY COMMITTEE

While no specific date or tactical plan for the uprising was adopted by the Bolsheviks, the Petrograd Soviet under Trotsky's leadership did vote on October 16 [29] to create a "Military-Revolutionary Committee" responsible for liaison with revolutionary army and navy units in Petrograd. The Committee first met on October 20 [November 2], and two days later challenged the authority of the Provisional Government over the Petrograd garrison.

Bulletin of the Petrograd Military-Revolutionary Committee (October 20 [November 2], 1917)

In connection with the alarming political situation and to take the appropriate measures in this regard for the defense of Petrograd against counter-revolutionary moves and pogroms, the Petrograd Soviet of Workers' and Soldiers' Deputies has mobilized all its forces.

Confirmed by a general meeting of the Soviet, the Military-Revolutionary Committee got organized as of the 20th of this October and proceeded with the most intensive activity, while maintaining contact with the Headquarters of the Petrograd Military District.

In the make-up of the Military-Revolutionary Committee, besides members of the Soviet and representatives of the garrison, representatives have been brought in from the Central Committee of the Baltic Fleet, the Finland regional committee, local government, the Factory and Mill Committees and the trade unions, the Soviet of Peasants' Deputies, party military organizations, and others.

Uninterrupted guard duty by the members of the Military-Revolutionary Committee and the closest liaison with the district soviets and military units of the garrison of Petrograd and its environs were decided upon.

In the Military-Revolutionary Committee there is one representative from each of the regimental committees to serve as liaison.

Every morning at the report desk reports are to be presented by the representatives of the district and troop committees on the mood and state of affairs in each locality.

October 20

The first session of the Military-Revolutionary Committee has taken place. A report was presented by the organizing bureau on a series of basic

FROM: Bulletins of the Military-Revolutionary Committee, October 20 and 22 [November 2 and 4], 1917, in G. N. Golikov et al., eds., *Oktiabrskoe Vooruzhennoe Vosstanie v Petrograd* [The October Armed Uprising in Petrograd] (Moscow, USSR Academy of Sciences, 1957, pp. 226, 234; editor's translation).

tasks subject to decision by the meetings, and on the establishment of liaison service with units around the city and in the suburbs.

Also at a session of the bureau today a series of measures was adopted to guard against possible excesses in connection with the scheduled Holy Procession of Cossacks, and also for the defense of Petrograd.

Agitators have been dispatched around the city. Liaison with the brigade committees has been organized. A report on the state of affairs at Headquarters was heard.

Commissars have been dispatched to the line units of the garrison, certain institutions and storehouses, for observation, guidance, and organization of the appropriate measures of defense.

The Petrograd Soviet of Workers' and Peasants' Deputies has issued an appeal to the Cossacks explaining the political situation and the efforts of the counter-revolution.

Proclamation of the Military-Revolutionary Committee
(October 22 [November 4], 1917)

At its meeting on the 21st of October the revolutionary garrison of Petrograd rallied around the Military-Revolutionary Committee of the Petrograd Soviet of Workers' and Soldiers' Deputies as its leading organ.

In spite of this, on the night of October 21-22 the headquarters of the Petrograd Military District failed to recognize the Military-Revolutionary Committee and refused to conduct its work in cooperation with the representatives of the soldiers' section of the Soviet.

By this act the headquarters breaks with the revolutionary garrison and the Petrograd Soviet of Workers' and Soldiers' Deputies.

By breaking with the organized garrison of the capital, the headquarters is becoming a direct instrument of the counter-revolutionary forces.

The Military-Revolutionary Committee disclaims all responsibility for the actions of the headquarters of the Petrograd Military District.

Soldiers of Petrograd!

1. The protection of the revolutionary order from counter-revolutionary incursions rests on you, under the direction of the Military-Revolutionary Committee.

2. Any directives for the garrison that are not signed by the Military-Revolutionary Committee are invalid.

3. All directives for today – the Day of the Petrograd Soviet of Workers' and Soldiers' Deputies – remain in full force.

4. Every soldier in the garrison has the obligation of vigilance, restraint, and undeviating discipline.

5. The revolution is in danger. Long live the revolutionary garrison!

TRIGGERING THE UPRISING

The actual Bolshevik seizure of power was precipitated by an abortive move of Provisional Government troops to seize the Bolshevik newspapers early in the morning of October 24 [November 6], on the eve of the Second Congress of Soviets. The Bolshevik leaders took emergency defensive measures which soon turned into a successful offensive.

a) CIRCULAR OF THE MILITARY-REVOLUTIONARY COMMITTEE (October 24 [November 6], 1917)

Soldiers! Workers! Citizens!

The enemies of the people have gone over to the offensive during the night. The Kornilovites* at Headquarters are trying to pull cadets and shock battalions in from the outskirts. The Oranienbaum cadets and the shock troops at Tsarskoe Selo have refused to move. A traitorous blow is being devised against the Petrograd Soviet of Workers' and Soldiers' Deputies. The newspapers "Rabochi Put" [Worker's Path] and "Soldat" [Soldier] have been closed and the printing plant sealed up. The campaign of the counter-revolutionary plotters is directed *against the All-Russian Congress of Soviets* on the eve of its opening, *against the Constituent Assembly, against the people.* The Petrograd Soviet of Workers' and Soldiers' Deputies is standing up to defend the revolution. The Military-Revolutionary Committee is leading the resistance to the attack of the plotters. The whole garrison and the whole proletariat of Petrograd are ready to deal a crushing blow to the enemies of the people.

The Military-Revolutionary Committee decrees:

1. All regimental, company, and crew committees, together with the commissars of the Soviet, and all revolutionary organizations must meet in constant session, and concentrate in their hands all information about the plans and actions of the plotters.

2. Not a single soldier shall become separated from his unit without the permission of the committee.

3. Two representatives from each unit and five from each district soviet shall immediately be sent to the Smolny Institute.†

FROM: Golikov, p. 290 (editor's translation); *Protokoly Tsentralnogo Komiteta RSDRP-B,* avgust 1917-fevral 1918 [Minutes of the Central Committee of the RSDWP-B, August 1917-February 1918] (2nd ed., Moscow, 1958, pp. 119-21; editor's translation).

*Kornilovites: supposed followers of General Kornilov—Ed.

†Smolny Institute: former girls' school used as headquarters for the Petrograd Soviet—Ed.

4. Report all actions of the plotters immediately to the Smolny Institute.

5. All members of the Petrograd Soviet and all delegates to the All-Russian Congress of Soviets are summoned immediately to the Smolny Institute for a special session.

The counter-revolution has raised its criminal head.

All the gains and hopes of the soldiers, workers, and peasants are threatened with great danger. But the forces of the revolution immeasurably surpass the forces of its enemies.

The people's cause is in firm hands. The plotters will be crushed.

No vacillation or doubts. Firmness, steadfastness, perseverance, decisiveness. Long live the revolution!

b) MINUTES OF THE BOLSHEVIK CENTRAL COMMITTEE
(October 24 [November 6], 1917)

Attending: Dzerzhinsky, Kamenev, Nogin, Lomov (Oppokov), Miliutin, Ioffe, Uritsky, Bubnov, Sverdlov, Trotsky, Vinter (Berzin)

Comrade Kamenev proposes that today no member of the Central Committee be allowed to leave Smolny without the special decision of the Central Committee. Adopted.

To arrange with the Executive Commission [of the Petrograd Bolshevik Committee] regarding their duty watch both at Smolny and at the Petrograd Committee. Adopted.

AGENDA

1. Report of the Military-Revolutionary Committee.

2. The Congress of Soviets.

3. On the plenary meeting of the Central Committee.

1. Report of Comrade Kamenev.

Reports on the negotiations with the representatives of Headquarters.

2. On the printing plant and the newspaper.

Decided: To immediately send a guard detail to the printing plant and take care of the immediate issue of the regular number of the newspaper.

3. On the relation to the Bureau of the Central Executive Committee.*

Comrade Nogin insists on the necessity of clarifying the relation to the Bureau of the Central Executive Committee, since the railroad workers are following the decisions of the Central Executive Committee, and in case of disagreement with the latter we will be cut off from the rest of Russia.

The other comrades protest against this fear concerning the railroad workers.

*Central Executive Committee: the moderate leadership body set up by the First Congress of Soviets in June, 1917 – Ed.

Comrade Trotsky proposes putting two members of the Central Committee at the disposal of the Military-Revolutionary Committee to organize liaison with the postal and telegraph and railroad workers; a third member of the Central Committee, for observation of the Provisional Government. In regard to the Central Executive Committee with whatever of its delegates are present at today's session, to declare that the Central Executive Committee, whose mandate has long ago expired, is undermining the cause of revolutionary democracy.

Comrade Vinter expresses the view that it is risky to scatter the Central Committee, therefore it is better to bring in not just members of the Central Committee.

Comrade Kamenev considers it necessary to make use of yesterday's negotiations with the Central Executive Committee, which now have been violated by the closing of *Rabochi Put*, therefore the break with the Central Executive Committee must be accomplished on just this basis. He further considers it necessary to enter into negotiations with the Left SR's and enter into political contact with them.

Comrade Sverdlov considers it necessary to assign Comrade Bubnov for liaison with the railroad workers and with the postal and telegraph employees. He proposes that our comrades in the Bureau of the Central Executive Committee quickly declare their nonsolidarity with the latter.

The vote is taken on Comrade Trotsky's first proposal on delegating members of the Central Committee for specified functions: (1) the railroad workers; (2) the post office and telegraph; (3) the food supply. Adopted.

Comrade Bubnov – to the railroad workers.

Comrade Dzerzhinsky – the post office and telegraph.

Comrade Dzerzhinsky speaks and proposes Comrade Liubovich, who has contact with the post office and telegraph.

Comrade Dzerzhinsky is made responsible; he is to organize this matter.

Comrade Miliutin is assigned to organize food supply affairs.

Comrade Podvoisky is assigned to organize observation of the Provisional Government and the disposition of its forces.

(A view expressed against Comrade Podvoisky.)

It is assigned to Comrade Sverdlov.

It is proposed to assign three men for negotiations with the Left SR's; one is proposed.

Comrade Kamenev and Comrade Vinter are assigned.

Comrades Lomov and Nogin are assigned to inform Moscow immediately about everything that is happening here.

The Moscow people report that at least one man needs to go to Moscow.

Comrade Miliutin proposes to establish permanent contact with Moscow; therefore not to send Lomov and Nogin, but only one of them; tomorrow one will go, and in a few days the other.

Comrade Trotsky proposes setting up a reserve headquarters at the Peter-Paul Fortress and to this end assigning one member of the Central Committee there.

Comrade Kamenev considers that in case of the destruction of Smolny, it is necessary to have a support point on the "Aurora,"* but Uritsky introduces a correction regarding a torpedo boat.

Comrade Trotsky insists that the political point be at the Peter-Paul Fortress.

Comrade Sverdlov proposes assigning over-all observation to Comrade Lashevich, not to a member of the Central Committee.

It is decided to furnish all members of the Central Committee with passes to the Fortress.

General observation to be assigned to Lashevich and Blagonravov.

Sverdlov is assigned to maintain constant liaison with the Fortress.

THE OCTOBER REVOLUTION

By the morning of October 25 [November 7] most of Petrograd had fallen into the hands of Bolshevik soldiers and sailors and workers' Red Guards, with scarcely a shot being fired. Lenin appeared publicly for the first time since July to proclaim the overthrow of the Provisional Government, whose leaders were beseiged and captured that evening in the Winter Palace of the Tsars.

To The Citizens of Russia!

The Provisional Government has been deposed. State power has passed into the hands of the organ of the Petrograd Soviet of Workers' and Soldiers' Deputies – the Revolutionary Military Committee, which heads the Petrograd proletariat and the garrison.

The cause for which the people have fought, namely, the immediate offer of a democratic peace, the abolition of landed proprietorship, workers' control over production, and the establishment of Soviet power – this cause has been secured.

Long live the revolution of workers, soldiers and peasants!

FROM: Proclamation of the Military-Revolutionary Committee, October 25 [November 7], 1917 (English translation in Lenin, *Collected Works*, Moscow, 1964, Vol. 26, p. 236).

*"Aurora": cruiser in Petrograd Harbor with a pro-Bolshevik crew – Ed.

THE SOVIET GOVERNMENT

Simultaneously with the capture of the Winter Palace, the Second All-Russian Congress of Soviets convened with a pro-Bolshevik majority. Over the protests of the anti-Bolshevik minority the Congress endorsed the "October Revolution" and voted to make the system of local and national soviets the official government of Russia. Executive authority was given to a new Bolshevik cabinet, the Council of People's Commissars.

The All-Russian Congress of Soviets of Workers', Soldiers', and Peasants' Deputies decrees:

To form, for the administration of the country until the convocation of the Constituent Assembly, a provisional workers' and peasants' government, which will be called the Council of People's Commissars. The conduct of the particular branches of governmental activity is entrusted to commissions, whose make-up must guarantee the carrying out of the program proclaimed by the Congress, in close combination with the mass organizations of the workers, working women, sailors, soldiers, peasants, and white-collar workers. Governmental power is vested in the collegium of the representatives of these commissions, i.e., the Council of People's Commissars.

Control over the activity of the People's Commissars and the right to remove them are vested in the All-Russian Congress of Soviets of Workers', Peasants', and Soldiers' Deputies and its Central Executive Committee.

At the present time the Council of People's Commissars consists of the following persons:

Chairman of the Council – Vladimir Ulianov (Lenin)
People's Commissar for Internal Affairs – A. I. Rykov
Agriculture – V. P. Miliutin
Labor – A. G. Shliapnikov
For Military and Naval Affairs – a committee consisting of V. A. Ovseyenko (Antonov), N. V. Krylenko, and P. E. Dybenko.
For Commercial and Industrial Affairs – V. P. Nogin
Public Education – A. V. Lunarcharsky
Finance – I. I. Skvortsov (Stepanov)
For Foreign Affairs – L. D. Bronshtein (Trotsky)
Justice – G. I. Oppokov (Lomov)
For Food Supply – I. A. Teodorovich
Posts and Telegraphs – N. P. Avilov (Glebov)
Chairman for Nationality Affairs – I. V. Dzhugashvili (Stalin)

FROM: *Decree on the Formation of a Workers' and Peasants' Government*, Golikov (p. 432; editor's translation).

The post of People's Commissar for Railroad Affairs temporarily remains unfilled.

BOLSHEVIK REVOLUTIONARY LEGISLATION

In a quick series of decrees, the new Soviet government instituted a number of sweeping reforms, some long overdue and some quite revolutionary. They ranged from democratic reforms such as the disestablishment of the church and equality for the national minorities, to the recognition of the peasants' land seizures and to openly socialist steps such as the nationalization of the banks. The Provisional Government's commitment to the war effort was repudiated. This was followed by the ominous gesture of suppressing the "bourgeois" press.

a) DECREE ON THE LAND

1. Landlord ownership of land is abolished forthwith without any compensation.

2. The landed estates, as also all crown, monasterial and church lands, with their livestock, implements, buildings and everything pertaining thereto, shall be placed at the disposal of the volost [township] Land Committees and the uyezd [county] Soviets of Peasants' Deputies pending the convocation of the Constituent Assembly. . . .

4. The following peasant Mandate, compiled by the *Izvestia of the All-Russian Soviet of Peasants' Deputies* from 242 local peasant mandates and published in No. 88 of the *Izvestia* (Petrograd, No. 88, August 19, 1917), shall serve everywhere to guide the implementation of the great land reforms until a final decision on the latter is taken by the Constituent Assembly.

5. The land of ordinary peasants and ordinary Cossacks shall not be confiscated.

Peasant Mandate on the Land

"The land question in its full scope can be settled only by the popular Constituent Assembly.

"The most equitable settlement of the land question is to be as follows:

"1) *Private ownership of land shall be abolished forever*; land shall not be sold, purchased, leased, mortgaged, or otherwise alienated.

"All land, whether *state, appanage, crown, monasterial, church, factory, primogenitary, private, public, peasant, etc., shall be alienated without compensation* and become the property of the whole people, and pass into the use of all those who cultivate it.

"Persons who suffer by this property revolution shall be deemed to be entitled to public support only for the period necessary for adaptation to the new conditions of life.

"2) All mineral wealth, e.g., ore, oil, coal, salt, etc., as well as all forests and waters of state importance, shall pass into the exclusive use of the state. All the small streams, lakes, woods, etc., shall pass into the use of the communities, to be administered by the local self-government bodies.

"3) Lands on which *high-level scientific* farming is practised, e.g., orchards, plantations, seed plots, nurseries, hot-houses, etc. *shall not be divided up, but shall be converted into model farms*, to be turned over for exclusive use *to the state or to the communities*, depending on the size and importance of such lands.

"Household land in towns and villages, with orchards and vegetable gardens shall be reserved for the use of their present owners, the size of the holdings, and the size of tax levied for the use thereof, to be determined by law. . . .

"6) The right to use the land shall be accorded to all citizens of the Russian state (without distinction of sex) desiring to cultivate it by their own labour, with the help of their families, or in partnership, but only as long as they are able to cultivate it. The employment of hired labour is not permitted. . . .

"7) Land tenure shall be on an equality basis, i.e., the land shall be distributed among the toilers in conformity with a labour standard or a consumption standard, depending on local conditions.

"There shall be absolutely no restriction on the forms of land tenure: household, farm, communal, or cooperative, as shall be decided in each individual village and settlement.

"8) All land, when alienated, shall become part of the national land fund. Its distribution among the toilers shall be in charge of the local and central self-government bodies, from democratically organized village and city communities, in which there are no distinctions of social rank, to central regional government bodies.

"The land fund shall be subject to periodical redistribution, depending on the growth of population and the increase in the productivity and the scientific level of farming. . . ."

b) DECREE ON SUPPRESSION OF HOSTILE NEWSPAPERS

In the serious decisive hour of the revolution and the days immediately following it the Military-Revolutionary Committee was compelled to adopt a whole series of measures against the counterrevolutionary press of all shades.

FROM: Decree on the Land, October 26 [November 8], 1917 (written by Lenin); *Selected Works*, Vol. II, book 1, pp. 339-41.

Immediately on all sides cries arose that the new socialistic authority was violating in this way the essential principles of its program by an attempt against the freedom of the press.

The Workers' and Soldiers' Government draws the attention of the population to the fact that in our country behind this liberal shield there is practically hidden the liberty for the richer class to seize into their hands the lion's share of the whole press and by this means to poison the minds and bring confusion into the consciousness of the masses.

Everyone knows that the bourgeois press is one of the most powerful weapons of the bourgeoisie. Especially in this critical moment when the new authority, that of the workers and peasants, is in process of consolidation, it was impossible to leave this weapon in the hands of the enemy at a time when it is not less dangerous than bombs and machine guns. This is why temporary and extraordinary measures have been adopted for the purpose of cutting off the stream of mire and calumny in which the yellow and green press would be glad to drown the young victory of the people.

As soon as the new order will be consolidated, all administrative measures against the press will be suspended; full liberty will be given it within the limits of responsibility before the laws, in accordance with the broadest and most progressive regulations in this respect.

Bearing in mind, however, the fact that any restrictions of the freedom of the press, even in critical moments, are admissible only within the bounds of necessity, the Council of People's Commissaries decrees as follows:

General rules on the press.

1. The following organs of the press shall be subject to be closed: (a) those inciting to open resistance or disobedience towards the Workers' and Peasants' Government; (b) those sowing confusion by means of an obviously calumniatory perversion of facts; (c) those inciting to acts of a criminal character punishable by the penal laws.

2. The temporary or permanent closing of any organ of the press shall be carried out only by a resolution of the Council of People's Commissaries.

3. The present decree is of a temporary nature and will be revoked by special *ukaz* when the normal conditions of public life will be reestablished.

Chairman of the Council of People's Commissars
Vladimir Ulianov (Lenin).

FROM: Decree on Suppression of Hostile Newspapers, October 27 [November 9], 1917 (English translation in *Bolshevik Propaganda:* Hearings before a Subcommittee of the Committee on the Judiciary, U. S. Senate, 65th Congress, 3rd Session, Feb. 11, 1919, to Mar. 10, 1919, Washington, Government Printing Office, p. 1243).

c) DECLARATION OF THE RIGHTS OF THE PEOPLES OF RUSSIA

The October revolution of the workmen and peasants began under the common banner of emancipation.

The peasants are being emancipated from the power of the landowners, for there is no longer the landowner's property right in the land – it has been abolished. The soldiers and sailors are being emancipated from the power of autocratic generals, for generals will henceforth be elective and subject to recall. The workingmen are being emancipated from the whims and arbitrary will of the capitalists, for henceforth there will be established the control of the workers over mills and factories. Everything living and capable of life is being emancipated from the hateful shackles.

There remain only the peoples of Russia, who have suffered and are suffering oppression and arbitrariness, and whose emancipation must immediately be begun, whose liberation must be effected resolutely and definitely.

During the period of czarism the peoples of Russia were systematically incited against one another. The results of such a policy are known: massacres and pogroms on the one hand, slavery of peoples on the other.

There can be and there must be no return to this disgraceful policy of instigation. Henceforth the policy of a voluntary and honest union of the peoples of Russia must be substituted.

In the period of imperialism, after the February revolution, when the power was transferred to the hands of the Cadet bourgeoisie, the naked policy of instigation gave way to one of cowardly distrust of the peoples of Russia, to a policy of fault-finding and provocation, of "freedom" and "equality" of peoples. The results of such a policy are known: the growth of national enmity, the impairment of mutual trust.

An end must be put to this unworthy policy of falsehood and distrust, of fault-finding and provocation. Henceforth it must be replaced by an open and honest policy which leads to complete mutual trust of the people of Russia. Only as the result of such a trust can there be formed an honest and lasting union of the peoples of Russia. Only as the result of such a union can the workmen and peasants of the peoples of Russia be cemented into one revolutionary force able to resist all attempts on the part of the imperialist-annexationist bourgeoisie.

Starting with these assumptions, the first Congress of Soviets, in June of this year, proclaimed the right of the peoples of Russia to free self-determination.

The second Congress of Soviets, in October of this year, reaffirmed this inalienable right of the peoples of Russia more decisively and definitely.

The united will of these Congresses, the Council of the People's Commissars, resolved to base their activity upon the question of the nationalities of Russia, as expressed in the following principles:

1. The equality and sovereignty of the peoples of Russia.

2. The right of the peoples of Russia to free self-determination, even to the point of separation and the formation of an independent state.

3. The abolition of any and all national and national-religious privileges and disabilities.

4. The free development of national minorities and ethnographic groups inhabiting the territory of Russia.

The concrete decrees that follow from these principles will be immediately elaborated after the setting up of a Commission on Nationality Affairs . . . .

In the name of the Russian Republic,

Chairman of the Council of People's Commissars,
V. Ulianov (Lenin).
People's Commissar on Nationality Affairs,
Iozef Dzhugashvili (Stalin).

COALITION OR ONE-PARTY GOVERNMENT

Immediately after the overthrow of the Provisional Government, many Bolsheviks, together with most members of the other socialist parties, hoped that a multi-party coalition government, based on the soviets, could be agreed upon. The Mensheviks and Right Socialist Revolutionaries, however, would not accept Lenin as head of the government, while Lenin was in no mood to make any concessions at all. Nonetheless, the cautious wing of the Bolshevik leadership – again headed by Zinoviev and Kamenev, together with the future premier Rykov – were so alarmed at the risky prospect of a one-party government that they threatened to resign in protest. Lenin's reply was to have the Central Committee condemn the supporters of the coalition as traitorous deviators, and the latter in turn resigned as they had threatened from the Bolshevik Central Committee and from the Council of People's Commissars. A few weeks later a coalition was actually arrived at between the Bolsheviks and the Left Socialist Revolutionaries, and representatives of the latter party received three posts in the Council of People's Commissars.

By early 1918 the Bolshevik critics individually made their peace with Lenin, and were accepted back into the party and governmen-

FROM: Declaration of the Rights of the Peoples of Russia, November 2 [15], 1917 (English translation in *The Nation*, December 28, 1919).

tal leadership. At the same time, the Left SR's, incensed over the signing of the Treaty of Brest-Litovsk with Germany, resigned from the cabinet in disgust, and the Soviet administration thus acquired the exclusively Communist character which it has had ever since. The Left SR's, like the Right SR's and the Mensheviks, continued to function in the soviets as a more or less legal opposition until the outbreak of large-scale civil war in the middle of 1918. At that point the opposition parties took positions which were either equivocal or openly anti-Bolshevik, and one after another they were suppressed.

a) RESOLUTION OF THE CENTRAL COMMITTEE ON THE OPPOSITION (November 2 [15], 1917)

The Central Committee recognizes that the present session has historic importance and that it is therefore essential to define the two positions which have been revealed here.

1) The Central Committee recognizes that the opposition within the Central Committee who are resigning have completely departed from all the fundamental positions of Bolshevism and the proletarian class struggle in general; they are repeating profoundly un-Marxist remarks about the impossibility of a socialist revolution in Russia, about the necessity of giving in to the ultimatums and threats which come from a conscious minority in the soviet organization; in this manner they are undermining the will and decision of the Second All-Russian Congress of Soviets; in this manner they are sabotaging the dictatorship of the proletariat and the poorest peasantry just after it has begun.

2) The Central Committee charges this opposition with full responsibility for slowing down revolutionary work and for the vacillation which at the present moment is criminal; it invites it to shift its controversy and its skepticism to the press, away from the practical work in which it does not believe. In this opposition there is nothing, except for the fright of the bourgeoisie and the reflection of tendencies of the backward (but nonrevolutionary) part of the population.

3) The Central Committee asserts that it is impossible to refuse a purely Bolshevik government without treason to the slogan of the power of the Soviets, since a majority at the Second All-Russian Congress of Soviets, without excluding anyone from the congress, handed power over to this government.

4) The Central Committee asserts that it is impossible, without betraying the Soviets of Workers', Soldiers', and Peasants' Deputies, to turn to petty bargaining and join to the Soviets organizations of a nonsoviet type,

i.e., organizations which are not voluntary unions of the masses' revolutionary vanguard which is struggling to overthrow the landlords and the capitalists.

5) The Central Committee asserts that concessions in the face of the ultimatums and threats by the minority in the Soviets is equivalent to full renunciation not only of the power of the Soviets, but also of democratism, for such concessions are equivalent to the majority's fear of using its majority, are equivalent to submitting to anarchy and to the repetition of ultimatums on the part of any minority.

6) The Central Committee asserts that without excluding anyone from the Second All-Russian Congress of Soviets, it is now quite ready to restore those who walked out and to accept a coalition with these people within the framework of the Soviets; it is accordingly absolutely false to speak as though the Bolsheviks do not want to share power with anyone. . . .

9) The Central Committee asserts, finally, that the victory of communism both in Russia and in Europe is guaranteed in spite of all difficulties, but only if the policy of the present government is continued undeviatingly. The Central Committee expresses full confidence in the victory of this socialist revolution and calls on all skeptics and vacillators to throw off all their hesitation and support the activity of this government with all their souls and the utmost energy.

b) BOLSHEVIK STATEMENTS OF RESIGNATION (November 4 [17], 1917)

On November 1 the Central Committee of the RSDWP (Bolsheviks) adopted a resolution which in actuality rejects agreement with the parties making up the Soviet of Workers' and Soldiers' Deputies for the formation of a socialist soviet government.

We consider that only immediate agreement on the conditions indicated by us would make it possible for the proletariat and the revolutionary army to consolidate the conquests of the October Revolution, to consolidate themselves in their new positions and gather their forces for the further struggle for socialism.

We consider that the creation of such a government is essential to avert further bloodshed, the imminent famine, and the destruction of the revolution by the Kaledinites,* and also to guarantee the summoning of the Constituent Assembly at the appointed time and the real execution of the

FROM: Resolution of the Central Committee of the RSDWP (Bolsheviks), November 2 [15], 1917, "On the Question of the Opposition within the Central Committee" (CPSU in Resolutions, I, 401-02; editor's translation).

*Kaledin: Cossack general who organized the first White resistance to the Bolsheviks—Ed.

program of peace adopted by the All-Russian Congress of Soviets of Workers' and Soldiers' Deputies.

By incredible effort we have succeeded in winning reconsideration of the decision of the Central Committee and of the new resolution, which could become the basis for creating a soviet government.

However, this new decision evoked on the part of the leading group in the Central Committee a series of actions which clearly show that it has firmly decided not to allow the formation of a government of the soviet parties but to fight for a purely Bolshevik government however it can and whatever the sacrifices this costs the workers and soldiers.

We cannot assume responsibility for this ruinous policy of the Central Committee, carried out against the will of a large part of the proletariat and soldiers, who crave the earliest cessation of bloodshed between the separate parts of the democratic forces.

We resign, therefore, from the posts of members of the Central Committee, so that we will have the right to speak our minds openly to the mass of workers and soldiers and to call on them to support our slogan! Long live the Government of the Soviet Parties! Immediate agreement on this condition!

We leave the Central Committee at the moment of victory, at the moment of our party's domination; we leave because we cannot watch quietly as the policy of the leading group in the Central Committee leads to the workers' parties' losing the fruits of this victory, to the destruction of the proletariat.

Remaining in the ranks of the proletarian party, we hope that the proletariat will overcome all obstacles and will recognize that our step was compelled by our consciousness of our burden of responsibility to the socialist proletariat.

INDUSTRIAL DEMOCRACY

The ideal which commanded the loyalty of most Russian workers at the time of the October Revolution was that of direct administration of industry by elected committees of workers. Such control was often put into effect by direct seizures, just as the peasants were seizing landlords' property. For the moment, the Bolshevik party acknowledged the practice of workers' control, though Lenin was soon to change his attitude. The ideal continued to animate the ultra-left

FROM: Kamenev, Rykov, Miliutin, Zinoviev, and Nogin, Declaration to the Central Committee of the RSDWP (Bolsheviks), November 4 [17], 1917 (*Protocols of the Central Committee of the RSDWP*, 1917-1918, Moscow, State Press, 1929, pp. 167-68; editor's translation).

groups among the Communists, and was revived again in Yugoslavia after Tito's break with Stalin in 1948.

1. In the interests of a systematic regulation of national economy, Workers' Control is introduced in all industrial, commercial, agricultural (and similar) enterprises which are hiring people to work for them in their shops or which are giving them work to take home. This control is to extend over the production, storing, buying and selling of raw materials and finished products as well as over the finances of the enterprise.

2. The workers will exercise this control through their elected organizations, such as factory and shop committees, soviets of elders, etc. The office employees and the technical personnel are also to have representation in these committees.

3. Every large city, province and industrial area is to have its own Soviet of Workers' Control, which, being an organ of the S(oviet) of W(orkers'), S(oldiers'), and P(easants') D(eputies), must be composed of representatives of trade-unions, factory, shop and other workers' committees and workers' co-operatives. . . .

6. The organs of Workers' Control have the right to supervise production, fix the minimum of output, and determine the cost of production.

7. The organs of Workers' Control have the right to control all the business correspondence of an enterprise. Owners of enterprises are legally responsible for all correspondence kept secret. Commercial secrets are abolished. The owners have to show to the organs of Workers' Control all their books and statements for the current year and for the past years.

8. The rulings of the organs of Workers' Control are binding on the owners of enterprises and can be annulled only by decisions of the higher organs of Workers' Control.

V. Ulianov (Lenin) – President of the Council of People's Commissars
A. Shliapnikov – People's Commissar of Labor

THE SECRET POLICE

Police action by the Bolsheviks to combat political opposition commenced with the creation of the "Cheka" (so called from the Russian initials of the first two terms in its official name, "Extraordinary Commission to Fight Counter-Revolution"). Under the direction of Felix Dzerzhinsky, the Cheka became the

FROM: Decree on Workers' Control, November 14 [27], 1917 (English translation in James Bunyan and H. H. Fisher, *The Bolshevik Revolution, 1917-1918*, pp. 308-10; this and subsequent selections reprinted by permission of the publisher, Stanford University Press. Copyright 1934 by the Board of Trustees of Leland Stanford Junior University).

prototype of totalitarian secret police systems, enjoying at critical times the right of unlimited arrest and summary execution of suspects and hostages. The principle of such police surveillance over the political leanings of the Soviet population has remained in effect ever since, despite the varying intensity of repression and the organizational metamorphoses of the police – from Cheka to GPU (1922, from the Russian initials for "State Political Administration") to NKVD (1934 – the "People's Commissariat of Internal Affairs") to MVD and MGB (after World War II – "Ministry of Internal Affairs" and "Ministry of State Security," respectively) to KGB (since 1953 – the "Committee for State Security").

The Commission is to be named the All-Russian Extraordinary Commission and is to be attached to the Council of People's Commissars. [This commission] is to make war on counter-revolution and sabotage. . . .

The duties of the Commission will be:

1. To persecute and break up all acts of counter-revolution and sabotage all over Russia, no matter what their origin.

2. To bring before the Revolutionary Tribunal all counter-revolutionists and saboteurs and to work out a plan for fighting them.

3. To make preliminary investigation only – enough to break up [the counter-revolutionary act]. The Commission is to be divided into sections: (a) the information section, (b) the organization section (in charge of organizing the fight against counter-revolution all over Russia) with branches, and (c) the fighting section.

The Commission will be formed tomorrow (December 21). . . . The Commission is to watch the press, saboteurs, strikers, and the Socialist-Revolutionists of the Right. Measures [to be taken against these counter-revolutionists are] confiscation, confinement, deprivation of [food] cards, publication of the names of the enemies of the people, etc.

Council of People's Commissars.

THE DISSOLUTION OF THE CONSTITUENT ASSEMBLY

In December, 1917, the Bolsheviks permitted, as they had promised, the election of a Constituent Assembly. This was the only reasonably free and democratic general election which Russia has ever had. The Bolsheviks placed second with some nine million votes, but an overwhelming majority was won by the Right SR's with their

FROM: Decree on Establishment of the Extraordinary Commission to Fight Counter-Revolution [the "Cheka"], December 7 [20], 1917 (English translation in Bunyan and Fisher, pp. 297-98).

peasant backing. Lenin permitted the Assembly to meet for only one day, and then forcibly banned its continuation on the ground that it was a counterrevolutionary threat to the soviets.

. . . The Constituent Assembly, elected on the basis of lists drawn up prior to the October Revolution, was an expression of the old relation of political forces which existed when power was held by the compromisers and the Kadets. When the people at that time voted for the candidates of the Socialist-Revolutionary Party, they were not in a position to choose between the Right Socialist-Revolutionaries, the supporters of the bourgeoisie, and the Left Socialist-Revolutionaries, the supporters of Socialism. Thus the Constituent Assembly, which was to have been the crown of the bourgeois parliamentary republic, could not but become an obstacle in the path of the October Revolution and the Soviet power.

The October Revolution, by giving the power to the Soviets, and through the Soviets to the toiling and exploited classes, aroused the desperate resistance of the exploiters, and in the crushing of this resistance it fully revealed itself as the beginning of the socialist revolution. The toiling classes learnt by experience that the old bourgeois parliamentarism had outlived its purpose and was absolutely incompatible with the aim of achieving Socialism, and that not national institutions, but only class institutions (such as the Soviets), were capable of overcoming the resistance of the propertied classes and of laying the foundations of a socialist society. To relinquish the sovereign power of the Soviets, to relinquish the Soviet republic won by the people, for the sake of bourgeois parliamentarism and the Constituent Assembly, would now be a retrograde step and cause the collapse of the October workers' and peasants' revolution.

Owing to the circumstances mentioned above, the majority in the Constituent Assembly which met on January 5 was secured by the party of the Right Socialist-Revolutionaries, the party of Kerensky, Avksentyev and Chernov. Naturally, this party refused to discuss the absolutely clear, precise and unambiguous proposal of the supreme organ of Soviet power, the Central Executive Committee of the Soviets, to recognize the program of the Soviet power, to recognize the "Declaration of Rights of the Toiling and Exploited People," to recognize the October Revolution and the Soviet power. Thereby the Constituent Assembly severed all ties with the Soviet Republic of Russia. The withdrawal from such a Constituent Assembly of the groups of the Bolsheviks and the Left Socialist-Revolutionaries, who now patently constitute the overwhelming majority in the Soviets and

FROM: Lenin, Draft Decree on the Dissolution of the Constituent Assembly (January 6 [19], 1918; *Selected Works*, Vol. II, book 1, pp. 382-84).

enjoy the confidence of the workers and the majority of the peasants, was inevitable.

The Right Socialist-Revolutionary and Menshevik parties are in fact waging outside the walls of the Constituent Assembly a most desperate struggle against the Soviet power, calling openly in their press for its overthrow and characterizing as arbitrary and unlawful the crushing by force of the resistance of the exploiters by the toiling classes, which is essential in the interests of emancipation from exploitation. They are defending the saboteurs, the servitors of capital, and are going to the length of undisguised calls to terrorism, which certain "unidentified groups" have already begun to practise. It is obvious that under such circumstances the remaining part of the Constituent Assembly could only serve as a screen for the struggle of the counterrevolutionaries to overthrow the Soviet power.

Accordingly, the Central Executive Committee resolves: The Constituent Assembly is hereby dissolved.

TROTSKY ON THE RED ARMY

Trotsky resigned as Foreign Commissar during the Brest-Litovsk crisis, but he was immediately appointed Commissar of Military Affairs and entrusted with the creation of a new Red Army to replace the old Russian army which had dissolved during the revolution. Many Communists wanted the new military force to be built up on strictly revolutionary principles, with guerrilla tactics, the election of officers, and the abolition of traditional discipline. Trotsky set himself emphatically against this attitude and demanded an army organized in the conventional way and employing "military specialists" – experienced officers from the old army.

. . . As regards politics and direct fighting, the October Revolution has come about with unexpected and incomparable successfulness. There has been no case in history of such a powerful offensive of an oppressed class which with such deliberateness and speed overthrew the rule of the propertied ruling classes in all parts of the country and extended its own rule from Petrograd and Moscow to every far-flung corner of Russia.

This successfulness of the October uprising has shown the political weakness of the bourgeois classes, which is rooted in the peculiarities of the development of Russian capitalism. . . .

If, as the working class, following what Marx said, we cannot simply

FROM: Trotsky, "Labor, Discipline, Order" (Speech to a Moscow City Conference of the Russian Communist Party, March 27, 1918; *Works*, Vol. 17, part 1, Moscow, 1926, pp. 157-58, 161-62, 170-71; editor's translation).

take over mechanically the old apparatus of state power, this does not at all mean that we can do without all of those elements which helped make up the old apparatus of state power.

The misfortune of the working class is that it has always been in the position of an oppressed class. This is reflected in everything: both in its level of education, and in the fact that it does not have those habits of rule which the dominant class has and which it bequeaths to its heirs through its schools, universities, etc. The working class has none of this, but must acquire it.

Having come to power, it has had to view the old state apparatus as an apparatus of class oppression. But at the same time it must draw from this apparatus all the worthwhile skilled elements which are technically necessary, put them where they belong, and heighten its proletarian class power by using these elements. This, Comrades, is the task which now stands before us for our overall growth. . . .

Here I turn to a ticklish point which to a familiar degree has now assumed major importance in our party life. This is one of the questions of the organization of the army, specifically the question of recruiting military specialists – i.e., to speak plainly, former officers and generals – to create the army and to run it. All basic, guiding institutions of the army are now set up so that they consist of one military specialist and two political commissars. Such is the present basic type of the leading organs of the army.

I have more than once had to say at open meetings that in the area of command, operations and fighting we will place full responsibility on the military specialists, and therefore will grant them the necessary rights. Many among us are afraid of this, and their misgivings find expression in the resolutions of certain party organizations. . . . Here again the task of the party is to handle such phenomena in our own midst with complete mercilessness, for they ruin the country and disgrace and disrupt our party. . . .

There is still another question in the area of the organization of the army: the so-called elective principle. In general, all it means is to struggle against the old officers' corps, to control the commanding staff.

As long as power was in the hands of a class that was hostile to us, when the commanding staff was an instrument in the hands of this power, we were obliged to strive to smash the class resistance of the commanding personnel by way of the elective principle. But now political power is in the hands of that same working class from whose ranks the army is recruited.

Under the present regime in the army – I tell you this in all frankness – the elective principle is politically pointless and technically inexpedient, and has in fact already been set aside by decree. . . .

The question of creating the army is now a question of life and death for us. You yourselves understand this as well as I. But we cannot create the army only by means of the administrative mechanism which we have as long as it is so very poor. If we have a powerful mechanism, it is an ideological mechanism – this mechanism is our party. It will create the army, Comrades, and do everything to uproot the prejudices of which I spoke; it will help us fill up the cadres of the revolutionary army with militant and devoted workers and peasants, it will apply itself in conducting obligatory military training in the mills, factories and villages, and in this way will create the military apparatus for the defense of the Soviet Republic.

LENIN ON ECONOMIC EXPEDIENCY

Once firmly established in power, Lenin began to reconsider the utopianism which characterized the Bolsheviks in 1917 as regards both internal and international revolution. After the conclusion of peace he prepared an extensive statement on the transitional forms which he felt the Soviet economic order would have to adopt, with emphasis on the principal features of large-scale capitalistic industry – individual managerial authority, labor discipline and piecework incentives, and the employment of "bourgeois" managers and technical experts.

Thanks to the peace which has been achieved – notwithstanding its extremely onerous character and extreme instability – the Russian Soviet Republic has received an opportunity for a certain period of time to concentrate its efforts on the most important and most difficult aspect of the socialist revolution, namely, the organizational task. . . .

. . . In every socialist revolution – and consequently in the socialist revolution in Russia which we began on October 25, 1917 – the principal task of the proletariat, and of the poor peasantry which it leads, is the positive or constructive work of setting up an extremely intricate and delicate system of new organizational relationships extending to the planned production and distribution of the goods required for the existence of tens of millions of people. Such a revolution can be successfully carried out only if the majority of the population, and primarily the majority of the toilers, engage in independent creative work as makers of history. Only if the proletariat and the poor peasantry display sufficient class consciousness, devo-

FROM: Lenin, "The Immediate Tasks of the Soviet Government: The International Position of the Russian Soviet Republic and the Fundamental Tasks of the Socialist Revolution" (April, 1918; *Selected Works*, Vol. II, book 1, pp. 448, 450, 458-59, 468-71, 475-77, 481-82, 488).

tion to principles, self-sacrifice and perseverance will the victory of the socialist revolution be assured. By creating a new, Soviet type of state, which gives the opportunity to the toiling and oppressed masses to take an active part in the independent building up of a new society, we solved only a small part of this difficult problem. The principal difficulty lies in the economic sphere, viz., the introduction of the strictest and universal accounting and control of the production and distribution of goods, raising the productivity of labour and *socializing* production *in actual practice.* . . .

This is a peculiar epoch, or rather stage of development, and in order to utterly defeat capital, we must be able to adapt the forms of our struggle to the peculiar conditions of this stage.

Without the guidance of specialists in the various fields of knowledge, technology and experience, the transition to Socialism will be impossible, because Socialism calls for a conscious mass advance to greater productivity of labour compared with capitalism, and on the basis achieved by capitalism. Socialism must achieve this advance *in its own way*, by its own methods – or, to put it more concretely, by *Soviet* methods. And the specialists, because of the entire environment of the social life which made them specialists, are, in the main, unavoidably bourgeois. Had our proletariat, after capturing power, quickly solved the problem of accounting, control and organization on a national scale (which was impossible owing to the war and the backwardness of Russia), then we, after breaking the sabotage, would have also completely subordinated these bourgeois specialists to ourselves by means of universal accounting and control. . . .

Now we have to resort to the old bourgeois method and to agree to pay a very high price for the "services" of the biggest bourgeois specialists. All those who are familiar with the subject appreciate this, but not all ponder over the significance of this measure being adopted by the proletarian state. Clearly, such a measure is a compromise, a departure from the principles of the Paris Commune and of every proletarian power, which call for the reduction of all salaries to the level of the wages of the average worker, which call for fighting careerism, not with words, but with deeds.

Moreover, it is clear that such a measure not only implies the cessation – in a certain field and to a certain degree – of the offensive against capital (for capital is not a sum of money, but a definite social relation); it is also *a step backward* on the part of our socialist Soviet state power, which from the very outset proclaimed and pursued the policy of reducing high salaries to the level of the wages of the average worker. . . .

. . . It becomes immediately clear that while it is possible to capture the central government in a few days, while it is possible to suppress the military resistance (and sabotage) of the exploiters even in different parts of a great country in a few weeks, the capital solution of the problem of raising the productivity of labour requires, at all events (particularly after a most terrible and devastating war), several years. The protracted nature of the work is certainly dictated by objective circumstances. . . .

. . . We must raise the question of piecework and apply and test it in practice; we must raise the question of applying much of what is scientific and progressive in the Taylor system, we must make wages correspond to the total amount of goods turned out, or to the amount of work done by the railways, the water transport system, etc., etc.

The Russian is a bad worker compared with the advanced peoples. Nor could it be otherwise under the tsarist regime and in view of the tenacity of the remnants of serfdom. The task that the Soviet government must set the people in all its scope is – learn to work. The Taylor system, the last word of capitalism in this respect, like all capitalist progress, is a combination of the refined brutality of bourgeois exploitation and a number of greatest scientific achievements in the field of analyzing mechanical motions during work, the elimination of superfluous and awkward motions, the elaboration of correct methods of work, the introduction of the best system of accounting and control, etc. The Soviet Republic must at all costs adopt all that is valuable in the achievements of science and technology in this field. The possibility of building Socialism is conditioned precisely upon our success in combining the Soviet power and the Soviet organization of administration with the up-to-date achievements of capitalism. We must organize in Russia the study and teaching of the Taylor system and systematically try it out and adapt it to our purposes. . . .

. . . It would be extremely stupid and absurdly utopian to assume that the transition from capitalism to Socialism is possible without coercion and without dictatorship. Marx's theory very definitely opposed this petty-bourgeois-democratic and anarchist absurdity long ago. And Russia of 1917-18 confirms the correctness of Marx's theory in this respect so strikingly, palpably and imposingly that only those who are hopelessly dull or who have obstinately decided to turn their backs on the truth can be under any misapprehension concerning this. Either the dictatorship of Kornilov (if we take him as the Russian type of bourgeois Cavaignac*), or the dictatorship of the proletariat – any other choice is *out of the question* for a country which has gone through an extremely rapid development with extremely sharp turns and amidst desperate ruin created by one of the most horrible wars in history. . . .

*Cavaignac: general who put down the uprising of the Paris working class in June, 1848–Ed.

. . . Firstly, capitalism cannot be defeated and eradicated without the ruthless suppression of the resistance of the exploiters, who cannot at once be deprived of their wealth, of their advantages of organization and knowledge, and consequently for a fairly long period will inevitably try to overthrow the hated rule of the poor; secondly, every great revolution, and a socialist revolution in particular, even if there were no external war, is inconceivable without internal war, i.e., civil war, which is even more devastating than external war, and involves thousands and millions of cases of wavering and desertion from one side to another, implies a state of extreme indefiniteness, lack of equilibrium and chaos. And of course, all the elements of disintegration of the old society, which are inevitably very numerous and connected mainly with the petty bourgeoisie (because it is the petty bourgeoisie that every war and every crisis ruins and destroys first) cannot but "reveal themselves" during such a profound revolution. And these elements of disintegration *cannot* "reveal themselves" otherwise than in the increase of crime, hooliganism, corruption, profiteering and outrages of every kind. To put these down requires time and *requires an iron hand. . . .*

. . . There is absolutely *no* contradiction in principle between Soviet (*that is*, socialist) democracy and the exercise of dictatorial powers by individuals. The difference between proletarian dictatorship and bourgeois dictatorship is that the former strikes at the exploiting minority in the interests of the exploited majority, and that it is exercised – *also through individuals* – not only by the toiling and exploited masses, but also by organizations which are built in such a way as to rouse these masses to the work of history-making. (The Soviet organizations are organizations of this kind.)

In regard to the second question concerning the significance of precisely individual dictatorial powers from the point of view of the specific tasks of the present moment, it must be said that large-scale machine industry – which is precisely the material source, the productive source, the foundation of Socialism – calls for absolute and strict *unity of will*, which directs tha joint labours of hundreds, thousands and tens of thousands of people. The technical, economic and historical necessity of this is obvious, and all those who have thought about Socialism have always regarded it as one of the conditions of Socialism. But how can strict unity of will be ensured? – by thousands subordinating their will to the will of one.

Given ideal class consciousness and discipline on the part of those taking part in the common work, this subordination would rather remind one of the mild leadership of a conductor of an orchestra. It may assume the sharp forms of a dictatorship if ideal discipline and class consciousness are lacking. But be that as it may, *unquestioning subordination* to a single will is absolutely necessary for the success of processes organized on the pattern of large-scale machine industry. On the railways it is twice and three times as necessary. In this transition from one political task to another, which *on the surface* is totally dissimilar to the first, consists the peculiar nature of the present situation. The revolution has only just smashed the oldest, strongest and heaviest fetters to which the masses submitted under duress. That was yesterday. But today the same revolution demands – precisely in the interests of its development and consolidation, precisely in the interests of Socialism – that the masses *unquestioningly obey the single will* of the leaders of the labour process. Of course, such a transition cannot be made at one step. Clearly, it can be achieved only as a result of tremendous jolts, shocks, reversions to old ways, the enormous exertion of effort on the part of the proletarian vanguard, which is leading the people to the new ways. . . .

The fight against the bureaucratic distortion of the Soviet form of organization is assured by the firmness of the connection between the Soviets and the "people," meaning by that the toilers and exploited, and by the flexibility and elasticity of this connection. Even in the most democratic capitalist republics in the world, the poor never regard the bourgeois parliament as "their own" institution. But the Soviets are "their own" and not alien institutions to the masses of workers and peasants. . . .

THE LEFT COMMUNISTS ON A PROLETARIAN ECONOMIC POLICY

Lenin's espousal of the forms of capitalist industry was a rude shock to the anarchistic hopes of the Communist left wing. The Left Communist opposition which had fought the Treaty of Brest-Litovsk now organized to resist, in the name of the working class, the "petty-bourgeois" policy of "state capitalism" as a menace to the ideals of the revolution.

. . . 8. The economic situation and the grouping of classes in Russia have changed since the conclusion of peace. A situation has arisen which provides the foundation for two opposite tendencies (toward the weakening and toward the growth of revolutionary forces), of which the first was immediately strengthened by the conclusion of the peace and for the time being may prevail. . . .

FROM: "Theses on the Present Moment," presented by the faction of Left Communists to a conference of party leaders, April 4, 1918 (*Kommunist*, No. 1, April, 1918; editor's translation).

9. . . . . In spite of the temporary weakening of the forces of the revolution, in spite of the serious international position of the Soviet Republic, there is no serious support within the limits of the present Soviet state for the restoration either of the monarchy or of the power of the compromiser parties. . . .

On the contrary, there is a basis for the strengthening and development of the dictatorship of the proletariat and the poorest peasants, and for the socialist reform of society which they have begun. . . . Above all, the preliminary smashing of the bourgeois-compromiser governmental system, of the old relations of production, and of the material class forces of the bourgeoisie and its allies is almost complete. Further, the class education of the proletariat in the course of civil war will give it a great supply of class solidarity, energy and consciousness. Also, the real conquests which it has made have strengthened these revolutionary forces and energy in resisting the enemy who threatens the conquests of the proletariat. The energetic organization of production on socialist lines will on the one hand strengthen the economic base of the proletariat as a revolutionary force, and on the other will be a new school of class organization and activity for it. Finally, the preservation of a link with the international and all-Russian proletarian movement will also increase the class activity of the proletariat and protect it from disruption and tiring.

But in connection with the most imminent, immediate consequences of the peace: the reduction of class activeness and the increasing de-classing of the proletariat in the main revolutionary centers, in connection with the increasing class fusion of the proletariat and poorest peasants (which since the signing of the peace must, under the pressure of their demands and influence, become a bulwark of the soviet power), it is quite possible for a tendency to arise toward a deviation by the majority of the Communist Party and the soviet power directed by it into the channel of a petty-bourgeois policy of a new form.

In the event that this tendency becomes a reality, the working class will cease to be the director, the exerciser of hegemony over the socialist revolution, leading the poorest peasantry toward the destruction of the rule of finance capital and the landlords; it will show itself to be a force sprinkled into the ranks of the semiproletarian-petty-bourgeois masses, a force which sets itself the task not of the proletarian struggle in union with the West-European proletariat for the overthrow of the imperialist system, but the defense of the farmers' fatherland from the oppression of imperialism, which is possible to achieve by means of compromise with it. In the event of the rejection of an actively proletarian policy, the conquests of the workers' and peasants' revolution would begin to freeze into a system of state capitalism and petty-bourgeois economic relations.

10. Before the party of the proletariat two paths stand open. One of these paths is to guard and strengthen the intact part of the Soviet state, which now with respect to the economic process – since the revolution is not complete – is only an organization for the transition to socialism (with incomplete nationalization of the banks, with capitalistic forms of financing enterprises, with the partial nationalization of enterprises, with the predominance of small-scale farming and small property-holding in the village, with the effort of the peasants to solve the agrarian question by dividing the land; and in the political respect can be transformed from the framework of the dictatorship of the proletariat supported by the poorest peasantry, into an instrument for the political domination of the semiproletarian-petty-bourgeois masses, and become merely a transition stage to the full domination of finance capital.

This path can be justified – verbally – as an effort to preserve for the international revolution, in any way at all, the revolutionary forces and soviet power even if in "Great Russia" alone.* In this case every effort will be directed toward the strengthening and development of the forces of the revolution, toward "organic construction," with the rejection of further smashing of capitalistic production relations and even with the partial restoration of them. . . .

11. . . . . The economic policy which corresponds to such a course will have to develop in the direction of agreements with capitalistic businessmen, both the "patriotic" ones and the international ones who stand behind them. . . .

With the policy of administering enterprises on the basis of broad participation by capitalists and semibureaucratic centralization it is natural to combine a labor policy directed toward the installation among the workers of discipline under the banner of "self-discipline," toward the introduction of obligatory labor for workers (such a program was proposed by the rightist Bolsheviks), piecework payment, lengthening of the working day, etc.

The form of governmental administration will have to develop in the direction of bureaucratic centralization, the rule of various commissars, the deprivation of local soviets of their independence, and in practice the rejection of the type of "commune state" administered from below. . . .

12. The path described above, taken as a whole, as well as the tendency to deviate along this path, is dangerous in the highest degree to the interests of the Russian and international proletariat. This path strengthens the separation begun by the Brest peace between the "Great-Russian" Soviet Republic and the all-Russian and international revolutionary movement,

* I.e., in Russia minus its non-Russian-speaking western regions – Ed.

locking up the Soviet Republic in the frame of a national state with a transitional economy and a petty-bourgeois political order. . . .

The line of policy sketched above may strengthen the influence of foreign and domestic counterrevolutionary forces in Russia, break down the revolutionary might of the working class, and, by cutting the Russian revolution off from the international revolution, have a ruinous effect on the interests of both.

13. Proletarian Communists consider another course of policy essential: not the course of preserving a soviet oasis in the north of Russia with the help of concessions that transform it into a petty-bourgeois state; not the transition to "organic internal work," fortified by the consideration that the "acute period" of the civil war is over.

The acute period of civil war is over only in the sense of the absence of an objective necessity to apply predominantly the sharpest physical measures of revolutionary violence. Once the bourgeoisie is beaten and is no longer capable of open fighting, "military" methods for the most part subside. But the sharpness of the class contradiction between the proletariat and the bourgeoisie cannot diminish; as before, the position of the proletariat in relation to the bourgeoisie reduces to the complete negation of it, the annihilation of it as a class. The end of the acute period of the civil war cannot signify that deals are possible with the remaining forces of the bourgeoisie, and the "organic construction" of socialism, which is undoubtedly the key task of the moment, can be accomplished only by the efforts of the proletariat itself, with the participation of skilled technicians and administrators, and not with some form or other of collaboration with the "privileged elements" as such.

The Russian workers' revolution cannot "save itself" by leaving the international revolutionary path, steadily avoiding a fight, retreating in the face of the pressure of international capital, and making concessions to "patriotic capital.". . .

The administration of enterprises must be placed in the hands of mixed collegia of workers and technical personnel, under the control and direction of the local economic councils. All economic life must be subordinated to the organized influence of these councils, which are chosen by the workers without the participation of the "privileged elements," but with the participation of the unions of the technical and service personnel of the enterprises.

No capitulation to the bourgeoisie and its petty-bourgeois intellectual henchmen, but the finishing off of the bourgeoisie and the final smashing of sabotage. Final liquidation of the counterrevolutionary press and counterrevolutionary bourgeois organizations. Introduction of labor duty for skilled specialists and intellectuals; organization of consumption communes; limitation of consumption by the well-to-do classes and confiscation of their surplus possessions. In the village, organization of pressure by the poorest peasants on the rich ones, the development of large-scale social agriculture, and the support of forms of working the land by the poorest peasants in the transition to social farming. . .

15. The proletarian Communists define their attitude toward the majority of the party as the position of the left wing of the party and the vanguard of the Russian proletariat, which preserves full unity with the party insofar as the policy of the majority does not create an unavoidable split in the ranks of the proletariat itself. They define their attitude toward the Soviet power as the position of unqualified support of this power at a time of necessity, by way of participating in it insofar as the confirmation of the peace has removed from the agenda the question of responsibility for this decision and has created a new objective situation. This participation is possible only on the basis of a definite political program which would prevent the deviation of the Soviet power and the majority of the party on the ruinous path of petty-bourgeois policies. In the event of such a deviation the left wing of the party will have to stand in the position of an effective and responsible proletarian opposition.

ONE-PARTY DICTATORSHIP

With the rapid spread of armed resistance to the Communists in the spring of 1918 and the organization of the "White" armies, the relatively moderate phase of Soviet rule came to an end. The anti-Communist socialist parties were ousted from the soviets and in effect outlawed. In July, 1918, the Left SR's abandoned the role of a loyal opposition and tried to overthrow the Communists in the hope of forcing a resumption of the war. With their defeat, the Soviet government became a completely one-party affair. Political terror commenced in the summer of 1918 with widespread summary executions by both "Reds" and "Whites." Revolutionary emotion and violence swelled to a climax as bitter civil war raged from 1918 to 1920. Most Communists were filled with a fanaticism that combined utopian hopes for socialism with dictatorial violence against all who stood in their way.

FROM: Decree on the Expulsion of the Right Socialist Parties from the Soviets, June 14, 1918 (English translation in James Bunyan, *Intervention, Civil War, and Communism in Russia, April-December, 1918*, Baltimore, Johns Hopkins University Press, 1936, p. 191; this and following selection reprinted by permission of the publisher).

Taking into consideration that:

1. The Soviet Government is living through its most difficult period, having to withstand at the same time the attacks of international imperialism . . . and those of its allies within the Russian Republic, who spare no means, from the most shameless calumny to conspiracy and armed uprisings, in the struggle against the Workers' and Peasants' Government.

2. The presence in Soviet organizations of representatives of parties which are obviously endeavoring to discredit and overthrow the Soviet Government is absolutely intolerable.

3. From previously published documents, as well as from those cited at the present meeting, it is clear that representatives of the Socialist-Revolutionists (of the Right and Center) and the Russian Social-Democratic Labor Party (Menshevik) . . . are guilty of organizing armed attacks against the workers and peasants, in association with notorious counter-revolutionists. . . .

The All-Russian Central Executive Committee of Soviets resolves: To exclude from its membership the representatives of the Socialist-Revolutionsts (of the Right and Center) and the Russian Social-Democratic Labor Party (Menshevik), and to urge all Soviets of Workers', Soldiers', Peasants' and Cossacks' Deputies to remove representatives of these parties from their ranks.

Y. Sverdlov
Chairman of the Central Executive Committee

WAR COMMUNISM

Upon the outbreak of civil war, radical changes were introduced in Soviet economic policy. Class strife was encouraged among the peasants, and food supplies were forceably "requisitioned" to keep the cities fed. Industry, up to this point under private ownership with "workers' control," was nationalized without compensation in a series of sweeping decrees, and placed under a highly centralized bureaucratic administration. With the breakdown of transportation and the monetary system, Russia approached a "natural economy" based on the equalization of poverty through rationing.

For the purpose of combating decisively the economic disorganization and the breakdown of the food supply, and of establishing more firmly the dictatorship of the working class and the village poor, the Soviet of People's Commissars has resolved:

FROM: Decree on Nationalization of Large-Scale Industry, June 28, 1918 (English translation in Bunyan, pp. 397-99).

1. To declare all of the following industrial and commercial enterprises which are located in the Soviet Republic, with all their capital and property, whatever they may consist of, the property of the Russian Socialist Federated Soviet Republic. [At this point there is given a long list of the most important mines, mills, factories, etc.]

2. The administration of the nationalized industries shall be organized . . . by the different departments of the Supreme Council of National Economy. . . .

3. Until the Supreme Council of National Economy issues special rulings for each enterprise, the enterprises which have been declared the property of the R.S.F.S.R. by this decree shall be considered as leased rent-free to their former owners; the boards of directors and the former owners shall continue to finance the enterprises . . . and also to receive the income from them . . . .

4. Beginning with the promulgation of this decree, the members of the administration, the directors, and other responsible officers of the nationalized industries will be held responsible to the Soviet Republic both for the intactness and upkeep of the business and for its proper functioning. Those who leave their posts without the permission of the . . . Supreme Council of National Economy, or are found guilty of negligence in the management of the business, are liable both civilly and criminally to the Republic.

5. The entire personnel of every enterprise – technicians, workers, members of the board of directors, and foremen – shall be considered employees of the Russian Socialist Federated Soviet Republic; their wages shall be fixed in accordance with the scales existing at the time of nationalization and shall be paid out of the funds of the respective enterprises. Those who leave their posts . . . are liable to the Revolutionary Tribunal and to the full penalty of the law.

6. All private capital belonging to members of the boards of directors, stockholders, and owners of the nationalized enterprises will be attached pending the determination of the relation of such capital to the turnover capital and resources of the enterprises in question.

7. All boards of directors of the nationalized enterprises must prepare at once a financial statement of their respective businesses as of July 1, 1918.

8. The Supreme Council of National Economy is authorized to formulate at once and send to all nationalized plants detailed instructions on the organization connected with the carrying out of the present decree.

9. Enterprises belonging to consumers' cooperative societies . . . are not to be nationalized.

10. The present decree becomes effective on the day it is signed.

V. Ulianov (Lenin)
Chairman of the Council of People's Commissars
Tsiurupa, Nogin, Rykov
People's Commissars.

WESTERN RADICALS ON THE COMMUNISTS

At the time of the Russian Revolution Rosa Luxemburg was in jail in Germany for her activity in the antiwar wing of the German Social-Democratic Party. She wrote a remarkably objective pamphlet appraising the new Soviet regime and prophetically indicating its fundamental defects.

The Russian Revolution is the mightiest event of the World War. Its outbreak, its unexampled radicalism, its enduring consequences, constitute the clearest condemnation of the lying phrases which official Social-Democracy so zealously supplied at the beginning of the war as an ideological cover for German imperialism's campaign of conquest. . . .

Moreover, for every thinking observer, these developments are a decisive refutation of the doctrinaire theory which Kautsky shared with the Government Social-Democrats,* according to which Russia, as an economically backward and predominantly agrarian land, was supposed not to be ripe for social revolution and proletarian dictatorship. This theory, which regards only a *bourgeois* revolution as feasible in Russia, is also the theory of the opportunist wing of the Russian labor movement, of the so-called Mensheviks. . . .

. . . According to this view, if the revolution has gone beyond that point and has set as its task the dictatorship of the proletariat, this is simply a mistake of the radical wing of the Russian labor movement, the Bolsheviks. And all difficulties which the revolution has met with in its further course, and all disorders it has suffered, are pictured as purely a result of this fateful error. . . .

The fate of the revolution in Russia depended fully upon international events. That the Bolsheviks have based their policy entirely upon the world proletarian revolution is the clearest proof of their political farsightedness

FROM: Luxemburg, *The Russian Revolution* (1918; English translation by Bertram D. Wolfe, New York, Workers Age Publishers, 1940, pp. 1-4, 11-12, 44-48, 53-54, 56).

*I.e., the wing of the German Social-Democratic Party which supported the government's war effort—Ed.

and firmness of principle and of the bold scope of their policies. . . .

The real situation in which the Russian Revolution found itself, narrowed down in a few months to the alternative: victory of the counter-revolution or dictatorship of the proletariat–Kaledin or Lenin. . . . The Russian Revolution has but confirmed the basic lesson of every great revolution, the law of its being, which decrees: either the revolution must advance at a rapid, stormy and resolute tempo, break down all barriers with an iron hand and place its goals ever farther ahead, or it is quite soon thrown backward behind its feeble point of departure and suppressed by counter-revolution. To stand still, to mark time on one spot, to be contented with the first goal it happens to reach, is never possible in revolution. . . .

Lenin says: the bourgeois state is an instrument of oppression of the working class; the socialist state, of the bourgeoisie. To a certain extent, he says, it is only the capitalist state stood on its head. This simplified view misses the most essential thing: bourgeois class rule has no need of the political training and education of the entire mass of the people, at least not beyond certain narrow limits. But for the proletarian dictatorship that is the life element, the very air without which it is not able to exist. . . .

. . . The very giant tasks which the Bolsheviks have undertaken with courage and determination . . . demand the most intensive political training of the masses and the accumulation of experience.

Freedom only for the supporters of the government, only for the members of one party–however numerous they may be–is no freedom at all. Freedom is always and exclusively freedom for the one who thinks differently. Not because of any fanatical concept of "justice" but because all that is instructive, wholesome and purifying in political freedom depends on this essential characteristic, and its effectiveness vanishes when "freedom" becomes a special privilege. . . .

The tacit assumption underlying the Lenin-Trotsky theory of the dictatorship is this: that the socialist transformation is something for which a ready-made formula lies completed in the pocket of the revolutionary party, which needs only to be carried out energetically in practice. This is, unfortunately–or perhaps fortunately–not the case. Far from being a sum of ready-made prescriptions which have only to be applied, the practical realization of socialism as an economic, social and juridical system is something which lies completely hidden in the mists of the future. . . .

. . . Socialism by its very nature cannot be decreed or introduced by *ukaz*. It has as its prerequisite a number of measures of force–against property, etc. The negative, the tearing down, can be decreed; the building up, the positive, cannot. New territory. A thousand problems. Only experience is capable of correcting and opening new ways. Only unobstructed, effervescing life falls into a thousand new forms and improvisations, brings to light creative force, itself corrects all mistaken attempts. The public life of countries with limited freedom is so poverty-stricken, so miserable, so rigid, so unfruitful, precisely because, through the exclusion of democracy, it cuts off the living sources of all spiritual riches and progress. . . .

. . . Socialism in life demands a complete spiritual transformation in the masses degraded by centuries of bourgeois class rule. Social instincts in place of egotistical ones, mass initiative in place of inertia, idealism which conquers all suffering, etc., etc. No one knows this better, describes it more penetratingly, repeats it more stubbornly than Lenin. But he is completely mistaken in the means he employs. Decree, dictatorial force of the factory overseer, draconic penalties, rule by terror – all these things are but palliatives. The only way to a rebirth is the school of public life itself, the most unlimited, the broadest democracy and public opinion. It is rule by terror which demoralizes.

When all this is eliminated, what really remains? In place of the representative bodies created by general, popular elections, Lenin and Trotsky have laid down the soviets as the only true representation of the laboring masses. But with the repression of political life in the land as a whole, life in the soviets must also become more and more crippled. Without general elections, without unrestricted freedom of press and assembly, without a free struggle of opinion, life dies out in every public institution, becomes a mere semblance of life, in which only the bureaucracy remains as the active element. Public life gradually falls asleep, a few dozen party leaders of inexhaustible energy and boundless experience direct and rule. Among them, in reality only a dozen outstanding heads do the leading and an elite of the working class is invited from time to time to meetings where they are to applaud the speeches of the leaders, and to approve proposed resolutions unanimously – at bottom, then, a clique affair – a dictatorship, to be sure, not the dictatorship of the proletariat, however, but only the dictatorship of a handful of politicians, that is a dictatorship in the bourgeois sense, in the sense of the rule of the Jacobins. . . . Yes, we can go even further: such conditions must inevitably cause a brutalization of public life: attempted assassinations, shooting of hostages, etc. . . .

"As Marxists," writes Trotsky, "we have never been idol worshippers of formal democracy." . . . All that that really means is: We have always distinguished the social kernel from the political form of *bourgeois* democracy; we have always revealed the hard kernel of social inequality and lack of freedom hidden under the sweet shell of formal equality and freedom – not in order to reject the latter but to spur the working class into not being satisfied with the shell, but rather, by conquering political power, to create a socialist democracy to replace bourgeois democracy – not to eliminate democracy altogether. . . .

Yes, dictatorship! But this dictatorship consists in the *manner of applying democracy*, not in its *elimination*, in energetic, resolute attacks upon the well-entrenched rights and economic relationships of bourgeois society, without which a socialist transformation cannot be accomplished. But this dictatorship must be the work of the *class* and not of a little leading minority in the name of the class – that is, it must proceed step by step out of the active participation of the masses; it must be under their direct influence, subjected to the control of complete public activity; it must arise out of the growing political training of the mass of the people. . . .

What is in order is to distinguish the essential from the non-essential, the kernel from the accidental excrescences in the policies of the Bolsheviks. In the present period, when we face decisive final struggles in all the world, the most important problem of socialism was and is the burning question of our time. It is not a matter of this or that secondary question of tactics, but of the capacity for action of the proletariat, the strength to act, the will to power of socialism as such. In this, Lenin and Trotsky and their friends were the *first*, those who went ahead as an example to the proletariat of the world; they are still the *only ones* up to now who can cry with Hutten:* "I have dared!"

This is the essential and *enduring* in Bolshevik policy. In *this* sense theirs is the immortal historical service of having marched at the head of the international proletariat with the conquest of political power and the practical placing of the problem of the realization of socialism, and of having advanced mightily the settlement of the score between capital and labor in the entire world. In Russia the problem could only be posed. It could not be solved in Russia. And in *this* sense, the future everywhere belongs to "Bolshevism."

THE PARTY PROGRAM OF 1919

An official statement of the aims and principles of the Communist Party was issued by the Eighth Party Congress in 1919. It is noteworthy for its stress on the superior "democratic" character of the Soviet state, the importance of education and anti-religious propaganda, and the economic role of the trade unions, together with the necessary expedients of economic incentives and "bourgeois" experts.

*Ulrich von Hutten: German humanist and early follower of Luther – Ed.

. . . 2. In contrast to bourgeois democracy, which concealed the class character of the state, the Soviet authority openly acknowledges that every state must inevitably bear a class character until the division of society into classes has been abolished and all government authority disappears. By its very nature, the Soviet state directs itself to the suppression of the resistance of the exploiters, and the Soviet constitution does not stop short of depriving the exploiters of their political rights, bearing in mind that any kind of freedom is a deception if it is opposed to the emancipation of labor from the yoke of capital. The aim of the Party of the proletariat consists in carrying on a determined suppression of the resistance of the exploiters, in struggling against the deeply rooted prejudices concerning the absolute character of bourgeois rights and freedom, and at the same time explaining that deprivation of political rights and any kind of limitation of freedom are necessary as temporary measures in order to defeat the attempts of the exploiters to retain or to reestablish their privileges. With the disappearance of the possibility of the exploitation of one human being by another, the necessity for these measures will also gradually disappear and the Party will aim to reduce and completely abolish them. . . .

8. The proletarian revolution, owing to the Soviet organization of the state, was able at one stroke finally to destroy the old bourgeois, official and judicial state apparatus. The comparatively low standard of culture of the masses, the absence of necessary experience in state administration on the part of responsible workers who are elected by the masses, the pressing necessity, owing to the critical situation of engaging specialists of the old school, and the calling up to military service of the more advanced section of city workmen, all this led to the partial revival of bureaucratic practices within the Soviet system.

The All-Russian Communist Party, carrying on a resolute struggle with bureaucratism, suggests the following measures for overcoming this evil:

(1) Every member of the Soviet is obliged to perform a certain duty in state administration.

(2) These duties must change in rotation, so as gradually to embrace all the branches of administrative work.

(3) All the working masses without exception must be gradually induced to take part in the work of state administration.

The complete realization of these measures will carry us in advance of the Paris Commune, and the simplification of the work of administration,

FROM: *The Program of the All-Russian Communist Party (Bolsheviks)* (1919; English translation, Moscow, Communist Library [1920], reprinted in James H. Meisel and Edward S. Kozera, *Materials for the Study of the Soviet System*, Ann Arbor, Mich., Wahr, 1950, pp. 105, 107-8, 110-15).

together with the raising of the level of culture of the masses, will eventually lead to the abolition of state authority. . . .

Jurisprudence

11. Proletarian democracy, taking power into its own hands and finally abolishing the organs of domination of the bourgeoisie – the former courts of justice – has replaced the formula of bourgeois democracy: "judges elected by the people" by the class watchword: "judges elected from the working masses and only by the working masses," and has applied the latter in the organization of law courts, having extended equal right to both sexes, both in the election of judges and in the exercise of the functions of judges.

In order to induce the broad masses of the proletariat and the poorest peasantry to take part in the administration of justice, a bench of jury-judges sitting in rotation under guidance of a permanent judge is introduced and various labor organizations and trade unions must impanel their delegates. . . .

Public Education

12. The All-Russian Communist Party in the field of education sets itself the task of bringing to fulfillment the work begun by the October Revolution of 1917, of transforming the school from an instrument of class domination of the bourgeoisie into an instrument for the abolition of the class divisions of society, into an instrument for a communist regeneration of society.

In the period of the dictatorship of the proletariat, i.e., in the period of preparation of conditions suitable for the realization of communism, the school must be not only the conductor of communist principles, but it must become the conductor of the intellectual, organizational and educational influences of the proletariat, to the semi-proletariat and non-proletarian sections of the toiling masses, in order to educate a generation capable of establishing communism. . . .

Religion

13. With reference to religion, the All-Russian Communist Party does not content itself with the already decreed separation of church from state, i.e., measures which are one of the items of the programs of bourgeois democracy, which was, however, never fulfilled owing to many and various ties binding capital with religious propaganda.

The All-Russian Communist Party is guided by the conviction that only the realization of conscious and systematic social and economic activity of the masses will lead to the disappearance of religious prejudices. The aim of the Party is finally to destroy the ties between the exploiting classes and the organization of religious propaganda, at the same time helping the toiling masses actually to liberate their minds from religious superstitions, and organizing on a wide scale scientific-educational and anti-religious propaganda. It is, however, necessary carefully to avoid offending the religious susceptibilities of believers, which leads only to the strengthening of religious fanaticism.

Economics

1. Undeviatingly to continue and finally to realize that expropriation of the bourgeoisie which was begun and which has already been largely completed, the transforming of all means of production and exchange into the property of the Soviet republic, i.e., the common property of all toilers.

2. All possible increase of the productive forces of the country must be considered the fundamental and principal point upon which the economic policy of the Soviet Government is based. In view of the disorganization of the country, everything in other spheres of life must be subordinated to the practical aim immediately and at all costs to increase the quantity of products required by the population. The successful functioning of every Soviet institution connected with public economy must be gauged by the practical results in this direction.

At the same time it is necessary in the first place to pay attention to the following:

3. The decaying imperialist system of economy left to the Soviet state a heritage of chaos in the organization and management of production, which hampered it in the first period of construction. The more imperative therefore becomes the fundamental task of concentrating all the economic activity of the country according to a general state plan; the greatest concentration of production for the purpose of amalgamating it into various branches and groups of branches, and centralizing it in the most productive units, and for the purpose of rapidity in carrying out economic achievements; the most efficient arrangement of the productive apparatus and a rational and economical utilization of all material resources of the country. . . .

5. The organizing apparatus of socialized industry must first of all rest upon the trade unions. The latter must free themselves from their narrow guild outlook and transform themselves into large productive combinations which will unite the majority, and finally all the workmen of a given branch of production.

Trade unions, being already, according to the laws of the Soviet Republic and established practice, participants in all local and central organs for managing industry, must actually concentrate in their hands the management of the whole system of public economy as an economic unit. The trade unions, thus securing an indissoluble union between the central state administration, the public system of economy and the masses of toilers must induce the latter to take part in the immediate management of production. The participation of trade unions in the management of production and the attraction by them of the broad masses are, moreover, the principal means to carry on a struggle against bureaucracy in the economic apparatus of the Soviet state, and afford the opportunity of establishing a really democratic control over the results of production.

6. A maximum utilization of all labor power existing in the state, its regular distribution and redistribution among various territorial regions as well as among various branches of production, is necessary for the systematic development of public economy, and must be the immediate aim in the economic policy of the Soviet Government. This aim can be attained in closest co-operation with the trade unions. For the purpose of performing certain social duties, a general mobilization of all capable of work must be carried out by the Soviet Government, aided by the trade unions, on a much wider scale and more systematically than has been done hitherto.

7. In the state of the complete disorganization of the capitalist system of labor, the productive forces of the country can be restored and developed, and a socialist system of production strengthened, only on the basis of the comradely discipline of toilers, maximum activity on their part, responsibility and the strictest mutual control over the productivity of labor.

Persistent systematic effort directed to the re-education of the masses is necessary to attain this aim. This work is now made easier as the masses in reality see the abolition of capitalists, landowners, and merchants, and from their own experience draw the conclusion that the level of their prosperity depends entirely upon the productivity of their own labor.

The trade unions play the principal part in the work of establishing a new socialist discipline. Breaking with old conventions, they must put into practice and try various measures, such as the establishment of control, standards of production, the introduction of responsibility of the workmen before special labor tribunals, etc., for the realization of this aim.

8. Moreover, for the development of the productive forces the immediate, wide and full utilization of all specialists in science and technology left to us by capitalism, is necessary, in spite of the fact that the majority of the latter are inevitably imbued with bourgeois ideas and habits. The Party considers that the period of sharp struggle with this group, owing to organized sabotage on their part, is ended as the sabotage is in the main subdued. The Party, in closest contact with the trade unions, will follow its former

line of action, i.e., on the one hand it will make no political concessions to this bourgeois section and mercilessly suppress any counter-revolutionary moves on its part, and on the other hand it will carry on a merciless struggle against the pseudo-radical, but in reality, ignorant and conceited opinion that the working class can overcome capitalism and the bourgeois order without the aid of bourgeois specialists or taking advantage of their knowledge, without passing, together with them, through a thorough schooling of hard work.

While striving toward equal remuneration of labor and to realize communism, the Soviet Government does not regard the immediate realization of such equality possible at the moment, when only the first steps are being taken towards replacing capitalism by communism. It is therefore necessary to maintain a higher remuneration for specialists in order that they should work not worse but better than before, and for that purpose it is not possible to abandon the system of bonuses for the most successful, particularly for work of organization.

To the same degree, it is necessary to place the bourgeois experts in a setting of comradely common effort, working hand in hand with the mass of average workers, led by class-conscious Communists, and thus to assist the mutual understanding and unity between manual and intellectual workers formerly separated by capitalism. . . .

CENTRALIZATION OF THE COMMUNIST PARTY

Under the stress of civil war the Communist leaders had to put a premium on swift decision-making and on the development of a disciplined body of party secretaries to carry out decisions. The Eighth Party Congress accordingly approved the creation of new executive organs for the party—the Politbureau, the Orgbureau, and the Secretariat—and gave these central bodies full authority over the membership (including Communists in nominally separate countries like the Ukraine). With this step the Communist Party began to approximate the organizational ideal laid down by Lenin in 1902.

. . . *1. The Growth of the Party:*

The numerical growth of the party is progressive only insofar as healthy proletarian elements of town and country flow into the ranks of the party. The doors of the party should be wide open to workers and to worker and

FROM: Resolution of the Eighth Congress of the Russian Communist Party, March, 1919, "On the Organizational Question," (CPSU in Resolutions, I, 441-44; editor's translation).

peasant youth. But the party must always follow attentively the progressive changes in its social composition. . . . It is important to handle the admission into the party of non-worker and non-peasant elements by careful selection. . . .

2. The Link with the Masses:

The Russian Communist Party, since it is in power and holds in its hands the whole apparatus of the soviets, has naturally had to turn tens of thousands of its members over to the work of administering the country. One of the party's most important tasks at the present moment is to place new thousands of its best functionaries in the network of the governmental administration (the railroads, provisioning, control, the army, the courts, etc.).

However, in connection with the fulfillment of this substantial task a serious danger has arisen. Many members of the party who have been placed in this governmental work are divorcing themselves from the masses and becoming infected with bureaucratism, which very often applies to many workers who are members of the soviets. It is necessary to begin the most determined struggle against this evil immediately. . . .

4. The Internal Structure of the Central Committee:

The Central Committee has no less than two plenary sessions a month on previously arranged days. All the most important political and organizational questions which do not demand the most hasty decision are considered at these plenary meetings of the Central Committee.

The Central Committee organizes firstly a *Political Bureau*, secondly an *Organizational Bureau*, and thirdly a *Secretariat*.

The Political Bureau consists of five members of the Central Committee. All the other members of the Central Committee who find it possible to participate in one or another of the sessions of the Political Bureau enjoy a consultative voice at the sessions of the Political Bureau. The Political Bureau makes decisions on questions which do not permit delay, and it gives a report on all its work in the two weeks' period to the following meeting of the Central Committee.

The Organizational Bureau consists of five members of the Central Committee. Each of the members of the Organizational Bureau conducts his respective branch of the work. The Organizational Bureau assembles not less than three times a week. The Organizational Bureau directs all the organizational work of the party. The Organizational Bureau reports to the Plenum of the Central Committee every two weeks.

The Secretariat of the Central Committee is composed of one responsible secretary, a member of the Organizational Bureau of the Central Committee, and five technical secretaries from among the experienced party functionaries. The Secretariat organizes a series of departments. The Secretariat reports to the Plenum of the Central Committee every two weeks.

5. Nationality Organizations:

At the present time the Ukraine, Latvia, Lithuania and Byelorussia exist as special Soviet republics. Thus, the question of their forms of *governmental* existence is decided at the present moment.

But this does not at all mean that the Russian Communist Party in its turn should be organized on the basis of a federation of independent Communist parties.

The Eighth Congress of the Russian Communist Party decides that the existence of a *unitary* centralized Communist Party with a unitary Central Committee directing all the work of the party in all parts of the RSFSR is essential. All decisions of the Russian Communist Party and its leading institutions are unconditionally binding on all parts of the party, regardless of their nationality composition. The Central Committees of the Ukrainian, Latvian, and Lithuanian Communists enjoy the rights of regional committees of the party and are wholly subordinated to the Central Committee of the Russian Communist Party. . . .

7. Centralism and Discipline:

The party finds itself in a position where the strictest centralism and the most rigorous discipline are absolute necessities. All decisions of a higher jurisdiction are absolutely binding for lower ones. Each decision must above all be fulfilled, and only after this is an appeal to the respective party organ permissible. In this sense outright military discipline is essential for the party at the present time. . . .

8. The Assignment of Party Forces:

At the present time the correct assignment of party forces is the main guarantee of success and one of the most important tasks. The whole matter of the assignment of party functionaries is in the hands of the Central Committee of the party. Its decision is binding for everyone. In each province the forces are assigned by the provincial committee of the party; in the capitals, by the city committees under the general direction of the Central Committee. The Central Committee is commissioned to wage the most determined struggle against any local privilege or separatism in these questions.

The Central Committee is commissioned to transfer party functionaries systematically from one branch of work to another and from one region to another with the aim of utilizing them the most productively. . . .

THE CIVIL WAR

Hostilities between the Communists and the Whites reached a decisive climax in 1919. Intervention by the Allied powers on the side of the Whites almost brought them victory. Facing the most serious White threat led by General Denikin in Southern Russia, Lenin appealed to his followers for a supreme effort, and threatened ruthless repression of any opposition behind the lines. By early 1920 the principal White forces were defeated.

Comrades,

This is one of the most critical, probably even the most critical moment for the socialist revolution. The defenders of the exploiters, of the landlords and capitalists, Russian and foreign (and in the first instance the British and French), are making a desperate effort to restore the power of the robbers of the people's labour, the landlords and exploiters, in Russia, in order to bolster up their declining power all over the world. The British and French capitalists have failed in their plan to conquer the Ukraine with their own troops; they have failed in their support of Kolchak* in Siberia; the Red Army, heroically advancing in the Urals with the help of the Urals workers, who are rising to a man, is nearing Siberia with the purpose of liberating it from the incredible tyranny and brutality of the overlords there, the capitalists. Lastly, the British and French imperialists have failed in their plan to seize Petrograd by means of a counterrevolutionary conspiracy, in which there took part Russian monarchists, Kadets, Mensheviks and Socialist-Revolutionaries, not even excluding Left Socialist-Revolutionaries.

The foreign capitalists are now making a desperate effort to restore the yoke of capital with the help of an onslaught by Denikin, whom they have helped, as they once had helped Kolchak, with officers, supplies, shells, tanks, etc., etc.

All the forces of the workers and peasants, all the forces of the Soviet Republic, must be harnessed to repulse Denikin's onslaught and to defeat him, without suspending the Red Army's victorious advance into the Urals and Siberia. That is the

Main Task of the Moment

All Communists first and foremost, all sympathizers with them, all hon-

FROM: Lenin, "All Out for the Fight Against Denikin!" (Letter of the Central Committee of the Russian Communist Party (Bolsheviks) to the Party Organizations, July, 1919; *Selected Works*, Vol. II, book 2, pp. 240-41, 257, 259-60).

* Admiral Kolchak: leader of the White forces in Siberia, and a military dictator, until his capture and execution in 1920 – Ed.

est workers and peasants, all Soviet officials, must *display military efficiency* and concentrate *to the maximum their work*, their efforts and their concern *directly on the tasks of war*, on the speedy repulse of Denikin's onslaught, curtailing and rearranging all their other activities in subordination to this task.

The Soviet Republic is besieged by the enemy. It must become *a single military camp*, not in word but in deed.

. . . Counterrevolution is raising its head in our rear, in our midst.

Counterrevolution has been vanquished, but it is far from having been destroyed, and it is naturally taking advantage of Denikin's victories and of the aggravation of the food shortage. And, as always, in the wake of direct and open counterrevolution, in the wake of the Black Hundreds and the Kadets, whose strength lies in their capital, their direct connections with Entente imperialism, and their understanding of the inevitability of dictatorship and their ability to exercise it (on Kolchak lines), follow the wavering, spineless Mensheviks, Right Socialist-Revolutionaries and Left Socialist-Revolutionaries, who embellish their deeds with words. . . .

Our task is to put the question bluntly. What is better? To ferret out, to imprison, sometimes even to shoot hundreds of traitors from among the Kadets, nonparty people, Mensheviks and Socialist-Revolutionaries, who "come out" (some with arms in hand, others with conspiracies, others still with agitation against mobilization, like the Menshevik printers and railwaymen, etc.) *against* the Soviet power, *in other words, in favour of Denikin?* Or to allow matters to reach a pass enabling Kolchak and Denikin to slaughter, shoot and flog to death tens of thousands of workers and peasants? The choice is not difficult to make. . . .

The Soviet Republic is a fortress besieged by world capital. We can concede the right to use it as a refuge from Kolchak, and the right to live in it generally, only to those who take an active part in the war and help us in every way. Hence our right and our duty to mobilize the whole population for the war to a man, some for military duties in the direct meaning of the term, others for subsidiary activities of every kind in aid of the war. . .

BUKHARIN'S APOLOGY FOR WAR COMMUNISM

Bukharin took it upon himself to justify in Marxist terms the collapse of the Russian economy which occurred during the period of War Communism, and the utilization of the "technical intelligentsia" and the conventional hierarchical organization of industry. The key, for him, was the possession of power by the allegedly "proletarian" state, under which no expedients could possibly harm the interests of the workers.

It is absolutely clear that the disintegration and revolutionary loosening of the links of the system as essential characteristics of the breakdown means a collapse of the "technical apparatus" of society, insofar as we are considering the technical organization of the people of this society.

But from this it follows that one cannot simply "take possession" of the old economic apparatus. Anarchy in production, or . . . the "revolutionary disintegration of industry" is a historically inevitable stage, which cannot be escaped by lamentation. Certainly, from the absolute standpoint it would be fine if the revolution and the breakdown of the old production relationships were not accompanied by any collapse of the technical relations of production. But the considered judgment of the actual processes, the scientific analysis of them, tells us that the period of this collapse is historically inevitable and historically necessary.

The collapse of the *technical* hierarchy, which appears at a certain stage of the process of broadened negative reproduction,* exerts pressure in turn on the condition of the forces of production. The forces of production are fused with the relationships of production in a definite system of the social organization of labor. Consequently, the collapse of the "apparatus" must inevitably be followed by a further decline in the forces of production. In this way the process of further negative reproduction is extraordinarily accelerated.

From the above analysis it follows that the "restoration of industry" which capitalistic Utopians dream about is impossible on the basis of the old capitalistic relationships, which are flying apart. The only remedy is for the lower links of the system, the basic productive force of capitalist society, the working class, to assume a dominant position in the organization of social labor. In other words, the establishment of communism is the prerequisite for a re-birth of society. . . .

We have seen that that which for society as a whole constitutes a condition of its further existence represents for the proletariat an organizational problem which it must solve in practice. In this period the proletariat must *actively build* socialism and at the same time, in the process of this building, educate itself anew. This task can be met only with the help of specific methods, with methods of *organized* labor. But these methods have already been prepared in the development of capitalism. . . .

Socialism as an organized system must be built by the proletariat as the

FROM: Bukharin, *The Economics of the Transformation Period* (1920; German edition, Hamburg, Hoym, 1922, pp. 55-56, 71-72, 76, 78-80, 85; editor's translation).

*Reproduction: Marx's concept of the maintenance and expansion of capital; "negative reproduction" would be to allow the industrial plant to wear out – Ed.

organized collective subject. Whereas the process of the growth of capitalism was elemental nature, the process of building communism is to a high degree a conscious, i.e., organized process. For communism will be created by a class which in the womb of capitalism has grown up into that "revolutionary association" of which Marx spoke. The epoch of building communism will therefore inevitably be the epoch of planned and organized labor; the proletariat will fulfill its tasks as social-technical tasks of building a new society, tasks which are consciously posed and consciously fulfilled. . . .

In this period the proletariat educates itself, closes ranks, and organizes itself as a class with tremendous intensity and swiftness. The proletariat as the totality of production relations accordingly builds the scaffolding of the whole structure. But the problem of the social organization of production consists of *new combinations of the old elements*. And indeed what elements? . . .

The ex-bourgeois group of organizers and the *technical* intelligentsia which stands beneath it are material which is obviously necessary for the reconstruction period: it is the social deposit of organizational and technical-scientific experience. It is indeed apparent that both these categories must be regrouped. How and under what circumstances is this possible?

We wish to point out above all that this is the decisive – one could say basic – question for our structure. It is no accident that in the mature period of the Russian socialist revolution the problem of the "specialist" played so important a role.

We know that earlier types of social ties survive in the heads of the people in these categories, in the form of an ideological and physiological residue. "Healthy capitalism" hovers before them with the persistency of a fixed idea. The prerequisite for the possibility of a new social combination of production is therefore to dissolve the earlier types of associations in the heads of this technical intelligentsia. . . .

How, in general, is another combination of personal and technical elements of production possible if the logic of the production process itself requires associations of a completely determined kind? Must an engineer or technician indeed give orders to the workers and consequently stand *over* them? In just the same way the former officers in the Red Army must stand over the common soldiers. Here we pose an inner, purely technical, factual logic, which must be observed in any social order whatsoever. How can this contradiction be solved?

Here a whole series of circumstances must be considered, and we will now attack their study.

Above all: Under the proletarian state power and with the proletarian nationalization of production the process of creating surplus value, a specific feature of bourgeois society, ceases. . . . With the dialectical transformation of the bourgeois dictatorship into the proletarian, the technical function of the intelligentsia changes from a capitalistic to a social function of labor, and the creation of surplus value changes (under the conditions of expanded reproduction) into the creation of surplus product, which is applied to the expansion of the reproduction fund. Paralleling this, the *basic type of association* changes, *although in the hierarchical scheme the intelligentsia occupies the same "middle" place.* For the highest authority in the state economy is the concentrated social power of the proletariat. Here the technical intelligentsia on the one hand stands above the great mass of the working class, but on the other is in the last analysis *subordinated* to its collective will, the expression of which is found in the proletariat's organization of the state economy. The transformation of the process of producing surplus value into a process of planned satisfaction of social needs finds expression in the regrouping of production relations, notwithstanding the formal retention of the same place in the hierarchical system of production, which in principle assumes as a whole a different character, the character of the dialectic negation of the structure of capitalism and which, insofar as it destroys the social-caste character of the hierarchy, leads toward the abolition of the hierarchy altogether. . . .

We must now pose the question of the general principle of the system of organization of the proletarian apparatus, i.e., the interrelations between the various forms of proletarian organization. It is indeed clear that formally the same method is necessary for the working class as for the bourgeoisie of the era of state capitalism. This organizational method consists of the coordination of all proletarian organizations by means of the most all-embracing organization possible, i.e., by means of the state organization of the working class, by means of the *proletarian Soviet state.* The "governmentalization" of the trade unions and in practice the governmentalization of all the mass organizations of the proletariat result from the inner logic of the transformation process itself. The smallest germ cell of the labor apparatus must become a support for the general process of organization, which is planfully led and conducted by the collective reason of the working class, which has its material embodiment in the highest, all-embracing organization, its state power. Thus the system of state capitalism is dialectically transformed into its own opposite, into the governmental form of workers' socialism. . . .

TROTSKY ON TERROR AND MILITARIZATION

During the Civil War years Trotsky was surpassed by none in his advocacy of dictatorial ruthlessness and authoritarianism. He frankly defended every means of violence and intimidation for the compelling end of revolutionary victory, and insisted that tight control and strict discipline of the entire population were essential for the success of the socialist economy. Trotsky was the earliest articulate exponent of the all-embracing totalitarian approach to economic development which Stalin made his own in 1929.

. . . The problem of revolution, as of war, consists in breaking the will of the foe, forcing him to capitulate and to accept the conditions of the conqueror. The will, of course, is a fact of the physical world, but in contradistinction to a meeting, a dispute, or a congress, the revolution carries out its object by means of the employment of material resources – though to a less degree than war. The bourgeoisie itself conquered power by means of revolts, and consolidated it by the civil war. In the peaceful period, it retains power by means of a system of repression. As long as class society, founded on the most deep-rooted antagonisms, continues to exist, repression remains a necessary means of breaking the will of the opposing side.

Even if, in one country or another, the dictatorship of the proletariat grew up within the external framework of democracy, this would by no means avert the civil war. The question as to who is to rule the country, i.e., of the life or death of the bourgeoisie, will be decided on either side, not by references to the paragraphs of the constitution, but by the employment of all forms of violence. . . .

The question of the form of repression, or of its degree, of course, is not one of "principle." It is a question of expediency. . . .

. . . Terror can be very efficient against a reactionary class which does not want to leave the scene of operations. *Intimidation* is a powerful weapon of policy, both internationally and internally. War, like revolution, is founded upon intimidation. A victorious war, generally speaking, destroys only an insignificant part of the conquered army, intimidating the remainder and breaking their will. The revolution works in the same way: it kills individuals, and intimidates thousands. In this sense, the Red Terror is not distinguishable from the armed insurrection, the direct continuation

FROM: Trotsky, *Terrorism and Communism* (1920; English translation, *Dictatorship vs. Democracy: A Reply to Karl Kautsky*, New York, Workers' Party of America, 1922, pp. 54, 57-59, 106-7, 136-37, 141-43).

of which it represents. The State terror of a revolutionary class can be condemned "morally" only by a man who, as a principle, rejects (in words) every form of violence whatsoever – consequently, every war and every rising. For this one has to be merely and simply a hypocritical Quaker.

"But, in that case, in what do your tactics differ from the tactics of Tsarism?" we are asked, by the high priest of Liberalism and Kautskianism.

You do not understand this, holy men? We shall explain to you. The terror of Tsarism was directed against the proletariat. The gendarmerie of Tsarism throttled the workers who were fighting for the Socialist order. Our Extraordinary Commissions shoot landlords, capitalists, and generals who are striving to restore the capitalist order. Do you grasp this – distinction? Yes? For us Communists it is quite sufficient. . . .

If the organization of the new society can be reduced fundamentally to the reorganization of labor, the organization of labor signifies in its turn the correct introduction of general labor service. This problem is in no way met by measures of a purely departmental and administrative character. It touches the very foundations of economic life and the social structure. It finds itself in conflict with the most powerful psychological habits and prejudices. The introduction of compulsory labor service pre-supposes, on the one hand, a colossal work of education, and, on the other, the greatest possible care in the practical method adopted. . . .

The introduction of compulsory labor service is unthinkable without the application, to a greater or less degree, of the methods of militarization of labor. This term at once brings us into the region of the greatest possible superstitions and outcries from the opposition. . . .

The foundations of the militarization of labor are those forms of State compulsion without which the replacement of capitalist economy by the Socialist will forever remain an empty sound. Why do we speak of *militarization*? Of course, this is only an analogy – but an analogy very rich in content. No social organization except the army has ever considered itself justified in subordinating citizens to itself in such a measure, and to control them by its will on all sides to such a degree, as the State of the proletarian dictatorship considers itself justified in doing, and does. Only the army – just because in its way it used to decide questions of the life or death of nations, States, and ruling classes – was endowed with powers of demanding from each and all complete submission to its problems, aims, regulations, and orders. And it achieved this to the greater degree, the more the problems of military organization coincided with the requirements of social development.

The question of the life or death of Soviet Russia is at present being settled on the labor front; our economic, and together with them our professional and productive organizations, have the right to demand from their members all that devotion, discipline, and executive thoroughness, which hitherto only the army required. . . .

. . . We can have no way to Socialism except by the authoritative regulation of the economic forces and resources of the country, and the centralized distribution of labor-power in harmony with the general State plan. The Labor State considers itself empowered to send every worker to the place where his work is necessary. And not one serious Socialist will begin to deny to the Labor State the right to lay its hand upon the worker who refuses to execute his labor duty. But the whole point is that the Menshevik path of transition to "Socialism" is a milky way, without the bread monopoly, without the abolition of the market, without the revolutionary dictatorship, and without the militarization of labor.

THE "DEMOCRATIC CENTRALISTS" IN OPPOSITION TO CENTRALIZATION

The "Democratic Centralist" group, led by V. V. Osinsky, was an offshoot of the Left Communist movement of early 1918 which held to the original anti-bureaucratic line. They were significant as a group dedicated to the observance of revolutionary principle, in opposition to the expedients promoted by Lenin and Trotsky; they spoke out on many occasions to protest the trend toward centralization and hierarchical authority in the party, the government, the army, and industry. Their ideals were local autonomy and administration of every sort of activity by elected boards or "collegia." At the Ninth Party Congress in 1920, Osinsky spoke against Trotsky's scheme of militarization as a violation of basic revolutionary principles of democracy and collective decision-making.

I propose to make a series of amendments and additions to Comrade Trotsky's theses. . . . First of all I want to give the basis for the amendment which we are introducing on the question of militarization.

What is happening now at the congress is the clash of several cultures, for our setup has given birth to different cultures. We have created a military-Soviet culture, a civil Soviet culture, and, finally, the trade-union movement has created its own sphere of culture. Each of these forms of our movement has its own approach to things, has created its own practices.

FROM: Osinsky, Minority Report on Building the Economy, Ninth Party Congress, March, 1920 (*Protocols of the Ninth Congress of the Russian Communist Party [of Bolsheviks]*, Moscow, Party Press, 1934, pp. 123-26, 128, 130-33; editor's translation).

Comrade Trotsky has posed the question from the point of view of a man coming from the sphere of military culture; we approach it from the point of view of the civil sphere, and, finally, the trade-union comrades have posed it in their own way. They have posed it the most poorly, insofar as they have for a long time been considering only the need to protect the workers from militarization and to keep labor free, etc.

I want first of all to establish the fact that we approached the question of militarization earlier than the people from the other cultures, and from the other side. . . . I radically reject the proposition that we oppose militarization *per se*. . . . We are against the excessive extension of the concept of militarization, we are against the blind imitation of military models. . . .

The collegium is not the only means for drawing the broad working masses into administration. There are many other ways, such as, for example, the appointment of probationary workers and participation in the Workers' and Peasants' Inspection. But there is no doubt that the collegium is an essential higher-level school of administration, given final preparation and the broadest outlook. The collegium is the proper means to prepare workers for the most responsible work and for completely taking over the state apparatus. . . .

Comrade Lenin reproaches here on the grounds that we approach the question of individual authority vs. the collegial principle not in a practical way but purely "in principle." . . . In the developed socialist system, when the division of labor and skills has been abolished, the collegial principle will be essential for people to be able to replace each other continuously in the organs of administration. . . .

We must not put the question of the collegial principle vs. individual authority on a purely technical plane and seek the absolute technical advantages of one form or another of administration. . . . We must approach the matter from the social-political side. Then we can reach concrete conclusions, including some less favorable to individual authority. . . .

Comrade Lenin has revealed here today a very original understanding of democratic centralism. . . . Comrade Lenin says that all democratic centralism consists of is that the congress elects the Central Committee, and the Central Committee governs. . . . With such an original definition we cannot agree. We consider that democratic centralism – a very old concept, a concept clear to every Bolshevik and fixed in our rules – consists of carrying out the directives of the Central Committee through local organizations; the autonomy of the latter; and their responsibility for individual spheres of work. If party work is broken down into several branches with special departments, and if these departments are under the general direction of the local organization, just as the soviets' departments are under the power and direction of the provincial executive committee – this is democratic centralism, i.e., the execution of the decisions of the center through local organs which are responsible for all the particular spheres of work in the provinces. This is the definition of democratic centralism, a system of administration preserved from bureaucratism and closely connected with the principle of collegia. . . .

If you reduce the collegial principle to nothing in our institutions, bear in mind that this signifies the downfall of the whole system of democratic centralism. I advise careful thought about this, although the speakers following me may try to "smear" this argument. Bearing this in mind, we will conduct an unyielding struggle against the principle of individual authority. . . .

In the unpublished part of his theses Comrade Trotsky raised the question, what to do with democratic centralism in the area of the party, and the answer was – replace the party organizations with political departments, not only on the railroads, but in all the basic branches of industry. Comrade Stalin, whom I deeply respect, but with whom I do not go along on this question, has already surpassed Comrade Trotsky's idea, and has established a political department for coal in the Donets coal industry. In general we need to take all this into account as a manifestation of familiar tendencies. We will also recall how Comrade Lenin, speaking of democratic centralism the first day of the congress, called everyone who spoke of democratic centralism an idiot, and called democratic centralism itself antediluvian and obsolete, etc. If the separate facts are connected, the tendency for me is clear. The ultimate tendency leads to setting up individual administration in every link of the soviet apparatus. We ask ourselves a serious question, what does this mean? This means that once we take this path and go far enough on it, we will collapse under the weight of bureaucracy, which will emasculate all our work, for the basic slogan which we should proclaim at the present time is the unification of military work, military forms of organization and methods of administration, with the creative initiative of the conscious workers. If, under the banner of military work, you in fact begin to implant bureaucratism, we will disperse our own forces and fail to fulfill our tasks.

The unrestrained application of complete formal militarization can also lead to this. To apply it generally is enticing – under the banner of militarization it is all the easier to implant individual bureaucratic authority. Meanwhile, what character does our economic work have to assume? It has to assume a shock-work character, and we can apply complete militarization only in certain branches. Complete militarization is bound up with the limitation of the civil and political rights of man, with his complete bondage in production, etc. Complete militarization means that man is removed to a situation where they tell him: for the moment you are not a citizen, you are only a functionary, you must fulfill your civic duty not at meetings but in the workshop. . . .

LENIN ON REVOLUTIONARY PURISM

Stung by criticisms directed against his policies of centralization and expediency by Communist critics both in Russia and in the newly-founded Communist International, Lenin delivered a diatribe against the "petty-bourgeois childishness" of people who objected to compromises. In his characteristic manner he denounced opponents of party discipline as virtual agents of capitalism.

Certainly, almost everyone now realizes that the Bolsheviks could not have maintained themselves in power for two and a half months, let alone two and a half years, unless the strictest, truly iron discipline had prevailed in our Party, and unless the latter had been rendered the fullest and unreserved support of the whole mass of the working class, that is, of all its thinking, honest, self-sacrificing and influential elements who are capable of leading or of carrying with them the backward strata.

The dictatorship of the proletariat is a most determined and most ruthless war waged by the new class against a *more powerful* enemy, the bourgeoisie, whose resistance is increased *tenfold* by its overthrow (even if only in one country), and whose power lies not only in the strength of international capital, in the strength and durability of the international connections of the bourgeoisie, but also in the *force of habit*, in the strength of *small production*. For, unfortunately, small production is still very, very widespread in the world, and small production *engenders* capitalism and the bourgeoisie continuously, daily, hourly, spontaneously, and on a mass scale. For all these reasons the dictatorship of the proletariat is essential, and victory over the bourgeoisie is impossible, without a long, stubborn and desperate war of life and death, a war demanding perseverance, discipline, firmness, indomitableness and unity of will.

I repeat, the experience of the victorious dictatorship of the proletariat in Russia has clearly shown even to those who are unable to think, or who have not had occasion to ponder over this question, that absolute centralization and the strictest discipline of the proletariat constitute one of the fundamental conditions for victory over the bourgeoisie. . . .

FROM: Lenin, " 'Left-Wing' Communism: An Infantile Disorder" (April, 1920; *Selected Works*, Vol. II, book 2, pp. 344, 359-60, 366-67).

. . . To reject compromises "on principle," to reject the admissibility of compromises in general, no matter of what kind, is childishness, which it is difficult even to take seriously. A political leader who desires to be useful to the revolutionary proletariat must know how to single out *concrete* cases when such compromises are inadmissible, when they are an expression of opportunism and *treachery*, and direct all the force of criticism, the full edge of merciless exposure and relentless war, against *those concrete* compromises. . . .

There are compromises and compromises. One must be able to analyze the situation and the concrete conditions of each compromise, or of each variety of compromise. One must learn to distinguish between a man who gave the bandits money and firearms in order to lessen the damage they can do and facilitate their capture and execution, and a man who gives bandits money and firearms in order to share in the loot. In politics this is by no means always as easy as in this childishly simple example. But anyone who set out to invent a recipe for the workers that would provide in advance ready-made solutions for all cases in life, or who promised that the policy of the revolutionary proletariat would never encounter difficult or intricate situations, would simply be a charlatan. . . .

Repudiation of the party principle and of party discipline . . . is tantamount to completely disarming the proletariat *in the interest of the bourgeoisie*. It is tantamount to that petty-bourgeois diffuseness, instability, incapacity for sustained effort, unity and organized action, which, if indulged in, must inevitably destroy every proletarian revolutionary movement. From the standpoint of Communism, the repudiation of the party principle means trying to leap from the eve of the collapse of capitalism (in Germany), not to the lower, or the intermediate, but to the higher phase of Communism. We in Russia (in the third year since the overthrow of the bourgeoisie) are going through the first steps in the transition from capitalism to Socialism, or the lower stage of Communism. Classes have remained, and will remain everywhere *for years after* the conquest of power by the proletariat. Perhaps in England, where there is no peasantry (but where there are small owners!), this period may be shorter. The abolition of classes means not only driving out the landlords and capitalists – that we accomplished with comparative ease – it also means *abolishing the small commodity producers*, and they *cannot be driven out*, or crushed; we *must live in harmony* with them; they can (and must) be remoulded and re-educated only by very prolonged, slow, cautious organizational work. They encircle the proletariat on every side with a petty-bourgeois atmosphere, which permeates and corrupts the proletariat and causes constant relapses among the proletariat into petty-bourgeois spinelessness, disunity, individualism, and alternate moods of exaltation and dejection. The strictest centralization and discipline are required within the political party of the proletariat in order to counteract this, in order that the *organizational* role of the proletariat (and this is its *principal* role) may be exercised correctly, successfully, victoriously. The dictatorship of the proletariat is a persistent struggle – bloody and bloodless, violent and peaceful, military and economic, educational and administrative – against the forces and traditions of the old society. The force of habit of millions and tens of millions is a most terrible force. Without an iron party tempered in the struggle, without a party enjoying the confidence of all that is honest in the given class, without a party capable of watching and influencing the mood of the masses, it is impossible to conduct such a struggle successfully. It is a thousand times easier to vanquish the centralized big bourgeoisie than to "vanquish" the millions and millions of small owners; yet they, by their ordinary, everyday, imperceptible, elusive, demoralizing activity, achieve the *very* results which the bourgeoisie need and which tend to *restore* the bourgeoisie. Whoever weakens ever so little the iron discipline of the party of the proletariat (especially during the time of its dictatorship), actually aids the bourgeoisie against the proletariat. . . .

THE REACTION AGAINST BUREAUCRACY

By the fall of 1920 the Communists had crushed most of the White opposition and the Soviet regime was fairly secure. Within the Communist Party there was an upsurge of feeling against the extremes of hierarchical centralization and discipline which had become the rule for the organization of the party during the Civil War. At the Ninth Party Conference the leadership felt it necessary to acknowledge this sentiment by accepting a resolution on the need for more equality and democracy in the party.

The unprecedentedly difficult position of the Soviet Republic in the first years of its existence, extreme devastation, and the greatest military danger have made it essential to separate "shock" (and therefore actually privileged) offices and groups of functionaries. This was essential, for it was impossible to save the ruined country without concentrating forces and means in such offices and in such groups of functionaries, without which the combined imperialists of the whole world certainly would have crushed us and would not have let our Soviet Republic even begin economic construction. This circumstance, together with the heritage of capi-

FROM: Resolution of The Ninth Conference of the Russian Communist Party, September, 1920, "On the Coming Tasks of Building the Party" (CPSU in Resolutions, I, 507, 509, 511-12; editor's translation).

talistic and private-property habits and tendencies which we are enduring with difficulty, explains the necessity of directing the attention of the whole party again and again toward putting more equality into practice, firstly within the party, secondly within the proletariat and among all the toiling masses, and thirdly for the various offices and various groups of functionaries especially the "spetsy" [specialists] and responsible functionaries, in relation to the masses. Distinguishing members of the party only by the degree of their consciousness, devotion, endurance, political vision, revolutionary experience, readiness for self-sacrifice – the party struggles with any attempts to make distinctions among members of the party on any other lines: higher-ups and rank-and-file, intellectuals and workers, on nationality lines, etc. . . .

It is essential to realize in the internal life of the party broader criticism of the central as well as local institutions of the party; to commission the Central Committee to point out by circulars the means for broadening intraparty criticism at general meetings; to create publications which are capable of realizing broader and more systematic criticism of the mistakes of the party and general criticism within the party (discussion sheets, etc.). . . .

Recognizing in principle the necessity of appointment to responsible offices in exceptional cases, it is necessary to propose to the Central Committee that in the assignment of functionaries in general it replace appointment with recommendation.

[It is necessary] to point out that in the mobilization of comrades it is not permissible for party organs and individual comrades to be guided by any considerations except business ones. Any repression whatsoever against comrades because they dissent about some question or another decided by the party is not permissible. . . .

[It is necessary] to work out fully effective practical measures to eliminate inequality (in conditions of life, the wage scale, etc.) between the "spetsy" and the responsible functionaries on the one hand and the toiling masses on the other. . . . This inequality violates democratism and is the source of disruption in the party and of reduction in the authority of Communists. . . .

It is essential to create a Control Commission alongside the Central Committee; this must consist of comrades who have the highest party preparation, who are the most experienced, impartial, and capable of realizing strict party control. The Control Commission, elected by the party congress, must have the right to receive any complaints and examine them. . . .

Bureaucratism, which rules in many of our head offices and centers, often strikes painfully at the entirely legal interests of the mass of the people and serves as one of the most important sources of dissatisfaction within the party, for which the head offices and centers bear the responsibility.

The Central Committee of the party must take the most serious measures against this. The local organizations must help the Central Committee in this struggle, above all by communicating the pertinent facts to it.

THE COMMUNIST IDEAL IN FAMILY LIFE

While the world was shocked by rumors of the "nationalization of women," much Communist thought exhibited a glowing idealism about the future free and equal relationship of the sexes after abolition of the "slavery" of the "bourgeois" family. The most famous exponent of this ideal – in practice as well as theory – was Alexandra Kollontai, a paragon of revolutionary idealism and the first Commissar of Social Welfare. She was a leader in the ultra-left "Workers' Opposition" movement of 1920-21, but later made her peace with Stalin and enjoyed a long career as a Soviet diplomat.

. . . There is no escaping the fact: the old type of family has seen its day. It is not the fault of the communist State, it is the result of the changed conditions of life. *The family is ceasing to be a necessity of the State, as it was in the past*; on the contrary, it is worse than useless, since it needlessly holds back the female workers from more productive and far more serious work. Nor is it any longer necessary to the members of the family themselves, since the task of bringing up the children, which was formerly that of the family, is passing more and more into the hands of the collectivity. But on the ruins of the former family we shall soon see a new form rising which will involve altogether different relations between men and women, and which will be *a union of affection and comradeship, a union of two equal members of the communist society, both of them free, both of them independent, both ot them workers*. No more domestic "servitude" of women. No more inequality within the family. No more fear on the part of the woman lest she remain without support or aid with little ones in her arms if her husband should desert her. The woman in the communist city no longer depends on her husband but on her work. It is not her husband but her robust arms which will support her. There will be no more anxiety as to the fate of her children. The State of the Workers will assume responsibility for these. Marriage will be purified of all its material elements, of all money

FROM: Kollontai, *Communism and the Family* (1920; excerpts translated in Rudolf Schlesinger, ed., *The Family in the USSR*, London, Routledge and Kegan Paul, 1949, pp. 67-69; reprinted by permission of the publisher).

calculations, which constitute a hideous blemish on family life in our days. Marriage is henceforth to be transformed into a sublime union of two souls in love with each other, each having faith in the other; this union promises to each working man and to each working woman, simultaneously, the most complete happiness, the maximum of satisfaction which can be the lot of creatures who are conscious of themselves and of the life which surrounds them. *This free union,* which is strong in the comradeship with which it is inspired, *instead of the conjugal slavery of the past – that is what the communist society of to-morrow offers to both men and women.* Once the conditions of labour have been transformed, and the material security of working women has been increased, and after marriage such as was performed by the Church – that so-called indissoluble marriage which was at bottom merely a fraud – after this marriage has given place to the free and honest union of men and women who are lovers and comrades, another shameful scourge will also be seen to disappear, another frightful evil which is a stain on humanity and which falls with all its weight on the hungry working woman: prostitution.

This evil we owe to the economic system now in force, to the institution of private property. Once the latter has been abolished, the trade in women will automatically disappear.

Therefore let the women of the working class cease to worry over the fact that the family as at present constituted is doomed to disappear. They will do much better to hail with joy the dawn of a new society which will liberate woman from domestic servitude, which will lighten the burden of motherhood for woman, and in which, finally, we shall see the disappearance of the most terrible of the curses weighing upon women, prostitution.

The woman who is called upon to struggle in the great cause of the liberation of the workers – such a woman should know that in the new State there will be no more room for such petty divisions as were formerly understood: "These are my own children; to them I owe all my maternal solicitude, all my affection; those are your children, my neighbour's children; I am not concerned with them. I have enough to do with my own." Henceforth the worker-mother, who is conscious of her social function, will rise to a point where she no longer differentiates between *yours* and *mine*; she must remember that there are henceforth only *our* children, those of the communist State, the common possession of all the workers.

The Workers' State has need of a new form of relation between the sexes. The narrow and exclusive affection of the mother for her own children must expand until it embraces all the children of the great proletarian family. In place of the indissoluble marriage based on the servitude of woman, we shall see rise the free union, fortified by the love and mutual respect of the two members of the Workers' State, equal in their rights and in their obligations. In place of the individual and egotistic family, there will arise a great universal family of workers, in which all the workers, men and women, will be, above all, workers, comrades. Such will be the relation between men and women in the communist society of to-morrow. This new relation will assure to humanity all the joys of so-called free love ennobled by a true social equality of the mates, joys which were unknown to the commercial society of the capitalist regime.

Make way for healthy blossoming children: make way for a vigorous youth that clings to life and to its joys, which is free in its sentiments and in its affections. Such is the watchword of the communist society. In the name of equality, of liberty, and of love, we call upon the working women and the working men, peasant women and peasants, courageously and with faith to take up the work of the reconstruction of human society with the object of rendering it more perfect, more just, and more capable of assuring to the individual the happiness which he deserves. The red flag of the social revolution which will shelter, after Russia, other countries of the world also, already proclaims to us the approach of the heaven on earth to which humanity has been aspiring for centuries. . . .

THE TRADE UNION CONTROVERSY AND THE WORKERS' OPPOSITION

In the fall of 1920 sharp controversy broke out in the Communist Party over the role of the trade unions and their relation to the party and the government. Trotsky, with Bukharin's support, pressed his plan for militarizing or "governmentalizing" the unions as agencies of industrial administration. Lenin and the cautious wing of the party, including Zinoviev, Kamenev, Rykov, and Stalin, decided to eliminate the unions from administration altogether and relegate them to a social-service and educational role. At the other extreme, the left-wing enthusiasts in the trade unions, organized into the "Workers' Opposition," demanded that industrial administration be made the independent responsibility of the unions themselves. One of the most fervent spokesmen for the Workers' Opposition was Alexandra Kollontai, who bewailed the trend to bureaucracy and pleaded for trust in the "class instinct" of the proletariat.

. . . the Workers' Opposition is composed of the most advanced part of

FROM: Kollontai, *The Workers' Opposition* (1921; English translation, Chicago, Industrial Workers of the World, 1921, pp. 3-4, 7, 11, 20, 22-23, 32-33, 37-41, 44).

our class-organized proletarian-Communists. The opposition consists almost exclusively of members of the trade unions, and this fact is attested by the signatures of those who side with the opposition under the theses on the role of industrial unions. Who are these members of the trade unions? Workers – that part of the advanced guard of the Russian proletariat which has borne on its shoulders all the difficulties of the revolutionary struggle, and did not dissolve itself into the soviet institutions by losing contact with the laboring masses, but on the contrary, remained closely connected with them. . . .

Through their class instinct, these comrades standing at the head of the Workers' Opposition became conscious of the fact that there was something wrong: they understood that even though during these three years we have created the soviet institutions and reaffirmed the principles of the workers' republic, yet the working class, *as a class*, as a self-contained social unit with identical class aspirations, tasks, interests, and, hence, *with a uniform, consistent, clear-cut policy*, becomes an ever less important factor in the affairs of the Soviet republic. . . .

Why was it that none but the unions stubbornly defended the principle of collective management, even without being able to adduce scientific arguments in favor of it; and why was it that the specialists' supporters at the same time defended the "one man management"? The reason is that in this controversy, though both sides emphatically denied that there was a question of principle involved, two historically irreconcilable points of view had clashed. The "one-man management" is a product of the individualist conception of the bourgeois class. The "one man management" is in principle an unrestricted, isolated, free will of one man, disconnected from the collective.

This idea finds its reflection in all spheres of human endeavor – beginning with the appointment of a sovereign for the state and ending with a sovereign director of the factory. This is the supreme wisdom of bourgeois thought. The bourgeoisie do not believe in the power of a collective body. They like only to whip the masses into an obedient flock, and drive them wherever their unrestricted will desires. . . .

Rejection of a principle – the principle of collective management in the control of industry – was a tactical compromise on behalf of our party, an act of adaptation; it was, moreover, an act of deviation from that class policy which we so zealously cultivated and defended during the first phase of the revolution.

Why did this happen? How did it happen that our party, matured and tempered in the struggle of the revolution, was permitted to be carried away from the direct road in order to journey along the round-about path of adaptation, formerly condemned severely and branded as "opportunism"?. . .

Beside peasant-owners in the villages and burgher elements in the cities, our party in its soviet state policy is forced to reckon with the influence exerted by the representatives of wealthy bourgeoisie now appearing in the form of specialists, technicians, engineers, and former managers of financial and industrial affairs, who by all their past experience are bound to the capitalist system of production. They can not even imagine any other mode of production but only that one which lies *within the traditonal bounds of capitalist economics.*

The more Soviet Russia finds itself in need of specialists in the sphere of technique and management of production, the stronger becomes the influence of these elements, foreign to the working class elements, on the development of our economy. Having been thrown aside during the first period of the revolution, and being compelled to take up an attitude of watchful waiting or sometimes even open hostility toward the soviet authorities, particularly during the most trying months (the historical sabotage by the intellectuals), this social group of brains in capitalist production, of servile, hired, well-paid servants of capital, acquire more and more influence and importance in politics with every day that passes. . . .

The basis of the controversy is namely this: whether we shall realize communism through workers or over their heads, by the hands of soviet officials. And let us, comrades, ponder whether it is possible to attain and build a communist economy by the hands and creative abilities of the scions from the other class, who are imbued with their *routine of the past?* If we begin to think as Marxians, as men of science, we shall answer categorically and explicitly – no. . . .

The solution of this problem as it is proposed by the industrial unions, consists in giving complete freedom to the workers as regards experimenting, class training, adjusting and feeling out the new forms of production, as well as expression and development of their creative abilities, that is, to that class which alone can be the creator of communism. This is the way the Workers' Opposition handles the solution of this difficult problem from which follows the most essential point of their theses. "Organization of control over the social economy is a prerogative of the All-Russian Congress of Producers, who are united in the trade and industrial unions which elect the central body directing the whole economic life of the republic" (Theses of the Workers' Opposition). This point secures freedom for the manifestation of class creative abilities, not restricted and crippled by the bureaucratic machine which is saturated with the spirit of routine of the bourgeois capitalist system of production and control. The Workers'

Opposition relies on the creative powers of its own class – the workers. From this premise is deduced the rest of the program.

But right at this point there begins the deviation of the Workers' Opposition from the line that is followed by the party leaders. Distrust toward the working class (not in the sphere of politics, but in the sphere of economic creative abilities) is the whole essence of the theses signed by our party leaders. They do not believe that by the rough hands of workers, untrained technically, can be created those basic outlines of the economic forms from which in the course of time shall develop a harmonious system of communist production. . . .

There can be no self-activity without freedom of thought and opinion, for self-activity manifests itself not only in initiative, action, and work, but in *independent thought* as well. We are afraid of mass-activity. We are afraid to give freedom to the class activity, we are afraid of criticism, we have ceased to rely on the masses, hence, *we have bureaucracy with us.* That is why the Workers' Opposition considers that bureaucracy is our enemy, our scourge, and the greatest danger for the future existence of the Communist Party itself.

In order to do away with the bureaucracy that is finding its shelter in the soviet institutions, *we must first of all get rid of all bureaucracy in the party itself.* . . .

The Workers' Opposition, together with a group of responsible workers in Moscow, in the name of party regeneration and elimination of bureaucracy from the soviet institutions, demands complete realization of all democratic principles, not only for the present period of respite, but also for times of internal and external tension. This is the first and basic condition of the party regeneration, of its return to the principles of the program, from which in practice it is more and more deviating under the pressure of elements that are foreign to it.

The second condition, fulfillment of which with all determination is insisted upon by the Workers' Opposition, is the *expulsion from the party* of all non-proletarian elements. . . .

The third decisive step toward democratization of the party is the elimination of all non-workers' elements from all the administrative positions; in other words, the central, provincial, and county committees of the party must be composed so that workers closely connected with the working masses would have the preponderant majority therein. . . .

The fourth basic demand of the Workers' Opposition is this: *the party must reverse its policy to the elective principle.*

Appointments must be permissible only as exceptions, but lately they began to prevail as a rule. Appointments are very characteristic of bureaucracy, and yet at present they are a general, legalized and well recognized daily occurrence. The procedure of appointments produces a very unhealthy atmosphere in the party, and disrupts the relationship of equality among the members by rewarding friends and punishing enemies as well as by other no less harmful practices in our party and soviet life. . . .

Wide publicity, freedom of opinion and discussion, right to criticize within the party and among the members of the trade unions – such is the decisive step that can put an end to the prevailing system of bureaucracy. Freedom of criticism, right of different factions to freely present their views at party meetings, freedom of discussion – are no longer the demands of the Workers' Opposition alone. Under the growing pressure from the masses a whole series of measures that were demanded by the rank and file long before the All-Russian conference* was held, are recognized and promulgated officially at present. . . . However, we must not overestimate this "leftism," for it is only a declaration of principles to the congress. It may happen, as it has happened many a time with the decisions of our party leaders during these years, that this radical declaration will be forgotten for, as a rule, they are accepted by our party centres only just as the mass impetus is felt, and as soon as life again swings into normal channels the decisions are forgotten. . . .

The Workers' Opposition has said what has long ago been printed in "The Communist Manifesto" by Marx and Engels, viz.: "Creation of communism can and will be the work of the toiling masses themselves. Creation of communism belongs to the workers.". . .

THE KRONSTADT REVOLT

By early 1921 it was becoming clear to the Communist leaders that the system of "War Communism" had reached an impasse of economic breakdown and mass discontent. The seriousness of the situation was brought home to them by the outbreak of armed defiance of the Soviet government at the Baltic naval base of Kronstadt, a stronghold of anarchistic radicalism. For a few days Kronstadt appealed to the Russian populace to carry out a "third revolution" against the bureaucratic dictatorship of the Communists, in the name of the original ideals of the October Revolution. No effective response was forthcoming, and the rebels were soon overwhelmed by government troops.

*The Ninth Party Conference, September, 1920 – Ed.

FROM: "What We Are Fighting For," *News* of the Kronstadt Temporary Revolutionary Committee, March 8, 1921 (reprinted in *The Truth about Kronstadt*, Prague, Volia Rossii, 1921, pp. 82-83; editor's translation).

After carrying out the October Revolution, the working class hoped to achieve emancipation. The result has been to create even greater enslavement of the individual man.

The power of the police-gendarme monarchy has gone into the hands of the Communist-usurpers, who instead of freedom offer the toilers the constant fear of falling into the torture-chambers of the Cheka, which in their horrors surpass many times the gendarme administration of the czarist regime.

Bayonets, bullets, and the harsh shouts of the *oprichniki** of the Cheka, are what the working man of Soviet Russia has got after a multitude of struggles and sufferings. The glorious arms of labor's state – the sickle and hammer – have actually been replaced by the Communist authorities with the bayonet and the barred window, for the sake of preserving the calm, carefree life of the new bureaucracy of Communist commissars and officials.

But the most hateful and criminal thing which the Communists have created is moral servitude: they laid their hands even on the inner life of the toilers and compelled them to think only in the Communist way.

With the aid of militarized trade unions they have bound the workers to their benches, and have made labor not into a joy but into a new slavery. To the protests of the peasants, expressed in spontaneous uprisings, and of the workers, who are compelled to strike by the circumstances of their life, they answer with mass executions and bloodthirstiness, in which they are not surpassed by the czarist generals.

Labor's Russia, the first country to raise the banner of the liberation of labor, has been continuously covered with the blood of the people who have been tortured for the glory of Communist domination. In this sea of blood the Communists are drowning all the great and glowing pledges and slogans of labor's revolution.

It has been sketched out more and more sharply, and now has become obvious, that the Russian Communist Party is not the defender of the toilers which it represents itself to be; the interests of the working nation are alien to it; having attained power, it is afraid only of losing it, and therefore all means are allowed: slander, violence, deceit, murder, vengeance on the families of rebels.

The enduring patience of the toilers has reached its end.

Here and there the glow of insurrection has illuminated the country in its struggle against oppression and violence. Strikes by the workers have flared

---

*"Oprichniki": originally, members of the sixteenth-century police force of Czar Ivan the Terrible – Ed.

up, but the Bolshevik *okhrana** has not slept and has taken every measure to forestall and suppress the unavoidable third revolution. . . .

There can be no middle ground. Victory or death!

Red Kronstadt gives this example, threatening the counterrevolutionaries of the right and of the left.

The new revolutionary upheaval has been accomplished here. Here the banner of insurrection has been raised for liberation from the three-year violence and oppression of Communist domination, which has overshadowed the three-century yoke of monarchism. Here at Kronstadt the first stone of the third revolution has been laid, to break off the last fetters on the toiling masses and open a new broad road for socialist creativity.

This new revolution will rouse the laboring masses of the East and of the West, since it shows an example of the new socialist construction as opposed to the Communists' barrackroom "creativity" and directly convinces the laboring masses abroad that everything created here up to now by the will of the workers and peasants was not socialism.

The first step has been completed without a single shot, without a drop of blood. The toilers do not need blood. They will shed it only at a moment of self-defense. Firmness is enough for us, in spite of the outrageous actions of the Communists, to confine ourselves to isolating them from social life, so that their evil false agitation will not interfere with revolutionary work.

The workers and peasants unreservedly go forward, abandoning behind them the Constituent Assembly with its bourgeois stratum and the dictatorship of the party of the Communists with its Cheka men, its state capitalism, its hangman's noose encircling the neck of the masses and threatening to strangle them for good.

The present overturn at last makes it possible for the toilers to have their freely elected soviets, working without any violent party pressure, and remake the state trade unions into free associations of workers, peasants and the laboring intelligentsia. At last the policeman's club of the Communist autocracy has been broken.

INSTITUTION OF THE MONOLITHIC PARTY

Lenin's response to the Kronstadt rebellion was to change his course drastically, in two respects. For the country at large, he ordered a "strategic retreat" to the much more moderate "New Economic Policy." For the Communist Party he demanded a much more rigorous system of discipline, and the Tenth Party Congress in March, 1921, accepted the resolutions which he proposed to this

*"Okhrana": originally, the Czarist secret police – Ed.

effect – prohibition of organized factions within the party, and condemnation of the ultra-Left Workers' Opposition as an un-Communist deviation. As Alexandra Kollontai had predicted, the democratic concessions of 1920 were abruptly retracted. To enforce the new line of discipline, the personnel of the party Secretariat was shaken up; the old secretaries, who had supported Trotsky, were replaced by a new group including Molotov and influenced by Stalin as the leading figure in the Orgbureau.

a) ON PARTY UNITY

1. The Congress calls the attention of all members of the Party to the fact that the unity and solidarity of the ranks of the Party, ensuring complete mutual confidence among Party members and genuine team work, genuinely embodying the unanimity of will of the vanguard of the proletariat, are particularly essential at the present juncture when a number of circumstances are increasing the vacillation among the petty-bourgeois population of the country.

2. Notwithstanding this, even before the general Party discussion on the trade unions, certain signs of factionalism had been apparent in the Party, viz., the formation of groups with separate platforms, striving to a certain degree to segregate and create their own group discipline. Such symptoms of factionalism were manifested, for example, at a Party conference in Moscow (November 1920) and in Kharkov, both by the so-called "Workers' Opposition" group, and partly by the so-called "Democratic-Centralism" group.

All class-conscious workers must clearly realize the perniciousness and impermissibility of factionalism of any kind, for no matter how the representatives of individual groups may desire to safeguard Party unity, in practice factionalism inevitably leads to the weakening of team work and to intensified and repeated attempts by the enemies of the Party, who have fastened themselves onto it because it is the governing Party, to widen the cleavage and to use it for counterrevolutionary purposes.

The way the enemies of the proletariat take advantage of every deviation from the thoroughly consistent Communist line was perhaps most strikingly shown in the case of the Kronstadt mutiny, when the bourgeois counterrevolutionaries and Whiteguards* in all countries of the world immediately expressed their readiness to accept even the slogans of the

FROM: Resolution of the Tenth Congress of the Russian Communist Party, "On Party Unity," March, 1921 (Lenin, *Selected Works*, Vol. II, book 2, pp. 497-501).

*Whiteguards: anti-Bolshevik units in the Civil War; applied to anti-Communists anywhere – Ed.

Soviet system, if only they might thereby secure the overthrow of the dictatorship of the proletariat in Russia, and when the Socialist-Revolutionaries and the bourgeois counterrevolutionaries in general resorted in Kronstadt to slogans calling for an insurrection against the Soviet government of Russia ostensibly in the interest of Soviet power. These facts fully prove that the Whiteguards strive, and are able, to disguise themselves as Communists, and even as the most Left Communists, solely for the purpose of weakening and overthrowing the bulwark of the proletarian revolution in Russia. . . .

4. In the practical struggle against factionalism, every organization of the party must take strict measures to prevent any factional actions whatsoever. Criticism of the Party's shortcomings, which is absolutely necessary, must be conducted in such a way that every practical proposal shall be submitted immediately, without any delay, in the most precise form possible, for consideration and decision to the leading local and central bodies of the Party. Moreover, everyone who criticizes must see to it that the form of his criticism takes into account the position of the Party, surrounded as it is by a ring of enemies, and that the content of his criticism is such that, by directly participating in Soviet and Party work, he can test the rectification of the errors of the Party or of individual Party members in practice. . . .

5. . . . . While ruthlessly rejecting unpractical and factional pseudo-criticisms, the Party will unceasingly continue – trying out new methods – to fight with all the means at its disposal against bureaucracy, for the extension of democracy and initiative, for detecting, exposing and expelling from the Party elements that have wormed their way into its ranks, etc.

6. The Congress therefore hereby declares dissolved and orders the immediate dissolution of all groups without exception that have been formed on the basis of one platform or another (such as the "workers' opposition" group, the "democratic-centralism" group, etc.). Nonobservance of this decision of the Congress shall involve absolute and immediate expulsion from the Party.

7. In order to ensure strict discipline within the Party and in all Soviet work and to secure the maximum unanimity in removing all factionalism, the Congress authorizes the Central Committee, in cases of breach of discipline or of a revival or toleration of factionalism, to apply all Party penalties, including expulsion, and in regard to members of the Central Committee to reduce them to the status of alternate members and even, as an extreme measure, to expel them from the Party. A necessary condition for the application of such an extreme measure to members of the Central Committee, alternate members of the Central Committee and members of the Control Commission is the convocation of a plenum of the Central

Committee, to which all alternate members of the Central Committee and all members of the Control Commission shall be invited. If such a general assembly of the most responsible leaders of the Party, by a two-thirds majority, deems it necessary to reduce a member of the Central Committee to the status of alternate member, or to expel him from the Party, this measure shall be put into effect immediately.

b) ON THE SYNDICALIST AND ANARCHIST DEVIATION IN OUR PARTY

1. In the past few months a syndicalist and anarchist deviation has been definitely revealed in our Party, and calls for the most resolute measures of ideological struggle and also for purging and restoring the health of the Party.

2. The said deviation is due partly to the influx into the Party of former Mensheviks and also of workers and peasants who have not yet fully assimilated the Communist world outlook; mainly, however, this deviation is due to the influence exercised upon the proletariat and on the Russian Communist Party by the petty-bourgeois element, which is exceptionally strong in our country, and which inevitably engenders vacillation towards anarchism, particularly at a time when the conditions of the masses have sharply deteriorated as a consequence of the crop failure and the devastating effects of war, and when the demobilization of the army numbering millions releases hundreds and hundreds of thousands of peasants and workers unable immediately to find regular means of livelihood.

3. The most theoretically complete and formulated expression of this deviation (*or:* one of the most complete, etc., expressions of this deviation) are the theses and other literary productions of the so-called "workers' opposition" group. Sufficiently illustrative of this is, for example, the following thesis propounded by this group: "The organization of the administration of the national economy is the function of an All-Russian Producers' Congress organized in industrial trade unions, which elect a central organ for the administration of the entire national economy of the Republic."

The ideas at the bottom of this and numerous analogous statements are radically wrong in theory, and represent a complete rupture with Marxism and Communism as well as with the practical experience of all semiproletarian revolutions and of the present proletarian revolution. . . .

Marxism teaches – and this tenet has not only been formally endorsed

FROM: Resolution of the Tenth Congress of the Russian Communist Party, "On the Syndicalist and Anarchist Deviation in Our Party," March, 1921 (Lenin, *Selected Works*, Vol. II, book 2, pp. 502-06).

by the whole of the Communist International in the decisions of the Second (1920) Congress of the Comintern on the role of the political party of the proletariat, but has also been confirmed in practice by our revolution – that only the political party of the working class, i.e., the Communist Party, is capable of uniting, training and organizing a vanguard of the proletariat and of the whole mass of the working people that alone will be capable of withstanding the inevitable petty-bourgeois vacillations of this mass and the inevitable traditions and relapses of narrow craft unionism or craft prejudices among the proletariat, and of guiding all the united activities of the whole of the proletariat, i.e., of leading it politically, and through it, the whole mass of the working people. Without this the dictatorship of the proletariat is impossible. . . .

5. In addition to theoretical fallacies and a radically wrong attitude towards the practical experience of economic construction already begun by the Soviet government, the Congress of the Russian Communist Party discerns in the views of these and analogous groups and persons a gross political mistake and a direct political danger to the very existence of the dictatorship of the proletariat.

In a country like Russia, the overwhelming preponderance of the petty-bourgeois element and the devastation, impoverishment, epidemics, crop failures, extreme want and hardship inevitably resulting from the war, engender particularly sharp vacillations in the moods of the petty-bourgeois and semiproletarian masses. At one moment the wavering is in the direction of strengthening the alliance between these masses and the proletariat, and at another moment in the direction of bourgeois restoration. The whole experience of all revolutions in the eighteenth, nineteenth, and twentieth centuries shows with utmost and absolute clarity and conviction that the only possible result of these vacillations – if the unity, strength and influence of the revolutionary vanguard of the proletariat is weakened in the slightest degree – can be the restoration of the power and property of the capitalists and landlords.

Hence, the views of the "workers' opposition" and of like-minded elements are not only wrong in theory, but in practice are an expression of petty-bourgeois anarchist wavering, in practice weaken the consistency of the leading line of the Communist Party, and in practice help the class enemies of the proletarian revolution.

6. In view of all this, the Congress of the Russian Communist Party, emphatically rejecting the said ideas which express a syndicalist and anarchist deviation, deems it necessary

Firstly, to wage an unswerving and systematic ideological struggle against these ideas;

Secondly, the Congress regards the propaganda of these ideas as being incompatible with membership of the Russian Communist Party.

Instructing the Central Committee of the Party strictly to enforce these decisions, the Congress at the same time points out that space can and should be devoted in special publications, symposiums, etc., for a most comprehensive interchange of opinion among Party members on all the questions herein indicated.

THE NEW ECONOMIC POLICY

To allay the dangers of popular hostility, particularly among the peasants, Lenin suspended the War Communism policy of requisitioning food, substituted a definite tax system, and began the restoration of a normal money economy qualified only by state ownership of the "commanding heights" of large-scale industry, transportation, communications, etc. He justified the broad use of capitalistic methods – "state capitalism" – as the only way to restore production. Thus, in 1921, the period of utopian revolutionary fervor came to an end.

... The most urgent thing at the present time is to take measures that will immediately increase the productive forces of peasant farming. Only in *this way* will it be possible to improve the conditions of the workers and strengthen the alliance between the workers and peasants, to strengthen the dictatorship of the proletariat. The proletarian or representative of the proletariat who *refused* to improve the conditions of the workers in *this way* would *in fact* prove himself to be an accomplice of the Whiteguards and the capitalists; because to refuse to do it in this way would mean putting the craft interests of the workers above their class interests, would mean sacrificing the interests of the whole of the working class, of its dictatorship, its alliance with the peasantry against the landlords and capitalists, its leading role in the struggle for the emancipation of labour from the yoke of capital, for the sake of the immediate, momentary and partial gain of the workers.

Thus, the first thing required is immediate and serious measures to raise the productive forces of the peasantry.

This cannot be done without a serious modification of our food policy. Such a modification was the substitution of the surplus-appropriation system by the tax in kind, which implies free trade, at least in local economic exchange, after the tax has been paid.

What, in essence, is the substitution of the surplus-appropriation system by the tax in kind? ...

The tax in kind is one of the forms of transition from that peculiar "War

FROM: Lenin, "The Tax In Kind" (April, 1921; *Selected Works*, Vol. II, book 2, pp. 540-44; 565-66).

Communism," which we were forced to resort to by extreme want, ruin and war, to the proper socialist exchange of products. The latter, in its turn, is one of the forms of transition from Socialism, with the peculiar features created by the predominance of the small peasantry among the population, to Communism.

The essence of this peculiar "War Communism" was that we actually took from the peasant all the surplus grain – and sometimes even not only surplus grain, but part of the grain the peasant required for food – to meet the requirements of the army and sustain the workers. . . . We were forced to resort to "War Communism" by war and ruin. It was not, nor could it be, a policy that corresponded to the economic tasks of the proletariat. It was a temporary measure. The correct policy of the proletariat which is exercising its dictatorship in a small-peasant country is to obtain grain in exchange for the manufactured goods the peasant requires. Only such a food policy corresponds to the tasks of the proletariat; only such a policy can strengthen the foundations of Socialism and lead to its complete victory. . . .

The effect will be the revival of the petty bourgeoisie and of capitalism on the basis of a certain amount of free trade (if only local). This is beyond doubt. It would be ridiculous to shut our eyes to it.

The question arises: Is it necessary? Can it be justified? Is it not dangerous? . . .

. . . What is to be done? Either to try to prohibit entirely, to put the lock on, all development of private, nonstate exchange, i.e., trade, i.e., capitalism, which is inevitable amidst millions of small producers. But such a policy would be foolish and suicidal for the party that tried to apply it. It would be foolish because such a policy is economically impossible. It would be suicidal because the party that tried to apply such a policy would meet with inevitable disaster. We need not conceal from ourselves the fact that some Communists sinned "in thought, word and deed" in this respect and dropped precisely into *such* a policy. We shall try to rectify these mistakes. They must be rectified without fail, otherwise things will come to a very sorry state.

Or (and this is the last *possible* and the only sensible policy) not to try to prohibit, or put the lock on the development of capitalism, but to try to direct it into the channels of *state capitalism*. This is economically possible, for state capitalism – in one form or another, to some degree or other – exists wherever the elements of free trade and capitalism in general exist.

Can the Soviet state, the dictatorship of the proletariat, be combined, united with state capitalism? Are they compatible? Of course they are . . . .

Chapter Three
Soviet Communism: The Era of Controversy,
1922-1929

For nearly a decade after the consolidation of Communist power Soviet Russia was ruled by a collective dictatorship of the top party leaders. At the top level individuals still spoke for themselves, and considerable freedom for factional controversy remained despite the principles of unity laid down in 1921.

The scope of political difference among the Communists was restricted, however, by certain severe limiting conditions. Under the New Economic Policy ("NEP"), the party was in power in a situation of postrevolutionary compromise, where reality made the serious application of its theory very difficult. The party was, however, dogmatically committed to the theoretical premises of the "proletarian revolution" and the "workers' state." Finally, the Civil War had bequeathed a military form of party organization, which put decisive political power in the hands of Stalin's Secretariat. While controversy raged between Right, Center, Left, and Ultra-Left groups about the proper way to advance toward the socialist ideal, the course of events was really dictated by the realities of economic backwardness and organizational power.

The uncertainties of the era of controversy came to an end with the successive victories of Stalin's party machine over Trotsky's Left Opposition and Bukharin's Right Opposition. By this time, the most important enduring features of the Soviet regime were laid down – a new system of personal power resting on total party control; a new use of doctrine as unchallengeable justification for the expediencies of government; and a new attack on the problems of backwardness, to accomplish economic development through dictatorial compulsion and violence.

PROTESTS AGAINST THE NEW ECONOMIC POLICY

The 1921 ban on factions did not immediately check the complaints of leftwing Communists that the NEP was a betrayal of the proletariat. The Workers' Opposition made their last stand in appealing to the Communist International (the "Declaration of the Twenty-Two") against bureaucratic muzzling of working-class sentiment in Russia. Another group, styling itself the "Workers' Truth," formed around Lenin's one-time second-in-command Alexander

145

Bogdanov and attacked the Communist Party for its "state capitalism" under which the workers were exploited for the benefit of the "organizers." Groups such as the "Workers' Truth," with their tone reminiscent of the old revolutionary protest against czarism, were naturally intolerable to the Soviet leaders and were quickly suppressed by the G.P.U.

a) THE DECLARATION OF THE TWENTY-TWO

Dear Comrades:

We have learned from our newspapers that the International Conference of the Communist International is considering the question of the "united Workers' front," and we consider it our Communist duty to make it known to you that in our country things stand unfavorably with the united front, not only in the broad sense of the term, but even in applying it to the ranks of our party.

At a time when the forces of the bourgeois element press on us from all sides, when they even penetrate into our party, whose social content (40% workers and 60% nonproletarians) favors this, our leading centers are conducting an unrelenting, disruptive struggle against all, especially proletarians, who allow themselves to have their own judgment, and against the expression of this within the party they take all kinds of repressive measures.

The effort to draw the proletarian masses closer to the state is declared to be "anarcho-syndicalism," and its adherents are subjected to persecution and discredit.

In the area of the trade-union movement there is the very same picture of suppression of the workers' independence and initiative, and a struggle using every means against heterodoxy. The combined forces of the party and trade-union bureaucracies, taking advantage of their position and power, are ignoring the decisions of our congresses about carrying out the principles of workers' democracy. Our [Communist] fractions in the unions, even the fractions of entire [trade-union] congresses, are deprived of the right to express their will in the matter of electing their centers. Tutelage and pressure by the bureaucracy lead to the members of the party being constrained by the threat of expulsion and other repressive measures to elect not whom these Communists themselves want, but those whom the higher-ups, ignoring them, want. Such methods of work lead to careerism, intrigue, and toadying, and the workers answer this by quitting the party.

FROM: Declaration of Twenty-Two Members of the Russian Communist Party to the International Conference of the Communist International (February, 1922; in *Izvestiya TsK* (News of the Central Committee), March, 1922, pp. 69-70; editor's translation).

Sharing the idea of a united workers' front . . . we turn to you in the sincere hope of ending all the abnormalities which stand in the way of the unity of this front, above all within our Russian Communist Party. . . .

b) APPEAL OF THE "WORKERS' TRUTH" GROUP

> "The liberation of the workers can only be the deed of the working class itself." [Marx]

Message to the Revolutionary Proletariat and to All Revolutionary Elements Who Remain Faithful to the Struggling Working Class:

. . . The working class of Russia, small in numbers, unprepared, in a peasant country, accomplished in October, 1917, the historically necessary October Revolution. Led by the Russian Communist Party, it has overthrown and destroyed the power of the ruling classes; during long years of revolution and civil war it has firmly contained the pressure of international and Russian reaction.

In spite of the unprecedentedly heavy losses sustained by the working class, the October Revolution remains a decisive and heroic event in the history of the struggle of the Russian proletariat. The Russian October Revolution has given the struggling international proletariat an experience of tremendous value for its struggle against capital.

As a result of the October Revolution all the barriers in the path of the economic development were eliminated; there is no longer any oppression by the landlords, the parasitic czarist bureaucracy, and the bourgeoisie, which relied on reactionary groups of European capitalists. After the successful revolution and civil war, broad perspectives opened before Russia, of rapid transformation into a country of progressive capitalism. In this lies the undoubted and tremendous achievement of the revolution in October.

But what has changed in the position of the working class? The working class of Russia is disorganized; confusion reigns in the minds of the workers: are they in a country of the "dictatorship of the proletariat," as the Communist Party untiringly reiterates by word of mouth and in the press? Or are they in a country of arbitrary rule and exploitation, as life tells them at every step? The working class is leading a miserable existence at a time when the new bourgeoisie (i.e., the responsible functionaries, plant directors, heads of trusts, chairmen of executive committees, etc.) and the Nepmen* live in luxury and recall in our memory the picture of the life of the bourgeoisie of all times. And again long and difficult years of the struggle

FROM: Appeal of the "Workers' Truth" Group (1922; in *Sotsialisticheskii Vestnik* (The Socialist Herald), Berlin, Jan. 31, 1923, pp. 12-14; editor's translation).

*Nepmen: private traders allowed to operate under the NEP—Ed.

for existence lie ahead. But the more complicated the circumstances, the more clarity and organization are necessary for the struggling proletariat. To introduce class clarity into the ranks of the working class of Russia, to aid in every way the organization of the revolutionary powers of the struggling proletariat – this is our task. . . .

The Communist Party, which during the years of the revolution was a party of the working class, has become the ruling party, the party of the organizers and directors of the governmental apparatus and economic life on capitalistic lines, with the general backwardness and lack of organization of the working class. The party has more and more lost its tie and community with the proletariat. The soviet, party, and trade-union bureaucracies and organizers find themselves with material conditions which are sharply distinguished from the conditions of existence of the working class. Their very well-being and the stability of their general position depend on the degree to which the toiling masses are exploited and subordinated to them. All this makes a contradiction between their interests and a break between the Communist Party and the working class inevitable.

The social existence of the Communist Party itself inevitably determines the corresponding social consciousness, interests and ideals, which contradict the interests of the struggling proletariat.

The Russian Communist Party has become the party of the organizer intelligentsia. The abyss between the Russian Communist Party and the working class is getting deeper and deeper, and this fact cannot be glossed over by any resolutions or decisions of the Communist congresses and conferences, etc. . . .

The NEP, i.e., the rebirth of normal capitalistic relations and intensive economic differentiation among the peasantry, intensified by the famine of 1920-21, has contributed to the pronounced growth of the big kulak stratum in the Russian village. The small-scale, unorganized character of peasant farming, together with the disruption of the means of communication, makes it definite that commercial capital will have a dominant role in the immediate future. At the same time the state is growing in influence as the representative of the nation-wide interests of capital and as the mere directing apparatus of political administration and economic regulation by the organizer intelligentsia. The proletariat – broken up in consequence of the destruction of industry; weakened by losses, the detaching (by bourgeois captivation) of part of the most active elements, and ideological confusion; and lacking a proletarian party and revolutionary workers' organizations of its own – is incapable of playing any sort of influential role. . . .

LENIN'S "TESTAMENT"

Lenin began to suffer strokes in May, 1922, and relinquished active leadership of the Soviet state. His lieutenants, particularly Zinoviev, Kamenev and Stalin, banded together to prevent Trotsky from assuming power. Stalin had meanwhile been appointed to the new post of General Secretary of the Communist Party in April, 1922, and was working to get effective control over the party into his own hands. Toward the end of 1922 Lenin recovered sufficiently to make certain acute observations on the Soviet political scene. His comments on the successor leadership were embodied in notes which became known abroad in 1926 as his "testament," and which were finally published in the USSR after Khrushchev's attack on Stalin's record in 1956.

By the stability of the Central Committee of which I spoke before, I mean measures to prevent a split, so far as such measures can be taken. For, of course, the White Guard in *Russkaya Mysl** (I think it was S. E. Oldenburg) was right when, in the first place, in his play against Soviet Russia he banked on the hope of a split in our party, and when, in the second place, he banked for that split on serious disagreements in our party.

Our party rests upon two classes, and for that reason its instability is possible, and if there cannot exist agreement between those classes its fall is inevitable. In such an event it would be useless to take any measures or in general to discuss the stability of our Central Committee. In such an event no measures would prove capable of preventing a split. But I trust that is too remote a future, and too improbable an event, to talk about.

I have in mind stability as a guarantee against a split in the near future, and I intend to examine here a series of considerations of a purely personal character.

I think that the fundamental factor in the matter of stability – from this point of view – is such members of the Central Committee as Stalin and Trotsky. The relation between them constitutes, in my opinion, a big half of the danger of that split, which might be avoided, and the avoidance of which might be promoted, in my opinion, by raising the number of members of the Central Committee to fifty or one hundred.

Comrade Stalin, having become General Secretary, has concentrated an

FROM: Lenin, Continuation of Notes, December 24, 1922 (in Lenin, *Pismo syezdu* [Letter to the Congress], Moscow, State Press for Political Literature, 1956; English translation by Max Eastman, *The New York Times*, November 19, 1926).

*"Russian Thought": an emigré journal – Ed.

enormous power in his hand; and I am not sure that he always knows how to use that power with sufficient caution. On the other hand Comrade Trotsky, as was proved by his struggle against the Central Committee in connection with the question of the People's Commissariat of Ways of Communication,* is distinguished not only by his exceptional abilities – personally he is, to be sure, the most able man in the present Central Committee – but also by his too far-reaching self-confidence and disposition to be too much attracted by the purely administrative side of affairs.

These two qualities of the two most able leaders of the present Central Committee might, quite innocently, lead to a split; if our party does not take measures to prevent it, a split might arise unexpectedly.

I will not further characterize the other members of the Central Committee as to their personal qualities. I will only remind you that the October episode of Zinoviev and Kamenev was not, of course, accidental, but that it ought as little to be used against them personally as the non-bolshevism of Trotsky.

Of the younger members of the Central Committee I want to say a few words about Bukharin and Piatakov. They are, in my opinion, the most able forces (among the youngest), and in regard to them it is necessary to bear in mind the following: Bukharin is not only the most valuable and biggest theoretician of the party, but also may legitimately be considered the favorite of the whole party, but his theoretical views can only with the very greatest doubt be regarded as fully Marxist, for there is something scholastic in him (he never has learned, and I think never has fully understood, the dialectic).

And then Piatakov – a man undoubtedly distinguished in will and ability, but too much given over to administration and the administrative side of things to be relied on in a serious political question.†

Of course, both these remarks are made by me merely with a view in the present time, in the assumption that these two able and loyal workers may not find an occasion to supplement their knowledge and correct their one-sidedness.

Postcript, January 4, 1923:

Stalin is too rude, and this fault, entirely supportable in relations among us Communists, becomes insupportable in the office of General Secretary. Therefore, I propose to the comrades to find a way to remove Stalin from that position and appoint to it another man who in all respects differs from Stalin only in superiority – namely, more patient, more loyal, more polite

* Lenin is referring to a controversy of 1920, when Trotsky tried to shake up the administration of transport in a particularly high-handed manner – Ed.

† Piatakov sided with Trotsky in the controversies of the twenties, and was tried and shot in 1937 – Ed.

and more attentive to comrades, less capriciousness, etc. This circumstance may seem an insignificant trifle, but I think that from the point of view of preventing a split and from the point of view of the relation between Stalin and Trotsky which I discussed above, it is not a trifle, or it is such a trifle as may acquire a decisive significance.

Lenin

LENIN ON NATIONALITY POLICY

The issue which had most to do with turning Lenin against Stalin was the nationality question, particularly as it arose in the Soviet Republic of Georgia. Lenin was extremely cautious about observing the forms of national autonomy; he reacted against Stalin's excessively centralist handling of the plan for a Union of Soviet Socialist Republics, as the "Great-Russian chauvinism" of the "Russified non-Russian."

. . . We call our own an apparatus which is still completely alien to us and represents a bourgeois and czarist jumble. To overcome this in five years, in the absence of the help of other countries and with the prevalence of military "take-overs" and the struggle with hunger, was in no way possible.

Under such conditions it is quite natural that "the freedom to secede from the Union," by which we justify ourselves, should prove to be an empty scrap of paper, incapable of defending the other nationalities of Russia from the aggression of that truly Russian man, the Great-Russian chauvinist, in reality a scoundrel and man of violence, which the typical Russian bureaucrat reveals himself to be. There is no doubt that an insignificant percentage of Soviet and Sovietized workers will sink in this sea of chauvinistic Great-Russian filth, like flies in milk.

They say in defense of this measure [the formation of the Union] that they have divided up the People's Commissariats which touch immediately on national psychology, national education. But here appears a question: is it possible to divide up these commissariats completely? and a second question: have we taken measures with sufficient care really to defend the other nationalities from the truly Russian Derzhimorda?* I think we have not taken these measures, although they can and must be taken.

I think that here Stalin's haste and administrative enthusiasm have played a fatal role, and also his anger against the notorious "social-nationalism." Anger in general plays the very worst role in politics.

FROM: Lenin, "On the Question of the Nationalities or of 'Autonomization'" (December 30-31, 1922; in Lenin, *Letter to the Congress*, pp. 22-25, 27-28; editor's translation).

*"Derzhimorda": a policeman in Gogol's play, *The Inspector General*—Ed.

I fear also that Comrade Dzerzhinsky, who went to the Caucasus to investigate the matter of the "crimes" of these "social-nationalists," was also distinguished here only by his truly Russian tendency (it is known, that the russified non-Russian always overdoes things in the truly Russian direction), and that the impartiality of his whole commission is sufficiently illustrated by Ordzhonikidze's resort to force, and that Comrade Dzerzhinsky is unforgiveably guilty for approaching this resort to force light-mindedly . . . .

. . . Internationalism on the part of the oppressor or so-called "great" nation (although great only in its violence, great only as the great Derzhi-morda) must consist not only in the observance of the formal equality of nations, but also in the inequality which offsets on the part of the oppressor nation, the large nation, that inequality which actually is built up in life. Whoever has not understood this has really not understood the proletarian attitude toward the national question; essentially he retains the petty-bourgeois point of view and therefore cannot but slide continually toward the bourgeois point of view.

What is important for the proletariat? For the proletariat it is not only important, but essentially necessary, to guarantee the maximum confidence in the proletarian class struggle on the part of the other nationalities. What is necessary for this? For this we need not only formal equality. For this it is necessary to compensate, in one way or another by our treatment or concessions in regard to the non-Russian, for that distrust, that suspiciousness, those wrongs, which in the historical past were inflicted upon him by the ruling "great-power" nation.

I think that for the Bolsheviks, for the Communists, it is not necessary to explain this further and in detail. I think that in the present case regarding the Georgian nation we have a typical example of what extreme care, foresight and conciliation are required on our part for a truly proletarian approach to the matter. . . .

We should, of course, make Stalin and Dzerzhinsky politically responsible for this whole truly Great-Russian nationalist campaign. . . .

The harm for our state which can rise from the absence of national commissariats united with the Russian apparatus is immeasurably less, infinitely less, than the harm which can develop not only for us but for the whole International, for the hundreds of millions of the peoples of Asia, who are ready to make their appearance on the historical stage in the very near future, following us. It would be unforgiveable opportunism if, on the eve of this appearance of the East and at the beginning of its awakening, we undermined our prestige among the peoples of the East by even the slightest rudeness and injustice in regard to our own minorities. The necessity for solidarity of the forces against the imperialists of the West, who defend the capitalist world, is one thing. Here there can be no doubt, and it is superfluous for me to say that I approve of these measures unconditionally. It is another matter when we ourselves fall, even on a small scale, into an imperialistic relationship toward the oppressed nationalities. But tomorrow, in world history, will be the very day when the aroused peoples, oppressed by imperialism, will finally awake, and when the long, severe, decisive battle for their liberation will begin.

LENIN ON THE PREREQUISITES FOR SOCIALISM

Lenin was prepared to admit, as he did in commenting on the memoirs of the Menshevik Sukhanov, that Russia lacked the conditions for socialism, but he saw no reason why the Communist government could not proceed to create them. Here again he revealed his real philosophy, hardly compatible with Marxism, that political power determined all else.

. . . "Russia has not attained the level of development of productive forces that makes Socialism possible." Of this proposition, all the heroes of the Second International, including, of course, Sukhanov, are as proud as a peacock. They keep repeating this incontrovertible proposition over and over again in a thousand different keys, and imagine that it is the decisive criterion of our revolution.

But what if peculiar circumstances drew Russia, first, into the world imperialist war in which every more or less influential West-European country was involved, and brought her development to the verge of the revolutions that were maturing and had partly already begun in the East, in conditions which enabled us to achieve precisely that union of a "peasant war" with the working-class movement which no less a "Marxist" than Marx himself had in 1856 suggested as a possible prospect for Prussia?

What if the complete hopelessness of the situation, by stimulating the efforts of the workers and peasants tenfold, offered us the possibility of creating the fundamental requisites of civilization in a different way from that of the West-European countries? Has that altered the general line of development of world history? Has that altered the basic relations between the basic classes of all the countries that are, or have been, drawn into the general course of world history?

If a definite level of culture is required for the building of Socialism (although nobody can say just what that definite "level of culture" is, for it

FROM: Lenin, "Our Revolution: Apropos of the Notes of N. Sukhanov" (January, 1923; *Selected Works*, Vol. II, book 2, pp. 726-27).

differs in every West-European country), why cannot we begin by first achieving the prerequisites for that definite level of culture in a revolutionary way, and *then*, with the aid of the workers' and peasants' government and the Soviet system, proceed to overtake the other nations?

You say that civilization is necessary for the building of Socialism. Very good. But why could we not first create such prerequisites of civilization in our country as the expulsion of the landlords and the Russian capitalists, and then start moving towards Socialism? Where, in what books, have you read that such variations of the customary historical order of events are impermissible or impossible?

Napoleon, one recalls, wrote: *On s'engage et puis – on voit*. Rendered freely this means: One must first join a serious battle and then see what happens. Well, we did first join serious battle in October 1917, and then we saw such details of development (from the standpoint of world history they were certainly details) as the Brest-Litovsk Peace, the New Economic Policy, and so forth. And now there can be no doubt that in the main we have been victorious. . . .

LENIN ON ADMINISTRATIVE REFORM

In his last articles, early in 1923, Lenin turned his attention to the quality of the Soviet governmental administration, which he found sorely lacking. He proposed various schemes of reform to meet the expectations of the nation and enable the Soviet regime to hold power firmly until the next international revolutionary upsurge. The latter, significantly, Lenin now expected to come from the nations of Asia.

. . . The situation as regards our machinery of state is so deplorable, not to say disgusting, that we must first of all think very carefully how to eliminate its defects, bearing in mind that the roots of these defects lie in the past, which, although it has been overturned, has not yet been overcome, does not yet belong to the culture of the dim and distant past. I say culture deliberately, because in these matters we can regard as achievements only what have become part and parcel of our culture, of our social life, our habits. We can say that what is good in the social system of our country has not been properly studied, understood, felt; it has been hastily grasped at; it has not been tested, tried by experience, made durable, etc. Of course, it could not be otherwise in a revolutionary epoch, when development proceeded at

FROM: Lenin, "Better Fewer, But Better" (March, 1923; *Selected Works*, Vol. II, book 2, pp. 735-39, 746, 748-51).

such breakneck speed that we passed from tsarism to the Soviet system in a matter of five years.

We must come to our senses in time. We must be extremely skeptical of too rapid progress, of boastfulness, etc. We must think of testing the steps forward which we proclaim to the world every hour, which we take every minute, and which later on we find, every second, to be flimsy, superficial and not understood. The most harmful thing here would be haste. The most harmful thing would be to rest on the assumption that we know anything, or on the assumption that we possess to any degree the elements necessary for building a really new state machine that would really deserve to be called socialist, Soviet, etc.

No, the machine of this kind, and even the elements of it that we do possess, are ridiculously small; we must remember that we must not stint time on building this machine, and that it will take many, many years to build.

What elements have we for building this machine? Only two. First, the workers who are absorbed in the struggle for Socialism. These elements are not sufficiently educated. They would like to build a better machine for us, but they do not know how. They cannot build one. They have not yet developed the culture which is required for this; and it is precisely culture that is required. Here nothing will be achieved by doing things in a rush, by assault, by being smart or vigorous, or by any other of the best human qualities in general. Secondly, we have the element of knowledge, education and training, but to a ridiculously low degree compared with all other countries.

Here, too, we must not forget that we are too prone to compensate (or imagine that we can compensate) our lack of knowledge by zeal, haste, etc. . . .

. . . Let us say frankly that the People's Commissariat for Workers' and Peasants' Inspection does not enjoy the slightest prestige at present. Everybody knows that a more badly organized institution than our Workers' and Peasants' Inspection does not exist, and that under present conditions nothing can be expected from this People's Commissariat. We must have this firmly fixed in our minds if we really want to set out to create within a few years an institution that will, firstly, be an exemplary institution, secondly, win everybody's absolute confidence, and, thirdly, prove to all and sundry that we have really justified the work of such a high institution as the Central Control Commission. In my opinion, we must utterly and irrevocably reject all general numerical standards for office staffs. We must make a particularly careful selection of the employees of the Workers' and

Peasants' Inspection and put them to the strictest test. Indeed, what is the use of establishing a People's Commissariat which carries on anyhow, which does not enjoy the slightest confidence, and whose word carries scarcely any weight? I think that our main object in launching the work of reconstruction we now have in mind is to change all this. . . .

In all spheres of social, economic and political relationships we are "frightfully" revolutionary. But as regards precedence, the observation of the forms and rites of office routine, our "revolutionariness" often gives way to the mustiest routine. Here, on more than one occasion, we have witnessed the very interesting phenomenon of a great leap forward in social life being accompanied by amazing timidity whenever the slightest changes are proposed. . . .

. . . At the present time we are confronted with the question: Shall we be able to hold on with our small and very small peasant production, and in our present state of ruin, while the West-European capitalist countries are consummating their development towards Socialism? But they are consummating it not as we formerly expected. They are not consummating it by the gradual "maturing" of Socialism, but by the exploitation of some countries by others, by the exploitation of the first of the countries to be vanquished in the imperialist war combined with the exploitation of the whole of the East. On the other hand, precisely as a result of the first imperialist war, the East has been definitely drawn into the revolutionary movement, has been definitely drawn into the general maelstrom of the world revolutionary movement.

What tactics does this situation prescribe for our country? Obviously the following: We must display extreme caution so as to preserve our workers' government and enable it to retain its leadership and authority over our small and very small peasantry. We have the advantage in that the whole world is now passing into a movement that must give rise to a world socialist revolution. . . .

. . . The outcome of the struggle as a whole can be foreseen only because we know that in the long run capitalism itself is educating and training the vast majority of the population of the globe for the struggle.

In the last analysis, the outcome of the struggle will be determined by the fact that Russia, India, China, etc., account for the overwhelming majority of the population of the globe. And it is precisely this majority that, during the past few years, has been drawn into the struggle for emancipation with extraordinary rapidity, so that in this respect there cannot be the slightest shadow of doubt what the final outcome of the world struggle will be. In this sense, the complete victory of Socialism is fully and absolutely assured.

But what interests us is not the inevitability of this complete victory of

Socialism, but the tactics which we, the Russian Communist Party, we, the Russian Soviet government, should pursue to prevent the West-European counterrevolutionary states from crushing us. To ensure our existence until the next military conflict between the counterrevolutionary imperialist West and the revolutionary and nationalist East, between the most civilized countries of the world and the Orientally backward countries, which, however, account for the majority, this majority must become civilized. We, too, lack sufficient civilization to enable us to pass straight on to Socialism, although we have the political requisites for this. We must adopt the following tactics, or pursue the following policy to save ourselves.

We must strive to build up a state in which the workers retain their leadership in relation to the peasants, in which they retain the confidence of the peasants, and, by exercising the greatest economy, remove every trace of extravagance from our social relations.

We must reduce our state apparatus to the utmost degree of economy. We must remove from it all traces of extravagance, of which so much has been left over from tsarist Russia, from its bureaucratic capitalist apparatus.

Will not this be the reign of peasant narrowness?

No. If we see to it that the working class retains its leadership of the peasantry, we shall be able, by exercising the greatest possible economy in the economic life of our state, to use every kopek we save to develop our large-scale machine industry, to develop electrification, the hydraulic extraction of peat, to finish the construction of Volkhovstroi, etc.

In this, and this alone, lies our hope. Only when we have done this will we, speaking figuratively, be able to change horses, to change from the peasant, muzhik horse of poverty, from the horse of economy fit for a ruined peasant country, to the horse which the proletariat is seeking and cannot but seek – the horse of large-scale machine industry, or electrification, of Volkhovstroi, etc.

That is how I link up in my mind the general plan of our work, of our policy, of our tactics, of our strategy, with the functions of the reorganized Workers' and Peasants' Inspection. . . .

TROTSKY ON INDUSTRIALIZATION

In the early years of the NEP Trotsky devoted himself to problems of economic planning, and urged systematic efforts by the Soviet government to build and improve industry on the basis of a clear hierarchy of authority, ostensibly as the foundation for the "proletarian" dictatorship.

FROM: Trotsky, "Theses on Industry," March 6, 1923 (editor's translation from copy in the Trotsky Archive, Houghton Library, Harvard University, document T2964).

The interrelationship which we have between the working class and the peasantry rests in the last analysis on the interrelationship between industry and agriculture. In the last analysis the working class can maintain and strengthen its guiding position not through the apparatus of government, not through the army, but through industry, which reproduces the proletariat itself. The party, the trade unions, the youth league, our schools, etc., have their tasks of educating and preparing new generations of the working class. But all this work would prove to be built on sand if it did not have a growing industrial base under it. Only the development of industry creates an unshakable foundation for the proletarian dictatorship. . . .

. . . The preparation of our budget, the state's credit policy, the system of measures for the military security of the state, all state activity in general, must give primary concern to the planned development of state industry.

The regeneration of state industry, in the general economic structure of our country, will necessarily be closely dependent on the development of agriculture; the necessary means of exchange must be formed in agriculture, by way of the excess of the agricultural product over the consumption of the village, before industry can take a decisive step forward. But it is just as important for state industry not to lag behind agriculture; otherwise, on the foundation of the latter private industry would be created, which, in the last analysis, would swallow up state industry or suck it dry.

Only such industry can be victorious which gives more than it swallows up. Industry which lives off the budget, i.e., off agriculture,* could not create a firm and lasting support for the proletarian dictatorship. The question of creating surplus value within state industry is the question of the fate of the Soviet power, that is, the fate of the proletariat.

The expanded reproduction of state industry, which is unthinkable without the accumulation of surplus value by the state, is in turn the condition for the development of our agriculture in the socialistic rather than the capitalistic direction.

Thus, through state industry lies the road to the socialist social order. . . .

The interrelationship between light and heavy industry cannot be decided through the market alone, for this would actually threaten heavy industry with destruction in the next few years, with the prospect of its restoration afterward on the basis of private property, as a result of the spontaneous work of the market.

Thus, in contrast to capitalist countries, the area of the planning principle is not limited here to the framework of individual trusts or syndicates, but extends to all industry as a whole. Not only that: the state must

* I.e., financed by taxing the peasants – Ed.

embrace the interrelationship of industry on the one hand and of agriculture, finance, transport, domestic and foreign trade, on the other. . . .

The system of actual one-man management must be applied in the organization of industry from top to bottom. For the leading economic organs really to direct industry and to be able to bear responsibility for its fate, it is essential for them to have authority over the selection of functionaries and their transfer and removal. Recommendations and attestations by the trade-union organs must be considered with full attention, but this can in no case remove responsibility from the corresponding economic organs, which in actual practice have full freedom of selection and appointment.

The weak side of state industry and trade is their ponderousness, immobility, lack of enterprise. The cause of this, above all, is still the inadequate selection of business executives, in their lack of experience, in their lack of incentives to succeed in their own work. We need correct systematic measures in all these directions. In particular, the payment of the directors of enterprises must be made to depend on their balance sheets, like wages depend on output. . . .

FORMATION OF THE TROTSKYIST OPPOSITION

In the fall of 1923, after a variety of issues and personal frictions had accumulated, Trotsky launched a behind-the-scenes attack on his colleagues in the party leadership, with particular stress on the abuses being committed by Stalin's Secretariat. This was followed by a collective statement, signed by various former oppositionists, which took the leadership severely to task for their failures in economic policy as well as their violation of party democracy.

a) TROTSKY PROTESTS BUREAUCRATIZATION

In the fiercest moment of War Communism, the system of appointment within the party did not have one-tenth of the extent that it has now. Appointment of the secretaries of provincial committees is now the rule. That creates for the secretary a position essentially independent of the local organization . . . .

The Twelfth Congress of the party was conducted under the sign of democracy. Many of the speeches at that time spoken in defense of workers' democracy seemed to me exaggerated, and to a considerable extent demagogish, in view of the incompatibility of a fully developed workers' democracy with the regime of dictatorship. But it was perfectly clear that

FROM: Trotsky, Letter to the Central Committee and the Central Control Commission, October 8, 1923 (Excerpts [translated by Max Shachtman] in Trotsky, *The New Course*, New York, New International, 1943, pp. 153-56).

the pressure of the period of War Communism ought to give place to a more lively and broader party responsibility. However, this present regime, which began to form itself before the Twelfth Congress, and which subsequently received its final reinforcement and formulation – is much farther from workers' democracy than the regime of the fiercest period of War Communism. The bureaucratization of the party apparatus has developed to unheard-of proportions by means of the method of secretarial selection. There has been created a very broad stratum of party workers, entering into the apparatus of the government of the party, who completely renounce their own party opinion, at least the open expression of it, as though assuming that the secretarial hierarchy is the apparatus which creates party opinion and party decisions. Beneath this stratum, abstaining from their own opinions, there lies the broad mass of the party, before whom every decision stands in the form of a summons or a command. In this foundation-mass of the party there is an unusual amount of dissatisfaction. . . . This dissatisfaction does not dissipate itself by way of influence of the mass upon the party organization (election of party committees, secretaries, etc.), but accumulates in secret and thus leads to interior strains. . . .

It is known to the members of the Central Committee and the Central Control Commission that while fighting with all decisiveness and definiteness within the Central Committee against a false policy, I decisively declined to bring the struggle within the Central Committee to the judgment even of a very narrow circle of comrades, in particular those who in the event of a reasonably proper party course ought to occupy prominent places in the Central Committee. I must state that my efforts of a year and a half have given no results. This threatens us with the danger that the party may be taken unawares by a crisis of exceptional severity. . . . In view of the situation created, I consider it not only my right, but my duty to make known the true state of affairs to every member of the party whom I consider sufficiently prepared, matured and self-restrained, and consequently able to help the party out of this blind alley without factional convulsions. . . .

b) DECLARATION OF THE FORTY-SIX

To the Politbureau of the Central Committee of the Russian Communist Party – Secret:

The extreme seriousness of the situation compels us (in the interests of our party, in the interests of the working class) to tell you openly that the continuation of the policy of the majority of the Politbureau threatens serious harm for the whole party. The economic and financial crisis which began at the end of July of this year, together with all the political (including intra-party) consequences which have stemmed from it, has unmercifully uncovered the unsatisfactoriness of the party leadership, in the area of the economy and especially in the area of intra-party relations.

The casualness, thoughtlessness, lack of system in the decisions of the Central Committee, not making ends meet in the area of the economy, has led to this, that with undoubted large successes in the area of industry, agriculture, finance and transport, successes achieved by the country's economy essentially not thanks to, but in spite of the unsatisfactory leadership, or rather, in the absence of any leadership – we face the prospect not only of the cessation of this success, but of a serious general economic crisis. . . .

If broad, considered, planned and energetic measures are not taken quickly, if the present absence of direction continues, we will face the possibility of an unusually sharp economic shock, unavoidably linked with internal political complications and with complete paralysis of our external activity and strength. And the latter, as anyone understands, we need now more than ever; on it depends the fate of the world revolution and of the working class of all countries.

Similarly, in the area of intraparty relations, we see the incorrectness of direction, paralyzing and disrupting the party, which has appeared with special clarity during the recent crisis.

We explain this not by the political incompetence of the present directors of the party; on the contrary, however we may differ with them in evaluating the situation and in the choice of measures to change it – we consider that the present leadership under any conditions cannot but be kept by the party in the leading posts of the workers' dictatorship. But we explain the crisis thus: that under the external form of official unity we actually have a selection of people and a guiding of action which are one-sided and adapted to the views and sympathies of a narrow circle. As a result of the party leadership being distorted by such narrow considerations, the party is to a significant degree ceasing to be the living, self-acting collective, which really embraces living activity, being linked by thousands of threads with this activity. Instead of this we observe a more and more progressive division of the party, no longer concealed by hardly anyone, into the secretarial hierarchy and the "laymen," into the professional party functionaries, selected from above, and the simple party masses, who do not participate in its group life.

This is a fact which every member of the party knows. Members of the party who are dissatisfied by this or that decision of the Central Commit-

FROM: The Declaration of the Forty-Six, October 15, 1923 (editor's translation from copy in the Trotsky Archive, T802a).

tee or even of a provincial committee, who have in mind certain doubts, who have noticed "by themselves" certain mistakes, confusions and disorders, are afraid to speak of these at party meetings; further, they are afraid to converse with each other, unless their conversants appear to be completely reliable men in the sense of keeping quiet. Free discussion within the party has in fact disappeared; the party's social mind has been choked off. In these times the broad masses of the party do not nominate and elect the provincial committees and the Central Committee of the RCP. On the contrary, the secretarial hierarchy of the party to an ever greater degree selects the membership of conferences and congresses, which to an ever greater degree are becoming executive consultations of this hierarchy.

The regime which has been set up within the party is absolutely intolerable; it kills initiative in the party, subjects the party to an apparatus of appointed officials, which undeniably functions in normal times, but which unavoidably misfires in moments of crisis, and which threatens to reveal itself as completely bankrupt in the face of the serious events which are approaching.

THE "NEW COURSE" CONTROVERSY OF DECEMBER, 1923

The first and most decisive public debate between the Trotskyists and the adherents of the party leadership took place in December, 1923, after some months of behind-the-scenes maneuver. The Politbureau had passed a resolution—largely drafted by Trotsky—promising broad reform in the direction of democracy within the party, and Trotsky then published an open letter warning that the party bureaucracy would try to sabotage the reform. This was the signal for a month-long press and agitational campaign against Trotsky's "factionalism."

In the debates and articles of recent times, it has been underlined that "pure," "complete," "ideal" democracy is not realizable and that in general for us it is not an end in itself. That is incontestable. But it can be stated with just as much reason that pure, absolute centralism is unrealizable and incompatible with the nature of a mass party, and that it can no more be an end in itself than can the party apparatus. Democracy and centralism are two faces of party organization. The question is to harmonize them in the most correct manner, that is, the manner best corresponding to the situation. During the last period there was no such equilibrium. The center of gravity wrongly centered in the apparatus. The initiative of the party was

FROM: Trotsky, "The New Course" (Open letter to a party meeting, December 8, 1923; English translation by Max Schachtman in Trotsky, *The New Course*, pp. 89-95).

reduced to the minimum. Thence, the habits and the procedures of leadership, fundamentally contradicting the spirit of revolutionary proletarian organization. The excessive centralization of the apparatus at the expense of initiative engendered a feeling of *uneasiness*, an uneasiness which, at the extremities of the party, assumed an exceedingly morbid form and was translated, among other things, in the appearance of illegal groupings directed by elements indubitably hostile to communism. At the same time, the whole of the party disapproved more and more of apparatus-methods of solving questions. The idea, or at the very least the feeling, that bureaucratism threatened to get the party into a blind alley, had become pretty general. Voices were raised to point out the danger. The resolution on the new course is the first official expression of the change that has taken place in the party. It will be realized to the degree that the party, that is, its four hundred thousand members, will want to realize it and will succeed in doing so. . . .

Bureaucratism kills initiative and thus prevents the elevation of the general level of the party. That is its cardinal defect. As the apparatus is made up inevitably of the most experienced and most meritorious comrades, it is upon the political training of the young Communist generations that bureaucratism has its most grievous repercussions. Also, it is the youth, the most reliable barometer of the party, that reacts most vigorously against party bureaucratism. . . .

. . . We, the "elders," we ought to say to ourselves plainly that our generation, which naturally enjoys the leading role in the party, is not *absolutely* guaranteed against the gradual and imperceptible weakening of the revolutionary and proletarian spirit in its ranks if the party were to tolerate the further growth and stabilization of bureaucratic methods which transform the youth into the passive material of education and inevitably create an estrangement between the apparatus and the mass, the old and the young. The party has no other means to employ against this indubitable danger than a serious, profound, radical change of course toward party democracy and the increasingly large flow into its midst of working-class elements. . . .

Before the publication of the decision of the Central Committee on the "new course," the mere pointing out of the need of modifying the internal party regime was regarded by bureaucratic apparatus functionaries as heresy, as factionalism, as an infraction of discipline. And now the bureaucrats are ready formally to "take note" of the "new course," that is, to *nullify it bureaucratically*. The renovation of the party apparatus – naturally within the clear-cut framework of the statutes – must aim at replacing the mummified bureaucrats with fresh elements closely linked with the life of the collectivity, or capable of assuring such a link. And before anything else, the leading posts must be cleared out of those who, at the first word of criticism, of objection, or of protest, brandish the thunderbolts of penalties before the critic. The "new course" must begin by making everyone feel that from now on nobody will dare terrorize the party.

THE CONDEMNATION OF THE TROTSKYIST OPPOSITION

By organizational pressure and some rigging of elections the party leadership scored an overwhelming success against the Opposition. At the Thirteenth Party Conference in January, 1924, this was registered in a resolution denouncing the Opposition's defiance of party authority as a Menshevik-like deviation. This was the end of the Trotsky movement as a serious organizational threat to the leadership, though top-level controversy continued.

. . . The opposition, headed by Trotsky, came forth with the slogan of smashing the party apparatus, and tried to shift the center of gravity of the struggle against bureaucratism in the governmental apparatus to "bureaucratism" in the apparatus of the party. Such wholesale criticism and attempts at directly discrediting the party apparatus cannot objectively lead to anything else than the emancipation of the governmental apparatus from influence upon it on the part of the party, to the divorce of the governmental organs from the party. . . .

Trotsky came out with vague insinuations about the degeneration of the basic cadres of our party and thereby tried to undermine the authority of the Central Committee, which between congresses is the only representative of the whole party. Trotsky not only tried to counterpose himself to all the rest of the Central Committee, but also permitted accusations which could not but evoke unrest in broad circles of the working class and a stormy protest in the ranks of our party. . . .

The opposition in all its shades has revealed a completely un-Bolshevik view on the significance of party discipline. The moves of a whole series of representatives of the opposition represent a crying violation of party discipline, and recall the times when Lenin had to struggle against the "anarchism of the intellectuals" in organizational questions and defend the foundations of proletarian discipline in the party.

The opposition clearly violated the decision of the Tenth Congress of the Russian Congress Party which prohibited the formation of factions within

FROM: Resolution of the Thirteenth Conference of the Russian Communist Party, January, 1924, "On the Results of the Controversy and on the Petty-Bourgeois Deviation in the Party" (CPSU in Resolutions, I, 780-782; editor's translation).

the party. The opposition has replaced the Bolshevik view of the party as a monolithic whole with the view of the party as the sum of all possible tendencies and factions. These tendencies, factions and groupings, according to the "new" view of the opposition, must have equal rights in the party, and the Central Committee of the party must not be so much the leader of the party as a simple registrar and intermediary between the tendencies and groupings. Such a view of the party has nothing in common with Leninism. The factional work of the opposition cannot but become a threat to the unity of the state apparatus. The factional moves of the opposition have enlivened the hopes of all enemies of the party, including the West-European bourgeoisie, for a split in the ranks of the Russian Communist Party. These factional moves again pose before the party in all its sharpness the question whether the Russian Communist Party, since it is in power, can allow the formation of factional groupings within the party.

Adding up the sum of these differences and analyzing the whole character of the moves by the representatives of the opposition, the All-Union Party Conference comes to the conclusion that in the person of the present opposition we have before us not only an attempt at the revision of Bolshevism, not only a direct departure from Leninism, but also a clearly expressed *petty-bourgeois deviation*. There is no doubt that this 'opposition' objectively reflects the pressure of the petty bourgeoisie on the position of the proletarian party and its policy. The principle of intraparty democracy is already beginning to be interpreted broadly beyond the limits of the party, in the sense of weakening the dictatorship of the proletariat and extending political rights to the new bourgeoisie.

In the situation where the Russian Communist Party, embodying the dictatorship of the proletariat, enjoys a monopoly of legality in the country, it is unavoidable that the least stable groups of Communists should sometimes give in to nonproletarian influences. The party as a whole must see these dangers and watchfully guard the proletarian line of the party.

A systematic and energetic struggle of our whole party against this petty-bourgeois deviation is essential. . .

THE FORMATION OF THE USSR: THE UNION CONSTITUTION

The Union of Soviet Socialist Republics officially came into being in January, 1924, as a federal union of four states which had been nominally independent though controlled by the single Russian Communist Party: the Russian Republic, the Ukraine, White Russia, and the Transcaucasian Federation. The forms of national autonomy, complete with the right of secession, were carefully observed, but in point of fact language was the only real distinction among the Soviet nationalities, who remain to the present under the strictly centralized control of the Communist Party.

Part I: Declaration

Since the foundation of the Soviet Republics, the States of the world have been divided into two camps; the camp of Capitalism and the camp of Socialism.

There, in the camp of Capitalism: national hate and inequality, colonial slavery and chauvinism, national oppression and massacres, brutalities and imperialistic wars.

Here, in the camp of Socialism: reciprocal confidence and peace, national liberty and equality, the pacific co-existence and fraternal collaboration of peoples.

The attempts made by the capitalistic world during the past ten years to decide the question of nationalities by bringing together the principle of the free development of peoples with a system of exploitation of man by man have been fruitless. In addition, the number of national conflicts becomes more and more confusing, even menacing the capitalistic regime. The bourgeoisie has proven itself incapable of realizing a harmonious collaboration of the peoples.

It is only in the camp of the Soviets; it is only under the conditions of the dictatorship of the proletariat that has grouped around itself the majority of the people, that it has been possible to eliminate the oppression of nationalities, to create an atmosphere of mutual confidence and to establish the basis of a fraternal collaboration of peoples. . . .

. . . National economic reestablishment is impossible as long as the Republics remain separated.

On the other hand, the instability of the international situation and the danger of new attacks make inevitable the creation of a united front of the Soviet Republics in the presence of capitalistic surroundings.

Finally, the very structure of Soviet power, international by nature of class, pushes the masses of workers of the Soviet Republics to unite in one socialist family.

All these considerations insistently demand the union of the Soviet Republics into one federated State capable of guaranteeing security against the exterior, economic prosperity internally, and the free national development of peoples.

FROM: Constitution of the USSR, Ratified by the Second Congress of Soviets of the USSR, January 13, 1924 (English translation in Milton H. Andrew, *Twelve Leading Constitutions*, Compton, Cal., American University Series, 1931, pp. 327 ff.).

The will of the peoples of the Soviet Republics recently assembled in Congress, where they decided unanimously to form the "Union of Socialist Soviet Republics," is a sure guarantee that this Union is a free federation of peoples equal in rights, that the right to freely withdraw from the Union is assured to each Republic, that access to the Union is open to all Republics already existing, as well as those that may be born in the future, that the new federal state will be the worthy crowning of the principles laid down as early as October 1917, of the pacific co-existence and fraternal collaboration of peoples, that it will serve as a bulwark against the capitalistic world and mark a new decisive step towards the union of workers of all countries in one World-Wide Socialist Soviet Republic.

Part II: Treaty

The Russian Socialist Federated Soviet Republic, the Socialist Soviet Republic of the Ukraine, the Socialist Soviet Republic of White Russia, and the Socialist Soviet Republic of Transcaucasia (including the Socialist Soviet Republic of Azerbaijan, the Socialist Soviet Republic of Georgia, and the Socialist Soviet Republic of Armenia) unite themselves in one federal State – "The Union of Soviet Socialist Republics." . . .

Chapter II: Sovereign Rights of the Member Republics

Article 3. The Sovereignty of the member Republics is limited only in the matters indicated in the present Constitution, as coming within the competence of the Union. Outside of those limits, each member Republic exerts its public powers independently; the Union of S.S.R. protects the rights of member Republics.

Article 4. Each one of the member Republics retains the right to freely withdraw from the union. . . .

STALIN ON LENINISM AND THE PARTY

Lenin died on January 21, 1924. He was succeeded as Chairman of the Council of Peoples' Commissars of the USSR by Alexei Rykov, but the real leadership of the Communist Party was temporarily shared by Stalin and Zinoviev. Stalin had the decisive advantage with his control of the party Secretariat, and in the spring of 1924 began to assert himself in the theoretical field with a series of lectures on "Leninism." Stalin proved to be Lenin's most adept pupil in both the theory and practice of the disciplined party organization.

FROM: Stalin, "The Foundations of Leninism" (April, 1924; English translation in J. Stalin, *Problems of Leninism*, Moscow, Foreign Languages Publishing House, 1953, pp. 100, 102-12).

. . . The Party is not only the *vanguard* detachment of the working class. If it desires really to direct the struggle of the class it must at the same time be the *organized* detachment of its class. The Party's tasks under the conditions of capitalism are immense and extremely varied. The Party must direct the struggle of the proletariat under the exceptionally difficult conditions of internal and external development; it must lead the proletariat in the offensive when the situation calls for an offensive; it must lead the proletariat in retreat when the situation calls for retreat in order to ward off the blows of a powerful enemy; it must imbue the millions of unorganized non-Party workers with the spirit of discipline and system in the struggle, with the spirit of organization and endurance. But the Party can fulfil these tasks only if it is itself the embodiment of discipline and organization, if it is itself the *organized* detachment of the proletariat. Without these conditions there can be no talk of the Party really leading the proletarian millions. . . .

. . . The Party is the organized detachment of the working class. But the Party is not the only organization of the working class. The proletariat has also a number of other organizations, without which it cannot properly wage the struggle against capital: trade unions, cooperative societies, factory organizations, parliamentary groups, non-Party women's associations, the press, cultural and educational organizations, youth leagues, revolutionary fighting organizations (in times of open revolutionary action), Soviets of deputies as the form of state organization (if the proletariat is in power), etc. The overwhelming majority of these organizations are non-Party, and only some of them adhere directly to the Party, or represent its offshoots. All of these organizations, under certain conditions, are absolutely necessary for the working class, for without them it would be impossible to consolidate the class positions of the proletariat in the diverse spheres of struggle; for without them it would be impossible to steel the proletariat as the force whose mission it is to replace the bourgeois order by the socialist order. . . . The question then arises: who is to determine the line, the general direction, along which the work of all these organizations is to be conducted? Where is that central organization which is not only able, because it has the necessary experience, to work out such a general line, but, in addition, is in a position, because it has sufficient prestige, to induce all these organizations to carry out this line, so as to attain unity of leadership and to preclude the possibility of working at cross purposes?

This organization is the Party of the proletariat.

The Party possesses all the necessary qualifications for this because, in the first place, it is the rallying centre of the finest elements in the working class, who have direct connections with the non-Party organizations of the proletariat and very frequently lead them; because, secondly, the Party, as the rallying centre of the finest members of the working class, is the best school for training leaders of the working class, capable of directing every form of organization of their class; because, thirdly, the Party, as the best school for training leaders of the working class, is, by reason of its experience and prestige, the only organization capable of centralizing the leadership of the struggle of the proletariat, thus transforming each and every non-Party organization of the working class into an auxiliary body and transmission belt linking the Party with the class.

The Party is the highest form of class organization of the proletariat . . . .

. . . The Party is the principal guiding force within the class of the proletarians and among the organizations of that class. But it does not by any means follow from this that the Party can be regarded as an end in itself, as a self-sufficient force. The Party is not only the highest form of class association of the proletarians; it is at the same time an *instrument* in the hands of the proletariat *for* achieving the dictatorship when that has not yet been achieved and *for* consolidating and expanding the dictatorship when it has already been achieved. The Party could not have risen so high in importance and could not have overshadowed all other forms of organization of the proletariat, if the latter had not been confronted with the problem of power, if the conditions of imperialism, the inevitability of wars, and the existence of a crisis had not demanded the concentration of all the forces of the proletariat at one point, the gathering of all the threads of the revolutionary movement in one spot in order to overthrow the bourgeoisie and to achieve the dictatorship of the proletariat. The proletariat needs the Party first of all as its General Staff, which it must have for the successful seizure of power. It need hardly be proved that without a Party capable of rallying around itself the mass organizations of the proletariat, and of centralizing the leadership of the entire movement during the progress of the struggle, the proletariat in Russia could never have established its revolutionary dictatorship.

But the proletariat needs the Party not only to achieve the dictatorship; it needs it still more to maintain the dictatorship, to consolidate and expand it in order to achieve the complete victory of socialism.

"Certainly, almost everyone now realizes," says Lenin, "that the Bolsheviks could not have maintained themselves in power for two-and-a-half months, let alone two-and-a-half years, unless the strictest, truly iron discipline had prevailed in our Party, and unless the latter had been rendered the fullest and unreserved support of the whole mass of the working class, that is, of all its thinking, honest, self-sacrificing and influential elements who are capable of leading or of carrying with them the backward strata."

Now, what does to "maintain" and "expand" the dictatorship mean? It means imbuing the millions of proletarians with the spirit of discipline and organization; it means creating among the proletarian masses a cementing force and a bulwark against the corrosive influences of the petty-bourgeois elements and petty-bourgeois habits; it means enhancing the organizing work of the proletarians in re-educating and re-moulding the petty-bourgeois strata; it means helping the masses of the proletarians to educate themselves as a force capable of abolishing classes and of preparing the conditions for the organization of socialist production. But it is impossible to accomplish all this without a party which is strong by reason of its solidarity and discipline.

"The dictatorship of the proletariat," says Lenin, "is a persistent struggle – bloody and bloodless, violent and peaceful, military and economic, educational and administrative – against the forces and traditions of the old society. The force of habit of millions and tens of millions is a most terrible force. Without an iron party tempered in the struggle, without a party enjoying the confidence of all that is honest in the given class, without a party capable of watching and influencing the mood of the masses, it is impossible to conduct such a struggle successfully."

The proletariat needs the Party for the purpose of achieving and maintaining the dictatorship. The Party is an instrument of the dictatorship of the proletariat.

But from this it follows that when classes disappear and the dictatorship of the proletariat withers away, the Party will also wither away.

. . . The achievement and maintenance of the dictatorship of the proletariat is impossible without a party which is strong by reason of its solidarity and iron discipline. But iron discipline in the Party is inconceivable without unity of will, without complete and absolute unity of action on the part of all members of the Party. This does not mean, of course, that the possibility of contests of opinion within the Party is thereby precluded. On the contrary, iron discipline does not preclude but presupposes criticism and contest of opinion within the Party. Least of all does it mean that discipline must be "blind." On the contrary, iron discipline does not preclude but presupposes conscious and voluntary submission, for only conscious discipline can be truly iron discipline. But after a contest of opinion has been closed, after criticism has been exhausted and a decision has been arrived at, unity of will and unity of action of all Party members are the necessary conditions without which neither Party unity nor iron discipline in the Party is conceivable. . . .

. . . It follows that the existence of factions is incompatible either with the Party's unity or with its iron discipline. It need hardly be proved that the existence of factions leads to the existence of a number of centres, and the existence of a number of centres connotes the absence of one common centre in the Party, the breaking up of the unity of will, the weakening and disintegration of discipline, the weakening and disintegration of the dictatorship. . . .

. . . The source of factionalism in the Party is its opportunist elements. The proletariat is not an isolated class. It is constantly replenished by the influx of peasants, petty bourgeois and intellectuals proletarianized by the development of capitalism. . . .

The Party is strengthened by purging itself of opportunist elements. . . .

. . . Leninism is a school of theory and practice which trains a special type of Party and state worker, creates a special Leninist style in work.

What are the characteristic features of this style? What are its peculiarities?

It has two specific features:

a) the Russian revolutionary sweep and

b) American efficiency.

The style of Leninism is a combination of these two specific features in Party and state work.

The Russian revolutionary sweep is an antidote to inertness, routine, conservatism, mental stagnation and slavish submission to ancestral traditions. The Russian revolutionary sweep is the life-giving force which stimulates thought, impels things forward, breaks the past and opens up perspectives. Without it no progress is possible.

But Russian revolutionary sweep has every chance of degenerating in practice into empty "revolutionary" Manilovism if it is not combined with American efficiency in work. . . .

. . . American efficiency is that indomitable force which neither knows nor recognizes obstacles; which with its businesslike perseverance brushes aside all obstacles; which continues at a task once started until it is finished, even if it is a minor task; and without which serious constructive work is inconceivable.

But American efficiency has every chance of degenerating into narrow and unprincipled commercialism if it is not combined with the Russian revolutionary sweep. . . .

The combination of the Russian revolutionary sweep with American efficiency is the essence of Leninism in Party and state work.

This combination alone produces the finished type of Leninist worker, the style of Leninism in work.

STALIN ON SOCIALISM IN ONE COUNTRY

In the fall of 1924 some critical publications by Trotsky were taken as the signal for the party leaders to direct a series of scathing denunciations at him for his alleged ideological heresies. The "theory of permanent revolution" figured prominently as the basis for asserting a fundamental opposition between Trotsky and Lenin, although the more immediate reason for scotching the theory was its implication that the Soviet regime, unsupported by international revolution, was in danger of losing its socialist qualities. Stalin's contribution to the defense against Trotsky was the theory of "socialism in one country," which he contrived out of one distorted quotation from Lenin.

. . . According to Lenin, the revolution draws its strength primarily from among the workers and peasants of Russia itself. According to Trotsky, the necessary strength can be found *only* "in the arena of the world proletarian revolution."

But what if the world revolution is fated to arrive with some delay? Is there any ray of hope for our revolution? Trotsky offers no ray of hope, for "the contradictions in the position of a workers' government . . . can be solved *only* . . . in the arena of the world proletarian revolution." According to this plan, there is but one prospect left for our revolution: to vegetate in its own contradictions and rot away while waiting for the world revolution. . . .

. . . "Permanent revolution" is not a mere underestimation of the revolutionary potentialities of the peasant movement. "Permanent revolution" is an underestimation of the peasant movement which leads to the *repudiation* of Lenin's theory of the dictatorship of the proletariat.

Trotsky's "permanent revolution" is a variety of Menshevism. . . .

The second peculiar feature of the October Revolution lies in the fact that this revolution represents a model of the practical application of Lenin's theory of the proletarian revolution.

He who has not understood this peculiar feature of the October Revolution will never understand either the international nature of this revolution, or its colossal international might, or the specific features of its foreign policy.

FROM: Stalin, "The October Revolution and the Tactics of the Russian Communists" (December, 1924; *Problems of Leninism*, pp. 121-130).

"Uneven economic and political development," says Lenin, "is an absolute law of capitalism. Hence, the victory of socialism is possible first in several or even in one separate capitalist country. The victorious proletariat of that country, having expropriated the capitalists and organized socialist production, would stand up *against* the rest of the world, the capitalist world, attracting to its cause the oppressed classes of other countries, raising revolts in those countries against the capitalists, and in the event of necessity coming out even with armed force against the exploiting classes and their states." For "the free union of nations in socialism is impossible without a more or less prolonged and stubborn struggle of the socialist republics against the backward states."

The opportunists of all countries assert that the proletarian revolution can begin – if it is to begin anywhere at all, according to their theory – only in industrially developed countries, and that the more highly developed these countries are industrially the more chances there are for the victory of socialism. Moreover, according to them, the possibility of the victory of socialism in one country, and in a country little developed in the capitalist sense at that, is excluded as something absolutely improbable. As far back as the period of the war, Lenin, taking as his basis the law of the uneven development of the imperialist states, opposed to the opportunists his theory of the proletarian revolution on the victory of socialism in one country, even if that country is less developed in the capitalist sense.

It is well known that the October Revolution fully confirmed the correctness of Lenin's theory of the proletarian revolution.

How do matters stand with Trotsky's "permanent revolution" in the light of Lenin's theory of the victory of the proletarian revolution in one country?

Let us take Trotsky's pamphlet *Our Revolution* (1906).

Trotsky writes:

"Without direct state support from the European proletariat, the working class of Russia will not be able to maintain itself in power and to transform its temporary rule into a lasting socialist dictatorship. This we cannot doubt for an instant."

What does this quotation mean? It means that the victory of socialism in one country, in this case Russia, is impossible "*without* direct state support from the European proletariat," i.e., before the European proletariat has conquered power.

What is there in common between this "theory" and Lenin's thesis on the possibility of the victory of socialism "in one separate capitalist country"?

Clearly, there is nothing in common. . . .

It goes without saying that for the *complete* victory of socialism, for *complete* security against the restoration of the old order, the united efforts of the proletarians of several countries are necessary. It goes without saying that, without the support given to our revolution by the proletariat of Europe, the proletariat of Russia could not have held out against the general onslaught, just as without the support the revolution in Russia gave to the revolutionary movement in the West the latter could not have developed at the pace at which it has begun to develop since the establishment of the proletarian dictatorship in Russia. It goes without saying that we need support. But what does support of our revolution by the West-European proletariat imply? Is not the sympathy of European workers for our revolution, their readiness to thwart the imperialists' plans of intervention – is not all this support? Is this not real assistance? Unquestionably it is. . . .

. . . Let us take, for example, Trotsky's "postscript," written in 1922, for the new edition of his pamphlet *Peace Program*. Here is what he says in this "Postscript":

> "The assertion reiterated several times in the *Peace Program* that a proletarian revolution cannot culminate victoriously within national bounds may perhaps seem to some readers to have been refuted by the nearly five years' experience of our Soviet republic. But such a conclusion would be unwarranted. The fact that the workers' state has held out against the whole world in one country, and a backward country at that, only testifies to the colossal might of the proletariat, which in other, more advanced, more civilized countries will be truly capable of performing miracles. But while we have held our ground as a state politically and militarily, we have not arrived, or even begun to arrive, at the building of a socialist society. . . . As long as the bourgeoisie remains in power in the other European countries we will be compelled, in our struggle against economic isolation, to strive for agreement with the capitalist world, at the same time it may be said with certainty that these agreements may at best help us to mitigate some of our economic ills, to take one or another step forward, but real progress of a socialist economy in Russia will become possible *only after the victory* of the proletariat in the major European countries." [Stalin's italics.]

Thus speaks Trotsky, plainly sinning against reality and stubbornly trying to save his "permanent revolution" from final shipwreck.

It appears, then, that, twist and turn as you like, we not only have "not arrived," but we have "not even begun to arrive" at the building of a socialist society. It appears that some people have been hoping for "agreements with the capitalist world," but it also appears that nothing will come of these agreements, for, twist and turn as you like, a "real progress of a socialist economy" will not be possible until the proletariat has been victorious in the "major European countries."

Well, then, since there is still no victory in the West, the only "choice" that remains for the revolution in Russia is: either to rot away or to degenerate into a bourgeois state.

It is no accident that Trotsky has been talking for two years now about the "degeneration" of our Party. . . .

. . . Trotsky's "permanent revolution" is the negation of Lenin's theory of the proletarian revolution; and conversely, Lenin's theory of the proletarian revolution is the negation of the theory of "permanent revolution."

Lack of faith in the strength and capabilities of our revolution, lack of faith in the strength and capabilities of the Russian proletariat–that is what lies at the root of the theory of "permanent revolution."

Hitherto only *one* aspect of the theory of "permanent revolution" has usually been noted–lack of faith in the revolutionary potentialities of the peasant movement. Now, in fairness, this must be supplemented by *another* aspect–lack of faith in the strength and capabilities of the proletariat in Russia.

What difference is there between Trotsky's theory and the ordinary Menshevik theory that the victory of socialism in one country, and in a backward country at that, is impossible without the preliminary victory of the proletarian revolution "in the principal countries of Western Europe"?

As a matter of fact, there is no difference.

There can be no doubt at all. Trotsky's theory of "permanent revolution" is a variety of Menshevism. . . .

PREOBRAZHENSKY ON THE ECONOMICS OF INDUSTRIALIZATION

While organizationally defeated, the Trotskyists remained intellectually active. Evgeny Preobrazhensky, the leading Opposition economist, worked out a penetrating analysis of the obstacles standing in the way of the industrial progress on which all the Communists set their hopes. In his view only a systematic exploitation of the peasant majority could support industrialization by the socialist state. Essentially this was the analysis on which Stalin later based the Five-Year Plans and the collectivization of the peasants.

... It will be no exaggeration to say that for all our theoreticians, and practitioners as well, the most interesting, vital, exciting question since the October coup of 1917 and the military victory of the revolution is the question of what the Soviet system represents, in what direction it is developing, what the basic laws of this development are, and, finally, what relation this first experience of an economy whose main links go outside the limits of capitalism has to our old and habitual images of socialism. The last question could be correctly phrased thus: How after eight years of the dictatorship of the proletariat in a vast country, should we view our former images of socialism? ...

... The complex of state socialist production can appear only as the result of breaking up the old system on all fronts, only as the result of social revolution. This fact has colossal significance for understanding not only the genesis of socialism but also the socialist construction that follows. On the other hand, insufficient understanding or neglect of the essence of what socialism is has more than once led and is leading a series of comrades to purely Philistine and sometimes outright reformist notions about the Soviet economy and the paths of its development. ...

Primary socialist accumulation, as the period of creating the material prerequisites for socialist production in the proper sense of the word, can only begin with the seizure of power and nationalization. ...

... On a private or limited scale socialist accumulation is not able to resolve the basic problem of the socialist organization of the economy. In particular, insofar as we are concerned with the economy of the Soviet Union, it is essential to have: 1) accumulation which makes it possible for the state economy to achieve the technical level of contemporary capitalism wherever it is not possible to move gradually on to the base of the new technology; 2) accumulation which makes possible the change in the technological base of the state economy, the scientific organization of labor, the planned direction of the whole complex of the state economy, everything that is not possible without large supplies for insurance and planned reserves; 3) accumulation which guarantees progress for the whole complex, not just its individual parts, since the chain of dependence in the movement of the whole complex makes progress on different levels, in the manner of capitalist "partisan warfare," individual initiative, and competition, completely impossible. ...

We term *socialist* accumulation the assimilation to the functioning

FROM: Preobrazhensky, *Novaya ekonomiya* (The New Economics, second edition, Moscow, Communist Academy, 1926, pp. 86, 89-90, 92-94, 99, 136-37; editor's translation).

means of production of the surplus product which is created within the amalgamated socialist economy and which is not distributed as a supplement among the agents of socialist production and the socialist state, but contributes to expanded reproduction.* On the other hand, we term *primary socialist* accumulation the accumulation in the hands of the state of most or all of the material resources from sources lying outside the complex of the state economy. In a backward peasant country this accumulation must play a colossally important role, to a vast degree hastening the arrival of the moment when the technological and scientific reconstruction of the state economy can begin and when this economy can finally achieve purely economic predominance over capitalism. . . . The basic law of our Soviet economy, which at the present moment is coursing through this stage, is precisely the law of primary or preliminary socialist accumulation. To this law are subordinated all the basic processes of economic life in the sphere of the state economy. This law, on the other hand, changes and partly liquidates the law of value and all the laws of the commodity and commodity-capitalistic economy insofar as they manifest themselves or can manifest themselves in our system of economy. Consequently, *we can not only speak of primary socialist accumulation, we cannot even understand the essence of the Soviet economy unless we understand the central role which the law of primary socialist accumulation plays in this economy, how it determines, in the struggle with the law of value, the distribution of the means of production in the economy, the distribution of the working force, and the extent of alienation of the country's surplus product for the expansion of socialist reproduction.* . . .

In regard to alienation of part of the surplus product for the benefit of socialism, matters are entirely different from all pre-socialist economic forms. Exactions from the non-socialist forms must not only have a place inevitably in the period of primary socialist accumulation – they must inevitably assume a vast, directly decisive role in peasant countries like the Soviet Union. . . .

In the period of primary socialist accumulation the state economy cannot do without alienating part of the surplus product of the village and of craft production, in sum, without deductions from capitalistic accumulation for the benefit of socialist accumulation. We do not know to what extent other countries will emerge devastated from the civil war in which the dictatorship of the proletariat triumphs. But a country like the U.S.S.R., with its devastated and in general rather backward economy, must go through the period of primary accumulation with very broad use of the sources of the presocialist forms of the economy. We should not forget that

*I.e., an increased investment in industrial plant – Ed.

the period of primary socialist accumulation is the most critical period in the life of the socialist state after the termination of the civil war. In this period the socialist system is not yet in a condition to develop organically all its own advantages, while at the same time it inevitably liquidates a series of economic advantages which are characteristic of the developed capitalist system. To traverse this period rapidly, to reach quickly the moment when the socialist system will have developed all its natural advantages over capitalism – this is a question of life or death for the socialist state. At least this is how the question stands right now for the U.S.S.R., and perhaps it will stand thus for some time in a series of European countries where the proletariat is victorious. Under such conditions to rely only on accumulation within the socialist sphere means to risk the very existence of socialist economics, or to extend indefinitely the period of preliminary accumulation. . . .

. . . At the moment of its victory the working class changes from the object of exploitation into the subject of it. It cannot regard its own working power, health, labor and conditions as the capitalists regard them. This constitutes the definition of the limit to the tempo of socialist accumulation, a limit which capitalistic industry in the first period of its development did not know. . . .

. . . In this period the law of wages is subordinated to the law of socialist accumulation, which finds its expression in conscious self-restraint by the working class. . . . Socialist accumulation is a necessity for the working class, but now it proceeds as a consciously understood necessity . . . .

SOVIET CULTURAL POLICY – THE LIBERAL PERIOD

While the Communists were firmly wedded to the Marxian proposition that all aspects of life are affected by the class struggle and must be considered in waging class war, the party leaders during the first decade after the revolution did not imagine that they had the competence to make commanding decisions in the artistic realm. They dealt severely with overtly anti-Communist political opinions, but otherwise they were content to give encouragement to "proletarian" cultural contributions, and, as the 1925 party statement on literature illustrates, allow a variety of aesthetic currents to exist.

FROM: Resolution of the Central Committee of the Russian Communist Party, "On the Policy of the Party in the Field of Literature," July 1, 1925 (English translation in Edward J. Brown, *The Proletarian Episode in Russian Literature*, 1928-1932, New York, Columbia University Press, 1952, pp. 235-40; reprinted by permission of the publisher).

. . . As the class war in general has not ended, neither has it ended on the literary front. In a class society there is not, nor can there be a neutral art, though the class nature of art generally and of literature in particular is expressed in forms which are infinitely more various than, for instance, in politics. . . .

It must be remembered, however, that this problem is infinitely more complicated than other problems being solved by the proletariat. Even within the limitations of a capitalist society the working class could prepare itself for a victorious revolution, build cadres of fighters and leaders and produce a magnificent ideological weapon for the political struggle. But it could work out neither the problems of natural science nor the tasks of technical development; and by the same token the proletariat, the class which was culturally deprived, was unable to develop its own literature, its own characteristic artistic forms, its own style. Although the proletariat has ready infallible criteria regarding the sociopolitical content of any literary work, it does not have such definite answers to all questions of artistic form. . . .

With relation to the "fellow-travelers" we must bear in mind: (1) their differentiation, (2) the importance of many of them as qualified specialists of literary technique; and (3) the presence of vacillation in this group of writers. The general directive should be for tactful and careful relations with them, and for such an approach as will guarantee all the conditions for their earliest possible movement in the direction of Communist ideology. While discouraging antiproletarian and antirevolutionary elements (now quite insignificant), and while fighting to expose the ideology of the new *bourgeoisie* which is taking form among a part of the fellow-travelers—those of the "change-of-landmarks" stripe—the Party should have a patient attitude toward intermediate ideological formations, patiently aiding those inevitably numerous formations to develop in the process of ever closer comradely coöperation with the cultural forces of communism. . . .

Communist criticism should fight mercilessly against counterrevolutionary phenomena in literature; and yet at the same time show the greatest tact, attention and patience toward all those groups which can and will join the proletariat. Communist criticism must drive out the tone of literary command. Such criticism can have deep educational significance only when it relies on its own ideological superiority. Marxist criticism should once and for all drive out of its midst all pretentious, half-literate, and self-satisfied Communist conceit. Marxist criticism should have as its slogan "to learn," and should resist every appearance of cheap judgment and ignorant arrogance in its own milieu.

While it has infallible criteria of judgment regarding the class content of literary tendencies, the Party as a whole must not bind itself to any one tendency in the field of literary form. Giving general leadership to literature, the Party cannot support any one faction in literature (classifying these factions according to their different views on form and style), just as it cannot by resolutions settle questions of the form of the family, though in general it does and should lead in the development of new ways of life. Everything indicates that a style proper to the epoch will be created, but it will be created by different methods, and the solution of this problem has not yet been begun. In the present phase of cultural development any attempt to bind the Party in this direction must be repulsed.

Therefore the Party should declare itself in favor of the free competition of various groups and tendencies in this province. Any other solution of the problem would be an official, bureaucratic pseudo-solution. In the same way it is inadmissible to legalize by a decree the monopoly of the literary printing business by any one group or literary organization. While morally and materially supporting proletarian and proletarian-peasant literature, and aiding the fellow-travelers, the Party cannot offer a monopoly to any of these groups, even the one most proletarian in its ideology. For this would be to destroy proletarian literature itself. . . .

SOVIET EDUCATIONAL POLICY – THE REVOLUTIONARY PERIOD

The early Communist position on social problems held, according to Marxian logic, that individual development or defects were the product of social and economic conditions. The ideal was the spontaneous blossoming of the individual proletarian, freed from legal, family and educational restraints. (Industrial and political discipline would also have been eliminated had the early left-wing opposition groups had their way.) In education the authority of school and teacher was deëmphasized in favor of letting the child develop freely amid the proper conditioning influences. This was closely akin to the "learning by doing" of American progressive education, as A. P. Pinkevich, one of the leading Soviet educational theorists, freely conceded.

. . . The mere enumeration of the names of Hall, Dewey, Russell, Monroe, Judd, Thorndike, Kilpatrick, and many others, known to every

FROM: Pinkevich, *Outlines of Pedagogy* (1927; translated as *The New Education in the Soviet Republic* by Mucia Perlmutter and edited by George S. Counts, New York, The John Day Co., 1929, pp. vi, 198-99, 202, 214, 288, 301-2; reprinted by permission of Martha L. Counts).

educator in our country, is a sufficient reminder of the tremendous influence which American education has exerted upon us. In spite of the undoubted differences in ideology which divide Soviet from western educational leaders, mutual understanding and recognition of scientific attainments are indispensable. . . .

In his volume entitled *Fundamental Questions of Social Education* Shulgin* has given an excellent exposition of the demands of the party. He presents the Communist conception of the role of labor in education and the role of the labor school in society as follows:

"To our mind labor is the best method of so introducing young children to the laboring class and of so merging them with the class-builder that they may not only understand the proletarian ideology, but may actually begin to live, to strive, and to build according to that ideology. But this is not all. Labor to us is a means of inducting children into the working world family in order that they may participate in and understand the struggle of the masses, follow the history of human society, acquire working, organizing, and collective habits, and come into possession of the discipline of work. To us labor, because of its superior integrating power, is the best method of teaching children how to live the contemporary life. The factory is the first and most sensitive place of modern society. Since labor, self-government, and contemporary life merge into an inseparable union, the march of economic events calls for schools which will train the warrior and builder of life. . . ."

In every school a distinction may be drawn between the teaching of the materials of instruction and the teaching of behavior. In our schools the latter could more properly be called the organization of the children's collective or the organization of behavior. The term behavior is used here in the sense in which it is employed by the psychologist.

At the beginning of our discussion of the question of the organization of conduct we wish to emphasize one guiding principle of Soviet pedagogy. We assign to the teacher the role of organizer, assistant, instructor, and older comrade, but not the role of superior officer. In the old school the teacher was a dictator. In the liberal bourgeois school he is at best a leader. With us he is primarily an organizer. . . .

In our opinion the children should organize their own social life in school in order to develop those collectivistic traits which are indispensable for the creation of new forms of social life. Naturally they should not be left entirely to themselves. In order to make full pedagogical use of the

*Shulgin: an early Soviet educational theorist—Ed.

efforts of children at self-organization the teacher should place certain limitations on their social activity. . . .

The most fundamental characteristic, however, which distinguishes our theory of self-government from that obtained in other countries is its communistic coloring, or at least its communistic foundation. We need organizers and builders of a new society, we need warriors for a new way of life. Self-government is our most effective educational instrument for producing such organizers, builders, and warriors. . . .

Our aim is to take the project method and put our own content into it. All forms of our community purposeful undertakings are as a matter of fact "projects." . . . The bourgeois American school fails to give to the method that community quality which is characteristic of our socialistic school. There is no doubt, however, that of all the contemporary attempts to reform the school, the project system with appropriate changes is best adapted to the nature and purposes of the Soviet school. It affords the children greater freedom of activity, encourages them to engage in practical work, demands of them independent planning, and trains them in the methods of investigation. . . .

The center of all the work of the school should be human labor. Every school activity is consequently closely related to this central aim. But an understanding of labor requires a penetrating study of the productive forces which man utilizes as well as those social relations which grow out of the particular organization of labor in a given society. These considerations have led us to adopt as a fundamental scheme for organizing the curriculum of the labor school the three-fold concept of nature, labor, and society, or, to put it another way, productive energies, productive relations, and superstructure. And all teaching is unified through one central synthetic theme of colossal importance – *human labor*. Obviously this scheme is distinctly Marxian. Moreover, it is the first truly Marxian educational plan; and, regardless of the extent to which the program itself may change, we are confident that the basic scheme of the Soviet school will remain unshaken.

In complete harmony with the content of the new program are the methods of instruction which it suggests. First of all, it calls for a completely objective method of teaching, understanding the term in the light of our discussion above. This means that children are not to study verbal descriptions of phenomena and things but rather the phenomena and things themselves. In other words the program of the [State Scientific] Council calls for direct contact with the surrounding nature, labor, and society in which the child lives. This environment is the starting point of all the work of the school. . . .

THE ZINOVIEV-KAMENEV OPPOSITION

In 1925 the party leadership split. Zinoviev and Kamenev, with the Leningrad party organization which Zinoviev controlled, went into opposition against the party majority led by Stalin, Bukharin and Rykov. At the Fourteenth Party Congress in December 1925, the new opposition vainly attacked the leadership. Zinoviev raised again the theoretical problem of "state capitalism" and progress toward socialism, while Kamenev bluntly warned of the danger of Stalin's becoming a personal dictator. Stalin's dominance in the party organization decided the issue, and Zinoviev and Kamenev were overwhelmingly defeated.

a) ZINOVIEV ON STATE CAPITALISM

What are the chief difficulties in our work? In my opinion there are three. They form, as it were, the background of the whole picture of our construction. *The first difficulty* is the delay of the world revolution. At the beginning of the October Revolution we were convinced that the workers of other countries would provide us with direct support in a matter of months, or in any case within a few years. Now, unfortunately, it has been demonstrated that the delay of the world revolution is a fact, that the partial stabilization of capitalism characterizes a whole period, and that a new, more complicated set of difficulties is connected with this stabilization.

The second difficulty is well known – this is the building of socialism in a backward country with such an enormous predominance of the peasantry. This is a difficulty for which we gave ourselves the answer in the first days of the revolution and which we have been successfully overcoming.

The third difficulty is the creation of a collective leadership for our party after the death of Vladimir Ilich. Only now, it seems to me, is this being drawn in full clarity. This difficulty is not unimportant, because leading the party means at the same time directing the state. This is not only an organizational question – this is a political problem of the most profound importance. . . .

Recently a dispute about the question of *state capitalism* descended upon us quite unexpectedly, out of a clear blue. . . . To take the bull by the horns, Comrades, I think it is first of all necessary to answer those who are now trying to represent the matter as though we have no state capitalism and practically nothing of capitalism in general. I feel that the thing here is

FROM: Zinoviev, Minority Report to the Fourteenth Party Congress, December, 1925 (*Fourteenth Congress of the All-Union Communist Party [of Bolsheviks]: Steno-graphic Report*, Moscow, Party Press, 1926, pp. 98, 101, 108–9; editor's translation).

really the attempt of certain comrades to declare that the NEP is socialism. (*Laughter, noise*) Such a point of view, such a position represents the idealization of the NEP, the idealization of capitalism. (*Voice: "Who thinks so?"*) It is indisputable that the NEP is the *road* to socialism, but the assertion that the NEP is not socialism also seems to me indisputable. (*Voice: "These are questions from political grammar school."*) So, Comrades, it appears to me that this is just what the dispute is about. Of course, he who idealizes the NEP cannot but dispute Lenin's formulation on the question of state capitalism. . . .

So, Comrades, I think it is indisputable . . . that our state industry consists of enterprises which are of a type consistent with socialism but are not yet fully socialist, as Bukharin admitted in the spring of 1922. Finally, it is indisputable that the simplest and clearest example of state capitalism in a country like ours is concessions and leases. But it must be just as indisputable for us that this does not exhaust state capitalism, that we cannot forget about free trade and its forms, about planning and distribution, about the revival of capitalism in individual farms. We cannot forget that all this, insofar as it is subordinated to the control of the state – all this Vladimir Ilich called state capitalism, adding the qualification that this is a *unique* state capitalism, radically distinguished from the state capitalism of the bourgeois countries in that it is subordinated and limited by the working class, by the proletarian state. But at the same time Vladimir Ilich said that in order for the workers to see that we do have capitalism we must not idealize or gloss over reality.

b) KAMENEV ON STALIN

I turn to intraparty questions. To these questions I give three answers.

The first concerns the organizational forms of our intraparty life. Comrade Bukharin has said that we bought the controversy with Comrade Trotsky at the price, as he expressed it, of a convulsion in intraparty life. You must resolve this question in the sense that in the background of a general enlivening and heightening of the activity of all strata of the population, intraparty democracy is essential, its further development is essential. According to the testament of Lenin this has now become possible precisely because the de-classing of the proletariat has ceased.

In the contrary case with this background you will inevitably have a new convulsion in intraparty life. This will be a phenomenon on a catastrophic order. I appeal to you not to choose this path, but the other path.

FROM: Kamenev, Speech to the Fourteenth Party Congress, December, 1925 (Stenographic Report, pp. 273-75; editor's translation).

The things you hear about that path at the congress – about defeatists, liquidators, Axelrodists, etc. – cannot be true; such things had not entered the party's head even after it assembled at the congress. *This must be avoided. This can be avoided only if the minority, which is not made up of newcomers, which you know about fully – if this minority is given an opportunity to defend its views in the party, of course with the full responsibility which the party and the dictatorship impose upon us.*

Second: Besides the invigoration of party discussion, besides granting the minority an opportunity to express its views to the whole party, as becomes Bolsheviks, within those limits which are set by the party statutes and the dictatorship of the party and the proletariat – it seems to me that you must *resist this new tendency in the party which I have tried to sketch out to you.* I am sure that if you find it impossible to do this now because of some organizational consideration or another – the facts of life, the course of the class struggle in our country, the growth of differentiation in the village will compel you to do this, and to say that the school which Bukharin has established is based on a departure from Lenin. What we need right now is in the slogan, back to Lenin! (Voice from a seat: "Why back?") Because this is going forward. Comrades, I know that in the first part of my speech you tried to attribute the matter to malice. We see that the matter is not one of malice, and I hope you will say this after a few months.

And finally, the third point: *We are against creating a theory of the "Chief,"* * *we are against establishing a "Chief."* We are against the Secretariat, which has in practice combined both policy and organization, standing over the political organ. *We are for our upper level being organized in such a fashion that there would be a really all-powerful Politbureau, bringing together all our party's policies, and at the same time the Secretariat would be subordinate to it and execute the technical aspects of its decisions.* (Noise) We cannot consider it normal but think it harmful to the party, if such a situation is continued where the Secretariat combines both policy and organization, and in fact predecides policy. (Noise) Here, Comrades, is what we need to do. Everyone who does not agree with me will draw his own conclusions. (Voice from a seat: "You should have begun with this.") The speaker has the right to begin with what he wants. You think I ought to have begun with what I have said, that personally I assert that our General Secretary is not the kind of figure that can unite the old Bolshevik staff around himself. I don't consider this a basic political question. I don't consider this question more important than the question of the theoretical line. I feel that if the party adopted (Noise) a definite political

*Russian *vozhd* – "leader," in a then derogatory sense – Ed.

line which was clearly marked off from those deviations which part of the Central Committee is now supporting, this question would not now be on the agenda. But I must say this out to the end. Precisely because I more than once told Comrade Stalin this, precisely because I more than once told a group of Leninist comrades, I repeat it here at the congress: *I have arrived at the conviction that Comrade Stalin cannot fulfill the role of unifier of the Bolshevik staff.* (Voices from the audience: "Untrue!" "Nonsense!" "So that's what it is!" "He's shown his cards!" Noise. Applause by the Leningrad delegation. Shouts: "We won't surrender the commanding heights to you." "Stalin! Stalin!" The delegates stand and cheer Comrade Stalin. Stormy applause. Shouts: "Here's where the party has become united. Now the Bolshevik staff must be united.")

(Yevdokimov, from his seat) "Long live the Russian Communist Party! Hurrah! Hurrah!" (The delegates stand and shout "Hurrah!" Noise. Stormy, long-sustained applause)

(Yevdokimov, from his seat) "Long live the Central Committee of our party! Hurrah!" (The delegates shout "Hurrah!") "The party above all! Right!" (Applause and shouts, "Hurrah!")

(Voice from a seat) "Long live Comrade Stalin!" (Stormy, continued applause, shouts) "Hurrah!" (Noise)

(Chairman) "Comrades, I beg you to quiet down. Comrade Kamenev will now finish his speech."

I began this part of my speech with the words, "We are against the theory of individual preeminence, we are against creating a Chief!" With these same words I end my speech. (Applause by the Leningrad delegation)

(Voice from a seat) "And who do you propose?"

(Chairman) "I declare a ten minute recess." . . .

THE UNITED OPPOSITION

In 1926, the two defeated opposition groups, Trotskyist and Zinovievist, merged and undertook a major appeal to the party rank-and-file against the leadership. They had to resort to conspiratorial organization, and when this activity was detected (the "Lashevich affair"), the leadership prepared a new condemnation of the Opposition's factionalism. In reply, the leaders of the Opposition drew up a detailed statement of their case which they vainly tried to present to the party membership.

FROM: The Declaration of the Thirteen, July, 1926 (editor's translation from copy in the Trotsky Archive, T880a).

. . . 1. *Bureaucratism as the Source of Factionalism*

The immediate cause of all of the sharpening crises in the party is in bureaucratism, which has grown amazingly in the period following the death of Lenin, and continues to grow.

The Central Committee of the ruling party has at its disposal for action upon the party not only ideological and organizational, i.e., not only party means, but also governmental and economic means. Lenin always took into account the danger that the concentration of administrative power in the hands of the party would lead to bureaucratic pressure on the Party. Precisely from this arose Vladimir Ilich's idea about organizing the Control Commission, which, while it had no administrative power in its hands, would have all the power essential for the struggle with bureaucratism, for the defense of the right of a party member to express his convictions freely and to vote according to his conscience without fearing any punitive consequences. . . .

Meanwhile, in fact – and this must be said here before anything else – the Central Control Commission itself has become a purely administrative organ, which assists the repression conducted by other bureaucratic organs, executing for them the punitive part of the work, prosecuting any independent thought in the party, any voice of criticism, any concern expressed aloud about the fate of the party, any critical remarks about certain leaders of the party. . . .

An official show prevails in the meetings, together with the apathy which is unavoidably connected with it. Frequently only an insignificant minority remains at the time of voting; the participants in the meeting hasten to leave so that they will not be compelled to vote for decisions dictated earlier. No resolutions anywhere are ever adopted otherwise than "unanimously." All this is gravely reflected in the internal life of the Party organizations. Members of the Party are afraid openly to express aloud their most cherished thoughts, wishes and demands. This is what constitutes the cause of the "affair" of Comrade Lashevich et al.

2. *The Cause of the Growth of Bureaucratism*

It is completely obvious that the more difficult it is for the ruling centres to carry through their decisions by the methods of party democracy, the less the vanguard of the working class sees their policy as its own.

The divergence between the direction of economic policy and the direction of the feelings and thoughts of the proletarian vanguard inevitably strengthens the need for repression and gives all policy an administrative-bureaucratic character. Any other explanation of the growth of bureaucratism is secondary and does not encompass the essence of the question.

The lag of industry behind the economic development of the country as a whole signifies, in spite of the growth in the number of workers, a lowering of the specific gravity of the proletariat in the society. The lag in the influence of industry on agriculture and the rapid growth of the *kulaks** lowers in the village the specific gravity of the hired workers and poor peasants and their trust in the state and in themselves. The lag of wage raises behind the rising living standard of the nonproletarian elements of the city and the upper groups of the village inevitably signifies the lowering of the political and cultural self-esteem of the proletariat as the ruling class. From this, in particular, comes the clear decrease in the activity of the workers and poor peasants in the elections to the soviets, which is a most serious warning for our Party. . . .

4. The Question of Industrialization

The present year again reveals with all clarity that state industry is lagging behind the development of the economy as a whole. The new harvest again catches us without supplies of goods. But movement toward socialism is assured only when the tempo of development of industry does not lag behind the general development of the economy, but leads it, systematically bringing the country closer to the technical level of the advanced capitalist countries. Everything must be subordinated to this task, equally vital both for the proletariat and for the peasantry. . . .

The question of the *smychka* is under present conditions above all a question of industrialization.

Meanwhile the party sees with alarm that the resolution of the Fourteenth Congress on industrialization in reality draws back more and more, following the example of what was not carried out in the party's resolution on democracy. In this fundamental question, on which the life and death of the October Revolution depend, the party cannot and does not want to live with official "cribs," which are dictated, frequently, not by the interests of the matter but by the interests of factional struggle. The party wants to know, to think, to check, to decide. The present regime prevents this, and precisely from this stems the secret distribution of party documents on the "affair" of Lashevich, etc.

5. Policy in the Village

In questions of agricultural policy in the village the danger of shifts to the side of the upper groups in the village is all the more clearly defined. . . .

The fact is that under the guise of a union of the poor peasantry with the

---

Kulak: Russian "fist," colloquial expression for a prosperous peasant—Ed.

middle peasant, we observe steadily and regularly the political subordination of the poor peasantry to the middle peasants, and through them to the
kulaks.

6. The Bureaucratic Perversion of the Workers' State

The number of workers in our state industry does not now reach two
million; together with transport, it is less than three million. The soviet,
trade-union, coöperative and all other employees certainly do not number
less than that figure, and this comparison alone testifies to the colossal
political and economic role of the bureaucracy; it is entirely obvious that
the state apparatus, in its composition and level of life, is to an overwhelming degree bourgeois and petty-bourgeois, and inclines away from the proletariat and the village poor, on the one hand, toward the displaced
intelligentsia, and on the other toward the land-leaser, the merchant, the
kulak, the new bourgeois. How many times did Lenin remind us of the
bureaucratic perversion of the state apparatus and about the frequent
necessity for the trade unions to defend the workers from the state, while
the party bureaucrat in just this region is infected with the most dangerous
self-deception. . . .

7. The Bureaucratic Perversion of the Party Apparatus

In 1920 a party conference under Lenin's direction considered it essential to point out the impermissibility of the fact that in the mobilization of
the comrades, party organs and individual comrades were guided by some
considerations other than business ones. Any repression whatever against
comrades because they think differently about one or another question or
party decision is impermissible. The whole present practice contradicts this
decision at every step. Genuine discipline is shaken apart and replaced by
subordination to the influential figures in the apparatus. The comrades on
whom the party can rely in the most difficult days are pushed out of the
staff in ever greater numbers, they are thrown around, exiled, persecuted,
and replaced steadily and regularly by casual people, untested, but who are
distinguished by silent obedience. Now these bureaucratic sins of the party
regime are transferred to the accused comrades Lashevich and Belenki,
whom the party has known in the course of more than two decades as
devoted and disciplined members. The act of accusing them is therefore an
act of accusing the bureaucratic perversion of the party apparatus.

The significance of a firmly welded, centralized apparatus in the Bolshevik Party needs no explanation. Without this skeleton the proletarian revolution would be impossible. The party apparatus in its majority is

composed of devoted and irreproachable party members who have no stimulus other than the struggle of the working class. Under the correct regime and the proper distribution of forces the very same party workers could successfully help realize party democracy.

8. Bureaucratism and the Everyday Life of the Working Masses

... The bureaucratic regime has spread like rust into the life of every plant and workshop. If the members of the party are in fact deprived of the right to criticize by the district committee, the provincial committee, or the Central Committee, in the plant, they are deprived of the right to subject the immediate authorities to criticism. Party members are scared. The administrator who is able as a loyal person to guarantee himself the support of the secretary of the next higher organization thus insures himself against criticism from below and not infrequently also from responsibility for mismanagement or actual stupidity.

In a socialist economy which is under construction, the fundamental condition for economic expenditure of the nation's resources is vigilant control by the masses, above all by the workers in the factories and plants. As long as they cannot move openly against disorders and abuses and expose their perpetrators by name, without the danger of being counted in the Opposition, among the "dissidents," among the troublemakers, or of being driven out of the cell and even from the plant, the struggle for a regime of economy as well as for the productivity of labor will inevitably be viewed on bureaucratic lines, i.e., they will most often strike at the vital interests of the workers. Precisely this is observed right now.

Clumsy or slovenly rate-setting work, harshly striking the workers, is in nine cases out of ten the direct result of bureaucratic inattention to the most elementary interests of the workers and even of production itself. It is to this that we must account the delayed payment of wages, i.e., relegating to the last consideration that which ought to constitute the prime concern.

The question of the so-called excesses at the top is fully linked to the repression of criticism. Many circulars are written against the excesses. Not a few cases against them are conducted in the Control Commissions. But the masses are suspicious of this kind of office-routine struggle with the excesses. There is one serious solution here – the masses must not be afraid to say what they think.

Where are these burning questions being discussed? Not in official party meetings but in corners and alleys, under cover, always in danger. From these intolerable conditions has stemmed the affair of Comrades Lashevich et al. The basic conclusion from this affair is: it is necessary to change conditions. . . .

10. *The Comintern*

Straightening out the class line of the Party means straightening out its international line. We must cast aside all doubting survivals of the innovation which represents the matter as though the victory of socialist construction in our country is not linked indissolubly with the course and outcome of the struggle of the European and world proletariat for power. We are building socialism and will go on building it. The European proletariat will struggle for power. The colonial peoples are struggling for independence. This is the common front. Each unit in each sector must give the maximum that it can give without waiting for the initiative of the others. Socialism will be victorious in our country in direct connection with the revolution of the European and world proletariat and with the struggle of the East against the imperialist yoke. . . .

11. *On Factionalism*

. . . The idea that by mechanically settling with the so-called opposition, it is possible to broaden the frame of party democracy is a crude self-deception; on the basis of all its experience the party cannot believe these lullabies any more. The methods of mechanical adjudication are preparing new splits and cleavages, new removals, new expulsions, new pressure with respect to the party as a whole. This system inevitably constricts the leading summit, reduces its authority and compels it to replace its ideological authority with doubled and tripled pressure. Whatever it does, the party must put a stop to this pernicious process. Lenin showed that firm leadership of the party does not mean strangling it.

12. *For Unity*

There cannot be the slightest doubt that the Party is able to straighten out its difficulties. The idea that there is no way out for the Party on the path of unity would be the supreme nonsense. There is a way out—moreover, only on the path of unity. . . .

Only on the foundation of party democracy is healthy, collective leadership possible. There is no other path. In struggle and in work on this, the only correct path, our unrecriminating support is guaranteed to the Central Committee wholly and in full.

BUKHARIN ON THE OPPOSITION

Bukharin was the main spokesman of the party leadership on matters of theory during the controversy of 1926-27. In the summer of 1926 he replied to the Opposition with a defense of the cautious economics of the NEP and a warning that Opposition challenges to the unity of the party endangered the Soviet regime as a whole. The latter argument prepared the ground for the expulsion of the Opposition in 1927.

. . . The first thesis advanced by the opposition is the assertion that our industry is retrogressing, and that the disproportion between agriculture and city industry is increasing, to the detriment of city industry. . . . The total balance is undoubtedly in favor of the growth of industry as compared with agriculture.

The second thesis advanced by the opposition in the sphere of economic policy in its relation to the industrialization of the country is the thesis that we must now carry on a greatly intensified industrial policy, this to be accomplished in the first place by increasing the prices of our industrial products. . . .

We believe this policy to be entirely *wrong*, and we cannot agree to its pursuance. . . .

Every *monopoly* runs a *certain danger of rusting*, of resting on its laurels. The private capitalist and private owner is constantly being spurred onward by competition. . . . But if we, who have practically all big industry in our hands, who have a state super-monopoly and own all essentials, do not stimulate the leading staff of our industry to cheapen production, and to produce on more rational lines, then indeed we have arrived at the prerequisite stage for the rusting of our industry on the basis of its monopoly. That which is accomplished by competition . . . in a capitalist state, we must attain by conscious pressure under the impetus of the needs of the masses: *produce better and cheaper, supply better goods, supply cheap goods!* . . .

It would be entirely wrong to say industry should develop solely upon what is produced within this industry itself. On the contrary, the whole question is; *How much* can we take away from the peasantry, *to what extent* and *by what methods* can we accomplish the pumping-over process, what are the limits of the pumping-over, and how shall we calculate in order to arrive at favorable results? This is the question. Here lies the difference between us and the opposition, a difference which may be defined by saying that the comrades of the opposition are in favor of an immoderate amount of pumping-over, and are desirous of putting so severe a pressure upon the peasantry that in our opinion the result would be economically irrational and politically unallowable . . . .

FROM: Bukharin, "The Party and the Opposition Bloc" (Report to the Leningrad Party Organization, July 28, 1926; slightly adapted from English translation in *International Press Correspondence*, no. 58, August 26, 1926, pp. 978-81, 983-84, 986-87).

Now the character, the class character of our soviet power in our country is being questioned. This is another step in the development of the oppositional idea, another step away from the true Leninist standpoint.

Comrade Trotsky, in one of his speeches at the Plenum of the Central Committee, advanced the thesis of the "extremely non-proletarian character" of the soviet power existing in our country. When the peasant question came under discussion, in connection with the results of the elections, the opposition stated that we are threatened by a deviation in the direction of the rich peasantry, and demanded decisive intervention on the part of the party, in order to prevent any further shifting in a state already far from being proletarian. . . .

Our proletarian dictatorship, our workers' state, has the peculiarities of working in an agricultural country and of having its state apparatus burdened with various bureaucratic aberrations.

This is perfectly true. But what is the *class character* of the state? It is a *workers' state.* To state that our state is not a workers' state, that it is already semi-bourgeois, is to assert that our state is already in a condition of degeneration, and to throw doubts upon the existence of the proletarian dictatorship in our country. . . . If this were really the case, it would be a very serious matter indeed. If we really had no proletarian dictatorship, then we should have to pursue a very different line, and our party, in so far as it is a proletarian party, would obviously place questions on the agenda aiming at a radical purging of the present Soviet power. . . .

This brings us to the thesis of the degeneration of our whole state apparatus, and of the deviation of our policy, and of the policy of the present Soviet state, from the interests of the broad proletarian masses. . . . The opposition has pointed out that the numerous bureaucratic groups in our state apparatus are complemented by the equally numerous bureaucratic groups in the economic organs, the cooperatives, the trade unions, etc. It would thus seem that the whole of the groups composing our apparatus have practically nothing in common with the interests of the broad masses.

We have been believing in our simplicity that our party is the vanguard of the proletariat; but now it turns out that it is a bureaucratic clique entirely detached from the masses. We believe the soviet power to represent a form of the dictatorship of the proletariat, but it appears that all we have is an extremely non-proletarian state, headed by a completely declassed caste. The logical continuance of this train of thought is bound to lead sooner or later to the idea of the overthrow of the soviet power – it can lead nowhere else. . . .

You are aware that up to now we Leninists have regarded the unity and coherence of our party as the first prerequisite for the maintenance and firmer establishment of the proletarian dictatorship. We Leninists have always imagined that the proletarian dictatorship can only be secure in our country if our party plays its role properly and when this party is in the first place the *sole* party in our country, that is, when the legal existence of other parties is made impossible, and in the second place the party is *unitary* in its structure, that is, represents a structure excluding any independent and autonomous groups, factions, organized currents, etc. . . . Now this has all changed at one blow. Now the whole opposition, the whole oppositional bloc – Trotsky, Kamenev, Zinoviev, Krupskaia,* etc. – demands freedom for factions within the party. . . .

. . . The Central Committee and the Central Control Commission have been faced by the fact that a number of comrades, including some holding extremely responsible positions, had actually taken such steps as the convocation of an illegal meeting against the party and its leaders. *Were we to tolerate such actions, our party would cease to exist tomorrow as a Leninist party.* We cannot tolerate this. We say to these comrades: Defend your principles, declare your standpoint, *speak in the party meetings*; but if you take to the forest, if you will not reply to our questions, if you refuse to make statements before the Control Commission, if you choose the method of organizing a new party within our party, the method of illegal organization, then we shall fight you relentlessly. . . .

THE THEORETICAL DEBATE ON SOCIALISM IN ONE COUNTRY

At the Fifteenth Party Conference in November, 1926, the opposition leaders tried to expose the forced nature of Stalin's theoretical innovations. A battle of quotations and hair-splitting distinctions ensued, indicative of the new Communist scholasticism. Stalin had the last word, thanks to his control of the party organization, and the manipulation of scripture to fit the political needs of the moment became a permanent feature of communism.

a) KAMENEV'S CRITICISM OF STALIN

. . . Our whole Party holds the standpoint that our revolution is a socialist revolution, that it represents the basis for the further development of

---

*Nadezhda Krupskaia: Lenin's widow, who sided with the opposition in 1925 and 1926 – Ed.

FROM: Kamenev, Speech at the Fifteenth Party Conference (English translation in *International Press Correspondence*, no. 79, November 25, 1926, pp. 1365-67).

international revolution, and that it forms the transitional period from capitalism to socialism. . . .

Why is it then necessary, comrades, to invent differences of opinion on the character of our revolution and its future, since we are able to agree wholly and entirely with everything expressed in this resolution as the point of departure of the Party in the question of the nature of our revolution? (A voice: "Can socialism be established?") Wait, comrades, I cannot say everything at once. Wait till I come to that. . . .

Yes, in the course of the transition period between capitalism and Communism the proletariat will be able to establish the completely socialist state of society, provided it pursues a correct policy in its relations with the peasantry. . . .

. . . But why did Comrade Rykov write, and why did you unanimously decide – we are in perfect agreement with this standpoint – that we must catch up to and pass the level of development in the advanced capitalist countries within a historically comparative minimum of time? . . .

The point is, comrades, that this speed is necessary, and we must ask why it is considered necessary. It is necessary because the Soviet Union, as the first country of Socialism, must prove to the millions of the working people, the workers and peasants, the real superiority of socialist economy. This means that this country must and can provide for the needs of the population much more completely and cheaply than capitalist economics are capable of doing. (Comrade: "Thank God for that!" Laughter.)

. . . It is not only military intervention which may prove an obstacle in the path of the realisation of the completely socialist state of society, but the failure to carry out the above instructions. For this reason we raise the question of the rate of development of our economics, and not only the question of military intervention. The rate of our economic development, as compared with the rate of capitalist development, the necessity of rapidly attaining and passing the level of capitalism, is as important a prerequisite for the final victory of Socialism in our country as the necessity of safeguarding against military intervention. . . .

Comrade Stalin has here given us a detailed analysis of Lenin's views on the possibility of the realisation of Socialism in one country. In this he referred to an article of Lenin published in 1915. He proved that the theory and practice of the establishment of Socialism in the Soviet Union arise, so to speak, from his quotations, and from this law of the inequality of capitalist development. I cannot deal with this in detail, as the time is too short, and I must still speak of a number of other questions. But I cannot but observe that one must not refer to this quotation as indicating how Lenin conceived the tasks of the revolution in Russia at that time.

The simple duty of being perfectly accurate with respect to quotations from Lenin forces me to this explanation. This quotation, adduced correctly and completely by Comrade Stalin, was published in the "Social Democrat," the then central organ of our Party, on 25 August 1915. The article from which it is taken contains a general criticism of the standpoint of those social traitors who had said: We cannot begin the social revolution in Germany or in England or in Italy, we must begin everywhere at once. Lenin replied to them: You are traitors, for under the cloak of this theory, which compels one country to wait for another, you wish to avoid fulfilling your duty of kindling the proletarian revolution in every country. This was during the epoch of the imperialist war, in 1915. A month and a half later, in number 47 of the "Social Democrat," published on 13 October, exactly six weeks afterwards, Lenin wrote an article dealing specially with the tasks then confronting the Bolsheviki in Russia. Since Lenin stated in September that the victory of Socialism is possible in one country, even a backward country, and since he stated that it was the duty of every proletarian revolutionist to maintain this standpoint, we should naturally expect that he would apply the standpoint first of all to Russia.

But, comrades, this is not the case. We must not carelessly represent the true history of Lenin's views in order to score points in debate. Six weeks after the publication of the passage quoted by comrade Stalin, Lenin wrote in his famous article "Some Theses":

"While paying due regard to the demands made by our comrades from Russia, we formulate some theses on the actual questions of our present work."

A number of these are then enumerated, of which the fifth runs as follows:

"The social import of the next revolution in Russia can only be the revolutionary democratic dictatorship of the proletariat and the peasantry."

The sixth thesis reads:

"It is the task of the proletariat of Russia to carry through the bourgeois democratic revolution to its end, in order to arouse socialist revolution in Europe. This second task is now following very closely upon the first, but it still continues to remain a special and second task."

(Voices: "What of it?" "We have read that for ourselves." "That will not do. Nothing can be made of that!") Comrades, I cannot help it if it is disagreeable for you to hear these sentences. (Voices: "We not only hear them, but we understand them as well!")

If you will accord a straightforward consideration to the declaration of Lenin, made six weeks after the appearance of the article correctly quoted by Comrade Stalin, you will be bound to admit that Lenin's words in 1915 on the establishment of Socialism in one country referred clearly to the West European States . . . (A voice: "Nothing of the sort!") and that at the same time he pointed out another urgent task for Russia. That which I have read to you is his definition of the social import of the impending revolution. . . .

We regard our State as a proletarian State, not only because it is a State ruled by the dictatorship of the proletariat, but because the proletariat is utilising state power and state organisation as an instrument for raising up to Socialism the whole of the non-proletarian strata of the workers.

But, comrades, we must add – and it is our duty to do this – all that Lenin said on this question. Were we to state that we have a proletarian State and nothing more, then we should not be stating the truth, nor what Lenin said. For Lenin told us that we have a proletarian State in a double sense: the dictatorship of the proletariat, and the rising of the whole stratum of the workers to an ever higher level; but we have a proletarian State in a country with a preponderant peasant population and with bureaucratic deformations. . . .

And precisely as this fact is the inevitable consequence of the realisation of the dictatorship of the proletariat and of the proletarian State in an agrarian country, in the same manner the bureaucratic deformations of the state apparatus are an expression of class.

What does this mean? In my opinion it means that the state apparatus, viewed from the class standpoint, is endeavouring to oust the workers from immediate participation in the administration of the State. . .

b) STALIN'S REPLY TO KAMENEV

. . . Engels said that the proletarian revolution . . . could not succeed in one single country alone. The facts, however, show that under the new conditions of imperialism, such a revolution in its most essential parts has already been carried through in one single country alone, for we have carried out nine tenths of this programme in our country.

Comrade Zinoviev may say that we have committed a mistake by carrying out the points of this programme (laughter). It is very easily possible that in carrying out these points we have shown a certain "national limitedness" (laughter). That is very easily possible. One thing is nevertheless true;

FROM: Stalin, Concluding Remarks at the Fifteenth Party Conference (English translation in *International Press Correspondence*, no. 78, November 25, 1926, pp. 1350, 1353-54).

that which Engels wrote in the forties of the last century under the conditions of pre-monopolistic capitalism and which was impossible for one country alone has become possible under the conditions of imperialism in our own country.

Naturally, if Engels were alive today, he would not cling to the old formula. On the contrary, he would welcome our revolution and say: To hell with all old formulas! Long live the victorious revolution in the Soviet Union! The gentlemen in the ranks of the Social Democracy, however, do not think like that. They cling to the old formulation of Engels in order to facilitate their struggle against the revolution, against the Bolsheviks. That is naturally their affair. It is only serious when Comrade Zinoviev attempts to imitate these gentlemen and in this matter to go the way of the Social Democracy . . . .

One must recognise, comrades, that it was Lenin and no other who first of all established the proof of the possibility of the victory of socialism in one country alone. One may not deny Lenin that which is due to him. One must not be afraid of the truth, one must have the courage to speak the truth, one must have the courage to declare that Lenin was the first Marxist who formulated the question of the victory of socialism in one country alone in a new form and answered it in the affirmative.

I do not wish with this to say that Lenin as a thinker stood higher than Marx or Engels. I only wish to say two things: First of all, one must not demand of Marx and Engels, although they were tremendous thinkers and geniuses, that in the period of pre-monopolistic capital they could foresee all the possibilities of the proletarian class struggle and the proletarian revolution which developed half a century later in the period of developed monopolistic capitalism. Secondly, there is nothing particularly wonderful in the fact that Lenin, himself a genius and a follower of Engels and Marx, should have understood the new possibilities of the proletarian revolution under the new conditions of capitalist development and thus establish the truth that the victory of socialism in one country alone is possible.

. . . Comrade Kamenev took the "trouble" to prove that the basic article of Comrade Lenin (1915) which deals with the possibility of socialism in one country alone, allegedly did not refer to Russia, but that when Lenin spoke of such a possibility he was thinking not of Russia but of other capitalist countries. Comrade Kamenev took this doubtful "trouble" in order to clear the way for Comrade Trotsky whose "scheme" was refuted by the article of Lenin written in 1915.

To put it vulgarly, Comrade Kamenev has played the role of housemaid to Comrade Trotsky by cleaning the way for him (laughter). It is naturally a sad sight to observe the director of the Lenin Institute in the role of Housemaid to Comrade Trotsky. Not that there is anything undignified in the work of a housemaid, but because Comrade Kamenev is without doubt a capable person who might very well concern himself with more qualified work. He adopted this role, however, perfectly voluntarily, as of course he was fully entitled to do, so that nothing is to be done in the matter. How has Comrade Kamenev carried out this peculiar role? Comrade Kamenev declared in his speech that the chief theses of Lenin in his article written in 1915, the theses which have determined the whole policy of our revolution and its work of reconstruction, the theses which speak of the possibility of the victory of socialism in one country alone, do not refer to Russia and could not refer to Russia and that when Lenin spoke of the victory of socialism in one country alone, he was not thinking of Russia but of other capitalist countries. That is unbelievable and unheard of, that sounds like a direct slander against Comrade Lenin. But Comrade Kamenev evidently does not care what the party thinks about such a falsification of Lenin. He is only concerned to clear the way for Comrade Trotsky at any price.

How has he attempted to justify this peculiar contention?

He said that two weeks after the publication of the article mentioned, Comrade Lenin published his well-known theses concerning the character of the coming revolution in which he said that the task of Marxists would be exhausted with the efforts to achieve the victory of the bourgeois democratic revolution in Russia and that Lenin, when he said this, spoke on the assumption that the Revolution in Russia would retain its bourgeois stage and not develop into a socialist revolution. As, however, the article of Lenin upon the possibility of the victory of socialism in one country alone deals not with the bourgeois revolution but with the socialist revolution, it is clear that Lenin in his article could not have been thinking of Russia.

According to Kamenev it turns out that Lenin interpreted the extent of the Russian revolution just as a left bourgeois revolutionary or a reformist of the social democratic type would have done, according to whose opinions a bourgeois revolution would not develop into a socialist revolution and that between a bourgeois and a socialist revolution a long historical interval, a long pause of at least several decades must intervene whilst capitalism develops and the proletariate vegetates.

According to Kamenev it turns out that in 1915 when he wrote his article, Lenin did not think and did not conceive of directly going on to the socialist revolution after the victory of the bourgeois revolution. You will say, this is unbelievable and unheard of. Yes, this contention of Comrade Kamenev is really unbelievable and unheard of. But Kamenev does not mind about that in the least.

Permit me to mention a few documents which prove that Comrade

Kamenev has vulgarly falsified the opinions of Comrade Lenin in this question. . . .

. . . Where are we to fit in the theses of Lenin from 1915 to which Comrade Kamenev appealed in his speech and which deal with the tasks of the bourgeois democratic revolution in Russia? Do not these theses contradict the idea of the development of the bourgeois revolution into a socialist revolution? No, they do not, on the contrary. The basis of these theses is just the idea of the development of the bourgeois revolution into the socialist revolution, the idea of the development of the first stage of the Russian revolution into its second stage.

First of all Lenin by no means says in these theses that the extent of the Russian revolution and the tasks of the Marxists in Russia are exhausted with the fall of the Czar and the landowners, by the fulfilment of the tasks set by the bourgeois democratic revolution. Secondly, Lenin in these theses limited himself to characterising the tasks of the bourgeois democratic revolution because he regarded this revolution as the first stage and as the immediate task of the Russian Marxists. Thirdly, Lenin proceeds from the assumption that the Russian Marxists must not commence their task with the second stage (as comrade Trotsky proposed with his slogan "down with the Czar, form a workers government") but with the first stage, with the stage of the bourgeois democratic revolution.

Is there any contradiction here? Is even the shadow of a contradiction with the idea of the development of the bourgeois revolution into the socialist revolution here? The opposite is the case.

We see that Comrade Kamenev has definitely falsified the standpoint of Lenin. . . .

STALIN ON THE EXPULSION OF THE LEFT OPPOSITION

Bitter controversy between the Opposition and the party leadership raged from the summer of 1926 to the fall of 1927, though Stalin's control of the party organization left no doubt as to the outcome of the contest. The Opposition leaders were removed from one post after another, and at the Fifteenth Party Congress in December, 1927, the active oppositionists were expelled from the party. Stalin justified this as the elimination of deviant individualists who refused to respect the principle of party discipline. Zinoviev and Kamenev with their followers thereupon recanted, and were temporarily reinstated in the party. The Trotskyists were exiled to remote points in Siberia and elsewhere. A year later, in February, 1929, Trotsky was ousted from the country altogether.

How could it happen that the entire Party, as a whole, and following it the working class too, so thoroughly isolated the opposition? After all, the opposition are headed by well-known people with well-known names, people who know how to advertise themselves (*voices:* "Quite right!"), people who are not afflicted with modesty (*applause*) and are able to blow their own trumpets.

It happened because the leading groups of the opposition proved to be a group of petty-bourgeois intellectuals divorced from life, divorced from the revolution, divorced from the Party, from the working class. (*Voices:* "Quite right!" *Applause*). . . .

Have we the dictatorship of the proletariat or not? Rather a strange question. (*Laughter*) Nevertheless, the opposition raise it in every one of their statements. The opposition say that we are in a state of Thermidor degeneration. What does that mean? It means that we have not the dictatorship of the proletariat, that our economics and our politics are a failure, are going backwards, that we are not going towards Socialism, but towards capitalism. This, of course, is strange and foolish. But the opposition insist on it. . . .

. . . The opposition utterly break away from the Leninist principle of organization and take the path of organizing a second party, the path of organizing a new International. . . . On all these questions the opposition have slipped into Menshevism. Can these Menshevik views of the opposition be regarded as compatible with the Party's ideology, with our Party's program, with its tactics, with the tactics of the Comintern, with the organizational principles of Leninism?

Under no circumstances; not for a single moment!

You will ask: how could such an opposition come into being among us; where are their social roots? I think that the social roots of the opposition lie in the fact that the urban petty-bourgeois strata are being ruined under the conditions of our development, in the fact that these strata are discontented with the regime of the dictatorship of the proletariat, in the striving of these strata to change this regime, to "improve" it in the spirit of establishing bourgeois democracy.

I have already said that as a result of our progress, as a result of the growth of the relative weight of the socialist forms of economy, a section of the petty-bourgeoisie, particularly the urban bourgeoisie, is being ruined

FROM: Stalin, *Political Report of the Central Committee to the Fifteenth Congress of the C.P.S.U.(B.)* (December 3, 1927; English translation, Moscow Foreign Languages Publishing House, 1950, pp. 92, 99, 105-6, 110-11).

and is going under. The opposition reflect the grumbling and discontent of these strata with the regime of the proletarian revolution.

Such are the social roots of the opposition. . . .

Why did the Party expel Trotsky and Zinoviev? Because they are the *organizers* of the entire anti-Party opposition (*voices:* "Quite right!"), because they set themselves the aim of breaking the laws of the Party, because they thought that nobody would dare to touch them, because they wanted to create for themselves the privileged position of nobles in the Party. . . .

If the opposition want to be in the Party let them submit to the will of the Party, to its laws, to its instructions, without reservations, without equivocation. If they refuse to do that, let them go wherever they please. (*Voices:* "Quite right!" *Applause*). We do not want new laws providing privileges for the opposition, and we will not create them. (*Applause*).

The question is raised about terms. We have only one set of terms: the opposition must disarm wholly and entirely, in ideological and organizational respects. (*Voices:* "Quite right!" *Prolonged applause*).

They must renounce their anti-Bolshevik views openly and honestly, before the whole world. (*Voices:* "Quite right!" *Prolonged applause*). . . .

STALIN ON THE GRAIN CRISIS

In 1928, after disposing of the Trotsky-Zinoviev opposition, Stalin began to turn to a more vigorous policy of industrial development and exploitation of the peasants. While there is evidence that he was at least partly motivated in this by the desire to embarrass Bukharin and Rykov, Stalin nonetheless put his case effectively.

. . . The underlying cause of our grain difficulties is that the increase in the production of grain for the market is not keeping pace with the increase in the demand for grain.

Industry is growing. The number of workers is growing. Towns are growing. And, lastly, the regions producing industrial crops (cotton, flax, sugar beet, etc.) are growing, creating a demand for grain. All this leads to a rapid increase in our requirements as regards grain – grain available for the market. But the production of grain for the market is increasing at a disastrously slow rate. . . .

. . . Is it not a fact that the grain crop area has already reached the pre-war mark? Yes, it is a fact. Is it not a fact that already last year the gross

FROM: Stalin, "On the Grain Front" (*Talk to Students of the Institute of Red Professors, the Communist Academy and the Sverdlov University, May 28, 1928; Problems of Leninism*, pp. 248-249, 251-59).

production of grain was equal to the prewar output, i.e., 5,000,000,000 *puds?* * Yes, it is a fact. How, then, is it to be explained that, in spite of these facts, the amount of grain we are producing for the market is only one-half, and the amount we are exporting is only about one-twentieth of what it was in prewar times?

The reason is primarily and chiefly the change in the structure of our agriculture brought about by the October Revolution, the change from large-scale landlord and large-scale kulak farming, which provided the largest proportion of marketed grain, to small- and middle-peasant farming, which provides the smallest proportion of marketed grain. The mere fact that before the war there were fifteen to sixteen million individual peasant farms, whereas at present there are 24,000,000 to 25,000,000 peasant farms, shows that now the basis of our agriculture is essentially small-peasant farming, which provides a minimum amount of grain for the market. . . .

. . . The abolition of landlord (large-scale) farming, the reduction of the kulak (large-scale) farming to less than one-third, and the change to small-peasant farming with only 11 per cent of its output available for the market, in the absence, in the sphere of grain growing, of any more or less developed large-scale socialized farming (collective farms and state farms), was bound to lead, and in fact has led, to a sharp reduction in the output of grain for the market as compared with prewar times. It is a fact that the amount of marketed grain in our country is now half of what it was before the war, although the gross output of grain has reached the prewar level. . . .

What is the way out of this situation?

Some people see the way out of this situation in a return to kulak farming, in the development and extension of kulak farming. These people dare not advocate a return to landlord farming, for they realize, evidently, that such talk is dangerous in our times. All the more eagerly, therefore, do they urge the necessity of the utmost development of kulak farming in the interest of – Soviet power. These people think that the Soviet power can simultaneously rely on two opposite classes – the class of the kulaks, whose economic principle is the exploitation of the working class, and the class of the workers, whose economic principle is the abolition of all exploitation. A trick worthy of reactionaries.

There is no need to prove that these reactionary "plans" have nothing in common with the interests of the working class, with the principles of Marxism, with the tasks of Leninism. . . .

What, then, is the way out of the situation?

*One *pud* = approximately 36 lbs. – Ed.

1. The way out lies, firstly, in the transition from the small, backward and scattered peasant farms to amalgamated, large-scale socialized farms, equipped with machinery, armed with scientific knowledge and capable of producing a maximum of grain for the market. The solution lies in the transition from individual peasant farming to collective, socialized farming. . . .

2. The way out lies, secondly, in expanding and strengthening the old state farms, and in organizing and developing new, large state farms. . . .

3. Finally, the way out lies in systematically increasing the yield of the small and middle individual peasant farms. We cannot and should not lend any support to the individual large kulak farms. But we can and should assist the individual small- and middle-peasant farms, helping them to increase their crop yields and drawing them into the channel of cooperative organizations. . . .

Thus, if all these tasks are fulfilled, the state can in three or four years' time have at its disposal 250,000,000 to 300,000,000 additional *puds* of marketable grain – a supply more or less sufficient to enable us to manoeuvre within the country as well as abroad. . . .

Should not, in addition to these measures, a number of other measures be adopted – measures, say, to reduce the rate of development of our industry, the growth of which is causing a considerable increase in the demand for grain which at present is outstripping the increase in the production of grain for the market? No, not under any circumstances! To reduce the rate of development of industry would mean to weaken the working class; for every step forward in the development of industry, every new factory, every new works, is, as Lenin expressed it, "a new stronghold" of the working class, which strengthens its position in the fight against the petty-bourgeois element, in the fight against the capitalist elements in our economy. On the contrary, we must maintain the present rate of development of industry; we must at the first opportunity speed it up in order to pour goods into the rural districts and obtain from them more grain, in order to supply agriculture, primarily the collective farms and state farms, with machines, in order to industrialize agriculture and to increase the proportion of its output for the market.

Should we, perhaps, for the sake of greater "caution," retard the development of heavy industry and make light industry, which produces chiefly for the peasant market, the basis of our industry as a whole? Not under any circumstances! That would be suicidal; it would undermine our whole industry, including light industry. It would mean abandoning the slogan of industrializing our country, it would transform our country into an appendage of the world capitalist system of economy. . . .

How will the measures proposed affect the alliance between the workers and the peasants? I think that these measures can only help to strengthen the alliance between the workers and the peasants.

Indeed, if the collective farms and the state farms develop at increased speed; if, as a result of direct assistance given to the small and middle peasants, the yield of their farms increases and the cooperative societies embrace wider and wider masses of the peasantry; if the state obtains the hundreds of millions of *puds* of additional marketable grain required for the purposes of manoeuvering; if, as a result of these and similar measures, the kulaks are curbed and gradually overcome – is it not clear that the contradictions between the working class and the peasantry within the alliance of workers and peasants will thereby be smoothed out more and more; that the need for emergency measures in the purchase of grain will disappear; that the large masses of peasantry will turn more and more to collective forms of farming and that the fight to overcome the capitalist elements in the rural districts will assume an increasingly mass and organized character?

Is it not clear that the cause of the alliance between the workers and the peasants can only benefit by these measures? . . .

. . . The alliance of the proletariat with the peasantry under the conditions of the dictatorship of the proletariat should not be regarded as an alliance with the whole of the peasantry. The alliance of the proletariat with the peasantry is an alliance of the working class with the labouring masses of the peasantry. Such an alliance cannot be effected without a struggle against the capitalist elements of the peasantry, against the kulaks. . . .

THE RIGHT OPPOSITION

Stalin's political tactics and his desire for stepped-up industrialization and increased pressure on the peasants produced acute anxiety among many of his colleagues. Bukharin, together with Rykov and the trade-union chief Tomsky, formed a "Right Opposition" which endeavored to check Stalin in behind-the-scenes maneuvers. In July, 1928, Bukharin addressed the Central Committee with a vain plea for caution, and then turned to the broken Left Opposition to reveal his fears and seek help.

FROM: Bukharin, Speech to the Central Committee, July 10, 1928 (editor's translation from partial copy of the minutes of the meeting in the Trotsky Archive, T1901).

a) BUKHARIN ON PEASANT POLICY

. . . If we want to catch up with Western Europe – and we want to do this – if we want to increase the tempo of accumulation for socialist industry – and we want to do this – if we take into account our general economic backwardness, our poverty, then it is perfectly clear that great difficulties for our building stem from all this. We want to solve a series of great tasks at once: the maximum accumulation in socialist industry, the maximum increase in agriculture, the maximum consumption for the working class and the toiling masses in general, their maximum uplift, etc. These tasks cannot be solved simultaneously. We solve them as we come to them, heeling over now to one side, now to the other, contradicting ourselves. We are moving all the time in contradictions. It stands to reason that difficulties of such a kind really lie in the nature of our reconstruction period. I call your attention, for example, to the curious fact that we complain of economic disproportions now from one end and now from the other.

Voroshilov: Give us your panacea.

Bukharin: I don't want to give a panacea, and you, please, don't make fun of me. I want to say that the reconstruction period quite naturally evokes a series of complications and difficulties, but at the same time there is no doubt in my mind that there are different kinds of difficulties. . . . When, taking Comrade Stalin's formulation, we say now, "We have a threat to the *smychka*," does this fit into the category of circumstances from which a split could issue? Of course it does. A threat to the *smychka* is a circumstance from which a split could issue. But Lenin wrote that the main task of our Central Committee and Central Control Commission, as of our party as a whole, consists of not allowing these disagreements to grow to the level of serious class disagreements. . . . To undertake the slightest campaign in the country reversing our election instruction means to mobilize against us to an ever greater degree the *kulak* element, the petty bourgeoisie of a whole series of cities, the middle bourgeoisie, petty-bourgeois strata, etc. The reserves of these forces remain very great, and the slightest vacillation on this question in the ranks of our party will have a disproportionately great political significance. . . . Should we correct the situation we now have as a result of the grain collections by making concessions in the direction of the *kulak*, by dropping the slogan of an intensified offensive against the *kulaks*? Absolutely not. The problem at the present time is to remove the threat to the alliance with the middle peasant which we now find. We are dropping the extraordinary measures,* and in no case do we identify the extraordinary measures with the decisions of the Fifteenth Congress.

*I.e., the pressure applied to the peasants to get grain during the winter of 1928-29 – Ed.

... Can we have such difficulties this year as we had last year? We can. How will we react to this? We will turn to the application of extraordinary measures if such difficulties are met within the coming year, but if we apply them, will we do so to the same extent or not? It seems to me that this is the most agonizing and important question that faces us. As a preliminary I would like to suggest a consideration or analogy which at first glance will appear wild or joking.

Imagine that you are the proletarian power in a petty-bourgeois country, but that you are forcibly driving the *muzhik* [peasant] into communes.
Voroshilov: As in 1918 and 1919, let's say.
Bukharin: Then you will get an uprising of the *muzhik*, of which the *kulak* is the driver; the *kulak* organizes and leads it.

The petty-bourgeois element rises against the proletariat, beats it on the head, and as the result of a cruel class war the proletarian dictatorship disappears. What do you get here?.
Stalin: The Son is terrifying but God is gracious. (Laughter). . . .
Bukharin: We must in no case turn toward allowing the expanded reproduction of extraordinary measures.
Kossior: This is true.
Lozovsky: Right now this doesn't depend on us.
Bukharin: Right now a great deal still depends on us. Therefore, the center of our policy is the following: We must in no case allow a threat to the *smychka*. Otherwise we will not fulfill the basic testament of Lenin. . . .

b) BUKHARIN ON THE MENACE OF STALIN

Kamenev: Is the struggle really serious?
Bukharin: That's just what I wanted to talk about. We feel that Stalin's line is ruinous for the whole revolution. We could be overthrown on account of it. The disagreements between us and Stalin are many times more serious than the disagreements which we used to have with you. Rykov, Tomsky and I agree on formulating the situation thus: "It would be much better if Zinoviev and Kamenev were in the Politbureau instead of Stalin." I have spoken with Rykov and Tomsky about this quite frankly. I have not spoken with Stalin for several weeks. He is an unprincipled intriguer, who subordinates everything to the preservation of his own power. He changes his theory according to whom he needs to get rid of. In the "seven"* our arguing with him reached the point of saying, "false," "you lie," etc. Now he has

FROM: Bukharin-Kamenev Talk, July 11, 1928 (Notes by Kamenev; editor's translation from copy in the Trotsky Archive, T1897).

*The informal leadership group, including most of the Politbureau – Ed.

made concessions, so that he can cut our throats. We understand this, but he maneuvers so as to make us appear to be the schismatics. . . . This is the line which he pronounced at the plenum: 1) Capitalism grew either on account of colonies, or loans, or the exploitation of the workers. We have no colonies, we can get no loans, therefore our basis is tribute from the peasantry. You understand that this is just what Preobrazhensky's theory is. 2) The more socialism grows, the greater will be the resistance [to it]. . . . This is idiotic illiteracy. 3) Since tribute is necessary and resistance will grow, we need firm leadership. Self-criticism must not apply to the leadership, but only to those who carry out orders. Self-criticism is in fact aimed at Tomsky and Uglanov.* As a result we are getting a police regime. This is not a "cuckoo" matter, but will really decide the fate of the revolution. With this theory everything can perish. . . .

The Petersburg [Leningrad] people are in general with us, but they got scared when the talk got to the possibility of removing Stalin. . . . Our potential forces are vast, but 1) the middle-ranking Central Committee member still does not understand the depth of the disagreements, 2) there is a terrible fear of a split. Therefore, when Stalin conceded on the extraordinary measures, he made it difficult for us to attack him. We don't want to come forth as schismatics, for then they would slaughter us. But Tomsky in his latest speech showed clearly that Stalin is the schismatic. . . .

KUIBYSHEV ON INDUSTRIALIZATION

Stalin's chief spokesman on industrial development was Valerian V. Kuibyshev, head of the Supreme Economic Council. In September, 1928, Kuibyshev set forth the basic intention of developing heavy industry at the maximum possible rate, and dismissed all criticism of this course as a "petty-bourgeois" deviation.

Is it right that we should particularly accelerate the rate of development of industry producing the means of production in regard both to the investment of funds and to an augmentation of the quantities produced, while the peasant question becomes more and more acute and there is an ever-increasing demand for mass-articles on the rural markets? I believe such a line of procedure to be absolutely correct. . . .

*Uglanov: pro-Bukharin secretary of the Moscow party organization, removed in the fall of 1928–Ed.
FROM: Kuibyshev, "The Economic Situation of the Soviet Union" (Report to the Leningrad Party Organization, September 19, 1928; English translation in *International Press Correspondence*, no. 73, October 19, 1928, pp. 1337-38, and no. 75, October 26, 1928, p. 1383).

Our economic development cannot be expected to proceed quite without failure, disproportions, or anomalies. We shall constantly be involved in anomalies, seeing that we had not the possibility during the first years of the existence of the Soviet Union to live in peace and to proceed smoothly and uninterruptedly with all branches of our development. We were deprived of this possibility because a great number of contradictions existed even in former times in our industry and in all other branches of our economy, in which connection it must be borne in mind that the more successfully we progress in our socialist development, the greater will be the difficulties that will be laid in our path by our opponents at home and abroad. The elimination of class differences, which is the final aim of our entire development, will and must be effected in the form of ever greater class struggle. Naturally we shall need more than a decade to eradicate these differences and to ensure a smooth and harmonious development of our economic organism without disproportions and anomalies. These differences and anomalies are inevitable and we shall be occupied with them for a long time to come. They will lead to new difficulties and complications in our economic life. But they will not hinder us, they must not be allowed to diminish the energy with which we carry on development along the lines laid down by our Party. The industrialisation of the country and the enhancement of the rate of industrialisation are both tasks continually confronting us. . . .

. . . We must be prepared to meet with discontent and active resistance in certain sections of the population, which will increase the difficulties with which we are faced in an economic respect. On the other hand, this same discontent penetrates through all sorts of channels even as far as certain parts of our Soviet apparatus, the result being doubts as to the possibility of executing such great tasks and as to the wisdom of aspiring to such difficult objectives as are involved in the industrialisation of agriculture and the industrialisation of our entire economy. By penetrating into our Soviet apparatus, such sentiments also find ingress in a small measure into our Party. The Party will have recourse to all available measures for the purpose of nipping in the bud such sentiments as pessimism or lack of confidence. The July plenum of the C[entral] C[ommittee] openly stated that, apart from its energetic struggle against pseudo-radical tendencies of the nature of Trotskyism, "left" tendencies which in reality hide a Social Democratic core, the Party must also combat such pessimistic currents as are occasioned by the existing difficulties and tend to diminish the energy and activity essential for the solution of the tremendous tasks with which we are faced. Seeing that the difficulties before us are very great and that the unity, discipline, and solidarity of our Party are our only guarantee of success, we must seek not only to combat the pessimistic tendencies, which are to a great part no more than the reflection of the discontent of the petty-bourgeois chaos at our policy of industrialisation, but also to combat the attitude of tolerance observed with regard to these tendencies. . . .

. . . We are told we are "over-industrialising" and "biting off more than we can chew." History, however, will not permit us to proceed more slowly, otherwise the very next year may lead to a series of even more serious anomalies than are apparent to-day. Any careful student of our economy will, I am sure, agree with me that the most serious misproportion, which is most disadvantageous in its effect on our economy, is that between the output of the means of production and the requirements of the country. . . .

The difficulty of the economic tasks before us upon the one hand and the growth of the hostile forces arrayed against us (both by international capitalism and by the capitalistic elements within our country) upon the other, are naturally reflected in the attitude of the engineers and other technical staffs.

The process of differentiation among the technical staffs has greatly increased, dividing them into a very small group of outright enemies of the Soviet authority and underminers of our economy on the one side, and upon the other such of the engineers and technical operatives as are wholly devoted to the object of socialist development and inspired with the [sense] of the grand task before us. This process of differentiation not only deserves our closest attention, but must also furnish us with various valuable conclusions. While most energetically opposing the enemies of our economy, who are direct agents of the bourgeoisie, we must give all possible aid and encouragement to the honest and devoted technical operatives and see to it that the conditions of their activity are such as will facilitate the execution of the tasks with which they are charged. . . .

All organisations that are in touch with the technical staffs are beginning to understand that without a healthy relationship and without the honest co-operation of the technical staffs with the Soviet authorities, we shall not be able to realise the gigantic plan of the reconstruction of our industry, which is not only completely indispensable to us but which is also the very best guarantee for our economy and for the development of socialism. Without technical staffs, the technical equipment of our industry is an impossibility. At the same time, however, all the necessary steps must naturally be taken to train new cadres of Red engineers. This side of the question deserves more attention than has ever been paid to it before. . . .

BUKHARIN ON EQUILIBRIUM

In reply to the Stalinists' new industrialization emphasis, Bukharin published a plea for caution and balance in which he opposed sacrificing the standard of living of the population. This "consumptionist" attitude has recurred from time to time in the Communist movement, particularly in the Communist regimes of Eastern Europe.

. . . The relative *planlessness* – or *relative planfulness* – of the economy of the transition period has its basis in the existence of small enterprises, of market connections, i.e., significant elements of . . . spontaneity. . . . Hence the very plan has a special nature: it is by no means the more or less 'finished' plan of a developed socialist society. In this plan there are many elements of the forecasting of the spontaneous or incalculable (for example, estimate of the crop, the amount of grain coming to market, the amount of products of peasant production as a whole that will be offered on the market, and, consequently, also the estimate of prices, etc. etc.), and these forecasts become the starting point of one or another directive. It is just for this reason that with us there is no possibility of an "ideal" plan. And just for this reason there is room up to a *certain* point for errors. But the fact that an error can be explained and may even be *unavoidable* does not prevent it from being an *error*. This is the first point. Secondly, the gravest violations of fundamental proportions (as was the case with us in the grain economy, of which more below), and the resultant miscalculations are *by no means unavoidable* errors. Thirdly, even if a good plan is not omnipotent, then a bad "plan" and bad economic maneuvering in general can ruin even a good cause. . . .

. . . For this reason, despite the relativism of our planning, its role is really *enormous*. Major errors in the directing of the economy which result in a violation of the basic economic proportions in the country, therefore, of themselves may engender a highly unfavorable change in the relations of the classes. The reverse side of such a violation of the necessary *economic* proportions would be a resultant upsetting of the *political* equilibrium in the country.

To avoid a "goods famine" and a "crisislike" violation of the basic economic proportions, which are by no means inevitable or absolute laws, it follows that:

FROM: Bukharin, "Notes of an Economist" (September 30, 1928; English translation by Bertram D. Wolfe in *Khrushchev and Stalin's Ghost*, New York, Praeger, 1957, pp. 299-302, 304-6, 309-11, 314-15; reprinted by permission of Mrs. Bertram D. Wolfe).

In order to attain the most favorable possible march of social reproduction (the most crisis-free), and to attain the systematic growth of socialism, and, in consequence, to attain the most favorable possible situation for the proletariat in the relations of class forces in the country – it is necessary to achieve a coordination of the basic elements of the national economy, to 'balance' them, arrange them, arrange them in such fashion that they best fulfill their respective functions, and actively influence the course of economic life and the class struggle so as to attain the best possible balance or equilibrium. . . .

In their simplicity, the ideologists of Trotskyism assume that the maximum annual pumping out of resources from the peasant economy into industry will assure the maximum tempo of the development of industry. But that is clearly not so. The greatest *not temporary but continuous* tempo can be attained by such a coordination in which industry develops on the foundation of a *rapidly growing* agricultural economy. It is then that industry attains its own record-breaking figures in its development. . . .

. . . What the Trotskyites fail to comprehend is that the *development of industry is dependent on the development of agriculture.* . . .

. . . *Along with a stormy growth of industry, along with a significant growth in the population and a rise in the needs of the population, the quanitity of grain has not grown in the country.* Isn't it clear that a contemptuous attitude to the grain problem under such conditions would be a real crime? And is it not clear . . . that a Trotskyist "solution" would lead straight to a real, and not an imaginary collapse? . . .

. . . One thing is clear: if any branch of production systematically fails to receive in return for its products the costs of production, plus a certain addition corresponding to a *part* of the surplus labor which can serve as a source of expanding reproduction, then that branch of industry either stagnates or *retrogresses.* This law "applies" to grain growing as it does to any other branch of the economy. . . .

Those who believe that the growth of the planned economy brings with it the possibility – as a result of the dying out of the law of value – of doing whatever one pleases, simply do not understand the ABC of economics. These considerations are sufficient to define the limit of the process of "pumping over" resources from agriculture to *industry. The opponents of industrialization* come out against any alienation even of a part of the surplus product, i.e. against all "pumping over" whatsoever. But in that case the tempo of industrialization will be slowed up. The Trotskyists define the magnitude of the pumping over by the limits of the "technically achievable," i.e., they go even beyond the limits of the entire surplus product. It is clear that in that case there can be no thought of the *development* of agriculture or its grain section, which in turn is required for the development of industry itself. Here the truth lies somewhere in between. . . .

The center of all our plan calculations, of all our economic policy, must be concern for the steadily developing *industrialization of our country* . . . . From every point of view – development of the productive forces, development of agriculture, growth of the specific gravity of socialism in the total economy, strengthening of the class alliances within the country, strengthening of our powers of self-defense, growth of mass consumption, etc. etc. – the industrialization of the country is for us a *law*.

But in carrying this out we must always remember that our socialist industrialization must differ from capitalist industrialization in that it is carried out *by the proletariat*, for the purposes of *socialism*, that its effect upon the peasant economy must be quite different and distinct in character, that its whole attitude towards the village economy must be different and distinct. Capitalism effected the *debasement* of agriculture. Socialist industrialization, however, is not a parasitic process in its relations with the village (under capitalism, despite the development of agriculture under the influence of industry, the elements of such a parasitism are present), but a means of its great *transformation and upswing*. The industrialization of the country therefore signifies also the industrialization of agriculture and thereby it prepares the abolition of the antagonism between city and village. . . .

We should strive for the fastest possible tempo of industrialization. Does that mean that we ought to put everything into capital construction? The question is quite a meaningless one. But behind this meaningless question there is hidden another that is quite meaningful: namely, the question of the limits of accumulation, of the upper limit for the sum of capital investment.

Above all, when we are drawing up our program of capital construction we must keep in mind the directive of the party on reserves (of valuta, gold, grain, goods). Of late it has become the fashion to keep quiet about the question of reserves. . . . Though silence may be golden and we short of gold, still we cannot afford to play at silence in this. We not only have no reserves; but in meeting the current supply problem itself "waiting one's turn" and "queuing up" have become our "way of life," which to a significant degree also disorganizes our *productive* life. . . .

. . . I have the impression that the People's Supreme Economic Council in drawing up its Five-Year Plan has forgotten the policy of reserves altogether . . . and that the excessive demands put upon the budget make it 'unrealistic.' But 'lack of realism' is 'quite' an essential deficiency in a plan.

It's clear that the question of reserves is tied up with the question of consumption, both productive consumption (including capital construction) and personal consumption (the personal consumption of the masses). And we all know that in this the bow is already drawn at high tension. *To increase this tension still further, and increase still more the goods famine, is impossible.* . . .

We must mobilize and put in motion the maximum number and kind of economic factors which work in favor of socialism. This requires a most complicated combination of personal, group, mass, social and state initiative. We have *too much* overcentralized everything. We must ask ourselves: ought we not now to take some steps in the direction of the Leninist commune-state? This does not by any means signify "letting go of the reins." Quite the contrary. The fundamental leadership, the solving of the more important problems, are matters which must be dealt with more firmly, more severely – *but for that reason more carefully thought out* "at the center." But within the strict framework of these decisions the lower organs must act on their own initiative and be responsible for *their own* range of problems, etc. Supercentralization in a number of fields had led to our depriving ourselves of *additional forces, means, resources and possibilities.* And we are in no position to utilize the entire mass of these possibilities, thanks to a number of bureaucratic barriers. We could act with more elasticity, more maneuverability, more successfully, if, beginning with the individual state enterprises, we were in a position to adapt ourselves to the real, concrete conditions, and thereby avoid the thousand small and large stupidities we are committing. . . .

Chapter Four
Soviet Communism: The Transformation under Stalin, 1929-1953

The Communist movement, despite the impersonal sociology contained in its doctrine, bears to an almost unique degree the impress of dominant individual personalities – specifically, Lenin and Stalin. Lenin launched the movement and gave it the qualities necessary for seizing and holding power; Stalin accomplished the permanent adaptation of the movement to the circumstances of its time and setting. The insane purging and self-glorification in which Stalin indulged were perhaps transitory, but the other changes for which he was responsible have been permanently assimilated into the Communist system in Soviet Russia – the priority of the industrialization effort and national power, the shift to conservative social and intellectual norms, and the monolithic control of all communication to enforce the pseudo-Marxist rationalization of the system. So constituted, the Soviet dictatorship proved itself in Stalin's eyes by emerging victorious from World War II, and he made every effort to keep it unchanged until his death in 1953.

STALIN'S REVOLUTION

Wielding the unchallenged personal control over the Communist Party and the Soviet state which he had attained with the defeat of the Right Opposition, Stalin commenced a drastic program of reconstructing the economic foundations of Soviet society. The two cardinal lines of effort, as he set them forth in his final attack on the Bukharin group in April, 1929, were the collectivization of the peasantry and the intensive development of heavy industry. Shortly afterward the First Five-Year Plan was formally approved by the Sixteenth Party Conference, with its commencement set retroactively back to October, 1928.

. . . What is the theoretical basis for the blindness and bewilderment of Bukharin's group?

I think that the theoretical basis for this blindness and bewilderment is Bukharin's incorrect, non-Marxian approach to the question of the class

FROM: Stalin, "The Right Deviation in the CPSU(B)" (Speech to the Central Committee, April, 1929; *Problems of Leninism*, pp. 309-13, 326-27, 331, 336-37, 371-72).

struggle in our country. I have in mind Bukharin's non-Marxian theory that the kulaks will grow into socialism, his failure to understand the mechanism of the class struggle under the dictatorship of the proletariat. . . .

Hitherto, we Marxist-Leninists thought that between the capitalists of town and country, on the one hand, and the working class, on the other, there is an *irreconcilable* antagonism of interest. This is exactly what the Marxian theory of the class struggle rests on. But now, according to Bukharin's theory that the capitalists will *peacefully grow* into socialism, all this is turned topsy-turvy; the irreconcilable antagonism of class interests between the exploiters and the exploited disappears, the exploiters grow into socialism. . . .

Either one thing or the other; either there is an irreconcilable antagonism of interests between the capitalist class and the class of the workers who have assumed power and have organized their dictatorship, or there is no such antagonism of interests, in which case only one thing remains: to proclaim the harmony of class interests. . . .

What can there be in common between Bukharin's theory that the kulaks will grow into socialism and Lenin's theory of the dictatorship as a fierce class struggle? Obviously, there is not, nor can there be, anything in common between them.

Bukharin thinks that under the dictatorship of the proletariat the class struggle must *subside* and *pass away* so that the abolition of classes may be brought about. Lenin, on the contrary, teaches us that classes can be abolished only by means of a stubborn class struggle, which under the dictatorship of the proletariat becomes *ever fiercer* than it was before the dictatorship of the proletariat. . . .

. . . In additon to the ordinary taxes, direct and indirect, which the peasantry is paying to the state, it also pays a certain supertax in the form of an overcharge on consumer goods, and in the form of low prices received for agricultural produce. . . .

. . . We also call it "the scissors," "drainage" of resources from agriculture into industry for the purpose of speeding up industrial development.

Is this "drainage" really necessary? Everybody agrees that it is, as a temporary measure, if we really wish to maintain a speedy rate of industrial development. Indeed, we must at all cost maintain a rapid growth of our industry, for this growth is necessary not solely for our industrial production, but primarily for our agriculture, for our peasantry, which at the present time needs most of all tractors, agricultural machinery and fertilizers.

Can we abolish this supertax at the present time? Unfortunately, we cannot. We must abolish it at the first opportune moment, in the coming years. But we cannot abolish it right now.

Now, as you see, this supertax obtained by means of "the scissors" is in fact "something like a tribute." Not a tribute, but "something like a tribute." It is "something like a tribute" which we are paying for our backwardness. We need this supertax to stimulate the development of our industry and to do away with our backwardness. . . .

. . . It was no accident that Bukharin and his friends took exception to the word "tribute" and began to speak of military-feudal exploitation of the peasants. Their outcry about military-feudal exploitation was undoubtedly an expression of their extreme discontent with the Party policy toward the kulaks, which is being applied by our organizations. Discontent with the Leninist policy of the Party in its leadership of the peasantry, discontent with our grain-purchasing policy, with our policy of developing collective and state farms to the utmost, and lastly, the desire to "unfetter" the market and to establish complete freedom of private trade – there you have the underlying reason for Bukharin's screams about military-feudal exploitation of the peasantry.

In the whole history of our party I cannot recall another single instance of the Party being accused of carrying on a policy of military-feudal exploitation. This anti-Party weapon was not borrowed from a Marxian arsenal. From where, then, was it borrowed? From the arsenal of Milyukov, the leader of the Constitutional-Democrats. . . .

. . . We have two different plans of economic policy.

The Party's Plan:

1. We are re-equipping industry (reconstruction).

2. We are beginning seriously to re-equip agriculture (reconstruction).

3. For this we must expand the development of collective farms and state farms, employ on a mass scale the contract system and machine and tractor stations as means of establishing a *bond* between industry and agriculture in the sphere of *production*.

4. As for the present grain-purchasing difficulties, we must admit the necessity for temporary emergency measures that are bolstered up by the popular support of the middle- and poor-peasant masses, as one of the means of breaking the resistance of the kulaks and of obtaining from them the maximum grain surplus necessary to be able to dispense with imported grain and to save foreign currency for the development of industry.

5. Individual poor- and middle-peasant farming plays, and will continue to play, a predominant part in supplying the country with food and raw materials; but alone it is no longer adequate – the development of individual poor- and middle-peasant farming must therefore be *supplemented* by the development of collective farms and state farms, by the contract system applied on a mass scale, by accelerating the development of machine-and-tractor stations, in order to facilitate the squeezing out of the capitalist

elements from agriculture and the gradual transfer of the individual peasant farms to large-scale collective farming, to collective labour.

6. But in order to achieve all this, it is necessary first of all to accelerate the development of industry, of metallurgy, chemicals, machine building, of tractor works, agricultural-machinery works, etc. Failing this it will be impossible to solve the grain problem just as it will be impossible to reconstruct agriculture.

Conclusion: *The key to the reconstruction of agriculture is the speedy rate of development of our industry.*

Bukharin's Plan:

1. "Normalize" the market; permit the free play of prices on the market and a rise in the price of grain, undeterred by the fact that this may lead to a rise in the price of manufactured goods, raw materials and bread.

2. The utmost development of individual peasant farming accompanied by a certain reduction of the rate of development of collective farms and state farms (Bukharin's theses of July and his speech at the July Plenum).

3. Grain purchasing on the spontaneity principle, precluding under all circumstances even the partial application of emergency measures against the kulaks, even though such measures are supported by the middle- and poor-peasant masses.

4. In the event of shortage of grain, to import about 100,000,000 rubles worth of grain.

5. And if there is not enough foreign currency to pay for imports of grain and equipment for industry, to reduce imports of equipment and, consequently, the rate of development of our industry – otherwise our agriculture will simply "mark time," or will even "directly decline."

Conclusion: *The key to the reconstruction of agriculture is the development of individual peasant farming.*

This is how it works out, comrades.

Bukharin's plan is a plan to *reduce* the rate of development of industry and to *undermine* the new forms of the [worker-peasant] bond.

Such are our divergencies. . . .

. . . The fight against the Right deviation is one of the most decisive duties of our Party. If we, in our own ranks, in our own Party, in the political General Staff of the proletariat, which is directing the movement and is leading the proletariat forward – if we in this General Staff should tolerate the free existence and the free functioning of the Right deviationists, who are trying to demobilize the Party, to demoralize the working class, to adapt our policy to the tastes of the "Soviet" bourgeoisie, and thus yield to the difficulties of our socialist construction – if we should tolerate all this, what would it mean? Would it not mean that we want to send the revolution downhill, demoralize our socialist construction, flee from difficulties, surrender our positions to the capitalist elements?

Does Bukharin's group understand that to refuse to fight the Right deviation is to betray the working class, to betray the revolution?

Does Bukharin's group understand that unless we overcome the Right deviation and the conciliationist tendency, it will be impossible to overcome the difficulties facing us, and that unless we overcome these difficulties it will be impossible to achieve decisive successes in socialist construction?

Compared with this, what is the value of this pitiful talk about the "civil execution" of three members of the Political Bureau?

No, comrades, the Bukharinites will not frighten the Party with liberal chatter about "civil execution." The Party demands that they should wage a determined struggle against the Right deviation and the conciliationist tendency side by side with all the members of the Central Committee of our Party. It demands this of the Bukharin group in order to help to mobilize the working class, to break down the resistance of the class enemies and to make sure that the difficulties of our socialist construction will be overcome.

Either the Bukharinites will fulfill this demand of the Party, in which case the Party will welcome them, or they will not, in which case they will have only themselves to blame. . . .

DISCIPLINING THE INTELLECTUALS

Simultaneously with his forceful new economic policies Stalin imposed stringent party controls over most fields of intellectual life. The toleration of variety came to an end with the silencing or imprisonment of large numbers of nonconforming thinkers, Communist and non-Communist alike. A spirit of class war, devotion to the interests of the party, and unqualified acceptance of the official version of Marxist orthodoxy became the guide lines for Soviet intellectual life, as was made clear in the 1929 purge of philosophers.

. . . 1. The Marxist-Leninist philosophy – dialectical materialism – is the only scientific theory which gives the proletariat a complete world view and weapon in the struggle for the proletarian dictatorship and the social-

FROM: Resolution of the Second All-Union Conference of Marxist-Leninist Scientific Research Institutions, April, 1929, "On Contemporary Problems of the Philosophy of Marxism-Leninism," *Pod Znamenem Marksizma* (Under the Banner of Marxism), No. 5, 1929, pp. 6-8; editor's translation.

ist reconstruction of society. It is the outcome of the whole accumulation of knowledge which mankind has achieved, and is confirmed by the everyday experience of the class struggle and every forward step of scientific research.

The significance of the materialistic dialectic in particular grows under the conditions of the present epoch – the epoch of dying capitalism, of proletarian revolution, and of socialism under construction. The deep contradictions of contemporary bourgeois society, the unusual complexity of all social phenomena, the rapid flux of events, the struggle of nascent social forms with dying ones, can be comprehended only from the point of view of dialectical materialism.

2. The condition of contemporary bourgeois philosophy reflects the disruption of capitalist society. Contemporary bourgeois philosophy not only does not fructify positive knowledge, but in every way retards its development. Sad epigonism, creeping empiricism, formalism, open acceptance of priests and mysticism – such is the philosophical countenance of the contemporary bourgeoisie. . . .

3. At the same time, in the USSR, dialectical materialism is steadily broadening its influence on the broadest masses and more and more is penetrating into all areas of scientific knowledge. . . . The solution of the problems of contemporary natural science from the point of view of dialectical materialism has begun. A cadre of Communist workers in the area of philosophy and natural science has been established and has grown.

4. Meanwhile, however, it is necessary to note that the successes which have been achieved are far from sufficient in comparison to the needs and great tasks facing Marxism-Leninism at the present time. In particular, in the area of natural science only the first steps have been taken to apply the Marxist method. It is essential to strengthen and deepen the connection of work in the field of philosophy with a series of actual problems in the field of social science; it is essential to develop to a significantly broader degree work in instilling the methodology of Marx, Engels and Lenin in the various fields of specialized knowledge. Finally, it is essential to adopt all measures to broaden the cadres of trained workers in the field of Marxist philosophy.

5. The class struggle which is going on under the conditions of developing socialist construction leads to the familiar invigoration of ideological tendencies openly inimical to Marxism-Leninism, as well as various revisionist deviations from it. The purest idealism and revisionism, adapting themselves to the conditions of the dictatorship of the proletariat, sometimes array themselves in Marxist dress and come forth under the flag of

specialized knowledge, or else they distort Marx, Engels and Lenin, and conceal themselves with incorrectly explained citations from their works.

On the other hand, the failure to understand all the complexity of the transitional period and the contradictory character of our development, and the consequences of this – narrow practicality, oversimplification, and failure to understand the vast theoretical tasks posed by our epoch – and on the other hand, the resistance to the penetration of Marxist-Leninism into new fields of knowledge, all feed the various anti- and pseudo-Marxist deviations in philosophy: positivism, the denial of the significance of the materialist dialectic or the distortion of it, deviations from the Marxist and Leninist understanding of the problems of historical materialism, etc. . . .

7. . . . The crisis which contemporary theoretical natural science is undergoing is a continuation of that crisis the analysis of which was made by Lenin. The latest successes of natural science cannot be fitted into the framework of the old, mechanistic and formally logical theories. Bourgeois philosophy lives on the crisis like a parasite, trying to utilize the crisis in natural science for its own ends. However, a real solution of the basic methodological difficulties in scientific research can be achieved only by applying the method of the materialist dialectic. Contemporary natural science "lies in child-birth. It is giving birth to dialectical materialism" (Lenin).

The conference observes that the solution of the tasks of working out the theory of the materialist dialectic and the methodology of contemporary natural science is possible only on the basis of the closest link of the work of Marxists in the field of philosophy and natural science.

8. The proletarian revolution, after shaking up old notions and prejudices among the broad masses, puts forth the task of working out a new world view among the broadest strata of the working class.

A decisive blow to religious ideology can be dealt only by disseminating the dialectical-materialist world view among the masses. Antireligious propaganda can be given positive content only by building it on the foundation of dialectical materialism.

Therefore the conference considers it essential to expand the publishing of atheistic literature, in order to satisfy the new stage of antireligious propaganda. . . .

RAKOVSKY ON BUREAUCRACY

Christian Rokovsky, a Rumanian-born Bulgarian who had served as prime minister of the Ukraine and Soviet ambassador to Great Britain, was one of the most articulate and determined critics of Stalin among the exiled Trotskyists. He began to analyze Soviet social trends in terms that recalled the warnings of the early left-wing Communist deviations: the "workers' state" had come under the domination of a bureaucratic social group which was well on the way to becoming a ruling class in its own right. This view was elaborated by Trotsky in his book *The Revolution Betrayed*, and paralleled later on in *The New Class* by Milovan Djilas.

a) LETTER ON THE CAUSES OF THE DEGENERATION OF THE PARTY AND GOVERNMENTAL APPARATUS

. . . When a class seizes power, a certain part of this class is transformed into agents of the power itself. In this way the bureaucracy arises. In the proletarian state, where capitalistic accumulation is not permitted for members of the ruling party, this differentiation is at first functional, but then it becomes social. I do not say class, but social. I mean that the social position of the Communist who has an automobile at his disposal, a good apartment, regular leaves, and earns the party maximum, is distinct from the position of that same Communist if he works in the coal mines where he gets fifty to sixty rubles a month. (While we are speaking of workers and employees, you know that they are classified among eighteen different grades.)

The second consequence is that part of those functions which formerly the whole party or the whole class itself carried out has now shifted to the power, i.e., to a certain number of people from this party, from this class.

The unity and solidarity which formerly were a natural consequence of the revolutionary class struggle can now be preserved only through a whole system of actions which have as their aim the preservation of the equilibrium between the different groups of that class and that party and their subordination to the common goal.

But this is a long, difficult process, comprising the political education of the ruling class and the knowledge which it must acquire to keep its hands on the governmental, party and union apparatuses, to control them and direct them.

I repeat, this is a matter of education. No one class has been born with the skill to rule – this is acquired only through experience, by making mistakes and learning from one's mistakes. The most ideal Soviet constitution is not in a position to guarantee to the working class the unimpeded application of its dictatorship and its class control, if it does not know how to make use of the constitutional rights granted to it. . . .

FROM: Rakovsky, Letter on the Causes of the Degeneration of the Party and Governmental Apparatus, August 2, 1928 , *Biuleten Oppozitsii* (Bulletin of the Opposition), No. 6, October, 1929, pp. 15,17; editor's translation.

I feel that we should note above all that when we manipulate the concepts "party" and "masses" we should not overlook the content with which a decade of history has invested them.

Neither the working class nor the party is *physically or morally* what it was ten years ago. I think I do not exaggerate when I say that the party member of 1917 would hardly recognize himself in the person of the party member of 1928. . . .

b) CIRCULAR OF THE BOLSHEVIK-LENINIST OPPOSITION

In our declaration to the Central Committee and the Central Control Commission of October 4 of last year the Bolshevik-Leninist opposition warned against extraordinary administrative measures in the villages because they are followed by negative political consequences.

We also warned against the harmful theory of the possibility of building a socialist society in one country, a theory which could arise only in the imagination of a bureaucracy believing in the omnipotence of the apparatus, the theory advanced by Stalin-Bukharin after Lenin's death. We wrote that this theory creates harmful illusions, that it leads to underestimation of the very great difficulties which stand in the path of socialist construction and thus leaves the party and the proletariat unprepared to overcome them. In our declaration we also pointed out that the correct assumptions of principle which were embodied in the decisions of the Sixteenth Party Conference on industrialization and collectivization lead, under conditions of bureaucratic administration, when the class has been replaced by officials who have been transformed into a specialized ruling stratum, not to the development but to the disruption of socialist construction.

We pointed out that the restoration and strengthening of party and workers' democracy is the primary condition for eliminating the avarice, irresponsibility, stubbornness and arbitrariness of the apparatus, the reverse side of which is the oppression, humiliation and lack of rights of the toiling masses. . . .

The Central Committe has issued a directive which is *per se the crudest deviation from socialism.* The slogan of *intensive* collectivization – no matter whether a term of fifteen years is assigned for this, as it was at first, or one year, as they have made it since – is *per se* the greatest economic absurd-

FROM: Rakovsky, Kossior, Muralov and Kasparova, "Circular of the Bolshevik-Leninist Opposition to the Central Committee, the Central Control Commission, and All Members of the CPSU," April, 1930 (*Bulletin of the Opposition*, No. 17-18, November-December, 1930, pp. 11-12, 16).

ity. We are Marxists, and we know that new forms of ownership can be created on the basis of new productive relations. But these productive relations still do not exist. . . .

Secretaries, chairmen of executive committees, procurement officials, heads of co-operatives, heads of state farms, party and nonparty directors of enterprises, specialists, foremen, who, following the line of least resistance, install in our industry the sweat-shop system and factory despotism – here is the real power in the period of the proletarian dictatorship which we are now experiencing. This stage can be characterized as domination by the corporative interests of the various categories of the bureaucracy, and internecine struggle between them.

From the workers' state with bureaucratic perversions – as Lenin defined our form of government – we have developed into *a bureaucratic state with proletarian-Communist survivals*.

Before our eyes a great *class of rulers* has been *taking shape* and is continuing to develop. It has its own internal subdivisions, and grows by way of calculated co-optation, through the direct or indirect appointment system (by way of bureaucratic promotion or the system of fictitious elections). The unifying factor of this unique class is that unique form of private property, governmental power. "The bureaucracy has the state in its possession," wrote Marx, "as rights of private property."

STALIN ON THE LIQUIDATION OF THE KULAKS

Late in 1929 the collectivization of the peasants was shifted from a relatively gradual and nonviolent basis to one of urgency and violence. There was much uneasiness in the party about this, but Stalin identified such qualms with the Right Opposition and denounced them as evidence of pro-capitalist sentiment. In the winter of 1929-30 over half of the Soviet peasantry was collectivized, but at the cost of such a growth in mass hostility to the regime that Stalin himself had to call a temporary retreat. Collectivization was then resumed at a more gradual pace and on the basis of a compromise that allowed small private plots to each peasant family, but the damage to agriculture which the program caused undoubtedly contributed to the grave famine of 1932-33. By the mid-1930's collectivization was virtually complete.

FROM: Stalin, "Problems of Agrarian Policy in the USSR" (Speech at a conference of Marxist students of the agrarian question, December 27, 1929; *Problems of Leninism*, pp. 391-93, 408-9, 411-12).

. . . The so-called theory of the "equilibrium" between the sectors of our national economy is still current among Communists. This theory has, of course, nothing in common with Marxism. Nevertheless, this theory is advocated by a number of people in the camp of the Right deviators.

This theory is based on the assumption that to begin with we have a socialist sector – which is one compartment, as it were – and that in addition we also have a nonsocialist or, if you like, capitalist sector – which is another compartment. These two "compartments" move on different rails and glide peacefully forward, without touching each other. Geometry teaches that parallel lines do not meet. But the authors of this remarkable theory believe that these parallel lines will meet eventually, and that when they do, we will have socialism. This theory overlooks the fact that behind these so-called "compartments" there are classes, and that these compartments move as a result of a fierce class struggle, a life-and-death struggle, a struggle on the principle of "who will win?"

It is not difficult to see that this theory has nothing in common with Leninism. It is not difficult to see that, objectively, the purpose of this theory is to defend the position of individual peasant farming, to arm the kulak elements with a "new" theoretical weapon in their struggle against the collective farms, and to destroy confidence in the collective farms. . . .

. . . Can we advance our socialized industry at an accelerated rate as long as we have an agricultural base, such as is provided by small-peasant farming, which is incapable of expanded reproduction, and which, in addition, is the predominant force in our national economy? No, we cannot. Can Soviet power and the work of socialist construction rest for any length of time on two *different* foundations: on the most large-scale and concentrated socialist industry, and the most scattered and backward, small-commodity peasant farming? No, they cannot. Sooner or later this would be bound to end in the complete collapse of the whole national economy.

What, then, is the solution? The solution lies in enlarging the agricultural units, in making agriculture capable of accumulation, of expanded reproduction, and in thus transforming the agricultural bases of our national economy.

But how are the agricultural units to be enlarged?

There are two ways of doing this. There is the *capitalist* way, which is to enlarge the agricultural units by introducing capitalism in agriculture – a way which leads to the impoverishment of the peasantry and to the development of capitalist enterprises in agriculture. We reject this way as incompatible with the Soviet economic system.

There is a second way: the *socialist* way, which is to introduce collective farms and state farms in agricultue, the way which leads to the amalgamation of the small-peasant farms into large collective farms, employing machinery and scientific methods of farming, and capable of developing further, for such agricultural enterprises can achieve expanded reproduction.

And so, the question stands as follows: either one way or the other, either *back* – to capitalism, or *forward* – to socialism. There is no third way, nor can there be.

The "equilibrium" theory is an attempt to indicate a third way. And precisely because it is based on a third (nonexistent) way, it is utopian and anti-Marxian. . . .

The characteristic feature in the work of our Party during the past year is that we, as a Party, as the Soviet power,

a) have developed an offensive along the whole front against the capitalist elements in the countryside;

b) that this offensive, as you know, has brought about and is bringing about very palpable, *positive* results.

What does this mean? It means that we have passed from the policy of *restricting* the exploiting proclivities of the kulaks to the policy of *eliminating* the kulaks as a class. This means that we have made, and are still making, one of the decisive turns in our whole policy.

Until recently the Party adhered to the policy of *restricting* the exploiting proclivities of the kulaks. . . .

. . . Could we have undertaken such an offensive against the kulaks five years or three years ago? Could we then have counted on success in such an offensive? No, we could not. That would have been the most dangerous adventurism. It would have been playing a very dangerous game at offensive. We would certainly have failed, and our failure would have strengthened the position of the kulaks. Why? Because we still lacked a wide network of state and collective farms in the rural districts which could be used as strongholds in a determined offensive against the kulaks. Because at that time we were not yet able to *substitute* for the capitalist production of the kulaks the socialist production of the collective farms and state farms. . . .

. . . Now we are able to carry on a determined offensive against the kulaks, to break their resistance, to eliminate them as a class and substitute for their output the output of the collective farms and state farms. Now, the kulaks are being expropriated by the masses of poor and middle peasants themselves, by the masses who are putting solid collectivization into practice. Now, the expropriation of the kulaks in the regions of solid collectivization is no longer just an administrative measure. Now, the expropriation of the kulaks is an integral part of the formation and development of the collective farms. Consequently it is now ridiculous and foolish to discourse on the expropriation of the kulaks. You do not lament the loss of the hair of one who has been beheaded.

There is another question which seems no less ridiculous: whether the kulaks should be permitted to join the collective farms. Of course not, for they are sworn enemies of the collective-farm movement. . . .

THE SOCIALIZED ECONOMY AND REVOLUTIONARY LAW

For the first two decades after the revolution the Communists took the Marxian view that law was a manifestation of the class struggle, and hence anticipated the eventual "withering away" of law. Meanwhile, jurists like Pashukanis argued, law was to be employed by the Soviet state not as a set of absolute norms but as a flexible instrument of policy in the transition from economic individualism to socialism.

. . . Our transition period cannot be regarded as a final social-economic conception but must be regarded as a movement – an ever accelerating movement – to socialism. The social-economic conception for whose sake the proletarian dictatorship exists and actively manifests itself is socialism and communism. Behind us lies capitalism. Now we are achieving the revolutionary transition from capitalism to socialism. The production of petty goods is being socialized and becoming socialist production. But we shall be told there is, of course, a "dominant leading sector." That is true. But, of course, when this dominant sector shall have absorbed everything, the disappearance of law will begin thereupon. How do you wish to build a final legal system when you start from social relationships which already comprise the necessity that law of every sort wither away? This is a task completely unthinkable. But if you reduce everything merely to the subjective will element – "to constraint" – then it is inconceivable why Marx and Engels spoke of the "bourgeois" form of law. It is specifically because we are starting from the objective relationships which the proletarian dictatorship is remaking every hour – it is specifically for this reason that we cannot be occupied with the creation of a system of proletarian law. . . .

The relationship of law to policy and to economics is utterly different among us from what it is in bourgeois society. In bourgeois-capitalist society, the legal superstructure should have maximum immobility –

FROM: Pashukanis, "The Soviet State and the Revolution in Law" (1930; English translation in Hugh W. Babb and John Newbold Hazard, *Soviet Legal Philosophy*, Cambridge, Mass., Harvard University Press, 1951, pp. 278–79; reprinted by permission of the publisher).

maximum stability – because it represents a firm framework for the movement of the economic forces whose bearers are capitalist entrepreneurs. Accordingly, the aspiration to create final and integrated systems of law, free from inner contradictions, is characteristic of bourgeois jurists. Among us it is different. We require that our legislation possess maximum elasticity. We cannot fetter ourselves by any sort of system, because every day we are demolishing the structure of production relationships and replacing them by new production relationships: we are doing this consciously and through the medium of the state – which the bourgeois state does not do. The bourgeois state is oriented in form. All the activity of the proletarian state is oriented in the attainment of results according to the essence of the matter. Accordingly, at a time when bourgeois political scientists are striving to depict policy itself as law – to dissolve policy in law – law occupies among us, on the contrary, a subordinate position with reference to policy. We have a system of proletarian policy, but we have no need for any sort of juridic system of proletarian law. The system of proletarian policy consists in this, that – resting upon our attainments in the economic and cultural fields – we transfer production relationships (utilizing the lever of state constraint) into another phase: we make them different. It is sufficient to enumerate such things as industrialization, grain collections under contract with the state, collectivization, the liquidation of the kulaks as a class, the struggle for an industrial and financial plan – all these are examples of how we are achieving a change of arrangements, drawing nearer to socialism and actively changing production relationships and replacing them by others. . . .

STALIN ON THE ENDS AND MEANS OF INDUSTRIALIZATION

In two speeches in 1931 Stalin spelled out some of the political and social implications of a socialist state dedicated to industrial development. He discarded the last pretenses of collectivistic equality in favor of a system of strict individual responsibility and incentives, with rewards in proportion to effort and skill. He recognized that the technical officialdom, properly trained, paid, and respected, is the backbone of a modern industrial system. At the same time he lent urgency to the industrialization effort by pointing to considerations of national power and defense.

FROM: Stalin, "The Tasks of Business Executives" (Speech at the First All-Union Conference of Managers of Socialist Industry, February, 1931; *Problems of Leninism*, pp. 454-58).

a) THE TASKS OF BUSINESS EXECUTIVES

. . . The underlying cause of wrecking activities is the class struggle. Of course, the class enemy is furiously resisting the socialist offensive. This alone, however, is not an adequate explanation for the luxuriant growth of wrecking activities.

How is it that sabotage has assumed such wide dimensions? Who is to blame for this? We are to blame. Had we handled the business of industrial management differently, had we started much earlier to learn the technique of the business, to master technique, had we more frequently and efficiently intervened in the management of production, the wreckers could not have done so much damage.

We must ourselves become experts, masters of the business; we must turn to technical science – such was the lesson life itself was teaching us. But neither the first warning nor even the second brought about the necessary change. It is time, it is high time that we turned towards technique. It is time we cast aside the old slogan, the obsolete slogan of nonintereference in technique, and ourselves become specialists, experts, complete masters of our economy.

It is frequently asked: Why have we not one-man management? We do not have it and will not have it until we have mastered technique. Until there are among us Bolsheviks a sufficient number of people thoroughly familiar with technique, economics and finance, we will not have real one-man management. You can write as many resolutions as you please, take as many vows as you please, but, unless you master the technique, economics and finance of the mill, factory or mine, nothing will come of it, there will be no one-man management.

Hence, the task is for us to master technique ourselves, to become the masters of the business ourselves. This is the sole guarantee that our plans will be carried out in full, and that one-man management will be established.

This, of course, is no easy matter; but it can certainly be accomplished. Science, technical experience, knowledge, are all things that can be acquired. We may not have them today, but tomorrow we will. The main thing is to have the passionate Bolshevik desire to master technique, to master the science of production. Everything can be achieved, everything can be overcome, if there is a passionate desire to do so.

It is sometimes asked whether it is not possible to slow down the tempo somewhat, to put a check on the movement. No, comrades, it is not possible! The tempo must not be reduced! On the contrary, we must increase it as much as is within our powers and possibilities. This is dictated to us by our obligations to the workers and peasants of the U.S.S.R. This is dictated to us by our obligations to the working class of the whole world.

To slacken the tempo would mean falling behind. And those who fall behind get beaten. But we do not want to be beaten. No, we refuse to be beaten! One feature of the history of old Russia was the continual beatings she suffered because of her backwardness. She was beaten by the Mongol khans. She was beaten by the Turkish beys. She was beaten by the Swedish feudal lords. She was beaten by the Polish and Lithuanian gentry. She was beaten by the British and French capitalists. She was beaten by the Japanese barons. All beat her – because of her backwardness, military backwardness, cultural backwardness, political backwardness, industrial backwardness, agricultural backwardness. They beat her because to do so was profitable and could be done with impunity. Do you remember the words of the prerevolutionary poet: "You are poor and abundant, mighty and impotent, Mother Russia."* Those gentlemen were quite familiar with the verses of the old poet. They beat her, saying: "You are abundant," so one can enrich oneself at your expense. They beat her, saying: "You are poor and impotent," so you can be beaten and plundered with impunity. Such is the law of the exploiters – to beat the backward and the weak. It is the jungle law of capitalism. You are backward, you are weak – therefore you are wrong; hence, you can be beaten and enslaved. You are mighty – therefore you are right; hence, we must be wary of you.

That is why we must no longer lag behind.

In the past we had no fatherland, nor could we have one. But now that we have overthrown capitalism and power is in our hands, in the hands of the people, we have a fatherland, and we will defend its independence. Do you want our socialist fatherland to be beaten and to lose its independence? If you do not want this you must put an end to its backwardness in the shortest possible time and develop genuine Bolshevik tempo in building up its socialist system of economy. There is no other way. That is why Lenin said on the eve of the October Revolution: "Either perish, or overtake and outstrip the advanced capitalist countries."

We are fifty or a hundred years behind the advanced countries. We must make good this distance in ten years. Either we do it, or we shall be crushed.

This is what our obligations to the workers and peasants of the U.S.S.R. dictate to us.

But we have other, still more serious and more important obligations. They are obligations to the world proletariat. They coincide with our obli-

*From Nekrasov's "Who Is Happy in Russia?" (1876) – Ed.

gations to the workers and peasants of the U.S.S.R. But we place them higher. The working class of the U.S.S.R. is part of the world working class. We achieved victory not solely through the efforts of the working class of the U.S.S.R., but also thanks to the support of the working class of the world. Without this support we would have been torn to pieces long ago. It is said that our country is the shock brigade of the proletariat of all countries. This is a fitting definition. But this imposes very serious obligations upon us. Why does the international proletariat support us? How did we merit this support? By the fact that we were the first to hurl ourselves into the battle against capitalism, we were the first to establish a working-class state, we were the first to start building socialism. By the fact that we are doing work which, if successful, will change the whole world and free the entire working class. But what is needed for success? The elimination of our backwardness, the development of a high Bolshevik tempo of construction. We must march forward in such a way that the working class of the whole world, looking at us, may say: This is my vanguard, this is my shock brigade, this is my working-class state, this is my fatherland; they are promoting their cause, which is *our* cause, and they are doing this well; let us support them against the capitalists and promote the cause of the world revolution. Must we not live up to the hopes of the world's working class, must we not fulfill our obligations to them? Yes, we must if we do not want utterly to disgrace ourselves.

Such are our obligations, internal and international.

As you see, they dictate to us a Bolshevik tempo of development.

I will not say that we have accomplished nothing in regard to economic management during these years. In fact, we have accomplished a good deal. We have doubled our industrial output as compared with the prewar level. We have created the largest-scale agricultural production in the world. But we could have accomplished more had we tried hard during this period really to master production, the technique of production, the financial and economic side of it.

In ten years at most we must make good the distance which separates us from the advanced capitalist countries. We have all the "objective" possibilities for this. The only thing lacking is the ability to take proper advantage of these possibilities. And that depends on us. *Only* on us! It is time we learned to take advantage of these possibilities. It is time to put an end to the rotten policy of noninterference in production. It is time to adopt a new policy, a policy adapted to the present times – the policy of *interfering in everything*. If you are a factory manager, then interfere in all the affairs of the factory, look into everything, let nothing escape you, learn and learn again. Bolsheviks must master technique. It is time Bolsheviks themselves became experts. In the period of reconstruction technique decides everything. And a business executive who does not want to study technique, who does not want to master technique, is a joke and not an executive.

It is said that it is hard to master technique. That is not true! There are no fortresses which Bolsheviks cannot capture. We have solved a number of most difficult problems. We have overthrown capitalism. We have assumed power. We have built up a huge socialist industry. We have swung the middle peasants to the path of socialism. We have already accomplished what is most important from the point of view of construction. What remains to be done is not so much: to study technique, to master science. And when we have done that we will develop a tempo of which we dare not even dream at present.

And we will do that if we really want to.

b) NEW CONDITIONS – NEW TASKS IN ECONOMIC CONSTRUCTION

. . . What is the cause of the heavy turnover of labour power?

The cause is the wrong structure of wages, the wrong wage scales, the "Leftist" practice of wage equalization. In a number of our factories wage scales are drawn up in such a way as to practically wipe out the difference between skilled and unskilled labour, between heavy and light work. The consequence of wage equalization is that the unskilled worker lacks the incentive to become a skilled worker and is thus deprived of the prospect of advancement; as a result he feels himself a "visitor" in the factory, working only temporarily so as to "earn a little" and then go off to "seek his fortune" elsewhere. The consequence of wage equalization is that the skilled worker is obligated to wander from factory to factory until he finds one where his skill is properly appreciated.

Hence, the "general" drift from factory to factory; hence, the heavy turnover of labour power.

In order to put an end to this evil we must abolish wage equalization and discard the old wage scales. In order to put an end to this evil we must draw up wage scales that will take into account the difference between skilled and unskilled labour, between heavy and light work. We canot tolerate a situation where a rolling-mill hand in a steel mill earns no more than a sweeper. We cannot tolerate a situation where a locomotive driver earns only as much as a copying clerk. Marx and Lenin said that the difference between skilled and unskilled labour would exist even under socialism,

FROM: Stalin, "New Conditions – New Tasks in Economic Construction" (Speech at a conference of business executives, June, 1931; *Problems of Leninism*, pp. 463-64, 466-67, 471-73).

even after classes had been abolished; that only under communism would this difference disappear and that, consequently, even under socialism "wages" must be paid according to work performed and not according to needs. But the equalitarians among our business executives and trade union officials do not agree with this and believe that under our Soviet system this difference has already disappered. Who is right, Marx and Lenin, or the equalitarians? We must take it that it is Marx and Lenin who are right. But if that is so, it follows that whoever draws up wage scales on the "principle" of wage equalization, without taking into account the difference between skilled and unskilled labour, breaks with Marxism, breaks with Leninism. . . .

. . . Can it be said that the present organization of labour in our factories meets the modern requirements of production? Unfortunately, this cannot be said. At all events, there are still a number of factories where work is organized abominably, where instead of order and coordination of work there is disorder and confusion, where instead of responsibility for the work there is absolute irresponsibility, absolute *lack of personal responsibility*.

What does lack of personal responsibility mean? It means complete lack of responsibility for work that is entrusted to anyone, lack of responsibility for machinery and tools. Naturally, when there is not personal responsibility we cannot expect a tangible increase in productivity of labour, and improvement in the quality of the goods, the exercise of care in handling machinery and tools. You know what lack of personal responsibility led to on the railways. It is leading to the same result in industry. We have abolished the system under which there was lack of personal responsibility on the railways and have thus improved their work. We must do the same in industry in order to raise its work to a higher level.

Formerly, we could "manage" somehow or other with bad organization of labour, which gets on quite nicely without personal responsibility, without every man being responsible for the job entrusted to him. Now it is a different matter. Conditions have entirely changed. With the present vast scale of production and the existence of giant enterprises, lack of personal responsibility has become the plague of industry which is jeopardizing all our achievements in our factories in the sphere of production and organization. . . .

. . . We can no longer manage our industry with the very small engineering, technical and administrative staffs with which we managed it formerly. It follows that the old centres for training engineering and technical forces are no longer adequate, that we must create a network of new centres – in the Urals, in Siberia and in Central Asia. We must now ensure the supply of three times, five times the number of engineering, technical and administrative staffs for industry if we really intend to carry out the program of the socialist industrialization of the U.S.S.R.

But we do not need just *any kind* of administrative, engineering and technical forces. We need *such* administrative, engineering and technical forces as are capable of understanding the policy of the working class of our country, are capable of assimilating that policy and are ready to carry it out conscientiously. And what does this mean? This means that our country has entered a phase of development in which the *working class must create its own industrial and technical intelligentsia*, one that is capable of upholding the interests of the working class in production as the interests of the ruling class.

No ruling class has managed without its own intelligentsia. There are no grounds for believing that the working class of the U.S.S.R. can manage without its own industrial and technical intelligentsia.

The Soviet government has taken this fact into account and has opened wide the doors of all the higher educational institutions in every branch of national economy to members of the working class and labouring peasantry. You know that tens of thousands of working class and peasant youths are now attending higher educational institutions. Formerly, under capitalism, the higher educational institutions were the monopoly of the scions of the rich – today, under the Soviet system, the working class and peasant youth predominate in these institutions. There is no doubt that our educational institutions will soon be turning out thousands of new technicians and engineers, new leaders for our industries.

But that is only one side of the matter. The other side is that the industrial and technical intelligentsia of the working class will be recruited not only from among those who have passed through the institutions of higher learning, but also from among practical workers in our factories, from the skilled workers, from among the working-class cultural forces in the mills, factories and mines. The initiators of socialist emulation, the leaders of shock brigades, those who inspire in practice labour enthusiasm, the organizers of work in the various sections of our construction – such is the new stratum of the working class that, together with the comrades who have passed through the institutions of higher learning, must form the core of the intelligentsia of the working class, the core of the administrative staffs of our industry. It is our duty not to discourage these "rank-and-file" comrades who show initiative, but boldly to promote them to responsible positions; to give them the opportunity to display their organizing abilities and the opportunity to supplement their knowledge; to create suitable conditions for their work, not stinting money for this purpose. . . .

STALIN ON THE SANCTITY OF LENINISM

In 1931, reacting to an article which cast doubt on Lenin's infallibility, Stalin made it clear that the pursuit of truth – "rotten liberalism" – would henceforth be subordinated to considerations of the glory and discipline of the party.

Dear Comrades!

I emphatically protest against the publication in *Proletarskaya Revolyutsia* (No. 6, 1930) of Slutsky's anti-Party and semi-Trotskyite article, "The Bolsheviks on German Social-Democracy in the Period of its Prewar Crisis," as a discussion article.

Slutsky asserts that Lenin (the Bolsheviks) underestimated the danger of *centrism* in German Social-Democracy and in pre-war Social-Democracy in general; that is, he underestimated the danger of camouflaged opportunism, the danger of conciliation with opportunism. In other words, according to Slutsky, Lenin (the Bolsheviks) did not wage a relentless struggle against opportunism, for, in essence, underestimation of centrism is tantamount to the renunciation of a forceful struggle against opportunism. Thus, it is suggested that in the period before the war Lenin was not yet a real Bolshevik; that it was only in the period of the imperialist war, or even at the close of that war, that Lenin became a real Bolshevik.

This is the tale Slutsky tells in his article. And you, instead of branding this new-found "historian" as a slanderer and falsifier, enter into discussion with him, provide him with a forum. I cannot refrain from protesting against the publication of Slutsky's article in your journal as a discussion article, for the question of Lenin's *Bolshevism*, the question as to whether Lenin *did* or *did not* wage a relentless principled struggle against centrism as a certain form of opportunism, the question as to whether Lenin *was* or *was not* a real Bolshevik, cannot be made the subject of discussion. . . .

Everyone knows that Leninism was born, grew up and became strong in its ruthless struggle against opportunism of every brand, including centrism in the West (Kautsky) and centrism in our country (Trotsky, etc.). This cannot be denied even by the outspoken enemies of Bolshevism. It is an axiom. But you are trying to drag us back by turning an axiom into a problem requiring "further analysis." Why? On what grounds? Perhaps through ignorance of the history of Bolshevism? Perhaps for the sake of a rotten liberalism, so that the Slutskys and other disciples of Trotsky may not be able to say that they are being gagged? A rather strange sort of

FROM: Stalin, "Some Questions Concerning the History of Bolshevism" (Letter to the Editorial Board of *Proletarian Revolution*, 1931; *Problems of Leninism*, pp. 483-84, 493-94).

liberalism, this, exercised at the expense of the vital interests of Bolshevism. . . .

. . . The more reliable method of testing the Bolseviks by their deeds would have upset Slutsky's whole position in a flash.

Because a test of the Bolsheviks by their deeds would have shown that the Bolsheviks are the *only* revolutionary organization in the world which has completely smashed the opportunists and centrists and driven them out of the Party.

Because the real deeds and the real history of the Bolsheviks would have shown that Slutsky's teachers, the Trotskyites, were the *principal* and *basic* group which fostered centrism in Russia, and for this purpose created a special organization – the August Bloc,* which was a hotbed of centrism.

Because a test of the Bolsheviks by their deeds would have exposed Slutsky once and for all as a falsifier of the history of our Party, who is trying to cover up the centrism of prewar Trotskyism by slanderously accusing Lenin and the Bolsheviks of underestimating the danger of centrism.

That, comrade editors, is how matters stand with Slutsky and his article.

As you see, the editorial board made a mistake in permitting a discussion with a falsifier of the history of our Party.

What induced the editorial board to take this wrong road?

I think that they were induced to take that road by the rotten liberalism which has spread to some extent among a section of the Bolsheviks. Some Bolsheviks think that Trotskyism is a faction of communism – one which makes mistakes, it is true, which does many foolish things, is sometimes even anti-Soviet, but which, nevertheless, is a faction of communism. Hence, there is a somewhat liberal attitude towards the Trotskyites and Trotskyite-minded people. It need hardly be proved that such a view of Trotskyism is profoundly wrong and pernicious. As a matter of fact, Trotskyism has long ceased to be a faction of communism. As a matter of fact, Trotskyism is the vanguard of the counterrevolutionary bourgeoisie which is fighting communism, fighting the Soviet regime, fighting the building of socialism in the U.S.S.R. . . .

THE NEW EDUCATIONAL POLICY

The impact of the industrialization drive was quickly felt in various areas of social policy, where revolutionary notions about conditioning the ideal man gave way to the practical necessity for imparting knowledge and evoking effort. In a series of decrees beginning

*"August Bloc": the largely Menshevik group which met in Vienna in August, 1912 – Ed.

in 1931, the experiment in progressive education was repudiated in favor of academic education of the traditional disciplinarian type.

The "polytechnical" approach stressed at this time (to combine regular instruction with practical labor training) was abandoned between the late thirties and Stalin's death. Khrushchev failed in his effort to revive it in the 1950s.

. . . The Soviet school, taking as its task "the preparation of the all-around developed member of communist society," gives the children an incomparably broader social-political outlook and more general development than the pre-revolutionary and bourgeois school. In the last few years the level of general education of the children in the Soviet school has risen.

Especially significant successes have been achieved by the school since the historic decision of the Sixteenth Party Congress [July, 1930] on the introduction of universal primary education. Just in the last year the number of students in the primary and secondary school has risen from 13.5 million to 20 million. In addition to this the factory-plant schools and technicums have 1,400,000 students.

Together with decisive steps toward the realization of compulsory instruction for children of school age the school has moved significantly forward on the path of combining school instruction with productive labor and social work, thanks to which the fundamental reconstruction of the school on the basis of polytechnicism has been started. . . .

However, in spite of all these achievements, the Central Committee states that the Soviet school is still far from meeting the tremendous demands which are placed upon it in the present stage of socialist construction. The Central Committee considers that a radical inadequacy of the school at the present moment lies in the fact that instruction in the school does not give sufficient breadth of general educational knowledge, and does not satisfactorily meet the task of preparing literate people who have mastered the basic sciences (physics, chemistry, mathematics, the native language, geography, etc.), for the technicums and higher schools. As a result of this, the polytechnicization of the school in many cases acquires a formal character and does not prepare children as all-around developed builders of socialism who have tied theory and practice together and have mastered technique. . . .

While applying in the Soviet school various new methods of instruction which can facilitate the education of energetic and initiative-possessing

FROM: Decision of the Central Committee of the All-Union Communist Party on the Primary and Secondary School, September 5, 1931, *V Puti k Novoi Shkole* (On the Way to the New School), October, 1931, pp. 3-4, 8; editor's translation.

participants in the building of socialism, it is essential to unleash a decisive struggle against light-minded methodological projectism, the dissemination on a mass scale of methods not verified in preliminary practice, which has recently been revealed with special clarity in the application of the so-called "project method." Attempts, stemming from the anti-Leninist theory of the "withering-away of the school," to put all school work on the basis of the so-called "project method" have actually led to the ruin of the school. . . .

In the period of socialism, when the proletariat is accomplishing the final destruction of classes under conditions of sharpened class struggle, sustained communist education in the Soviet school and intensification of the struggle against all attempts to inoculate children in the Soviet school with elements of anti-proletarian ideology assume exceptionally weighty significance.

In connection with this the Central Committee proposes that the party organizations strengthen their guidance of the school and take under their immediate supervision the setting up of the teaching of social-political discipline in the seven-year schools, pedagogical technicums and higher pedagogical institutes.

Confirming the necessity of the timely fulfillment of the decision of the Central Committee of July 25, 1930, on universal compulsory primary instruction, the Central Committee proposes, toward the end of the quickest realization of the demands of the party program on general and polytechnical education for all children and youth up to 17 years of age, that the Council of People's Commissars of the USSR work out a plan of *universal compulsory seven-year instruction.* . . .

The Central Committee underscores the growing significance and role of the school in the building of socialism. The Central Committee proposes that all organizations systematically and undeviatingly conduct a struggle against opportunist anti-Leninist perversions of the policy of the party in the region of school work. The success of the struggle with the chief danger on the path of setting up the polytechnical school – the right-opportunist claimants of party policy, who would lead it to reject the polytechnicization of the school, to attempt to preserve the old, verbalistic school, to divorce theoretical instruction and practice – requires the intensification of the struggle against left-opportunist perversions, against theories of the "withering-away of the school" and reduction of the role of the teacher.

The Central Committee directs the attention of all party organizations to the necessity of decisively heightening attention on the mass school, the work of the teacher, and the strengthening of day-to-day concrete guidance of the school.

STALIN'S SOCIAL IDEAL

At the Seventeenth Party Congress in 1934, Stalin set forth his revised conception of the positive virtues of socialism – class struggle instead of the withering away of the state, inequality instead of equality, and the decisiveness of individual effort instead of the sway of economic circumstances. By this time Stalin's reinterpretation of doctrine under cover of a pretended orthodoxy had cut the Communist movement entirely off from any guiding influence of Marxist principle.

. . . It goes without saying that a classless society cannot come of itself, spontaneously, as it were. It has to be achieved and built by the efforts of all the working people, by strengthening the organs of the dictatorship of the proletariat, by intensifying the class struggle, by abolishing classes, by eliminating the remnants of the capitalist classes, and in battles with enemies both internal and external.

The point is clear, one would think.

And yet, who does not know that the promulgation of this clear and elementary thesis of Leninism has given rise to not a little confusion and to unhealthy sentiments among a section of Party members? The thesis that we are advancing towards a classless society – which was put forward as a slogan – was interpreted by them to mean a spontaneous process. And they began to reason in this way: If it is a classless society, then we can relax the class struggle, we can relax the dictatorship of the proletariat, and get rid of the state altogether, since it is fated to wither away soon in any case. They dropped into a state of moon-calf ecstasy, in the expectation that soon there will be no classes, and therefore no class struggle, and therefore no cares and worries, and therefore we can lay down our arms and retire – to sleep and to wait for the advent of a classless society. (*General laughter*). . . .

It goes without saying that if this confusion of mind and these non-Bolshevik sentiments obtained a hold over the majority of our Party, the Party would find itself demobilized and disarmed.

Now take the question of the agricultural *artel* and the agricultural *commune*. Everybody admits now that under present conditions the artel is the only proper form of the collective-farm movement. . . .

Unlike the artel, where only the means of production are socialized, the communes, until recently, socialized not only the means of production, but also the appurtenances of life of every member of the commune; that is to say, the members of a commune, unlike the members of an artel, did not

FROM: Stalin, Report on the Work of the Central Committee, to the Seventeenth Congress of the CPSU(B) (January, 1934; *Problems of Leninism*, pp. 631-32, 634-35, 643-45).

individually own poultry, small livestock, a cow, grain, or household land. This means that in the commune the individual, everyday interests of the members have not so much been taken into account and combined with the public interests as they have been eclipsed by the latter in the pursuit of petty-bourgeois equalization. . . .

. . . There are those who think that in declaring the artel to be the fundamental form of the collective-farm movement the Party has drifted away from socialism, has retreated from the commune, from the higher form of the collective-farm movement, to a lower form. The question arises – why? Because, it is suggested, there is no equality in the artel, since differences in the requirements and in the individual lives of the members of the artel are preserved; whereas in the commune there is equality, because the requirements and the individual life of all its members have been made equal. But in the first place, there are no longer any communes which practise levelling, equalization in requirements and in individual life. Practice has shown that the communes would certainly have been doomed had they not abandoned equalization and had they not actually assumed the status of artels. Hence, it is useless talking about what no longer exists. Secondly, every Leninist knows (that is, if he is a real Leninist) that equalization in the sphere of requirements and individual life is a piece of reactionary petty-bourgeois absurdity worthy of a primitive sect of ascetics, but not of a socialist society organized on Marxian lines; for we cannot expect all people to have the same requirements and tastes, and all people to live their individual lives on the same model. And, finally, are not differences in requirements and in individual life still preserved among the workers? Does that mean that the workers are more remote from socialism than the members of the agricultural communes?

These people evidently think that socialism calls for equalization, for levelling the requirements and the individual lives of the members of society. Needless to say, such an assumption has nothing in common with Marxism, with Leninism. By equality Marxism means, not equalization of individual requirements and individual life, but the abolition of classes, i.e., a) the equal emancipation of all working people from exploitation after the capitalists have been overthrown and expropriated; b) the equal abolition for all of private property in the means of production after they have been converted into the property of the whole of society; c) the equal duty of all to work according to their ability, and the equal right of all working people to receive remuneration according to the amount of work performed (*socialist* society); d) the equal duty of all to work according to their ability, and the equal right of all working people to receive remuneration according to their needs (*communist* society). Furthermore, Marxism proceeds from the assumption that people's tastes and requirements are not, and cannot be, identical, equal, in regard to quality or quantity, either in the period of socialism or in the period of communism.

That is the Marxian conception of equality. . . .

. . . Victory never comes of itself – it usually has to be attained. Good resolutions and declarations in favour of the general line of the Party are only a beginning; they merely express the desire for victory, but not the victory itself. After the correct line has been laid down, after a correct solution of the problem has been found, success depends on how the work is organized; on the organization of the struggle for the application of the Party line; on the proper selection of personnel; on the way a check is kept on the fulfilment of the decisions of the leading bodies. Otherwise the correct line of the Party and the correct solutions are in danger of being seriously prejudiced. Furthermore, after the correct political line has been laid down, organizational work decides everything, including the fate of the political line itself, its success or failure.

As a matter of fact, victory was achieved and won by a stern and systematic struggle against all sorts of difficulties that stood in the way of carrying out the Party line; by overcoming the difficulties; by mobilizing the Party and the working class for the purpose of overcoming the difficulties; by organizing the struggle to overcome the difficulties; by removing inefficient executives and choosing better ones, capable of waging the struggle against difficulties.

What are these difficulties; and wherein are they lodged?

They are difficulties attending our organizational work, difficulties attending our organizational leadership. They are lodged in ourselves, in our leading people, in our organizations, in the apparatus of our Party, state, economic, trade union, Young Communist League, and all other organizations.

We must realize that the strength and prestige of our Party, state, economic, and all other organizations, and of their leaders, have grown to an unprecedented degree, and precisely because their strength and prestige have grown to an unprecedented degree, it is their work that now determines everything, or nearly everything. There can be no justification for references to so-called objective conditions. Now that the correctness of the Party's political line has been confirmed by the experience of a number of years, and that there is no longer any doubt as to the readiness of the workers and peasants to support this line, the part played by so-called objective conditions has been reduced to a minimum; whereas the part played by our organizations and their leaders has become decisive, exceptional. What does this mean? It means that from now on nine tenths of the responsibility for the failures and defects in our work rest, not on "objective" conditions, but on ourselves, and on ourselves alone. . . .

Bureaucracy and red tape in the administrative apparatus; idle chatter about "leadership in general" instead of real and concrete leadership; the functional structure of our organizations and lack of individual responsibility; lack of personal responsibility in work, and wage equalization; the absence of a systematic check upon the fulfilment of decisions; fear of self-criticism – these are the sources of our difficulties; this is where our difficulties are now lodged. . . .

THE NEW HISTORY

In keeping with Stalin's stress on individual responsibility, the old ultra-Marxist line of economic determinism in history and social science was sharply criticized in 1934. A much more conventional presentation of history, with emphasis on individuals and nations, was enjoined upon Soviet schools and historians. This was followed by the repudiation of anti-nationalist attacks on the past of Czarist Russia.

The Council of People's Commissars of the USSR and the Central Committee of the All-Union Communist Party (Bolsheviks) find that the teaching of history in schools of the USSR is not conducted satisfactorily. The textbooks and the instruction have an abstract, schematic character. Instead of the teaching of civic history in a lively, engaging form with an exposition of the most important events and facts in their chronological sequence, with characterizations of historical personages, the pupils are presented with abstract definitions of socio-economic formations, which thus replace the connected exposition of civic history with abstract sociological schemes.

The decisive condition of a firm mastery of the history course by the pupils is the observance of historical and chronological sequence in the exposition of historical events, with mandatory consolidation in the pupils' memory of important historical events, historical personages, and chronological dates. Only such a history course can ensure to the pupils the necessary understanding, clarity, and concreteness of historical material, on which basis alone is it possible to have the correct analysis and correct generalizations about historical events that will lead pupils to a Marxist understanding of history. . . .

FROM: Decree of the Council of People's Commissars of the USSR and the Central Committee of the All-Union Communist Party (Bolsheviks), "On the Teaching of Civic History in Schools of the USSR," May 16, 1934; *Pravda*, May 17, 1934 (editor's translation).

THE NEW NATIONALISM

After an accumulation of hints about the paramountcy of national interest, the Soviet government proclaimed the supreme virtue of national tradition and patriotism – which, incidentally, served as the justification for intensifying the penalties for treason.

. . . The country of the October Revolution is endlessly dear to the workers, the kolkhozniks [collective farmers] and the Soviet intelligentsia. The working people are bound to their factories, sovkhozes [state farms] and kolkhozes [collective farms], to their soil and to their culture by the indissoluble links of blood, heroism and love. For proletarians and kolkhozniks, for honest Soviet specialists, there is nothing more beautiful and more clear than their own country liberated from the yoke of landowners and capitalists.

The best traditions of the Civil War and of the struggle with the interventionists, when the workers and peasants were armed to defend their right to a new life, are now being multiplied in the progress of techniques and Socialistic culture. That is why the Soviet Union has become an impregnable fortress and is capable of crushing all those who would dare to attempt to violate the sanctity of its boundaries.

For our fatherland! This call fans the flame of heroism, the flame of creative initiative in pursuits and all fields of our rich life. For our fatherland! This call arouses millions of workers and alerts them in the defence of their great country.

The defence of the fatherland is the supreme law of life. And he who raises his hand against his country, he who betrays his country should be destroyed.

Today we publish the decree of the Central Executive Committee of the U.S.S.R. regarding the supplementing of the statutes of the state criminal code with articles on treason. The Soviet country is very dear to the workers and kolkhozniks. They have paid for it dearly in blood and suffering in their struggle with exploiters and interventionists and they will not allow anyone to betray their country and will not allow anyone to bargain with her interests.

For high treason, for acts detrimental to the country's military might, or state independence, or inviolability of her territories, for espionage, for divulging military or state secrets, for deserting to the enemy, or escaping

FROM: "For the Fatherland!" *Pravda*, June 9, 1934 (English translation in *The Communist Conspiracy, Part I: Communism outside the U. S., Section B: the USSR*; U. S. House of Representatives Report No. 2241, 84th Congress, 2nd Session, Washington, Government Printing Office, 1956, pp. 287-88).

across the border, the Soviet court will punish the guilty by shooting or by confiscating all his property. In the case of a civilian, some leniency will be shown according to circumstances, and for the death penalty will be substituted the confiscation of his property or imprisonment for ten years. For a person in military service, however, for treason there will be only one measure of punishment – execution by shooting with confiscation of all his property. Individual members of his family are also responsible for the acts of traitors. In the case of the escape or flight across the border of a person in military service, all mature members of his family, if they are implicated in aiding the criminal, or knew of his intentions and did not report them to the authorities, are punished by imprisonment for five to ten years with confiscation of all their property.

The other members of the family of the traitor and all his dependents at the time he committed treason are subject to disfranchisement and exile to some remote region in Siberia for five years.

Traitors should be punished unmercifully. On the other hand, if a person in military service was aware of a plot to betray the government or of an act of betrayal and did not report this to the authorities, he is subject to imprisonment for ten years. One cannot be a neutral observer where the interests of the country or the workers and peasants are concerned. This is a terrible crime; this is complicity in the crime.

This decree of the Central Executive Committee gives the workers of the great Soviet Union a new weapon in their hands in the struggle against the enemies of the proletariat dictatorship. The one hundred and seventy million working people who regard the Soviet land as their own mother who has nursed them to a happy and joyous life will deal with the traitors of their fatherland with all their force.

For the fatherland, for its honor and glory, might and well-being!

SOCIALIST REALISM

Artistic activity, like other fields of intellectual endeavor in the USSR, was subjected to stringent party control from 1929 on. After a dismal experiment in "proletarian" art the party line shifted to conservative nineteenth-century fashions which were applied to the task of propagandizing an official optimism. The famous revolutionary writer Maxim Gorky was restored to favor as the leading exponent of the "new" literature, which he extolled at a writer's congress in 1935 as "socialist realism." With some variation in the rigor of its enforcement, this has been the Communist line in the arts ever since, while modernistic experiments have been systematically condemned as "bourgeois formalism."

The Communist-Leninist Party, the workers' and peasants' government of the Union of Socialist Soviets, which have destroyed capitalism throughout the length and breadth of tsarist Russia, which have handed over political power to the workers and the peasants, and which are organizing a free classless society, have made it the object of their daring, sage and indefatigable activity to free the working masses from the age-old yoke of an old and outworn history, of the capitalist development of culture, which today has glaringly exposed all its vices and its creative decrepitude. And it is from the height of this great aim that we honest writers of the Union of Soviets must examine, appraise and organize our work. . . .

. . . We must grasp and fully realize the fact that in our country the socially organized labour of semi-literate workers and a primitive peasantry has in the short space of ten years created stupendous values and armed itself superbly for defence against an enemy's attack. Proper appreciation of this fact will reveal to us the cultural and revolutionary power of a doctrine which unites the whole proletariat of the world.

All of us – writers, factory workers, collective farmers – still work badly and cannot even fully master everything that has been made by us and for us. Our working masses do not yet quite grasp the fact that they are working only for themselves. This feeling is smouldering everywhere, but it has not yet blazed up into a mighty and joyous flame. But nothing can kindle until it has reached a certain temperature, and nobody ever was so splendidly capable of raising the temperature of labour energy as is the party organized by the genius of Vladimir Lenin, and the present-day leader of this party.

As the principal hero of our books we should choose labour, i.e., a person, organized by the processes of labour, who in our country is armed with the full might of modern technique, a person who, in his turn, so organizes labour that it becomes easier and more productive, raising it to the level of an art . . . .

The party leadership of literature must be thoroughly purged of all philistine influences. Party members active in literature must not only be the teachers of ideas which will muster the energy of the proletariat in all countries for the last battle for its freedom; the party leadership must, in all its conduct, show a morally authoritative force. This force must imbue literary workers first and foremost with a consciousness of their collective responsibility for all that happens in their midst. Soviet literature, with all

FROM: Gorky, "Soviet Literature" (Speech at The First All-Union Congress of Soviet Writers, August, 1934; English translation in H. G. Scott, ed., *Problems of Soviet Literature*, Moscow, Cooperative Publishing Society of Foreign Workers in the U.S.S.R., 1935, pp. 53-54, 64-67).

its diversity of talents, and the steadily growing number of new and gifted writers, should be organized as an integral collective body, as a potent instrument of socialist culture.

The Writers' Union is not being created merely for the purpose of bodily uniting all artists of the pen, but so that professional unification may enable them to comprehend their corporate strength, to define with all possible clarity their varied tendencies, creative activity, guiding principles, and harmoniously to merge all aims in that unity which is guiding all the creative working energies of the country.

The idea, of course, is not to restrict individual creation, but to furnish it with the widest means of continued powerful development.

It should be realized that critical realism originated as the individual creation of "superfluous people," who, being incapable of the struggle for existence, not finding a place in life, and more or less clearly realizing the aimlessness of personal being, understood this aimlessness merely as the senselessness of all phenomena in social life and in the whole historical process.

Without in any way denying the broad, immense work of critical realism, and while highly appreciating its formal achievements in the art of word painting, we should understand that this realism is necessary to us only for throwing light on the survivals of the past, for fighting them, and extirpating them.

But this form of realism did not and cannot serve to educate socialist individuality, for in criticizing everything, it asserted nothing, or else, at the worst, reverted to an assertion of what it had itself repudiated.

Socialist individuality, as exemplified by our heroes of labour, who represent the flower of the working class, can develop only under conditions of collective labour, which has set itself the supreme and wise aim of liberating the workers of the whole world from the man-deforming power of capitalism.

Life, as asserted by socialist realism, is deeds, creativeness, the aim of which is the uninterrupted development of the priceless individual faculties of man, with a view to his victory over the forces of nature, for the sake of his health and longevity, for the supreme joy of living on an earth which, in conformity with the steady growth of his requirements, he wishes to mould throughout into a beautiful dwelling place for mankind, united into a single family. . . .

The high standard demanded of literature, which is being rapidly remoulded by life itself and by the cultural revolutionary work of Lenin's party, is due to the high estimation in which the party holds the importance of the literary art. There has never been a state in the world where science and literature enjoyed such comradely help, such care for the raising of professional proficiency among the workers of art and science.

The proletarian state must educate thousands of first-class "craftsmen of culture," "engineers of the soul." This is necessary in order to restore to the whole mass of the working people the right to develop their intelligence, talents and faculties – a right of which they have been deprived everywhere else in the world. This aim, which is a fully practicable one, imposes on us writers the need of strict responsibility for our work and our social behaviour. This places us not only in the position, traditional to realist literaure, of "judges of the world and men," "critics of life," but gives us the right to participate directly in the construction of a new life, in the process of "changing the world." The possession of this right should impress every writer with a sense of his duty and responsibility for all literature, for all the aspects in it which should not be there. . . .

THE NEW FAMILY IDEAL

Together with the rejection of most other early revolutionary social norms in the mid-1930's, the Soviet government discarded the ideal of sexual freedom in favor of the stable family and parental responsibility.

The published draft of the law prohibiting abortion and providing material assistance to mothers has provoked a lively reaction throughout the country. It is being heatedly discussed by tens of millions of people and there is no doubt that it will serve as a further strengthening of the Soviet family. Parents' responsibility for the education of their children will be increased and a blow will be dealt at the lighthearted, negligent attitude toward marriage.

When we speak of strengthening the Soviet family, we are speaking precisely of the struggle against the survivals of a bourgeois attitude toward marriage, women and children. So-called "free love" and all disorderly sex life are bourgeois through and through, and have nothing to do with either socialist principles or the ethics and standards of conduct of the Soviet citizen. Socialist doctrine shows this, and it is proved by life itself.

The *elite* of our country, the best of the Soviet youth, are as a rule also excellent family men who dearly love their children. And *vice versa*: the man who does not take marriage seriously, and abandons his children to

FROM: Discussion of the Law on Abolition of Legal Abortion, *Pravda*, Editorials of May 28 and June 9, 1936 (English translation in Rudolf Schlesinger, ed., *Changing Attitudes in Soviet Russia: The Family in the USSR*, London, Routledge & Kegan Paul, 1949, pp. 251-54, 268-69; reprinted by permission of the publisher).

the whims of fate, is usually also a bad worker and a poor member of society.

Fatherhood and motherhood have long been virtues in this country. This can be seen at the first glance, without searching enquiry. Go through the parks and streets of Moscow or of any other town in the Soviet Union on a holiday, and you will see not a few young men walking with pink-cheeked, well-fed babies in their arms.

The rise in the standard of living has brought the joy of parenthood within the reach of all adults. The Soviet land cannot complain of too low a birth-rate. The birth-rate is rising steadily, and the mortality rate is as steadily going down. . . .

More than once the enemies of the people suggested to us the foul and poisonous ideal of liquidating the family and disrupting marriage. The bourgeoisie has tried to use it as a weapon in the struggle against socialist progress. It is enough to recall with what persistence they spread the slander about the "nationalization of women." And during the great move to collectivize the villages, the *kulaks* again broadcast this favourite bourgeois allegation. The *kulaks* used it to scare the peasants: "In the collective farms you will all sleep under the same 30-yard-wide blanket."

The bourgeois who establishes his family order with the aid of a knout, the bourgeois for whom his own family is but a thin veneer covering prostitution and sexual debauchery, naturally thought that everyone would fall for his lie about "free love" in the country where the exploitation of man by man has been abolished and women have been liberated. But he failed. This weapon, too, was shattered by the stubborn facts of Soviet reality. . . .

There is no point in denying that in towns and villages there are still men and women whose attitude towards family and children is superficial and devil-may-care. Marriage and divorce are, of course, private affairs – but the State cannot allow anyone to mock at women or to abandon his children to the mercy of fate. The irresponsible profligate who gets married five times a year cannot enjoy the respect of Soviet youth. Nor can a girl who flutters from one marriage into the next with the swiftness of a butterfly enjoy respect. Men and women of this sort merely deserve social contempt. Marriage is a serious, responsible business and one that must not be approached lightheartedly . . . .

Social education is being widely developed in this country. The State is coming to the aid of the family. But the State in no wise relieves the mother or the father of their care of the children. Under Soviet conditions the father is the social educator. He has to prepare good Soviet citizens: that is his duty, that is also his pride – and the Soviet land has heard many proud declarations by fathers and mothers about the sons and daughters they gave to the Soviet fatherland, about gallant pilots and parachutists, engineers, doctors, teachers. . . .

A man who cowardly and basely abandons his children, shuns his responsibility, hides in corners and puts all the paternal duties on the mother's shoulders, shames the name of a Soviet citizen. Evading the payment of alimony is not a weakness, though it is treated with such leniency by some of our institutions. It is a crime, and not only the man who befouls the name of Soviet citizen, but all those who protect him are guilty of this crime. . . .

A Soviet child has a right to a real father, an educator and friend. A father who abandons his children is guilty both before them and before the socialist State which has entrusted the children to his care. An irresponsible attitude towards marriage and family is a bad recommendation as a citizen.

Socialism provides every toiler with a happy, beautiful life. For the first time in history it creates for the workers a possibility of fatherhood and motherhood in the fullest sense of the word. It therefore makes serious demands on mother and father. A bourgeois attitude towards the family cannot be tolerated.

The published law-project and its widespread discussion are signs of a new socialist morality, imbued with force, confidence and vitality. It lies in the flowering and enrichment of human personality, in love for Man. In the light of this morality, the mother wears a new face, and so does the father. "Paternal pride" – these words sound real only in the Soviet land, because a father who has raised new builders of socialism can feel a worthy citizen of his country. . . .

THE KIROV AFFAIR

By 1933 the rigors of the Five Year Plan, collectivization, and famine had produced a new wave of opposition to Stalin among the party officialdom, crystallizing around the Leningrad party chief Sergei M. Kirov. Stalin allowed a brief period of political and economic relaxation, rudely interrupted by the assassination of Kirov in December, 1934. Though Stalin later became suspected of complicity in the murder, he took it as the pretext to launch his purge of the Old Bolsheviks.

The behind-the-scenes story of this episode was related by Bukharin to the Menshevik emigré Boris I. Nicolaevsky, who published it anonymously in 1936.

Kirov played an important part in the Politburo. He was a 100 percent supporter of the "general line," and distinguished himself during its operation by great energy and inflexibility. This caused Stalin to value him highly. But there was always a certain independence in Kirov's attitude which annoyed Stalin. The story is that Stalin had prevented Kirov from attending the meetings of the Politburo in Moscow for several months under the pretext that his presence in Leningrad was indispensable. However, Stalin could never make up his mind to take strong measures against Kirov. It would have been folly to add to the already large number of the dissatisfied an important party leader such as Kirov, especially since Kirov had succeeded in surrounding himself in Leningrad with reliable and devoted aides. A new conflict with the Leningrad party might have been more fatal now than in Zinoviev's day. In the winter of 1933-1934, Kirov had so strengthened his position that he could afford to follow his own line. He aimed not only at a "Western orientation" in foreign policy, but also at the conclusions which would follow logically from this new orientation as far as home policy was concerned.

The task, therefore, was not only that of creating a mighty army in preparation for the impending military conflict, a conflict which appeared inevitable, but also, politically speaking, of creating the proper psychologic frame of mind on the home front. There were two alternatives: to pursue the former policy of crushing all dissenters, with the adminstrative pressure ruthlessly tightened and the terror intensified, or to try "reconciliation with the people," to gain their voluntary cooperation in the political preparation of the country for the coming war. The most convinced and most prominent advocates of the *second alternative* were *Kirov* and *Gorki* [Maxim Gorki, the writer]. It would be worthwhile to describe in greater detail Gorki's influence in the life of the party, particularly as it is now possible to speak more openly since his death. But that is another matter, and would take us too far afield. Gorki had exercised a great and beneficent influence upon Stalin. But, despite all his influence, Gorki was *not a member* of the Politburo, and had no direct part in the making of its decisions. Kirov's part became, therefore, all the more important.

Kirov stood for the idea of *abolition of the terror*, both in general and inside the party. We do not desire to exaggerate the importance of his proposals. It must not be forgotten that when the First Five-Year Plan was being put into effect, Kirov was one of the heads of the party, that he was

FROM: *Letter of an Old Bolshevik* (New York, The Rand School, and London, George Allen and Unwin, 1938), pp. 22-25, 27-29, 69-71; reprinted by permission of Allen Unwin, Inc.

among those who inspired and carried through the notoriously ruthless measures against the peasants and the wiping out of the kulaks. The Kem and Murmansk coasts, with their prison camps, and so forth, were under his jurisdiction. Furthermore, he was in charge of the construction of the Baltic-White Sea Canal. This is enough to make it clear that Kirov could not be reproached with any undue tenderness in the manner in which he disposed of human lives. But this very fact added to his strength in the official circles in which he had to defend his point of view. That he had so large a share of responsibility in the horrors of the First Five-Year Plan made it possible for him to come forward as a leader and protagonist of the policy of moderating the terror during the Second Five-Year Plan. Kirov's line of thought ran as follows: The period of destruction, which was necessary to extirpate the small proprietor elements in the villages, was now at an end; the economic position of the collectives was consolidated and made secure for the future. This constituted a firm basis for future development, and as the economic situation continued to improve, the broad masses of the population would become more and more reconciled to the government; the number of "internal foes" would diminish. It was now the task of the party to rally those forces which would support it in the new phase of economic development, and thus to broaden the foundation upon which Soviet power was based. Kirov, therefore, strongly advocated reconciliation with those party elements who, during the period of the First Five-Year Plan, had gone over to the Opposition, but who might be induced to cooperate on the new basis, now that the "destructive" phase was over. . . .

. . . Early in the summer of 1933, when it became certain that the harvest would be good, Kamenev, Zinoviev and a number of other former members of the Opposition were once again readmitted as members of the party. They were even permitted to choose their spheres of work, and some of them actually received invitations to the party congress (February 1934).

At that congress Kirov appeared in triumph. Previously, his election in Leningrad had been celebrated as was no other. At district conferences in various parts of the city, all of which he toured on the same day, he had been received with wild cheers. "Long live our Mironich!"* the delegates shouted; it had been an exceedingly impressive demonstration and it showed that the entire Leningrad proletariat was behind Kirov. At the party congress, too, Kirov received an extraordinarily enthusiastic reception. He was cheered, the entire assembly rising to its feet on hearing his

*Mironich: Kirov's middle name (patronymic), a respectful-familiar form of address—Ed.

report. During the recesses there was discussion as to who had had the more tumultuous reception, Kirov or Stalin. This very comparison shows how strong Kirov's influence had already become.

Not only was Kirov reelected to the Politburo, but he was also chosen a secretary of the Central Committee, making it necessary for him to move to Moscow within a short time to take over direction of a whole group of departments which had heretofore been under Postyshev and Kaganovich. This was to insure putting into effect the new line which Kirov had inspired. His removal to Moscow was delayed, however. The official reason given was that his presence in Leningrad was indispensable; a substitute was supposedly being sought in Leningrad, but until someone could be found fit to take his place, his transfer to Moscow had to be postponed. In spite of this, he took part in the work of the Politburo, and his influence there continued to grow. . . .

. . . [Kirov's assassination put an end to any chance for liberalization within the party. Thereafter] the trend was in quite the opposite direction: not toward reconciliation inside the party, but toward intensification of the terror inside the party to its logical conclusion, to the stage of *physical extermination of all those whose party past might make them opponents of Stalin or aspirants to his power*. Today, I have not the slightest doubt that it was at that very period, between the murder of Kirov and the second Kamenev Trial, that Stalin made his decision and mapped out his plan of "reforms," an essential component part of which was the trial of the *sixteen* and *other trials yet to come*. If, before the murder of Kirov, Stalin still had some hesitation as to which road to choose, he had now made up his mind.

The determining reason for Stalin's decision was his realization, arrived at on the basis of reports and information reaching him, that *the mood of the majority of the old party workers was really one of bitterness and hostility toward him*.

The trials and investigations which followed the Kirov affair had demonstrated unmistakably that the party had not reconciled itself to Stalin's personal dictatorship; that, in spite of all their solemn declarations, the old Bolsheviks rejected Stalin in the depths of their hearts, that this attitude of hostility, instead of diminishing, was growing, and that the majority of those who cringed before him, protesting devotion, would betray him at the first change of the political atmosphere.

This was the basic fact that emerged for Stalin from the documents compiled in the course of the investigation of Nikolayev's act [the assassination of Kirov]. It must be conceded that Stalin was able to provide a reasonable basis for this deduction, and from it he fearlessly drew his ultimate conclusions. As Stalin perceived it, the reasons for the hostility toward t *the basic psychology of the old Bolsheviks.* Having grown up conditions of revolutionary struggle against the old regime, we t trained in the psychology of oppositionists, of irreconcilable no ists. Involuntarily, our minds work in a direction *critical* of the exis... order; we seek everywhere its weak sides. In short, we are all critics, destructionists – not builders. This was all to the good – in the past; but now, when we must occupy ourselves with constructive building, it is all hopelessly bad. It is impossible to build anything enduring with such human materials, composed of skeptics and critics. What must be considered now, first and foremost, is the necessity of enduring Soviet construction, particularly because Soviet Russia is facing tremendous perturbations, such as will arise inevitably with the coming of war. It was thus that Stalin reasoned.

The conclusion that he drew from all this was certainly daring: if the old Bolsheviks, the group constituting today the ruling caste in the country, are unfit to perform this function, it is necessary to remove them from their posts, to create a new ruling caste. Kirov's plans presupposed reconciliation with the nonparty intelligentsia and enlistment of nonparty workers and peasants in the tasks of social and political life, as a means of widening the social basis of the Soviet regime and promoting its cooperation with the democratic elements of the population. Under Stalin's plan these very same proposals acquired quite a different significance; they were to facilitate a complete revision of the personnel of the ruling caste by expelling from its midst all those infected with the spirit of criticism, and the substitution of a new ruling caste, governed by a new psychology aiming at positive construction. . . .

TROTSKY ON THE NEW SOVIET SOCIETY

In 1937 Trotsky published a general critique of Stalin's regime, "The Revolution Betrayed." He elaborated Rakovsky's argument, with the thesis that the bureaucracy dominated the Soviet state and had raised Stalin to power as a "Bonaparte" to protect its group interests. While Trotsky explained this phenomenon as the inevitable result of Russian backwardness, he nonetheless defended the "socialist" character of the Soviet economy and expressed hope that a new proletarian movement would restore the ideals of the revolution.

FROM: Trotsky, *The Revolution Betrayed: What Is the Soviet Union and Where Is It Going?* (English translation by Max Eastman, Garden City, N. Y., Doubleday, Doran & Co., 1937, pp. 47, 51-52, 89, 93, 111-13, 255, 277-78, 288-90; reprinted by permission of the copyright holder, Pioneer Publishers).

... Marx expected that the Frenchman would begin the social revolution, the German continue it, the Englishman finish it; and as to the Russian, Marx left him far in the rear. But this conceptual order was upset by the facts. Whoever tries now mechanically to apply the universal historic conception of Marx to the particular case of the Soviet Union at the given stage of its development, will be entangled at once in hopeless contradictions.

Russia was not the strongest, but the weakest link in the chain of capitalism. The present Soviet Union does not stand above the world level of economy, but is only trying to catch up to the capitalist countries. If Marx called that society which was to be formed upon the basis of a socialization of the productive forces of the most advanced capitalism of its epoch, the lowest stage of communism, then this designation obviously does not apply to the Soviet Union, which is still today considerably poorer in technique, culture and the good things of life than the capitalist countries. It would be truer, therefore, to name the present Soviet regime in all its contradictoriness, not a socialist regime, but a *preparatory* regime *transitional* from capitalism to socialism. . . .

However you may interpret the nature of the present Soviet state, one thing is indubitable: at the end of its second decade of existence, it has not only not died away, but not begun to "die away." Worse than that, it has grown into a hitherto unheard of apparatus of compulsion. The bureaucracy not only has not disappeared, yielding its place to the masses, but has turned into an uncontrolled force dominating the masses. The army not only has not been replaced by an armed people, but has given birth to a privileged officers' caste, crowned with marshals, while the people, "the armed bearers of the dictatorship," are now forbidden in the Soviet Union to carry even nonexplosive weapons. With the utmost stretch of fancy it would be difficult to imagine a contrast more striking than that which exists between the schema of the workers' state according to Marx, Engels and Lenin, and the actual state now headed by Stalin. While continuing to publish the works of Lenin (to be sure, with excerpts and distortions by the censor), the present leaders of the Soviet Union and their ideological representatives do not even raise the question of the causes of such a crying divergence between program and reality. We will try to do this for them. . . .

The proletarian character of the October revolution was determined by the world situation and by a special correlation of internal forces. But the classes themselves were formed in the barbarous circumstances of tsarism and backward capitalism, and were anything but made to order for the demands of a socialist revolution. The exact opposite is true. It is for the very reason that a proletariat still backward in many respects achieved in the space of a few months the unprecedented leap from a semifeudal monarchy to a socialist dictatorship, that the reaction in its ranks was inevitable. . . .

Before he felt out his own course, the bureaucracy felt out Stalin himself. He brought it all the necessary guarantees: the prestige of an old Bolshevik, a strong character, narrow vision, and close bonds with the political machine as the sole source of his influence. The success which fell upon him was a surprise at first to Stalin himself. It was the friendly welcome of the new ruling group, trying to free itself from the old principles and from the control of the masses, and having need of a reliable arbiter in its inner affairs. A secondary figure before the masses and in the events of the revolution, Stalin revealed himself as the indubitable leader of the Thermidorian bureaucracy, as first in its midst. . . .

The present Soviet society cannot get along without a state, nor even – within limits – without a bureaucracy. But the cause of this is by no means the pitiful remnants of the past, but the mighty forces and tendencies of the present. The justification for the existence of a Soviet state as an apparatus of compulsion lies in the fact that the present transitional structure is still full of social contradictions, which in the sphere of consumption – most close and sensitively felt by all – are extremely tense, and forever threaten to break over into the sphere of production. The triumph of socialism cannot be called either final or irrevocable.

The basis of bureaucratic rule is the poverty of society in objects of consumption, with the resulting struggle of each against all. When there is enough goods in a store, the purchasers can come whenever they want to. When there is little goods, the purchasers are compelled to stand in line. When the lines are very long, it is necessary to appoint a policeman to keep order. Such is the starting point of the power of the Soviet bureaucracy. It "knows" who is to get something and who has to wait.

A raising of the material and cultural level ought, at first glance, to lessen the necessity of privileges, narrow the sphere of application of "bourgeois law," and thereby undermine the standing ground of its defenders, the bureaucracy. In reality the opposite thing has happened: the growth of the productive forces has been so far accompanied by an extreme development of all forms of inequality, privilege and advantage, and therewith of bureaucratism. That too is not accidental.

In its first period, the Soviet regime was undoubtedly far more equalitarian and less bureaucratic than now. But that was an equality of general poverty. The resources of the country were so scant that there was no opportunity to separate out from the masses of the population any broad privileged strata. At the same time the "equalizing" character of wages, destroying personal interestedness, became a brake upon the development of the productive forces. Soviet economy had to lift itself from its poverty to a somewhat higher level before fat deposits of privilege became possible. The present state of production is still far from guaranteeing all necessities to everybody. But it is already adequate to give significant privileges to a minority, and convert inequality into a whip for the spurring on of the majority. That is the first reason why the growth of production has so far strengthened not the socialist, but the bourgeois features of the state.

But that is not the sole reason. Alongside the economic factor dictating capitalistic methods of payment at the present stage, there operates a parallel political factor in the person of the bureaucracy itself. In its very essence it is the planter and protector of inequality. It arose in the beginning as the bourgeois organ of a workers' state. In establishing and defending the advantages of a minority, it of course draws off the cream for its own use. Nobody who has wealth to distribute ever omits himself. Thus out of a social necessity there has developed an organ which has far outgrown its socially necessary function, and become an independent factor and therewith the source of great danger for the whole social organism.

The social meaning of the Soviet Thermidor now begins to take form before us. The poverty and cultural backwardness of the masses has again become incarnate in the malignant figure of the ruler with a great club in his hand. The deposed and abused bureaucracy, from being a servant of society, has again become its lord. On this road it has attained such a degree of social and moral alienation from the popular masses, that it cannot now permit any control over either its activities or its income. . . .

The Soviet Union is a contradictory society halfway between capitalism and socialism, in which: (a) the productive forces are still far from adequate to give the state property a socialist character; (b) the tendency toward primitive accumulation created by want breaks out through innumerable pores of the planned economy; (c) norms of distribution preserving a bourgeois character lie at the basis of a new differentiation of society; (d) the economic growth, while slowly bettering the situation of the toilers, promotes a swift formation of privileged strata; (e) exploiting the social antagonisms, a bureaucracy has converted itself into an uncontrolled caste alien to socialism; (f) the social revolution, betrayed by the ruling party, still exists in property relations and in the consciousness of the toiling masses; (g) a further development of the accumulating contradictions can as well lead to socialism as back to capitalism; (h) on the road to capitalism the counterrevolution would have to break the resistance of the workers; (i) on the road to socialism the workers would have to overthrow the bureaucracy. In the last analysis, the question will be decided by a struggle of living social forces, both on the national and the world arena. . . .

The increasingly insistent deification of Stalin is, with all its elements of caricature, a necessary element of the regime. The bureaucracy has need of an inviolable superarbiter, a first consul if not an emperor, and it raises upon its shoulders him who best responds to its claim for lordship. That "strength of character" of the leader which so enraptures the literary dilettantes of the West, is in reality the sum total of the collective pressure of a caste which will stop at nothing in defense of its position. Each one of them at his post is thinking: *l'état – c'est moi*. In Stalin each one easily finds himself. But Stalin also finds in each one a small part of his own spirit. Stalin is the personification of the bureaucracy. That is the substance of his political personality.

Caesarism, or its bourgeois form, Bonapartism, enters the scene in those moments of history when the sharp struggle of two camps raises the state power, so to speak, above the nation, and guarantees it, in appearance, a complete independence of classes – in reality, only the freedom necessary for a defense of the privileged. The Stalin regime, rising above a politically atomized society, resting upon a police and officers' corps, and allowing of no control whatever, is obviously a variation of Bonapartism – a Bonapartism of a new type not before seen in history.

Caesarism arose upon the basis of a slave society shaken by inward strife. Bonapartism is one of the political weapons of the capitalist regime in its critical period. Stalinism is a variety of the same system, but upon the basis of a workers' state torn by the antagonism between an organized and armed Soviet aristocracy and the unarmed toiling masses.

As history testifies, Bonapartism gets along admirably with a universal, and even a secret, ballot. The democratic ritual of Bonapartism is the *plebiscite*. From time to time, the question is presented to the citizens: *for* or *against* the leader? And the voter feels the barrel of a revolver between his shoulders. Since the time of Napoleon III, who now seems a provincial dilettante, this technique has received an extraordinary development. The new Soviet constitution which establishes *Bonapartism on a plebiscite basis* is the veritable crown of the system.

In the last analysis, Soviet Bonapartism owes its birth to the belatedness of the world revolution. But in the capitalist countries the same cause gave rise to fascism. We thus arrive at the conclusion, unexpected at first glance, but in reality inevitable, that the crushing of Soviet democracy by an all-powerful bureaucracy and the extermination of bourgeois democracy by fascism were produced by one and the same cause: the dilatoriness of the world proletariat in solving the problems set for it by history. . . .

This is the first time in history that a state resulting from a workers' revolution has existed. The stages through which it must go are nowhere written down. It is true that the theoreticians and creators of the Soviet Union hoped that the completely transparent and flexible Soviet system would permit the state peacefully to transform itself, dissolve, and die away, in correspondence with the stages of the economic and cultural evolution of society. Here again, however, life proved more complicated than theory anticipated. The proletariat of a backward country was fated to accomplish the first socialist revolution. For this historic privilege, it must, according to all evidences, pay with a second supplementary revolution – against bureaucratic absolutism. . . .

It is not a question of substituting one ruling clique for another, but of changing the very methods of administering the economy and guiding the culture of the country. Bureaucratic autocracy must give place to Soviet democracy. A restoration of the right of criticism, and a genuine freedom of elections, are necessary conditions for the further development of the country. This assumes a revival of freedom of Soviet parties, beginning with the party of Bolsheviks, and a resurrection of the trade unions. The bringing of democracy into industry means a radical revision of plans in the interests of the toilers. Free discussion of economic problems will decrease the overhead expense of bureaucratic mistakes and zigzags. Expensive playthings – palaces of the Soviets, new theaters, show-off subways – will be crowded out in favor of workers' dwellings. "Bourgeois norms of distribution" will be confined within the limits of strict necessity, and, in step with the growth of social wealth, will give way to socialist equality. Ranks will be immediately abolished. The tinsel of decorations will go into the melting pot. The youth will receive the opportunity to breathe freely, criticize, make mistakes, and grow up. Science and art will be freed of their chains. And, finally, foreign policy will return to the traditions of revolutionary internationalism. . . .

THE GREAT PURGE

The era of the purges commencing after the assassination of Kirov was distinguished by the elaborately staged "Moscow Trials" of 1936, 1937 and 1938, in which most of the old opposition leaders were sentenced to death after confessing to a fantastic series of imaginary crimes. By 1937 the purge began to spread from the ranks of old opposition sympathizers to the government, the army, and the party itself, as more and more people were implicated in the false confessions of "plots" which the NKVD under N. I. Yezhov extracted from its victims. Stalin apparently convinced himself that the menace of "Trotskyist wreckers" employed by "intelligence services of foreign states" was real, and warned the party to prepare for ever sharper struggle with the hidden enemies of socialism.

Comrades!

From the reports and the discussions of them heard at this Plenum it is obvious that we have to deal here with the following three basic facts.

In the first place, the wrecking and diversionary-spying work of agents of foreign states, among whom a rather active role has been played by the Trotskyists, has touched to one degree or another all or almost all of our organizations, administrative and party as well as economic.

In the second place, agents of foreign states, including Trotskyists, have penetrated not only into the lower organizations, but even into certain responsible posts.

In the third place, certain of our leading comrades, at the center as well as in the provinces, have not only been unable to see the real face of these wreckers, diversionists, spies and murderers, but have proved to be careless, indifferent and naïve about it, and not uncommonly have coöperated in promoting agents of foreign states to some responsible post or other. . . .

. . . Our party comrades . . . have forgotten that the Soviet power has won only in one-sixth of the earth, that five-sixths of the earth constitute the realm of the capitalist states. They forget that the Soviet Union finds itself in the circumstances of a capitalistic encirclement . . . .

Capitalistic encirclement means that there is one country, the Soviet Union, which has established the socialist order, and that apart from this there are many countries – bourgeois countries – which continue to lead the capitalistic way of life and which surround the Soviet Union, awaiting the chance to attack it and destroy it, or in any case to undermine its might and weaken it . . . .

Is it not clear that as long as the capitalist encirclement exists we will have wreckers, spies, diversionists and murderers sent into our interior by agents of foreign states?

Our party comrades have forgotten about all this, and having forgotten this, have been caught completely off guard.

This is why the spying and diversionary work of the Trotskyist agents of the Japanese-German police force has proved to be a complete surprise for some of our comrades.

Further: While struggling with Trotskyist agents our party comrades did

FROM: Stalin, "On Inadequacies of Party Work and Measures for Liquidating Trotskyist and Other Double-Dealers" (Speech to the Plenum of the Central Committee of the CPSU, March 3, 1937; *Pravda*, March 29, 1937; editor's translation).

not notice – they overlooked the fact – that present-day Trotskyism is no longer what it was, say, seven or eight years ago; that during this time Trotskyism and the Trotskyists have undergone an important evolution which has radically changed the face of Trotskyism; that in view of this the struggle with Trotskyism and the methods of struggle with it must be radically changed. Our party comrades have not noticed that Trotskyism has ceased to be a political tendency in the working class . . . and has turned into a frantic and unprincipled band of wreckers, diversionists, spies and murderers working under the orders of the intelligence organs of foreign states. . . .

At the 1937 trial Piatakov, Radek and Sokolnikov* . . . admitted that they had a definite political platform . . . , an antipopular and antiproletarian platform. The restoration of capitalism, the liquidation of the collective farms and state farms, the restoration of the system of exploitation, alliance with the fascist forces of Germany and Japan to bring war to the Soviet Union, the struggle for war and against the policy of peace, the territorial dismemberment of the Soviet Union with the cession of the Ukraine to the Germans and of the Maritime Province to Japan, preparations for the military defeat of the Soviet Union in the event of an attack on it by hostile powers, and – as the means of fulfilling these tasks – wrecking, diversion, individual terror against the leaders of the Soviet government, espionage in the service of the Japanese-German fascist forces – such is the political platform of present-day Trotskyism set forth by Piatakov, Radek and Sokolnikov. . . .

. . . Now that we have technically well-trained Bolshevik cadres, the role of wrecker is played not by openly alien people . . . but by people who possess party cards and enjoy all the rights of party members. Now the weakness of our people consists not in technical backwardness but in political carelessness, in blind trust of people who have accidentally acquired party cards, in the absence of checkups on people not just on the basis of their political declarations but according to the results of their work. Now the key question for us is not the liquidation of the technical backwardness of our cadres, for this has basically already been liquidated, but the liquidation of political carelessness and political trustingness toward wreckers who have accidentally acquired party cards. . . .

We must smash and throw out the rotten theory that with each forward movement we make the class struggle will die down more and more, that in proportion to our successes the class enemy will become more and more domesticated.

*Radek: a Comintern leader and Trotsky supporter in the twenties; Sokolnikov: Commissar of Finance, 1922-26, and a follower of Zinoviev – Ed.

This is not only a rotten theory but a dangerous theory, for it lulls our people to sleep, leads them into a trap, and makes it possible for the class enemy to rally for the struggle against the Soviet power.

On the contrary, the more we move forward, the more success we have, then the more wrathful become the remnants of the beaten exploiter classes, the more quickly they turn to sharper forms of struggle, the more mischief they do the Soviet state, the more they grasp at the most desperate means of struggle, as the last resort of the doomed. . . .

We must smash and throw out a second rotten theory which says that he who does not always wreck things and sometimes may be successful in his work cannot be a wrecker.

This strange theory reveals the naïveté of its authors. No wrecker wrecks things all the time if he doesn't want to be exposed very quickly. On the contrary, the real wrecker must from time to time be successful in his work, for this is the only way for the wrecker to get people's confidence and continue his wrecking work. . . .

We must smash and throw out a third rotten theory which says that the systematic fulfillment of the economic plans reduces wrecking and the results of wrecking to nothing.

Such a theory can serve only one end – to tickle the bureaucratic conceit of our functionaries, soothe them and weaken their struggle against wrecking. . . .

We must smash and throw out [another] rotten theory which says that the Trotskyist wreckers do not have large reserves, that they are assembling their last cadres, as it were.

This is untrue, comrades. Only naïve people could think up such a theory. The Trotskyist wreckers have their reserves. They consist above all of the remnants of the beaten exploiter classes in the USSR. They consist of a whole series of groups and organizations outside the borders of the USSR which are hostile to the Soviet Union.

Take, for example, the Trotskyist counterrevolutionary Fourth International, which is two-thirds made up of spies and diversionists. Isn't this a reserve? Is it not clear that this International of spies will spawn cadres for the spying and wrecking work of the Trotskyists? . . .

THE GULAG

The most infamous feature of Stalinism was its vast expansion of the system of forced labor camps to accommodate the millions of victims of the collectivization drive and the purges. During World War II and after the death of Stalin when many surviving inmates were amnestied, reports of the camp regime finally found their way to the West. One of these documents, first published in the *Socialist Messenger* in 1961, was an eyewitness account of the Trotskyists who were incarcerated at the far northern coal-mining center of Vorkuta.

During the middle and at the end of the 1930s, the Trotskyists formed a quite disparate group at Vorkuta; one part of them kept its old name of "Bolshevik-Leninists." There were almost 500 at the mine, close to 1,000 at the camp of Ukhta-Pechora, and certainly several thousands altogether around the Pechora district.

The Orthodox Trotskyists were determined to remain faithful to the end to their platform and their leaders. In 1927, following the resolutions of the fifteenth congress of the party, they were excluded from the Communist Party and, at the same time, arrested. From then on, even though they were in prison, they continued to consider themselves Communists; as for Stalin and his supporters, "the apparatus men," they were characterized as renegades from communism.

Among these "Trotskyists" were also found people who had never formally belonged to the CP and did not join the Left Opposition, but who tied their own fate with it to the very end – even when the struggle of the Opposition was most acute.

In addition to these genuine Trotskyists, there were in the camps of Vorkuta and elsewhere more than 100,000 prisoners who, members of the party and the youth, had adhered to the Trotskyist Opposition and then at different times and for diverse reasons (of which the principal were, evidently, repressions, unemployment, persecutions, exclusion from schools and university facilities, etc.) were forced to "recant their errors" and withdraw from the Opposition. . . .

In the autumn of 1936, soon after the frame-up trials against the leaders of the Opposition, Zinoviev, Kamenev, and the others, the entire group of "Orthodox" Trotskyists at the mine got together to confer with one another.

Opening the meeting, Gevorkian addressed those present: "Comrades! Before beginning our meeting, I ask you to honor the memory of our comrades, guides, and leaders who have died as martyrs at the hands of the Stalinist traitors to the revolution."

The entire assembly stood up. Then, in a brief and very trenchant speech, Gevorkian explained that it was necessary to examine and resolve the key problem: what should be done and how should they conduct themselves from now on.

FROM: "M.B.", "Trotskyists at Vorkuta: An Eyewitness Report" (English translation in *International Socialist Review*, Summer, 1963, pp. 206, 210-16; reprinted by permission of Monad Press, copyright 1974 by The Anchor Foundation, Inc.).

"It is now evident that the group of Stalinist adventurers have completed their counterrevolutionary coup d'etat in our country. All the progressive conquests of our revolution are in mortal danger. Not twilight shadows, but those of deep black night envelop our country. No Cavaignac spilled as much working class blood as has Stalin. Physically annihilating all the opposition groups within the party, he aims at total personal dictatorship. The party and the whole people are subjected to surveillance and to summary justice by the police apparatus. The predictions and the direst fears of our Opposition are fully confirmed. The nation slides irresistibly into the Thermidorian swamp. This is the triumph of the centrist petty-bourgeois forces, of which Stalin is the interpreter, the spokesman, and the apostle.

"No compromise is possible with the Stalinist traitors and hangmen of the revolution. Remaining proletarian revolutionaries to the very end, we should not entertain any illusion about the fate awaiting us. But before destroying us, Stalin will try to humiliate us as much as he can. By throwing political prisoners in with common criminals, he strives to scatter us among the criminals and to incite them against us. We are left with only one means of struggle in this unequal battle: the hunger strike. With a group of comrades, we have already drawn up a list of our demands of which many of you are already informed. Therefore, I now propose to you that we discuss them together and make a decision."

The meeting lasted only a short time; the question of the hunger strike and of concrete demands had already been debated for some months by the Trotskyists. Some Trotskyist groups in other camps (Usa station, Chib-Yu, Kochmes, etc.) had also been discussing the matter and had sent their agreement to support the demands and to participate in the hunger strike. These demands were ratified unanimously by those present. They stipulated:

1. Abrogation of the illegal decision of the NKVD, concerning the transfer of all Trotskyists from administrative camps to concentration camps. Affairs relating to political opposition to the regime must not be judged by special NKVD tribunals, but in public juridical assemblies.

2. The work day in the camp must not exceed eight hours.

3. The food quota of the prisoners should not depend on their norm of output. A cash bonus, not the food ration, should be used as a production incentive.

4. Separation, at work as well as in the barracks, of political prisoners and common criminals.

5. The old, the ill, and women political prisoners should be moved from the polar camps to camps where the climatic conditions were more favorable.

It was recommended, at the time of the meeting, that the sick, the invalids, and the old should not participate in the hunger strike; however, all those in question energetically rejected this proposal.

The meeting did not decide the day on which the hunger strike should begin; a five-member directorate, headed by Gevorkian, was delegated to inform the other Trotskyist groups spread over the immense territory containing the camps of Ukhta-Pechora.

Three weeks later, October 27, 1936, the massive hunger strike of the political prisoners began, a strike without precedent and a model under Soviet camp conditions. In the morning, at reveille, in almost every barrack, prisoners announced themselves on strike. The barracks occupied by the Trotskyists participated 100 percent in the movement. Even the orderlies struck. Close to 1,000 prisoners, of whom half worked in the mine, participated in this tragedy, which lasted more than four months.

Having begun the end of October 1936, the hunger strike lasted 132 days, ending in March 1937. It culminated with the complete victory of the strikers who received a radiogram from the headquarters of the NKVD, drawn up in these words: "Inform the hunger strikers held in the Vorkuta mines that all their demands will be satisfied."

The Trotskyists were then taken back to the mine, received food reserved for the sick and, after a period of time, they went back to work, but only above ground; certain of them worked in the office of the director of the mine, in the capacity of paid workers, bookkeepers, economists, etc. Their work day did not exceed eight hours; their food ration was not based on their production norm.

But little by little the other prisoners' interest in the strikers began to diminish. Everyone's interest was now focused on the new trial at Moscow, which was being broadcast by radio; besides, new prisoners began arriving at the end of June. Their stories described mass arrests, outrages, executions without trial behind the walls of the NKVD, and this all over the country. At the beginning, no one wanted to believe this, particularly since the new arrivals spoke unwillingly and rather enigmatically. But little by little, the bonds between them became tighter and the conversations franker. Without letup, new prisoners arrived from Russia; old friends and acquaintances discovered each other: it no longer was possible not to believe the stories.

In spite of these obvious facts, a certain number of prisoners waited with impatience for the autumn of 1937 and the twentieth anniversary of the October Revolution; they hoped, on this occasion as in 1927, that the government would declare a large-scale amnesty, particularly since a little while earlier the very promising "Stalinist Consitution" had been adopted. But the autumn brought bitter disillusions.

The harsh regime of the camps grew abruptly worse. The sergeants and their assistants in maintaining order – common criminals – having received new orders from the camp director, armed themselves with clubs and pitilessly beat the prisoners. The guards, the watchmen close to the barracks, tormented the prisoners. To amuse themselves during the night they fired on those who went to the toilets. Or else, giving the order "*On your bellies*," they forced the prisoners to stretch out, naked, for hours on the snow. Soon there were massive arrests. Almost every night, GPU agents appeared in the barracks, called out certain names and led away those called.

Certain Trotskyists, including Vladimir Ivanov, Kossior, and Trotsky's son, Sergei Sedov, a modest and likeable youth, who had imprudently refused to follow his parents into exile in 1928, were taken in a special convoy to Moscow. We can only believe that Stalin was not satisfied simply to hurl them into the tundra; his sadistic nature thirsted not only for blood; he wished first to immeasurably humiliate them and torture them, coercing them into false self-accusations. Ivanov and Kossior disappeared without trace behind the walls of the Lubyanka prison. As for Sergei Sedov, after a "treatment" at the Lubyanka he was "tried" at Sverdlovsk, where he had worked as an engineer at the electric station; according to the newspaper stories, "he recalled having devoted himself to acts of sabotage" and other "crimes," for which he was condemned to be shot. . . .

The whole winter of 1937-38 some prisoners, encamped in barracks at the brickyard, starved and waited for a decision regarding their fate. Finally, in March, three NKVD officers, with Kashketin at their head, arrived by plane at Vorkuta, coming from Moscow. They came to the brickyard to interrogate the prisoners. Thirty to forty were called each day, superficially questioned five to ten minutes each, rudely insulted, forced to listen to vile name-calling and obscenities. Some were greeted with punches in the face; Lt. Kashketin himself several times beat up one of them, the Old Bolshevik Virap Virapov, a former member of the Central Committee of Armenia.

At the end of March, a list of twenty-five was announced, among them Gevorkian, Virapov, Slavin, etc. . . . To each was delivered a kilo of bread and orders to prepare himself for a new convoy. After fond farewells to their friends, they left the barracks, and the convoy departed. Fifteen or twenty minutes later, not far away, about half a kilometer, on the steep bank of the little river Verkhnyaya Vorkuta (Upper Vorkuta), an abrupt volley resounded, followed by isolated and disorderly shots; then all grew quiet again. Soon, the convoy's escort passed back near the barracks. And it was clear to all in what sort of convoy the prisoners had been sent.

Two days later, there was a new call, this time of forty names. Once more there was a ration of bread. Some, out of exhaustion, could no longer move; they were promised a ride in a cart. Holding their breath, the prisoners remaining in the barracks heard the grating of the snow under the feet of the departing convoy. For a long time there was no sound; but all, on the watch, still listened. Nearly an hour passed in this way. Then, again, shots resounded in the tundra; this time, they came from much further away, in the direction of the narrow railway which passed three kilometers from the brickyard. The second "convoy" definitely convinced those remaining behind that they had been irremediably condemned.

The executions in the tundra lasted the whole month of April and part of May. Usually one day out of two, or one day out of three, thirty to forty prisoners were called. It is characteristic to note that each time, some common criminals, repeaters, were included. In order to terrorize the prisoners, the GPU, from time to time, made publicly known by means of local radio, the list of those shot. Usually broadcasts began as follows: "For counter-revolutionary agitation, sabotage, brigandage in the camps, refusal to work, attempts to escape, the following have been shot . . ." followed by a list of names of some political prisoners mixed with a group of common criminals.

One time, a group of nearly a hundred, composed mainly of Trotskyists, was led away to be shot. As they marched away, the condemned sang the "Internationale," joined by the voices of hundreds of prisoners remaining in camp.

At the beginning of May, a group of women were shot. Among them were the Ukrainian Communist, Chumskaya, the wife of I. N. Smirnov, a Bolshevik since 1898 and ex-peoples' commissar; (Olga, the daughter of Smirnov, a young girl, apolitical, passionately fond of music, had been shot a year before in Moscow); the wives of Kossior, of Melnais, etc. . . . one of these women had to walk on crutches. At the time of execution of a male prisoner, his imprisoned wife was automatically liable to capital punishment; and when it was a question of well-known members of the Oppositon, this applied equally to any of his children over the age of twelve.

In May, when hardly a hundred prisoners remained, the executions were interrupted. Two weeks passed quietly; then all the prisoners were led in a convoy to the mine. There it was learned that Yezhov had been dismissed, and that his place had been taken by Beria. . . .

THE MOSCOW TRIALS

Bukharin and Rykov were brought to trial in 1938 together with the Trotskyists Rakovsky and Krestinsky and the former secret police chief Yagoda. Andrei Vyshinksy was prosecutor in this as in the earlier trials; new heights of fantasy were reached in the charges which he pressed, ranging from a conspiracy to kill Lenin in 1918 to a recent plot with Germany and Japan to partition the USSR and restore capitalism. All the defendants except Krestinsky confessed readily, probably as the result of promises, threats, torture, and ideological arguments in combination. Bukharin's last plea is interesting evidence of the latter factor. As in the previous trials most of the defendants were shot, and those who received prison terms were never heard of again.

The Indictment

. . . The investigation instituted by the organs of the People's Commissariat of Internal Affairs has established that on the instructions of the intelligence services of foreign states hostile to the U.S.S.R. the accused in the present case organized a conspiratorial group named the "bloc of Rights and Trotskyites," the object of which was to overthrow the Socialist social and state system existing in the U.S.S.R., to restore capitalism and the power of the bourgeoisie in the U.S.S.R., to dismember the U.S.S.R. and to sever from it for the benefit of the aforementioned states the Ukraine, Byelorussia, the Central Asiatic Republics, Georgia, Armenia and Azerbaijan and the Maritime Region. . . .

Lacking all support within the U.S.S.R., the members of the "bloc of Rights and Trotskyites" in their struggle against the Socialist social and state system existing in the U.S.S.R. and for seizing power placed all their hopes exclusively upon the armed assistance of foreign aggressors, who promised the conspirators this assistance on the condition that the U.S.S.R. was to be dismembered and that the Ukraine, the Maritime region, Byelorussia, the Central Asiatic Republics, Georgia, Armenia and Azerbaijan were to be severed from the U.S.S.R.

This agreement between the "bloc of Rights and Trotskyites" and the representatives of the aforementioned foreign states was facilitated by the fact that many of the leading participants of this conspiracy had long been agents of foreign intelligence services and had for many years carried on espionage activities on behalf of these intelligence services.

This applies first of all to one of the inspirers of the conspiracy, enemy of the people TROTSKY. His connection with the Gestapo was exhaustively

FROM: *Report of Court Proceedings: The Case of the Anti-Soviet Bloc of Rights and Trotskyites* (Moscow, People's Commissariat of Justice of the USSR, 1938, English edition, pp. 5-6, 36, 626, 648, 696-97, 767, 778-79).

proved at the trials of the Trotskyite-Zinovievite Terrorist Centre in August 1936, and of the Anti-Soviet Trotskyite Centre in January 1937.

However, the materials in the possession of the investigating authorities in the present case establish that the connections between the enemy of the people TROTSKY and the German political police and the intelligence services of other countries were established at a much earlier date. The investigation has definitely established that TROTSKY has been connected with the German intelligence service since 1921, and with the British Intelligence Service since 1926. . . .

The Pleas

THE PRESIDENT: Accused Bukharin, do you plead guilty to the charges brought against you?

BUKHARIN: Yes, I plead guilty to the charges brought against me.

THE PRESIDENT: Accused Rykov, do you plead guilty to the charges brought against you?

RYKOV: Yes, I do.

THE PRESIDENT: Accused Yagoda, do you plead guilty to the charges brought against you?

YAGODA: Yes, I do.

THE PRESIDENT: Accused Krestinsky, do you plead guilty to the charges brought against you?

KRESTINSKY: I plead not guilty. I am not a Trotskyite. I was never a member of the bloc of Rights and Trotskyites, of whose existence I was not aware. Nor have I committed any of the crimes with which I personally am charged, in particular I plead not guilty to the charge of having had connections with the German intelligence service.

THE PRESIDENT: Do you corroborate the confession you made at the preliminary investigation?

KRESTINSKY: Yes, at the preliminary investigation I confessed, but I have never been a Trotskyite.

THE PRESIDENT: I repeat the question, do you plead guilty?

KRESTINSKY: Before my arrest I was a member of the Communist Party of the Soviet Union (Bolsheviks) and I remain one now.

THE PRESIDENT: Do you plead guilty to the charge of participating in espionage activities and of participating in terrorist activities?

KRESTINSKY: I have never been a Trotskyite, I have never belonged to the bloc of Rights and Trotskyites and have not committed a single crime.

THE PRESIDENT: Accused Rakovsky, do you plead guilty to the charges brought against you?

RAKOVSKY: Yes, I do. . . .

Vyshinsky's Summation

... The Trotskyites and Bukharinites, that is to say, the "bloc of Rights and Trotskyites," the leading lights of which are now in the prisoners' dock, is not a political party, a political tendency, but a band of felonious criminals, and not simply felonious criminals, but of criminals who have sold themselves to enemy intelligence services, criminals whom even ordinary felons treat as the basest, the lowest, the most contemptible, the most depraved of the depraved. ...

The investigation established, and I deem it necessary to remind you of this here in its full scope, Comrades Judges, that in 1918, immediately following the October Revolution, in the period of the conclusion of the Brest-Litovsk Peace, Bukharin and his group of so-called "Left Communists," and Trotsky with his group, together with the "Left" Socialist-Revolutionaries, organized a conspiracy against Lenin as the head of the Soviet government.

Bukharin and the other conspirators, as can be seen from the materials of the investigation, aimed at frustrating the Brest-Litovsk Peace, overthrowing the Soviet government, arresting and killing Lenin, Stalin and Sverdlov,* and forming a new government made up of Bukharinites, who then for purposes of camouflage called themselves "Left Communists," and of Trotskyites and "Left" Socialist-Revolutionaries. ...

All the accused stand convicted of having, according to the indictment, in 1932-33 organized, on the instructions of intelligence services of foreign states, a conspiratorial group called the "bloc of Rights and Trotskyites," which set itself the aim of committing the crimes which have been fully proved here.

It has been proved that this bloc consisted of agents of the intelligence services of several foreign states, it has been proved that the "bloc of Rights and Trotskyites" maintained regular illegitimate relations with certain foreign states with the object of obtaining their help for putting into effect its criminal designs, for the overthrow of the Soviet government and for establishing the power of the landlords and capitalists in the U.S.S.R.

It has been proved that the "bloc of Rights and Trotskyites" regularly engaged in espionage on behalf of these states and supplied their intelligence services with most important state secret material.

It has been proved that in pursuance of the same aims the "bloc of Rights and Trotskyites" systematically perpetrated wrecking and diversionist acts in various branches of our national economy – in the sphere of industry, agriculture, finance, municipal economy, railways, etc.

It has been proved that the "bloc of Rights and Trotskyites" organized a

*Sverdlov: Secretary of the party from 1917 until his death in 1919 – Ed.

number of terrorist acts against leaders of the Communist Party of the Soviet Union (Bolsheviks) and of the Soviet government, that this "bloc of Rights and Trotskyites" perpetrated terrorist acts against S. M. Kirov, V. R. Menzhinsky,* V. V. Kuibyshev, A. M. Gorky, and also brought about the death of M. A. Peshkov.†

It has been proved that the bloc had organized, but fortunately for us had not succeeded in effecting, a number of terrorist acts against the leaders of our Party and government.

Such are the circumstances of the present case. Such is the part taken in this case by each of the accused who are now awaiting your verdict, Comrades Judges.

There exist no words with which one could depict the monstrousness of the crimes committed by the accused. But, I ask, do we need any more words for that? No, Comrades Judges, these words are not needed. All the words have already been spoken. Everything has been analysed to the minutest details. The entire people now sees what these monsters are.

Our people and all honest people throughout the world are waiting for your just verdict. May this verdict of yours resound through the the the whole of our great country like a bell calling to new feats of herosim and to new victories! May your verdict resound as the refreshing and purifying thunderstorm of just Soviet punishment!

Our whole country, from young to old, is awaiting and demanding one thing: the traitors and spies who were selling our country to the enemy must be shot like dirty dogs!

Our people are demanding one thing: crush the accursed reptile!

Time will pass. The graves of the hateful traitors will grow over with weeds and thistle, they will be covered with eternal contempt of honest Soviet citizens, of the entire Soviet people. But over us, over our happy country, our sun will shine with its luminous rays as bright and as joyous as before. Over the road cleared of the last scum and filth of the past, we, our people, with our beloved leader and teacher, the great Stalin, at our head, will march as before onwards and onwards, towards communism!

Bukharin's Last Plea

Citizen President and Citizens Judges, I fully agree with Citizen the Procurator regarding the significance of the trial, at which were exposed our dastardly crimes, the crimes committed by the "bloc of Rights and Trotsky-

---

*Menzhinsky: Head of the GPU, 1922-34. He and the following men had apparently died natural deaths, but were now alleged to be the victims of medical murders. – Ed.

†Peshkov: Gorky's son – Ed.

ites," one of whose leaders I was, and for all the activities of which I bear responsibility.

This trial, which is the concluding one of a series of trials, has exposed all the crimes and the treasonable activities, it has exposed the historical significance and the roots of our struggle against the Party and the Soviet government.

I have been in prison for over a year, and I therefore do not know what is going on in the world. But, judging from those fragments of real life that sometimes reached me by chance, I see, feel and understand that the interests which we so criminally betrayed are entering a new phase of gigantic development, are now appearing in the international arena as a great and mighty factor of the international proletarian phase.

We, the accused, are sitting on the other side of the barrier, and this barrier separates us from you, Citizens Judges. We found ourselves in the accursed ranks of the counter-revolution, became traitors to the Socialist fatherland. . . .

. . . At such moments, Citizens Judges, everything personal, all the personal incrustation, all the rancour, pride, and a number of other things, fall away, disappear. And, in addition, when the reverberations of the broad international struggle reach your ear, all this in its entirety does its work, and the result is the complete internal moral victory of the U.S.S.R. over its kneeling opponents. I happened by chance to get Feuchtwanger's book* from the prison library. There he refers to the trials of the Trotskyites. It produced a profound impression on me; but I must say that Feuchtwanger did not get at the core of the matter. He stopped half way, not everything was clear to him; when, as a matter of fact, everything is clear. World history is a world court of judgment: A number of groups of Trotskyite leaders went bankrupt and have been cast into the pit. That is true. But you cannot do what Feuchtwanger does in relation to Trotsky in particular, when he places him on the same plane as Stalin. Here his arguments are absolutely false. For in reality the whole country stands behind Stalin; he is the hope of the world; he is a creator. Napoleon once said that fate is politics. The fate of Trotsky is counter-revolutionary politics.

I am about to finish. I am perhaps speaking for the last time in my life.

I am explaining how I came to realize the necessity of capitulating to the investigating authorities and to you, Citizens Judges. We came out against the joy of the new life with the most criminal methods of struggle. I refute the accusation of having plotted against the life of Vladimir Ilyich, but my counter-revolutionary confederates, and I at their head, endeavoured to

*Evidently Lion Feuchtwanger, *Moscow, 1937: A Travel Report for My Friends* (original German edition, Amsterdam, 1937) – Ed.

murder Lenin's cause, which is being carried on with such tremendous success by Stalin. The logic of this struggle led us step by step into the blackest quagmire. And it has once more been proved that departure from the position of Bolshevism means siding with political counter-revolutionary banditry. Counter-revolutionary banditry has now been smashed, we have been smashed, and we repent our frightful crimes. . . .

. . . I am kneeling before the country, before the Party, before the whole people. The monstrousness of my crimes is immeasurable especially in the new stage of the struggle of the U.S.S.R. May this trial be the last severe lesson, and may the great might of the U.S.S.R. become clear to all. Let it be clear to all that the counter-revolutionary thesis of the national limitedness of the U.S.S.R. has remained suspended in the air like a wretched rag. Everbody perceives the wise leadership of the country that is ensured by Stalin.

It is in the consciousness of this that I await the verdict. What matters is not the personal feelings of a repentant enemy, but the flourishing progress of the U.S.S.R. and its international importance. . . .

THE PURGES AND TORTURE

In 1939 Stalin issued in the name of the Central Committee his retroactive approval of the methods of torture which the NKVD used to obtain confessions.

The Central Committee of the All-Union Communist Party (Bolsheviks) explains that the application of methods of physical pressure in NKVD practice is permissible from 1937 on in accordance with permission of the Central Committee of the All-Union Communist Party (Bolsheviks). . . . It is known that all bourgeois intelligence services use methods of physical influence against the representatives of the socialist proletariat and that they use them in their most scandalous form. The question arises as to why the socialist intelligence service should be more humanitarian against the mad agents of the bourgeoisie, against the deadly enemies of the working class and the kolkhoz workers. The Central Committee of the All-Union Communist Party (Bolsheviks) considers that physical pressure should still be used obligatorily, as an exception applicable to known and obstinate enemies of the people, as a method both justifiable and appropriate.

FROM: Stalin, Telegram to regional and republic secretaries of Communist Party committees, to the People's Commissars of Internal Affairs, and to the heads of NKVD organizations, January 20, 1939 (quoted by Khrushchev in his secret speech of February 25, 1956; English translation by the United States Department of State in *The Anti-Stalin Campaign*, New York, Columbia University Press, 1956, p. 41).

THE PLEA OF A PURGE VICTIM

The secret purges of 1937-38 struck the party hierarchy severely. A large majority of the Central Committee, all but one of the six candidate members of the Politbureau, and two members of the Politbureau itself – all tested Stalinists – were secretly arrested, tortured and shot. The statement by one of the candidate members of the Politbureau, Robert Eikhe, repudiating the confession extorted from him, was revealed by Khrushchev in 1956.

I have not been guilty of even one of the things with which I am charged and my heart is clean of even the shadow of baseness. I have never in my life told you a word of falsehood and now, finding my two feet in the grave, I am also not lying. My whole case is a typical example of provocation, slander and violation of the elementary basis of revolutionary legality. . . .

. . . The confessions which were made part of my file are not only absurd but contain some slander toward the Central Committee of the All-Union Communist Party (Bolsheviks) and toward the Council of People's Commissars because correct resolutions of the Central Committee of the All-Union Communist Party (Bolsheviks) and of the Council of People's Commissars, which were not made by my initiative and without my participation, are presented as hostile acts of counter-revolutionary organizations made at my suggestion. . . .

I am now alluding to the most disgraceful part of my life and to my really grave guilt against the Party and against you. This is my confession of counter-revolutionary activity. . . . The case is as follows: not being able to suffer the tortures to which I was submitted by Ushakov and Nikolayev – and especially by the first one – who utilized the knowledge that my broken ribs have not properly mended and have caused me great pain – I have been forced to accuse myself and others.

The majority of my confession has been suggested or dictated by Ushakov, and the remainder is my reconstruction of NKVD materials from western Siberia for which I assumed all responsibility. If some part of the story which Ushakov fabricated and which I signed did not properly hang together, I was forced to sign another variation. The same thing was done to Rukhimovich,* who was at first designated as a member of the reserve net and whose name later was removed without telling me anything about it; the same was also done with the leader of the reserve net, supposedly

FROM: Eikhe, Declaration to Stalin, October 27, 1939 (quoted by Khrushchev in his secret speech of February 25, 1956; in *The Anti-Stalin Campaign*, pp. 32-33).

*Rukhimovich: a member of the Central Committee who fell in the purge – Ed.

created by Bukharin in 1935. At first I wrote my name in, and then I was instructed to insert Mezhlauk. *There were other similar incidents.

... I am asking and begging you that you again examine my case and this not for the purpose of sparing me but in order to unmask the vile provocation which like a snake wound itself around many persons in a great degree due to my meanness and criminal slander. I have never betrayed you or the Party. I know that I perish because of vile and mean work of the enemies of the Party and of the people, who fabricated the provocation against me.

STALIN AS A PHILOSOPHER

A new history of the Communist Party of the Soviet Union, written under Stalin's direction, was published in 1938 to bring the past into line with the purge charges. Stalin personally contributed a chapter on the philosophy of Marxism, in which he put special stress on the historical role of the proper ideas and theories.

... The strength and vitality of Marxism-Leninism lies in the fact that it does base its practical activity on the needs of the development of the material life of society and never divorces itself from the real life of society.

It does not follow from Marx's words, however, that social ideas, theories, political views and political institutions are of no significance in the life of society, that they do not reciprocally affect social being, the development of the material conditions of the life of society. We have been speaking so far of the *origin* of social ideas, theories, views and political institutions, of *the way they arise*, of the fact that the spiritual life of society is a reflection of the conditions of its material life. As regards the *significance* of social ideas, theories, views and political institutions, as regards their *role* in history, historical materialism, far from denying them, stresses the important role and significance of these factors in the life of society, in its history.

There are different kinds of social ideas and theories. There are old ideas and theories which have outlived their day and which serve the interests of the moribund forces of society. Their significance lies in the fact that they hamper the development, the progress of society. Then there are new and advanced ideas and theories which serve the interests of the advanced forces of society. Their significance lies in the fact that they facilitate the development, the progress of society; and their significance is the greater the more accurately they reflect the needs of development of the material life of society.

FROM: Stalin, "Dialectical and Historical Materialism" (from the *History of the CPSU(B): Short Course*, 1938; in *Problems of Leninism*, pp. 726-28).

*Mezhlauk: a vice-premier and purge victim – Ed.

New social ideas and theories arise only after the development of the material life of society has set new tasks before society. But once they have arisen they become a most potent force which facilitates the carrying out of the new tasks set by the development of the material life of society, a force which facilitates the progress of society. It is precisely here that the tremendous organizing, mobilizing and transforming value of new ideas, new theories, new political views and new political institutions manifests itself. New social ideas and theories arise precisely because they are necessary to society, because is is *impossible* to carry out the urgent tasks of development of the material life of society without their organizing, mobilizing and transforming action. Arising out of the new tasks set by the development of the material life of society, the new social ideas and theories force their way through, become the possession of the masses, mobilize and organize them against the moribund forces of society, and thus facilitate the overthrow of these forces, which hamper the development of the material life of society.

Thus social ideas, theories and political institutions, having arisen on the basis of the urgent tasks of the development of the material life of society, the development of social being, themselves then react upon social being, upon the material life of society, creating the conditions necessary for completely carrying out the urgent tasks of the material life of society, and for rendering its further development possible.

In this connection, Marx says: "Theory becomes a material force as soon as it has gripped the masses."

Hence, in order to be able to influence the conditions of material life of society and to accelerate their development and their improvement, the party of the proletariat must rely upon such a social theory, such a social idea as correctly reflects the needs of development of the material life of society, and which is therefore capable of setting into motion broad masses of the people and of mobilizing them and organizing them into a great army of the proletarian party, prepared to smash the reactionary forces and to clear the way for the advanced forces of society.

The fall of the "Economists" and Mensheviks was due, among other things, to the fact that they did not recognize the mobilizing, organizing and transforming role of advanced theory, of advanced ideas and, sinking to vulgar materialism, reduced the role of these factors almost to nothing, thus condeming the Party to passivity and inanition.

The strength and vitality of Marxism-Leninism is derived from the fact that it relies upon an advanced theory which correctly reflects the needs of development of the material life of society, that it elevates theory to a proper level, and that it deems it its duty to utilize every ounce of the mobilizing, organizing and transforming power of this theory.

That is the answer historical materialism gives to the question of the relation between social being and social consciousness, between the conditions of development of material life and the development of the spiritual life of society. . . .

VYSHINSKY ON THE NEW LAW

The final step in the enunciation of the new Soviet set of social ideals was the purge of Pashukanis and his theory of the diminishing role of law. In place of this Vyshinsky proclaimed that law of the socialist type would remain firmly in effect until that distant date when the state withered away.

The proletariat requires the state, state apparatus, a definite state order—the socialist legal order, which signifies the stability of socialist social relationships and of socialist discipline, respect for the rules of socialist life in common, respect and preservation inviolate of social, socialist property—the bases of the entire Soviet order, the observance of all Soviet laws. Special forms of the class struggle correspond to the epoch of the proletarian dictatorship, and the state during this period is confronted with special problems related to those forms and responsive to the demands of this period. . . .

The dictatorship of the proletariat solves the problems of the proletarian revolution both with the aid of law and with the assistance of measures strictly defined by statute, through administrative and judicial organs. The dictatorship of the proletariat is authority unlimited by any statutes whatever. But the dictatorship of the proletariat, creating its own laws, makes use of them, demands that they be observed, and punishes breach of them. Dictatorship of the proletariat does not signify anarchy and disorder but, on the contrary, strict order and firm authority which operates upon strict principles, set out in the fundamental law of the proletarian state—the Soviet Constitution. . . .

The greatest expression of the development of proletarian democracy—and at the same time of the organic synthesis of the principles thereof and of the proletarian dictatorship—is the Stalin Constitution, which records in the form of law the brilliant and epoch-making triumphs of socialism. It is at the same time the greatest monument of Soviet socialist law, the greatest historical act, in which is expressed the will of the Soviet people, the will of the working classes. The Stalin Constitution signifies the ultimate strengthening of the Soviet order, of the proletarian dictatorship, which

FROM: Vyshinsky, ed., *The Law of the Soviet State* (1938; English translation by Hugh W. Babb, New York, 1948, pp. 47-48, 52, 54-57; copyright 1948 by the American Council of Learned Societies. Reprinted with permission of The Macmillan Co.

rests on a still more mighty socialist basis than had ever existed in the previous twenty years of the history of our socialist revolution. It reveals the ultimate essence of socialist democracy, which is the direct consequence of the triumph of the proletarian dictatorship and the integration of the development of the Soviet socialist state order. . . .

As a means of control on the part of society, a means of regulating social relationships, a method and means of preserving the interests of socialist society and the rights and interests of citizens, Soviet law carries out a social function of gigantic importance – without which the socialist state could not get along until that time when it completely withers away.

Law – like the state – will wither away only in the highest phase of communism, with the annihilation of the capitalist encirclement; when all will learn to get along without special rules defining the conduct of people under the threat of punishment and with the aid of constraint; when people are so accustomed to observe the fundamental rules of community life that they will fulfill them without constraint of any sort. Until then, however, there is necessity for general control, firm discipline in labor and in community life, and complete subordination of all the new society's work to a truly democratic state . . . .

Stuchka* characterized Soviet civil law and the Soviet Civil Code as basically bourgeois phenomena. He flatly declared all the law of the period of the New Economic Policy to be bourgeois, asserting that we have simply "imported, borrowed, bourgeois law."

Our new (and we may say here our first) codes were to him the result of "concessions to bourgeois law," as "landmarks of retreat" – thus repeating the anti-Leninist fabrications of Zinoviev and Bukharin and transferring Trotskyist-Zinovievist principles into the field of legal theory. In *The Revolutionary Role of Soviet Law*, Stuchka wrote that he had succeeded "with the help of his comrades" in formulating a new revolutionary dialectic conception of civil law in general and of our Soviet civil law in particular. This new conception, for whose invention Stuchka takes special credit, was the notorious theory of so-called "economic" law whereby, as everyone knows, Stuchka and some of his pupils understood a part of the civil law embracing questions of an administrative-economic character. . . .

The "new, revolutionary-dialectic conception," proudly proclaimed by Stuchka, dwindled to the right-opportunist "theory" of "two-section law," merely contrasting the interests of socialist economy with those of the socialist man, and underestimating the civil law as law which regulates, affirms, and preserves the individual and property interests of the toiling citizens of the USSR, the builders of socialism.

---

*Stuchka: a leading Soviet jurist of the nineteen-twenties – Ed.

This is a coarse perversion of the Marx-Engels-Lenin-Stalin theory of socialism – as to the place and part of individuality in socialist society.

"Socialism does not deny individual interests – it amalgamates them with those of the group. Socialism cannot be isolated from individual interests – only socialist society can most completely satisfy them. Moreover, socialist society represents the only firm guarantee that individual interests will be preserved" (Stalin).

These teachings of Stalin define also the path of development of Soviet civil law and the problems before us in this field – problems of developing and reinforcing Soviet civil law.

The extent of the perversions in the field of the Marxist-Leninist theory of law is particularly apparent in the liquidation of the discipline of Soviet civil law by Stuchka and his followers, who have now come actually to be wreckers and traitors. The whole depth of these perversions is particularly conspicuous in our time, when the greatest of human constitutions, the Stalin Constitution, allots a particularly honored place to the civil rights of Soviet people, when civil legal relationships are raised, in conditions of socialist society, to the highest degree of their development. Unfortunately the perversions of the Marxist theory of law went far deeper than would be inferred from the foregoing. A group of traitors, headed by Pashukanis and others, sat for a number of years in the former Institute of Soviet Construction and Law, and systematically practiced the distortion of the fundamental and most important principles of Marxist-Leninist methodology in the field of law . . . .

. . . Each in his field wrought not a little to pervert the great doctrine of Marx-Engels-Lenin-Stalin, so as to disarm Soviet jurists and expose them to the putrid vapor of all kinds of anti-Marxist, anti-Leninist "theories" whereby our enemies sought to sully the pure source of great and truly scientific thought. Because of the work of these wreckers over a period of years, the extremely rich scientific inheritance of Marx-Engels-Lenin, and the equally rich works of Stalin, which guarantee the further development of Soviet legal science, remained unutilized and insufficiently elaborated. . . .

They denied the very possibility of the development of Soviet law as socialist law. They tried mechanically to transfer the legal institutions of one epoch (that of imperialistic capitalism) into another (that of socialism), perverting the basic methodological settings of Marxism-Leninism, which teaches that law, or the legal superstructure, can and must be explained in the last analysis out of the economic structure of society, out of its relationships of production. . . .

STALIN ON THE STATE AND THE INTELLIGENTSIA

At the Eighteenth Party Congress in March, 1939, Stalin undertook to explain theoretically the role of the Soviet state (to all intents and purposes permanent), both in developing the country and in protecting it against the "capitalist encirclement." He added a defense of the "Soviet intelligentsia"—meaning all the middle and upper strata of white-collar, technical, and managerial employees of the government—which confirmed that political preference for "proletarians" had come to an end.

. . . The state arose because society split up into antagonistic classes; it arose in order to keep in check the exploited majority in the interests of the exploiting minority. The instruments of state power became concentrated mainly in the army, the penal organs, the intelligence service, the prisons. Two basic functions characterize the activity of the state: at home (the main function), to keep in check the exploited majority; abroad (not the main function), to extend the territory of its class, the ruling class, at the expense of the territory of other states, or to defend the territory of its own state from attack by other states. Such was the case in slave society and under feudalism. Such is the case under capitalism.

In order to overthrow capitalism it was necessary not only to remove the bourgeoisie from power, not only to expropriate the capitalists, but also to smash entirely the bourgeois state machine, its old army, its bureaucratic officialdom and its police force, and to substitute for it a new, proletarian form of state, a new, socialist state. And that, as we know, is exactly what the Bolsheviks did. But it does not at all follow that the new, proletarian state may not retain certain functions of the old state, modified to suit the requirements of the proletarian state. Still less does it follow that the forms of our socialist state must remain unchanged, that all the original functions of our state must be fully retained in the future. As a matter of fact, the forms of our state are changing and will continue to change in line with the development of our country and with the changes in the international situation.

Lenin was absolutely right when he said:

"The forms of bourgeois states are extremely varied, but their essence is the same: all these states, whatever their form, in the final analysis are inevitably the *dictatorship of the bourgeoisie*. The transition from capitalism to communism certainly cannot but yield a

FROM: Stalin, Report on the Work of the Central Committee, to the Eighteenth Congress of the CPSU(B) (March, 1939; *Problems of Leninism*, pp. 795-800).

great abundance and variety of political forms, but the essence will inevitably be the same: *the dictatorship of the proletariat.*"

Since the October Revolution, our socialist state has in its development passed through two main phases.

The first phase was the period from the October Revolution to the elimination of the exploiting classes. The principal task in that period was to suppress the resistance of the overthrown classes, to organize the defence of the country against the attack of the interventionists, to restore industry and agriculture, and to prepare the conditions for the elimination of the capitalist elements. Accordingly, in this period our state performed two main functions. The first function was to suppress the overthrown classes within the country. In this respect our state bore a superficial resemblance to previous states, whose functions had also been to suppress recalcitrants, with the fundamental difference, however, that our state suppressed the exploiting minority in the interests of the labouring majority, while previous states had suppressed the exploited majority in the interests of the exploiting minority. The second function was to defend the country from foreign attack. In this respect it likewise bore a superficial resemblance to previous states, which also undertook the armed defence of their countries, with the fundamental difference, however, that our state defended from foreign attack the gains of the labouring majority, while previous states in such cases defended the wealth and privileges of the exploiting minority. Our state had yet a third function: this was economic and organizational work and cultural and educational work performed by our state bodies with the purpose of developing the young shoots of the new, socialist economic system and re-educating the people in the spirit of socialism. But this new function did not attain any considerable development in that period.

The second phase was the period from the elimination of the capitalist elements in town and country to the complete victory of the socialist economic system and the adoption of the new Constitution. The principal task in this period was to organize socialist economy throughout the country and to eliminate the last remnants of the capitalist elements, to organize a cultural revolution, and to organize a thoroughly modern army for the defence of the country. And the functions of our socialist state changed accordingly. The function of military suppression inside the country ceased, died away; for exploitation had been abolished, there were no more exploiters left, and so there was no one to suppress. In place of this function of suppression the state acquired the function of protecting socialist property from thieves and pilferers of the property of the people. The function of armed defence of the country from foreign attack fully remained; consequently, the Red Army and the Navy also fully remained, as did the penal organs and the intelligence service, which are indispensable for the detection and punishment of the spies, assassins and wreckers sent into our country by foreign intelligence services. The function of the state organs as regards economic and organizational work, and cultural and educational work, remained and was developed to the full. Now the main task of our state inside the country lies in peaceful economic and organizational work, and cultural and educational work. As for our army, penal organs, and intelligence service, their edge is no longer turned to the inside of the country but to the outside, against external enemies.

As you see, we now have an entirely new, socialist state, one without precedent in history and differing considerably in form and functions from the socialist state of the first phase.

But development cannot stop there. We are moving ahead, towards communism. Will our state remain in the period of communism also?

Yes, we will, if the capitalist encirclement is not liquidated, and if the danger of foreign military attack is not eliminated, although naturally, the forms of our state will again change in conformity with the change in the situation at home and abroad.

No, it will not remain and will wither away if the capitalist encirclement is liquidated and is replaced by a socialist encirclement.

That is how the question stands with regard to the socialist state. . . .

In spite of the fact that the position of the Party on the question of the Soviet intelligentsia is perfectly clear, there are still current in our Party views hostile to the Soviet intelligentsia and incompatible with the Party position. As you know, those who hold these false views practise a disdainful and contemptuous attitude toward the Soviet intelligentsia and regard it as a force alien and even hostile to the working class and the peasantry. True, during the period of Soviet development the intellgentsia has undergone a radical change both in composition and status. It has become closer to the people and is honestly collaborating with it, in which respect it differs fundamentally from the old, bourgeois intelligentsia. But this apparently means nothing to these comrades. They go on harping on the old tune and wrongly apply to the Soviet intelligentsia views and attitudes which were justified in the old days when the intelligentsia was in the service of the landlords and capitalists. . . .

But the position with regard to the intelligentsia has radically changed since the October Revolution, since the defeat of the foreign armed intervention, and especially since the victory of industrialization and collectivization, when the abolition of exploitation and the firm establishment of the socialist economic system made it effectively possible to give the country a new Constitution and to put it into effect. . . . Parallel with this painful process of differentiation and break-up of the old intelligentsia there was going on a rapid process of formation, mobilization and mustering of forces of a new intelligentsia. Hundreds of thousands of young people from the ranks of the working class, the peasantry and the working intelligentsia entered the universities and technical colleges, from which they emerged to reinforce the attenuated ranks of the intelligentsia. They infused fresh blood into it and animated it with a new, Soviet spirit. They radically changed the whole aspect of the intelligentsia, moulding it in their own form and image. The remnants of the old intelligentsia were dissolved in the new, Soviet intelligentsia, the intelligentsia of the people. There thus arose a new, Soviet intelligentsia, intimately bound up with the people and, for the most part, ready to serve them faithfully and loyally.

As a result, we now have a numerous, new, popular, socialist intelligentsia, fundamentally different from the old, bourgeois intelligentsia both in composition and in social and political character.

The old theory about the intelligentsia, which taught that it should be distrusted and combated, fully applied to the old prerevolutionary intelligentsia, which served the landlords and capitalists. That theory is now out-of-date and does not fit our new, Soviet intelligentsia. A new theory is needed for our new intelligentsia, one teaching the necessity for a cordial attitude towards it, solicitude and respect for it, and cooperation with it in the interests of the working class and the peasantry. . . .

THE IMPACT OF THE SECOND WORLD WAR

The German invasion of 1941 and the imperatives of total mobilization had a colossal material impact on the Soviet people, yet the Soviet political and economic system as fashioned by Stalin was reaffirmed as the optimum framework for the national struggle. This was the thesis of the appraisal of the war years published in 1947 by the State Planning Chief Nikolai A. Voznesensky. Shortly afterwards, Voznesensky perished in the purge of supporters of Stalin's lieutenant Andrei Zhdanov following the death of the latter in 1948.

The Great Patriotic War of 1941-45 has radically transformed the national economy of the USSR, converted the Soviet economy in the interests of a victorious war, and created peculiar laws of the war period. It is a special

FROM: Nikolai A. Voznesensky, *The Economy of the USSR during World War II* (Washington, D. C., Public Affairs Press, 1948), pp. 1, 3-4, 12-13, 21-22, 32, 97-98; reprinted by permission of the publisher.

period of socialist economics, a period of war economies in the history of the USSR. A separate chapter in the political economy of socialism corresponds to it – the political economy of the Patriotic War.

The unity of the national interests of the peoples of the Union of Soviet Socialist Republics exhibited itself with all its force in the Great Patriotic War; socialism against fascism, the Soviet people against Germans infected with Nazism. The war against Fascist Germany became the holy war of all the peoples inhabiting the Soviet Union – for their national existence, for their homeland, for socialism.

The great unity of the peoples of the Soviet Union during the Patriotic War, which is admired by the whole world, grew up on the basis of the victory of the socialist method of production and the annihilation of exploiting classes in the USSR. Long before the beginning of the Patriotic War, the roots of the parasitical classes and groups were eradicated from the soil of Soviet Society, which created a firm basis of moral and political unity of the Soviet people. . . .

The war against the USSR in 1941 was begun by Hitlerite Germany, the country of most rapacious imperialism. In the very first days of the Patriotic War, Stalin armed the peoples of the Soviet Union with the program of a holy war of liberation against German imperialism. Comrade Stalin said that "the Germans are now leading an aggressive, unjust war calculated to grab foreign territory and to subjugate foreign nations. Therefore, all honorable men rise against the German aggressors as against enemies."

"In contrast to Hitlerite Germany, the Soviet Union and its allies are waging a just war of liberation aimed at freeing the enslaved nations of Europe and the USSR from Hitlerite tyranny. Therefore, all honorable men must support the armies of the USSR, Great Britain and of other allies as armies of liberation."

Stalin called upon the Soviet army and the peoples of the Soviet Union to crush the military might of the German aggressors, to destroy the German occupiers who had transgressed on the territory of our homeland for its enslavement, to liberate the Soviet lands and peoples from the fascist German yoke, and then to kill off the fascist beast in its own territory.

Following the directives of Comrade Stalin, the Soviet army and the armed nation of the Soviet Union, led by the party of Communists-Bolsheviks, fought for every inch of Soviet soil, for our cities and villages, exhibiting the greatest valor and endurance. During the forced retreat of units of the Soviet army in the initial period of the Patriotic War, Soviet railroad men drove back rolling stock; workers, engineers and mechanics moved out equipment and went east; collective farmers drove back livestock and moved grain into rear areas. In the regions of the USSR occupied by the enemy during the Patriotic War guerrilla forces and diversionist groups were organized to fight against units of the enemy army. Everywhere the flames of guerrilla warfare was spreading, creating unbearable conditions for the German occupiers and their collaborators. This feat of the Soviet people in the regions occupied by Hitlerite Germany will remain for many ages a monument to valor, heroism and devotion to the homeland.

During the Patriotic War, the front and the rear were welded into a single undefeatable camp in which the union of workers and peasants and the friendship of the peoples of the multi-national Soviet Union were strengthened ever further. Comrade Stalin said that any other state suffering such losses as our homeland would not have stood the tests and would have collapsed. The Soviet system has proved its great durability based on the leadership of our battle-tested party of Lenin-Stalin, on the victory of socialism, on the union of workers and peasants, on the unity of the peoples of the Soviet Union.

Bearing firmly and valiantly the war-time privations, the working class, kolkhoz peasantry, and the Soviet intelligentsia created with their heroic labor during the Patriotic War a solid war economy and assured our Soviet Army and our Navy of excellent war equipment, food, material supplies and fuel. The peoples of the Soviet Union furnished to their army continuous replacements from the ranks of their best sons and daughters, who multiplied the honor and glory of Soviet arms. The Soviet nation has demonstrated itself before the whole world to be an heroic nation, a warrior nation.

During the most difficult period of the Patriotic War, Comrade Stalin was inspiring the peoples of the Soviet Union and its armed forces for a struggle and victory. Endurance in the struggle with German hordes and confidence in the victory of our just cause emanated from the Great Stalin throughout the whole land, welding together the nation and the army and transforming the USSR into an unassailable fortress. . . .

The Patriotic War demanded an immediate conversion of the Soviet economy to a wartime economic basis. Resolutions of the All-Union Communist Party (of Bolsheviks) and of the Soviet government, and the directives of Comrade Stalin during the very first days of the Great Patriotic War defined the program of conversion of peacetime socialist economics to wartime socialist economics.

The creation of the State Defense Committee, which had merged Soviet executive and legislative authority and the party leadership in the country, assured the orderliness and unity of action in the mobilization of all resources of the economy for the needs of the Great Patriotic War.

A comparison of the features of the war economy of pre-revolutionary Russia during 1914-17 and the war economy of the USSR during 1941-45 shows the great superiority of the war economy of the USSR which permitted the Soviet state to assure the supplying of the front with war equipment and foodstuffs, in spite of the temporary loss of a number of industrial and agricultural regions.

The war economy of the USSR was based on the predominance of socialist ownership of the means of production. The concentration of the basic means of production in the hands of the Soviet state assured a rapid conversion of the economy of the USSR to a wartime footing. The predominance of private ownership of the means of production in pre-revolutionary Russia, a low level of development of productive powers, and the dependence on foreign capital created unsurpassable difficulties for Russia in the waging of the war of 1914-17.

The socialist revolution had destroyed the dependence of our country on foreign capital and had radically altered the class composition of the population of the USSR. While in pre-revolutionary Russia in 1913 urban and rural workers and employees constituted less than 17 percent of the whole population, in the USSR in 1939 they comprised 48 percent, i.e. almost half of the whole population. As is known, there was no *kolkhoz* peasantry and there were no cooperatives of handicraftsmen and artisans in Russia prior to the socialist revolution of 1917, while in the USSR in 1939 they comprised 46 percent, or the basic and predominant part of the other half of the population of the country. Private peasants, workers outside of cooperatives, and handicraftsmen and artisans comprised 65 percent of the population of Russia in 1913, and in the USSR in 1939 they were only 2.6 percent.

The bourgeoisie – estate owners, the large and petty urban bourgeoisie, traders and *kulaks* – comprised 16 percent of the whole population of Russia in 1913. Long before the beginning of the Patriotic War exploiting classes – estate owners, the urban bourgeoisie, and *kulaks* – had been annihilated in the USSR. This change in the class compositon of the population of the USSR in comparison with the population of pre-revolutionary Russia assured the moral and political unity of the peoples of the USSR, the firm union of the working class and peasantry, and the inviolable friendship of all peoples forming the Great Soviet Union. . . .

The wartime conversion of the economy of the USSR was carried out under the direction of the organizer of our victories, the Great Stalin, in the course of the second half of 1941 and the first half of 1942. The nucleus of economic and political personnel, created and trained by the party of Lenin-Stalin during the period of peacetime construction, assured the wartime conversion of the economy without which our victory would have been impossible. The people of the Soviet Union who had given their heroic labor to the Soviet Army, had organizers and leaders that were devoted to their people and to their party until the end.

The wartime conversion of the economy of the USSR found its expression in the war economy plans. A week after the beginning of the Patriotic War, the Soviet government adopted the first wartime plan – "the mobilizational economic plan" for the third quarter of 1941. This plan was one of the first attempts to convert the economy of the USSR and to transfer socialist economics to a wartime economic basis. It supplanted the plan for the development of the economy for the third quarter of 1941 which was intended for a relatively peaceful period and was adopted by the government before the beginning of the Patriotic War.

In comparison with the plan adopted before the war, the schedule of output of war equipment in the mobilizational economic plan for the third quarter of 1941 was increased by 26 percent. The volume of capital projects was decreased and the reduction in capital projects was primarily connected with the redistribution of metals in favor of war production. A list of priority construction was confirmed, which included war enterprises, electric stations, enterprises of the fuel, metallurgical, and chemical industries, and the construction of railroads. The plan provided for the concentration of capital projects and material resources in the construction of defense enterprises in the regions of the Volga, the Urals, and Western Siberia. Railroad car loading was retained at the prewar volume only for coal, petroleum products, metals, and grain, as, owing to the increase in military hauls, it was impossible to guarantee the fulfillment of the plan with respect to the rest of commercial freight. The plan for retail trade was reduced by 12 percent, which was caused by the diversion of the retail stocks of commodities to the Soviet Army. Of 22 thousand metal-cutting machine tools manufactured domestically, the production of which was called for by the quarterly plan, about 14 thousand machine tools were allocated to the enterprises of the Ministeries of Ammunition, Armaments, and Aviation Industry. The mobilization plan for the third quarter of 1941 converted the economy for service to the Great Patriotic War. However, experience had shown that this change was insufficient. The war was penetrating the economy more decisively and more extensively all the time.

On August 16, 1941, the Soviet government adopted the "war economic plan" for the fourth quarter of 1941 and for 1942 for the regions of the Volga, the Urals, Western Siberia, Kazakhstan, and Central Asia, which was prepared under assignment from Comrade Stalin. This plan was drawn up with the intention of relocating industry to the eastern regions of the USSR, and of intensifying war production, essential for the needs of the Patriotic War, in those regions. . . .

While the process of wartime increasing socialist reproduction was taking place in the eastern regions of the USSR, a heroic process of reconstructing the socialist economy destroyed by Hitlerite Germany was taking place in the course of the Patriotic War in the northwestern, western, central, southeastern, and southern economic regions of the USSR.

This process of reconstruction was proceeding in the regions liberated from German occupation in which the red banner of the Soviets was planted anew after the defeat of the enemy. Reconstruction of the economy was taking place in the frontal regions as well, where a part of the enterprises was either destroyed as a result of enemy bombing and artillery fire or evacuated to the eastern regions of the country and then reconstructed after the front had moved to the west.

The reconstruction of the economy in the liberated and frontal regions in the course of the Patriotic War represents a heroic feat by the peoples of the Soviet Union. In the general balance sheet of the war economy of the USSR, the reconstruction and growth in production in the frontal and liberated regions had a tremendous importance for the supplying of the needs of the front and especially for the raising of the political and the material levels of the population of the liberated regions. . . .

The material damage inflicted on the economy of the USSR by Hitlerite Germany and her accomplices can be expressed in terms of the loss of output and income by the population and the state as a result of the cessation of production in the occupied territory of the USSR. Production in state and cooperative enterprises had ceased on a considerable part of the territory of the USSR occupied by the Germans during the Patriotic War. After the liberation of the occupied regions by the Soviet Army, the volume of production still continued to be below the prewar volume for a long time. As a result, a tremendous amount of goods failed to be produced in the USSR.

The following failed to be produced, and consequently were lost to the economy, in the occupied regions and enterprises of the USSR during the period of the Patriotic War only: 307 million tons of hard coal, 72 billion kilowatt-hours of electric power, 38 million tons of steel, 136 thousand tons of aluminum, 58 thousand tractors, 90 thousand metal-cutting machine tools, 63 million quintals of sugar, 11 billion poods of grain, 1,922 million quintals of potatoes, 68 million quintals of meat, and 567 million quintals of milk. This colossal quantity of goods would have been produced in the occupied regions and enterprises of the USSR even if the production in these regions and enterprises had remained at the 1940 level.

Not a single capitalist country in all its past history or in modern war has sustained such losses and barbaric destruction on the part of aggressors, as has our homeland.

The Soviet people is reconstructing the national economy of the USSR with its heroic efforts, and will surpass the prewar level of production and overtake economically the main capitalist countries. The peoples of the USSR, manifesting an extraordinary will to work and straining their spiritual and physical powers, will successfully solve these historic problems.

The material loss inflicted by Hitlerite Germany on the peoples of the Soviet Union is being to a negligible extent compensated by the relocation of industrial equipment from Germany to the USSR in the form of reparations. The value of this equipment amounts to only 0.6 percent of the magnitude of just the "direct property losses" borne by the USSR during the Patriotic War. To reattain and to surpass the prewar blossoming of material and spiritual culture – this is the problem which the peoples of the Soviet Union are solving with their creative and heroic labor. The restoration of production in the liberated regions of the USSR, and the liquidation of the effects of German occupation, are proceeding on the basis of socialist production, which had demonstrated during the Patriotic War its stability and its great superiority over the capitalist economy. "We must liquidate completely the effects of German economic management in the regions liberated from German occupation. This is a great problem for the whole people. We can and we must solve this difficult problem in the shortest time." (Stalin).

STALIN AND THE ORTHODOX CHURCH

In 1943, as a further step to mobilize traditionalist support for his regime, as well as to counteract collaborationist sentiment in the German-occupied part of the country, Stalin extended a measure of recognition to the Russian Orthodox Church and allowed restoration of the office of the Patriarch (defunct since the time of Peter the Great except for a brief period during the Revolution). Since then the Orthodox Church has functioned legally despite restrictions on its expansion and on the religious education of children. Other faiths – Catholic, Protestant, Jewish, Moslem – have continued to suffer harassment, especially where they are associated with international allegiance or minority separatism.

FROM: *Zhurnal Moskovskoi Patriarkhii* (Journal of the Moscow Patriarchate), No. 1, September 12, 1943, pp. 5, 6, 11, 16 (editor's translation).

Stalin Receives Metropolitan Sergei

On September 4 the Chairman of the Council of People's Commissars of the USSR, Comrade J. V. Stalin, held a reception, during which a conversation took place with the Acting Patriarch Metropolitan Sergei, Metropolitan Aleksei of Leningrad, and Metropolitan Nikolai of Kiev and Galicia, Exarch of the Ukraine.

During the conversation Metropolitan Sergei made it known to the Chairman of the Council of People's Commissars that in the governing circles of the Orthodox Church there is an intention in the near future to convene a Council of Bishops to elect a Patriarch of Moscow and all Russia and to form a Holy Synod under the Patriarch.

Head of government Comrade J. V. Stalin responded sympathetically to this proposal and stated that on the part of the government there will be no obstacles to this.

Also present in the conversation was Deputy Chairman of the Council of People's Commissars of the USSR Comrade V. M. Molotov.

The Council of Bishops of the Orthodox Church

On 8 September in Moscow there was held the Council of Bishops of the Orthodox Church, convened to elect a Patriarch of Moscow and All Russia and to form a Holy Synod under the Patriarch.

The Council of Bishops unanimously elected Metropolitan Sergei as Patriarch of Moscow and All Russia.

The Council furthermore adopted unanimously the statement addressed by Metropolitan Sergei to the Government of the USSR expressing thanks for its attention to the needs of the Russian Orthodox Church. Archbishop Grigory of Saratov read a statement to the Christians of the whole world. This document, containing an appeal for the unification of all forces in the struggle against Hitlerism, was also adopted unanimously by the Council. . . .

Statement of the Council of the Most Reverend Hierarchy of the Russian Orthodox Church to the Soviet Government (September 8, 1943)

Deeply moved by the sympathetic attitude of our national Leader and Head of the Soviet Government, J. V. STALIN, toward the needs of the Russian Orthodox Church and toward our modest works, we, his humble servants, express to the Government our council's sincere gratitude and joyful conviction that, encouraged by this sympathy, we will redouble our share of work in the nationwide struggle for the salvation of the motherland.

Let the Heavenly Head of the Church bless the works of the Government with the Creator's blessing and let him crown our struggle in a just cause with the victory we long for and the liberation of suffering humanity from the dark bondage of fascism.

(Signed by Sergei, Metropolitan of Moscow and Kolomna, and eighteen other metropolitans, archbishops and bishops.)

Condemnation of Traitors to the Faith and the Fatherland (September 8, 1943)

Alongside the gratifying manifestations of patriotic activity by the Orthodox clergy and laity it is all the sadder to see manifestations of a contrary character. Among the clergy and laity there are those who, forgetting their fear of God, dare to take advantage of the common misfortune: they meet the Germans like invited guests, make themselves available for service, and sometimes commit outright treason, for example betraying to the enemy their fellows among the partisans and others who are sacrificing themselves for the motherland. An obliging conscience, of course, is always ready to suggest justification even for such conduct. But the treachery of Judas will never cease to be the treachery of Judas. Just as Judas destroyed his own soul and bodily bore an exceptional punishment even here on earth, so these traitors, preparing themselves to perish for eternity, do not avoid the fate of Cain on earth. The Fascists will suffer just retribution for their plunder, murder and other evil needs. Nor can mercy be expected by these stooges of the Fascists who do well for themselves at the expense of their brothers and behind their backs.

The Holy Orthodox Church, Russian and Eastern, has already pronounced its condemnation of traitors to the Christian cause and betrayers of the Church. And today, gathered in the name of the Father, the Son and the Holy Spirit, we affirm this condemnation and declare that anyone guilty of betraying the cause of the Church and going over to the side of Fascism is an enemy of Christ the Lord and is excommunicated, and if a bishop or cleric is removed from office. Amen.

(Signed by Metropolitan Sergei of Moscow and eighteen other metropolitans, archbishops and bishops.)

WARTIME DEFECTIONS: THE VLASOV MOVEMENT

In 1941 the German invaders were met with mass surrenders and widespread collaboration on the part of people who had been terrorized by Stalinism or demoralized by Red Army reverses. Among their prisoners the Nazis allowed a limited political and military organization to be formed under the leadership of Andrei Vlasov, a lieutenant general in the Red Army who had been captured in 1942 while attempting to break the siege of Leningrad. Formalized in

1944 as the "Committee for the Liberation of the Peoples of Russia," the Vlasov movement proclaimed in the so-called "Prague Manifesto" (influenced by the captured political commissar and Bukharinist Milenty Zykov) a program for a democratic Russia harking back to the policies of the NEP. Ironically, the only major action in which Vlasov troops were involved was when they turned against the Germans to help in the liberation of Prague in May, 1945. Nevertheless, after they were rounded up by the Red Army or forcibly repatriated by the Americans and British, Vlasov and other leaders were executed for treason and the rank and file were sentenced to the labor camps.

Countrymen! Brothers, and Sisters!

In this hour of great trials we must decide the fate of our homeland, our peoples, and our own fate.

Mankind is going through an era of the greatest upheavals. The present world war is a fight to the finish of opposing political systems.

It is fought by the powers of imperialism, led by the plutocrats of England and the USA, whose power is based on the suppression and exploitation of other countries and peoples. It is fought by the powers of internationalism, led by the Stalin clique, dreaming of world revolution and the destruction of the national independence of other countries and peoples. It is fought by freedom-loving nations, who thirst to live their own way of life, determined by their historical and national development. . . .

For more than a quarter of a century the peoples of Russia have experienced the burden of Bolshevik tyranny.

In the Revolution of 1917 the peoples who inhabited the Russian Empire sought to realize their aspirations for justice, general welfare, and national freedom. They revolted against the spent regime of the Tsar, which did not and could not abolish the causes of social injustice, the remnants of serfdom, and the economic and cultural backwardness. But after the Tsarist empire was overthrown by the peoples of Russia in February 1917, the parties and leaders were unable to decide on bold and consequent reforms. With their ambiguous policy, their compromises and their unwillingness to assume responsibility before the future, they failed to justify themselves before the people. The people spontaneously followed those who promised them immediate peace, land, freedom, and bread, those who advanced the most radical slogans. The Bolshevik Party prom-

FROM: Manifesto of the Committee for the Liberation of the Peoples of Russia, November 14, 1944 (English translation in George Fischer, *Soviet Opposition to Stalin*, Cambridge, Mass., Harvard University Press, 1952, pp. 194-97). Reprinted by permission.

ised the people a social-order system, where the people could live happily and, for this, the people made incalculable sacrifices. It is not the fault of the people that this party, after seizing power, not only failed to realize the demands of the people but, strengthening their repressive organs more and more, robbed the people of the rights they had won, and forced the people into permanent misery, into lawlessness, and into the most unscrupulous exploitation. . . .

The Bolsheviks condemned the peoples of our homeland to permanent misery, hunger, and extinction, to spiritual and physical slavery, and, finally, they forced them into a criminal war for causes foreign to them.

All this is being camouflaged with the lie about the democratism of the Stalin constitution and the building of a socialist society. No other country in the world has or ever had such a low standard of living, while the material wealth of the country is so enormous. No other country has had such trammeling of rights and humiliation of the individual personality as there has been and remains under the Bolshevik system.

The peoples of Russia have lost forever their faith in Bolshevism, where the state is an all-devouring machine and the people have become impoverished slaves without any rights. . . .

The Committee for the Liberation of the Peoples of Russia has as its aim:

(a) The overthrow of Stalin's tyranny, the liberation of the peoples of Russia from the Bolshevik system, and the restitution of those rights to the peoples of Russia which they fought for and won in the people's revolution of 1917;

(b) Discontinuation of the war and an honorable peace with Germany;

(c) Creation of a new free People's political system without Bolsheviks and exploiters.

As the basis for the new political system of the peoples of Russia the committee lays down the following main principles:

(1) Equality of all peoples of Russia and their real right for national development, self-determination, and state independence;

(2) Establishment of a national labor system where the interests of the state are subordinated to the task of raising the welfare and the development of the nation;

(3) Maintenance of peace, establishment of friendly relations with all countries, and international coöperation to the greatest possible extent;

(4) Extensive government measures to strengthen family and marriage; real equality of rights for women;

(5) Liquidation of forced labor and guarantee to all laboring people of the right to free labor as the basis for their material well-being; determina-

tion of wages for all types of labor that provide for a civilized standard of living;

(6) Liquidation of the kolkhozes, and gratuitous turnover of the land to the peasants as their private property; free choice of forms of land use; freedom to dispose of the products of one's own labor, abolition of forced deliveries, and annulment of debts to the Soviet government;

(7) Establishment of inviolable private property earned by work; reestablishment of trade, crafts, artisan enterprises, and furnishing to private initiative the right and opportunity to participate in the economic life of the country;

(8) Providing the intellectuals with the opportunity to create freely for the well-being of their people;

(9) The guarantee of social justice and protection for laboring people against any kind of exploitation, regardless of their origin and their former activity;

(10) Establishment for all, without exceptions, of a real right to free education, medical care, vacation, and old-age security;

(11) Destruction of the system of terror and tyranny; liquidation of forced resettlement and mass deportation; establishment of genuine freedom of religion, conscience, speech, assembly, and press; guarantee of inviolability of persons, their property, and homes: equality of all before the law, independence and public proceedings of the courts;

(12) Release of all political prisoners of Bolshevism, and the return home of those in the prisons and camps who suffered reprisals for their struggle against Bolshevism; no vengeance or persecution whatsoever of those who discontinue their fight for Stalin and Bolshevism, regardless of whether they fought from conviction or coercion;

(13) Rehabilitation of national property destroyed during the war — towns, villages, factories, and plants – at the expense of the government;

(14) Support of war invalids and their families by the state.

The destruction of Bolshevism is an urgent task of all progressive forces. The Committee for the Liberation of the Peoples of Russia is convinced that the united efforts of the peoples of Russia will receive support from all the freedom-loving nations of the world. . . .

STALIN ON THE GREAT-RUSSIANS

One aspect of Stalin's later conservatism was his acknowledgment of the national pride of the "Great-Russian" (i.e., Russian-speaking) majority of the Soviet population, together with considerable Russification of the cultures of the minorities. At the close of

World War II Stalin singled out the Great-Russians to credit them with the victory.

Comrades, permit me to propose another toast, the last one.

I would like to propose that we drink to the health of the Soviet people, and primarily of the Russian people. (Loud and prolonged appluase and cheers)

I drink primarily to the health of the Russian people because it is the most outstanding of all the nations that constitute the Soviet Union.

I drink to the health of the Russian people, because, during this war, it has earned universal recognition as the guiding force of the Soviet Union among all the peoples of our country.

I drink to the health of the Russian people, not only because it is the leading people, but also because it is gifted with a clear mind, a staunch character, and patience.

Our Government committed no few mistakes; at times our position was desperate, as in 1941-42, when our army was retreating, abandoning our native villages and towns in the Ukraine, Byelorussia, Moldavia, the Leningrad Region, the Baltic Region, and the Karelo-Finnish Republic, abandoning them because there was no other alternative. Another people might have said to the government: You have not come up to our expectations. Get out. We shall appoint another government, which will conclude peace with Germany and ensure tranquillity for us. But the Russian people did not do that, for they were confident that the policy their Government was pursuing was correct; and they made sacrifices in order to ensure the defeat of Germany. And this confidence which the Russian people displayed in the Soviet Government proved to be the decisive factor which ensured our historic victory over the enemy of mankind, over fascism.

I thank the Russian people for this confidence!

To the health of the Russian people! (Loud and prolonged applause)

STALIN'S ANALYSIS OF VICTORY

In February, 1946, Stalin took the occasion of a "campaign" meeting preceding the usual single-slate election to claim that victory in World War II vindicated his policies of intensive industrialization, collectivization, and purging.

FROM: Stalin, Speech at the Reception in the Kremlin in Honour of the Commanders of the Red Army Troops, May 24, 1945 (English translation in Stalin, *On the Great Patriotic War of the Soviet Union*, Moscow, Foreign Languages Publishing House, 1954, pp. 241-42).

FROM: Stalin, Pre-Election Speech of February 9, 1946 (English translation in *The Strategy and Tactics of World Communism: Supplement I*, "One Hundred Years of Communism, 1848-1948," U. S. House of Representatives Document No. 619, 80th Congress, 2nd Session, Washington, Government Printing Office, 1948, pp. 170-78).

Our victory means, first of all, that our Soviet social order has triumphed, that the Soviet social order has successfully passed the ordeal in the fire of war and has proved its unquestionable vitality. . . .

. . . The point now is that the Soviet social order has shown itself more stable and capable of enduring than a non-Soviet social order, that the Soviet social order is a form of organization, a society superior to any non-Soviet social order. . . .

Of course, victory cannot be achieved without gallantry. But gallantry alone is not enough to vanquish an enemy who has a large army, first-class armaments, well-trained officer cadres, and a fairly good organization of supplies. To meet the blow of such an enemy, to repulse him and then to inflict utter defeat upon him required, in addition to the matchless gallantry of our troops, fully up-to-date armaments and adequate quantitites of them as well as well-organized supplies in sufficient quantities.

But that, in turn, necessitated having – and in adequate amounts – such elementary things as metal for the manufacture of armaments, equipment and machinery for factories, fuel to keep the factories and transport going, cotton for the manufacture of uniforms, and grain for supplying the Army.

Can it be claimed that before entering the Second World War our country already commanded the necessary minimum material potentialities for satisfying all these requirements in the main? I think it can. In order to prepare for this tremendous job we had to carry out three Five-Year Plans of national economic development. It was precisely these three Five-Year Plans that helped us to create these material potentialities. At any rate, our country's position in this respect before the Second World War, in 1940, was several times better than it was before the First World War, in 1913. . . .

Such an unprecedented increase in production cannot be regarded as the simple and usual development of a country from backwardness to progress. It was a leap by which our Motherland was transformed from a backward into an advanced country, from an agrarian into an industrial country. . . .

By what policy did the Communist Party succeed in providing these material potentialities in the country in such a short time?

First of all, by the Soviet policy of industrializing the country.

The Soviet method of industrializing the country differs radically from the capitalist method of industrialization. In capitalist countries industrialization usually begins with light industry. . . .

. . . Naturally, the Communist Party could not take this course. The Party knew that a war was looming, that the country could not be defended without heavy industry, that the development of heavy industry must be undertaken as soon as possible, that to be behind with this would mean to lose out. The Party remembered Lenin's words to the effect that without heavy industry it would be impossible to uphold the country's independence, that without it the Soviet order might perish.

Accordingly the Communist Party of our country rejected the "usual" course of industrialization and began the work of industrializing the country by developing heavy industry. It was very difficult, but not impossible. A valuable aid in this work was the nationalization of industry and banking, which made possible the rapid accumulation and transfer of funds to heavy industry.

There can be no doubt that without this it would have been impossible to secure our country's transformation into an industrial country in such a short time.

Second, by a policy of collectivization of agriculture.

In order to do away with our backwardness in agriculture and to provide the country with greater quanitities of marketable grain, cotton, and so forth, it was essential to pass from small-scale peasant farming to large-scale farming, for only large-scale farming can make use of new machinery, apply all the achievements of agronomical science and yield greater quantities of marketable produce.

There are, however, two kinds of large farms – capitalist and collective. The Communist Party could not adopt the capitalist path of development of agriculture, and not as a matter of principle alone but also because it implies too prolonged a development and involves preliminary ruination of the peasants and their transformation into farm hands. Therefore, the Communist Party took the path of the collectivization of agriculture, the path of creating large-scale farming by uniting peasant farms into collective farms.

The method of collectivization proved a highly progressive method not only because it did not involve the ruination of the peasants but especially because it permitted, within a few years, the covering of the entire country with large collective farms which are able to use new machinery, take advantage of all the achievements of agronomic science and give the country greater quantities of marketable produce.

There is no doubt that without a collectivization policy we could not in such a short time have done away with the age-old backwardness of our agriculture.

It cannot be said that the Party's policy encountered no resistance. Not only backward people, such as always decry everything new, but many prominent members of the Party as well, systematically dragged the Party backward and tried by hook or by crook to divert it to the "usual" capitalist path of development. All the anti-Party machinations of the Trotskyites and the Rightists, all their "activities" in sabotaging the measures of our Government, pursued the single aim of frustrating the Party's policy and obstructing the work of industrialization and collectivization. But the Party did not yield either to the threats from one side or the wails from the other and advanced confidently regardless of everything. . . .

The Communist Party's plans of work for the immediate future . . . are set forth in the new Five-Year Plan which is shortly to be endorsed. The principal aims of the new Five-Year Plan are to rehabilitate the ravaged areas of the country, to restore the prewar level in industry and agriculture, and then to surpass this level in more or less substantial measure. To say nothing of the fact that the rationing system will shortly be abolished (*stormy, prolonged applause*), special attention will be devoted to extending the production of consumer goods, to raising the living standard of the working people by steadily lowering the prices of all goods (*stormy, prolonged applause*), and to the widespread construction of all manner of scientific research institutions (*applause*) that can give science the opportunity to develop its potentialities. (*Stormy applause*)

I have no doubt that if we give our scientists proper assistance they will be able in the near future not only to overtake but to surpass the achievements of science beyond the boundaries of our country. (*Prolonged applause*)

As regards the plans for a longer period ahead, the Party means to organize a new mighty upsurge in the national economy, which would allow us to increase our industrial production, for example, three times over as compared with the prewar period. We must achieve a situation where our industry can produce annually up to 50 million tons of pig iron (*prolonged applause*), up to 60 million tons of steel (*prolonged applause*), up to 500 million tons of coal (*prolonged applause*), and up to 60 million tons of oil. (*Prolonged applause*) Only under such conditions can we consider that our homeland will be guaranteed against all possible accidents. (*Stormy applause*) That will take three more Five-Year Plans, I should think, if not more. But it can be done and we must do it. (*Stormy applause*)

Such is my brief report on the Communist Party's work in the recent past and its plans of work for the future.

It is for you to judge how correctly the Party has been working and whether it could not have worked better. . . .

. . . The Communist Party is prepared to accept the electors' verdict. (*Stormy applause*)

In the election struggle the Communist Party is not alone. It goes to the polls in a bloc with non-Party people. In by-gone days the Communists treated non-Party people and non-Party status with some mistrust. This was due to the fact that the non-Party flag was not infrequently used as a camouflage by various bourgeois groups for whom it was not advantageous to face the electorate without a mask.

That was the case in the past. But now we have different times. Our non-Party people are now divided from the bourgeoisie by a barrier known as the Soviet social order. This same barrier unites non-Party people with the Communists in a single community of Soviet men and women. Living in this single community they struggled together to build up the might of our country, fought and shed their blood together on the battle fronts for the sake of our country, and in greatness worked together to forge a victory over the enemies of our country and did forge that victory. The only difference between them is that some belong to the Party, others do not. But that is a formal difference. The important thing is that both are furthering the same common cause. Therefore the bloc of Communists and non-Party people is a natural and vital thing. (*Stormy, prolonged applause*)

In conclusion, allow me to thank you for the confidence you have shown me (*prolonged, unabating applause; shout from the audience: "Hurrah for the great captain of all victories, Comrade Stalin!"*) in nominating me to the Supreme Soviet. You need not doubt that I shall do my best to justify your trust.

(*All rise. Prolonged, unabating applause turning into an ovation. From all parts of the hall come cheers: "Long live our great Stalin! Hurrah!" "Hurrah for the great leader of the peoples!" "Glory to the great Stalin!" "Long live Comrade Stalin, the candidate of the entire nation!" "Glory to Comrade Stalin, the creator of all our victories!"*)

THE ZHDANOV MOVEMENT

Stalin's heir apparent from the end of the war until his death in 1948 was Andrei Zhdanov, who figured particularly in the ideological sphere. In August, 1946, Zhdanov launched an intensive campaign of ideological retightening, in a savage attack on certain writers and literary journals for allowing themselves to fall under "bourgeois" influences. Such criticism was then extended to virtually every other field of culture and learning, and until Stalin's death Soviet intellectual life was at its most regimented and barren.

FROM: Zhdanov, Report to the Leningrad Branch of the Union of Soviet Writers and the Leningrad City Committee of the Communist Party, August 21, 1946 (English translation in George S. Counts and Nucia Lodge, *The Country of the Blind: the Soviet System of Mind Control*, Boston, 1949, pp. 86-90, 95-96. Copyright 1949 by George S. Counts and Nucia Lodge. Copyright renewed 1977 by Martha Counts. Reprinted by permission of Houghton Mifflin Company).

. . . We demand that our comrades, both as leaders in literary affairs and as writers, be guided by the vital force of the Soviet order – its politics. Only thus can our youth be reared, not in a devil-may-care attitude and a spirit of ideological indifference, but in a strong and vigorous revolutionary spirit.

It is known that Leninism incarnated all the best traditions of the Russian revolutionary democrats of the nineteenth century and that our Soviet culture has risen, developed, and flowered on the basis of a critical working over of the cultural heritage of the past. In the sphere of literature our Party, through the words of Lenin and Stalin, has recognized more than once the tremendous significance of the great Russian revolutionary-democratic writers and critics – Belinsky, Dobroliubov, Chernyshevsky, Saltykov-Shchedrin, and Plekhanov. Beginning with Belinsky, all of the best representatives of the revolutionary-democratic Russian intelligentsia repudiated so-called "pure art" and "art for art's sake." They were heralds of art for the people, of art of high ideological and social significance. Art cannot separate itself from the fate of the people. . . .

V. I. Lenin was the first to formulate with utmost precision the attitude of advanced social thought toward literature and art. I remind you of Lenin's well-known article, "Party Organization and Party Literature," written at the end of 1905, in which he showed with characteristic force that literature cannot be non-Party, that it must be an important component part of the general proletarian cause. In this article Lenin lays the foundations on which the development of our Soviet literature is based. He wrote as follows:

"Literature must become Party. As a counterpoise to bourgeois morals, to the bourgeois commercial press, to bourgeois literary careerism and individualism, to 'manorial anarchism' and the pursuit of gain, the socialist proletariat must promote and develop the principle of *Party literature* and bring this principle to life in the most complete and integral form possible. . . ."

Leninism proceeds from the fact that our literature cannot be politically indifferent, cannot be "art for art's sake." On the contrary, it is called upon to play an important leading role in social life.

From this position issues the Leninist principle of partisanship in literature – a most important contribution of V. I. Lenin to the science of literature. . . .

Leninism recognizes the tremendous socially-transforming significance of our literature. For our Soviet literature to permit a lowering of its vast educational role would mean a development backward, a return "to the stone age."

Comrade Stalin called our writers engineers of human souls. This definition has profound meaning. It speaks of the enormous responsibility of Soviet writers for the education of the people and for the education of Soviet youth. It says that wastage in literary work is intolerable. . . .

Recently large gaps and weaknesses have been exposed on the ideological front. It suffices to remind you of the backwardness of our cinema, of the littering of our theatrical-dramatic repertoire with inferior productions, not to mention what happened in the journals *Zvezda* ["star"] and *Leningrad*. The Central Committee was compelled to interfere and introduce decisive corrections. It had no right to soften its blow against those who forget their obligations to the people and for the education of the young. If we want to turn the attention of our active members to questions of ideological work and bring order here, if we want to give clear direction in this work, we must be quick, as befits Soviet people and Bolsheviks, to criticize mistakes and weaknesses in ideological work. Only then will we be able to correct matters. . . .

Our successes within our country as well as in the international arena do not please the bourgeois world. As a result of the second world war the positions of socialism have been strengthened. The question of socialism has been placed on the order of the day in many countries of Europe. This is unpleasant to imperialists of all colors. They are afraid of socialism. They fear socialism and our socialist country, which is a model for all progressive mankind. Imperialists and their ideological servants, their writers and journalists, their politicians and diplomats, strive in every way to defame our country, to present it in a wrong light, to slander socialism. Under these conditions the task of Soviet literature is not only to reply, blow for blow, to all this base calumny and to the assaults on our Soviet culture and on socialism, but also to lash out boldly and attack bourgeois culture which is in a state of emaciation and depravity.

However outwardly beautiful the form that clothes the creative work of the fashionable contemporary bourgeois West-European and American writers, and also film and theatrical producers, still they can neither redeem nor lift up their bourgeois culture. That culture is putrid and baneful in its moral foundations. It has been put at the service of private capitalist property, at the service of the egotistic and selfish interests of the highest stratum of bourgeois society. The entire host of bourgeois writers, of film and theatrical producers, is striving to divert the attention of the advanced strata of society from acute questions of the political and social struggle and to shift attention into the channel of vulgar and ideologically empty literature and art, crowded with gangsters, chorus girls, praise of adultery, and the affairs of adventurers and rogues of every kind.

Is the role of worshipers or pupils of bourgeois culture becoming to us,

Soviet patriots and representatives of the most advanced Soviet culture? Certainly our literature, which reflects a social order higher than any bourgeois-democratic order and a culture many times higher than bourgeois culture, has the right to teach others this new universal morality. Where will you find such people and such a country as ours? Where will you find the magnificent qualities which our people displayed in the Great Patriotic War and which they display in their daily work as they pass to the peaceful restoration and development of economy and culture? Every day our people rise higher and ever higher. Today we are not what we were yesterday, and tomorrow we shall not be as we are today. Already we are not the same Russians we were before 1917, our Russia is different, our character is not the same. We have changed and grown along with the great reforms which have profoundly changed the face of our country.

To reveal these new high qualities of Soviet persons, not only to reveal our people in their today, but also to give a glimpse of them in their tomorrow, to help light the way ahead with a searchlight–such is the task of every conscientious Soviet writer. The writer cannot trudge along at the tail of events; he must march in the front ranks of the people, pointing out to them the road of their development. Guided by the method of socialist realism, studying conscientiously and attentively our reality, striving to penetrate more deeply into the essence of the processes of our development, the writer must educate the people and arm them ideologically. While selecting the best sentiments and qualities of Soviet man and revealing his tomorrow, we must at the same time show our people what they must not be and scourge the vestiges of yesterday, vestiges which hamper the Soviet people in their forward march. Soviet writers must assist the people, the state, and the Party in the education of our youth to be cheerful, confident of their own strength, and fearful of no difficulties. . . .

PARTY CONTROL OF SCIENCE–GENETICS

Since the 1930's the conventional study of genetics in the USSR had been challenged by a pseudo-scientific quack, Trofim D. Lysenko, who claimed to speak in the name of Marxism. In 1948 Lysenko's "Michurinist" doctrine of the inheritance of acquired characteristics received party sanction, and biologists who refused to accept this were summarily purged on grounds of "reactionary bourgeois idealism."

FROM: Resolution of the Presidium of the Academy of Sciences of the USSR, August 26, 1948, "On the Question of the Status and Problems of Biological Science in the Institutes and Institutions of the Academy of Sciences of the USSR" (English translation in Conway Zirkle, ed., *Death of a Science in Russia*, Philadelphia, University of Pennsylvania Press, 1949, pp. 285-86, 288; reprinted by permission of the publisher).

The Session of the V. I. Lenin All-Union Academy of Agricultural Sciences (LAAAS) has placed a number of important problems before Soviet biological science, whose solution must contribute to the great work of socialistic construction. The Session of the LAAAS has revealed the reactionary, anti-national nature of the Weismann-Morgan-Mendel movement in biological science,* and has exposed its actual bearers. The destruction of the anti-Michurinist movement has opened new possibilities for the creative development of all branches of advanced biological science.

The materials of the LAAAS Session have shown, with all transparency, that there has been in progress a struggle between two diametrically opposite, according to their ideological and theoretical concepts, movements in biological science: the struggle of a progressive, materialistic, Michurinist movement against a reactionary, idealistic, Weismannist-Morganist movement.

The Michurinist movement, having creatively enriched the theory of evolution and revealed the laws of development of living nature, has through its methods of controlled alteration of the nature of plants and animals made an outstanding contribution to the practice of socialistic agriculture. The Weismannist-Morganist movement, maintaining the independence of hereditary changes of an organism from its characteristics of form and its conditions of life, has supported the idealistic and metaphysical views, torn apart from life; has disarmed practical workers in agriculture from their goal of improving existing and creating new varieties of plants and animal breeds; and has occupied itself with fruitless experiments.

The Academy of Sciences not only failed to take part in the struggle against the reactionary bourgeois movement in biological science, but actually supported representatives of formal-genetic pseudoscience in the Institute of Cytology, Histology, and Embryology; in the Institute of Morphological Evolution; in the Institute of Plant Physiology; in the Main Botanical Gardens; and in other biological institutions of the Academy of Sciences.

The Praesidium of the Academy of Sciences, USSR, admits that its work in directing the Academy's biological institutes was unsatisfactory. . . .

The brilliant transformer of nature, I. V. Michurin, created by his efforts a new epoch in the development of Darwinism. The teaching of I. V. Michurin is founded on the great creative force of Marxist-Leninist philosophy. Michurinist teaching sets for itself the most important task of controlling organic nature; of creating new forms of plants and animals necessary for a socialistic society.

*I.e., the standard conception of inheritance through the genes – Ed.

Czarist Russia was incapable of evaluating the significance and transforming force of I. V. Michurin's scientific creative genius.

Michurin was discovered for our people and for advanced science through the genius of Lenin and Stalin. In an epoch of Socialism, Michurin's teaching has proved to be a powerful lever in the matter of the transformation of nature. It has received wide opportunities for its development, and popular acclaim.

If in its old form Darwinism set before itself only the problem of explanation of the evolutionary process, then Michurin's teaching, receiving further development through the works of T. D. Lysenko, has set and solves the problem of controlled alteration of hereditary characteristics of plants and animals, has set and solves the problem of controlling the process of evolution.

T. D. Lysenko and his adherents and students have made an essential contribution to Michurinist biological science, to the goal of the development of socialistic agricultural economy, to the concern of the struggle for abundant yields of agricultural crops and productivity of animal husbandry.

The Praesidium of the Academy of Sciences, USSR, obliges the Divison of Biological Sciences, biologists, and all naturalists working in the Academy of Sciences to reorganize their work radically; to assume the leadership in the struggle against idealistic and reactionary teachings in science; against toadyism and servility to foreign pseudoscience. The natural-history scientific institutes of the Academy of Sciences must fight actively for a continual progress of native biological science and, in the first place, for the further development of the teachings established by I. V. Michurin, V. V. Dokuchayev, and V. R. Williams, continued and developed by T. D. Lysenko.

THE CAMPAIGN AGAINST "COSMOPOLITANISM"

A new wave of ideological tightening-up swept the Soviet Union in 1949. Historians and literary critics in particular were attacked for the "denationalized cosmopolitanism" which failed to assert the superiority of Russian culture and facilitated contamination by "imperialist" influences. History was reduced to a device for national glorification of Russia. The campaign had a marked anti-Jewish aspect; Yiddish-language culture in the USSR was virtually obliterated, while the other minorities were forced to acknowledge the past and present virtues of Great-Russian domination.

FROM: Editorial, "On the Tasks of Soviet Historians in the Struggle with Manifestations of Bourgeois Ideology," *Voprosy Istorii* (Questions of History), No. 2, 1949, pp. 3-6, 13 (editor's translation; this number did not appear until July, 1949).

Historical science plays a great role in the cause of educating and uplifting the mass of the people, and it is the strongest instrument of class struggle on the ideological front. The exploiting classes have always tried and are trying to utilize historical science for the purpose of making their class domination eternal. In the interests of the ruling classes bourgeois historians falsify history. Only in the Soviet socialist society has history been transformed into a genuine science, which, using the sole scientific method of historical materialism, studies the laws of the development of human society and in the first instance the history of its productive forces and productive relations, the history of the toiling mass of the people.

Soviet historical science not only explains the past, but also gives the key to the correct understanding of contemporary political events and aids in understanding the perspectives of the development of society, nations, and states.

The creators of Soviet historical science, the teachers and educators of the Soviet cadres of historians, are Lenin and Stalin. In the works of Lenin and Stalin the foundations of historical science are laid down, the classical evaluations of the most important questions of world history are given, the most important questions of modern and contemporary history and especially of the history of the peoples of the USSR are worked out. Lenin and Stalin are the foundation-layers of the study of the Soviet period of the history of our country. . . .

A bunch of nationless cosmopolitans have been preaching a national nihilism hostile to our world view. Defending the anti-scientific and reactionary idea of a "single world stream" of the development of culture, the cosmopolitans declared that such concepts as national culture, national traditions, national priority in scientific and technical discoveries, were antiquated and outlived. They denied and bemoaned the national forms of socialist culture, and refused to admit that the best traditions and cultural achievements of the peoples of the USSR – above all, the traditions and cultural achievements of the Russian people – provided the basis for Soviet socialist culture. The nationless cosmopolitans have slandered the great Russian people and have propagated a false assertion about its centuries-old backwardness, about the foreign origin of Russian culture and about the absence of national traditions among the Russian people. They have denied and discredited the best achievements of Soviet culture and have tried to deprecate it in favor of the corrupt culture of the bourgeois West.

In this manner nationless cosmopolitanism is closely bound up with subservience toward things foreign. The preaching of cosmopolitan ideas is harmful and dangerous because they are aimed against Soviet patriotism, they undermine the cause of educating the Soviet people in a spirit of patriotic pride in our socialist motherland, in the great Soviet people. Therefore, it is a matter of special importance and immediacy to uproot all manifestations of cosmopolitanism from our literature, art and science.

Bourgeois cosmopolitanism, moreover, represents a special danger because at the present time it is an ideological weapon of the struggle of international reaction against socialism and democracy, an ideological cover for the efforts of the American imperialists to establish world domination.

The events of the last few years show what a dangerous enemy cosmopolitanism is of the freedom and independence of nations. Screening themselves with ideas about the "world economy," a "world state," and "world government," and proclaiming the idea of getting rid of national sovereignty supposedly as antiquated, the cunning businessmen and politicians of Wall Street are operating in the countries of Europe and Asia to suppress the national independence of the nations and prepare war against the Soviet Union and the countries of People's Democracy. . . .

Since it is a manifestation of bourgeois ideology, cosmopolitanism does not at all stand in contrast to its other forms, but finds in them – in bourgeois objectivism and bourgeois nationalism, in Kadet liberalism and social-reformism – its allies, and a nutritious milieu and the basis for its development. The bourgeois objectivist castrates the historical process of its class content, extols the reactionary sides of the historical past, worships the old conservative principles, and hates the new revolutionary principles. The bourgeois cosmopolitan castrates the historical process not only of its class content, but also of its national form. To the clear Marxist-Leninist class analysis of the historical process, which teaches about national factors as well as social-economic ones, he counterposes flimsy idealistic schemes of cultural borrowing and the affiliation of ideas as the foundation of the historical process.

This is why we must not weaken our struggle against other forms of the manifestation of bourgeois ideology.

Individual manifestations of the conceptions of bourgeois cosmopolitanism take place even in Soviet historical science.

In their time cosmopolitan ideas were implanted by M. N. Pokrovsky* and his anti-historical "school." Replacing historical materialism with vulgar sociologism, the "school" of Pokrovsky falsified and distorted historical events, blackened the great past of the peoples of our country, and ridiculed the national traditions of the Russian people. The party destroyed the Pokrovsky movement, but some notions of this "school" have been

*Pokrovsky: the leading Soviet historian until his death in 1932. In 1936 he was posthumously condemned for his ultramaterialist and antinationalist views – Ed.

current in historical science to the present time. The manifestation of cosmopolitan ideas has also been facilitated by the as yet not completely outlived influence of the traditions of the old, pre-revolutionary aristocratic and bourgeois historiography, which, as is known, cultivated all kinds of cosmopolitan "theories." Finally, cosmopolitan conceptions penetrate our historical science from the bourgeois-imperialist encirclement, for cosmopolitanism is one of the ideological instruments directed from Wall Street and its agencies and aimed at weakening Soviet patriotism, at weakening the will of the Soviet people to struggle for communism.

Such are the roots of bourgeois cosmopolitanism manifested in the field of historical science by a bunch of nationless cosmopolitans who are divorced from the people and their strivings.

The nationless cosmopolitans of our day distort the history of the heroic struggle of the Russian people against their oppressors and foreign usurpers, they deprecate the leading role of the Russian proletariat in the history of the revolutionary struggle of the whole world as well as of Russia, they shade over the socialist character and international significance of the Great October Socialist Revolution, they falsify and distort the world-historical role of the Russian people in the construction of a socialist society and in the victory over the enemy of mankind – German fascism – in the Great Patriotic War. . . .

Soviet historians must be impassioned, militant Bolshevik propagandists, they must pose the substantive problems of history and boldly work them out. The Soviet historical front must not resemble a quiet creek or a rear-area bivouac. Soviet historians have all the foundations for fulfilling those present tasks which our party, the government and Comrade Stalin personally have set before us.

Soviet historians must march in the front ranks of the fighters against the bourgeois ideology of Anglo-American imperialism, to expose Anglo-American imperialism and its reactionary essence, to expose social-reformism, which falsifies and adapts history in the interests of its bosses, the imperialists.

With the active participation of the whole army of Soviet historians the journal "Problems of History" must become a militant organ, directing the development of Soviet historical thought, generalizing its achievements, and organizing the Soviet historians, educated and led by the party of Lenin-Stalin, for the struggle to build a communist society.

STALIN ON LANGUAGE AND SOCIETY

In 1950 the party line on the subject of linguistics changed in a way paralleling other fields of thought, as extreme Marxist notions were replaced by traditional ideas bearing the Marxist label. Stalin intervened to dismiss the class theory of language promoted by the late N. Y. Marr. In so doing Stalin further revised his conception of Marxism, by suggesting that the political and ideological "super-structure" of society enjoyed a measure of independence from the economic "base," and that governments could bring about decisive changes without revolution.

The base is the economic structure of society at a given stage of its development. The superstructure consists of the political, legal, religious, artistic, and philosophical views of society and the political, legal, and other institutions corresponding to them.

Every base has its own superstructure corresponding to it. The base of the feudal system has its superstructure – its political, legal, and other views and the corresponding institutions; the capitalist base has its own super-structure, and so has the socialist base. If the base changes or is eliminated, then following this its superstructure changes or is eliminated; if a new base arises, then following this a superstructure arises corresponding to it.

In this respect language radically differs from superstructure. Take, for example, Russian society and the Russian language. During the past thirty years the old, capitalist base was eliminated in Russia and a new, socialist base was built. Correspondingly, the superstructure on the capitalist base was eliminated and a new superstructure created corresponding to the socialist base. The old political, legal, and other institutions were consequently supplanted by new, socialist institutions. But in spite of this the Russian language has remained essentially what it was before the October Revolution.

What has changed in the Russian language in this period? To a certain extent the vocabulary of the Russian language has changed, in the sense that it has been supplemented by a large number of new words and expressions, which have arisen in connection with the rise of a new socialist production, of a new state – a new socialist culture, a new public spirit and ethics, and lastly, in connection with the development of technology and science; a number of words and expressions have changed their meaning; a number of obsolete words have fallen out of the vocabulary. As to the basic vocabulary and grammatical structure of the Russian language, which constitute the foundation of the language, they, after the elimination of the capitalist base, far from having been eliminated and supplanted by a new

FROM: Stalin, *Marxism and Linguistics* (1950; English translation, New York, International Publishers, 1951, pp. 9-10, 27-28; reprinted by permission of the publisher).

basic vocabulary and a new grammatical system of the language, have been preserved in their entirety and have not undergone any serious changes – have been preserved precisely as the foundation of modern Russian.

Further, the superstructure is a product of the base; but this does not mean that it merely reflects the base, that it is passive, neutral, indifferent to the fate of its base, to the fate of the classes, to the character of the system. On the contrary, no sooner does it arise than it becomes an exceedingly active force, actively assisting its base to take shape and consolidate itself, and doing everything it can to help the new system finish off and eliminate the old base and the old classes.

It cannot be otherwise. The base creates the superstructure precisely in order that it may serve it, that it may actively help it to take shape and consolidate itself, that it may actively strive for the elimination of the old, moribund base and its old superstructure. The superstructure has only to renounce its role of auxiliary, it has only to pass from a position of active defense of its base to one of indifference toward it, to adopt the same attitude to all classes, and it loses its virtue and ceases to be a superstructure. . . .

Marxism holds that the transition of a language from an old quality to a new does not take place by way of an explosion, by the destruction of an existing language and the creation of a new one, but by the gradual accumulation of the elements of the new quality, and, hence, by the gradual dying away of the elements of the old quality.

It should be said in general for the benefit of comrades who have an infatuation for such explosions that the law of transition from an old quality to a new by means of an explosion is inapplicable not only to the history of the development of languages; it is not always applicable to some other social phenomena of a basal or superstructural character. It is compulsory for a society which has no hostile classes. In a period of eight to ten years we effected a transition in the agriculture of our country from the bourgeois individual-peasant system to the socialist, collective-farm system. This was a revolution which eliminated the old bourgeois economic system in the countryside and created a new, socialist system. But this revolution did not take place by means of an explosion, that is, by the overthrow of the existing power and the creation of a new power, but by a gradual transition from the old bourgeois system of the countryside to a new system. And we succeeded in doing this because it was a revolution from above, because the revolution was accomplished on the initiative of the existing power with the support of the overwhelming mass of the peasantry. . . .

THE LIMITS OF STALINISM – MALENKOV ON IMPERFECTIONS IN THE PARTY

At the Nineteenth Party Congress in October, 1952, Georgi Malenkov emerged as Stalin's successor-designate by delivering the political report of the Central Committee. Together with the usual glorification of Soviet achievements Malenkov made some sharp criticisms of inadequacies in the party's control work. This was followed by a typical example of the adulation of Stalin.

. . . The Soviet people's historic victory in the great patriotic war, the fulfillment of the Fourth Five-Year Plan ahead of schedule, the further development of the national economy, the improvement in the living and cultural standards of the Soviet people, the strengthening of the moral-political unity of Soviet society and of the friendship of peoples of our country, and the rallying of all the forces of the camp of peace and democracy around the Soviet Union – these are the principal results confirming the correctness of our party's policy. . . .

However, it would be a mistake not to see that the level of Party political work still lags behind the demands of life, the tasks put forward by the Party. It must be admitted that there are defects and errors in the work of the Party organizations and that there are still many negative and at times even unhealthy phenomena in the life of our Party organizations, which must be recognized, seen and brought to light in order to overcome and eliminate them and secure further progress. . . .

The role of criticism and self-criticism in the life of the Party and state is still underestimated in the party organizations; persecution and victimization for criticism occur. One can still meet officials who never stop shouting about their devotion to the party but actually tolerate no criticism from below, stifle it and take revenge on those who criticize them. . . .

Among our cadres there are many officials who react in a formal manner to decisions of the party and government, who do not display activeness or persistence in the struggle to carry them out and who are not concerned that things are going badly in their work and that harm is being done to the interests of the country. A formal attitude toward decisions of

FROM: Malenkov, Report of the Central Committee to the Nineteenth Party Congress, October, 1952 (English translation in *The Current Digest of the Soviet Press, IV*: 40 [1952], pp. 3-11). For this and subsequent selections, translation copyright 1952-4, 1956, 1962, 1966, 1977, 1981-82, by *The Current Digest of the Soviet Press*, published weekly at The Ohio State University; reprinted by permission.

the party and government and a passive attitude toward fulfilling them are vices which must be eradicated in the most merciless fashion. The party does not need hardened and indifferent bureaucrats who prefer their own peace of mind to the interests of work, but tireless and selfless fighters for fulfillment of the directives of the party and government who place the interests of the state above all else.

One of the most dangerous and vicious violations of party and state discipline is the concealment by certain officials of the truth about the state of affairs in enterprises and institutions in their charge, the embellishment of results in the work. . . .

One of the most widespread and deep-rooted defects in the practical work of Soviet, economic and Party organizations is poor organization of the factual fulfillment of directives from the center and of their own decisions, and absence of proper check on their execution. Our organizations and institutions issue far more decisions, directives and orders than required, but take little care to see whether or how they are being carried out. After all, the essence of the job is to carry them out correctly and not bureaucratically. An unconscientious, irresponsible attitude toward carrying out directives from the executive bodies is a most dangerous and vicious manifestation of bureaucracy. Experience shows that even good officials begin to grow spoiled and bureaucratic when left to themselves with no control or check on their activities. . . .

Ideological work is a paramount duty of the party and underestimation of it may do irreparable damage to the interests of the party and the state. We must always remember that any weakening of the influence of the socialist ideology signifies a strengthening of the influence of bourgeois ideology.

In our Soviet society there is not and cannot be any class basis for acceptance of bourgeois ideology. The socialist ideology reigns in our country; its indestructible foundation is Marxism-Leninism. But remnants of the bourgeois ideology, survivals of private-property mentality and morality are still with us. These survivals do not wither away by themselves. They are still very tenacious. They can grow, and a vigorous struggle must be waged against them. Nor are we guaranteed against the infiltration of alien views, ideas and sentiments from outside, from the capitalist states, and from inside, from the remnants of groups hostile to the Soviet regime and not yet completely destroyed by the party. It must not be forgotten that enemies of the Soviet state are trying to spread, fan and inflame all sorts of unhealthy sentiments, are trying to corrupt unstable elements of our society ideologically. . . .

Comrade Stalin's writings are a vivid indication of the outstanding importance our party attaches to theory. Revolutionary theory was, is and will remain the unfailing beacon which illumines the path of advance of our party and our people to the complete triumph of communism.

Comrade Stalin is constantly advancing Marxist theory. . . .

. . . Comrade Stalin's discoveries in the field of theory have world-historic importance and arm all peoples with knowledge of the ways of revolutionary transformation of society and with our party's wealth of experience in the struggle for communism.

The immense significance of Comrade Stalin's works of theory is that they warn us against skimming the surface, they penetrate the heart of phenomena, the very essence of the society's development, teach us to perceive in embryo the factors which will determine the course of events, which makes possible Marxist prognosis. . . .

Chapter Five
The Interval of Reform, 1953-1964

Stalin's death broke the spell of monolithic repression in Soviet society and opened the way for a more lenient and more innovative style of politics, briefly under the leadership of Malenkov, and then for nearly a decade under the ebullient Nikita Khrushchev. Although the system of Communist Party rule was not fundamentally changed, Khrushchev's "de-Stalinization" campaign forever altered the relation of the Soviet regime to its own past as well as to the outside world and Communism abroad. Though Khrushchev was ultimately repudiated by his own lieutenants, even the manner of his removal in 1964 showed that the Soviet Union had left the days of personal despotism behind.

THE DEATH OF STALIN AND COLLECTIVE LEADERSHIP

Immediately after Stalin's death on March 5, 1953, the Communist leadership was reorganized to prevent Malenkov from inheriting Stalin's dictatorial power. Malenkov became Chairman of the Council of Ministers (prime minister), but the post of First Secretary of the party was assumed by Nikita Khrushchev. The party Presidium (as the Politbureau had been renamed) became for the time being a real collective leadership. Praise of Stalin quickly gave way to enunciation of the new principle.

. . . The party committees are organs of political leadership. They cannot apply methods inherent in administrative-managerial agencies in their practical work. There were cases of this during the war. Wartime circumstances caused certain particular features in the methods of leadership which were to some extent justified for those conditions. But this led to serious shortcomings in the practical work of party organizations.

This is why in many very important cases of party work in the postwar period the party has set the task of raising the level of party leadership, of putting an end to such phenomena as the application in party organiza-

FROM: Slepov, "Collectivity Is the Highest Principle of Party Leadership" (*Pravda*, April 16, 1953; English translation in *The Current Digest of the Soviet Press*; V:13 [May 9, 1953], pp. 3, 30); this and subsequent selections reprinted by permission.

tions of administrative methods of leadership, which lead to bureaucratization of party work.

One of the fundamental principles of party leadership is collectivity in deciding all important problems of party work. It is impossible to provide genuine leadership if inner party democracy is violated in the party organization, if genuine collective leadership and widely developed criticism and self-criticism are lacking. Collectiveness and the collegium principle represent a very great force in party leadership. . . .

The principle of collectivity in work means, above all, that decisions adopted by party committees on all cardinal questions are the fruit of collective discussion. No matter how experienced leaders may be, no matter what their knowledge and ability, they do not possess and they cannot replace the initiative and experience of a whole collective. In any collegium, in any directing collective, there are people who possess diverse experience, without relying upon which the leaders cannot make correct decisions and exercise qualified leadership.

Individual decisions are always or almost always one-sided decisions. Hence, the very important requirement that decisions must rest on the experience of many, must be the fruit of collective effort. If this is not so, if decisions are adopted individually, serious errors can occur in work. Insofar as each person is able to correct the errors of individual persons and insofar as party agencies in the course of practice reckon with these corrections, the decisions which result are more correct. . . .

Leaders cannot consider criticism of themselves as a personal affront. They must be able to accept criticism courageously and show readiness to bend their will to the will of the collective. Without such courage, without the ability to overcome one's own vanity and to bend one's own will to the will of the collective, there can be no collective leadership, no collective. . . .

For correct training of cadres it is important that they be placed under the supervision of the party masses, that officials display readiness not only to teach the masses but to learn from the masses as well. Collectivity in work is called upon to play an important role in this connection. Where the collective principle is violated the necessary conditions for criticism and self-criticism are absent, the sense of responsibility is blunted and officials are infected by dangerous conceit and smugness. It is precisely in such a situation that some workers begin to behave as if they know everything, as if only they can say anything that makes sense, and as if the role of others is only to support their opinion.

Such a situation prepares the ground for unprincipled, alien habits of kowtowing and flattery. There are cases in which the head of a party committee behaves incorrectly and the party committee members accept this and, in order not to mar relations with the committee head, tolerate unprincipled behavior, do not think it necessary or possible to voice objections and even orient themselves to his views and defer to him in everything. Actually, the function of collective leadership is to correct and criticize one another. Where there is an intolerable atmosphere of kowtowing, which excludes businesslike, critical discussion of problems, where criticisms of comrades who are officials are not expressed, there are, as a rule, serious shortcomings in work.

It is necessary in discussing and solving problems to know how to combine the collective principle with personal responsibility in carrying matters through. Just as collectivity is essential in discussing basic problems, so individual responsibility is essential in carrying matters through in order to prevent evasion of responsibility for implementing resolutions. . . .

The method of collective leadership is the basic principle of party leadership, violation of which in party work cannot be viewed otherwise than as a manifestation of bureaucratic habits, which freeze the initiative and self-reliance of party organizations and party members. Strictest observance of this highest principle is the guarantee of correct leadership and a primary requisite for a further advance in party work for successful progress along the path of building communism in our country.

THE PURGE OF BERIA

In June 1953, the Soviet Minister of Internal Affairs, Lavrenty Beria, was removed and arrested on the not implausible charge that he planned to use the police to put himself in power and eliminate the collective leadership. In elaborating the case against Beria, however, the Soviet leaders revealed that they still had the habit of rewriting history in order to create an individual scapegoat.

Beria, a now exposed enemy of the people, through various careerist machinations wormed his way into a position of confidence, and threaded his way to the leadership. Whereas in the past his criminal anti-Party and anti-state work was carefully concealed and masked, Beria has lately become insolent and let himself go, exposing his real countenance, the countenance of a vicious enemy of the Party and the Soviet people. This intensification of Beria's criminal work is explained by the general intensi-

FROM: *Pravda* Editorial on the Dismissal of Beria, July 10, 1953 (English translation in *Soviet News*, July 16, 1953, reprinted in *Documents on International Affairs*, 1953 [London, Oxford University Press, 1956], pp. 19-20).

fication of subversive anti-Soviet activities by the international forces of reaction, hostile to our state. As international imperialism becomes more active, so also do its agents.

Beria began his foul machinations for the purpose of seizing power with his attempts to place the Ministry of Internal Affairs [MVD] above the Party and the government, and by using the MVD organs in the centre and in the localities against the Party and its leadership, against the government of the U.S.S.R., promoting workers in the Ministry of Internal Affairs on the basis of their personal devotion to him.

As has now been established, Beria used all sorts of invented pretexts for interfering in every way with the solution of the most important, urgent problems in agriculture. This was done in order to undermine the collective farms and to create food supply difficulties in the country.

In various treacherous ways Beria tried to undermine the friendship of the peoples of the U.S.S.R., the very basis of the multi-national socialist state and the main condition for all the successes of the fraternal Soviet republics, tried to sow discord among the peoples of the U.S.S.R., to intensify the activity of bourgeois nationalist elements in the union republics. . . .

. . . This adventurer and hireling of foreign imperialist forces was hatching plans to seize the leadership of the Party and the country, with the real object of destroying our Communist Party and substituting for the policy worked out by the Party over many years, a policy of capitulation which in the final analysis would have led to the restoration of capitalism.

Thanks to the timely and determined measures taken by the Presidium of the Central Committee of the C.P.S.U., approved unanimously and fully by a plenary meeting of the Central Committee of the Party, Beria's criminal designs against the Party and the state were exposed. The ending of Beria's criminal adventure shows again and again that any anti-Soviet plans of foreign imperialist forces have crushed and will crush against the unbreakable might and great unity of the Party, the government and the Soviet people.

At the same time, the political lessons and necessary conclusions must be drawn from the Beria case.

The strength of our leadership lies in its collective nature and its solid and monolithic unity. Collective leadership is the highest principle of leadership in our Party. This principle accords entirely with Marx's well-known thesis that the cult of personality is harmful and impermissible . . . .

Any official, no matter what post he occupies, must be subject to the unrelaxed supervision of the Party. The Party organizations must regularly check the work of all organizations and departments, the activities of all leading workers. It is also necessary to exercise systematic and unrelaxed supervision over the work of the organs of the Ministry of Internal Affairs. This is not only the right, it is the direct duty of Party organizations.

THE "NEW COURSE" – MALENKOV ON AGRICULTURE

Under Malenkov's leadership the Soviet government relaxed its industrialization drive and gave long-overdue attention to agriculture and higher living standards.

. . . The urgent task is to secure in the next two or three years, by generally improving agriculture and further consolidating the collective farms organizationally and economically, the creation in our country of an abundance of 'food for the population and of raw materials for the light industries.

For the successful accomplishment of this task, the Government and the Central Committee of the Party consider it necessary to carry out a number of major measures to ensure the further swift progress of agriculture – measures, in the first place, which will provide a greater economic incentive to collective farms and collective farmers in developing lagging branches of agriculture. . . .

In addition to providing a greater material incentive to collective farmers to develop the common enterprises of their collective farms, the Government and the Central Committee of the Party have decided thoroughly to correct and revise the wrong attitude which has arisen towards the personal subsidiary husbandry of the collective farmer [the private plot]. . . .

Owing to the defects in our policy of taxing the personal subsidiary husbandry of the collective farmer, the latter's income from his personal subsidiary husbandry has diminished of late years, and there has also been a reduction in the amount of livestock, especially cows, in the personal possession of the collective farmers, which runs counter to our Party's policy in collective farming.

Accordingly, the Government and the Central Committee of the Party deem it necessary substantially to reduce the obligatory delivery quotas levied on the personal subsidiary husbandry of the collective farmers, and have decided, as Minister of Finance Comrade Zverev has already informed you, to change the system of levying the agricultural tax on collective farmers. The monetary tax payable by them is to be reduced by an

FROM: Malenkov, Speech to the Supreme Soviet of the USSR, August 8, 1953 (English translation in *Soviet News*, August 15, 1953, supplement; reprinted in *Documents on International Affairs*, 1953, pp. 22-25, 30).

average of about one-half, and also arrears in agricultural taxes incurred in past years are to be cancelled. . . .

THE RISE OF KHRUSHCHEV: THE VIRGIN LANDS PROGRAM

During 1953 and 1954 Khrushchev used his control of the party organization and his experience in agriculture to upstage Malenkov and lay the groundwork for his own takeover of the leadership. His first major initiative was to address the chronic grain harvest problem by plowing up the semi-arid steppes – the "virgin lands" – that stretched from the Volga River into Central Asia. Initial successes were followed by a serious dust-bowl problem and eventual stabilization of the program at a more modest level.

Comrades! The Communist Party of the Soviet Union is devoting all its efforts to peaceful construction and further improvement in the material well-being of the Soviet people.

From the first days of the Soviet regime, when the Communist Party became the ruling party, problems of economic development have been central in its domestic policy. The Party will always remember the statement by our inspired leader and teacher Vladimir Ilyich Lenin on the tremendous international importance of economic development in the U.S.S.R.

As far back as in 1921, when our people had ended the struggle against the interventionists and made the transition to peaceful construction, Lenin stated that we would now exert our main influence on the course of international events through our economic policies. "The struggle has been shifted to this sphere on a world scale," Vladimir Ilyich stated. "If we solve this task we will have won definitely and conclusively on an international scale. This is why problems of economic development are of quite extraordinary importance for us."

Many years have passed since these words were spoken. The land of the Soviets has been turned into a powerful industrial and collective farming socialist state. Every step in our progress has a profound effect on the course of international events. . . . The constant growth in the material welfare and cultural standards of the working people of the land of the Soviets helps honest men in all countries to appreciate still more the advantages of the socialist over the capitalist system.

FROM: N. S. Khrushchev, Report to the Central Committee, "On Further Increasing the Country's Grain Production and Putting Virgin and Idle Lands into Cultivation," February 23, 1954 (English translation, *Current Digest of the Soviet Press*, VI:12, May 4, 1954, pp. 3-4, 12-13).

Comrades! The Party Central Committee's plenary session set a nation-wide task of great urgency in the present situation – the task of meeting the growing need of our country's population for food products and providing the light and food industries with abundant raw materials within the next two to three years, on the basis of socialist industry's mighty growth. . . .

Comrades! The September plenary session of the Party Central Committee pointed out that grain farming is basic to all farm production. The level of grain production is a deciding factor in the development of all other branches of agriculture.

It was pointed out at the plenary session that on the whole our country is self-sufficient in grain.

However, grain requirements are constantly growing. . . .

It cannot be overlooked that until recently some of our personnel did not wage a sufficient struggle to increase grain production. Although grain growing shows improvement, yields in many areas are still low and the gross grain crop is inadequate. There is a disparity between the existing level of grain farming and the country's increasing need for grain.

The problem is to increase considerably the gross grain yield in 1954 and 1955 and to increase state procurements and purchases of grain at least 35% to 40% as compared with 1953. . . .

There are large amounts of undeveloped land in eastern areas. For example, there are up to 40,000,000 hectares of overgrown, idle and virgin lands, unirrigated hayfields and pastures in 14 provinces of the Russian Republic and eight of the Kazakh Republic.

The state farms of the U.S.S.R. Ministry of State Farms have great reserves of land suitable for development. Slightly more than 15,000,000 hectares of a total of 59,000,000 hectares of land, or 26% of all land on state farms of this ministry (not including northern districts and Central Asia), are planted or in summer fallow, while the area covered by pastures and hayfields, a considerable part of which could be planted to grain and other crops, totals more than 33,000,000 hectares, or more than 55% of all the land.

These figures indicate the tremendous reserves at the disposal of many districts of the country for expanding the acreage under grain crops and increasing grain production.

The most modest estimates show that in the northeastern provinces and certain other areas of the Kazakh Republic, in Western Siberia and the Urals, as well as the Volga area and to some extent the North Caucasus, grain planting can be expanded by 13,000,000 hectares in the next two years, 8,700,000 hectares on the collective farms and 4,300,000 on the state farms. The area under grain can be expanded by more than 2,300,000 hectares in 1954 alone. . . .

Production of grain on the new lands should be completely mechanized, making it possible to carry out field work during the best time periods and to do it well.

The new lands will be developed for planting to grain both by existing M.T.S. [machine-tractor stations] and state farms and through the organization of new state grain farms. Work has already begun to select lands suitable for organizing new state grain farms, as well as lands to be plowed up by existing state farms and M.T.S. Special attention should be devoted in the course of this work to the selection first of all of the more fertile and accessible lands near populated points.

Plans have been made to form special M.T.S. tractor detachments composed of two to four tractor brigades to develop idle and virgin lands on collective farms and sectors remote from populated points. Experienced engineers or agronomists should head the tractor detachments.

More than 120,000 tractors (in 15-h.p. units), 10,000 combines and the necessary number of plows, cultivators, disk harrows, seeders and other machinery and equipment are being allocated to the M.T.S. and state farms in the districts where new lands are to be developed in 1954. Much equipment is being provided. The problem will be to make correct use of it.

Equipment, as is known, is dead without people, without cadres. Consequently, cadres are a deciding factor in successful development of the new lands. Preliminary estimates show that a work force of about 70,000 persons, 30,000 of them tractor and combine operators, will be needed for the state farms alone.

The complexity of the manpower problem lies in the fact that new lands will be developed in relatively underpopulated areas. Only a part of the cadres can be selected locally. The bulk of them will have to be recruited from other parts of the country.

It is very important to select for the state farms and M.T.S. developing the new lands qualified directors, chief engineers and chief agronomists who have had much practical experience on state farms and M.T.S. and have proved their ability to manage large operations, overcome difficulties and carry out responsible assignments of the Party and government. . . .

We should not be seriously disturbed by the fact that in openly criticizing shortcomings we will for a time be supplying grist for the mill of the Soviet land's enemies, malicious persons of every type who, when we disclose our shortcomings, cry out about the weakness of the Soviet Union. But, as the saying goes: "The dog barks, but the horse gallops." We must pay no attention to our enemies' malicious gossip.

Criticism and self-criticism of our shortcomings is our tried and true weapon. Criticism of our shortcomings only strengthens us. . . .

Our socialist homeland is making a powerful, new advance. The Soviet Union's successes in peaceful construction are inspiring cheer and confidence in the hearts of our friends, and fierce anger and hatred in our enemies. The imperialists are starting to figure out what year the Soviet Union's economic level of development and per capita production in our country will surpass the highest indices of the most advanced capitalist countries. They no longer doubt that it will happen. And the prospect frightens them. . . .

The Communist Party is confidently leading the peoples of our country along the path of building communism!

THE FALL OF MALENKOV

By the beginning of 1955 a serious division had developed within the Soviet collective leadership on the issue of heavy industry versus consumer goods. The rising party theorist Dimitri Shepilov attacked the emphasis on consumer goods in harsh terms, and in February, 1955, Malenkov was forced to confess his errors and resign as prime minister. He was replaced by Nikolai Bulganin, who for a time appeared to share power with First Secretary Khrushchev as the collective leadership became a diarchy.

To the chairman of the joint meeting of the Soviet of the Union and the Soviet of Nationalities:

I ask you to bring to the notice of the Supreme Soviet of the U.S.S.R. my request to be relieved from the post of chairman of the Council of Ministers of the U.S.S.R. My request is due to business considerations on the necessity of strengthening the leadership of the Council of Ministers and the need to have at the post of chairman of the Council of Ministers another comrade with greater experience in state work.

I clearly see that the carrying out of the complicated and responsible duties of chairman of the Council of Ministers is being negatively affected by my insufficient experience in local work, and the fact that I did not have occasion, in a ministry or some economic organ, to effect direct guidance of individual branches of national economy.

I also consider myself bound to say in the present statement that now, when the Communist Party of the Soviet Union and the workers of our country are concentrating special efforts for the most rapid development of agriculture, I see particularly clearly my guilt and responsibility for the

FROM: Malenkov, Statement to the Supreme Soviet on his resignation from the post of Chairman of the Council of Ministers of the U.S.S.R., February 8, 1955 (English translation in *Current History*, March, 1955, pp. 185-186).

unsatisfactory state of affairs which has arisen in agriculture, because for several years past I have been entrusted with the duty of controlling and guiding the work of central agricultural organs and the work of local party and administrative organizations in the sphere of agriculture.

The Communist Party, on the initiative and under the guidance of the Central Committee of the C.P.S.U., has already worked out and is implementing a series of large-scale measures for overcoming the lagging behind in agriculture.

Among such important measures is, undoubtedly, the reform of agricultural taxation, regarding which I think it opportune to say it was carried out on the initiative of and in accordance with the proposals of the Central Committee of the C.P.S.U.

It is now evident what important role this reform played in the task of developing agriculture.

Now, as is known, on the initiative and under the guidance of the Central Committee of the C.P.S.U., a general program has been worked out for overcoming the lagging behind in agriculture and for its most rapid development.

This program is based on the only correct foundation: The further development, by every means, of heavy industry, and only its implementation will create the necessary conditions for a real upsurge in the production of all essential commodities for popular consumption.

It is to be expected that various bourgeois hysterical viragos will busy themselves with slanderous inventions in connection with my present statement, and the fact itself of my release from the post of chairman of the U.S.S.R. Council of Ministers, but we, Communists and Soviet people, will ignore this lying and slander.

The interest of the motherland, the people and the Communist Party stand above everything for every one of us.

Expressing the request of my release from the post of chairman of the U.S.S.R. Council of Ministers, I wish to assure the U.S.S.R. Supreme Soviet that, in the new sphere entrusted to me, I will, under the guidance of the Central Committee of the C.P.S.U., monolithic in its unity and solidarity, and the Soviet government, perform in the most conscientious manner my duty and the functions which will be entrusted to me. . . .

"DE-STALINIZATION"

In February, 1956, Khrushchev spoke at a closed session of the Twentieth Party Congress to attack some of the abuses of Stalin's rule, particularly the Great Purge of 1937-38 and the personal glorification of the dictator. The speech was read to party meetings throughout the Soviet Union, though never officially published; the text was obtained by the United States Department of State through an East European source.

At the present we are concerned with a question which has immense importance for the party now and for the future – [we are concerned] with how the cult of the person of Stalin has been gradually growing, the cult which became at a certain specific stage the source of a whole series of exceedingly serious and grave perversions of party principles, of party democracy, of revolutionary legality. . . .

When we analyze the practice of Stalin in regard to the direction of the party and of the country, when we pause to consider everything which Stalin perpetrated, we must be convinced that Lenin's fears were justified. The negative characteristics of Stalin, which, in Lenin's time, were only incipient, transformed themselves during the last years into a grave abuse of power by Stalin, which caused untold harm to our Party.

We have to consider seriously and analyze correctly this matter in order that we may preclude any possibility of a repetition in any form whatever of what took place during the life of Stalin, who absolutely did not tolerate collegiality in leadership and in work, and who practiced brutal violence, not only toward everything which opposed him, but also toward that which seemed to his capricious and despotic character, contrary to his concepts.

Stalin acted not through persuasion, explanation, and patient co-operation with people, but by imposing his concepts and demanding absolute submission to his opinion. Whoever opposed this concept or tried to prove his viewpoint, and the correctness of his position, was doomed to removal from the leading collective and to subsequent moral and physical annihilation. This was especially true during the period following the XVIIth Party Congress [1934], when many prominent party leaders and rank-and-file party workers, honest and dedicated to the cause of Communism, fell victim to Stalin's despotism.

We must affirm that the party had fought a serious fight against the Trotskyites, rightists and bourgeois nationalists, and that it disarmed ideologically all the enemies of Leninism. This ideological fight was carried on successfully, as a result of which the Party became strengthened and tempered. Here Stalin played a positive role. . . .

FROM: Khrushchev, Secret Speech on the "Cult of the Individual," delivered at the Twentieth Congress of the Communist Party of the Soviet Union, February 25, 1956 (*The Anti-Stalin Campaign*, New York, Columbia University, 1956, pp. 3, 9-13, 22-23, 39-40, 62-63, 81-82, 87-89).

Worth noting is the fact that even during the progress of the furious ideological fight against the Trotskyites, the Zinovievites, the Bukharinites and others, extreme repressive measures were not used against them. The fight was on ideological grounds. But some years later when socialism in our country was fundamentally constructed, when the exploiting classes were generally liquidated, when the Soviet social structure had radically changed, when the social basis for political movements and groups hostile to the party had violently contracted, when the ideological opponents of the party were long since defeated politically – then the repression directed against them began.

It was precisely during this period (1935-1937-1938) that the practice of mass repression through the government apparatus was born, first against the enemies of Leninism – Trotskyites, Zinovievites, Bukharinites, long since politically defeated by the party, and subsequently also against many honest Communists, against those party cadres who had borne the heavy load of the Civil War and the first and most difficult years of industrialization and collectivization, who actively fought against the Trotskyites and the rightists for the Leninist Party line.

Stalin originated the concept "enemy of the people." This term automatically rendered it unnecessary that the ideological errors of a man or men engaged in a controversy be proven; this term made possible the usage of the most cruel repression, violating all norms of revolutionary legality, against anyone who in any way disagreed with Stalin, against those who were only suspected of hostile intent, against those who had bad reputations. This concept, "enemy of the people," actually eliminated the possibility of any kind of ideological fight or the making of one's views known on this or that issue, even those of a practical character. In the main, and in actuality, the only proof of guilt used, against all norms of current legal science, was the "confession" of the accused himself; and, as subsequent probing proved, "confessions" were acquired through physical pressures against the accused.

This led to glaring violations of revolutionary legality, and to the fact that many entirely innocent persons, who in the past had defended the party line, became victims.

We must assert that in regard to those persons who in their time had opposed the party line, there were often no sufficiently serious reasons for their physical annihilation. The formula, "enemy of the people," was specifically introduced for the purpose of physically annihilating such individuals . . . .

. . . Many party, soviet and economic activists who were branded in 1937-1938 as "enemies" were actually never enemies, spies, wreckers, etc., but were always honest Communists; they were only so stigmatized, and often, no longer able to bear barbaric tortures, they charged themselves (at the order of the investigative judges – falsifiers) with all kinds of grave and unlikely crimes. The commission [for investigation of the purge] has presented to the Central Committee Presidium lengthy and documented materials pertaining to mass repressions against the delegates to the XVIIth Party Congress and against members of the Central Committee elected at that Congress. These materials have been studied by the Presidium of the Central Committee.

It was determined that of the 139 members and candidates of the Party's Central Committee who were elected at the XVIIth Congress, 98 persons, i.e., 70 percent, were arrested and shot (mostly in 1937-1938). (*Indignation in the hall*) . . . The same fate met not only the Central Committee members but also the majority of the delegates to the XVIIth Party Congress. Of 1,966 delegates with either voting or advisory rights, 1,108 persons were arrested on charges of anti-revolutionary crimes, i.e., decidedly more than a majority. This very fact shows how absurd, wild and contrary to common sense were the charges of counterrevolutionary crimes made out, as we now see, against a majority of participants at the XVIIth Party Congress. (*Indignation in the hall*) . . .

We have examined the cases and have rehabilitated Kossior, Rudzutak, Postyshev, Kosarev and others.* For what causes were they arrested and sentenced? The review of evidence shows that there was no reason for this. They, like many others, were arrested without the Prosecutor's knowledge. In such a situation there is no need for any sanction, for what sort of a sanction could there be when Stalin decided everything? He was the chief prosecutor in these cases. Stalin not only agreed to, but on his own initiative issued, arrest orders. We must say this so that the delegates to the Congress can clearly undertake and themselves assess this and draw the proper conclusions.

Facts prove that many abuses were made on Stalin's orders without reckoning with any norms of party and Soviet legality. Stalin was a very distrustful man, sickly suspicious; we knew this from our work with him. He could look at a man and say: "Why are your eyes so shifty today?" or "Why are you turning so much today and avoiding to look me directly in the eyes?" The sickly suspicion created in him a general distrust even toward eminent party workers whom he had known for years. Everywhere and in everything he saw "enemies," "two-facers" and "spies."

*S. V. Kossior: Politburo member; Y. E. Rudzutak and P. P. Postyshev, Politburo alternates; A. V. Kosarev, member of the Central Committee; all secretly purged, 1937-38 – Ed.

Possessing unlimited power he indulged in great willfulness and choked a person morally and physically. A situation was created where one could not express one's own will.

When Stalin said that one or another should be arrested, it was necessary to accept on faith that he was an "enemy of the people." Meanwhile, Beria's gang, which ran the organs of state security, outdid itself in proving the guilt of the arrested and the truth of materials which it falsified. And what proofs were offered? The confessions of the arrested, and the investigative judges accepted these "confessions." And how is it possible that a person confesses to crimes which he has not committed? Only in one way – because of application of physical methods of pressuring him, tortures, bringing him to a state of unconsciousness, deprivation of his judgment, taking away of his human dignity. In this manner were "confessions" acquired. . . .

The willfulness of Stalin showed itself not only in decisions concerning the internal life of the country but also in the international relations of the Soviet Union.

The July Plenum of the Central Committee studied in detail the reasons for the development of conflict with Yugoslavia. It was a shameful role which Stalin played here. The "Yugoslav Affair" contained no problems which could not have been solved through party discussions among comrades. There was no significant basis for the development of this "affair"; it was completely possible to have prevented the rupture of relations with that country. This does not mean, however, that the Yugoslav leaders did not make mistakes or did not have shortcomings. But these mistakes and shortcomings were magnified in a monstrous manner by Stalin, which resulted in a break of relations with a friendly country.

I recall the first days when the conflict between the Soviet Union and Yugoslavia began artificially to be blown up. Once, when I came from Kiev to Moscow, I was invited to visit Stalin who, pointing to the copy of a letter lately sent to Tito, asked me, "Have you read this?" Not waiting for my reply he answered, "I will shake my little finger – and there will be no more Tito. He will fall.". . .

But this did not happen to Tito. No matter how much or how little Stalin shook, not only his little finger but everything else that he could shake, Tito did not fall. Why? The reason was that, in this case of disagreement with the Yugoslav comrades, Tito had behind him a state and a people who had gone through a severe school of fighting for liberty and independence, a people which gave support to its leaders.

You see to what Stalin's mania for greatness led. He had completely lost consciousness of reality; he demonstrated his suspicion and haughtiness not only in relation to individuals in the USSR, but in relation to whole parties and nations. . . .

Some comrades may ask us: Where were the members of the Political Bureau of the Central Committee? Why did they not assert themselves against the cult of the individual in time? And why is this being done only now?

First of all we have to consider the fact that the members of the Political Bureau viewed these matters in a different way at different times. Initially, many of them backed Stalin actively because Stalin was one of the strongest Marxists and his logic, his strength and his will greatly influenced the cadres and party work. . . .

Later, however, Stalin, abusing his power more and more, began to fight eminent party and government leaders and to use terroristic methods against honest Soviet people. As we have already shown, Stalin thus handled such eminent party and government leaders as Kossior, Rudzutak, Eikhe, Postyshev and many others.

Attempts to oppose groundless suspicions and charges resulted in the opponent falling victim of the repression. This characterized the fall of Comrade Postyshev.

In one of his speeches Stalin expressed his dissatisfaction with Postyshev and asked him, "What are you actually?"

Postyshev answered clearly, "I am a Bolshevik, Comrade Stalin, a Bolshevik."

This assertion was at first considered to show a lack of respect for Stalin; later it was considered a harmful act and consequently resulted in Postyshev's annihilation and branding without any reason as a "people's enemy."

In the situation which then prevailed I have talked often with Nikolai Alexandrovich Bulganin; once when we two were traveling in a car, he said, "It has happened sometimes that a man goes to Stalin on his invitation as a friend. And when he sits with Stalin, he does not know where he will be sent next, home or to jail."

It is clear that such conditions put every member of the Political Bureau in a very difficult situation. And when we also consider the fact that in the last years the Central Committee plenary sessions were not convened and that the sessions of the Political Bureau occurred only occasionally, from time to time, then we will understand how difficult it was for any member of the Political Bureau to take a stand against one or another injust or improper procedure, against serious errors and shortcomings in the practices of leadership. . . .

Comrades: We must abolish the cult of the individual decisively, once and for all; we must draw the proper conclusions concerning both ideological-theoretical and practical work.

It is necessary for this purpose: . . . to return to and actually practice in all our ideological work the most important theses of Marxist-Leninist science about the people as the creator of history and as the creator of all material and spiritual good of humanity, about the decisive role of the Marxist Party in the revolutionary fight for the transformation of society, about the victory of Communism.

In this connection we will be forced to do much work in order to examine critically from the Marxist-Leninist viewpoint and to correct the widely spread erroneous views connected with the cult of the individual in the sphere of history, philosophy, economy and of other sciences, as well as in literature and the fine arts. . . .

[It is necessary] to restore completely the Leninist principles of Soviet socialist democracy, expressed in the Constitution of the Soviet Union, to fight willfulness of individuals abusing their power. The evil caused by acts violating revolutionary socialist legality, which have accumulated during a long time as a result of the negative influence of the cult of the individual, has to be completely corrected. Comrades! The XXth Congress of the Communist Party of the Soviet Union has manifested with a new strength the unshakable unity of our party, its cohesiveness around the Central Committee, its resolute will to accomplish the great task of building Communism. (*Tumultuous applause*) And the fact that we present in all their ramifications the basic problems of overcoming the cult of the individual which is alien to Marxism-Leninism, as well as the problem of liquidating its burdensome consequences, is an evidence of the great moral and political strength of our party. (*Prolonged applause*)

We are absolutely certain that our party, armed with the historical resolutions of the XXth Congress, will lead the Soviet people along the Leninist path to new successes, to new victories. (*Tumultuous, prolonged applause*)

Long live the victorious banner of our party – Leninism! (*Tumultuous, prolonged applause ending in ovation. All rise.*)

THE "THAW" IN CULTURAL LIFE

Stalin's death and Khrushchev's de-Stalinization campaign signalled a significant loosening of the political straightjacket imposed on Soviet writers and artists prior to 1953. The new spirit was articulated by the official theoretical journal *Problems of Philosophy*, citing the more liberal party line of the 1920's, although the writers in question were soon censured for excessive ideological laxity. Party controls and intellectual individualism then continued in an uneasy standoff until Khrushchev's successors threw their weight to the side of enforced orthodoxy and drove the nonconformists underground.

It is well known that the problem of freedom of creative endeavor is one of great importance in the arts. Bourgeois esthetics interprets this freedom anarchistically as complete freedom of the artist from society and even from any kind of reality at all. In his essay on "Party Organization and Party Literature," V. I. Lenin convincingly demonstrated that there is not and cannot be any real freedom in bourgeois society because "the freedom of any bourgeois writer, artist or actress is only a disguised (or hypocritically veiled) dependence on the moneybags, on bribes, on being kept."

The October revolution freed artists from these invisible fetters, of which they were often unaware, and gave them real instead of imaginary freedom. In a talk with Clara Zetkin, V. I. Lenin explained the essence of the question with the utmost clarity: "Every artist, everyone who regards himself as an artist, has the right to create freely, according to his ideal, independently of everything." . . .

The principle of freedom of creative endeavor was regarded as the grounds for the existence of various trends and schools of thought in literature. In 1925 the Russian Communist Party Central Committee resolution "On the Party Policy in the Sphere of Literature" said: "While faultlessly discerning the social and class content of literary trends, the Party as a whole can by no means bind itself by adherence to any one trend in *the sphere of literary form.* . . . The Party therefore must express itself in favor of free competition of various groupings and trends in this sphere. Any other decision of the question would be a formal-bureaucratic pseudo-decision."

The same viewpoint was voiced in the resolution adopted by a 1927 theater conference held under auspices of the Agitation and Propaganda Department of the Party Central Committee. This resolution declared: "As in the sphere of literature, the Party and the Soviet government cannot bind themselves to any of the theater trends. . . . There can be no place for attempts to obliterate the distinction among theater trends, for attempts to dissolve all trends into one, even a highly artistic one, or to support one trend at the expense of others. Only in the process of competition and interaction can all these forms win the maximum attention of the mass of

FROM: B. A. Nazarov and O. V. Gridneva, "On the Problem of the Lag in Drama and Theater," *Voprosy Filosofii* [Problems of Philosophy], no. 5, 1956 (English translation in *The Current Digest of the Soviet Press*, VIII:45, December 19, 1956, pp. 3-4, 6-8).

spectators and enhance their own social-artistic importance."

Of course, the acknowledgment of complete freedom of creative endeavor did not mean that the formation of a new, socialist art proceeded spontaneously. In the talk with Clara Zetkin,* immediately after the words quoted above about creative freedom, Lenin added: "But, of course, we are Communists. By no means should we stand by with folded arms and let chaos develop. We must direct this process in fully planned fashion and shape its results."

How, then, did the Party direct this process?

In respect to the proletarian cadres that had entered the arts, the method was the same as in the case of Party and Soviet cadres: mastery of the ideology of Marxism-Leninism. Matters were more complicated as they concerned the cadres of pre-revolutionary intelligentsia in the arts. The above-mentioned Central Committee resolution on literature said that a tactful and conserving approach should be employed toward the old cadres in the arts, that is, an approach "ensuring every condition for them to come over to the side of the communist ideology as fast as possible. While sifting out antiproletarian and antirevolutionary elements (now quite insignificant), . . . the Party must be tolerant of intermediate ideological forms, patiently helping to eliminate these inevitably numerous forms gradually in the process of ever closer friendly cooperation with the cultural forces of communism." . . .

Free competition is a manifestation of freedom of creative endeavor; bossing and the rejection of free competition violate this freedom and make creative endeavor a matter of a kind of dependence. What kind of dependence, and dependence upon what? To answer this question, let us examine the article "Confusion Instead of Music," published in Pravda, No. 27, 1936, and the circumstances which caused the banning of D. Shostakovich's opera "Lady Macbeth of Mtsensk District."

Let us recall this article's characterization of the music: "From the very first moment of the opera the listener is flabbergasted by a deliberately disjointed, confused torrent of sound. Fragments of melodies, snatches of musical phrases are drowned, reappear and then again vanish in the general din, rattle and screeching. . . . On the stage, screams substitute for singing. If the composer happens to slip onto the path of simple and comprehensible melody, he promptly . . . dives back into the jungle of musical confusion, which at times turns into cacophony. Expressiveness . . . is replaced by frenzied rhythm. Musical noise is supposed to express passion. . . . This is music deliberately composed 'upside down' – so that nothing in it might suggest classical opera. . . . This is some sort of leftist confusion

*Klara Zetkin: a leading German Communist – Ed.

instead of natural human music. . . . The music croaks, squeals, puffs and gasps in order to make the love scenes as naturalistic as possible."

There you have the whole basic characterization given to the music. Is it not clear that this is not an example of "businesslike and serious criticism," on the need for which *Pravda* insists in the same article, but an expression of the critic's personal attitude to the opera?

D. Shostakovich's opera played at the K. S. Stanislavsky – V. I. Nemirovich-Danchenko Music Theater for about two years. In December, 1935, it was produced by the Bolshoi Theater. After it was seen in January, 1936, by some leading personalities, it was removed from the repertoire. The same thing happened to the ballet "Bright Stream" at the same theater and to the production of "Bogatyri" at the Kamerny Theater. All the other plays were banned in approximately the same way. These were plays licensed by the Repertoire Committee and included in the repertoire of the theaters either by the Committee itself or with its knowledge. Then someone saw the production and used his "veto." Matters finally reached a stage at which the members of the Repertoire Committee were given the right to decide the fate of a production singlehanded.

Thus, beginning with the case of the Shostakovich opera in 1936, individual persons were given the right to elevate their personal esthetic likes and dislikes to the rank of guiding ideas and to make the creative endeavors of artists, playwrights and actors dependent on them. Consequently, views diametrically opposed to those of Lenin were established; moreover, the right to claim these views to be those of the people as a whole and to speak about each individual work of art in the name of the people was established. . . .

It is true that the masses of the people had definitely spoken in favor of realism. But realism is a general, broad concept which takes concrete form in individual works of art. And, while the masses of the people had shown that they favor realism as a whole, this did not at all mean that they had given up their right "to judge of everything" and to enjoy all the fruits of art and not merely those that someone else had deemed fit for consumption. . . .

Then why should all questions be settled for the people by the discretion of any administrative official?

As we see, along with the encroachment on the personal initiative and personal inclinations of workers of the arts, a sharp violation of democratic principles of art guidance took place in 1936. Depriving the people of the right to "judge of everything" and turning the opinions of individuals into "guiding ideas" fundamentally contradicted Lenin's attitude toward the people and eliminated their opportunity to exert active influence on the shaping of Soviet theater art. At the same time the establishment of rigid control over both works of art and the creative process itself signified loss of confidence in the intelligentsia working in the arts.

The Party had trusted this intelligentsia in the years when it consisted exclusively of prerevolutionary intellectuals and when its ideals could not possibly have been called proletarian, and the intelligentsia had justified the confidence of the Party. The intelligentsia ceased to be trusted at a time when a numerous new Soviet intelligentsia had emerged from the ranks of the working class, the peasantry and Soviet employees, an intelligentsia which is flesh of the flesh and blood of the blood of the Soviet people. The only Soviet intellectuals to be trusted at that time were those who occupied administrative posts, among whom there were many over-cautious or simply insufficiently cultured individuals.

A natural question arises: What phenomena in public life caused such a sharp departure from Lenin's attitude to art?

The transformation of individuals' opinions into "guiding ideas" was one of the manifestations of the cult of the individual leader, which became widespread in the thirties. It was in the soil of this cult that the conviction arose and grew in the mid-thirties that success in art could be achieved by orders, instructions, decrees and decisions.

This conviction fundamentally contradicts the views held by V. I. Lenin. Speaking of the need of reforming literary work, V. I. Lenin said: "We are far from the idea of preaching any kind of uniform system or of solving the problem by issuing a set of decisions." In his speech at the Second Congress of Political Education Workers in 1921 V. I. Lenin spoke still more definitely and sharply, describing as "Communist swagger" the assumption that all problems can be solved by "Communist decree-passing." . . .

Until the mid-thirties the Party, proceeding on Leninist principles, had fought tirelessly for a realistic art. The principal method in this struggle was leadership based on patient, comradely criticism aimed at implanting communist ideals in the intelligentsia working in the arts. From the mid-thirties onward, the concept of "leadership" began to be identified more and more with the concept of "command"; bossing and wide application of all kinds of repression became the principal method of influencing the arts. After the war the influence of the cult of the individual leader increased even more. On the basis of an exaggerated idea of the role of the individual in history, some theoreticians even evolved a theory of the absence of objective laws of social development in the U.S.S.R. and the possibility of "creating" such laws at will. The result was that literature and the arts were guided by variable day-to-day instructions, and artificial schemes were passed off for life, instead of truthfully portraying reality and instead of following the objective laws of art. This, in turn, led to adapting art to the current political situation, to "varnishing" and distorting reality. It is hardly necessary to cite examples, so well known are they to everybody.

Our party is now conducting a sharp and systematic struggle against the harmful consequences of the cult of the individual leader. The positive results of this struggle have already become manifest in many aspects of our life, but in the theater field these consequences still play a considerable role. Just as before, from time to time some leaders "veto" a work on the basis of their personal impressions, disregarding public opinion and proclaiming their viewpoint to be the only correct one and beyond appeal, and describing all who disagree as nitwits. For example, only exceptional persistence by the management of the Vakhtangov Theater blocked the effort of the Central Theater Administration to "veto" the play "A Woman Alone."

Confidence in the intelligentsia in the arts has not been fully restored to this day. Only the officials of government agencies, among whom there are still many over-cautious people, enjoy full trust even now. There is hardly any need to demonstrate that in 1956 our intelligentsia of the arts has more right to this trust than it had in 1931. True, some improvement has been noticeable quite recently: The theaters have been given the right to select their own repertoire, and the repertoire has become more interesting, although, unfortunately, this change for the better has been achieved mainly by revivals of classics and not by plays about modern life. However, these steps are not enough to restore complete trust, such as the intelligentsia of the arts enjoyed when Leninist views on art were still strong in the Party. A determined reorganization of the whole work of guidance of the arts is needed.

The organizational aspect, of course, is extremely important in any matter. If we look at this aspect from the vantage point of historical perspective, it is not difficult to note some quite interesting circumstances. First, it is characteristic that the drama is in a less satisfactory state than any other art, not to mention science; second, this lag in the theater began immediately after the formation of the Committee on Affairs of the Arts.

In a brief note entitled "On the Work of the People's Commissariat of Education," V. I. Lenin wrote: "A Communist leader must prove his right to leadership by – and only by – his ability to *find many* – always more and more – helpers among the practical teachers; by his *ability* to help *them* in their work, to promote *them*, to make the most of *their* experience and to take it into account.

"In *this* respect our motto should certainly be: *Less* 'leadership,' more practical work."

Since 1936 this method has been abandoned and replaced by the demand for more "leadership." As the end result, administrators and not the workers of the arts have come to determine the destinies of the theater. Public organizations have found themselves completely excluded from leadership of the theater.

Our state is a state of a new type. It exists for the very purpose of advancing the welfare of the people with the help of the people themselves. Therefore there can be no situation in our country wherein the state would remove itself from the guidance and control of any sphere of public life. But the forms of state leadership or control may be various; leadership and control may be exercised directly by government enterprises and institutions, but they may also be effected through public organizations. In the theater direct government leadership has been established since 1936. In literature state control is exercised through a public organization, the Writers' Union. Life shows that in the field of literature and the arts, self-government methods best ensure application of Lenin's call for "*less* 'leadership,' more practical work." In the theater, too, the method of direct and constant "leadership" from above must be rejected, and the theater arts should be granted extensive self-government. What form this self-government should take is a matter for discussion. It seems most expedient to remove matters of the arts from the jurisdiction of the Ministry of Culture and to set up an Academy of Arts or even an Academy of Literature and the Arts. As demonstrated by the experience of the Academy of Sciences, this form or organization sensibly combines leadership and self-government. One thing is beyond doubt – granting self-government to the theater arts will make it easier to put Lenin's ideas into effect, and without this a new and mighty flowering of theater arts is impossible.

THE "ANTI-PARTY GROUP"

In June, 1957, the final stage in the succession to Stalin was reached when Khrushchev's colleagues in the party Presidium, alarmed over his power and perhaps genuinely opposed to some of his economic policies, attempted to remove him from the Secretariat. Khrushchev successfully appealed to the Central Committee, which was made up largely of party secretaries loyal to him, and had his opponents denounced for the old familiar sin of factionalism. Malenkov, Molotov, Kaganovich and Shepilov were removed from all their party and government offices, and were followed the next year by Bulganin. Khrushchev then took over as prime minister in addition to his post as First Secretary of the party, and emerged as the unchallenged individual leader of the USSR.

At its meetings of June 22 to June 29, 1957, the plenary session of the Party Central Committee considered the question of the anti-Party group of Malenkov, Kaganovich and Molotov which had formed within the Presidium of the Party Central Committee.

At a time when the Party, led by the Central Committee and supported by the people as a whole, is doing tremendous work to carry out the historic decisions of the 20th Congress – intended to develop the national economy further and steadily raise the living standard of the Soviet people, to re-establish Leninist norms of inner-Party life, to eliminate violations of revolutionary legality, to expand the Party's ties with the masses, to develop Soviet socialist democracy, to strengthen the friendship of the Soviet peoples, to pursue a correct nationality policy and, in the sphere of foreign policy, to relax international tension in order to secure a lasting peace – and when notable progress, well known to every Soviet citizen, has been made in all these fields, the anti-Party group of Malenkov, Kaganovich and Molotov came out against the Party line.

Seeking to change the Party's political line, this group used anti-Party, factional methods in an attempt to change the composition of the Party's leading bodies, elected by the plenary session of the Party Central Committee. . . .

This group persistently opposed and sought to frustrate so vastly important a measure as the reorganization of industrial management and the setting up of economic councils in the economic regions, a measure approved by the entire Party and the people. They refused to understand that at the present stage, when progress in socialist industry has assumed a tremendous scale and continues to grow rapidly, with the development of heavy industry receiving priority, it was essential to find new, more perfect forms of industrial management which would uncover great reserves and assure an even more powerful rise in Soviet industry. This group went so far as to continue its struggle against the reorganization of industrial management, even after the approval of these measures in the course of the nation-wide discussion and the subsequent adoption of the law at a session of the U.S.S.R. Supreme Soviet.

With regard to agricultural questions, the members of this group failed to understand the new and vital tasks. They did not acknowledge the need to increase material incentives for the collective farm peasantry in increasing the output of agricultural products. They opposed abolition of the old

FROM: Resolution of the Central Committee of the CPSU, "On the Anti-Party Group of G. M. Malenkov, L. M. Kaganovich, and V. M. Molotov," June 29, 1957 (English translation in *The Current Digest of the Soviet Press*, IX:23, July 17, 1957, pp. 5-7).

bureaucratic system of planning on the collective farms and the introduction of the new system of planning which unleashes the initiative of the collective farms in managing their own affairs – a measure which has already yielded positive results. They have become so divorced from life that they cannot understand the real opportunity which makes it possible to abolish obligatory deliveries of farm products from collective farm households at the end of this year. Implementation of this measure, which is of vital importance for the millions of working people of the land of the Soviets, has been made possible by substantial progress of communal animal husbandry on the collective farms and by the development of the state farms. Instead of supporting this pressing measure, the members of the anti-Party group opposed it.

They waged an entirely unwarranted struggle against the Party's appeal – actively supported by the collective farms, provinces and republics – to overtake the U.S.A. in per capita output of milk, butter and meat in the next few years. Thereby the members of the anti-Party group demonstrated lordly indifference to the vital life interests of the broad masses of the people and lack of faith in the enormous potentialities inherent in the socialist economy, in the nationwide movement now going on for a faster increase in milk and meat production.

It cannot be considered accidental that Comrade Molotov, a participant in the anti-Party group, manifesting conservatism and a stagnant attitude, not only failed to realize the need for developing the virgin lands but even opposed the plowing up of 35,000,000 hectares of virgin land, which has been of such tremendous importance in our country's economy.

Comrades Malenkov, Kaganovich and Molotov stubbornly opposed those measures which the Central Committee and our entire party carried out to eliminate the consequences of the cult of the individual leader, to eliminate the violations of revolutionary law which had occurred and to create conditions which would preclude their recurrence.

Whereas the workers, collective farmers, our glorious youth, our engineers and technicians, scientists, writers, the entire intelligentsia, unanimously supported the measures promulgated by the Party in accordance with the decisions of the 20th Party Congress, whereas the entire Soviet people joined the active struggle to carry out these measures, and whereas our country is experiencing a mighty increase in the active part played by the people and a fresh surge of new creative forces, the participants in the anti-Party group remained deaf to this creative movement of the masses.

In the sphere of foreign policy, this group, in particular Comrade Molotov, showed stagnation and hampered in every way implementation of new and pressing measures intended to alleviate international tension and strengthen world peace. As Minister of Foreign Affairs, Comrade Molotov for a long time not only failed to take any measures through the Ministry of Foreign Affairs to improve relations between the U.S.S.R. and Yugoslavia but repeatedly came out against those measures which the Presidium of the Central Committee carried out to improve relations with Yugoslavia. Comrade Molotov's erroneous stand on the Yugoslav question was unanimously condemned by the July, 1955, plenary session of the Party Central Committee as "not corresponding to the interests of the Soviet state and the socialist camp and not conforming to the principles of Leninist policy." . . .

Seeing that their erroneous statements and actions were constantly rebuffed in the Presidium of the Central Committee, which has been consistently carrying out the line of the 20th Party Congress, Comrades Molotov, Kaganovich and Malenkov embarked on a group struggle against the Party leadership. Reaching agreement among themselves on an anti-Party basis, they set out to change the policy of the Party, to return the Party to those erroneous methods of leadership which were condemned by the 20th Party Congress. They resorted to methods of intrigue and reached a secret agreement against the Central Committee. The facts revealed at the Plenary session of the Central Committee show that Comrades Malenkov, Kaganovich and Molotov, as well as Comrade Shepilov, who joined them, having embarked on the path of factional struggle, violated the Party Statutes and the "On Party Unity" decision of the Tenth Party Congress, drafted by Lenin. . . .

. . . Guided by the interests of comprehensively strengthening the Leninist unity of the Party, the plenary session of the Party Central Committee resolves:

1. To condemn as incompatible with the Leninist principles of our party the factional activities of the anti-Party group of Malenkov, Kaganovich and Molotov, and of Shepilov, who joined them.

2. To exclude Comrades Malenkov, Kaganovich and Molotov from membership in the Presidium of the Central Committee and from the Central Committee; to remove Comrade Shepilov from the post of Secretary of the Central Committee and to exclude him from the list of candidates for membership in the Presidium of the Central Committee and from membership in the Central Committee. . . .

THE PROMISE OF A COMMUNIST FUTURE

In 1961, for the first time since the Civil War year of 1919, the Communist Party officially adopted a new program. The document reflected Khrushchev's grandiose aspirations to overtake the U.S.A. economically and proclaim the transition to the Communist utopia within two decades. It proved to be the last great effort to square the Marxian ideal of stateless equalitarianism with the realities of bureaucratic industrialism under the management of the Party.

Communism – The Bright Future of all Mankind

The building of a communist society has become an immediate practical task for the Soviet people. The gradual development of socialism into communism is an objective law; it has been prepared by the development of Soviet socialist society throughout the preceding period.

What is communism?

Communism is a classless social system with one form of public ownership of the means of production and full social equality of all members of society; under it, the all-round development of people will be accompanied by the growth of the productive forces through continuous progress in science and technology; all sources of public wealth will gush forth abundantly, and the great principle "From each according to his ability, to each according to his needs" will be implemented. Communism is a highly organised society of free, socially conscious working people in which public self-governement will be established, a society in which labour for the good of society will become the prime vital requirement of everyone, a necessity recognised by one and all, and the ability of each person will be employed to the greatest benefit of the people.

A high degree of communist consciousness, industry, discipline, and devotion to the public interest are intrinsic qualities of the man of communist society.

Communism ensures the continuous development of social production and rising labour productivity through rapid scientific and technological progress; it equips man with the best and most powerful machines, greatly increases his power over nature and enables him to control its elemental forces to an ever greater extent. The social economy reaches the highest stage of planned organisation, and the most effective and rational use is made of the material wealth and labour reserves to meet the growing requirements of the members of society.

Under communism there will be no classes, and the socio-economic and cultural distinctions, and differences in living conditions, between town and countryside will disappear; the countryside will rise to the level of the town in development of productive forces and nature of work, forms of production relations, living conditions and well-being of the population.

FROM: *Programme of the Communist Party of the Soviet Union*, adopted by the Twenty-Second Congress of the Communist Party of the Soviet Union, October 31, 1961 (English translation in *New Times*, November 29, 1961, supplement, pp. 27-28, 41, 47-49, 54, 56).

With the victory of communism mental and physical labour will merge organically in the production activity of people. The intelligentsia will no longer be a distinct social stratum. Workers by hand will have risen in cultural and technological standards to the level of workers by brain.

Thus, communism will put an end to the division of society into classes and social strata, whereas the whole history of mankind, with the exception of its primitive period, was one of class society. Division into opposing classes led to the exploitation of man by man, class struggle, and antagonisms between nations and states.

Under communism all people will have equal status in society, will stand in the same relation to the means of production, will enjoy equal conditions of work and distribution, and will actively participate in the management of public affairs. Harmonious relations will be established between the individual and society on the basis of the unity of public and personal interests. For all their diversity, the requirements of people will express the sound, reasonable requirements of the fully developed person.

The purpose of communist production is to ensure uninterrupted progress of society and to provide all its members with material and cultural benefits according to their growing needs, their individual requirements and tastes. People's requirements will be satisfied from public sources. Articles of personal use will be in the full ownership of each member of society and will be at his disposal.

Communist society, which is based on highly organised production and advanced technology, alters the character of work, but it does not release the members of society from work. It will by no means be a society of anarchy, idleness and inactivity. Every able-bodied person will participate in social labour and thereby ensure the steady growth of the material and spiritual wealth of society. Thanks to the changed character of labour, its better technical equipment and the high degree of consciousness of all members of society, the latter will work willingly for the public benefit according to their own inclinations.

Communist production demands high standards of organisation, precision and discipline, which are ensured, not by compulsion, but through an understanding of public duty, and are determined by the whole pattern of life in communist society. Labour and discipline will not be a burden to people: labour will no longer be a mere source of livelihood – it will be a genuinely creative process and a source of joy.

Communism represents the highest form or organisation of public life. All production units and self-governing associations will be harmoniously united in a common planned economy and a uniform rhythm of social labour.

Under communism the nations will draw closer and closer together in all spheres on the basis of a complete identity of economic, political and spiritual interests, of fraternal friendship and co-operation.

Communism is the system under which the abilities and talents of free man, his best moral qualities, blossom forth and reveal themselves in full. Family relations will be freed once and for all from material considerations and will be based solely on mutual love and friendship.

In defining the basic tasks to be accomplished in building a communist society, the Party is guided by Lenin's great formula: "*Communism is Soviet power plus the electrification of the whole country.*"

The C.P.S.U. being a party of scientific communism, proposes and fulfils the tasks of communist construction in step with the preparation and maturing of the material and spiritual prerequisites, considering that it would be wrong to jump over necessary stages of development, and that it would be equally wrong to halt at an achieved level and thus check progress. The building of communism must be carried out by successive stages.

In the current decade (1961-70) the Soviet Union, in creating the material and technical basis of communism, will surpass the strongest and richest capitalist country, the U.S.A. in production per head of population; the people's standard of living and their cultural and technical standards will improve substantially; everyone will live in easy circumstances; all collective and state farms will become highly productive and profitable enterprises; the demand of Soviet people for well-appointed housing will, in the main, be satisfied; hard physical work will disappear; the U.S.S.R. will have the shortest working day.

The material and technical basis of communism will be built up by the *end of the second decade* (1971-80), ensuring an abundance of material and cultural values for the whole population; Soviet society will come close to a stage where it can introduce the principle of distribution according to needs, and there will be a gradual transition to one form of ownership – national ownership. Thus, *a communist society will in the main be built in the USSR*. The construction of communist society will be fully completed in the subsequent period.

The majestic edifice of communism is being erected by the persevering effort of the Soviet people – the working class, the peasantry and the intelligentsia. The more successful their work, the closer the great goal – communist society. . . .

The Tasks of the Party in the Spheres of State Development and the Further Promotion of Socialist Democracy

The dictatorship of the proletariat, born of the socialist revolution, played an epoch-making role by ensuring the victory of socialism in the

U.S.S.R. In the course of socialist construction, however, it underwent changes. After the exploiting classes had been abolished, the function of suppressing their resistance ceased to exist. The chief functions of the socialist state – organisation of the economy, culture and education – developed in full measure. The socialist state entered a new period of its development. The state began to grow over into a nation-wide organisation of the working people of socialist society. Proletarian democracy was growing more and more into a socialist democracy of the people as a whole.

The working class is the only class in history that does not aim to perpetuate its power. Having brought about the complete and final victory of socialism – the first phase of communism – and the transition of society to the full-scale construction of communism, the dictatorship of the proletariat has fulfilled its historic mission and has ceased to be indispensable in the U.S.S.R. from the point of view of the tasks of internal development. The state, which arose as a state of the dictatorship of the proletariat, has, in the new, contemporary stage, become a state of the entire people, an organ expressing the interests and will of the people as a whole. Since the working class is the foremost and best organised force of Soviet society, it plays a leading role also in the period of the full-scale construction of communism. The working class will have completed its role of leader of society after communism is built and classes disappear.

The Party holds that the dictatorship of the working class will cease to be necessary before the state withers away. The state as an organisation of the entire people will survive until the complete victory of communism. Expressing the will of the people, it must organise the building up of the material and technical basis of communism, and the transformation of socialist relations into communist relations, must exercise control over the measure of work and the measure of consumption, promote the people's welfare, protect the rights and freedoms of Soviet citizens, socialist law and order and socialist property, instil in the people conscious discipline and a communist attitude to labour, guarantee the defence and security of the country, promote fraternal co-operation with the socialist countries, uphold world peace, and maintain normal relations with all countries.

All-round extension and perfection of socialist democracy, active participation of all citizens in the administration of the state, in the management of economic and cultural development, improvement of the government apparatus, and increased control over its activity by the people constitute the main direction in which socialist statehood develops in the building of communism. As socialist democracy develops, the organs of state power will gradually be transformed into organs of public self-government. The

Leninist principle of democratic centralism, which ensures the proper combination of centralised leadership with the maximum encouragement of local initiative, the extension of the rights of the Union republics and greater creative activity of the masses, will be promoted. It is essential to strengthen discipline, constantly control the activities of all the sections of the administrative apparatus, check the execution of the decisions and laws of the Soviet state and heighten the responsibility of every official for the strict and timely implementation of these laws. . . .

The Tasks of the Party in the Spheres of Ideology, Education, Instruction, Science and Culture

Soviet society has made great progress in the socialist education of the masses, in the moulding of active builders of socialism. But even after the socialist system has triumphed there persist in the minds and behavior of people survivals of capitalism, which hamper the progress of society.

In the struggle for the victory of communism, ideological work becomes an increasingly powerful factor. The higher the social consciousness of the members of society, the more fully and broadly their creative activities come into play in the building of the material and technical basis of communism, in the development of communist forms of labour and new relations between people, and, consequently, the more rapidly and successfully the building of communism proceeds.

The Party considers that the paramount task in the ideological field in the present period is to educate all working people in a spirit of ideological integrity and devotion to communism, and cultivate in them a communist attitude to labour and the social economy; to eliminate completely the survivals of bourgeois views and morals; to ensure the all-round, harmonious development of the individual; to create a truly rich spiritual culture. Special importance is attached by the Party to the moulding of the rising generation.

The moulding of the new man is effected through his own active participation in communist construction and the development of communist principles in the economic and social spheres, under the influence of the educational work carried out by the Party, the state, and various social organisations, work in which the press, radio, cinema, and television play an important part. As communist forms of social organisation are created, communist ideas will become more firmly rooted in life and work and in human relations, and people will develop the ability to enjoy the benefits of communism in a rational way. Joint planned labour by the members of society, their daily participation in the management of state and public affairs, and the development of communist relations of comradely cooperation and mutual support, recast the minds of people in a spirit of collectivism, industry, and humanism.

Increased communist consciousness of the people furthers the ideological and political unity of the workers, collective farmers, and intellectuals and promotes their gradual fusion in the single collective of the working people of communist society.

The Party sets the following tasks in the field of development of Communist consciousness:

(a) *The Shaping of a Scientific World Outlook.* Under socialism and at a time when a communist society is being built, when spontaneous economic development has given way to the conscious organisations of production and social life as a whole, and when theory is daily translated into practice, it is of prime importance that a scientific world outlook be shaped in all working people of Soviet society on the basis of Marxism-Leninism, an integral and harmonious system of philosophical, economic and sociopolitical views. The Party calls for the education of the whole population in the spirit of scientific communism and strives to ensure that all working people fully understand the course and perspectives of world development. . . .

(b) *Labour Education.* The Party sees the development of a communist attitude to labour in all members of society as its chief educational task. Labour for the benefit of society is the sacred duty of all. Any labour for society, whether physical or mental, is honourable and commands respect. Exemplary labour and management in the social economy should serve to educate all working people. . . .

(c) *The Affirmation of Communist Morality.* In the course of transition to communism, the moral principles of society become increasingly important; the sphere of action of the moral factor expands and the importance of the administrative control of human relations diminishes accordingly. The Party will encourage all forms of conscious civic self-discipline leading to the assertion and promotion of the basic rules of the communist way of life.

The Communists reject the class morality of the exploiters; in contrast to the perverse, selfish views and morals of the old world, they promote communist morality, which is the noblest and most just morality, for it expresses the interests and ideals of the whole of working mankind. Communism makes the elementary standards of morality and justice, which were distorted or shamelessly flouted under the rule of the exploiters, inviolable rules for relations both between individuals and between peoples. Communist morality encompasses the fundamental norms of human morality which the masses of the people evolved in the course of millenniums as they fought against vice and social oppression. The revolutionary morality of the working class is of particular importance to the moral advancement of society. As socialist and communist construction progresses, communist morality is enriched with new principles, a new content.

The Party holds that *the moral code of the builder of communism* should comprise the following principles:

devotion to the communist cause; love of the socialist motherland and of the other socialist countries;

conscientious labour for the good of society—he who does not work, neither shall he eat;

concern on the part of everyone for the preservation and growth of public wealth;

a high sense of public duty; intolerance of actions harmful to the public interest;

collectivism and comradely mutual assistance: one for all and all for one;

humane relations and mutual respect between individuals—man is to man a friend, comrade and brother;

honesty and truthfulness, moral purity, modesty, and unpretentiousness in social and private life;

mutual respect in the family, and concern for the upbringing of children;

an uncompromising attitude to injustice, parasitism, dishonesty, careerism and money-grubbing;

friendship and brotherhood among all peoples of the U.S.S.R; intolerance of national and racial hatred;

an uncompromising attitude to the enemies of communism, peace and the freedom of nations;

fraternal solidarity with the working people of all countries, and with all peoples.

(d) The Promotion of Proletarian Internationalism and Socialist Patriotism. The Party will untiringly educate Soviet people in the spirit of proletarian internationalism and will vigorously promote the international solidarity of the working people. In fostering the Soviet people's love of their country, the Party maintains that with the emergence of the world socialist system the patriotism of the members of socialist society is expressed in devotion and loyalty to their own country and to the entire community of socialist countries. Socialist patriotism and socialist internationalism necessarily imply proletarian solidarity with the working class and all working people of all countries. The Party will continue persever-

ingly to combat the reactionary ideology of bourgeois nationalism, racism, and cosmopolitanism.

(e) All-Round and Harmonious Development of the Individual. In the period of transition to communism, there are greater opportunities of *educating a new man, who will harmoniously combine spiritual wealth, moral purity and a perfect physique.*

All-round development of the individual has been made possible by historic social gains – freedom from exploitation, unemployment and poverty, from discrimination on account of sex, origin, nationality or race. Every member of society is provided with equal opportunities for education and creative labour. Relations of dependence and inequality between people in public affairs and in family life disappear. The personal dignity of each citizen is protected by society. Each is guaranteed an equal and free choice of occupation and profession with due regard to the interests of society. As less and less time is spent on material production, the individual is afforded ever greater opportunities to develop his abilities, gifts, and talents in the fields of production, science, engineering, literature, and the arts. People will increasingly devote their leisure to public pursuits, cultural intercourse, intellectual and physical development, scientific, technical and artistic endeavour. Physical training and sports will become part and parcel of the everyday life of people.

(f) Elimination of the Survivals of Capitalism in the Minds and Behaviour of People. The Party considers it an integral part of its communist education work to combat manifestations of bourgeois ideology and morality, and the remnants of private-owner psychology, superstitions, and prejudices.

The general public, public opinion, and extensive criticism and self-criticism must play a big role in combating survivals of the past and manifestations of individualism and selfishness. Comradely censure of anti-social behaviour will gradually become the principal means of doing away with manifestations of bourgeois views, customs and habits. The power of example in public affairs and in private life, in the performance of one's public duty, acquires tremendous educational significance.

The Party uses ideological media to educate people in the spirit of a scientific materialist world conception, to overcome religious prejudices without insulting the sentiments of believers. It is necessary to conduct regularly broad atheistic propaganda on a scientific basis, to explain patiently the untenability of religious beliefs, which were engendered in the past when people were overawed by the elemental forces and social oppression and did not know the real causes of natural and social phenomena. This can be done by making use of the achievements of modern science, which is steadily solving the mysteries of the universe and extending man's power over nature, leaving no room for religious inventions about supernatural forces.

(g) The Exposure of Bourgeois Ideology. The peaceful coexistence of states with different social systems does not imply any easing of the ideological struggle. The Communist Party will go on *exposing the antipopular, reactionary nature of capitalism* and all attempts to paint bright pictures of the capitalist system.

The Party will *steadfastly propagate the great advantages of socialism and communism over the declining capitalist system*.

The Party advances the scientific ideology of communism in contrast to reactionary bourgeois ideology. Communist ideology, which expresses the fundamental interests of the working class and all working people, teaches them to struggle, to live and work, for the happiness of all. It is the most humane ideology. Its ideals are to establish truly human relations between individuals and peoples, to deliver mankind from the threat of wars of extermination, and bring about universal peace and a free, happy life for all men on earth. . . .

The Party in the Period of Full-Scale Communist Construction

As a result of the victory of socialism in the U.S.S.R. and the consolidation of the unity of Soviet society, the Communist Party of the working class has become the vanguard of the Soviet people, a Party of the entire people, and extended its guiding influence to all spheres of social life. The Party is the brain, the honour and the conscience of our epoch, of the Soviet people, the people effecting great revolutionary transformations. It looks keenly into the future and shows the people scientifically motivated roads along which to advance, arouses titanic energy in the masses and leads them to the accomplishment of great tasks.

The period of full-scale communist construction is characterised by a further *enhancement of the role and importance of the Communist Party* as the leading and guiding force of Soviet society.

Unlike all the preceding socio-economic formations, communist society does not develop spontaneously, but as a result of the conscious and purposeful efforts of the masses led by the Marxist-Leninist Party. The Communist Party, which unites the foremost representatives of the working class, of all working people, and is closely connected with the masses, which enjoys unbounded prestige among the people and understands the laws of social development, provides proper leadership in communist construction as a whole, giving it an organised, planned and scientifically based character. . . .

There must be a new, higher stage in the development of the Party itself and of its political, ideological, and organisational work that is in conformity with the full-scale building of communism. The Party will continuously improve the forms and methods of its work, so that its leadership of the masses, of the building of the material and technical basis of communism, of the development of society's spiritual life will keep pace with the growing requirements of the epoch of communist construction. . . .

The achievement of communism in the U.S.S.R. will be the greatest victory mankind has ever won throughout its long history. Every new step made towards the bright peaks of communism inspires the working masses in all countries, renders immense moral support to the struggle for the liberation of all peoples from social and national oppression, and brings closer the triumph of Marxism-Leninism on a world-wide scale.

When the Soviet people will enjoy the blessings of communism, new hundreds of millions of people on earth will say: "We are for communism!" It is not through war with other countries, but by the example of a more perfect organisation of society, by rapid progress in developing the productive forces, the creation of all conditions for the happiness and well-being of man, that the ideas of communism win the minds and hearts of the masses.

The forces of social progress will inevitably grow in all countries, and this will assist the builders of communism in the Soviet Union.

The Party proceeds from the Marxist-Leninist proposition: history is made by the people, and communism is a creation of the people, of its energy and intelligence. The victory of communism depends on people, and communism is built for people. Every Soviet man brings the triumph of communism nearer by his labour. The successes of communist construction spell abundance and a happy life to all, and enhance the might, prestige and glory of the Soviet Union.

The Party is confident that the Soviet people will accept the new Programme of the C.P.S.U. as their own vital cause, as the greatest purpose of their life and as a banner of nation-wide struggle for the building of communism. The Party calls on all Communists, on the entire Soviet people – all working men and women, collective farmers and workers by brain – to apply their energies to the successful fulfilment of the historic tasks set forth in this Programme.

UNDER THE TRIED AND TESTED LEADERSHIP OF THE COMMUNIST PARTY, UNDER THE BANNER OF MARXISM-LENINISM, THE SOVIET PEOPLE HAVE BUILT SOCIALISM.

UNDER THE LEADERSHIP OF THE PARTY, UNDER THE BANNER OF MARXISM-LENINISM, THE SOVIET PEOPLE WILL BUILD COMMUNIST SOCIETY.

*THE PARTY SOLEMNLY PROCLAIMS: THE PRESENT GEN-
ERATION OF SOVIET PEOPLE SHALL LIVE IN COMMUNISM!*

HAREBRAINED SCHEMES – KHRUSHCHEV'S DIVISION OF THE PARTY APPARATUS

In his efforts to drive the Soviet economy forward and outmaneuver his neo-Stalinist opponents in the party hierarchy, Khrushchev undertook a number of rash initiatives in the domestic as well as the foreign policy realm. One of his most disruptive moves, immediately cancelled by his successors, was to divide the provincial organizations of the Communist Party into separate urban-industrial and rural-agricultural branches.

The 22nd Party Congress set forth the further improvement of guidance of the national economy as one of the primary and most important of the Party's tasks. It is now necessary also to bring Party guidance of industry, construction and agriculture into line with the demands of the time. In conditions of full-scale communist construction, when the Party's role is growing immeasurably, the organizational restructuring of the guidance of the national economy has great political significance.

In our time what is required of the Party is the ability not only to issue the proper slogan at the proper time but also to give knowledgeable day-by-day, concrete guidance to production, to the development of industry, agriculture and all branches of the economy.

The rate of the development of the country's national economy depends chiefly on the labor efforts of the millions and on an ability to organize the implementation of Party policy and of plans for economic construction.

However, the organizational forms for guidance of the national economy that took shape earlier, and that played in their time a positive role, now are preventing a more closely planned and concrete treatment of all branches of industry and agriculture and the taking of timely, effective measures to remove existing shortcomings, are engendering the guidance of the economy by proclamation and in "campaign style," and are preventing the proper placement of Party cadres and the better employment of their knowledge and experience.

To overcome the above-mentioned shortcomings and to improve the guidance of the national economy, *it is necessary to shift to the production principle in the structure of the guiding Party agencies from bottom to top*.

FROM: Resolution of the Central Committee of the CPSU, "On the Development of the USSR Economy and Reorganization of Party Guidance of the National Economy," November 23, 1962 (English translation in *Current Digest of the Soviet Press*, XIV:48, December 26, 1962, pp. 12-14).

The organization of Party agencies according to the production principle will present an opportunity to ensure more concrete and closely planned guidance of industry, construction and agriculture and to concentrate the principal attention on production questions. Such a reorganization will stimulate all aspects of the Party's activity and will link organizational and ideological work still more closely to the tasks of creating the material and technical base for communism and of rearing the new man.

The creation of the material and technical base for communism requires acceleration of the rate of technical progress. At present the guidance of a large part of the research and design organizations is dispersed among economic councils, ministries and departments, which hampers the pursuit of a unified technical policy in the branches of the national economy and slows down the introduction of new technology.

The plenary session of the C.P.S.U. Central Committee deems it necessary to reorganize the guidance of research and design organizations, to eliminate parallelism and lack of coordination in their activity and to carry out measures for the centralization of the guidance of technical policy.

The plenary session of the C.P.S.U. Central Committee calls the attention of Party, Soviet and economic agencies to the shortcomings that exist in the organization of industrial, housing and cultural and service construction. Certain economic councils, Union-republic State Planning Committees and local Party agencies frequently undertake the construction of new projects without considering general state interests and without taking into account the possibilities for providing their projects with designs, materials, manpower and equipment, and they scatter funds among a multitude of construction projects. . . .

The plenary session of the Central Committee of the Communist Party of the Soviet Union resolves:

I. – In the sphere of Party guidance of the national economy:

1. To approve the measures for the reorganization of the Party guidance of the national economy worked out by the Presidium of the C.P.S.U. Central Committee and set forth in Comrade N. S. Khrushchev's report at the present plenary session.

2. To recognize it as necessary to reorganize the leading Party agencies from bottom to top on the basis of the production principle, and thereby to censure more concrete guidance of industrial and agricultural production.

To form within the limits of the existing territories and provinces, as a rule, two independent Party organizations:

– a territory or province Party organization uniting Communists who work in industry, construction and transport, in educational institutions and research institutes, and in design organizations and other institutions that serve industrial production and construction;

– a territory or province Party organization uniting Communists who work on collective and state farms, at experimental stations, in agricultural educational institutions and research institutes, at enterprises that process agricultural raw materials, and in procurement and other institutions and organizations connected with agricultural production.

In the territory and province Party organizations to have, correspondingly:

– a territory or province Party committee for guiding industrial production;

– a territory or province Party committee for guiding agricultural production.

3. For purposes of improving the guidance of the national economy, to recognize as expedient the formation in the C.P.S.U. Central Committee and the Central Committees of the Union-republic Communist Parties of Central Committee Bureaus for Guiding Industrial Production and Central Committee Bureaus for Guiding Agricultural Production.

To elect a Presidium of the Central Committee in the Central Committees of the Union-republic Communist Parties for deciding questions of republic-wide significance and for coordination of the activities of the Bureaus. . . .

THE FALL OF KHRUSHCHEV

After four years of political maneuvering commencing with the U-2 affair in 1960 (when an American reconnaissance plane was shot down over Soviet territory) the neo-Stalinists inspired by Mikhail Suslov accomplished the unprecedented feat of removing the established leader according to the party rules. The gist of Suslov's speech at the Central Committee meeting where this action took place was reported in the underground press.

Khrushchev was consigned to political oblivion but lived on in quiet retirement until his death in 1971.

a) SUSLOV'S SECRET SPEECH

Generalizing all the information concerning M. Suslov's report that has come in from various sources, it is possible to reduce the charges made in

FROM: Report of M. Suslov at the Plenum of the Central Committee of the CPSU and Charges against Khrushchev, *Politicheskii Dnevnik* [Political Diary], no. 1 (1965), pp. 3-6 (editor's translation).

the report against Khrushchev to the following points:

Khrushchev allowed serious mistakes in his work, made thoughtless and hasty decisions, and played organizational leap-frog.

In recent years Khrushchev concentrated all the power in the country in his own hands and began to abuse it. He attributed all the achievements of the country to his own personal merits, completely ceased to consider the members of the Presidium, slighted them, insulted them, did not listen to their opinions, constantly lectured them and everyone else. In spite of repeated appeals to him by the members of the Presidium, he ignored all reproof.

In the press more and more was written about his merits. During 1963 in the central press his picture appeared 120 times, and in the first half of 1964, 140 times. Whereas even pictures of Stalin would be printed only ten times a year.

Khrushchev surrounded himself with advisors from among his relatives and journalists whose voice he heeded more than the voice of the members of the Presidium. The members of the Presidium had to handle a series of important measures through these people, since he did not want to listen to members of the Presidium and did not accept their proposals. Khrushchev often referred to the opinions of his son Sergei and his daughter Rada. He dragged his family into politics. He was surrounded by toadies and flatterers, in the press and on the radio as well.

To his son Sergei, who had recently finished the institute, they gave the title of laureate of the Lenin Prize and candidate of technical science.

Suslov called Khrushchev's son-in-law Adzhubei a toady, a lackey, and announced that the CC [Central Committee] had removed him from the office of chief editor of *Izvestia*. In Khrushchev's entourage Adzhubei was sort of a minister of foreign affairs, who tried to decide everything on the level of heads of government and disoriented the ambassadors. Gromyko was pushed into the second rank. Suslov recounted how Adzhubei, in West Germany, in a talk with members of the government and public figures of West Germany, referred to Ulbricht in an insulting tone. It took great effort to settle the conflict with the GDR [German Democratic Republic] that arose over this. The CC of the Socialist Unity [Communist] Party sent a protest against Adzhubei's gossip to West Germany, where he had come to sound out the basis for a possible trip there by Khrushchev. Adzhubei declared to the West Germans, "Why do you jump on Ulbricht, you know he won't live long, he has tuberculosis of the throat."

The creation at Khrushchev's initiative of two party organizations — industrial and rural — caused much confusion and represents the creation of two new parties, a workers' party and a peasants' party.

In a new note to the members of the Presidium (on the forthcoming November Plenum of the CC) Khrushchev proposed to liquidate the party organizations in rural food-supply administrations and to establish political departments in place of them. Besides this, he proposed to specialize the work of the food-supply administrations and create separate administrations – "Main Administration for Sheep," "Main Administration for Pigs," "Main Administration for Fowl," etc. The Presidium responded to this note by postponing the Plenum of the CC.

Khrushchev got the idea that he was a specialist in all areas – in agriculture, diplomacy, science, art – and lectured about all of them. In West Germany he lectured about how agriculture should be carried on, and acted as if he were in some one of the provinces of our own country.

Many materials on the CC and materials prepared by the apparatus of the CC he had printed under his own name. Circulating notes to the members of the Presidium, he demanded written comments from them and gave them 45 minutes for this. Naturally, when his notes were being considered at the CC none of the members of the Presidium was able to come forth with written conclusions.

The sessions of the Presidium of the CC under Khrushchev were turned into empty formality.

Khrushchev so confused the administration of industry by creating committees, the Economic Council of the USSR, the Supreme Economic Council of the USSR, that it appears very difficult to untangle all this. Industry is now doing worse.

Khrushchev carried on an incorrect policy in the area of price-setting. The rise in prices for meat, dairy products, and certain industrial goods was a blow to the material situation of the workers. He also carried on an incorrect policy in the area of stock-raising, as a result of which many cows were slaughtered and deliveries of meat were reduced and sales in the market were reduced.

Khrushchev was careless in his speeches and conversations. Thus, for example, in a conversation with Japanese parliamentarians he declared that here in Kazakhstan live Kazakhs and in Sinkiang there are also Kazakhs, and if a referendum were taken among them as to whether they wanted to remain in China or join the USSR, and if they voted for the USSR, we would unite them with us. Suslov said that in the USSR these phrases were deleted when the type was being set, but they were printed in Japan, which evoked a protest on the part of China. Although our differences with China are not going away, and will be considered at the conference of 26 Communist Parties, and later on at a conference of all Communist Parties, nevertheless it is necessary to emphasize that in the exacerbation of the position of the Chinese the conduct of Khrushchev also had an influence, when he slighted individual leaders of the socialist states. He called Mao Tse-tung an old galosh. This became known to him and caused bitterness. Khrushchev also conducted himself tactlessly in relation to Albania.

At a dinner after a session of Comecon* he hurled a retort at Zhivkov, that the Bulgarians were always dependents. Out of tactfulness Zhivkov kept quiet and swallowed this pill. At the dinner there were leaders of the socialist states and parties. This was a manifestation by Khrushchev of great-power chauvinism.

Through an understanding with Poland an aircraft factory was built there at which airplanes of the AN-2 type were produced. According to the agreement we were supposed to buy 500 planes from them. Khrushchev decided not to buy these planes, under the pretext that we could make them more cheaply. By this we let the Poles down and provoked great dissatisfaction. At the plant there are 15,000 workers.

We also provoked dissatisfaction in Rumania, compelling her to pump her oil into the "Friendship" oil pipe line at a time when Rumania was getting hard currency for her oil.

Khrushchev's petty tyranny was shown in the following. Learning that at the Timiryazev Agricultural Academy there were scholars who did not agree with his policy in the area of agriculture, he decided no matter what to move the academy out of Moscow and disperse its faculty completely in different places. On top of this he said, "There's no use their plowing up asphalt." The academy, as is well known, has existed in Moscow for a century. Suslov said that the members of the Presidium were in disagreement with Khrushchev, and under various pretexts stalled off the relocation of the academy, created various committees, and in a word, sabotaged his directive. But when the day came that he returned from a trip and learned that the academy was still in Moscow, he ordered that it cease accepting students. So for a period of two years the academy lacked the first class and then the second. Many professors had to leave the academy.

Without any explanation to the members of the Presidium he removed the Minister of Agriculture Comrade Pysin from his post.

After seeing fallow fields on one sovkhoz [state farm] in Kazakhstan, Khrushchev disregarded the explanation of the director of the sovkhoz that on this land fallow fields were absolutely necessary, and ordered the removal not only of the director but even of the secretary of the CC of Kazakhstan Comrade Kunaev.

Khrushchev did not refrain from reproaching Kosygin just because

*Council of Economic Mutual Assistance, comprising all the satellite governments – Ed.

somehow in a conversation with Yusupov* Kosygin asked how they were doing with the grain and said that they should get better grain yields. Khrushchev regarded this as interference by Kosygin in the direction of agriculture.

Khrushchev defended Lysenko,† without regard for the fact that many scholars had come out against Lysenko. Suslov related the following. At the insistence of Lysenko, Khrushchev proposed to the USSR Academy of Sciences to open up two vacancies for the election of Nuzhdin and Remeslo as academicians. At the session of the Academy of Sciences Academician Sakharov challenged both of these candidacies. Lysenko spoke out in regard to the rejection of these candidacies with an abusive speech and later reported what had happened to Khrushchev. The latter declared that if the Academy was getting into politics, then we would break up this kind of academy, this kind of academy we don't need. These pronouncements of Khrushchev's became known to the members of the academy.

We ordered some Finnish houses from Finland, in connection with which they built a special plant. Then at Khrushchev's insistence we refused these houses. Later on, when we ordered some ships from the Finns, they notified us that they would only build them in old plants. In ten years Khrushchev did not once receive the Minister of Foreign Trade Patolichev. Khrushchev never even called him up.

At Khrushchev's orders the private plots of the collective farmers were cut down. This caused irritation in the village, since the cut off portions could in no way be sown and grew up in weeds.

In regard to the decorating of Nasser things happened thus: the members of the Presidium objected to awarding Nasser the title Hero of the Soviet Union. However, Khrushchev insisted personally, and took the star and order of Lenin to Cairo. When Nasser said that they also had to give the title of hero to his vice-president Amer, Khrushchev without the agreement of the Presidium told Georgadze**to bring a star and order on the grounds that he had promised Nasser to do this.

When he returned from Cairo he told Ponomarev††to check what kind of Communists there were in the United Arab Republic who Nasser said were preventing him from building socialism.

---

*Evidently Ismail Yusupov, whom Khrushchev substituted for Kunaev in Kazakhstan in 1962, and was himself displaced again by Kunaev after Khrushchev was ousted – Ed.

†Trofim D. Lysenko, the quack geneticist – Ed.

**M. P. Georgadze, secretary to the Presidium of the Supreme Soviet – Ed.

†† Boris N. Ponomarev, head of the International Department of the Party Secretariat – Ed.

In one province he proposed to liquidate the kolkhozy and create sovkhozy, justifying this because the kolkhozy were unprofitable. In fact the kolkhozy were more profitable than the sovkhozy.

Khrushchev never allowed one member of the Presidium to go out to the provinces, declaring that it's useless for you to go there, they have to work!

He sometimes came down on a member of the Presidium for measures that had been carried out, forgetting that he had proposed these same measures in speeches that had been written for him earlier.

He was lavish and indiscriminate in his promises. Thus, for example, we are building 600 kilometers of railroad in Iraq, at the same time that here in the USSR our annual construction does not exceed 600 kilometers. In Indonesia, where incredible poverty rules, our builders erected a big stadium.

The crowning blow was his trip to the Scandinavian countries with his whole family, with his children and grandchildren, in all twelve people. Satiukov* took his daughter with him. In the Western press they wrote that it was a family picnic. This can't be called anything but a procession with a retinue. And the entire cost was a state expense.

Khrushchev insisted that the Party Program not make the reference "under the direction of the proletarian party." It was necessary to deceive him by saying that this was a typographical error; he discovered that this phrase was left in even at the last stage.

Khrushchev made his aide secretary of a province committee.

We bought ten million tons of grain, but even so because of losses we didn't complete the plan, although this was the biggest purchase of all time.

At the sessions of the Presidium Khrushchev shouted, swore, insulted members of the Presidium, and used dirty language.

Could we have called him to order sooner? The members of the Presidium did this, warned him, but except for coarse rebuffs and insults they heard nothing from him, although he did not employ repression in relation to the members of the Presidium. It is harder to struggle with a living cult than with a dead one. If Stalin destroyed people physically, Khrushchev destroyed them morally. The removal of Khrushchev from power is a sign not of the weakness but of the strength of the party, and this should be a lesson.

b) COMMUNIQUÉ OF THE CENTRAL COMMITTEE

On the 14th of October of this year a plenary session of the Central Committee of the CPSU took place.

*P. A. Satiukov, chief editor of *Pravda*, removed after Khrushchev was ousted – Ed.

The plenary session of the CC of the CPSU approved the request of Comrade N. S. Khrushchev to be released from the duties of First Secretary of the CC of the CPSU, member of the Presidium of the CC of the CPSU, and Chairman of the Council of Ministers of the USSR, in connection with his advanced age and worsening condition of health.

The plenary session of the CC of the CPSU elected as First Secretary of the CC of the CPSU Comrade L. I. Brezhnev.

FROM: Plenum of the Central Committee of the CPSU, Informational Communiqué, October 14, 1964, *Pravda*, October 16, 1964 (editor's translation).

Chapter Six
The Soviet Union Since Khrushchev

The years since 1964 have been for the Soviet Union the most stable period in its history, with rigid maintenance of institutions and ideology by an aging leadership unwilling to address creatively the country's fundamental problems. These are no longer problems of backwardness and revolution but of modernity and growth, for which the governing spirit in the Communist Party is increasingly anachronistic. This dilemma is the legacy bequeathed at the death of Brezhnev in 1982 to the new leadership of Yuri Andropov.

THE PROMISE OF THE BREZHNEV ERA

The palace coup of 1964, installing Leonid I. Brezhnev as First Secretary (after 1966, General Secretary) of the Party and Alexei N. Kosygin as prime minister, initiated the longest period of stable leadership and policy that the Soviet Union has experienced since the Revolution. Avoiding grand programmatic statements, the new leadership rescinded most of Khrushchev's administrative experiments and concentrated on the material enhancement of the nation's power and productivity.

In examining economic development we must see both the positive aspects of the results of our work and also the shortcomings. In recent years negative phenomena have appeared, such as a slowing down of the rates of growth of production and labor productivity and a reduction in the effectiveness of the utilization of production assets and capital investments. Unless we adopt a critical approach we cannot give a correct appraisal, without which our advance will be less successful.

After its October (1964) plenary session, the C.P.S.U. Central Committee analyzed the state of affairs in economics, exposed the reasons for the negative phenomena and outlined paths for overcoming them.

The rates of economic growth were affected by shortcomings in admin-

FROM: Brezhnev, "Report of the CPSU Central Committee to the 23rd Congress of the Communist Party of the Soviet Union," March 29, 1966, *Pravda*, March 30, 1966 (English translation in *Current Soviet Policies V*, Columbus, Ohio, American Association for the Advancement of Slavic Studies, 1973, pp. 14-16, 23-24, 29-30; this and subsequent selections reprinted by permission of *The Current Digest of the Soviet Press*).

istration and planning, by underestimation of the methods of economic accountability and by failure to make full use of material and moral incentives. The forms and methods of the management, planning and economic stimulation of production employed until recently did not conform to the new, higher level of productive forces in the country and had begun to hamper their development.

The crop failures of 1963 and 1965 had a negative effect on the national economy, and especially on raising the material well-being of the working people. The complications in the international situation must also be taken into account. The aggressive actions of the U.S. imperialists forced us to channel substantial additional funds into strengthening the country's defense might in recent years.

It must be admitted that, because of a subjectivist approach, certain miscalculations were made in working out the seven-year plan; running ahead was permitted. The expansion of production established for some branches did not always conform to actual possibilities.

The territorial system of industrial management led to the division of guidance of branches of industry among many economic regions; uniform technical policy was violated, research organizations were cut off from production, and this hampered the development and introduction of technology. . . .

First of all, it is necessary to say that the five-year plan for 1966-1970 is an important new stage in the Soviet people's struggle to create the material and technical base of communism. The C.P.S.U. Central Committee defined the *chief task* of the new five-year plan. It is *to ensure – on the basis of the comprehensive utilization of the achievements of science and technology, the industrial development of all social production and a rise in its effectiveness and in the productivity of labor – the further significant growth of industry and a high stable rate of agricultural development, and thereby to attain a substantial rise in the people's standard of living and the fuller satisfaction of the material and cultural needs of all Soviet people.*

New steps will be taken in the coming five-year period to solve such problems as overcoming the substantial differences between town and countryside and between mental and physical labor. The solution of major economic and social tasks will still further strengthen the political foundation and the material base of the alliance of the working class and the peasantry. The fraternal alliance of the peoples living in our country will be further developed. . . .

Primary significance is attached to the development of agriculture. The task is set of raising this very important sphere of material production so that the country's requirements for agricultural products may be more fully satisfied. It is planned to raise labor productivity in agriculture on the basis of mechanization, chemicalization and electrification and to bring agriculture step by step up to the level of technical equipment and organization of production that prevails in industry.

The substantial convergence of the rates of growth of the means of production (Group A) and the production of consumer goods (Group B) is an important feature of the coming five-year period.

This is one of the most important economic and political tasks, the fulfillment of which conforms to the interests of millions of people. And the Party, which holds the people's welfare above all else, is giving it a great deal of attention in the new five-year plan.

There was a time when we had to restrict our requirements deliberately in order to achieve high rates of development of heavy industry. Now we have powerful productive forces. They make it possible to develop more quickly the branches of social production that directly satisfy the material, cultural and other needs of the working people. It is this policy of the Party that has been given expression in the five-year-plan's provisions for the convergence of the rates of development of the production of means of production and the production of consumer goods, and of the rates of development of agriculture and industry. . . .

The Communist Party of the Soviet Union has always manifested and will continue to manifest concern for the development of literature and the arts. The Party has guided and will guide the activity of the creative organizations and institutions, rendering them all-round support and assistance. The Party opposes administration by fiat and arbitrary decisions on questions of art and literature. At the same time, we are unfailingly guided by the principle of Party spirit in art and a class approach to the evaluation of everything that is done in the sphere of culture. We shall always remember the words of Vladimir Ilyich Lenin that "literary matters must become *part* of the cause of the entire proletariat."

The Party will always support art and literature that affirms a faith in our ideals and will wage an implacable struggle against all manifestations of an ideology alien to us.

Socialist art is profoundly optimistic and life-affirming. It is able to look perceptively at what is new and progressive in our life and to show vividly and with talent the beauty of the world in which we live, the grandeur of the goals and ideals of the man of the new society. This does not mean, of course, that one must write only about the good things. As is known, there are quite a few difficulties and shortcomings in our country, and truthful criticism of them in works of art is useful and necessary and helps the Soviet people overcome these shortcomings.

Unfortunately, one also encounters those tradesmen in the arts who, instead of helping the people, select as their specialty the denigration of our system and slander against our heroic people. Of course, we have only a handful of such people. In no degree do they express the feelings and thoughts of our creative intelligentsia, which is indissolubly bound to the people and the Party. The renegades do not cherish what is most sacred for every Soviet man – the interests of the socialist homeland. It is perfectly obvious that the Soviet people cannot overlook the disgraceful activity of such individuals. They treat them as they deserve. (*Applause.*). . .

Our Leninist Communist Party is the guiding and directing force of Soviet society. It unites in its ranks the most advanced representatives of the working class and of all working people and is guided by the militant revolutionary ideology of the working class of the entire world – Marxism-Leninism; it is confidently leading the Soviet people forward along the path of the construction of communism, is channeling and organizing the life of socialist society and is successfully fulfilling the role of teacher, organizer and political leader of the entire Soviet people. (*Applause.*) The Party's political and organizational work among the masses and the selfless labor of the Soviet people have ensured the further growth of the country's economy and a rise in the well-being of the Soviet people, have made it possible to strengthen our socialist state still more and to increase the international prestige of the Soviet Union.

The October, 1964, plenary session of the C.P.S.U. Central Committee, which expressed the Party's unshakable will to develop and strictly observe Leninist norms of Party life and principles of leadership, was an important stage in the life of the Party and the country. On the basis of the decisions of the October plenary session, shortcomings in the sphere of economic and Party construction and errors linked with the unjustified restructuring of Party, Soviet and economic bodies are being corrected.

The October plenary session has exerted a positive influence on all aspects of the life and activity of the Party, the socialist state and the whole of Soviet society. It was a vivid testimonial to the monolithism and unity of the Party, its political maturity and ability to clear away boldly and decisively everything that impedes our advance. (*Applause.*) The Communist Party of the Soviet Union, armed with the great teaching of Marxism-Leninism, is confidently leading the Soviet people along the road to communism. (*Prolonged applause.*). . . .

The theoretical heritage of Marx, Engels and Lenin is the greatest wealth of our party and of the entire world Communist movement. It can be said with justice that the strongest and most remarkable feature of our party's entire activity throughout its history has been the creative development of the scientific theory of Marxism-Leninism and its organic combination with the revolutionary practice of the working class and of all the working masses. . . .

The struggle against bourgeois ideology, revisionism, dogmatism and reformism is of great importance. We must always remember that our class enemy is imperialism. It conducts subversive activities against the socialist system, its principles, ideology and morals. Imperialism's gigantic propaganda apparatus corrupts the individual and tries to divert the masses from politics. The struggle against bourgeois ideology must under all circumstances be uncompromising, for this is a class struggle, a struggle for man, for his dignity and freedom, for a consolidation of the positions of socialism and communism; it is a struggle in the interests of the international working class. (*Prolonged applause.*). . .

The Soviet people are carrying out the greatest social task in the history of mankind – the building of communism. Tens of millions of people are taking part in the active creative process of construction. We must teach first the majority and then all working people to work as our glorious shock workers and masters of labor are working today. This task is perfectly feasible. Today's shock workers and innovators of production are ordinary people. But they stand out because they have fully mastered technology, because they serve society consciously, display high moral and ethical qualities, a spirit of collectivism, and are carrying out their duties to the people self-sacrificingly and to the fullest of their abilities. These are people of the future, as it were. They work as all people will work under communism. This is of tremendous significance for the success of ideological work. Here is an example, a model that should be followed and from which it is possible to learn. Party organizations are called upon to do all in their power so that every Soviet person may see in the assignments of the new five-year plan a program for his own personal labor and may make a worthy contribution to its fulfillment.

Our party has always attached primary significance to instilling conscious discipline in all members of society. The strengthening of labor discipline and the demand for the unconditional observance of all the laws and rules of socialist society not only do not contradict the democratic principles of the Soviet system, but on the contrary, constitute a condition for the development and expansion of Soviet socialist democratism. The socialist organization of the whole of society for the sake of each individual and the socialist discipline of each individual for the sake of the whole society – such is the substance of socialist democracy. It is the task of the Party constantly to strengthen the high discipline and organization of all links of the Party and the state. . . .

Comrades! Our homeland, the great Soviet Union, is based on the fraternity, friendship and cooperation of all the peoples of the country, on a common socio-economic system, a common political system, a single socialist ideology. The economic and cultural ties of the peoples of the U.S.S.R. are becoming steadily closer and more varied. A great process of the rapprochement of peoples, of the strengthening of the unbreakable ties of their friendship and fraternity, unity and solidarity, is under way.

For almost half a century the Party has indefatigably strengthened, forged and perfected this alliance until it has turned into the inviolable and powerful force of our state that the friendship and fraternity of the peoples of the Soviet Union is today. (*Applause.*) Our enemies have repeatedly tried to undermine and to shake the strength of this friendship both by force of arms and by the poison of their bourgeois ideology. But all their hopes have been scattered like ashes, while the friendship of the Soviet peoples is confidently gathering force, flourishing, gaining strength and developing. (*Applause.*)

The Communist Party of the Soviet Union serves as the living embodiment of the ideas of proletarian internationalism, friendship and fraternity of the peoples. The finest sons and daughters of the 131 nations and peoples of our country are in its ranks. We are proud that all the national detachments of our party merge, as the waters of rivers merge in a mighty ocean, in the Communist Party of the Soviet Union – a union of likeminded Leninists, with one will, one aim, one ideology. (*Prolonged applause.*)

Our Congress is a remarkable example and proof of this. Look around the hall, comrades: Present here are representatives of many peoples and nationalities of our country. Each of them is the son of his own socialist nation, but at the same time he is a son of the Party, a soldier of it; he is an internationalist Communist for whom the interests of any of the other peoples of the Soviet Union are as dear, close and understandable as his own. Herein lies the strength of our party; herein is the strength of our multinational Soviet state, of our Soviet people. (*Prolonged applause.*)

The Party and all Communists, irrespective of their nationality, are called upon to continue to work indefatigably to bring about the further comprehensive rapprochement of the peoples of the Soviet Union and the strengthening of their friendship and fraternity, to make their economic, cultural and spiritual ties closer and more varied. In solving any problem, whether it be of the political, the economic or the cultural development of our country, the Party will continue to show solicitude for the interests and the national characteristics of each people, to instill in all Soviet people a spirit of the ideas of proletarian internationalism, a spirit of inviolable loyalty to the fraternity and friendship of the peoples of the U.S.S.R. This is the only correct national policy. The entire experience of the development of the U.S.S.R. confirms its viability and correctness. (*Applause.*)

THE END OF THE THAW – THE SINYAVSKY-DANIEL TRIAL

The limited relaxation of party controls over cultural life in the Khrushchev era was abruptly ended by the Brezhnev regime. The return to ideological conformity was signalled by the arrest and trial of the writers Andrei Sinyavsky and Yuli Daniel in 1966. Critical writing was thereafter forced into the underground dissident movement. Sinyavsky, like numerous other dissidents, was ultimately expelled from the Soviet Union.

The enemies of communism are not squeamish. With what gusto do they dish up any "sensation" gleaned from the garbage heap of anti-Sovietism! That was what happened some time ago. The bourgeois press and radio started coming out with reports of the "groundless arrest" in Moscow of two "men of letters" who had published anti-Soviet lampoons abroad. What a field day the unclean consciences and equally unclean imaginations of Western propagandists had! And here they are, already painting in sweeping strokes a mythical "purge in Soviet literary circles," alleging that these circles "are extremely alarmed at the threat of a new campaign" against "anticommunist-minded writers" and against "liberal intellectual circles" in general.

The question is: What really happened? What has so heartened the black host of anti-Sovieteers? Why have individual foreign intellectuals, who look out of place in this company, fallen into its embrace? Why do certain gentlemen strike the pose of mentors, all but protectors, of our morals, and pretend they are defending the two renegades "on behalf of" the Soviet intelligentsia? There is only one answer: In the ideological battles between the two worlds, the enemies of the new society are not particularly scrupulous as to means. And when a couple of turncoats turn up in their trenches, they hasten to heroize them, for want of something better. For those impoverished in spirit, such turncoats are a windfall they have longed for. After all, with their aid one can try to confuse public opinion, sow the poisonous seeds of unprincipledness, nihilism and morbid interest in shady "problems of life."

In brief, the enemies of communism found what they were looking for – two renegades, for whom duplicity and shamelessness had become a

FROM: D. Yeremin, "Turncoats," *Izvestia*, January 13, 1966 (English translation in *Current Digest of the Soviet Press*, XVIII:2, February 2, 1966, pp. 11-12).

credo. Hiding behind the pseudonyms of Abram Tertz and Nikolai Arzhak, for several years they had been secretly sending foreign publishing houses dirty libels against their country, against the Party and against the Soviet system, and having them published abroad. One of them, A. Sinyavsky, alias A. Tertz, published articles of literary criticism in Soviet magazines, wormed his way into the Writers' Union, and outwardly shared the aspirations of its Statutes – "to serve the people, to show in lofty artistic form the greatness of the ideas of communism" and "through all one's creative work and public activity to take an active part in the building of communism." The second, Yu. Daniel-N. Arzhak, did translations. But this was all just a false front for them. It concealed something else: hatred of our system and foul mockery of what is dearest to our motherland and people. . . .

They find nothing pleasing in our country, nothing in its multinational culture is sacred to them; they are ready to vilify and defame everything that is dear to Soviet man, whether it belongs to the present or the past. Just imagine what they wrote about Anton Pavlovich Chekhov, the outstanding Russian humanist, whose creative work stirs the good in man. Only the utmost shamelessness could move a pen that traces out such lines as: "Oh, to grab this Chekhov by his tubercular little beard and shove his nose into his consumptive phlegm!" And the Russian classics, the pride of world literature – what do they say about them? "The classics – those are what I hate most of all!"

These scribblers attempt to sling mud at and slander our Soviet Army, whose immortal exploit saved the peoples of Europe from extermination by Hitlerism.

For Soviet people, for the peoples of the earth, for all progressive mankind, no name is more sacred than the name of the leader of our revolution, Vladimir Ilyich Lenin. After all, Lenin is the age of socialist revolutions and national-liberation movements. He is our era, which has changed the world. He is scientific communism, which is being embodied in man's glorious deeds. Even prominent captains of capitalism have bowed their heads before Lenin – on more than one occasion they have had to admit that the 20th century found in him the greatest transformer of life.

To what a bottomless morass of abomination must a so-called man of letters sink to desecrate with his hooligan's pen this name that is sacred to us! It is impossible to repeat the relevant passages here, so malicious is this scribble, so outrageous and filthy! These blasphemous lines alone suffice for the diagnosis that the authors place themselves outside Soviet society . . . .

The lampoons by Sinyavsky-Tertz and Daniel-Arzhak can evoke only loathing and anger in us Soviet writers, profoundly devoted to the idea of the communist transformation of life and viewing the Leninist party as a firm bulwark and wise leader in the selfless struggle for peace and happiness – in us, as in all Soviet people. It is in vain that the trans-Atlantic patron of the turncoats, the White émigré poet B. Filippov, in prefaces to the vile books of Tertz and Arzhak tries to pass off his protégés as "well-known Soviet writers" – there are none like that in Soviet literature!

But let us leave the Western patrons of the two slanderers. If there is anything they can play upon, it is only ignorance of the foreign public regarding our Soviet life. But lies have short legs, one can't go far on them. I am sure that every sensible person in the West, comparing the facts he knows about the Soviet Union with the fabrications of the two renegades, will always draw a correct conclusion – he will consign the Sinyavsky-Tertz and Daniel-Arzhak lampoons to the rubbish heap.

It cannot be otherwise. The slanderers, after all, not only raise their hand against our Soviet society, they spew venom on all progressive mankind, on its ideals, on its sacred struggle for social progress, democracy and peace.

Today even many bourgeois journalists among our ideological adversaries speak with respect of the mighty power of socialism, which has become a "magnet of attraction" for Africa, Asia, Latin America and the entire world.

Sinyavsky and Daniel grew up in the Soviet Union. They enjoyed all the blessings of socialism. Everything that had been won by our elder brothers and fathers in the flaming years of the Revolution and the Civil War and in the difficult period of the first five-year plans was at their service.

Sinyavsky and Daniel began in a small way: They replaced honesty with unprincipledness, literary activity as understood by Soviet people with double-dealing, sincerity in their attitude to life with nihilism and with carping criticism of their fellowmen behind their backs. Having started with these petty mean tricks, they did not stop. They went on sliding down an inclined plane. And eventually they rolled as far as crimes against the Soviet regime. Thereby they placed themselves outside our literature, outside the community of Soviet people. From petty meanness to major betrayal – such was the route down which they marched. . . .

But is that all there is to it? It is, after all, not simply a question of the moral and political degeneration of two hooligans. It is a question of renegades in the service of the most rabid, most unbridled enemies of communism. In the West the story of Sinyavsky and Daniel is being spread because these two for their part have served as a tool for spreading psychological warfare against the Soviet Union.

Gentlemen, you rejoiced too soon! Your turncoats have themselves been turned on their backs. Their true visage has been recognized. These are not merely moral monsters but active henchmen of those who stoke the furnace of international tension, who wish to turn the cold war into a hot one, who have not abandoned the mad dream of raising their hand against the Soviet Union. No mercy can be shown to such henchmen. Our people have paid too dearly for the achievements of October, for the victory over fascism, for the blood and sweat shed for the homeland to be indifferent to these two scum.

As we have already seen, the "writings" of these two renegades, permeated through and through with malicious slander of our social system and our state, are specimens of anti-Soviet propaganda. Their entire content is aimed at inciting hostility between peoples and states, at aggravating the danger of war. Essentially, these are shots fired in the back of a people fighting for peace on earth and for universal happiness. Such actions cannot be regarded as other than hostile acts against the homeland.

Time will pass, and no one will even remember them. The pages steeped in bile will rot in the dump. After all, history has time and again confirmed that slander, however thick and venomous it be, inevitably evaporates under the warm breath of truth.

This will happen this time, too.

THE ATTEMPT AT ECONOMIC REFORM: LIBERMAN

Even in the Khrushchev years it was recognized by Soviet economists that Stalin-style methods of coercive centralism were beginning to outlive their usefulness for a sophisticated industrial economy. The economist Yevsei Liberman first proposed in 1962 a plan for enterprise autonomy, free market prices, and profit incentives. These ideas were endorsed by the Central Committee of the Party in 1965, as Liberman explained in his subsequent treatise. In practice, however, the system of central planning was not substantially altered.

a) LIBERMAN'S PROPOSAL

It is necessary to find a sufficiently simple and at the same time well-grounded solution to one of the most important problems set forth in the Party Program: the formation of a system for planning and assessing the work of enterprises so that they have a vital interest in higher plan assign-

FROM: Ye. G. Liberman, "Improve Economic Management and Planning: The Plan, Profits, and Bonuses," *Pravda*, September 9, 1962 (English translation in *Current Digest of the Soviet Press*, XIV:36, October 3, 1962, pp. 13-15).

ments, in the introduction of new technology and in improving the quality of output – in a word, in achieving the greatest production efficiency.

In our view, it is possible to accomplish this if the enterprises are given plans only for volume of output according to assortment of products and for delivery schedules. These must be drawn up with the maximum consideration for the direct ties between suppliers and consumers.

All other indices should be given only to the economic councils; they should not be apportioned among the enterprises.

On the basis of the volume and assortment assignments they receive, the enterprises themselves should draw up the final plan, covering labor productivity and number of workers, wages, production costs, accumulations, capital investments and new technology.

How is it possible to entrust the enterprises with the drafting of plans if all their calculations are, as a rule, far lower than their true potentials?

It can be done if the enterprises have the greatest possible moral and material interest in making full use of reserves not only in plan fulfillment but also in the very compilation of plans. To this end, planning norms of profitability must be worked out for each branch of industry and must be firmly established for an extended period. It would be most expedient to confirm these norms through a centralized procedure in the form of scales fixing the amounts of incentive payments to collectives of enterprises in accordance with the level of profitability achieved (in the form of profits expressed as percentages of production capital). . . .

One might naturally ask if the centralized basis of our planning would be retained and strengthened under this system.

There is every reason to assert that the proposed system would relieve centralized planning from petty tutelage over enterprises and from costly efforts to influence production through administrative measures rather than economic ones. The enterprise alone knows and can discover its reserves best. But in order to do this, they should not have to fear that through their own good work they will put themselves in a difficult position in the following year. All the basic levers of centralized planning – prices, finances, budget, accounting, large capital investments – and finally all the value, labor and major natural indices of rates and proportions in the sphere of production, distribution and consumption will be determined entirely at the center. . . .

At present, profitability is reduced if the enterprises are mastering many new products and a great deal of new technology. For this reason, we have worked out a scale of supplements to and reductions in incentive payments in accordance with the proportion of new products in the plan. The incentive payments will be somewhat reduced for the output of items long established in production and raised substantially for the introduction of new products.

Besides this, the very process of price formulation must be flexible. Prices for new products that represent more efficiency in production or consumption should be set to begin with so that the manufacturer can cover his additional expenditures. The consumer would not suffer from this at all but, on the contrary, would reap benefits for himself and for the national economy. In this way profitability incentives might become a flexible weapon in the struggle for rapid introduction of new technology and for increased quality (durability, reliability) of products. The present incentive system for inducing enterprises to reduce production costs and to increase output above the plan or above the figure for the previous years is a direct impediment to increasing product quality or mastering new products. . . .

Far be it from us, of course, to think that the proposed method is some sort of panacea, that by itself it will remove the shortcomings. Clearly the organizing, educational and controlling job done by the Party and economic apparatus will remain a decisive force. But this force will grow many times if it is supported from below by a firm stake in the success of the cause, and not for the sake of "indices" but in the name of true production efficiency. Then the apparatus of the administration will decrease sharply.

Let us note that the proposed procedure forces the enterprises to put out only products that are capable of being sold and of paying their way. Further, the enterprises will calculate the efficiency of new technology with some care and will stop thoughtlessly ordering any and all kinds of new equipment at state expense.

It is now common practice to assume that any evaluation of the enterprises' work and any incentive for them must proceed from plan fulfillment as the most trustworthy yardstick. Why is this so? Because the plan creates supposedly equal conditions for enterprises, takes into account different natural conditions, different degrees of mechanization and other "individual" circumstances. In actuality, the plans of enterprises are now set according to the so-called "record basis," i.e., proceeding from the level attained. What this creates is completely unequal conditions, privileged for those who work poorly and strenuous for those enterprises that really uncover and use their reserves. Why strive for good work in these conditions? Is it not simpler to try to obtain a "good" plan? It is time to amend this system!

Is it not clear that truly "equal conditions" can be created if there is the single standard of profitability for enterprises finding themselves in roughly the same natural and technical conditions? It is less dangerous to ignore a few differences in these objective conditions than to level off the quality of economic guidance. By such leveling, we are preserving backward methods of production. Let the enterprises themselves, having the production program from the center and the long-term standard of profitability to go by, show what they are capable of doing in competition for the best results. It is right that we have no rivalry, but this in no way means that we have no competition for the best methods of leadership. On the contrary, such competition must receive full scope here.

b) THE 1965 REFORM

The September (1965) Plenum of the Central Committee of the CPSU made a detailed examination of the state of affairs in USSR industry. It was noted that the organizational structure of management existing at that time and the methods of planning and of economic incentive in industry were not in keeping with present conditions and with the level of development of the productive forces.

Improvements in the system of management were outlined in the following basic directions: (1) raising the scientific level of planning, the optimization of planning, and the intensification of the role of long-term plans and norms; (2) eliminating excessive regulation of the economic activity of enterprises and allocating the necessary means to develop their production; (3) strengthening and developing cost-accounting and intensifying economic production incentives with the aid of prices, profits, bonuses, and credit; (4) converting to the branch principle of industrial management.

As we know, the economic reform was elaborated in a rather extensive, specific form. First, there was a substantial reduction in the range of obligatory plan indices communicated to enterprises on a centralized basis, a number of indices were replaced, and the new profitability index was introduced.

Plan targets for the volume of output to be sold are being established for enterprises instead of the gross output index. This substitution is very substantial: it places production under the economic control of purchasers and creates prerequisites for the establishment of organic unity between planning and cost-accounting. The basic product-mix [*nomenklatura*] is also confirmed from above.

In addition to other indices, profit and profitability calculated as the

FROM: Ye. G. Liberman, *Economic Methods and the Effectiveness of Production* (White Plains, N. Y., International Arts and Sciences Press, 1972), pp. 1 0-12, 14, 17-18. Reprinted by permission of M. E. Sharpe, Inc.

ratio of profit to fixed productive capital and to normed working capital have been established as indices for evaluating the effectiveness of the work of enterprises. Thus, yardsticks of effectiveness which, although they have existed in our country for a long time, have not played a large part in planning, to say nothing of the evaluation of the work of enterprises, have been brought into economic circulation.

In our opinion, the plan should confront production with ultimate goals but should not directly regulate the means of their attainment within the enterprise, which would deprive the enterprise of the necessary maneuverability in finding optimal solutions for the fulfillment of plan targets.

Although they retain their importance as accounting indices within the branch, such indices as the number of personnel, the average wage, labor productivity, and enterprise cost of production are not included in the number of obligatory indices that are confirmed for each enterprise. . . .

Naturally, the restriction of the number of plan indices confirmed by higher-echelon organizations considerably expands the economic autonomy of enterprises. In no small measure, this autonomy is also promoted by the Statute on the Socialist State Production Enterprise, which extends and legislatively confirms many rights to enterprise heads.

The September (1965) Plenum of the Central Committee of the CPSU outlined such a structure of the incentive system in order to arouse the enterprises' interest in elaborating and fulfilling higher plan targets and in making fullest use of internal reserves and resources. This goal is realized through the unity of the system of planning and economic incentives for enterprise collectives, which serves to increase the country's national income. In this instance, the interests of society and of enterprises are combined more harmoniously. . . .

The system of economic incentives makes provision for the formation of a special source of incentive payments above and beyond centrally established wage rates. The profit created at an enterprise is this source. It has been recognized that the amount of deductions paid from profits into the incentive fund depends on the fulfillment of the plan for increased sales or profits and on the profitability level contemplated in the annual plan (provided that the prescribed mix of key products stipulated in the plan is observed). In those instances when an increase in sales volume is not advisable, the size of the material incentive fund is determined as a function of increased profit . . . .

The September (1965) Plenum of the Central Committee of the CPSU emphasized that the price formation system must be improved if the reform is to be successful. Price must more completely reflect socially necessary labor outlays and must assure the compensation of production costs and the accumulation of profit by every normally functioning enterprise. At the same time, prices must also stimulate an improvement in the quality of production and in the expedient service life and reliability of products. Therefore, prices must take into account additional outlays by the producer for the improvement of the quality of goods as well as the effect of such improvement on productive or personal consumption. It has been emphasized that, as a rule, retail prices on consumer goods may be revised only in a downward direction. The reform of wholesale prices was carried out in 1967. The new prices reflect socially necessary outlays much more closely and completely. Nonetheless, in the future as well it will be necessary to conduct work to improve prices.

The reform of the system of planning and economic incentive in industry is inseparable from the simultaneous restructuring of industrial management. The national economic councils did a certain amount of useful work, especially in production cooperation locally, i.e., on a territorial level. But at the same time, administration based on the territorial principle has also carried negative effects: it has hindered the implementation of a single-branch technological policy; it has weakened intrabranch specialization and cooperation, which are no less important than territorial cooperation; it has led to a certain irresponsibility due to the lack of strict distribution of functions among national economic councils and branch committees; etc. After all the advantages and shortcomings of the branch and territorial systems of management were carefully weighed, a branch system of management was adopted and appropriate branch industrial ministries were created.

The September (1965) Plenum of the Central Committee of the CPSU emphasized the great importance of measures proposed to improve the organization of management and to intensify economic methods for industrial management. The importance of these measures is that they combine unified government planning with total cost-accounting operation of enterprises, centralized branch management with broad republic and local economic initiative, and the principle of one-man control with the enlargement of the role of production collectives. Moreover, democratic principles of management are further expanded and economic prerequisites are created for broader mass participation in production management and for mass influence on the results of the economic work of enterprises. As stated in the Decree of the September (1965) Plenum of the Central Committee of the CPSU, such a system of economic management more closely conforms to modern requirements and permits the better use of the advantages of the socialist system.

CURRENTS OF DISSENT

Following the advent of Brezhnev and Kosygin and the Sinyavsky-Daniel trial, the movements of quasi-legal political and cultural ferment that emerged under Khrushchev were forced underground. Numerous different political viewpoints were expressed in the typewritten literature of *samizdat* (literally "self-publishing") that was smuggled to the West for publication. Democratic Marxism was defended by the historian Roy Medvedev; traditionalist conservatism was espoused by the novelist Alexander Solzhenitsyn; and the values of pro-Western liberalism were represented by the physicist Andrei Sakharov. Solzhenitsyn was deported from the Soviet Union in 1974; Sakharov lives in internal exile; and Medvedev still lives and writes in Moscow.

a) LIBERAL DISSENT – SAKHAROV

The division of mankind threatens it with destruction. Civilization is imperiled by: a universal thermonuclear war, catastrophic hunger for most of mankind, stupefaction from the narcotic of "mass culture," and bureaucratized dogmatism, a spreading of mass myths that put entire peoples and continents under the power of cruel and treacherous demagogues, and destruction or degeneration from the unforeseeable consequences of swift changes in the conditions of life on our planet.

In the face of these perils, any action increasing the division of mankind, any preaching of the incompatibility of world ideologies and nations is madness and a crime. Only universal cooperation under conditions of intellectual freedom and the lofty moral ideals of socialism and labor, accompanied by the elimination of dogmatism and pressures of the concealed interests of ruling classes, will preserve civilization.

The reader will understand that ideological collaboration cannot apply to those fanatical, sectarian, and extremist ideologies that reject all possibility of rapprochement, discussion, and compromise, for example, the ideologies of fascist, racist, militaristic, and Maoist demagogy.

Millions of people throughout the world are striving to put an end to poverty. They despise oppression, dogmatism, and demagogy (and their more extreme manifestations – racism, fascism, Stalinism, and Maoism). They believe in progress based on the use, under conditions of social justice

FROM: Andrei Sakharov, "Progress, Coexistence, and Intellectual Freedom," in Harrison E. Salisbury, ed., *Sakharov Speaks* (New York, Knopf, 1974), pp. 58-61, 80-81, 112-13. Copyright ©1974 by Alfred A. Knopf, Inc. Reprinted by permission of the publisher and the editor.

and intellectual freedom, of all the positive experience accumulated by mankind. . . .

Intellectual freedom is essential to human society – freedom to obtain and distribute information, freedom for open-minded and unfearing debate, and freedom from pressure by officialdom and prejudices. Such a trinity of freedom of thought is the only guarantee against an infection of people by mass myths, which, in the hands of treacherous hypocrites and demagogues, can be transformed into bloody dictatorship. Freedom of thought is the only guarantee of the feasibility of a scientific democratic approach to politics, economy, and culture.

But freedom of thought is under a triple threat in modern society – from the deliberate opium of mass culture, from cowardly, egotistic, and philistine ideologies, and from the ossified dogmatism of a bureaucratic oligarchy and its favorite weapon, ideological censorship. Therefore, freedom of thought requires the defense of all thinking and honest people. This is a mission not only for the intelligentsia but for all strata of society, particularly its most active and organized stratum, the working class. The worldwide dangers of war, famine, cults of personality, and bureaucracy – these are perils for all of mankind.

Recognition by the working class and the intelligentsia of their common interests has been a striking phenomenon of the present day. The most progressive, internationalist, and dedicated element of the intelligentsia is, in essence, part of the working class, and the most advanced, educated, internationalist, and broad-minded part of the working class is part of the intelligentsia.

This position of the intelligentsia in society renders senseless any loud demands that the intelligentsia subordinate its strivings to the will and interests of the working class (in the Soviet Union, Poland, and other socialist countries). What these demands really mean is subordination to the will of the Party or, even more specifically, to the Party's central apparatus and its officials. Who will guarantee that these officials always express the genuine interests of the working class as a whole and the genuine interest of progress rather than their own caste interests? . . .

Fascism lasted twelve years in Germany. Stalinism lasted twice as long in the Soviet Union. There are many common features but also certain differences. Stalinism exhibited a much more subtle kind of hypocrisy and demagogy, with reliance not on an openly cannibalistic program like Hitler's but on a progressive, scientific, and popular socialist ideology.

This served as a convenient screen for deceiving the working class, for weakening the vigilance of the intellectuals and other rivals in the struggle for power, with the treacherous and sudden use of the machinery of torture, execution, and informants, intimidating and making fools of millions of people, the majority of whom were neither cowards nor fools. As a consequence of this "specific feature" of Stalinism, it was the Soviet people, its most active, talented, and honest representatives, who suffered the most terrible blow.

At least ten to fifteen million people perished in the torture chambers of the NKVD [secret police] from torture and execution, in camps for exiled kulaks [rich peasants] and so-called semi-kulaks and members of their families and in camps "without the right of correspondence" (which were in fact the prototypes of the fascist death camps, where, for example, thousands of prisoners were machine-gunned because of "overcrowding" or as a result of "special orders").

People perished in the mines of Norilsk and Vorkuta from freezing, starvation, and exhausting labor, at countless construction projects, in timbercutting, building of canals, or simply during transportation in prison trains, in the overcrowded holds of "death ships" in the Sea of Okhotsk, and during the resettlement of entire peoples, the Crimean Tatars, the Volga Germans, the Kalmyks, and other Caucasus peoples. . . .

In conclusion, I will sum up a number of the concrete proposals of varying degrees of importance that have been discussed in the text. These proposals, addressed to the leadership of the country, do not exhaust the content of the article.

The strategy of peaceful coexistence and collaboration must be deepened in every way. Scientific methods and principles of international policy will have to be worked out, based on scientific prediction of the immediate and more distant consequences.

The initiative must be seized in working out a broad program of struggle against hunger.

A law on press and information must be drafted, widely discussed, and adopted, with the aim not only of ending irresponsible and irrational censorship, but also of encouraging self-study in our society, fearless discussion, and the search for truth. The law must provide for the material resources of freedom of thought.

All anti-constitutional laws and decrees violating human rights must be abrogated.

Political prisoners must be amnestied and some of the recent political trials must be reviewed (for example, the Daniel-Sinyavsky and Ginzburg-Galanskov cases). The camp regime of political prisoners must be promptly relaxed.

The exposure of Stalin must be carried through to the end, to the complete truth, and not just to the carefully weighed half truth dictated by caste considerations. The influence of neo-Stalinists in our political life must be restricted in every way (the text mentioned, as an example, the case of S. Trapeznikov,* who enjoys too much influence).

The economic reform must be deepened in every way and the area of experimentation expanded, with conclusions based on the results.

b) CONSERVATIVE DISSENT – SOLZHENITSYN

. . . The murky whirlwind of *Progressive Ideology* swept in on us from the West at the end of the last century, and has tormented and ravaged our soul quite enough. . . .

A second danger is the multiple impasse in which Western civilization (which Russia long ago chose the honor of joining) finds itself, but it is not so imminent; there are still two or three decades in reserve. We share this impasse with all the advanced countries, which are in an even worse and more perilous predicament than we are, although people keep hoping for new scientific loopholes and inventions to stave off the day of retribution. I would not mention this danger in this letter if the solutions to both problems were not identical in many respects, if one and the same turnabout, a *single* decision, would not deliver us from *both* dangers. Such a happy coincidence is rare. Let us value history's gift and not miss these opportunities.

And all this has so "suddenly" come tumbling out at mankind's feet, and at Russia's! How fond our progressive publicists were, both before and after the Revolution, of ridiculing those *retrogrades* (there were always so many of them in Russia): people who called upon us to cherish and have pity on our past, even on the most Godforsaken hamlet with a couple of hovels, even on the paths that run alongside the railway track; who called upon us to keep horses even after the advent of the motorcar, not to abandon small factories for enormous plants and combines, not to discard organic manure in favor of chemical fertilizers, not to mass by the million in cities, not to clamber on top of one another in multistory apartment blocks. How they laughed, how they tormented those reactionary "Slavophiles" † (the jibe became the accepted term, the simpletons never

*S. P. Trapeznikov, head of the Science and Education Department of the Party Secretariat – Ed.

FROM: Aleksandr I. Solzhenitsyn, *Letter to the Soviet Leaders*, New York, 1974, pp. 19-21, 24-26, 41-43, 51-54, 56-57. Copyright 1974 by Aleksandr I. Solzhenitsyn. English translation by Hilary Sternberg. Copyright 1974 by Writers and Scholars International Ltd. Reprinted by permission of Harper & Row, Publishers, Inc.

† Slavophiles: nineteenth-century proponents of old Russian tradition—Ed.

managed to think up another name for themselves). They hounded the men who said that it was perfectly feasible for a colossus like Russia, with all its spiritual peculiarities and folk traditions, to find its own particular path; and that it could not be that the whole of mankind should follow a single, absolutely identical pattern of development.

No, we had to be dragged along the whole of the Western bourgeois-industrial and Marxist path in order to discover, toward the close of the twentieth century, and again from progressive Western scholars, what any village graybeard in the Ukraine or Russia had understood from time immemorial and could have explained to the progressive commentators ages ago, had the commentators ever found the time in that dizzy fever of theirs to consult him: that a dozen worms can't go on and on gnawing the same apple *forever;* that if the earth is a *finite* object, then its expanses and resources are finite also, and the *endless, infinite* progress dinned into our heads by the dreamers of the Enlightenment cannot be accomplished on it. No, we had to shuffle on and on behind other people, without knowing what lay ahead of us, until suddenly we now hear the scouts calling to one another: We've blundered into a blind alley, we'll have to turn back. All that "endless progress" turned out to be an insane, ill-considered, furious dash into a blind alley. A civilization greedy for "perpetual progress" has now choked and is on its last legs . . . .

But what about *us*? Us, with our unwieldiness and our inertia, with our flinching and inability to change even a single letter, a single syllable, of what Marx said in 1848 about industrial development? Economically and physically we are perfectly capable of saving ourselves. But there is a road-block on the path to our salvation – the sole Progressive World View. If we renounce industrial development, what about the working class, socialism, Communism, unlimited increase in productivity and all the rest? Marx is not to be corrected, that's revisionism. . . .

But you are already being called "revisionists" anyway, whatever you may do in the future. So wouldn't it be better to do your duty soberly, responsibly and firmly, and give up the dead letter for the sake of a living people who are utterly dependent on your power and your decisions? And you must do it without delay. Why dawdle if we shall have to snap out of it sometime anyway? Why repeat what others have done and loop the agonizing loop right to the end, when we are not too far into it to turn back? If the man at the head of the column cries, "I have lost my way," do we absolutely have to plow right on to the spot where he realized his mistake and only there turn back? Why not turn and start on the right course from wherever we happen to be?

As it is, we have followed Western technology too long and too faithfully.

We are supposed to be the "first socialist country in the world," one which sets an example to other peoples, in both the East and the West, and we are supposed to have been so "original" in following various monstrous doctrines – on the peasantry, on small tradesmen – so why, then, have we been so dolefully unoriginal in technology, and why have we so unthinkingly, so blindly, copied Western civilization? (Why? From military haste, of course, and the haste stems from our immense "international responsibilities," and all this because of Marxism again.)

One might have thought that, with the central planning of which we are so proud, we of all people had the chance *not* to spoil Russia's natural beauty, *not* to create antihuman, multimillion concentrations of people. But we've done everything the other way round: we have dirtied and defiled the wide Russian spaces and disfigured the heart of Russia, our beloved Moscow. (What crazed, unfilial hand bulldozed the boulevards so that you can't go along them now without diving down into degrading tunnels of stone? What evil, alien ax broke up the tree-lined boulevards of the Sadovoye Koltso and replaced them with a poisoned zone of asphalt and gasoline?) The irreplaceable face of the city and all the ancient city plan have been obliterated, and imitations of the West are being flung up, like the New Arbat; the city has been so squeezed, stretched and pushed upward that life has become intolerable – so what do we do now? Reconstruct the former Moscow in a new place? That is probably impossible. Accept, then, that we have lost it completely?

We have squandered our resources foolishly without so much as a backward glance, sapped our soil, mutilated our vast expanses with idiotic "inland seas" and contaminated belts of wasteland around our industrial centers – but for the moment, at least, far more still remains untainted by us, which we haven't had time to touch. So let us come to our senses in time, let us change our course! . . .

This Ideology that fell to us by inheritance is not only decrepit and hopelessly antiquated now; even during its best decades it was totally mistaken in its predictions and was never a science.

A primitive, superficial economic theory, it declared that only the worker creates value and failed to take into account the contribution of either organizers, engineers, transportation or marketing systems. It was mistaken when it forecast that the proletariat would be endlessly oppressed and would never achieve anything in a bourgeois democracy – if only we could shower people with as much food, clothing and leisure as they have gained under capitalism! It missed the point when it asserted that the prosperity of the European countries depended on their colonies – it was only after they had shaken the colonies off that they began to accomplish their "economic miracles." It was mistaken through and through in its prediction that socialists could never come to power except through an armed uprising. It miscalculated in thinking that the first uprisings would take place in the advanced industrial countries – quite the reverse. And the picture of how the whole world would rapidly be overtaken by revolutions and how states would soon wither away was sheer delusion, sheer ignorance of human nature. And as for wars being characteristic of capitalism alone and coming to an end when capitalism did – we have already witnessed the longest war of the twentieth century so far, and it was not capitalism that rejected negotiations and a truce for fifteen to twenty years; and God forbid that we should witness the bloodiest and most brutal of all mankind's wars – a war between two Communist superpowers. Then there was nationalism, which this theory also buried in 1848 as a "survival" – but find a stronger force in the world today! And it's the same with many other things too boring to list.

Marxism is not only not accurate, is not only not a science, has not only failed to predict a *single event* in terms of figures, quantities, time-scales or locations (something that electronic computers today do with laughable ease in the course of social forecasting, although never with the help of Marxism) – it absolutely astounds one by the economic and mechanistic crudity of its attempts to explain that most subtle of creatures, the human being, and that even more complex synthesis of millions of people, society. Only the cupidity of some, the blindness of others and a craving for *faith* on the part of still others can serve to explain this grim jest of the twentieth century: how can such a discredited and bankrupt doctrine still have so many followers in the West! In *our* country are left the fewest of all! We who have had a taste of it are only pretending willy-nilly. . . .

Here in Russia, for sheer lack of practice, democracy survived for only eight months – from February to October, 1917. The émigré groups of Constitutional Democrats and Social Democrats still pride themselves on it to this very day and say that outside forces brought about its collapse. But in reality that democracy was *their* disgrace; they invoked it and promised it so arrogantly, and then created merely a chaotic caricature of democracy, because first of all they turned out to be ill-prepared for it themselves, and then Russia was worse prepared still. Over the last half-century Russia's preparedness for democracy, for a multiparty parliamentary system, could only have diminished. I am inclined to think that its sudden reintroduction now would merely be a melancholy repetition of 1917.

Should we record as our democratic tradition the Land Assemblies of Muscovite Russia, Novgorod, the early Cossacks, the village commune? Or should we console ourselves with the thought that for a thousand years

Russia lived with an authoritarian order – and at the beginning of the twentieth century both the physical and spiritual health of her people were still intact?

However, in those days an important condition was fulfilled: that authoritarian order possessed a strong moral foundation, embryonic and rudimentary though it was – not the ideology of universal violence, but Christian Orthodoxy, the ancient, seven-centuries-old Orthodoxy of Sergei Radonezhsky and Nil Sorsky, before it was battered by Patriarch Nikon and bureaucratized by Peter the Great.* From the end of the Moscow period and throughout the whole of the Petersburg period, once this moral principle was perverted and weakened, the authoritarian order, despite the apparent external successes of the state, gradually went into a decline and eventually perished.

But even the Russian intelligentsia, which for more than a century has invested all its strength in the struggle with an authoritarian regime – what has it achieved for itself or the common people by its enormous losses? The opposite of what it intended, of course. So should we not perhaps acknowledge that for Russia this path was either false or premature? That for the foreseeable future, perhaps, whether we like it or not, whether we intend it or not, Russia is nevertheless destined to have an authoritarian order? Perhaps this is all that she is ripe for today? . . . Everything depends upon *what sort* of authoritarian order lies in store for us in the future.

It is not authoritarianism itself that is intolerable, but the ideological lies that are daily foisted upon us. Not so much authoritarianism as arbitrariness and illegality, the sheer illegality of having a single overlord in each district, each province and each sphere, often ignorant and brutal, whose will alone decides all things. An authoritarian order does not necessarily mean that laws are unnecessary or that they exist only on paper, or that they should not reflect the notions and will of the population. Nor does it mean that the legislative, executive and judicial authorities are not independent, any of them, that they are in fact not authorities at all but utterly at the mercy of a telephone call from the only true, self-appointed authority. May I remind you that the *soviets*, which gave their name to our system and existed until July 6, 1918, were in no way dependent upon Ideology: Ideology or no Ideology, they always envisaged the widest possible *consultation* with all working people.

Would it be still within the bounds of realism or a lapse into daydreams if we were to propose that at least some of the real power of the *soviets* be

---

*Sergei Radonezhsky: fourteenth-century Russian monastic leader and saint; Nil Sorsky: fifteenth-century Russian mystic and saint; Patriarch Nikon: seventeenth-century church reformer, opposed by traditionalist Old Believers – Ed.

restored? I do not know what can be said on the subject of our Constitution: from 1936 it has not been observed for a single day, and for that reason does not appear to be viable. But perhaps even the Constitution is not beyond all hope? . . .

So that the country and people do not suffocate, and so that they all have the chance to develop and enrich us with ideas, allow competition on an equal and honorable basis – not for power, but for truth – between all ideological and moral currents, in particular between *all religions:* there will be nobody to persecute them if their tormentor, Marxism, is deprived of its state privileges. But allow competition honestly, not the way you do now, not by gagging people; allow it to religious youth organizations (which are totally nonpolitical; let the Komsomol be the only political one), grant them the right to instruct and educate children, and the right to free parish activity. (I myself see Christianity today as the only living spiritual force capable of undertaking the spiritual healing of Russia. But I request and propose no special privileges for it, simply that it should be treated fairly and not suppressed.) Allow us a free art and literature, the free publication not just of political books – God preserve us! – and exhortations and election leaflets; allow us philosophical, ethical, economic and social studies, and you will see what a rich harvest it brings and how it bears fruit – for the good of Russia. Such an abundant and free flowering of inspiration will rapidly absolve us of the need to keep on belatedly translating new ideas from Western languages, as has been the case for the whole of the last fifty years – as you know.

What have you to fear? Is the idea really so terrible? Are you really so unsure of yourselves? You will still have absolute and impregnable power, a separate, strong and exclusive Party, the army, the police force, industry, transportation, communications, mineral wealth, a monopoly of foreign trade, an artificial rate of exchange for the ruble – but let the people breathe, let them think and develop! If you belong to the people heart and soul, there can be nothing to hold you back!

After all, does the human heart not still feel the need to atone for the past? . . .

c) MARXIST DISSENT – MEDVEDEV

How can we act to bring about democratization in the USSR?

The following observations can only be very general because the situation is constantly changing, which means that certain tactics used by the

FROM: Roy A. Medvedev, *On Socialist Democracy* (New York, Knopf, 1975; Nottingham, Spokesman, 1977, pp. 310-15, 331-32). Reprinted by permission of the publishers. Copyright 1975 by Alfred A. Knopf, Inc. and Macmillan London Ltd.

democratic movement at the beginning of its activity are no longer appropriate; on the other hand, new possibilities are constantly suggesting themselves.

At the outset it must be stressed that, in our conditions, the struggle for democratization must be a political one. It is unrealistic to suppose that neo-Stalinism, bureaucracy, and dogmatism can be overcome without a political fight. This is the only way that democracy can be achieved. However, we must make sure all our activities are strictly within the framework of the Constitution. In fact, the struggle has already begun at every level of society, taking different forms according to circumstances. And what is more, one can predict that with each extension of democratic rights, the political struggle will gain momentum, often reaching acute proportions. The transition from any authoritarian regime to a democratic one is always accompanied by an intensification of political passions and pressures.

There is no doubt about the fact that democratization is an objective necessity for our society. Its inevitability is related to economic and technical progress, the scientific and technological revolution and changes that have taken place in the social structure. The country cannot be governed in the old way, and this is beginning to be felt not only by many young government officials but also by certain seemingly dyed-in-the-wool bureaucrats. Yet the fact remains that democratization will not come about automatically nor will it be handed down "from above." It will occur only as a response to objective demands and determined efforts.

It is also unrealistic to suppose that a limited amount of democracy can be introduced which would apply to only one or two "approved" political trends or movements. Certainly all political groups, including all the conservative and reactionary ones, will try to use democratic freedoms to increase their own influence. The more circumstances seem to be turning against them, the harder they will struggle to maintain their political position. Therefore the presence of political conflict contains an element of risk, but risk is inevitable if there is to be a transition to a new and higher stage. Only the experience of struggle can foster the political activism and initiative of the masses and encourage democratic habits throughout the social fabric.

In democratic conditions, political struggle presupposes a comparatively free confrontation between different points of view, which obviously would provide a much better education in civic responsibility than does the present show of ostensible unity. We must only see to it that the political struggle is waged responsibly in forms that reasonable people can accept. Mutual destructiveness should be avoided; there must be a basic tolerance for those with whom one disagrees. Only this kind of open political contest can offer our people a proper political education, teaching them not only to express their own opinions but also to heed the views of others. This is the only way to establish a convention of ethical behavior in politics, to eliminate uncompromising sectarianism, intolerance, and elitist complacency. Only in conditions of overt political struggle will it be possible for genuine political figures to emerge, men who are capable of guiding the construction of a developed socialist and communist society in an efficient way. Thoughtful foreign observers who are sympathetic toward our country understand this very well. "Soviet society," wrote G. Boffa, the Italian communist, "stands in need of the establishment of democratic methods. The experience of the post-Stalin decades has shown that this cannot come about without political struggle, a struggle against those individuals and groups who openly or in secret have resisted and obstructed the policies initiated at the Twentieth Congress, a struggle against their theories and attitudes. But at all times there must be scrupulous regard for democratic principles. The words 'political struggle' evoke uneasiness in the Soviet Union, an out-of-date reaction, as if there were some real threat to the unity of society. But surely periods of political struggle are the greatest source of progress in both thought and action." This is an entirely reasonable view. If socialist democracy is to be firmly established, it must be defended by the whole people, possibly only after all have passed through the school of political struggle by actually participating in the fight to extend and strengthen socialist democracy.

I speak of struggle and pressure coming from the people and particularly from the intelligentsia; however, this does not exclude the possibility of initiative appearing at the top. If moves toward democratization were taken at the higher levels of party and state it would be an important guarantee that subsequent controversy involving so many difficult political problems would take place in the least painful manner and would be kept within bounds. But for the time being we do not have such a leadership; fine words about socialist democracy are not supported by actions. Yet the experience of Hungary, where over a period of years there has been a process of real democratization directed from "above," does show that cooperation between those "abvove" and those "below" is a perfectly viable possibility. Something similar happened in Poland in 1971-72 but only after a very bitter and dangerous political crisis, which could have been avoided by a more rational leadership. The Czechoslovak experience of 1968-69, its achievements and failures, must also be carefully studied.

It is by no means impossible that pressure from below could lead to various changes in the apparatus of power, to the appearance of influential groups that would support democratization. I have been criticized for expressing this view. One response to a preliminary version of this book was an accusation of utopianism: "You believe that the leadership would support a certain degree of democratization. But this would amount to the leadership liquidating itself, and the whole of political history confirms the unreality of such an expectation. No government withdraws of its own free will. . . . Your ideas are harmful, because they create illusions about the ease with which your proposed programme of reform might be realized. You suggest that because of changing social and political conditions, fresh forces will become part of the *apparat* and transform its bureaucratic style. But this only encourages the false idea of an automatic and spontaneous process – in reality these fresh forces will inevitably encounter fierce resistance."

Of course I know that democratization cannot come about automatically and have no illusions about the difficulty of the struggle. But all the same, it is wrong to exclude the possibility of an alliance between the best of the intelligentsia supported by the people and the most forward-looking individuals in the governing *apparat*. The author of "Words Are Also Deeds" writes:

> Because the language of the party-democrats' programme is loyal and will not shock, it can and should appeal to "consumers" within the party and state *apparat*. Our words can become their deeds, particularly in view of the growing emphasis on science and technology in the higher reaches of government. . . . Those endowed with expert qualifications, energy, and practical sense must be encouraged to revolt against the ignoramuses, scoundrels, and idlers who have no business being where they are.

But he also suggests that "we must promise a special approach to the problem of expropriating the exploiters within the bureaucracy, an approach that would on the whole avoid abrupt dismissals, let alone reprisals, but would rely instead on the mobility brought about by democratic reform."

The realization of a serious programme of democratic change must be a comparatively slow and gradual process. The actual time period will be determined by many factors, but it should take not less than ten or fifteen years. First of all, the democratic movement in our country is still too weak and would be unable to achieve rapid political changes. Secondly, we are still very much in the process of formulating political programmes. Therefore as the democratic movement evolves, there must also be a development of socialist political thought, the creation of new political doctrines on the basis of Marxism-Leninism which will analyze our changed political and economic circumstances. Without this kind of theoretical preparation, without a serious programme – even if it is discussed only in a relatively narrow circle – any kind of rapid political change would inevitably create overwhelming contradictions and disarray. Overhasty reform can also cause problems within the socialist bloc (as the experience of Czechoslovakia has shown). Improvisation in politics can easily result in anarchy. But although diametrically opposed to authoritarian abuse of power, anarchy offers little prospect for elementary human rights and freedoms.

Reform must also be gradual because of the peculiar nature of bureaucracy. As Lenin often pointed out, there is no way to "lance the bureaucratic boil, to wipe bureaucracy from the face of the earth" – the only possibility is cure. "Surgery in this case," wrote Lenin, "is absurd, it cannot work. There can only be a slow healing process – other alternatives are fraudulent or naïve." This advice should not be forgotten. It is essential for us to work out a democratic platform. But at the same time we must make an effort to accumulate information, educate people and win them over, step by step. And it all will take time.

There is now a very widespread feeling that the way we live and work has become untenable, and this applies not just to the intelligentsia but also to much of the working class, white collar workers, and perhaps some of the peasantry. But there is still no mass movement demanding change or democratic reform, and without this it is difficult to count on any rapid transformation of our political system or on a change of attitude at the top.

As for the ways and means of political struggle, they must be absolutely legal and constitutional. There are certain extreme groups that believe in the use of illegal methods including, for example, the organization of underground printing presses. Several years ago one group did manage this, not far from Moscow, and they succeeded in printing one or two leaflets. But very soon the press was discovered and its organizers arrested. Some dissident circles become involved with very dubious foreign groups and even tolerate indirect links with an émigré anti-Soviet organization like the NTS,* distributing journals and books published by them. In certain provincial cities popular discontent led to isolated acts of violence which can only be condemned. The use of unscrupulous means must be avoided at all cost, as a matter of principle and also because in practical terms it plays into the hands of the neo-Stalinists and reactionaries, making it easier for them to discredit absolutely valid demands in the eyes of public opinion. Of course we do not yet possess many of the most important rights and freedoms obligatory in a genuine socialist state which would make it easier

---

*Popular Labor Alliance, émigré organization based in West Germany. – Trans.

to struggle for democracy. However, it is to some extent the case that we still have not learned to make the most of those rights and freedoms that really do exist already. . . .

Coming to the end of this book on socialist democracy, I would like to compare our society and ideology with a building that continues to grow taller despite its antiquated, decayed, even rotten foundation. There are still firm supports, but they are becoming less reliable. One hardly needs to stress the dangers of such basic social and ideological weakness. There are, however, a number of people in the leadership who prefer to ignore all the cracks in the foundation of our social structure and all the flaws in our ideology. They tend simply to evade all difficult problems, dreading change and refusing to countenance repairs to the foundation of the house in which we live. Others in the leadership try to salvage and restore to their previous position in the structure totally rotted supports in the shape of dogmas long since discredited. And there are some who see only minor defects in our social fabric and attempt to put them right, but far too late and far too slowly. This means that new cracks constantly appear in the edifice even faster than existing ones can be eliminated.

There are, however, some bold spirits, well aware of all the faults of our society and ideology, who demand the *immediate* removal of all the flawed or weakened props that shore up our social system, even though they still have nothing with which to replace those dilapidated parts of the foundation that continue after a fashion, however badly, to support the enormous and still growing structure above. They can propose nothing better than to prop it up by makeshift, untried means, apparently untroubled by the possibility that the whole building might come tumbling down.

Finally, there are people who have no desire whatsoever to live in this particular building and would prefer to move to another one. They are therefore not interested in strengthening the foundation of our society or reconstructing it at any level. Such people should be allowed to change their place of residence.

But I cannot myself share any of these attitudes. Without being blind to the shortcomings and flaws in the very foundations of our social structure and ideology, we should fairly quickly, but also with the utmost caution, remove all the decayed elements at the base of the structure, replacing them with something much more durable. At the same time attempts must be made to improve conditions on all levels higher up. The whole process must take place gradually, step by step. Something new can only be fashioned out of what has come before in previous stages of social development. This painstaking and difficult task must, in my opinion, be the main objective of the democratic movement, which has arisen in the healthiest section of the party and includes a constantly growing number of honest individuals.

It is in no way a question of destroying the values of the October Revolution. Rather we must restore and purify them; they must be reinforced and built upon. Only if there is a systematic and consistent democratization of the whole of our political and social life on a socialist basis will our country be able to retain its role and influence among the progressive forces of the world.

SOVIET CONSUMERISM

While living standards for the Soviet population had been improving gradually since the privations of the 1930's and the Second World War, a major advance was promised with the adoption of the Ninth Five Year Plan in 1971. In part this was a response to sporadic protests among Soviet workers.

In the C.P.S.U. Central Committee's Report, Comrade Brezhnev set forth the Party's policy for raising the people's material well-being.

The draft Directives outline a broad program for raising the living standard of Soviet people and improving their working conditions and everyday life.

In the new five-year period, our people's material well-being will increase first of all as a result of increases in the wages and salaries of workers and office employees and in the incomes of collective farmers in step with growing labor productivity and the improved skills of personnel. This will provide the bulk of the increment in the population's incomes.

The program for raising the people's living standard envisages the implementation of a number of large-scale measures.

The C.P.S.U. Central Committee and the USSR Council of Ministers, with the participation of the Central Council of Trade Unions, after weighing our possibilities, have determined the sequence and schedule for implementing the planned program.

In accordance with this program, the minimum wage will be raised to 70 rubles a month in 1971, and at the same time the basic wage and salary rates of workers and office employees in the middle pay categories of railroad transport will be increased. The basic rates for machine operators in agriculture will be increased during the same year.

As of July 1, 1971, it is planned to raise the minimum size of the pension

FROM: Alexei N. Kosygin, "Report on the Directives of the 24th CPSU Congress for the Five-Year Plan for the Development of the USSR National Economy in 1971-1975," April 6, 1971 (English translation in *Current Soviet Policies*, VI, 1973, pp. 131-33).

for collective farmers and to extend to them the procedure for fixing pensions that has been established for workers and office employees.

At the same time, i.e., as of July 1, 1971, the minimum size of the old-age pension for workers and office employees will be increased. . . .

A high growth rate in the population's cash incomes is to be ensured by an increase in the production of consumer goods and by the growth of trade turnover. The draft Directives envisage that with a growth of 40% in the population's cash incomes, sales of goods to the population will increase by 42% and the volume of paid services will increase by 47%.

In the new five-year plan, market supplies of such products as meat, fish, vegetable oil, eggs and vegetables will increase by 40% to 60%. The sale of clothing will increase by 35%, that of knitwear by 56% and that of cultural and everyday goods by 80%. The rate at which the population is supplied with refrigerators will increase from 32 per 100 families in 1970 to 64 in 1975; for television sets, the corresponding figures will be 51 and 72, and for washing machines they will be 52 and 72. By the end of the five-year plan, the sale of automobiles to the population will have increased more than sixfold in comparison to 1970.

Given the volume of the increased production and sale to the population of consumer goods, it is necessary constantly to expand and improve their assortment. The task is not only to cover customer demand in terms of quantity; the most important thing is the kind of goods the customer finds in the stores and how well they satisfy him in terms of their diversity and quality. This increases the demands on industry and trade, which must respond efficiently to all changes in demand.

It is time to intensify the responsibility of trade organizations for the correct determination of the orders they file with industry and for making goods available to the consumer in good time. For its part, industry must influence the population's demand by producing new and improved goods.

The turnover of public catering will increase by 50% during the five-year period. We must continue expanding the network of dining rooms, restaurants and cafes, especially on construction sites, at enterprises and in educational institutions. The most important thing in the development of public catering is improving its quality and service standards.

As the draft Directives state, the stability of state retail prices will be ensured in the new five-year plan. As commodity resources accumulate, prices will be lowered on certain types of goods.

In the next few years, the production and sale of ready-to-cook products, precooked items, concentrates and other items that make the home preparation of food easier should be developed on a broad scale. We must substantially increase the production of packaged goods and develop the practice of advance orders, mail trade and other progressive trade forms.

Provision has been made for at least doubling the volume of *everyday services* to the population. To this end, we shall have to expand the network of workshops, tailoring shops, dry-cleaning plants, laundries and other everyday-service enterprises. In today's conditions, everyday services should be developed as a large-scale mechanized branch.

In connection with the growth in incomes, the cultural needs of broad strata of the population are rising and new requirements are appearing. For example, tourism is becoming more and more important. We must expand and strengthen its material base and build more hotels, campsites and other service facilities for tourists.

The draft Directives stipulate that housing with a total space of 565,000,000 to 575,000,000 square meters will be built in 1971-1975. *Housing construction* will to an increasing extent be carried out according to new designs that provide for more convenient layouts and better equipment and finishing in apartments.

We should develop housing-construction cooperatives and assist individual housing construction in cities and in rural areas.

It is necessary to devote great attention to improving communal services and the provision of communities with public services and amenities. The overwhelming majority of cities and large urban-type settlements will be provided with centralized water supply. The consumption of electric power for the population's everyday needs will increase. During the next five years, it is planned to provide 17,000,000 to 18,000,000 apartments with gas service. The level to which housing in cities is supplied with gas service will come to 65% to 75%, and in rural areas it will be 40% to 50%.

In the years of the first five-year plans, we put universal primary education into effect. In the new five-year plan, we shall *complete the introduction of universal secondary education*. The accomplishment of this task is of enormous political and social importance. The implementation of universal secondary education will give everyone broad possibilities for choosing an occupation that suits him, to employ his capabilities to the best advantage for the welfare of all society.

THE SCIENTIFIC-TECHNICAL REVOLUTION

With much fanfare the Brezhnev-Kosygin leadership endorsed a "scientific-technical revolution" to improve the education of the populace and the performance of the economy as well as the readiness of the armed forces.

The Ninth Five-Year Plan will be an important stage in the further advance of Soviet society along the path to communism, the construction of its material and technical base and the strengthening of the country's economic and defense might. The chief task of the five-year plan is to ensure a significant upswing in the material and cultural level of the people's life on the basis of high development rates in socialist production, its increased efficiency, scientific and technical progress and the accelerated growth of labor productivity.

In implementing the chief tasks of the five-year plan, it is necessary:

to ensure an improvement in the proportions of social production and high growth rates in agriculture and in the branches producing consumer goods; and significantly to increase the efficiency of all branches of the national economy. During the five-year period, to increase the country's national income by 34% to 40%, with 80% to 85% of the increment coming from increased labor productivity;

to accelerate the rates of scientific and technical progress through the all-round development of research in the most promising fields of science and the shortening of time periods for the introduction of the results of scientific research in production, to carry out the replacement of manual labor by machines on a broad scale, and to ensure the improvement of the branch and intrabranch structure of the national economy;

consistently to raise the level of the education and skills of the working people, to complete the changeover to the universal secondary education of young people, to carry out the necessary measures for the training of highly skilled specialists and workers and the retraining of cadres in connection with the introduction of new machinery and improvements in the organization of production;

to continue work on the improvement of management, planning and economic incentives to production in accordance with the requirements of the present stage of communist construction; to apply the latest techniques in management. To enlist the working people in the management of the economy on a broader scale;

to introduce the scientific organization of labor in every way, and to improve the forms and systems of pay and material and moral incentives to workers.

Proceeding from the basic tasks of the new five-year plan:

1. To carry out a broad program of social measures in the field of

FROM: "Directives of the 24th Congress of the CPSU on the Five-Year Plan of Development of the National Economy of the USSR for the Years 1971-1975," April 9, 1971 (English translation in *Current Soviet Policies*, VI, 1973, pp. 151-53).

increasing the population's income. To increase real income per capita by approximately 30%, bearing in mind that pay must continue to be the main source for an increase in the population's income. To provide for a further increase in minimum earnings. . . .

2. To accelerate the rates of scientific and technical progress and to ensure the implementation of a unified technical policy:

to make broader use of the possibilities created by the scientific and technological revolution for accelerating the development of productive forces;

to create and introduce fundamentally new implements of labor and material and technological processes that are superior in their technical and economic indices to the best domestic and world achievements;

to improve in every way the quality of output in all branches of the national economy;

more rapidly to raise the technical level of the inventory of technological equipment, and also to accelerate the replacement and modernization of obsolescent machinery and aggregates, providing for the necessary development of the requisite branches of machine building. To work out and gradually to introduce new and shorter time periods for the depreciation of production equipment, limiting the volume of ineffective capital repairs and increasing the share of depreciation allowances allocated for the replacement of worn-out obsolescent equipment;

to ensure a reduction in the materials-intensiveness of production through *the perfection of the branch structure of industry, improvements in the design of machinery, apparatus, instruments and other items, the application of progressive technology, a rise* in the qualitative characteristics of the intitial raw materials and other materials and their fuller and more integrated utilization, and also the development of finishing production lines in the branches of the processing industry. . . .

To provide for . . . the broad introduction of the scientific organization of labor, production and management, using up-to-date means of organizational and computer technology. To master the series production of highly productive means of computer technology, small computers and information-transmitting devices. To carry out the series production of electronic computers in complete sets with all the necessary devices for information input and output and sets of standard programs.

To raise the scientific and technical level of standards and their role in improving output quality. To carry out the updating of existing standards and technical specifications, ensuring the replacement of obsolete indices and the timely reflection of the requirements of the national economy that guarantee the high technical level and quality of output. . . .

To improve scientific and technical information and to ensure the systematic transmittal to the interested branches and enterprises of data on scientific and technical achievements and advanced experience in the fields of machinery, technology and the organization of production and management.

Broadly to develop the creative initiative of the working people in the technical improvement of production and to facilitate in every way the improvement of rationalization and invention work. To enhance the role of engineers and technicians as organizers and champions of scientific and technical progress in production.

3. To develop in every way basic and applied research and more rapidly to introduce the results of research in the national economy.

To ensure in the new five-year period:

the further elaboration of problems of theoretical and applied mathematics and cybernetics for the broader application in the national economy of mathematical methods and electronic-computer technology, the automation of production processes and the improvement of management;

the development of research in nuclear physics, solid-state physics and the physics of semiconductors, quantum electronics, plasma physics and low-temperature physics for the purpose of creating new materials and efficient methods of processing them; the further improvement of energy-transformation methods, the industrial assimilation of fast-neutron reactors, the broader utilization of nuclear and radiation processes in science and practice, further progress in electronics, radio engineering and computer technology, and the development of theoretical and applied mechanics;

the conduct of scientific work in outer space for the purpose of the development of *long-range* telephone and telegraph communications, television, meteorological forecasting and the study of natural resources, geographical research and the accomplishment of other national-economic tasks with the aid of satellites and automatic and piloted apparatus, and also the continuation of basic research on the moon and the planets of the solar system;

the conduct of research in the fields of geology, geophysics and geochemistry in order to ascertain the laws governing the geographical location of useful minerals, and an increase in the effectiveness of methods for finding, extracting and concentrating minerals;

the development of scientific work in oceanography, atmospheric physics and geography for the elaboration of problems of the broader and more rational utilization of natural resources, including the resources of the seas and oceans; the elaboration of scientific principles of the protection and transformation of nature for the purpose of improving the natural environment surrounding man and the better utilization of natural resources;

the further development of chemistry, especially in the field of improving the scientific principles of the creation of new polymer and inorganic materials and of highly effective chemical-engineering and electrochemical processes and economical methods for obtaining especially pure substances;

the development of scientific research in the fields of biology and medicine, aimed primarily at the prevention and treatment of cardiovascular, oncological and viral diseases and the creation of new physiologically active preparations for medicine, agriculture, light industry and the food industry; the elaboration of genetic methods of selection for the development of high-yield strains of plants and more productive breeds of animals; and the elaboration of the problems of the genetics of hereditary diseases;

the further development of the social sciences and the conduct of integrated research on the present-day processes of the development of society for the scientific guidance of the socialist economy and the accomplishment of the tasks of communist construction. In the field of economics, to concentrate attention on the elaboration of the most effective forms and methods for the utilization of objective laws in the practice of the planned management of the national economy, on the improvement of long-range planning, on the problems of the acceleration and technical progress and the intensification of and an all-round increase in the economic efficiency of social production, and also on the most important questions in the development of the socialist economic integration of the USSR with the other C.M.E.A. member-countries.*

Resolutely to enhance the effectiveness of the work of scientific institutions, to ensure the concentration of scientific forces and material and financial resources primarily on the leading areas of science and the solution of the most important scientific and technical problems, the further strengthening of the experimental and experimental-production base of research, and the application of economic-accountability methods in the organization of scientific research. To improve the planning of research and experimental-design work, providing in the plans for all stages of this work, up to and including the introduction of its results in production, and to intensify control over the fulfillment of plans. To strengthen the ties of science with production. To implement a system of organizational and eco-

* I.e., the East European Satellites plus Mongolia and Cuba—Ed.

nomic measures for the assimilation and introduction of new machinery and the realization of inventions and discoveries in the shortest possible periods. To enhance the stimulative role of patent work and patent information.

SOVIET JEWS AND THE EMIGRATION ISSUE

Labelled as a separate nationality but harassed in the exercise of their religion, Soviet Jews since Stalin's time were pressured to assimilate while at the same time subjected to discrimination in education and employment. In the 1970's many sought to emigrate to Israel or the West, prompting government measures to curb the outflow including a tax to collect from would-be émigrés the cost of their higher education.

a) SAMIZDAT ON DISCRIMINATION AND ASSIMILATION

1) Jews living in the USSR are a part of the Jewish people, who, as a whole are divided into those living in their state in Israel and those living in other countries – in the diaspora. To the extent that Jews living in the Soviet Union belong to that part of the Jewish people living in the diaspora, the Jewish question in the USSR can be viewed as part of the question of the Jewish diaspora. At the same time, the Soviet Jewish question is part of the problem of nationalities within the USSR.

2) The basic features of the Jewish question in the diaspora are:

a) Discrimination.

b) Assimilation.

3) The discrimination against Jews in the Soviet Union is a combination of all the basic forms of discrimination existing in the other countries of the diaspora, and includes official discrimination:

a) There are percentage norms limiting acceptance to higher educational institutions and limiting employment opportunities.

b) A circular has become known that declares those people not politically friendly to the USSR as undesirable for positions in the defense establishment, rocketry, nuclear work, and other secret undertakings. It is understood that this circular refers to Jews.

c) There is definite knowledge of discrimination against Jews in advancement in civilian work as well as in the military.

FROM: Mikhail Zand, "The Jewish Question in the USSR: Theses," *Politicheskii Dnevnik*, no. 67, April, 1970 (English translation in Stephen F. Cohen, ed., *An End to Silence: Uncensored Opinion in the Soviet Union*, New York, Norton, 1982, pp. 245-49; reprinted by permission).

d) The road to diplomatic service, foreign trade, and the central party apparatus is practically closed to Jews.

e) Exit, whether for a work assignment or for tourism, is extremely difficult for Jews.

f) Wide international publicity has been given to the many cases in which Jews who have received invitations from relatives in Israel to come there and live have been denied the right to leave. By doing this, Soviet agencies violate Point 5 of "The Declaration of Human Rights" (the right of each person to live where he wishes), which was signed by the Soviet Union. They likewise violate the public promise of the chairman of the Council of Ministers of the USSR that those so desiring could join their relatives in Israel.

4)   There are examples of unofficial discrimination in the USSR – ethnic, religious-confessional, ideological, and social.

For example, anti-Semitism in the Ukraine is much sharper and has more of a mass-movement character than in other republics of the Soviet Union (despite the decisive dissociation from it and struggle against it on the part of the nationalistically minded Ukrainian intelligentsia). This is obviously explained by the combination of an anti-Semitic tradition predating the USSR and administrative exploitation of this tradition.

Among these cases of intolerance, confessional in origin, we can also classify the swift growth of Judeophobic feelings among some of the youth of the USSR who come from Moslem backgrounds. Although most of these young people are not religious, Judeophobia in them stems from a feeling of Moslem solidarity. This is fanned by pan-Islamic propaganda, which closes ranks here with official pro-Arabic propaganda.

Judeophobia is part of the ideology of certain Nazi-type underground groups existing in the Soviet Union (whose existence is seen in the dissemination of anti-Semitic leaflets) and also of the almost legalized activities of the Great Russian chauvinists, the "men of the soil."

In regard to common, everyday anti-Semitism, every layer of Soviet society is diseased. Any Jew living in the USSR could tell of humiliations suffered in the most varied of situations – in the communal apartments, on the streets, in traveling, on store lines, in military barracks, or in city hospitals. Soviet laws calling for criminal punishment for such abuses are not applied. And the revitalization of anti-Semitic feelings is spurred in a large measure by the constant publication in the Soviet press of materials from Arabic sources concerning the "brutalities of the Israeli occupiers."

The national dignity of the Jew, a resident of the USSR, is no less mocked by an anti-Jew campaign that employs all the resources of mass propaganda. Like the one in Stalin's last years, this campaign is set up as a struggle against Zionism and not Judaism, and it even has the participation of some Jews. But this fact does not change the essence of the campaign. In all ages, Jewish apostates have participated in the persecution of Jews, using the weapons and the means of Judeophobia. The basic motivation for this campaign at the present is the sympathy of a significant portion of the Jews in the USSR for Israel, which is an uncompromising contradiction to the unconditionally anti-Israel foreign policy of the Soviet government. That this campaign is organized and directed from the top is indisputable, if only for the simple reason that nothing happens in the Soviet Union without the sanction of government and Party organs. Top-level direction is also apparent from the participation of highly placed government personnel. It is enough to recall the "witticism," expressed in the best tradition of Russian anti-Semitism, delivered by Foreign Minister Andrei Gromyko in a speech to the United Nations in 1967, about "the local bazaar." His deputy, V. Semenov, has written a book (under the pseudonym K. Ivanov and along with Z. Sheinis) entitled *The Government of Israel*. Yuri Ivanov, the leading specialist on Jewish affairs in the Central Committee apparatus of the CPSU, has also appeared as an author with *Beware of Zionism* and the contemporary *Protocols of the Elders of Zion*.

Discriminatory measures against the Jewish religion are well known: the closing of synagogues, the practical nonexistence of religious education, the ban on bringing in or producing objects for the cult. Under these conditions, the Jewish people as a community exist only as an object of discrimination, as all their rights and needs as a national community are rejected.

5) Discrimination is not a goal in itself. It is only the instrument of the rulers in their policy of assimilation.

6) Assimilation as a general feature of the life of Jews in the diaspora has a number of forms. Physical assimilation is expressed in the descendants of mixed marriages, the majority of whom include themselves in the basic population. In this case, the physical assimilation of Jews in the Soviet Union is wholly comparable to the physical assimilation of Jews in other countries of the diaspora. There are only three items that might be mentioned wherein this aspect of assimilation differs in the USSR from other countries of the diaspora:

a) According to Soviet law, at the age of sixteen, upon receiving their passports, children of mixed marriages must state their national affiliation. A growing, though still small, percentage of such children of Jewish descent are declaring themselves Jews as a gesture of protest against discrimination.

b) Administrative organs clearly do not wish to register such persons as

Jewish. They categorically refuse to register as Jews those descendants of mixed marriages who acknowledge themselves to be Jewish after receiving their initial passports. Such behavior by the administrative organs undoubtedly exposes their interests in bringing the descendants of mixed marriages into the national fold, i.e., in hastening the tempo of physical assimilation.

c) Descendants of mixed marriages who do list themselves in one of the basic national groupings serve the interests of the administration, yet such people find acceptance into agencies and establishments, where the cadres are recruited according to special social and national "purity" and where the application has questions about the nationality of each parent, very difficult or even closed.

7) Linguistic assimilation is a general phenomenon in the countries of the diaspora. But an essential difference between the linguistic assimilation of Jews in the USSR and that of Jews in other countries has been its speed and the force used to accomplish it. The closing of Jewish educational institutions in the late 1930s, the reduction in the number of Jewish journals, newspapers, and theaters in those same years, the later liquidation of the remnants of Jewish cultural institutions, and the physical destruction of the most famous cultural activities of the Jewish people at the end of the 1940s and the beginning of the 1950s – these are the phases of a forcible linguistic assimilation of the Jewish population in the USSR whose native language was Yiddish. This has led to a situation in which the overwhelming majority of Jews in the Soviet Union has ceased speaking in its native tongue.

8) Cultural assimilation has gone through the same stages as linguistic assimilation. An essential factor in the artificial acceleration of this assimilation was the deliberate identification of Jewish culture with the Yiddish language. As a result, culture in Hebrew was destroyed in the Soviet Union already in the 1920s. In the 1930s, the embryonic Jewish culture in the Georgian language was liquidated. At the end of the thirties, the literature of the Bukhara Jews was suppressed.

At a time when Jews in most of the other countries of the diaspora have had the opportunity of developing their culture in the language of the country in which they live, Jews in the USSR since the 1920s have been deprived of the opportunity of continuing their culture in the Russian language, which has become their sole means of communication. Practically speaking, at the present time in the Soviet Union there is only one Jewish culture – the culture of mountain Jews in the Tatsky language, and it continues to exist only because the bearers of this culture are forbidden to consider themselves Jews.

9) The remnants of Jewish culture in Yiddish in the USSR have no

chance for future survival, inasmuch as the sources nourishing this culture are drying up. The existence of one literary journal, the publication of a few books, and the work of a few traveling ensembles serve as a screen covering the real absence of Jewish culture in the USSR.

10) The religious community has always been a factor in determining who was a Jew. The idea of "Jewishness" coincided with the idea of "Judaism." But the situation changed after the Russian revolution. The general decline in religious life in the Soviet Union was expressed for the majority of the Jews either in a direct break with the synagogue or in indifference to it. In the postwar years, however, the situation changed again. Discrimination, together with the liquidation of all forms of national existence for Soviet Jews, led to a state in which national feelings turned to the sole legally preserved institution – the synagogue. Against its wishes, and even with open fear, the synagogue became the center of Jewish spiritual life. But it could not answer the people's questions or satisfy their needs, for the following basic reasons:

a) The active enmity of the government to all religions (and perhaps particularly to Judaism as the religion of the "internal enemy") led the synagogue into a servile humility, a constant fear of repression and therefore to submissive acquiescence in all of the demands of the rulers, no matter how unjust they were.

b) The deep assimilation put a wall of linguistic and cultural estrangement between the synagogue and the Jewish people in the USSR. The Jew, ignorant of his own language and history, raised in traditions of Russian culture, and, finally, with no chance for help and leadership from the Jewish religious community, had to move by groping in the dark, like a blind man. It is not surprising that an intellectual of Jewish descent looking for religion frequently turns to [Russian] Orthodoxy, which, in the final analysis, signifies yet another step in the assimilating process.

On the other hand, there can be no doubt that the longing of Soviet Jews for the synagogue has not so much a religious as a national character. Thus, even complete religious freedom in itself, no matter how important and also how unlikely it is under the Soviet system, cannot solve the Jewish problem.

11) At the present time two extremes can be discerned in Soviet Jewry:

a) Those Jews who have lost, or almost lost, all national consciousness and strive for complete assimilation into the basic population.

b) Those Jews who have come to realize the complete impossibility of a national existence as Jews in the USSR and strive for repatriation to Israel. Between these two extremes are those who have not yet realized the inevitability of a choice between assimilation and repatriation.

12) The sole possible solution of the Jewish question in the conditions of the Soviet Union lies in this: that the first group be given the real possibility of assimilation into the basic population and that the second group be given the unconditional right to repatriate. The third group must make its own decision.

b) THE EMIGRATION TAX

1. USSR citizens who depart for permanent residence abroad shall reimburse State expenditures for education at USSR institutions of higher learning in the following amounts: (in thousands of rubles)

In event of graduation from institutions of higher learning or study during the last year of the academic program

	In event of education for				
	one years	two years	three years	four years	five years
Moscow State University...	12.2	2.4	4.9	7.3	9.8	-
Other universities	6.0	1.2	2.4	3.6	4.8	-
Engineering-technical, engineering-economics, and higher military institutions of learning..............	7.7	1.5	3.1	4.6	6.1	-
Agricultural and Forestry ..	5.6	1.1	2.3	3.4	4.5	-
Medical, pharmaceutical, stomatological, and physical education............	8.3	1.4	2.8	4.2	5.6	7.0
Economics, law, pedagogical, history and library sciences institutes and cultural institutes	4.5	0.9	1.8	2.7	3.6	-
Institutes and departments of foreign languages	6.8	1.4	2.8	4.1	5.5	-
Institutes of arts (conservatories, theater, art, and literature).................	9.6	1.9	3.8	5.7	7.7	-

FROM: Directive of the USSR Council of Ministers, "On Reimbursement by USSR Citizens Who Depart for Permanent Residence Abroad of State Expenditures for Education," August 3, 1972 (English translation in Thomas Sawyer, *The Jewish Minority in the Soviet Union*, Boulder, Colo., Westview, 1979, pp. 312-14; reprinted by permission of the publisher).

2. Persons who have done graduate study, medical internship, graduate study at a higher military school or who have an academic degree shall, in addition to reimbursing State expenditures for receiving higher education, as provided in paragraph 1 of this Directive, be liable as follows:

(a) persons who have done graduate study, medical internship, or graduate study at a higher military school, but who have not successfully defended a dissertation – 1.7 thousand rubles for each year of education;

(b) persons who have been awarded the academic degree of Candidate of Sciences – 5.4 thousand rubles;

(c) persons who have been awarded the academic degree of Doctor of Sciences [in addition to the amounts stipulated in subparagraph (b) of this paragraph] – 7.2 thousand rubles.

3. The following USSR citizens who are departing for permanent residence abroad are exempted from reimbursement of State expenditures for education at an institution of higher learning, for graduate study, for medical internship, for graduate study at a higher military school and for receipt of the corresponding academic degree, as provided by paragraphs 1 and 2 of this Directive, as follows:

(a) invalids of groups One and Two – in full. Group Three invalids may be exempted from the above specified reimbursement in amounts up to 50 percent;

(b) men who have reached age 60 and women who have reached age 55 – in full;

(c) men with length of service of no less than 25, 15, and 8 years, and women with length of service of no less than 20, 12, and 6 years – in amounts of 75, 50, and 25 percent respectively;

(d) persons who have studied at an institution of higher learning, have done graduate work or graduate work at a higher military school without interruption of employment – in an amount of 50 percent;

(e) persons who have married citizens (subjects) of foreign states – in amounts between 25 and 50 percent with account being taken of their material situation, while persons who were married prior to 3 August 1972 – in full;

(f) persons who have graduated from institutions of higher learning on the basis of examinations without regular attendance at lectures, as well as those who have been awarded the academic degree of Candidate of Sciences without graduate study, medical internship or graduate study at a higher military school – in an amount of 75 percent.

USSR citizens who are departing for permanent residence in developing countries may be exempted from reimbursement of expenditures for education and receipt of an academic degree, in addition to the amounts of expenditure reimbursement reduction stipulated in this paragraph of the Directive, in an amount of up to 70 percent, while persons who have married citizens (subjects) of those countries in an amount of up to 80 percent, and in individual cases – in full.

A partial or full exemption from reimbursement of expenditures for education and receipt of an academic degree shall also be granted by the Ministry of Finance of the USSR, with the participation of the Ministry of Internal Affairs of the USSR, when there are other justifiable reasons.

4. The amounts specified in paragraphs 1 through 3 of the present Directive shall be accepted by branches of the State Bank of the USSR and credited to income in the Union budget.

5. Processing and issuance of exit visas to persons departing for permanent residence abroad shall be performed by agencies of the Ministry of Internal Affairs of the USSR upon presentation by said persons of receipts, issued by branches of the State Bank of the USSR, showing payment of amounts as reimbursement of State expenditures for education.

6. The present Directive does not pertain to USSR citizens who are departing for permanent residence in socialist countries.

BREZHNEV'S CONSTITUTION

In 1977 Brezhnev introduced a general revision of the Stalin Constitution of 1936, without however altering basic structural features or the political monoply of the Communist Party. Simultaneously Brezhnev removed Chief of State Nikolai Podgorny and took that title for himself in addition to his principal post as General Secretary of the Party.

Now for *the main features of the content of the draft of the new Constitution.*

First of all, one should mention that it gives *a detailed description of the guiding and directing role of the Communist Party* and clearly reflects our Party's actual place in Soviet society and the Soviet state. Unlike the 1936 Constitution, this role is treated more broadly, in a special article.

The draft of the new Constitution also states that *a developed socialist society has been created in the USSR and that the supreme goal of the Soviet state is the building of communism.* It is emphasized that *our state is a state of all the people and* that it expresses the will and interests of the working class, the peasantry and the intelligentsia, of all the country's

FROM: Brezhnev, Report to the Plenary Session of the CPSU Central Committee, "On the Draft Constitution of the USSR," May 24, 1977, *Pravda*, June 5, 1977 (English translation in *Current Digest of the Soviet Press*, XXIX:23, July 6, 1977, pp. 7-8).

nations and nationalities. In this connection, it is proposed to call our Soviets *Soviets of People's Deputies.*

The draft retains the fundamental provision to the effect that socialist ownership of the means of production is the basis of the USSR's economic system. At the same time, it is proposed that some clarifications, suggested by life itself, be made in the new Constitution. Along with state and collective farm-cooperative forms of ownership, ownership by trade union and other public organizations is now listed as well.

In general, it can be said that *the main guideline of the new elements contained in the draft is the broadening and deepening of socialist democracy.*

Above all, the democratic principles of the formation and activity of the Soviets have received further development. Provision has been made for increasing their role in the resolution of the most important questions in the life of society.

Art. 106 states that the USSR Supreme Soviet is empowered to resolve all questions placed within the jurisdiction of the USSR. The local Soviets not only resolve all questions of local importance but also, within the limits of their powers, control and coordinate the activity of all organizations in their territories. Special emphasis is given to the systematic nature of control by the Soviets over executive and administrative agencies and over the activity of organizations and officials.

The term of office of the Supreme Soviet has been increased to five years, and that of the local Soviets to two and a half years. Courts will be elected for the same terms.

The draft defines the main ways of strengthening the ties between the Soviets and their Deputies and the masses. The former are obliged to regularly inform the population about their activity, to report to the voters, and to consider carefully every proposal made by the working people. . . .

The draft gives significantly fuller formulation to *the political rights and liberties of USSR citizens.*

The right of every Soviet citizen to participate in the administration of state and public affairs is proclaimed, and the specific forms of such participation are indicated.

Freedom of speech, of the press, of assembly, of mass meetings and of street processions and demonstrations, which are included in the Constitution now in effect, are restated in full. The right of citizens to submit proposals to state and public agencies, to criticize shortcomings in work and to protest the actions of officials to court, as well as the right to legal protection against attempts on one's life, health, property, personal freedom, honor and dignity, are a significant addition to the constitutional guarantees of the rights of the individual.

Needless to say, comrades, the draft Constitution pro
premise that the rights and liberties of citizens cannot an'
against our social system or to the detriment of the S
ests. Therefore, the draft clearly states, for example, that
citizens of their rights and liberties must not injure the interes
and the state or the rights of other citizens and that political libe,
granted in accordance with the working people's interests and for the p
pose of strengthening the socialist system.

Every Soviet person should clearly realize that, in the final analysis, the chief guarantee of his rights is the might and prosperity of the homeland. To this end, every citizen should have a sense of his responsibility to society and should conscientiously fulfill his duty to the state and to the people.

THE THEORY OF "DEVELOPED SOCIALISM"

Soviet and East European ideologists put forth the notion in the 1970's that the Communist states had completed a definite stage along the Marxist road to the future, and now enjoyed the system of "developed socialism" or "real existing socialism" that distinguished them from the capitalist world, even though the transition to ideal communism lay much further ahead. Brezhnev affirmed this theme in 1977.

The main thing that life has given our people in the more than 40 years that have passed since the adoption of the previous Soviet Consitution is the building of a developed socialist society, the creation of the world's first state of the whole people.

A developed socialist society is a natural stage in the socio-economic maturing of the new system in the framework of the first phase of the communist formation. This, to use Lenin's words, is the fully established socialism from which the gradual transition to communism begins. This is precisely the stage in the development of socialism that has been achieved in our country.

When the Marxist-Leninist classics, lifting the curtain of time, charted the contours of socialism and communism they were extremely careful. Not a grain of Utopia. No flights of fantasy. Only what could be scientifically proved: the basic trends of development, the main, fundamental characteristics. Theoretically it was clear that the transition from capitalism to communism would embrace a long historical period, that the new society would rise from one stage of maturity to the next. But no one could tell in

FROM: Brezhnev, "A Historic Stage on the Road to Communism" (English translation in *World Marxist Review*, XX:12, December, 1977, pp. 3-5, 7; reprinted by permission of Progress Books).

ce what concretely these stages would be. Engels wrote that the question of the stages of transition to communist society "is the most difficult of any that exist. . . ."*

Lenin, the communists of Russia were the first who had to answer that question. It is understandable that Lenin's attention was focused mainly on the immediate tasks of that period, on creating the foundations of the new social system. But genius always anticipates its age. Already at the dawn of Soviet power Lenin spoke of "accomplished," "full" and "developed" socialism as the perspective, the goal of the socialist construction that had been launched. It was these ideas of Lenin's that formed the basis of the conception of developed socialist society evolved by the collective efforts of the CPSU and other fraternal parties.

The experience of the USSR, of other countries of the socialist community testifies to the fact that laying the foundations of socialism, that is, abolishing the exploiting classes and establishing public ownership of the means of production in all sectors of the national economy, does not yet make it possible to launch the direct transition to communism. Before this certain stages in the development of socialism on its own basis must be traversed. Moreover, practice has shown that the development, the perfecting of socialism is a task no less complex, no less responsible than the laying of its foundations.

It is self-evident that a mature socialist society must rest *on highly developed productive forces, on a powerful, advanced industry, on a large-scale, highly mechanized agriculture built on collectivist principles.* Such today is the Soviet economy which, both in scale and technical capability, differs fundamentally from what we had four decades ago, when socialist production relations had already prevailed in town and country.

In this period the gross social product increased 18-fold, the power-to-man ratio in industry nearly 8-fold, and in agriculture more than 15-fold. Our economy today is inconceivable without nuclear power, electronics, computers, transistors and many other industries that in 1936 we did not possess. The share of the industries determining technological progress and economic efficiency in the total volume of industrial output has more than tripled.

In the initial stages of socialist construction Soviet people had to concentrate their resources and efforts on the most urgent tasks, on things that the very existence of our state depended on. Today, in the conditions of developed socialism, on the basis of the constant growth of the whole national economy, the combination of the scientific and technological revolution with the advantages of the socialist organization of society, it has been pos-

*Letter to Konrad Schmidt, Zürich, July 1, 1891.

sible to achieve a perceptible swing of the economy toward ever fuller satisfaction of the people's many and diverse material and cultural requirements. In other words, the supreme goal of socialist production today is becoming directly central to the party's practical policy. The historical advantages of socialism as a mode of production and way of life, its genuinely humane essence are thus more fully and dramatically revealed. . . .

Thanks to the convergence of the diverse forms of socialist property, the gradual obliteration of any essential distinctions between town and country, between mental and physical labor, and adoption by all working people of the ideological and political positions of the working class, the interests and goals, the social ideals and psychology of all strata of the population have drawn closer together than ever before. On this basis substantial changes have also occurred in the political system. Essentially they consist *in the growing of the state of the dictatorship of the proletariat into a socialist state of all the people.*

Such are the objective processes that led our party to the conclusion that *developed socialism has now been built in the USSR, that is to say, a degree, a stage in the maturing of the new society has been reached when the repatterning of the totality of social relations on the collectivist principles intrinsically inherent in socialism is completed.* Full scope for the functioning of the laws of socialism, for the manifestation of its advantages in all spheres of social life, the organic integrity and dynamism of the social system, its political stability and indestructible intrinsic unity – such are the major distinguishing features of the developed socialist society. It stands to reason that the principle of distribution according to labor still holds good even at this stage of the development of the new system, and will continue to do so for some time.

We proceed from the fact that cognition and use of all the opportunities offered by developed socialism are, simultaneously, transition to the building of communism. In other words, the dialectics of development are such that as the mature socialist society perfects itself it gradually grows into a communist society. It is impossible to divide these two processes, to draw a line between them.

We are profoundly convinced that *no matter what the specific conditions in the countries building socialism may be, the stage of its perfection on its own basis, the stage of mature, developed socialism is an essential part of the social transformations, of the relatively long period of development on the road from capitalism to communism.* It stands to reason that this necessity, this regularity will be embodied in their own way in the conditions of the various socialist countries.

POPULATION AND THE BIRTHRATE

The 1979 Soviet census underscored falling birthrates and population growth in the European part of the country, and the non-Russian minorities collectively were on the verge of becoming a majority of the Soviet population. Official writers endeavored to address these trends together with the problems of an aging population and the failure to improve life expectancy.

Consideration of the specific features of demographic processes is mandatory for long-range social and economic planning. And the longer the period for which planning is undertaken, the better substantiated demographic policy – i.e., using a system of economic, social and legal measures and other ways of purposefully influencing the population's attitudes and its cultural and psychological standards to manage demographic processes – must be.

In other words, the developed socialist society requires that planned influence be applied to demographic phenomena. The exacerbation of the demographic situation makes this requirement a necessity.

2. – . . . The principal unit, the source of all demographic events, and hence the chief object of demographic policy, is the family. The attitude of married couples toward the problem of the birthrate determines its level in the country as a whole, and the moral climate in the family and the number of children it has largely determine success in the upbringing of the rising generation. The attitude toward health as a highly important social value, the ability to intelligently combine work and leisure, and young people's attitude toward migration are also formed "at home." . . .

Socialism's historic gains and the aforementioned trends in the social, economic and cultural process have brought about a change in women's position in society. Their legal equality has gradually been supplemented by social equality, economic independence from their husbands and, to all intents and purposes, equality of educational and cultural level. The role of children in the family has also changed – they no longer become workers at an early age, as they once did, and they are increasingly coming to have only a social, moral and psychological value for their parents. All this has brought about a mass shift of the Soviet family toward fewer children.

At present, the small family is prevalent among approximately 80% of the country's population. This includes practically the entire populations of the Russian Republic, the Ukraine, Latvia, Estonia, Lithuania, Belorussia

FROM: D. Valentei and A. Kvasha, "Questions of Theory: Population Problems and Demographic Policy," *Pravda*, June 19, 1981 (English translation in *Current Digest of the Soviet Press*, XXXIII:25, July 22, 1981, p. 12).

and Georgia. In some regions of these republics, and especially in the larger cities, the two-child or even one-child family predominates. . . .

But the shift toward population reproduction below replacement level (when succeeding generations are smaller than the preceding ones) may gradually lead to many negative consequences. These include a sharp increase in the rate of the population's aging, with all the complex social problems that this entails, future difficulties in developing new territories, and many others. The prevalence of the one-child family is also complicating the cultivation of a spirit of collectivism and comradeship in children and making marriages less stable. In short, the interests both of the family itself and of society are suffering.

In this connection, the existing situation in a number of rural areas of the Russian Republic, especially in the Non-Black-Earth Zone,* is cause for special concern. A low birthrate, in combination with a high rate of rural-to-urban migration among young people, has led to a deformation of the age-group structure there: The older age groups predominate in precisely those areas where manpower in the active age groups is very much needed.

One cannot fail to mention some of the negative phenomena that are encountered in other demographic processes. In particular, the population's life expectancy has changed very little in recent years. The gap between the life expectancy of men and that of women is not being lessened, which indicates that the work of public health agencies, the disease-prevention system and the struggle against job-related injuries and household accidents have not been sufficiently effective.

The exacerbation of the demographic situation is also manifest in the low rate of permanent settlement for new settlers in a number of regions of the country and in population migrations that are irrational from the standpoint of society's interests. The CPSU Central Committee's Report to the 26th Party Congress noted that people still prefer to move from north to south and from east to west, although movement in the opposite directions is preferable from the standpoint of the development of productive forces.

All these and certain other phenomena have increased the urgency of the scientific elaboration and implementation of an effective long-range demographic policy. . . .

Obviously, we should first of all reappraise women's social possibilities and obligations. . . . Developing and implementing a set of measures for creating the optimal combination of these two functions [reproductive and childbearing, on the one hand, and vocational and social, on the other] in

* I.e., the poor farming region of the North – Ed.

each family appears to be the main way for a developed socialist society to exercise a directed influence on demographic phenomena.

We must put special emphasis on the role of enterprises and organizations in implementing measures for helping families and children and protecting mother and child; this should be a mandatory element of their social development plans.

It's also necessary to set "psychological mechanisms" in motion. The press, movies, television and radio should devote more attention to problems of the family and to its lasting value. The point that the roles of father and mother are no less important to society than a married couple's work in production must be presented more clearly. . . .

THE LIMITS OF CENTRALISM

In the last years of Brezhnev, as the Soviet economy came up against limitations of resources, manpower and productivity, the promises of rapid economic expansion and rising living standards faltered, though the country's military potential continued to be built up. Soviet spokesmen, addressing the need for better management, tended to make a panacea of technical progress, even though it was the inability to accommodate innovation that was calling the central planning of the economy into question.

Let us attempt to analyze a number of data on the development of the national economy during the past 30 years, trying to assess the impact of various factors.

Figures indicate that, beginning in 1950, the national income and labor productivity rose at rapid rates, but that after 1958 these rates began to decline; by 1980, they had fallen by 67%.

What were the causes of this? One might think about unfavorable weather conditions; however, the climatic factor has not changed the curves' general pattern for a long time now. Declining growth rates are sometimes linked with the opening up of vast new territories and the need to create an infrastructure. But after all, these new territories were already inhabited. The scope of the development of the country's eastern regions has grown considerably, of course, but on the other hand, possibilities are different now.

One could look for the reason in the exhaustion of many raw-material sources. This certainly has an impact; however, new deposits – the Kursk

FROM: V. Trapeznikov, "The Essence, Ways and Means of Intensification: Management and Scientific and Technical Progress," *Pravda*, May 7, 1982 (English translation in *Current Digest of the Soviet Press*, XXXIV:18, June 2, 1982, pp. 1-4).

Magnetic Anomaly, the oil-and gas-bearing regions of Siberia, and others – are being brought into operation to replace worked-out deposits. As data for 1960-1980 show, the value of the extractive branches' output, based on nonrenewable raw-material sources, comes to nearly 5% of the gross social product; but, as calculations confirm, even if this figure were three times as high, the declining growth rates of labor productivity still could not be attributed to the raw-material factor. . . .

Outlays associated with the improvement of working conditions, as well as with environmental protection, have also been cited. But, calculations show, this factor has no appreciable influence either.

From 1958-1980, the change in the growth rate of assets available per worker was negligible; consequently, this too could not have had a noticeable impact on the rate of increase in labor productivity during that period. Thus, we must look for other, more important factors.

In my view, the principal reason lies in an underestimation of scientific and technical progress and in shortcomings in the management of the national economy. Let us recall that the switch in 1957 from the branch system to the territorial system of management (through economic councils) entailed the severance of many economic ties and the fragmentation of production complexes. As a result, the indices for national income, return on assets and rates of scientific and technical progress deteriorated sharply as early as 1958. The return to the branch system in 1965 led to a change for the better in 1966. However, the rates that had been obtained prior to 1958 could not be reached, owing to the difficulties of re-establishing severed economic ties and the need to train new cadres of economic managers and to have them gain experience.

In the period when the economic councils were in existence, every region began to build many production facilities – often without sufficient reason. Naturally, these construction projects had to be continued after that period had ended. This – along with new construction projects – scattered manpower and dragged out construction times. The nonfulfillment of plans for the construction of pilot-industrial plants and experimental shops and the assignment to them of the production of series-produced goods became a regular thing. Less than 1% of all capital investments in basic production was allocated for the creation of these plants and shops. The nonfulfillment of plans for the creation of new equipment became commonplace. Isn't this evidence of inattention to the utilization of the achievements of scientific and technical progress?!

The consequences were not slow in coming. In particular, while assets available per worker increased, the return on assets declined. From 1958 to 1980, the latter fell from 0.48 to 0.31. The return on new assets was 0.52 in

1958 but only 0.16 in 1980. This meant that, whereas in 1958 an increase of 1 ruble in production assets yielded 52 kopeks in additional income, in 1980 such an increase yielded only 16 kopeks. These figures should put us on guard. Their import becomes quite plain when one considers the fact that in a number of branches machinery and equipment have been replaced with more progressive models at an insufficient rate, which means that equipment in use is obsolescent and worn out. . . .

In my opinion, in view of the importance of scientific and technical progress and its insufficient pace, all measures to improve the economic mechanism should be evaluated primarily in terms of the following criteria: Will they accelerate or impede technical progress? Will they change the existing situation, in which it is advantageous for collectives to produce old goods and economically disadvantageous for them to put progressive goods into production?

In this connection, I shall touch on a number of requirements of management theory.

The first one is the proper selection of criteria in evaluating the efficacy of management. . . . The notorious "gross" [output] and "tons" indices have held sway in our country for decades. It is largely this circumstance that we can "thank" for the fact that our machinery and equipment are often heavier than analogous foreign models by dozens of percentage points.

The separate management of output quantity and output quality can serve as an example of the use of contradictory criteria. In both cases, the achievement of high indices requires additional outlays of labor and resources. What does an enterprise manager do when he runs into difficulties in fulfilling the plan? He chooses the alternative that will bring the enterprise the fewest problems; most often, it will be the production of large quantities of goods, to the detriment of their quality. . . .

Speaking about output quality, the question of its more rigorous evaluation by the USSR State Standards Committee should be raised. We're too liberal in assigning to the highest quality category manufactured goods that aren't on a par with the world's best models. . . . We must attach greater importance to exporting manufactured goods to the markets of technically advanced countries as a means of objectively verifying our products' merits, and we must provide better incentives for such exports. It's also time to evaluate the work of research institutes and design bureaus in comparision with the level reached by leading Soviet and foreign institutes and firms.

On the whole, we must devote paramount attention to the scientific and technical progressiveness of enterprises and ministries and rank this criterion as high (or perhaps higher) as plan fulfillment. Following this guideline is no simple matter, but there are ways to do it.

Another requirement of management theory is effective feedback – that is, the influence of succeeding segments of the management system on preceding ones. In the national economy, this includes the consumer's influence on the producer (which at present is negligible), the influence of results on management, etc. In our economy, feedback is extremely weak and operates only with great delays; when there is a scarcity of a particular product, feedback virtually disappears and output quality declines, since the rule "If you won't buy shoddy goods, someone else will" becomes operative.

A situation has come about in which the producer, in effect, bears no responsibility for the operational efficiency of his output. After officially turning over the product, the producer walks away, and the customer is forced to correct any defects on his own, in a makeshift fashion. Producer-enterprises should set up adjustment-service brigades that would eliminate defects at the producers' expense; this would stimulate higher output quality. In many countries, every reputable firm has service departments, but in our country they are still in a rudimentary stage. Their formation is one way of improving feedback in the customer-producer chain. . . .

Instead of active competition, frequently a directly opposite path is taken, one in which a given organization acquires a monopoly in its field. The saying "We'll mass our forces at one point" is offered as justification. However, a monopoly hinders technical progress and ultimately extinguishes scientific and technical initiative. Then the customer has nothing to choose from – he's forced to take what's offered, and the organization that has the monopoly, gradually abandoning an active search for new solutions, lives by the rule "If you don't like my product, make your own." A "lazy brains" syndrome is fostered, and technical progress is retarded.

Consideration for the human factor, in particular the all-out unleashing of people's initiative and its encouragement, is of enormous importance. Large numbers of instructions, explanations and restrictions of every kind have accumulated over the years. As a result, a manager who has been entrusted with an enterprise that produces hundreds of millions of rubles' worth of output can't make flexible use of a sum amounting to a few hundred rubles, especially where wages are concerned. These restrictions lead to a decline in initiative, sometimes to indifference, and usually to a search for detours.

In some countries of the socialist commonwealth, the director enjoys great confidence and is granted broad rights. Shouldn't we, as an experiment at individual enterprises where the director has won everyone's confidence, lift a number of financial restrictions and give him a field of activity for displaying initiative?

Cases are known, primarily in agriculture, in which resourceful people, thanks to the optimal organization of work, have raised productivity by 400% to 900%, with incentives in the form of substantial pay increases. However, there's no follow-through on such undertakings, as a rule. Shortages of goods to cover rising incomes are frequently cited as justification. But after all, it's necessary to look for ways of increasing productivity without capital investments, by making all-out use of people's abilities.

Given the shortage in the economic mechanism of factors that stimulate scientific and technical progress it is maintained largely by people's enthusiasm and by "forcible" measures. But that, of course, is not enough. . . .

THE FOOD PROGRAM

Throughout the Brezhnev years agriculture remained the most sluggish sector of the Soviet economy despite the shift from exploiting the collective farm peasantry to subsidizing them with substantial investments. The last important party initiative before Brezhnev's death was a much touted "food program" adopted by the Central Committee in May, 1982, which recognized severe managerial problems in the agricultural system.

The Party's present agrarian policy, as we know, originated with the Central Committee's March (1965) plenary session. By intently pursuing the course that it mapped out, the Party has succeeded in providing for the solution of a considerable number of agrarian problems in a relatively short time. Agriculture's productive forces and total output have grown substantially, and energetic efforts have been made to resolve the problems of the countryside's social development. . . .

These accomplishments could have been even more impressive if the advantages of a planned economy had been utilized more fully, untapped production potential had been put to use more actively, and shortcomings had been combated more persistently.

The chief cause of the difficulties that have arisen, we believe, was that the major reforms in productive forces have not been accompanied by corresponding changes in production relations.

It has become obvious that extensive factors for growth in agro-industrial production have been virtually exhausted. . . .

FROM: V. Miloserdov, "New Stage in the Management of the Agro-Industrial Complex," *Pravda*, August 6, 1982 (English translation in *Current Digest of the Soviet Press*, XXXIV: 31, September 1, 1982, pp. 1-3).

During the 1970s, a number of qualitative indices declined even though assets grew, and advanced research capabilities and skilled personnel were available. Outlays per unit of output produced rose, and the financial situation of many agricultural enterprises worsened.

The functions of economic management of the complex became fragmented, managerial work became narrowly specialized and the management function became isolated, making it impossible to manage food production as a single process.

Organizational disarray developed: Several specialized subdivisions performing the same type of work were set up in each district. Concentration of high-powered specialized machinery and equipment in these subdivisions was supposed to increase the efficiency of capital construction, equipment maintenance, and fertilizer procurement and application, and to gradually free the collective farms and state farms of these functions. However, even those farms that lacked the necessary buildings and equipment and were short of manpower continued to perform most of these operations themselves. Because the financial terms were too burdensome, farms often gave up the services of Selkhoztekhnika [the All-Union Farm Machinery Association], for example, and developed their own repair facilities. At the same time, a substantial proportion of the work the specialized organizations did was for other branches of the economy. The enterprises and organizations that serviced agriculture did not consider themselves responsible for the harvest. They fulfilled and overfulfilled their plans and received large profits even when the collective and state farms' harvests were dwindling and the production of meat, milk and other output was falling.

Narrow departmentalism has undermined the unified system for managing the food production process. For example, only three of the 17 state farms in Tula Province's Lenin District are subordinated to the district farm production administration; the rest are under eight different industrial associations. Confusion in the material and technical supply of collective farms and state farms has become appreciable. For example, tractors and combines have been arriving at specialized farms according to the allocation schedules of the trusts, while farm-machinery attachments and the equipment and supplies needed to perform maintenance have been arriving according to the schedules of the district farm production administration. Lack of coordination in the operations of these organizations has often resulted in certain farms' receiving tractors while other farms receive the ploughs and trailers that go with them, or in a district's plans for the procurement of certain products being increased while the trusts allocate resources to their farms for the development of other types of farming.

The fact that we are talking in the past tense about all the shortcomings listed above does not mean that they have already been surmounted, by any means. . . . Major efforts are being made and must continue to be made toward this end, along with efforts to surmount narrow departmentalism and regionalism, antiquated working methods, and inertia and sloth in economic thinking. The creative search for the effective methods for the planned guidance and management of the economy must also continue. . . .

The decisions [of the CPSU Central Committee's May (1982) plenary session], which are notable for their profound scientific grounding, contain a clear-cut system of carefully conceived measures aimed at an upswing in agro-industrial production and at the accomplishment of the USSR Food Program.

Appropriate management bodies are being set up to coordinate the work of the ministries and departments of the agro-industrial complex and their local agencies, enterprises and organizations, to mobilize efforts to make fuller use of resources, and to ensure that the branches of the agro-industrial complex operate in a highly efficient fashion. District agro-industrial associations have functioned in a number of the country's republics for many years. Their example attests to the fact that this form of management is the most acceptable and effective one. It has therefore been deemed advisable that agro-industrial associations be created in all districts, territories, provinces and autonomous republics and that agro-industrial commissions be formed in the Union republics and at the all-Union level. . . .

Bringing management closer to the production of the end product will enable the administrators of the relevant services to make day-to-day and long-term decisions more effectively and ensure that the appropriate resources are available for the specific steps they take. These conditions will provide realistic ways to increase the economic effectiveness of social production, make judicious use of production resources, decrease losses and upgrade the quality of output. . . .

In recent times there have been minimal improvements in the methods and forms of planning agro-industrial production. In fact, on certain positions there has been a retreat from points adopted at the CPSU Central Committee's March (1965) plenary session. Local planning and economic agencies have returned to using long-condemned methods. These include planning "from the achieved level"; failure to observe the territorial principle of planning; seeking to dictate to farms how much of what crops to sow and how many head of livestock of each type to raise; and imposing recommendations that do not take local conditions into account.

The Party has criticized such practices. . . .

Departmental barriers have promoted a scattering of capital investments and material resources among the various ministries and departments, which in turn have been distributing them among the enterprises of their own systems. These financial and material resources have been reaching the countryside through many separate channels. Inasmuch as there was no agency coordinating the work of the enterprises engaged in food production, disproportions and failures of coordination occurred in the development of the agro-industrial complex. They were especially significant at the local level. Local agencies saw these breakdowns in coordination but were unable to eliminate them because they lacked the authority to reallocate the investments among enterprises of different departments and could not maneuver resources as they needed to . . . .

Setting the agro-industrial complex apart as an independently planned and managed entity makes possible a better and more effective combination of territorial planning, branch planning, and special-program and specific-purpose planning. The point of departure for the planning is the end result, which is to provide an interrupted supply of food to the country.

Thus, the methodology for drawing up the Food Program contains fundamentally new approaches to planning. The planning reflects a systems approach and is geared to special programs and specific purposes, thereby making it possible to identify priorities for the utilization of capital investments and material resources.

THE MERGER OF NATIONALITIES

After the 1979 census showed that population growth among the Soviet minorities would soon make them collectively more numerous than the Russians, signs increased of pressure on the minorities to learn the Russian language and assimilate to the urban Russian way of life. The doctrine of cultivating the cultural distinctiveness of each nationality was restated by R. I. Kosolapov, editor of the party's main theoretical journal, as a theory of centralized development and eventual merger of nationalities.

The Soviet people constitute an unprecedented phenomenon in history. Internationalist in terms of its very essence, this new community of people has united in a single family over 100 nations and ethnic groups belonging

FROM: *Kommunist*, no. 12, 1982, editorial, "We are the Soviet People" (English translation, Washington, Joint Publications Research Service, no. 82130, November 1, 1982, pp. 1, 4-10).

to various races but has not submerged them within itself; on the contrary, it has secured the flourishing of each one of them while at the same time evolving numerous common psychological and moral features conditioned by the unity of their political, economic and ideological life. . . .

It is impossible not to single out the special role of the Russian people in the establishment and development of the Soviet people. The name of the first among equals of the fraternal peoples has been firmly and justly attributed to them. Not, of course, because the Russian people are numerically the strongest or possess some qualities which are unaccessible to others. They have won respect and authority for their revolutionary services, selflessness and spiritual generosity. It is no exaggeration to say that the Russian people have become the backbone of our new internationalist community of people.

The rulers of czarist Russia made great endeavors to instill in Russians a sense of "superiority" over a contemptuously hostile attitude toward "outsiders." But nothing could eliminate sensitivity to other people's troubles from the soul of the Russian people, who became a good friend to all the country's peoples, large and small. The misanthropic ideas of chauvinism and racism never took root in practice on Russian soil, and superpatriotic intoxication never turned the heads of indigenous Russians. . . .

The Russian people were undoubtedly the decisive force in the victory of the Great October Socialist Revolution, on the battlefields of the civil war and in the restoration of the national economy, the industrialization of the country and the collectivization of the countryside – that is, in the building of socialism as a whole – and subsequently in the victory over fascist Germany. They also made and are continuing to make an invaluable contribution to our society's postwar development.

As far as the first two decades of the Soviet Union's existence are concerned the Russian people rendered aid to all the USSR's other peoples which it is difficult to measure with conventional yardsticks. They shared literally everything they had with them, often giving away things they were in dire need of themselves, and taught them everything they had managed to learn before them. During this period the crux of the communist party's nationalities policy consisted simultaneously of establishing the national statehood of many Soviet peoples – there was an intensive process of the formation of new union and autonomous republics, autonomous oblasts and national okrugs – and effecting the accelerated economic and cultural development of all the backward regions of the country. The family of socialist nations and the peoples' uncrushable friendship and fraternal cooperation were formed on precisely this basis. The party relied primarily on the Russian people in implementing this nationalities policy. . . . The

Russian language became the means of communication between nationalities, which made a supreme contribution to the consolidation of the entire complex of internationalist ties. . . .

Under our country's specific conditions following the republics' voluntary unification in the Soviet Union it would have been a crime against the socialist revolution and the future of socialism and an irresponsible attitude to the peoples' destiny to have made centralized leadership of the union state formalistic, telling the republics "govern yourselves as you wish." This would have been a conscious deviation from the principles of proletarian internationalism to the benefit of national sovereignty interpreted in an egotistical, narrow and formalistic manner. Under such conditions it would have been extremely difficult if not impossible for many of our peoples to have extricated themselves from poverty and backwardness. But today it is common knowledge what national flourishing they have achieved under the conditions of comprehensive fraternal mutual aid attentively and skillfully administered by the central union authorities.

But maybe it is not a question of the past? Maybe now, when all the nations and ethnic groups comprising the Soviet people have achieved economic and cultural equality–they have had political equality from the start–when every union Soviet republic constitutes an economically strong and highly cultured state formation, maybe, proceeding from all this, we should weaken the bonds of democratic centralism for the sake of that notorious self-government? Of course we are talking about the present. All imperialism's ideological and psychological attacks on the Soviet people started with anti-Soviet "advisers," be they overt or covert, displaying touching "concern" for their "interests" and human and national rights, always treated in abstract terms. But we know that the age-old dream of all such "advisers" is to weaken by any means the great socialist power – the bastion of social progress and peace throughout the world – smash its economic and political system and weaken our invincible strength – the peoples' fraternal friendship. . . .

A unified policy also has to be pursued in all corners of the country in ideological work and the communist education of the Soviet people. A Marxist-Leninist world outlook, communist morality and socialist social awareness are class, not national phenomena. And therefore to deviate from them in favor of certain local traditions contradicting them means willy-nilly to slip from the world-outlook positions of the working class and communist ideology. There has never been a supraclass ideology in any class society. Certain champions of national uniqueness for some reason forget this elementary truth when it comes to attitudes toward certain spiritual values which appear to be strictly national. National nihilism is bad and harmful, but national conceit and tender feelings for "antiquity" and everything which has been carried down to our day from it is no better. As we say, we are not people who refuse to acknowledge our roots. It is just that for us the blood link with the past lies in the field of the material culture and democratic spiritual culture created by the people's intellect and talent. An uncritical and unthinking attitude to historically obsolete traditions, customs and morals leads as a rule to neglect of the new pan-Soviet spiritual values invested with a revolutionary, collectivist, communist content. And this manifestly does not promote the further consolidation of the Soviet people as a new historical community of people or, consequently, the spiritual health of each individual nation. . . .

The social structure of Soviet society is developing intensively in the direction of the intensification of its homogeneity: The working class, kolkhoz peasantry and people's intelligentsia are drawing closer together in terms of their qualitative indicators, mutual relations between them are improving, and their alliance is strengthening. "Under present-day conditions," the CPSU Central Committee resolution 'On the 60th Anniversary of the Founding of the USSR' notes, "the rapprochement of all the classes and social groups in Soviet society is continuing, leaning toward the establishment in its main and fundamental respects of a classless structure of society within the historical framework of mature socialism." This important scientifically substantiated tenet of creative Marxism-Leninism convinces us that new prospects are opening up for the Soviet people in the immediate future, particularly in the question – a natural question of the Soviet people – of the future merging [sliyaniye] of nations. This is not the place to examine this question in all its complexity. Let us just note that nobody intends to artificially accelerate this indubitably progressive process, which has nothing in common with the assimilation of some nations by others but benefits all the country's peoples. Time will tell what this projected new fusion of peoples of different ethnic groups and races will be like, but it seems perfectly clear that it will be a human community of an unprecedentedly high level since it will be effected on the threshold of the full implementation of the great humanist ideals of communism. . . .

THE ANDROPOV SUCCESSION

Upon Brezhnev's death in November, 1982, the Central Committee quickly endorsed the long-time secret police chief Yuri Vladimirovich Andropov as the new General Secretary of the party. A few months later he assumed the governmental title of Chief of State as well. Andropov immediately called for renewed discipline in addressing the country's economic problems, while reaffirming his ideological commitments in a programmatic article prepared for the hundredth anniversary of Marx's death. Summing up what Marxism means to the Soviet leadership, Andropov warned – half a century after Stalin made the same point – that the Soviet Union was not yet ready for the communist utopia. With his stress on incentives, efficiency and productivity, Andropov like his predecessors demonstrated the use of Marxism as "ideology" to justify the rigors of totalitarian modernization.

a) ANDROPOV ON THE ECONOMY

Comrades! This plenary session of the Party Central Committee is taking place at an important stage of the struggle to implement the plans of the 11th Five-Year Plan on the eve of its third year – its pivotal year, so to speak. We have done a good deal. But difficult and strenuous work lies ahead.

I would like to forcefully draw your attention to the fact that, for a number of highly important indices, the plan assignments for the first two years of the five-year plan were unfulfilled. Naturally, this has an effect on the draft we are discussing today.

The members of the Central Committee will remember Leonid Ilyich Brezhnev's last speeches and his memorandums to the Politburo of the Central Committee on questions of economic development. He put the question as follows: At Party Congresses and Central Committee plenary sessions, we have worked out a scientifically substantiated economic policy and embarked on a course aimed at improving the efficiency of production and its intensification. But the switching of our economy onto these tracks and the turn toward efficiency are still being carried out slowly.

The main index of the economy's efficiency – labor productivity – is growing at rates that cannot satisfy us. The lack of coordination in the development of the raw-materials and processing branches remains a problem. The materials-intensiveness of output shows virtually no decrease.

Plans continue to be fulfilled at the cost of large outlays and production expenses. There are still a good many economic managers who, while glibly quoting Leonid Ilyich's maxim that the economy should be economical, are in actuality doing little to accomplish this task.

Apparently the force of inertia and old habits are still at work. And some people, perhaps, simply don't know how to tackle the job. We must think

FROM: Andropov, Speech to the Central Committee of the CPSU, November 22, 1982, *Pravda*, November 23, 1982 (English translation in *Current Digest of the Soviet Press*, XXXIV:47, December 22, 1982, pp. 4-5).

about what kind of help should be given these comrades. The main thing is to accelerate work to improve the entire sphere of economic management – administration, planning and the economic mechanism.

It's necessary to create conditions – economic and organizational – that will stimulate good-quality, productive labor, initiative and enterprise. Conversely, poor work, sluggishness and irresponsibility should have an immediate and inescapable effect on the remuneration, job status and moral prestige of personnel. *(Applause.)*

It's necessary to enhance responsibility for observing the interests of the entire state and of all the people and to resolutely eradicate departmentalism and parochialism. It should be made a rule that any new decision on an old question is adopted only after past decisions have been fulfilled or some new circumstances have come up. We must wage a more resolute struggle against all violations of Party, state and labor discipline. I'm certain that in this we will have the full support of Party and trade union organizations and the support of all Soviet people. *(Applause.)* . . .

In general, comrades, there are many urgent tasks in the national economy. Needless to say, I have no ready-made recipes for accomplishing them. But all of us – the Party Central Committee – will have to find answers to them, by generalizing Soviet and world experience and collecting the knowledge of the best practical workers and scientists. In general, slogans alone won't get things moving. Large-scale organizational work by Party organizations, economic managers and engineering and technical personnel is needed if every one of these vast and important tasks is to be examined in the context not only of each branch but also of every plant, every shop and work sector and, if you will, every workplace.

I would like to stress that these questions are of paramount, vital importance for the country. If we resolve them successfully, the economy will continue to grow and the people's well-being will increase. . . .

b) ANDROPOV ON MARX AND THE LAWS OF SOCIALISM

A hundred years have gone by since the day when a man named Karl Marx departed this life. A whole century. A century of dramatic upheavals, revolutionary storms, radical changes in the fate of mankind. A century that upset and shattered a multitude of philosophical concepts, social theories, political doctrines. And a century of victories of Marxism, one after another, and its growing impact on the development of society. . . .

FROM: Yuri Andropov, "The Doctrine of Karl Marx and Certain Questions of Socialist Construction in the USSR," *Kommunist*, no. 3, February, 1983, pp. 9-13, 15-20, 22-23 (editor's translation).

It fell to the lot of the proletariat of Russia to be the revolutionary trail-blazer. Even in our time there are "critics" of the October Revolution who assert that somehow it came about contrary to all the wishes of Marx. They take the view that in his revolutionary forecasts Marx generally did not take Russia into account. But actually he showed a tremendous interest in Russian matters. In order to analyze them better, Marx studied the Russian language. An irreconcilable opponent of tsarism, he prophetically appraised the prospects of the social movement growing in Russia and saw that a "tremendous social revolution" (see K. Marx and F. Engels, *Works*, vol. 32, p. 549) was brewing there that would have worldwide significance. . . .

The concrete historical paths of the establishment of socialism have not gone entirely as the founders of our revolutionary theory expected. It was initially victorious in one country alone, and that one not the most economically developed. The point here is that the October Revolution took place under new historical conditions which did not exist during the lifetime of Marx, in the epoch of imperialism that was given expression in the Leninist theory of socialist revolution which has been completely confirmed by experience.

Bourgeois and reformist ideologists to this day build whole systems of conclusions in the effort to show that the new society created in the USSR and the other fraternal countries does not correspond to the model of socialism that Marx envisaged. They argue that the reality has supposedly diverged from the ideal. But consciously or in ignorance they overlook the fact that Marx himself in working out his doctrine was least of all guided by the demands of some sort of abstract ideal of pure, perfected "socialism." He derived his view of the future system from an analysis of the objective contradictions of large-scale capitalist production. It was this uniquely scientific approach that allowed him to define accurately the basic features of the society which were still waiting to be born in the cleansing storms of social revolution in the twentieth century.

The cornerstone of the socio-economic structure that was to replace capitalism was, according to Marx, social ownership of the means of production. . . . And in full correspondence with Marx's prediction, wherever proletarian revolutions have succeeded, social ownership of the means of production has been established in one form or another and has become the basic factor in the existence and maintenance of socialism and the main source of its progress.

On the basis of socialist ownership we have created a mighty economy, developed by planning, which has allowed us to pose and resolve large-scale, complex economic and social tasks. Obviously these possibilities do not get realized for us by themselves. Problems and serious difficulties arise. Their origins are various, but they are never tied to the essence of social, collective ownership that has confirmed and demonstrated its advantages. On the contrary, a significant part of the shortcomings disrupting the course of normal work in one sector or another of our economy has its cause in deviations from those norms and requirements of economic life whose ultimate basis is socialist ownership of the means of production.

Take for example the question of economizing, in the rational utilization of material, financial and labor resources. Fulfillment of the tasks of the current five-year plan and the long-term development of our economy depend in great measure on how this is answered. If you think about it, the point here is just this – to observe the essential norms of management which are prescribed by socialist ownership, the essence of which lies in a thrifty attitude toward the people's property and energy and initiative in augmenting it. Violations of this norm have to be paid for by society as a whole, and it is right in strictly callimg to account those who out of negligence, incompetence or considerations of self-interest squander its wealth.

Our concerns are now focused on raising the efficiency of production and of the economy as a whole. The party and the Soviet people are deeply conscious of the importance of this problem. However, as regards its practical solution things are not going as successfully as they should. What is interfering here? Why from vast capital investments do we now not get the return that we should, why is production characterized by an unsatisfactory pace of scientific technological achievement?

Many causes, of course, can be cited. Above all one cannot fail to see that our work directed at the perfection and restructuring of our economic mechanism and its forms and methods of administration has lagged behind the demands posed by the level now achieved in the material-technical, social and spiritual development of Soviet society. This is the main point. In addition, of course, one can cite the impact of such factors as, for example, the substantial shortfall in agricultural production over the last four years, and the need to direct ever-increasing financial and material resources into the extraction of fuel, energy and raw-material resources in the northern and eastern regions of the country. . . .

The so-called ABC truths of Marxism ought generally to be dealt with carefully, for life itself punishes one severely for misunderstanding or forgetting them. For example, only at the cost of much work and even mistakes was the full significance of Marx's views on distribution realized. He persistently pointed out that in the first phase of communism each laborer "receives back from society after all deductions exactly as much as he gives it," in other words, in exact correspondence with the quantity and quality of his labor (see K. Marx and F. Engels, *Works*, vol. 19, p. 18), which answers to the basic principle of socialism, "From each according to his abilities, to each according to his work." An irreproachable democrat and humanist, Marx was a determined opponent of levelling, and categorically rejected the common and in his day demagogic or naive arguments about socialism as "universal equality" in distribution and consumption.

Now from practice, from the experience of many socialist countries, the enormous political as well as social-economic impact of these judgments of the founder of scientific communism is clear. Of course relations of distribution directly and immediately affect the interests of each and everyone. The character of distribution is in essence one of the most important indicators of the degree of social equality that is possible under socialism. Any attempt arbitrarily to exceed this possible degree, to run ahead to the communist form of distribution, without an exact accounting of the labor contribution of each person in the creation of material and spiritual goods can and does generate undesirable phenomena.

Thus it has become absolutely clear that we cannot allow violation of the objective economic requirement of accelerated growth in the productivity of labor. Without a close link with this decisive factor the raising of wages, though it produces at the beginning an outwardly favorable impression, in the last analysis will inevitably have a negative effect on the whole of economic life. In particular it will generate demands which cannot be fully satisfied at the given level of production and will prevent the elimination of shortages with all the distorted consequences of this that evoke justifiable agitation among the toilers.

The correct solution of problems of distribution under socialism presumes, of course, the physical guarantee of the population's purchasing power by making available all kinds of items of consumption and services. Obviously it is impossible to satisfy demands which exceed our possibilities. At the same time our unalterable obligations have been and will be to work in two directions: first, the unswerving growth of social production and the lifting on this basis of the material and cultural level of life of the people; second, every sort of help to raise the material and spiritual demands of Soviet Man.

Complete social equality does not come about suddenly or in its final form. Society grows and works its way toward it for a rather long time, with difficulty, at the price of great effort. It must develop its productive forces to the level of the material-technical base of communism. For every toiler it must promote high consciousness and culture, professionalism, the capacity to use the benefits of socialism rationally.

Until we have these conditions, distributive relations and the strictest control in measuring labor and consumption must be at the center of the party's attention as it guides socialist society. And the CPSU is always concerned that the principle of socialist distribution discovered by Marx be carried out everywhere and unswervingly, or better, that it be more fully applied in practice. If it is violated, you have to deal with unearned income, with so-called drifters, strikers, loafers and incompetents, who essentially become social parasites living at the expense of the mass of conscientious workers. This is an intolerable phenomenon, a sort of parasitism living off the humanism of our system.

Work and only work, only its real results, and not someone's subjective wish or good will can determine the level of well-being of each citizen. Such an approach completely corresponds both to the spirit and the content of Marx's views on distribution under socialism. . . .

Obviously the party proceeds from the actual conditions of the administration of work that exist at the present stage of development of Soviet society. At present these conditions are such that the economic law that Marx considered the first basic law of collective production, the law of economizing working time, does not operate among us in full force. The cause of this to a significant degree is the presence of a large number of physically burdensome, unattractive, routine jobs, and the slow pace of their mechanization or rather their automation.

Meanwhile it is enough to consider the tense situation with labor resources and the demographic situation in the country, to make clear the economic necessity of further reducing by a significant proportion the amount of non-mechanized hand labor which even in industry reaches 40%. This is why the all-around acceleration of the tempo of scientific-technological progress and a more active utilization of its accomplishments are so relevant today, especially in those fields where labor costs are especially high. . . .

In the course of building a new society the content of socialist democracy is enriched, historically accumulated limitations fall away, and the forms of implementing the people's power become more diverse. This process unfolds in an unbreakable link with the development of socialist governance, which itself is undergoing qualitative changes. The most important of these is the transformation of the state of the dictatorship of the proletariat into the state of all the people. This is a shift of immense significance for the political system of socialism. It had its reflection in the Constitution of the USSR adopted by the people in 1977, which creates the legislative basis for the further deepening of socialist democratism.

We do not idealize what has been done and is being done in our country in this area. Soviet democracy has had, has, and one must expect, will have difficulties of growth conditioned by the material possibilities of society, by the level of mass consciousness and political culture, and even by the fact that our society is not developing under hothouse conditions, in isolation from a hostile world, but under the cold winds of the "psychological war" unleashed by imperialism. The perfection of our democracy demands the elimination of bureaucratic "over-organization" and formalism, of everything that stifles and undermines the initiative of the masses or fetters the creative thought and vigorous action of the toilers. With such phenomena we have struggled and will struggle with still more energy and persistence.

Sometimes one happens to hear that the present aspect of socialist governance and democracy supposedly does not correspond to the prospects indicated by Marx for communist self-administration. However, the path which we have trod, the experience we have had, say the reverse. . . .

Obviously, that version of self-administration that tends toward anarcho-syndicalism, and toward the fractionation of society into competing corporate bodies that do not depend on each other, toward democracy without discipline, toward the idea of rights without responsibilities, is profoundly alien to us. The tried and tested principle of organization of the whole life of socialist society is democratic centralism, which makes it possible to successfully combine the free creativity of the masses with the advantages of a unified system of scientific leadership, planning and administration. . . .

In his own time, analyzing Marx's methodological approach to the exposition of the basic features of the new society, Lenin wrote: "Marx did not make the slightest attempt to create a utopia, to make empty guesses about things that it is impossible to know. . . . In place of artificially contrived scholastic definitions and fruitless disputes over words (what is socialism, what is communism), Marx gives an analysis of what might be called the stages of the economic maturation of communism" (*Complete Collected Works*, vol. 33, pp. 85, 98). Precisely on the basis of such an analysis, as we know, Marx created his doctrine of the two phases of development of the single communist formation which is part of the armament of the CPSU and the other fraternal parties. Precisely on this basis, generalizing from new historical experience, Lenin broadly developed the theory of the building of socialism and communism. From these propositions we still proceed today to solve one of the most difficult questions, according to Marx, Engels and Lenin – the question of the concrete forms of the transition to communism.

The most important features of contemporary Soviet society have found reflection in the concept of developed socialism. It convincingly shows the dialectical unity both of real successes in socialist construction, in the fulfillment of many economic, social and cultural tasks of the first phase of communism, and of the growing seedlings of the communist future, and on the other hand of the problems left over from yesterday that we have still not solved. This means that a definite time is necessary to consolidate the lagging rear areas and move forward. We have to soberly consider where we are. To run ahead means to propose unrealizable tasks; to rest simply on what has been achieved means not utilizing everything that we have available. What is needed now is to see our society in its real dynamics, with all its opportunities and needs. . . .

Marxism is not a dogma but a living guide to action and independent work on those complex tasks which each new turn of history places before us. In order not to lag behind life, Communists must move and enrich the teaching of Marx in all directions, must put into practice the method of the materialist dialectic that he worked out and which is rightly called the living soul of Marxism. Only such an attitude toward our priceless ideological heritage whose pattern Lenin gave us, only such a continuous self-renewal of revolutionary theory under the influence of revolutionary practice, makes Marxism a genuine science and art of revolutionary creativity. In this lies the secret of the strength of Marxism-Leninism, its unfading freshness.

One may hear from time to time the notion that new phenomena in social life are "not listed" in the concept of Marxism-Leninism, that it is supposedly going through a "crisis," and that its influence needs, they say, to be "invigorated" with ideas drawn from western sociology, philosophy or political science. But the point here, however, is by no means any such "crisis" of Marxism. It is something else – the incapability of some theorists who call themselves Marxists to rise to the true scale of the theoretical thinking of Marx, Engels, Lenin, and their inability to apply the enormous intellectual power of their doctrine in the process of concrete study of concrete questions. It is not superfluous to add that not a few bourgeois theorists in the area of philosophy, sociology and political economy have made a name for themselves in large part by re-tailoring Marxist ideas in their own fashion. . . .

We Soviet Communists are proud to belong to the most influential ideological current in the whole history of world civilization – Marxism-Leninism. Open to all the best and most progressive that exists in contemporary science and culture, it finds itself today at the center of the world's spiritual life, and commands the minds of millions and millions of people. It is the ideological credo of the rising class that is liberating all humanity. It is the philosophy of social optimism, the philosophy of the present and the future.

At the present time a great distance has been traversed on the path of the social renewal of the world, on the path of the realization of the revolutionary goals and ideals of the working class. The political map of the globe has a new look. Great discoveries have been made by science; the achievements of technology take your breath away. At the same time mankind is confronted with many new and often very complex concerns. There is well-founded alarm connected with worsening problems of raw materials, energy, food, ecology, etc., on a global scale. And the most important thing that disturbs people today is the need to preserve peace and avoid a thermonuclear catastrophe. There is nothing more important than this on the international plane for our party, the Soviet state, and all peoples of the planet.

To deal with all the complexities of the contemporary world, to organize and direct the revolutionary social-historical creativity of the working class and all laboring people – this is the tremendous task that today is being resolved by the theory of Marxism-Leninism and the practice of struggle for the progress of mankind. That task, which Karl Marx posed for himself and for his ideological and political adherents and successors, is to explain and change the world.